CLSA ADVISORY OPINIONS
1984-1993

Edited by
PATRICK J. COGAN, S.A.

CANON LAW SOCIETY OF AMERICA

ACKNOWLEDGEMENTS

The professional canonical and editorial dedication of the editors of *CLSA Advisory Opinions* is gratefully acknowledged.

Editors of *CLSA Advisory Opinions*

Richard A. Hill, S.J. (1984)
J. James Cuneo (1985-1988)
Lynn Jarrell, O.S.U. (1989-1992)
James I. Donlon, (1990-1993)
Ann Keevan, C.S.J. (1993)

Special acknowledgement and gratitude is given to those who have participated in the preparation of this volume: Jennifer Miller, assistant to the executive coordinator, Joseph Carter, Daniel Kuntz and Michael Santistevan, student assistants.

TABLE OF CONTENTS

v

vi

BOOK III
THE TEACHING OFFICE OF THE CHURCH

BOOK IV
THE OFFICE OF SANCTIFYING IN THE CHURCH

BOOK V
THE TEMPORAL GOODS OF THE CHURCH

BOOK VI
SANCTIONS IN THE CHURCH

BOOK VII
PROCESSES

INTRODUCTION

The Canon Law Society of America, at the forty-fourth annual business meeting at Hartford in 1982, adopted a resolution "to establish a committee of canonists to issue advisory opinions on the meaning of the canons of the revised code after its promulgation." The publication of these advisory opinions was initiated in 1984 on an annual basis under the title *CLSA Advisory Opinions*.

A decade of the publication of advisory opinions has yielded a collection of more than 200 entries. These advisory opinions are collected in this volume in order to facilitate their access and reference for the canonist and other persons who are involved in the interpretation and application of canon law. This series of opinions has demonstrated to be a very useful and practical resource. A broad range of canonical topics are represented in the entries.

The reader is signaled to consider the relative weight of these unofficial interpretations. The canons on interpretation (CIC cc. 16-19; CCEO cc. 1498-1501) should be referred to for guidance in any evaluation of the contents of this volume.

Patrick J. Cogan, S.A.
Editor

BOOK I

GENERAL NORMS

CANONS 2; 87; AND 90

DISPENSATION FROM LITURGICAL LAWS

In our diocese the bishop recently dispensed from the liturgical law specifying that there can be no ritual Mass on November 2. All Souls Day fell on a Saturday. Many parishes had weddings scheduled for that day and they wanted to use the nuptial Mass rather than the Mass for All Souls. However, I discovered a 1985 reply from the Congregation for Divine Worship and the Discipline of Sacraments stating that the bishop may not grant permission for the nuptial Mass on All Souls Day (See Roman Replies and CLSA Advisory Opinions 1985, 3-5). By what right does a bishop dispense from a liturgical law when canon 2 excludes liturgical laws from the code?

OPINION

Liturgical law is not a different species of law from the law of the code. Both are ecclesiastical laws and are governed by the same rules of interpretation and dispensation. It just so happens that liturgical laws, "for the most part" (c. 2), are not found in the code. In fact, most church laws are not found in the code. Think of all the particular laws of episcopal conferences, dioceses, provinces, religious institutes, etc. None of these laws are in the code, yet all of them are interpreted and dispensed from in accord with the standard rules found in the code.

Liturgical laws are subject to the same rules for dispensation as are other ecclesiastical laws, namely, the rules found in canons 85-93. Therefore, all liturgical laws which are merely ecclesiastical and disciplinary in nature are subject to dispensation in accord with the law.

Canon 87, §2 says that the diocesan bishop can dispense from universal disciplinary laws [not excluding universal liturgical laws] "as often as he judges that a dispensation will contribute to the spiritual good of the faithful." However, a dispensation "may not be granted without a just and reasonable cause and without taking into consideration the circumstances of the case and the gravity of the law from which the dispensation is to be given" (c. 90). If this is not observed, a dispensation by the bishop from universal law is invalid.

The superior who grants the dispensation must consider the "gravity" of the law. The more important the matter treated by the law, the less readily can the law be dispensed. Those laws that govern integral parts of liturgical rites ought never to be dispensed. Other liturgical laws might be dispensed, again depending on their gravity and the circumstances of the case.

On the specific issue you raised, you are correct in noting that the bishop cannot grant permission for a nuptial Mass on All Souls Day. A "permission" is foreseen by the legislator as a routine occurrence, such as the permission that local ordinaries may give for priests to binate on weekdays and trinate on Sundays and holy days (c. 905, §2). A "dispensation," on the other hand, is exceptional in nature. It should not be routinely granted, but each case must be considered on its own merits.

In this case, your bishop, presumably having considered the circumstances of the case and the gravity of the law, determined that there was a just and reasonable cause for granting a dispensation. As for the gravity of this law, I concur that it is not such an important law that it could never be dispensed under any circumstance. As for the circumstances of the case, the bishop used his discretion. Another bishop might have reached a different conclusion.

Ignorance of the law does not excuse from its observance. Nevertheless, your bishop determined in this case that a dispensation would be beneficial because many priests are unaware of the rubric excluding ritual Masses on November 2, and they already scheduled wedding Masses for that day. However, when November 2 falls on a Saturday again, I would doubt whether a dispensation could be justified because there is sufficient time between now and then to educate the priests and engaged couples and to warn them well in advance that nuptial Masses or other ritual Masses are not permitted on November 2. Nor are they permitted on the Sundays of Advent, Lent, and the Easter season; solemnities; days within the octave of Easter; Ash Wednesday; and during Holy Week (*General Instruction of the Roman Missal*, n. 330). The reply of the Congregation for Divine Worship and the Discipline of Sacraments, mentioned above, offers sound pastoral advice in this regard:

> In order not to cause distress to those preparing for marriage it should be explained to them as soon as possible that the Ritual Mass for marriage may not be used on that day [November 2]. The faithful need some pastoral instruction on the deep spiritual significance of this celebration and [to] be shown why it is most unfitting that a marriage should be celebrated on the day when the Church commemorates all of the faithful departed (*Roman Replies and CLSA Advisory Opinions 1985*, 5).

John M. Huels, O.S.M. [1992]

THE TERM OF COUNCILORS CALCULATED ACCORDING TO
THE TIME OF LEGISLATION

See opinion under canon 627.

CANON 8

PROMULGATION OF NEW LAW

Canon 8, §1 states: "Universal ecclesiastical laws are promulgated by being published in the official commentary Acta Apostolicae Sedis *unless another form of promulgation is prescribed for individual cases." In light of experiences since the promulgation of the code (cf.* Roman Replies *and CLSA* Advisory Opinions *1988, 44-45), what is the meaning of "another form of promulgation prescribed for individual cases?"*

The situation in the case mentioned in the 1988 advisory opinion *involved a response of the Commission for the Authentic Interpretation of the Code which was published in* L'Osservatore Romano *at the time, but had not appeared in the AAS. It was accompanied by the note that "the Supreme Pontiff John Paul II was informed of the above decision, and on June 1, 1988, he ordered its publication in* L'Osservatore Romano." *Does the pope's order to publish it in* L'Osservatore Romano *amount to "another form of promulgation" in this case?*

Similarly, in the case discussed in the 1988 advisory opinion, *the Congregation for the Sacraments directed that the response be communicated to episcopal conferences through the papal representatives. The 1988* advisory opinion *points out the communication was not by sending an authentic copy of the response, but by a letter of information signed by the papal representative. Is this also "another form of promulgation" in this (or other) cases? It may actually be a more effective means than the publication in the AAS, which for some countries takes a long time to arrive.*

It seems that there are a number of questions yet to be answered in this matter.

OPINION

You have raised a number of serious questions from both a theoretical and practical point of view. Some of them require a more in-depth study than is possible in an "advisory opinion." But perhaps the following comments may be of some assistance.

The law is promulgated in a manner prescribed by the code, or in some other manner prescribed by the legislator. In the 1988 situation, the pope ordered that the authentic interpretation of the commission be published in *L'Osservatore Romano*. But he did not order that it be promulgated there. There is a distinction between publication and promulgation that needs to be respected, in order to protect the actions of the legislator.

Promulgation is the presenting of the official version of a law (or of an authentic interpretation made in the form of a law, which requires promulgation — c. 16, §2). It means the legislator has completed the full process of legislation, has reviewed the final version of the text, and is ready to bind the community to the law in this form.

Publication is the making public of something. Sometimes this is done in draft form, asking for comments (the publication of various drafts of pastoral letters by the U.S. bishops is one example; the circulation of various drafts of the code, or of the new universal catechism, are other examples). Publication may be to a restricted audience, as in the case of the drafts of the code and catechism; or it may be to a general audience, to help them prepare for a document which is coming in its final form.

Moreover, there have been examples of official documents made public (i.e., published) in *L'Osservatore Romano* which have been touched up, correcting minor mistakes, etc., when they finally are promulgated in the *AAS*. The 1988 authentic interpretation was itself eventually published in the *AAS*, although so far as I can tell without any significant changes from the version that appeared in *L'Osservatore Romano*.

The point is, however, that the legislator has specified that "promulgation" is required before a text is actually law, and that this promulgation must be done properly so there is no incertitude about the existence of the law. Another example, where there was considerable confusion at the time, was the imposition of the new obligation of an "oath of fidelity." It was first published in *L'Osservatore Romano* (February 25, 1989) with a very brief *vacatio legis* (the obligation was to take effect March 1, 1989). Later, in a rescript *ex audientia* which was published in the *AAS* (81 [1989] 1169), it became apparent that the pope had ordered the promulgation of this new obligation in the *AAS*, so that its publication in *L'Osservatore Romano* did not satisfy the requirements for promulgation set down by the legislator.

This raises the issue that in practice there has been less than rigorous attention to the promulgation of binding norms in the Church since the promulgation of the code. This is not limited to the organs of the Apostolic

See, and has raised complaints in several countries over the manner in which episcopal conference norms are promulgated. For example, in the United States this is done by letter to the members of the conference, even though the norms are particular law for all the United States, and not just for the bishops.

Finally, let me comment on the distribution of the 1988 authentic interpretation (and other documents) through papal representatives. First, it was not the competence of the Congregation for the Sacraments to determine the manner of promulgating the authentic interpretation in question. Its directive to communicate this through papal representatives is clearly an example of making something public, without it being thereby an official promulgation.

You observe quite rightly that it may be useful to communicate documents through papal representatives rather than awaiting the appearance (and distribution) of the *AAS*. But even in this situation, there appears to be a practice of some papal representatives not to send an authentic copy of the official decree, but rather to send a letter presenting the substance of the decree. This does not seem to be within the normal meaning of promulgation, for making known the text of the law itself is central to the notion of promulgation.

So you are correct to observe that the question is still to be answered as to how promulgation is really supposed to be done. Hopefully the experience of the past ten years since the promulgation of the Latin code will lead to more careful observance of its provisions in this regard, and greater certitude as to exactly what is the law.

James H. Provost [1993]

CANON 16

AUTHENTIC OR PRIVATE INTERPRETATION?

What is the legal force of the interpretation of canons 230 and 910 communicated in a letter from the Apostolic Pro-Nuncio to the bishops of the United States in a letter of September 21, 1987?

OPINION

The letter in question is similar to communications by papal representatives to the bishops of other countries, and the contents have been published in various diocesan bulletins in France according to a report by Michel Bonnnet, J.C.D., in *Les Cahiers du Droit Ecclesial* (4 [1987] 149-150). It may be helpful

5

to summarize the canonical analysis provided in that report.

The Pro-Nuncio's letter reported that the Pontifical Commission for the Authentic Interpretation of the Code had been asked whether extraordinary ministers of Holy Communion could distribute the Eucharist if ordinary ministers were present in the church, even though not participating in the Eucharistic celebration. The answer was negative: it was approved by the pope.

This interpretation was not published in the *AAS* until late in 1988. The Congregation for the Sacraments, however, received the faculty to communicate it to the bishops' conferences before that time.

Several questions arose from this situation.

1. Who has the power to interpret authentically?

Canon 16, §1 leaves no doubt: "Laws are authentically interpreted by the legislator and by the one to whom the legislator has granted the power to interpret them authentically."

This power of authentic interpretation was confided by the pope to the Pontifical Commission for the Authentic Interpretation of the Code of Canon Law (now the Pontifical Council for the Interpretation of Legislative Texts) by the motu proprio *Recognitio iuris* of January 2, 1984. The first article of the motu proprio is quite explicit: "Only this commission will have the right to give an authentic interpretation, which must be confirmed by our authority, of the canons of the Code of Canon Law and of other laws of the universal Latin Church - after seeking in matters of greater importance, however, the advice of the dicasteries competent in the matter."

Thus it is clear that the commission "interprets" and that the Roman dicasteries can only give their "advice" (of which the commission remains the judge). Any interpretation given by a dicastery would have, in law, only a private character (the same as for the approved authors — cf., c. 19). But by reason of the quality of the author of the interpretation, it could have a certain moral authority. It seems necessary, therefore, to verify clearly who gives the interpretation.

2. Obligatory character of interpretation

Once confirmed by the authority of the Roman Pontiff an authentic interpretation must be promulgated (cf., c. 8, §1), normally by its insertion in the *AAS* unless the legislator decides to use some other manner. But, for example, the simple publication of a reply in *L'Osservatore Romano* must not be confused with its official promulgation, and has no consequences in law.

In the case under consideration, the Pro-Nuncio's letter does not indicate that a special form of promulgation was decided in this instance, only that the

Congregation for Sacraments had been directed "to communicate the decision to the Episcopal Conferences." Moreover, the letter from the Congregation for Sacraments was not itself sent to the bishops, only a report about it in the Pro-Nuncio's letter. This procedure was followed in most countries.

Clearly then, this is not a normal promulgation in the canonical sense, but only an advance communication of the opinion prior to any legal enforcement. Before promulgation, even if it is known, it has no force of law and no one can be obliged to submit to it.

3. "Private" Interpretation

Any interpretation which does not come from the legislator or from those to whom this power has been granted, as well as any interpretation given outside the formalities described in canon 16, must be held as not "authentic" (i.e., not authoritative); these are sometimes called "private" interpretations. The officials of the commission itself have often given this type of response to questions posed to them.

Private interpretations, no matter what their source, cannot be imposed on anyone with the force of law. Certainly, if it comes from an important source and especially if it has been approved by the pope, such an interpretation ought not be disregarded in making a reasonable and equitable application of the law; but the source of authority responsible for the interpretation should always be clearly distinguished.

Thus, if a bishop followed the provisions in the Pro-Nuncio's letter he did so on his own authority, not on the basis of a provision of universal law, until the interpretation in the letter itself was formally promulgated. On the other hand, if there is a genuine doubt about the meaning of the law and the provisions of the letter were not observed, this would not constitute a violation of the law prior to the actual promulgation of the interpretation in the letter. This is not mere legal nicety; it is taking the provisions of the code seriously, as they are intended.

James H. Provost [1988, revised 1993]

CANONS 16; 17; AND 19

DISTINCTION BETWEEN
INTERPRETATION AND APPLICATION OF THE LAW

If a pastoral minister has limited training and limited resources, will his or her decision have a privileged legal status on the basis of canon 19, since the decision fills a lacuna?

Using a sports analogy, it is the difference between pine tar on a baseball bat and the first use of a radio receiver by a base runner.

When, in 1983, George Brett's game-winning home run against the Yankees was disallowed because he had smeared too much pine tar on his bat, the commissioner overruled the umpire's decision. He was the official interpreter of the rules, and his interpretation was that the minor infraction of pine tar on the bat handle was not sufficiently grave to nullify a home run.

When, sometime in the future, a base runner is detected using a miniature radio receiver in his cap in order to get steal signals from the dugout, then the umpire is going to have to improvise a rule to deal with the situation. He or she will draw upon other rules about unauthorized equipment, the general principle of fairness in baseball, or the opinion of learned sports writers, and come up with a ruling in the case, because there is no explicit rule that covers it.

Canon 16 on authoritative interpretation is about clarifications, declarations of the meaning of the rules, resolution of doubts, explanations of the content of existing rules. It refers only to authorized and official interpreters. Their rulings oblige all of those who are subject to the rule being interpreted.

Canon 19 tells what to do when there is no rule covering the situation at hand. It suggests a procedure to find appropriate guidance. The canon gives some possible sources from which a ruling might be derived when no explicit norm exists. Look, for example, to the Code of Canons of the Eastern Churches, to what other bishops' conferences have done, or to the policies of neighboring dioceses. These "private applications of the law" are also authoritative. That is, they are decisive for the case at hand. They result from the use of appropriate canonical procedure.

James A. Coriden [1991]

ANOTHER OPINION

As regards this issue, we are dealing with a real situation that certainly needs attention. I am not sure, however, that for this situation there is any answer in the law itself. There is a human (and common sense) answer: if you have limited training and limited access to authority, and you must make a decision, - do your best out of the resources that you have. At times this can turn out to be a good solution, at times an awful mistake that creates a mess. (I have come across both types of resolutions.) What one cannot say, though, is that the law gives a special status to decisions made by a pastoral minister in limited circumstances, as it does to the decisions made by judges, or by persons with *potestas regiminis* filling in a *lacuna*. I see behind the request a desire to find a rule on which the pastoral minister could rely, or a rule that absolves him or her from responsibility if a mistake was made — and there is really no such rule. (The issue is really not how to interpret the law, but how to give "legal" value to a decision when there is no firm and clear knowledge of the law. The answer is that in such circumstances the conditions for an assuredly correct legal solution do not exist. Note also that the majority of pastoral ministers have no *potestas*, hence technically their decisions are not made with "authority.")

The problem of handling complex cases with the help of limited resources is an everyday occurrence in mission territories, and a visiting canon lawyer cannot do much more than to encourage the pastoral minister who must make decisions to gather as much information as available, to be as wise as possible, and to check the correctness of the decisions when the opportunity to do so arises — and leave the rest to God. (God is more interested in faithful persons than in correct solutions.)

Similar situations, I think, can arise in any profession. For example, a physician who is a general practitioner, in a place where there is no access to specialists and books, has to make decisions that can turn out either way — yet, at the moment of need a decision must be made.

It seems that the correct response to the inquirer about this issue is to let him or her see that the law has no answer for this situation, which does not mean that there is no answer at some other level — moral or pastoral.

To sum it up: if I wrote anything on this, it would not be a legal opinion. It would be an encouragement to make decisions even if the resources are limited, check their correctness as soon as the opportunity arises, accept the possibility (probability) of occasional mistakes, and carry on with the work.

A couple of final remarks: the inquirer seems to indicate that a pastoral minister is continuously faced with important legal decisions. I do not think that is the case. Rarely, there can be serious issues, e.g., the validity of a sacrament. Otherwise the problems are of much lesser importance. Many of them arise in connection with episcopal directives, liturgical prescriptions, etc. Most of the time whatever a decision may be there are no great and dramatic consequences. Life goes on.

Even in such a case as the validity of a sacrament, while we have the absolute duty to do all that is necessary for the validity, we cannot bind the mercy of God by our mistakes. Catholic theology never taught that God cannot give all the graces of the sacrament intended whenever his ministers made a well meant but invalidating mistake. In divine wisdom (knowing us) and goodness, God must have foreseen such occurrences, must have thought of appropriate provisions. This remark, however, should not be taken as suggesting that the servants of God could be remiss in their duty, but only as saying that God takes care of the human family.

Ladislas M. Örsy, S.J. [1991]

CANON 57

ADMINISTRATIVE DECREES AND
THE DISCRETIONARY POWERS OF THE BISHOP

A group of parishioners is unhappy with decisions a pastor has made concerning the direction and focus of parish ministry. This group is upset specifically with the parish's becoming more involved in issues related to social justice, with a resulting lack of emphasis being placed on traditional prayers and devotions, which have had to be discontinued due to declining attendance. The group does not consider these changes proper or even "Catholic" in their vision of what the Church is. As a result of these "improper activities," one of the parishioners has placed a formally worded petition before the diocesan bishop based on canon 57, stating that the current direction of the parish is detrimental to his spiritual well-being and is not in the best interests of the parish in general. The petition is seeking "a preceptive decree or similar administrative act forbidding the continuation of these activities and reinstating the traditional prayers and devotions." The parishioner further indicates that if no response is received within three months, a negative decision will be presumed in accord with canon 57, §2, and recourse will be sought.

How should the bishop respond to this petition?

OPINION

The singular difficulty with the petition that this parishioner has placed before the diocesan bishop is a mistaken notion that this one canon provides a means by which any grievance whatsoever can be placed before a competent authority in the expectation of seeking redress. Such a notion does not consider the purpose of canon 57 and ignores the fact that Book VII contains the specialized processes in the code that address such contentious issues.

In the context in which it is found, canon 57 is part of a procedure permitting an interested party to place a petition before a competent authority for the purpose of obtaining a decree or other administrative act from that authority which will directly benefit the petitioner personally. A ready example of such a petition is the request an interested party would present for the purpose of obtaining a dispensation associated with marriage. The use of this procedure involves only two parties: the petitioner and the competent authority.

It is not the purpose of this canon or the procedure for the issuing of individual decrees contained in Book I (cc. 48-58) to provide for matters beyond this limited application, and it certainly is not their purpose to supplant or replace those procedures contained in Book VII. Hence, the attempt to present a petition on the basis of canon 57 for the purpose of settling a contention or dispute against a third party is clearly beyond the scope of this canon.

For a more detailed examination of canon 57, see the *Código de Derecho Canónico* (Universidad Pontificia de Salamanca, Biblioteca de Autores Cristianos, Segunda Edición [1983] 53), and the accompanying advisory opinion on this question prepared by Reverend Ladislas Örsy, S.J., J.C.D.

If the petitioning party in this case is clearly convinced that specific rights are being denied as a result of the actions or decisions of this pastor, a more suitable means of dealing with this issue might be to seek some form of conciliation to resolve the problems that have arisen rather than immediately invoking a formal process. Failing a satisfactory resolution by this means, the issue could be addressed through some other form of mediation or possibly even before a judicial forum utilizing the oral contentious process if a properly prepared petition is presented to the local tribunal addressing the rights allegedly denied this parishioner by the pastor.

In acting on the specific petition presented by the parishioner in this example, however, the diocesan bishop certainly can respond by stating that the petition as presented lacks a proper foundation in canon law due to the fact that it is beyond the purpose or scope of canon 57. Therefore, a formal response or decision is not possible. Having set aside the formal petition in this manner, the bishop could then deal with the entire issue in a less inflammatory and more conciliatory manner.

Gregory Ingels [1991]

ANOTHER OPINION

Canon 57 concerns the situation in which the person with administrative power has a legal duty to issue a decree. It does not deal with the situation when a superior issues a decree on his own initiative, nor does it deal with pastoral decisions which are within the discretion of the bishop.

The canon leaves no doubt that there are only two ways for such duty to come into existence: either because the law binds the superior to issue a decree in certain well-defined cases (*quoties lex iubeat*, whenever the law prescribes it); or because the law grants the subject the right in some specific cases to petition for a decree (to petition *legitime*, on the basis of a law).

A few examples can illustrate the meaning of the canon.

For the first situation: the law binds an ecclesiastical superior to grant the necessary canonical provision for an office to a person lawfully designated for that office (cf., c. 146 ff.); he has no right to refuse the decree if all conditions are fulfilled.

For the second situation: a public juridic person has the right to petition (he does it *legitime*, observing the prescriptions of the law) for an authorization to alienate property. By this very fact the superior is under obligation to respond either by issuing a decree of authorization or by denying it. Or, the faithful have a right to form associations. If they intend to form one and do everything according to the law, and they request approval, the bishop must respond. Or, if the right of a person has been violated, e.g., someone was unjustly barred from the sacraments, he or she has the right to petition for redress through a decree. The bishop has the duty to respond.

But the canon does not confer the right on the individual faithful to petition for a decree of his or her own choosing: the petition must start from an existing right on the part of the petitioner. No one is entitled to request from the bishop a declaration in the form of a decree concerning the canonical status of a third person, be it physical or legal, e.g., that X should be declared excommunicated, or that a university, hospital, association should be declared non-Catholic, even if the petitioner has some legitimate interest in the welfare of that third person.

Particular Situation Raised in the Inquiry

Mr. Smith has no right in canon law to compel the bishop to issue an administrative decree of his own choosing, or to compel the bishop to choose between issuing or not issuing such a decree in three months. He is mistaken about the meaning of the canon. It does not empower him to request a quasi-constitutional declaration about the official standing of a third person (in this case an institution) in the Church. It follows that the bishop is not bound in canon law to accept his petition, and of course still less is he bound to give a response in three months.

Mr. Smith is, of course, perfectly entitled according to canon 212, §§2 & 3 to make representation and offer suggestions to his bishop. In fact the canon encourages him to do so. The bishop would be within his right to examine the issue and form a pastoral judgment as to what to do, or what not to do, with no other duty to respond than what Christian charity and prudence dictate.

One cannot help but conjecture that the misunderstanding on the part of Mr. Smith concerning his right to an administrative decree arises from American constitutional or administrative law. Every taxpayer is considered an interested party in the transactions of the government, and has the right to petition a court to compel the government to take or omit certain actions. There is no such provision in canon law.

The absurdity of Mr. Smith's claim to an administrative decree can be shown also by the consequences that would follow if it were accepted. Any member of the faithful could bring down episcopal investigation on any Catholic institution — colleges, hospitals, associations, etc. — to be completed in three months! All that would be required is a petition with a charge sheet attached. If such interpretation of the law were admitted and made public, our episcopal chanceries would be inundated by "requests for a decree," the requests coming from persons and organizations of different persuasions. In all such matters the bishop has broad discretionary powers.

Ladislas M. Örsy, S.J. [1991]

Canons 85 and 87

Delegating Others to Grant Marriage Dispensations

The diocesan bishop has given general delegation to his chancellor to dispense from marriage impediments. Can the bishop delegate the chancellor to do this, even if the chancellor is not a cleric? Can the chancellor give general delegation to others to grant marriage dispensations? Can the chancellor do this if these others are not clerics?

Opinion

1. Marriage Dispensations

To dispense from marriage impediments is to exercise the power of governance. A dispensation is the "relaxation of a merely ecclesiastical law in a particular case" and "can be granted by those who enjoy executive power . . . as well as by those to whom the power of dispensing has been given explicitly or implicitly either by the law itself or by lawful delegation" (c. 85).

In virtue of their office, local ordinaries (diocesan bishop, vicars general and

13

episcopal) can dispense from a marriage impediment of ecclesiastical law unless this is restricted to the Apostolic See (c. 1078), and can even dispense from most of the restricted ones in danger of death situations (c. 1079, §1). The law grants the faculty to dispense from various marriage impediments under certain restricted circumstances to the pastor, the properly delegated sacred minister, and the priest or deacon who assists at matrimony when the extraordinary form is being used (cc. 1079, §2; 1080).

2. Delegation of Chancellors to Dispense

Anyone else who dispenses from marriage impediments must do so by lawful delegation. The office of chancellor does not itself include the power to dispense from ecclesiastical law. Unless he is an episcopal vicar or vicar general, the chancellor who is a cleric cannot validly dispense from marriage impediments unless he has been delegated to do this by an ordinary. In the United States there has been a long standing practice by diocesan bishops of granting general delegation to their diocesan chancellors (and at times, to other diocesan officials) to grant these dispensations. This is in keeping with the law that "ordinary executive power can be delegated both for a single act and for all cases, unless the law expressly provides otherwise" (c. 137, §1).

Whether a chancellor who is not a cleric can be so delegated has already been discussed in previous canonical opinions (see *Roman Replies and CLSA Advisory Opinions 1986*, 56-64). There it is argued on the basis of the distinction between ordinary and delegated power (c. 131, §1: "The ordinary power of governance is that which is joined to a certain office by the law; delegated power is that which is granted to a person, but not by means of an office") that "lay members of the Christian faithful can cooperate in the exercise of" the power of governance (c. 129, §2) when they have been delegated to do this. While only clergy can obtain offices for whose exercise is required the power of governance (c. 274, §1), the office of chancellor is not one of those offices. Moreover, since any chancellor who can grant dispensations from marriage impediments does so in virtue of delegation and not in virtue of office, canon 247, §1 does not impede persons who are not clerics from being so delegated.

One of the 1986 *Advisory Opinions* also notes that while some may not agree with the above opinion, it has sufficient strength to be a probable one. There is at least, therefore, a doubt of law involved, and in such cases even nullifying and disqualifying laws do not bind (c. 14). The power of a delegated chancellor who is not a cleric to dispense is secure, and the dispensations so granted are valid.

3. General Delegation by the Chancellor

The chancellor (whether a cleric or not a cleric) can dispense from marriage impediments only in virtue of delegation. In practice, the chancellor is usually delegated for all cases. This kind of delegation can itself be delegated, but only for individual cases. That is, if an authority (other than the Apostolic See) having ordinary power has delegated that power for all cases, "it can be subdelegated only for individual cases" (c. 137, §3).

The law is quite strong on this: "*tantum . . . potest.*" An attempt by the chancellor to delegate someone else "for all cases" to grant dispensations from marriage impediments is beyond the chancellor's power, and would not exist. It would be invalid. The dispensations so granted would themselves be invalid.

It does not matter whether the person to whom the chancellor attempted to extend the delegation was a cleric or not a cleric. The chancellor simply does not have the power to delegate for all cases, but can only subdelegate the power to dispense for individual cases. If for some reason this has been attempted, there is a pastoral problem of what to do about the invalid dispensations that were granted. The provisions on common error do not apply here, for the bases for common error (whether legal or factual common error) do not exist. Neither do the provisions for positive and probable doubt about law or about fact, for the law is quite clear. The dispensations are invalid, and marriages attempted without the proper dispensation are themselves invalid.

"Provided the consent of each party continues to exist," these marriages could be given a valid dispensation (cc. 1163, §1; 1165, §2). Careful records have presumedly been kept concerning the marriages so performed. It may therefore be possible to learn the present whereabouts of these couples. It would be necessary to determine discreetly from the appropriate parish ministers whether consent appears to continue. If so, the sanation can be granted without disturbing the couple. This may be preferable to approaching the couples directly and, having granted a valid dispensation, requiring them to give new consent according to the proper form (cc. 1156-1158).

James H. Provost [1990, revised 1993]

CANON 96

RECEPTION INTO THE CATHOLIC CHURCH OF A PERSON EXCOMMUNICATED FROM THE GREEK ORTHODOX CHURCH

Athena is a baptized member of the Greek Orthodox Church, but during adolescence she became a practicing Lutheran. She marries Martin, a non-Catholic, before a Lutheran minister. The marriage ends in divorce and a declaration of nullity is later obtained from a Catholic tribunal on the grounds of a lack of form: the defect of sacred rite, since Athena was obliged to marry in an Orthodox ceremony before an Orthodox priest.

Athena, now civilly married to a baptized Catholic, wishes to convalidate this union, and be received into the Catholic Church (Latin Rite). By virtue of her former invalid marriage, however, in the eyes of Eastern Orthodoxy, she has been excommunicated according to canon 72, par. 1 of the Synod of Trullo.

Can Athena make a profession of faith in Catholicism while this ban of excommunication from Orthodoxy remains in effect? Would the Roman Catholic Church, in either the internal/external forum, have the authority to remove this ban of excommunication? Would we recognize Orthodox discipline in this area as we do in terms of recognizing their own canonical form of marriage?

OPINION

1.   Can Athena make a profession of faith in Catholicism while this ban of excommunication from Orthodoxy remains in effect?

Athena incurred the censure of the Greek Orthodox Church in virtue of her attempted marriage before a Lutheran minister. She also incurred censure from the same church when she attempted a civil marriage with a member of the Catholic Church. Further, she will again incur a censure when this union is convalidated in the Catholic Church. None of these marriages (not even the convalidation in the Catholic Church) is regarded as valid by the Orthodox Church.

In virtue of her entrance into full communion with the Catholic Church, Athena *ipso facto* incurs excommunication from the Orthodox Church. Such an excommunication is quite logical since a person cannot be a member of both the Orthodox and Catholic Churches at the same time. The Catholic Church is obliged to ignore this excommunication since the person desires to enter into full communion with the Catholic Church. If the Catholic Church did not ignore this excommunication, it could never receive anyone from the Orthodox Church into full communion.

2.   Would the Roman Catholic Church, in either the internal/external forum, have the authority to remove this ban of excommunication?

The question is not a logical one. If Athena entered the Catholic Church and as a consequence, became subject to the authority of the Catholic Church, why would the Catholic Church want to lift the ban of excommunication and reinstate Athena's communion with the Orthodox Church? To do so would be to effectively "excommunicate" her from the Catholic Church.

16

3. Would we recognize Orthodox discipline in this area as we do in terms of recognizing their own canonical form of marriage?

The Catholic Church recognizes the validity of Orthodox orders. For this reason, Eastern and Latin Catholics can validly contract marriage with Eastern non-Catholics in the presence of an Orthodox minister. (See *Orientalium Ecclesiarum* 18 and *Crescens matrimoniorum*.) This accommodation should not be construed as a simple recognition of the canonical form of the Orthodox, since Catholics cannot lawfully be married before an Orthodox minister without a dispensation from canonical form.

The Church recognizes the jurisdiction of the Orthodox Churches over their own faithful:

> . . . this holy Synod solemnly declares that the Churches of the East, while keeping in mind the necessary unity of the whole Church, have the power to govern themselves according to their own disciplines, since these are better suited to the character of their faithful and better adapted to foster the good of souls (*Unitatis redintegratio*, 16.)

However, when a jurisdictional act affects the status of a member of the Catholic Church, the Catholic Church does not recognize certain acts. For example, the Catholic Church does not recognize divorces or annulments granted by an Orthodox Church on behalf of their faithful. A tribunal of the Catholic Church can adjudicate the validity of the marriage of two Orthodox or an Orthodox and a Protestant. (See decisions of the Apostolic Signatura of November 28, 1970 and November 23, 1974 and the norms dated May 10, 1976 regarding the procedure of defect of form cases.)

John D. Faris [1988]

CANON 127

NECESSITY OF CONSULTATION WITH THE ORDINARY OF THE PLACE OF MARRIAGE FOR THE SAKE OF VALIDITY OF DISPENSATION FROM CANONICAL FORM

See opinion under canon 1127.

Canons 164 ff.

Participation of Non-Delegates in the General Chapter

See opinion under canon 631.

Canon 167

Religious Institute Gathering Votes by Telephone

With reference to canon 167, is it ever permissible for a religious institute of diocesan right with limited funds to gather votes from electors by the telephone?

Opinion

The Church, traditionally, prefers that electors/delegates be present in a solemn convocation for the important elections. The Code of Canon Law has yet to give large credence to the modern means of communication such as the telephone, telegraph, fax, tele-conference, and other modern equipment that are used by the business community on a daily basis. Canon 167 admits to the possibility of a written ballot in case of serious and/or excusable absence of a legitimate elector who is present for the election assembly but suddenly takes ill and may be "next door" or "down the street." The law excludes the possibility of mail-vote or proxy-vote unless the constitutions of the religious institute provides for such. Be that as it may, the lawgiver prefers all electors to be physically present in assembly for the casting of votes. A strict interpretation would be called for in the more solemn elections such as officers of the community.

Consequently, votes taken by telephone would be unusual due to several potential problems: 1) the inability on the part of those who preside over the election to monitor and control the voting with regards to honesty, numbers of votes matching actual numbers of electors, without which the election can be invalid; 2) human error; 3) the inability to authenticate actual absentee votes, which should be validated by the signature of the absentee elector.

If not already contained in the constitutions of the institute, norms might be amended to include the possibility of voting through mail, making sure that each voting slip of an elector carries the authentic signature of the elector who is absent because of distance, and sent through secured mail/postal routes in time for the election; in other words, establishing a procedure for absentee ballots.

One conceivable difficulty here is the rare instance of loss of mail, which would hold up the solemn convocation of election. But there are various secured mail delivery services and couriers.

The general principle with absentee and proxy designation of ballots is authentication, that is, that these carry the signature of the lawful elector who cannot be present for the election assembly.

Regarding consultation by letter or telephone, the Congregation for Religious and Secular Institutes, in a private reply to the procurator general of the Conventual Franciscan Friars, said that it was permissible to consult with the provincial definitors (members of the provincial's council) on certain urgent matters in this manner when it was inconvenient to convene the members of the council, but with the exception of matters of election.

Now, private replies/clarifications of the general law are direct answers to queries presented by bishops, religious superiors, office holders and individuals throughout the Catholic world. Private replies are not meant to be law but they betray the thinking of the lawgiver and those responsible for interpreting the law regarding its implementation. Private replies are "informational."

Should the young diocesan institute believe that telephone consultation is a good mode of holding elections until it becomes more secure, consultation can be had with the diocesan bishop and his canon lawyers/vicar for religious, in pursuit of securing this in the constitutions. Attention will have to be paid to the usual cautions the Church has been concerned about, some of them mentioned here, regarding taking votes outside the voting assembly. A broad interpretation of this canon is called for when voting for electors/delegates and other minor business items for the institute.

Joseph N. Perry [1993]

Canon 184

Due Process Against the Loss of a Limited Tenured Office When the Predetermined Time Has Elapsed

What right to a due process is recognized on the part of a priest whose six-year term of office as a pastor has ceased?

Opinion

In reference to your question concerning the right to due process of pastors who have completed their six-year term of office, I would offer the following observations and conclusions:

1. If a pastor has not yet completed his six-year term, the process provided in canons 1740-1752 must be observed before removing him administratively against his will or transferring him to another parish or another office against his will.

2. A pastor whose six-year term is completed has lost his ecclesiastical office "by lapse of a predetermined time" (c. 184, §1). Note that such a loss of office does not take juridical effect until it has been *communicated in writing* by the competent authority (c. 186). In this case, the competent authority would be the diocesan bishop or his delegate (c. 523), unless the pastor is a religious, whose loss of office can be juridically intimated either by the diocesan bishop or by the religious superior (c. 682).

In fact, one of the ways of solving the situation in which an elderly pastor's six-year term expires one or two years before his retirement date is for the diocesan bishop simply to refrain from communicating to him in writing the fact of the loss of his office. I believe that this tactic is sometimes used in Rome with the prefects of the congregations and other officials whose terms have expired but who are left in office until a replacement is found.

3. Before addressing the substance of your question, please note that canonists are somewhat concerned about appointments of pastors that occurred between November 27, 1983, and September 24, 1984, since the Roman indults that permitted term appointments prior to the revised code lapsed on November 27, 1983, and no diocesan bishop had authority to appoint a pastor to a limited term against the norm of canon 522 until the decree of the NCCB was legitimately promulgated on September 24, 1984. No one has challenged a temporary appointment made during that time period; such a challenge might bring an interpretation supporting the diocesan bishop's action, but on what grounds I do not know. If your diocese appointed pastors to six-year terms between those dates, I would advise you to have them sign a resignation form when the six years elapse as a prelude to their reappointment to the same pastorate or assignment to another pastorate or office.

4. Once a pastor has been legitimately informed in writing that his term of office has expired, he immediately loses that office. Note that *loss* of office is not to be confused with *removal* from office or *transfer* from one office to another, even though in practice we normally think of it that way. (Actually, even the pastor appointed to a second term in the same parish *loses* his office when the first term expires. In fact, to comply with canon 186 the second appointment letter should probably state this fact: "Since your term of office expired [will expire] on mm/dd/yy, I write to inform you that I hereby reappoint you as pastor of the Parish of St. Joseph for a second term of six years. Your

term of office will extend until mm/dd/yy.")

5. Based on the above analysis, my principal conclusion is that a pastor whose office has been legitimately lost by lapse of predetermined time has no substantial right to due process about removal or transfer. His only right to due process would concern procedure about the juridic requirements for loss of office.

6. Such a pastor could file an administrative recourse about:

—lack of juridic empowerment of the diocesan bishop to appoint for a term (my point about 11/17/83-9/24/84);

—lack of advisement concerning the six-year term in the appointment letter;

—lack of written communication about the loss of office in accord with canon 186 (a violation that is quickly remedied);

—failure to follow any process which the diocese has mandated to be followed before the diocesan bishop makes his decision to communicate loss of office and to reappoint to the same office or reassign to another office. (In other words, a diocesan bishop may *bestow* due process, over and above the universal law, by establishing a particular procedure he wishes to see followed before he declares the office lost. If he then fails to follow that procedure, he has denied due process.);

—failure to provide him with due remuneration in accord with canon 281 and diocesan policy.

7. I would not call the bishop's written communication of loss of office a "decree." More properly, it is a "declaration," that is, a written confirmation of a fact. The diocesan bishop does not end a term; he merely puts the law's ending of a term into effect by communicating the fact in writing. (An analogy is the communication to a priest petitioner of a dispensation from celibacy. If the bishop does not communicate it, it is not in effect; but, when he communicates it, he does not grant the dispensation, he merely allows the pope's juridic act to be juridically effective.) I would also avoid the use of the word "terminated," since it again suggests that the bishop is *doing* some thing juridically rather than *declaring* what has occurred by force of the law itself.

8. Finally, I must make the usual lawyer's distinction between "suing" and "winning." We usually ask our diocesan attorneys, "Can he sue me?," and the attorney answers, "Anyone can sue anyone for anything. But in this particular case I don't think he can get anywhere by going to court." Just because canonists are in agreement that a particular situation does not involve aggrieved rights does not mean that a pastor cannot write to the Congregation for the Clergy and lodge a "recourse" against his loss of office. One hopes that the Congregation, however, after a quick perusal of the facts, will recognize that there is no ground for substantial recourse and will quickly inform the petitioner that his claim is without juridical foundation.

21

Moreover, since the bishop is not issuing a decree of removal or a decree of transfer, the bishop is not bound by canon 1747, §3's prohibition from naming a new pastor, even though the pastor who has lost his office has had recourse to the Congregation for the Clergy.

John A. Alesandro [1986]

BOOK II

THE PEOPLE OF GOD

CANON 205

RECEPTION INTO COMMUNION WITH
THE CATHOLIC CHURCH *POST MORTEM*

May a baptized non-Catholic person he received into the Catholic Church after his or her death? If the answer is affirmative, under what circumstances may it be done?

OPINION

The answer is negative. For Roman Catholics membership in the Church is a question of those who are alive. A person must be alive and, if an adult, be willing to become a member of the Catholic Church before they can do so.

James H. Provost [1985]

CANON 215

THE TRADITIONAL MASS SOCIETY

The "Vancouver Traditional Mass Society" was incorporated under the laws of the Province of British Columbia on July 13, 1989, in keeping with the Society Act of the Province. As such, it exists as a legitimate organization recognized in civil law. The question is, what is the status of this organization according to canon law?

OPINION

1. The Christian faithful enjoy a lawful freedom "to found and to govern associations for charitable and religious purposes" and may "hold meetings to pursue these purposes in common" (c. 215). However, in exercising this right the "faithful, both as individuals and when gathered in associations, must take account of the common good of the Church and of the rights of others as well as their own duties toward others" (c. 233, §1). Moreover, "in the interest of the common good, ecclesiastical authority has competence to regulate the

exercise of the rights which belong to the Christian faithful'' (c. 223, §2).

2. Ecclesiastical authority has made specific regulations concerning the competence of various persons to found certain types of associations in the Church. ''Competent ecclesiastical authority alone,'' and not the Christian faithful at large, ''has the right to erect associations of the Christian faithful which set out to teach Christian doctrine in the name of the Church or to promote public worship or which aim at other ends whose pursuit by their nature is reserved to the same ecclesiastical authority'' (c. 301, §1).

The ecclesiastical authority that is competent in a given situation depends on the founding purpose of an association. If its original purpose is directed for activity within a diocese, then the competent ecclesiastical authority is the diocesan bishop (c. 312, §1, 3°).

3. The purposes of the ''Vancouver Traditional Mass Society'' as set forth in their constitution filed with the Province of British Columbia include specific references to promoting public worship:

(1) to work towards the organic restoration of the liturgy in conformity with its nature and the tradition of the Church;

(2) to ensure that the Roman Mass codified by St. Pius V is maintained as one of the forms of Eucharistic celebration . . . in the universal liturgical life;

(3) to safeguard and restore the use of Latin . . . in the liturgy of the Roman Catholic Church;

(4) to enable the members of the Society and . . . all the faithful to better understand and more fruitfully participate in the Catholic liturgy as sacred action; . . .

Thus the major purposes for which this society was founded under civil law are specifically reserved to competent ecclesiastical authority for such a society to be erected under canon law. The Christian faithful are not competent under existing canon law to form such associations in the Church, but must request the competent ecclesiastical authority to do so.

4. Moreover, the competent ecclesiastical authority in this situation is the diocesan bishop.

a. The name of the society is specified to a particular locality: it is called ''*Vancouver* Traditional Mass Society'' (emphasis added). Entities should be taken as meaning what they call themselves, unless they make specific exception to this obvious reading.

b. There is nothing in its statement of purpose to indicate the society has a wider geographical intent than its title.

c. The incorporators all live within the territory of the Archdiocese of Vancouver, and its legal address is within the Archdiocese of Vancouver.

There can be no doubt, therefore, that by its name and purpose this Society would be considered diocesan in scope under canon law. In keeping with the 1983 Code of Canon Law, canon 312, it is therefore the diocesan bishop who is competent to erect such a society in canon law, and not some other ecclesiastical authority.

5. What should be the attitude of diocesan authorities toward such an organization?

a. If the archbishop determines the organization is to be promoted in the Church, then he is competent to erect it as an association of the faithful in the Church. In order to do this, he must issue a decree of erection since this kind of association cannot be formed in the Church by the simple initiative of the faithful but requires a definitive act of erection by the competent church authority.

b. If the archbishop determines the organization is not to be erected as an ecclesiastical association, but that it does not represent any danger to the common good of the Church, he may tolerate its existence as a civil law organization. In such circumstances, he needs to attend to the degree of publicity to be given to his toleration.

1) He may chose not to take any public stand in regard to the group. In such a circumstance, he would be judging that its existence poses no threat to the common good, and that taking a public stand may in fact do more harm to the common good than remaining quiet.

2) He may chose to take a public stand, notifying the public that the association is not recognized by the Church. In such a circumstance he would be judging that it is important for the faithful to know the status of the group insofar as the Church is concerned, without making any judgment on its merits or demerits. He may also wish to explain why the group is not recognized in the Church, since the formation of such associations in the Church is reserved to competent church authority and is not the proper object of private initiative.

c. If the archbishop determines the organization not only is not to be erected as an ecclesiastical association, but that it also poses a threat to the common good of the Church, then as the authority responsible for overseeing church discipline (c. 392) he may have an obligation to issue a warning (*monitum*) concerning the

"Vancouver Traditional Mass Society."

Such a warning might contain various elements, depending on the particulars of the situation and the judgment of the archbishop; for example:

1) the Society has not been organized properly according to canon law even though it is recognized in civil law;

2) the Society is not permitted to make use of church facilities, including church halls and other buildings, and no notices of its activities may be contained in any parish or diocesan publications;

3) persons who join the Society are to be advised that the group is not recognized by the Church and that its activities are not promoting the common good of the Church, etc.

d. If events become such that the activities of the Society become disruptive of the ecclesial community, the archbishop is advised under law to try to resolve the problem (cf., c. 1341). If that is not possible, and if the archbishop judges that the activities of the group are stirring up hostilities or disobedience to the Apostolic See (including liturgical decisions) or the local ordinary, he may begin penal proceedings (c. 1373). These begin with admonishment and rebuke (c. 1339), can extend to penance, and even lead to formal imposition of canonical penalties. Again, this last step is to be taken only as a last resort (c. 1341).

James H. Provost [1990]

CANON 216

CATHOLIC IDENTITY FOR A HOSPITAL

A hospital was founded by a community of Catholic sisters from another state about sixty years ago. In 1981 the sisters alienated the hospital to a local non-Catholic, not-for-profit corporation. The "alienation" was a true alienation of dominium *over the property as property, and the sisters did not retain any reserved powers. However, wishing to remain active in this health care ministry, the sisters did enter into an arrangement with the local board whereby the sisters would "sponsor" the hospital. Included in this concept of "sponsorship" were the following obligations accepted by the local board of the hospital:*

1. to operate the hospital in accordance with the teachings of the Catholic Church;

2. to operate the hospital in accordance with the ethical and religious directives of the U.S. bishops;

3. to operate the hospital in accordance with the Franciscan spirit;

4. to provide a strong pastoral care department.

Two years ago this local hospital board became affiliated with a not-for-profit corporation that is the parent corporation for various hospitals. The new holding corporation agreed to allow the hospital to function as agreed with the sisters, i.e., to continue to observe the provisions of the "sponsorship" worked out with the sisters. At the same time, the hospital retained its own governing board of trustees.

The holding corporation now wishes to restructure its hospital system, and to set up a governing board for the region of the state which would take over from the local board of trustees for the hospital, and would be responsible for three hospitals, including two non-Catholic hospitals.

The sisters and the holding corporation have proposed to retain the sponsorship arrangement whereby the hospital will operate according to the NCCB's Ethical and Religious Directives, including specifically the Catholic position on abortion and sterilization; will provide a strong pastoral care department; will have a sponsorship committee controlled by the sisters and including the local bishop or his representative to advise on these matters; etc.

Despite this a question has arisen concerning the "Catholic identity" of the hospital. While it has been considered "Catholic," and even continued to be listed in the Official Catholic Directory *after the sisters alienated the property to the local board, there are now two views. One view is that unless the hospital has a juridic relationship with church authority, it cannot be acknowledged as "Catholic." The other view is that the "sponsorship agreement" between the sisters and the hospital is sufficient to assure its "Catholic" identity.*

OPINION

This issue is a vexing one in many ways, and applies not only to hospitals, but to many other activities that traditionally express the Church's apostolate and witness in the world. As the number of religious who once operated these institutions dwindles, a serious issue arises as to the continued presence of the

Church in these important fields. Yet this is also a very complex issue of canon law, touching as it does on the debate between the positions advocated by Father McGrath[1] and by Bishop Maida.[2] I do not wish to engage in that debate, but rather to provide an interim response to your question pending further research by more competent persons on those fundamental questions.

I believe it is necessary to clarify some underlying concepts that seem to be intermingled in this case: ownership of property, control by a recognized authority of the Church, and recognition as "Catholic." The code does not deal directly with Catholic hospitals. However, it does deal with Catholic schools and here these concepts can be examined — see canon 803, §§1 and 2.

A school is a Catholic school (whatever its name may be — e.g., Hilltop Academy) if external and internal elements are met:

1. *The external element* (c. 803, §1) is in reference to who "runs" the school (*moderator*: "supervises" in the CLSA translation). The school could be run by an ecclesiastical authority (e.g., the bishop). It could be run by a public ecclesiastical juridic person (e.g., the diocese, parish, religious institute). Or it could be run by private individuals, as an apostolate in keeping with canon 216, or by a group of persons, a corporation, or even the state.

In the first two cases, the very fact of who runs (supervises, *moderator*) the school satisfies the external requirement. In the third case, a written document recognizing the school as a Catholic school is needed: "ecclesiastical authority" issues such a document.

2. *The internal element* (c. 803, §2) is that the formation and education in the school are based upon the principles of Catholic doctrine, and that the teachers are outstanding for their correct doctrine and integrity of life.

Application in Practice

It seems to me we can distinguish these factors:

1. To have a Catholic identity, an institution has to act that way (the *internal element*). No matter who owns, supervises or runs the institution, the internal reality is essential. This is as true for a hospital as it is for a school.

2. In addition, supervision of an institution by an entity which can act in the name of the Church, such as a public juridic person, clearly establishes the *external element* for Catholic identity of an institution. Generally, supervision follows from ownership, so a school or hospital that is owned by a diocese or religious institute is presumed to have a Catholic identity.

3. But it is conceivable that the property could be owned by a private person while the institution itself remains under the supervision of a public ecclesiastical juridic person. For example, in places where the Church cannot own property under secular law, some such arrangements have been made. Another example

is where a school building could be owned by the state, but the operation of the school could be under the supervision (*moderator*) of an ecclesiastical authority or public ecclesiastical juridic person.

This is not unknown for hospitals. For example, I know of one situation where the community built a new hospital building, then invited the sisters who had been running the old hospital (the building was now condemned and to be torn down) to manage the new building. While the hospital building was owned by the town, the sisters agreed to run it provided that Catholic ethical norms were observed (in other words, provided the internal element was met). In the case of a school, canon 803, §1 sets the presumption that such an institution has a Catholic identity even though it is not owned by the Church; a similar presumption would seem to hold for hospitals.

4. When ownership is not by an entity that can act in the name of the Church, and the institution is not run by an ecclesiastical authority or a public ecclesiastical juridic person, can it still have a Catholic identity? In the case of schools, it clearly can — provided ecclesiastical authority gives written recognition to this. Similarly, it would seem the same is possible for other institutions, such as hospitals.

The key to obtaining such written recognition, of course, is the assurance that the internal element (operating according to Catholic principles) will indeed be safeguarded. The easiest way to safeguard this is by controlling the property itself, but just as this is not always required when an institution is run (*moderator*) by the bishop, a religious institute or other public ecclesiastical juridic person, so it may not be necessary in this case, either. But here it becomes more difficult for the bishop to assure that the internal element will be assured, and so he will look for specific safeguards in keeping with the situation.

Comment on Other Views

Permit me to comment on the articles and letters you so thoughtfully enclosed. Underlying most of them is the concern that stems from the special situation of Catholic hospitals today — namely the loss of religious personnel who formerly staffed, managed, and exercised full control over the facilities. Short of getting out of the health care field, what alternatives are left?

1. Turn the facility over to someone else to manage, but retain reserved powers that assure the continued Catholic identity internally. This retains Catholic identity through a combination of Catholic ethical norms (internal element) and ownership through the "membership corporation" and reserved powers (external element). This is the position Bishop Myers advocates as the only solution;[3] however, others present further alternatives.

2. Sell the property, so that it is no longer owned by the diocese or a religious institute; but develop some canonical structure that assures a tie to the

Church. Morrisey and Howarth discuss two approaches: create a private juridic person (so the hospital itself has a juridic personality in the Church, albeit a private one);[4] or establish an association of the faithful to run the facility.[5] In either case, the statutes of the juridic person or of the association need to assure that Catholic ethical norms will be observed in the hospital (internal element). But also in either case, some written recognition of the Catholic identity of the hospital is needed (external element). This could be understood to be at least implicit in the written decree establishing the private juridic person (c. 114), or the written statement that the statutes of the association of the faithful have been reviewed by competent authority (c. 299, §3). It may even be stated explicitly in these documents.

3. Morrisey alludes to a third possibility. A group of Catholics operate a hospital that is generally considered by the public to be "Catholic," but in fact has no canonical status. He discusses what the bishop can do if they cease to observe Catholic ethical norms (internal element) — the bishop can declare in writing that the hospital has lost its Catholic identity (external element). Bishop Sheldon has done this in the Akron hospital situation.[6]

Morrisey discusses only what to do when the hospital ceases to observe Catholic ethical norms. Implicitly, however, his article recognizes that the situation could be the reverse — i.e., a hospital that has committed itself to follow Catholic ethical norms (internal element) seeks recognition of its Catholic identity (external element), which can be given by a written recognition from ecclesiastical authority.

Listing in Official Catholic Directory

Could such a hospital as this last case be listed in the *Official Catholic Directory*? There are several purposes for listing an institution in the *Directory*. It provides recognition of the Catholic identity of something — including entities that are not owned or operated by ecclesiastical authority or public ecclesiastical juridic persons. It also serves as the basis for tax exemption under the group ruling obtained each year by the USCC from the Internal Revenue Service.

The position of the USCC legal counsel's office is that hospitals such as the one in this example should not be listed in the *Official Catholic Directory* since it would be controlled by a non-Catholic organization (i.e., the holding corporation). But this position is based on a concern to safeguard the tax exempt ruling (which covers entities "operated, supervised, or controlled by or in connection with the Roman Catholic Church").

This standard has been applied quite broadly in regard to other organizations. The *Directory* includes various entities that are not established as private associations or juridic persons. For example, many of the organizations listed as "Associations" or even as "Corporate Entities Affiliated with USCC" right after the listing for the NCCB and USCC in the *Directory* do not meet the code's requirements for recognized associations of the faithful or juridic persons. In addition to the internal element for their Catholic nature, what constitutes the external element? It could be argued this is implicit by the listing in the *Directory!*

What of hospitals, schools, or other apostolates that fulfill the internal element for Catholic identity — should they be included or excluded from the *Directory*? The concern about the IRS recognition of the *Directory* for establishing tax exempt status is real, but it should not be allowed to be the only purpose for the *Directory*; historically it was not the primary purpose for the *Directory*, as I can tell. If a bishop decides to use this manner of recognizing the Catholic identity of such an entity, he should be able to do so. Arrangements can be made to clarify that these institutions do not seek tax exempt status through the *Directory* listing. This is already done for certain national level organizations (see "Catholic Organizations with Individual IRS Rulings" after the "Associations" mentioned above).

Of course, it is not essential for an institution with Catholic identity to be listed in the *Official Catholic Directory*; to meet the external element for Catholic identity it is sufficient that the bishop recognize this in writing.

Application to this Case

One view on this case, identified earlier, would require some form of juridic relationship with church authority to have a Catholic identity; the other sees the "sponsorship agreement" as adequate.

It should be clear from the above that I do not think the "sponsorship agreement" in itself would be sufficient; there needs to be some external recognition of the Catholic identity. But I do not think this external recognition requires some form of juridic relationship, such as ownership or supervision (*moderator*) or even the less immediate relationship provided by an association of the faithful or a private juridic person. It is sufficient to have the written recognition of an ecclesiastical authority.

In your specific case it seems to me the "sponsorship" arrangement the sisters have made with the hospital and which the holding corporation has agreed to observe may guarantee the internal element of being based upon the principles of Catholic doctrine. It is up to the prudent decision of the bishop whether to issue written recognition, supplying the external element.

It appears that the USCC is reluctant to have such institutions listed for tax exemption purposes in the *Directory*; if the bishop desires to continue to list it for purposes of recognition, he might discuss with the diocesan attorney how to do this in keeping with the current practice within the *Directory* itself as discussed above.

Notes

1. John J. McGrath, *Catholic Institutions in the United States, Canonical and Civil Law Status*, (Washington: Catholic University of America Press, 1968).
2. Adam J. Maida, *Ownership, Control and Sponsorship of Catholic Institutions* (Harrisburg, PA: Pennsylvania Catholic Conference, 1975); Adam J. Maida and Nicholas P. Cafardi, *Church Property, Church Finances, and Church-related Corporations* (St. Louis: Catholic Health Association of the United States, 1984).
3. See John J. Myers, "Church Approval Necessary for Activity to be Truly Catholic," *Health Progress* 68 (October 1987) 70, 74.
4. Francis G. Morrisey, *Health Progress* 67 (September 1986) 44.
5. Joseph Howarth, ibid., 51.
6. See news report, "Lay-run Akron hospital called 'no longer Catholic'" *The Catholic Times* of Columbus, Ohio, November 6, 1987.

James H. Provost [1988]

Canon 226

Right of Parents to Withdraw Children from Sex Education Classes in Catholic Schools or Religious Education Programs

The following facts and arguments are submitted for the purpose of seeking a canonical opinion from the Committee on Advisory Opinions of the Canon Law Society of America.

THE FACTS

The Benziger Family Life Program (hereinafter called "the Program") was published in 1958 and has since been the subject of controversy concerning its doctrinal and pedagogic adequacy. When the Program was introduced in the Archdiocese of Washington, D.C., the archbishop, who at the time was William Cardinal Baum and who had granted it an imprimatur, received so many complaints that he asked the Archdiocesan Committee for Doctrine to determine if the imprimatur should be withdrawn. While the committee did not recommend withdrawal, it did conclude that "the doctrinal content of the Benzinger (sic) Family Life Program is not adequate." The committee also stated that ". . . serious inadequacies exist in these books which render them inappropriate for use in the classrooms of Catholic schools and in CCD programs. These texts are inadequate not because of what they say, but because of what they fail to say."[1]

The Program was introduced three years ago at the school in question, later removed and reintroduced in the spring of 1987. Eight families approached the school principal and asked that their children be excused, and he agreed to do so. However, the superintendent of schools instructed the principal, "Do not release any child from the obligation to attend this officially approved part of the total curriculum of Elementary School if the reason presented by the parents is their personal reservations about the contents of the course or its implementation."

The parents have requested that the superintendent reconsider his position and are now awaiting a reply.

THE LAW

As one would ordinarily expect, the 1983 Code of Canon Law clearly reaffirms the sacramental nature of marriage. Thus it is not surprising that a definition of the duties of parents toward their children is to be found in Book IV, Title VII, canon 1136: "Along with the duty of providing for their children's education, the law also states that parents have a right to do so. This right is grounded in the essence of marriage itself and may not be usurped or curtailed by others, including the state. Only in extreme cases, when parents are incapable of fulfilling their duties to the extent that the good of the children is seriously threatened, is this right forfeited."[2]

The duties and rights of parents are similarly recognized in canon 226: In its struggle with civil authorities who wish to take over schools and to monopolize the educational enterprise, the Church has insisted that parents are the primary educators of their children, and therefore, have the primary right and duty to determine how that education will be carried out. The Council applied this position internally in the Church as well as in the Church-State struggle that occasioned it. Continuing this attention to parents within the Church's own activities, at various stages in the revision process canons have been added until now there is a veritable bill of parental rights and obligations scattered throughout the revised code.

"This canon is the foundation for the rest. Based on Gravissimum Educationis *3, it clearly applies within the Church's own legal system the principle that parents have the primary right and duty to see to the education of their own children. While this obligation and right are not absolute, but must respect the requirements of the common good (in the temporal order and in the Church), they are so fundamental as to lead to further specifications on behalf of parents."[3]*

Parental duties and rights within the context of the Catholic educational system are again noted in Book III, Title III. "The first paragraph (of c. 793) contains two fundamental assertions of parental rights and responsibilities regarding their children: (1) parents have both the obligation and the right to educate their offspring; this is a simple statement of the natural law, and it is derived from the fact that the parents conferred life on their children; . . . (2) Catholic parents have the duty and the right to select the most appropriate means and schools for the Catholic education of their children; the duty (officium) implies both the grave obligation to see to the formation of their children in the Catholic faith in the best way open to them, and the right to make the determination, among the means of schools available, of those which are most suitable for their children. For this duty and right of selection to be meaningful, there must exist some options from which to make choices."[4]

Canon 796 imposes the obligation of mutual collaboration on parents and teachers. It is presumed that the latter would include principals, superintendents and others who exercise authority in Catholic schools. "Both parents and teachers are admonished in the second paragraph to work as partners in the educational process; parents are urged to cooperate with the schoolteachers, and the teachers to collaborate with the parents, listening to them and starting associations for them."[5]

The Code of Canon Law is silent on education in human sexuality, but the subject is dealt with in other documents which have the force of law. The Apostolic Exhortation, Familiaris Consortio, *states quite clearly: "Sex education, which is a basic right and duty of parents, must always be carried out under their attentive guidance, whether at home or in educational centers chosen and controlled by them. In this regard, the Church reaffirms the law of subsidiarity, which the school is bound to observe when it cooperates in sex education, by entering into the same spirit that animates the parents."*[6]

In its Guidelines for Sex Education, Educational Guidance in Human Love, the Sacred Congregation for Catholic Education stated: "The family has an affective dignity which is suited to making acceptable without trauma the most delicate realities and to integrating them harmoniously in a balanced and right personality."[7] *The document thus places additional emphasis on the point: "From what has been said above . . . , the fact remains ever valid that with regard to the more intimate aspects, whether biological or affective, an individual education should be bestowed, preferably within the sphere of the family."*[8] *In recognizing that some parents may face difficulty in instructing their children in matters pertaining to sexuality, the Congregation also suggests, ". . . if parents do not feel able to perform this duty, they may have recourse to others who enjoy their confidence."*[9] *The use of the words "feel" and "may" would seem to clearly imply that the initiative in taking such recourse is the proper prerogative of parents.*

Should a difference of opinion arise between parents and school authorities over specific sex educations programs, the National Conference of Catholic Bishops has declared: "Parents have a right and duty to protest programs which violate their moral and religious convictions. If protests based on well-founded convictions and accurate information are unsuccessful, they have a right to remove their children from the classes, taking care to cause as little embarrassment to the children as possible."[10] This same principle was included in the charter of the Rights of the Family, issued by the Holy See. "Parents have the right to insure that their children are not compelled to attend classes which are not in agreement with their own moral and religious convictions. In particular, sex education is a basic right of the parents and must always be carried out under their close supervision, whether at home or in educational centers chosen and controlled by them."[11]

THE ARGUMENT

We feel compelled to state that the focus of our argument is not over the merits of the Benziger Family Life Program or whether it should be a part of the curriculum at school. Although we do agree with the conclusion of the Committee for Doctrine of the Archdiocese of Washington that the program is indeed unsuitable, the issue here is the exercise of our parental right to withdraw our children from a particular course, for what we believe are serious reasons, without having to remove them from school.

We would argue that the law is clearly in support of our position that parents have a duty and right to make important decisions with respect to the moral formation of their children, especially when sex education is involved. As the situation now is at school, concerned parents can only acquiesce to their children's participation in a program they believe is serious flawed or remove them from the school. If they choose the latter, the only alternatives are to place their children in public schools, enroll them in a Catholic school some thirty five miles distant, or attempt to educate them at home. In the face of such choices, parental rights become meaningless.

THE QUESTION

Are the parents correct in asserting a canonical right to withdraw their children from the sex education program in question without being required to withdraw them from the school?

Notes

35

[1] Archdiocese of Washington, D.C., Committee on Doctrine.

[2] Rev. Thomas P. Doyle, O.P., J.C.D., *The Code of Canon Law: A Text and Commentary*, Edited by James A. Coriden, Thomas J. Green and Donald E. Heintschel (New York/Mahwah: Paulist Press, 1985) 1136.

[3] Rev. James H. Provost, J.C.D., ibid., 162.

[4] Rev. James A. Coriden, S.T.L., J.C.D., J.D., ibid, 564.

[5] Ibid., 566.

[6] *Familiaris Consortio*, No. 37, St. Paul Edition, Boston, 1981, 61.

[7] *Educational Guidance in Human Love*, No. 48, St. Paul Edition, 1983, 19.

[8] Ibid., 22.

[9] Ibid., 22.

[10] *Sharing the Light of Faith*, National Catechetical Directory for Catholics of the United States, United States Catholic Conference, Washington, D.C., 1979, 115.

[11] *Charter of the Rights of the Family*, Article 5d, St. Paul Edition, Boston, 1983, 55.

OPINION

The above brief is well argued; it draws upon good authorities, and it has real merit. But it is not a convincing *canonical* argument. The canons do strongly assert the rights and responsibilities of parents for the nurture and education of their children, but they do not specify those rights and responsibilities to the extent or in the detail that the priest is trying to apply them. One will search in vain for *canonical* authority for actions so specific.

Permit me to comment briefly on the sources cited in this brief. The Committee on Doctrine of the Archdiocese of Washington has no special authority or standing. It is a group of people whom the Archbishop asked to advise him. The group was probably no more distinguished than the consultors used by the Benziger company on its *Family Life Program*.

The brief has cited some of the commentators (including me) on the Code of Canon Law (on cc. 1136, 226, 793, and 796). The commentators try to furnish explanations of the church's laws, but their opinions do not have the force of law nor any other special authority. Their comments do serve to highlight the code's attention to parental rights and responsibilities, but they do not suggest that parents have a right to pick and choose among the curricular offerings of a school.

The other four invoked in support of the argument for the right to withdraw do *not* have the force of law (as asserted in the brief). They are teaching documents with varying levels of *doctrinal* (as over against disciplinary or legal) authority. In my opinion one cannot deduce from those sources a strictly enforceable canonical right. However, the documents are authoritative and they are to the point. Indeed the National Catechetical Directory, *Sharing The Light of Faith*, is quite explicit (in number 191) on the issue under discussion here.

Even though I do not agree that parents are correct in asserting a canonical right to withdraw their children from the sex education program in question, I would conclude that parents have a strong and legitimate interest in this matter, an interest and a concern that should be attended to. There may be other remedies besides withdrawing their children from the program. Perhaps the program can be altered or supplemented so as to make its contents acceptable to the parents.

James A. Coriden [1988]

See also opinion under canon 890.

CANON 230

CONDITIONS FOR SERVING AS LECTOR

Our bishop has issued a directive interpreting this canon to say that lay men can be invested with the ministry of lector, and other lay persons can fulfill the office of lector by means of a temporary deputation when two conditions are both satisfied: (a) the necessity of the Church warrants it and (b) other ministers are lacking. But since at Mass there is always a minister present (e.g., the presiding priest), does the canon really exclude other lay persons from serving as lector?

OPINION

My interpretation of the canon is this. Section 1 refers specifically to lay men being installed after the age of eighteen (the age set by the NCCB for this country) and which puts them in a more supervisory role than the person who would serve as lector at Mass occasionally.

Section 2 deals with lay persons fulfilling the function of lector during liturgical actions, or reading the Scriptures as appropriate, according to the *Lectionary*. Their temporary deputation does not depend upon the availability or non-availability of installed lectors, but upon the qualifications which the *Lectionary* requires for people to be able to read.

Section 3 deals with other kinds of ministries and permits lay persons to be specially deputed when sacred ministers are lacking. Since the activities with which section 3 deals go beyond those normally permitted to lectors and acolytes (for example, to confer baptism), the canon in its present wording clearly does not require preference to be given lectors or acolytes. Rather, preference is to be given to those lay persons who are competent to do the activities concerned.

Earlier versions of this canon did specify that lectors and acolytes were to be preferred to other lay persons. This was changed before the pope promulgated the code. Since the activities involved are not those specific to lectors or acolytes, no special preference is given to them in section 3.

The difficulty seems to lie with section 2 and the restriction placed by your bishop on who can serve as lector. As I understand it, your bishop is stating that lay persons can fulfill the office of lector by means of a temporary deputation only when two conditions are verified: the necessity of the Church warrants it, and other "ministers" are lacking. This seems to go beyond what is required by canon 230, §2. Moreover, it would seem to be more restrictive than what is intended (and even stated) in the introduction to the *Lectionary*. The code, in canon 899, §2, calls for all who are present — whether clergy or laity — to participate actively in keeping with their own order and the diversity of liturgical functions. On the other hand, canon 838, §4 says that it pertains to the diocesan bishop within the church committed to his care and within the limits of his competence, to give norms concerning the liturgical matters by which all are bound.

So, it seems to me that what the bishop is doing is making a specific determination on his own authority in virtue of his role of establishing norms by which all are bound in the diocese. He is not giving an interpretation of canon 230, but rather a norm that applies the canon in the life of your particular diocese. Whether the norm is in keeping with the intention or even the words of the *Lectionary* is another question. It is certainly not merely an interpretation of canon 230 because section 2 of this canon does not place the same restrictions as he has placed on the role of lay persons fulfilling the function of lector. Essentially he has taken the conditions of section 3 and applied them to section 2; the law does not make that same application.

James H. Provost [1984]

CANON 230

A. NON-FUNCTIONING OF EXTRAORDINARY EUCHARISTIC MINISTERS WHEN CLERGY ARE PRESENT

A recent letter from the Cardinal Prefect of the Congregation of Sacraments to all Papal Representatives, subsequently communicated to the NCCB on September 21, 1987, advises: "After receiving numerous indications of such abuses, the Congregation decided to seek an authentic interpretation of the appropriate canons from the Pontifical Commission for the Authentic Interpreta-

tion of the Code of Canon Law . . . The reply of the Pontifical Commission indicates that, when ordinary ministers (Bishop, Priest, Deacon) are present at the Eucharist, whether they are celebrating or not, and are in sufficient number and are not prevented from doing so by other ministries, the extraordinary ministers of the Eucharist are not allowed to distribute Communion either to themselves or to the faithful."

The following cases have been submitted for canonical opinion in light of canon 230, §3, and the above mentioned Interpretation. "We have Sunday evening Masses which we try to plan and conduct seriously and in good order. For this reason we have lectors, song leaders and eucharistic ministers assigned. From time to time various permanent deacons will show up a few minutes before Mass with their families and expect to attend Mass just as any other Catholic would. If the priest doesn't see them walking in the door, he doesn't even know they are there. I presume that these men are not to be called out of the congregation to distribute Communion in the place of those who are already assigned. What is your opinion?"

Another case concerns planning celebrations or jubilees and anniversaries for parishes and religious. Many times these take place on Sunday afternoons when it is convenient for large numbers of the laity to attend. The clergy are always invited; however, it is never known how many will show up until just before the ceremony. In order to have a tasteful liturgy it is necessary to plan and assign roles. Are the assignments to extraordinary lay ministers done on a pro-tem or tentative basis, or may we go ahead and assign these without taking into account the possibility that there may be some or several concelebrants and deacons there?

OPINION

Your inquiry basically is examining the possibility of presumed exceptions to the norms of canon 230 and the recent interpretation promulgated by the Congregation of the Sacraments. The basic law states that when the necessity of the Church warrants it and when ministers are lacking, lay persons can supply even to distribute Holy Communion. The reported authentic interpretation explains that ordinary ministers are not to be considered lacking when they are present, even if not celebrating. The two cases that have been described are similar. The first concerns parish Masses in which there is the *possibility* of permanent deacons being present in the congregation unannounced. The second case concerns special celebrations in which there is the probability that invited clergy will attend and concelebrate. In both cases there is no accurate or certain knowledge, however, that either the permanent deacons or the invited clergy will actually be present. In the meantime, those planning the liturgy have assigned extraordinary ministers to be present in order to assist in the distribution of Communion. Such careful planning of participation would seem to be a fulfillment of canon 837: "Liturgical actions, to the extent that by their proper nature they involve a common celebration, are to be celebrated where possible with the presence and active participation of the Christian faithful."

My opinion is that lay eucharistic ministers should be assigned to liturgies with the understanding that their functioning is *extraordinary*. The notion of extraordinary is defined in canon 230 by the requirement that their ministry be limited only to circumstances both of necessity to the Church and lack of ordinary ministers. The functioning of the extraordinary eucharistic ministers is conditioned by the norm of law. The mere fact that someone has been assigned to a specifically scheduled Mass does not remove this condition from the definition of extraordinary minister and the norms for the exercise of the ministry.

On the other hand, it does seem to me that there could be a situation in which it is really not known until the beginning of the liturgy who may be present in the congregation. It would seem that this situation would be particularly true of the first case in this inquiry, involving a parish with permanent deacons, who may attend unannounced and unknown to the pastor or celebrant. If an extraordinary eucharistic minister has been assigned, and it really is not known to the pastor if any of the permanent deacons will be present, and if the permanent deacon arrives at church unannounced even by the time Mass begins, it seems there would be no obligation to confuse the order of worship by trying, during the Mass, to communicate to the extraordinary ministers that their conditional restriction to functioning is now being invoked, and the deacon called forward if he is present. It is possible, however, if this situation occurs regularly, that the pastor should establish some kind of program with the permanent deacons in the parish, requesting that they notify the parish ahead of time, if possible, or arrive earlier and make themselves known, or allow themselves to be scheduled, since the diaconate is a public ministry of the Church to be exercised when needed. The fact that they are seated with their families does not remove the constitutive public nature of their ministry.

In the case of the jubilee or special celebration described in the inquiry, where there are many clergy invited to concelebrate, and where there would probably be a presumption that several will attend, and where the attending and concelebrating clergy would need to have arrived early to vest, then it seems there would be sufficient time conveniently to communicate with the assigned extraordinary ministers that they will not be needed for the distribution of Communion since there are clergy present. The condition for their exercise of the function is not fulfilled.

This opinion is based on the notion that this function is defined as extraordinary by the norms of law. The interpretation, no doubt, is not a popular one, because extraordinary ministers of the Eucharist are very honored to be named to this task. They look forward to functioning. Furthermore, the functioning of various clergy and laity in the liturgy promotes the active participation of all persons in the celebration, as encouraged by canon 837, §1. It is pastorally and personally difficult to restrict ministers from doing what they very much wish to contribute to the Liturgy, especially if they have arranged their personal and family schedules to conform with the assignment given them. Nevertheless active participation by laity and clergy in the Liturgy "is carried out in the name of the Church by persons lawfully deputed and through acts approved by the authority of the Church (c. 834, §2)." Since the Church defines extraordinary ministers of the Eucharist by conditioning their functioning on the lack of clergy present, then the persons chosen for the ministry must be willing to accept this condition, which appears to be constitutive of the ministry according to the wording of the code of the Commission's interpretation. I do not believe that the code or the interpretation as written intend any exception to the definition of extraordinary ministry of the Eucharist.

Perhaps, however, there is room for some interpretation with regard to the question of "lacking" clergy and "presence" of clergy in a concrete, pastoral situation. As explained above, if it is probable and indeed anticipated that clergy will be present, there seems to be no reason not to advise the extraordinary ministers, when they are assigned, that they may not be called forward at the actual time of Communion. In the situation where the presence of clergy is truly an unknown factor up to the time of Mass, it does not seem that the law demands the impossible, namely a confusing or unsightly attempt to communicate with assigned extraordinary ministers after the Mass begins, when suddenly an unannounced cleric is spotted in the congregation. If the presence of the non-celebrating or merely attending clergy is truly unknown and is unable to be arranged or confirmed by the time the entrance procession is forming, then we are probably dealing with what could be called a "juridical non-presence" of clergy in the concrete situation.

J. James Cuneo [1988]

B. Authentic or Private Interpretation

See opinion under canon 16.

RECEPTION OF THE EUCHARIST THROUGH A NASO-GASTRIC TUBE

A patient in the hospital is unable to swallow food by mouth, so a naso-gastric (NG) tube was installed. Whatever is fed to the person must be dissolved sufficiently to go down the tube. Moreover, the hospital objects to Eucharistic ministers inserting anything in the tube, requiring instead that nursing staff perform this function.

The patient has a deep Eucharistic devotion and sincerely desires to receive Communion, and indeed in such a physical condition has special need of this spiritual help. On the other hand, the chaplain of the hospital has problems with how to administer the Eucharist in this situation.

OPINION

From a canon law point of view, there are several factors in this situation.

First, it is possible for a person to receive the Eucharist under either species of the Body and Blood of Christ. So in theory it would be possible for the person to receive under the form of the Precious Blood only. There can easily be medical problems, however, with people in this condition taking alcohol. If so, the practice of the Apostolic See has been to refuse permission for lay persons to receive the Eucharist using only *mustum* (see *Roman Replies and CLSA Advisory Opinions 1987*, 23). This refusal applies even to cases similar to this one, where health concerns have raised the question. I suspect that receiving the Eucharist under the form of the Precious Blood only is an unlikely solution to this situation.

While the host must be dissolved somewhat in order to be ingested through the NG tube, if there is still some appearance of bread the presumption is the sacramental Presence continues. It would seem that if this is done with proper precautions, it should be possible for the patient to continue to receive the Eucharist under the species of the Body of Christ.

A second issue concerns the minister of Communion in this situation. This would seem to be one of those occasions where necessity warrants the use of lay persons as the minister of Holy Communion (cc. 230, §3; 910). Arrangements should be made for a Catholic nurse to serve in this capacity for this individual.

A third issue brought up by the chaplain, but which is not a canonical issue, concerns the sacramental symbolism of receiving the Eucharist through a tube. It should be noted that one of the ways for receiving the Precious Blood is through a gold straw, and indeed for many years this was a common practice for the pope at certain Masses in Rome. So receiving the Eucharist through a tube is not foreign to Catholic tradition. Moreover, for this patient the only way of participating in a meal is through the NG tube. The symbolism of the Eucharistic meal would not necessarily be lost on this patient, assuming appropriate pastoral counselling is provided.

James H. Provost [1991]

CANON 231

SALARY GUIDELINES FOR DRES

What norms should be considered in drafting our diocesan salary guidelines for parishes that employ lay persons as directors or coordinators of religious education?

OPINION

Persons who are in ministry are covered by canon 231. They are to obtain an appropriate formation and to fulfill their service in a proper spirit. This would also seem to imply a right on their part to whatever is needed to obtain such a formation, including admission to appropriate formation programs, and a right to support in their ministry (moral support as well as financial support).

Those who are employed as wage earners by the Church are entitled to all the protection and benefits the civil law assures for workers (c. 1286), even if the Church in this country is exempted from some of those civil laws in virtue of our separation of Church and state. This is because those civil laws establish at least the standard of a "good householder" and can be enforced in the Church (c. 1284).

This applies in a special way to persons who are under contract. Even if separation of Church and state exempts the Church in some instances from civil enforcement of contracts (such as ministerial contracts), they may be enforceable within canon law on the same basis as they would have been considered in civil law (c. 1290).

The canons clearly apply to all types — ministers and wage earners — the Church's own social teaching on a just family wage. This is not a question of an optional ideal, but is stated quite clearly as a canonical minimum that must be provided. It applies not only to bishops and pastors, but to all administrators of church goods. It would not necessarily apply to certain institutions that are not church institutions (e.g., private institutions run by Catholics), but were they

43

to fail to observe this standard it would be cause for the bishop to withdraw their right to use the name "Catholic" in regard to the institution. Use of the "Catholic" name is restricted by the new code, and requires the permission of competent authority.

James H. Provost [1984, revised 1993]

CANON 241, §1

SEMINARY'S RESPONSIBILITIES WHEN TESTING FOR HIV/AIDS IS POSITIVE

A diocese has decided to make testing for HIV/AIDS a mandatory part of the application process for entrance into priesthood studies. What obligations does the diocese have to the applicant in the case where the test results are positive?

OPINION

Because the AIDS epidemic is a new crisis facing the Church, few precedents have been established regarding HIV testing of candidates for seminary and religious life. At present, approximately sixty-five dioceses of the United States require HIV testing for seminary applicants and seventy-three do not; twelve dioceses are in the process of establishing policy. Among the dioceses with no mandatory testing, some have not perceived a need to establish a policy; others have grappled with the question and have chosen not to make HIV testing a part of seminary admission requirements.

Dioceses that mandate HIV testing for seminary admission may or may not have procedures in place in the event that a candidate tests positive for HIV. Justice requires that there be a well thought out and consistent method for dealing with such information and the persons involved.

The first obligation a diocese has to an applicant is to review all test results fairly in light of vocational demands. Canon 241 lists the criteria by which the diocesan bishop should judge candidates for admission to the major seminary. Among the considerations are the candidate's human, moral, spiritual, and intellectual characteristics, as well as his physical and psychological health. Traditionally understood, health is not the absence of disease. If it were so, then dioceses would consider as unfit those candidates with controlled chronic conditions like diabetes and heart disease.

The dilemma that faces bishops, vocation directors, and formation personnel is the fact that many individuals infected with HIV are not physically impaired and meet the established health requirements for admission. Even though statistics are not conclusive about the latency period of the disease, some fear that HIV infected candidates will be unable to fulfill the duties of ministry and will eventually pose a significant financial strain on diocesan medical insurance programs. Therefore, in the evaluation of an HIV infected candidate, it is recommended that a diocese be assisted in its review of the individual's medical records by an expert in AIDS research and/or treatment. Because of rapidly changing developments in AIDS research and treatment, it would be presumptuous for a diocese to make a final determination about a candidate's health without expert advice.

Given the developments in civil legislation, which forbid discrimination in matters of housing, employment, and education, it would seem imprudent for a diocesan bishop to reject a candidate solely on the basis of his HIV seropositivity. Rather, a candidate's overall physical health should be evaluated along with the other requirements mentioned in the law.

At present, it would seem reasonable that dioceses not accept candidates manifesting symptoms of serious illness related to HIV infection. However, there seem to be no justifiable grounds for denying admission solely on the basis of a candidate's HIV status. If a candidate manifests good health, shows no signs of serious immunodeficiency, and is physically capable of assuming the rigors of seminary training and, eventually, the duties and obligations of ministry, then he should be admitted.

In discerning the suitability of an HIV seropositive candidate, the manner of exposure should not prejudice the choice to be made. Sexual transmission of HIV infection should not be concluded when seropositivity is evidenced. Many presume that seropositive candidates were infected through homosexual contact. It should not be forgotten, however, that other means of transmission include blood transfusion and intravenous drug use. And, given the changing trends of the disease, individuals are more and more likely to be infected with HIV through heterosexual contact.

The right to privacy demands that a candidate not be forced to divulge prior sexual history because of his HIV status. In addition to being inaccurate, it would be a violation of the right to privacy to employ HIV testing as a means of determining a person's sexual orientation. It is far more appropriate to use psychological testing to evaluate a candidate's psycho-sexual maturity.

In essence, one's history, sexual or otherwise, should not be the basis for determining whether to reject or accept an HIV infected candidate. For example, to accept a candidate infected through a blood transfusion and to reject another because he was infected by a previous sexual encounter would be unjust. Again, one's overall capacity for ministry should be the criterion used in making

45

a final decision.

Whether or not it accepts a candidate, a diocese also has an obligation to insure that several requirements are met when HIV testing is employed. Among these are informed consent and the conditions attached to it.

Informed consent to HIV testing means an agreement, without inducement, to undergo suggested tests for the presence of the HIV antibody following receipt of a fair explanation of the test, which includes: its purpose; potential use; limitations; the meaning of test results, including the possibility of false-positive and false-negative results; the procedures to be followed, including the voluntary nature of the test; the right to withdraw consent at any time during the testing process; the right to anonymity to the extent provided by law with respect to participation in the test and disclosure of test results; and the right to confidential treatment of information identifying the subject of the test and the results of the test to the extent provided by law.

Canon 220, flowing from the natural law, provides the canonical basis for a diocese's obligation in this regard. A candidate would have to be aware of and give written consent to HIV testing before submitting to it as a requirement for seminary admission. For a bishop or vocation director to order such tests without the individual's knowledge is a direct violation of one's right to privacy.

Secondly, a candidate should know who will have access to the test results and how these results will be used. This is particularly important if a candidate is subsequently rejected by a diocese. The release of such information to future employers or insurance companies could place a candidate in jeopardy and could conceivably be used for discriminatory purposes. Unfortunately, in our present social climate, HIV seropositivity has negative effects on a person's reputation.

Thirdly, a candidate has the right to refuse certain tests, even if this jeopardizes admission into the seminary or reception of orders. In other words, no individual can be forced to undergo a test; an individual must freely consent to all test procedures. These conditions for testing not only protect the individual's right to privacy and to a good reputation, but they also safeguard the Church against liability claims from a person charging violations of these rights.

If a diocese accepts a seropositive candidate into its formation program, it would be obliged to monitor the candidate's health and to assess on a regular basis the individual's overall capacity for priestly ministry. In addition, it should also provide counselling to the individual to assist him, if necessary, in dealing with his HIV status. It would be expected that the candidate himself would take an active role in this evaluation, and communicate honestly with formation personnel about any specific changes in his health status. The candidate would be responsible for medical insurance and pharmaceutical expenses until ordination to the diaconate, at which time the diocese would assist

46

with these financial obligations.

If a candidate is rejected by the diocese after he has tested positive for HIV, it would be expected that the diocese would assume the financial responsibility for providing any necessary post-test counselling needed by the individual. One can imagine the deep disappointment an individual might experience in being rejected by a diocese under such circumstances. If the candidate were previously unaware of his HIV status, he would have to deal not only with the pain of being rejected for priestly ministry in the Church, but also the trauma of knowing that he is HIV infected. Justice demands that these individuals be treated with compassion and understanding.

From a canonical perspective, the issue of HIV testing is an issue about rights — the right of a diocese to know about its candidates, the right of the Christian community to healthy candidates who are capable of living the demands of a vocation, and the right of a candidate to privacy, to a good reputation, to a fair judgment, and to know what is expected of him as part of admission procedures. In an effort to be sensitive to all of these rights, bishops, in collaboration with their vocation boards, must proceed cautiously in concert with canon and civil lawyers, as well as medical experts.

Jack D. Anderson [1992]

CANONS 241, §1; 1029; AND 1051, 1°

ADMISSION TO THE SEMINARY AND HIV TESTING

A diocese has established a policy determining that candidates seeking admission to the seminary must be tested for the human immunodeficiency virus (HIV). What are the canonical implications of such a policy?

OPINION

Canons 1029 and 1051, 1°, state that the proper bishop, competent major superior and seminary rector have the responsibility of assessing the physical and psychological suitability of candidates to the diaconate and the priesthood. Among the sources for these canons is the Second Vatican Council's *Decree on Priestly Formation*, which called for careful inquiry concerning the intention, freedom of choice, spiritual, moral and intellectual fitness, and the physical and mental suitability of a seminarian.[1] To make this assessment, dioceses and seminaries have required standard medical examinations and psychological testing as part of their admissions procedures. To require of applicants to a seminary testing for the human immunodeficiency virus (HIV) would appear to be a reasonable and prudent exercise of this responsibility to assess physical suitability. However, there are issues unique to HIV infection and the AIDS epidemic that warrant a consideration of the prudence and the justice of mandating HIV testing for admission to the seminary.

First of all, according to canon 220, "no one is permitted . . . to violate the right of another person to protect his or her own privacy." Absent jurisprudence on this canon, the code "appears to extend the right to privacy to cover many personal issues."[2] This right to protect against intrusion into one's privacy extends to limiting or restricting access to information about oneself, especially if the disclosure of information would harm or place a person at a disadvantage. In canon law, the exercise of this right is not absolute, but must be balanced with the common good of the Church and the rights and duties of others (c. 223, §1). Mandatory medical examinations and psychological testing in themselves are invasive of privacy and as such qualify the exercise of the right to privacy. Canon law allows for this restriction for the countervailing responsibility to assess suitability for orders so as to provide proper service to the Church. In applying to a seminary, an applicant voluntarily agrees to undergo a battery of tests with at least the presumed understanding that admission is neither a right nor an obligation. For this reason, mandatory testing does not necessarily violate a person's right to protect his privacy. However, in keeping with canon 220 and canon 642, the applicant still has a right to protect his privacy from any adverse effects resulting from testing. At the minimum, the applicant has the right to expect that the records of his testing will be kept confidential. Since "to protect one's privacy" presumes a person's initiative, it is reasonable to claim that the applicant also has the right to assess the guarantee of this confidentiality. Before consenting to testing, the applicant can seek information on who will have access to test results, how long they will be used in the admissions process, if and how long they will be kept in the seminary's files, if they will be used in future evaluations for orders, and their possible but unintended distribution (e.g., are they subject to subpoena?).

The issue of confidentiality and the right to assess its guarantee are particularly crucial to HIV testing. Knowledge of a person's HIV infection could seriously jeopardize one's employment, ability to obtain insurance, and relationships with family and friends. It also exposes a person to discrimination. The 1988 Presidential Commission on AIDS stated that "aside from the illness itself, it is discrimination that is most feared by the HIV infected."[3]

Since information about a person's HIV status could be potentially gravely damaging, the diocese and the seminary assume a particularly serious obligation to protect the confidentiality of HIV test results. The problem arises in regard to how many persons have access to the results of admissions tests.[4] Do the

48

seminary admissions committee (or the entire faculty), the rector, the diocesan vocation director (or vocations team), and the diocesan bishop all have access to this information? The fewer the number of persons authorized to receive this information the greater is the guarantee of confidentiality.

The problem of confidentiality extends beyond the seminary and the diocese. Once HIV test results become part of a person's medical records, this information is subject to routine distribution through the various "confidential" records of the health care system, insurance companies and even one's employer, if the employer is self-insured. In some states, HIV positive test results must be reported to the state health department.[5] The seminary or the diocese does not have any control over how or to whom this information is disseminated. However, requiring HIV testing for admissions potentially sets in motion this distribution of information.

Second, in assessing the reasonable protection of his privacy, an applicant to the seminary not only has the right to know the limitations of the seminary's guarantee of confidentiality, but also the right to know the purpose of the testing and its consequences.

Since HIV infected persons have often been stigmatized, a mandatory HIV testing policy must honestly and clearly state its purpose. Unless seropositive test results will be used as only one factor in assessing general physical suitability, a policy should state that an applicant will be excluded from admission if he is tested positive. The reasons for this exclusion should be given and based on current medical information. The policy should also state that test results will not be used as an index of moral character or capacity for celibacy. Testing for purposes other than determining physical health only confirms fears surrounding any mandatory testing, e.g., loss of good reputation, suspicion of immorality, discrimination. Clarity of purpose is needed because the purpose of mandatory HIV testing for admissions is exclusionary screening. This purpose does not share the goals of legislated mandatory testing, viz., curtailment of the spread of HIV, modification of unsafe behavior, or encouragement of individuals to seek advance treatment for HIV. Although positive HIV test results may encourage an applicant to seek treatment, this is not the primary purpose of testing for admissions. The purpose is screening to exclude and, for this reason, touches on the sensitive issue of discrimination.

Third, an applicant should be informed of the psychological consequences of testing seropositive. Given the fact that an HIV infected person will probably develop AIDS and die within a few years, the impact of testing seropositive can be psychologically devastating. A positive test result can enable an individual to seek available treatment and plan for the future. These advantages, however, do not mitigate the trauma of confronting probable death preceded by various opportunistic diseases and the loss of job and relationships. For an applicant to the seminary, rejection based on a positive test result can only compound this trauma.

Related to the impact of testing seropositive is the question of what obligation the seminary or diocese assumes in mandating HIV testing for admission. Is the seminary or diocese obligated to provide the applicant counseling or some system of support, especially since the applicant was required to be tested and otherwise may not have sought testing? The exclusionary purpose of mandatory HIV testing, the psychological devastation of testing HIV positive, and the potential stigmatization associated with HIV infection are compelling reasons to conclude that the seminary or the diocese is obligated in justice to provide some counseling.

In conclusion, this opinion has identified the canonical issues associated with the right to privacy in discussing the implications of mandatory HIV testing for seminary admission. Mandatory HIV testing opens a wide window of vulnerability — psychological, social, economic — for an individual against which the seminary and diocese can guarantee only limited protection. In this opinion, the need for a seminary to screen out HIV infected persons is not compelling enough to outweigh the established right of a person to protection against potentially damaging intrusion of privacy.

Notes

[1] *Optatam totius* 6.

[2] Francis G. Morrisey, O.M.I., "Issue of Confidentiality in Religious Life," *Bulletin of Religious Law* 4 (1988) 3. The author states that the 1917 code was more focused on the right to privacy in correspondence. Given that among the sources to canon 220 are *Pacem in terris* and *Gaudium et spes*, the issues under the umbrella of privacy can be extensive.

[3] *Report of the Presidential Commission on the Human Immunodeficiency Virus Epidemic* (Washington: U.S. Government Printing Office, 1988) 126.

[4] Morrisey, 5.

[5] For discussion of this topic, see Martin Gunderson, David J. Mayo and Frank S. Rhame, *AIDS: Testing and Privacy* (Salt Lake City: University of Utah Press, 1989) 43-46; 113-120. According to these authors, the states that require reporting are Alabama, Arizona, Colorado, Idaho, Minnesota, Montana, South Carolina, and Wisconsin.

Randolph R. Calvo [1991]

ANOTHER OPINION

The health of candidates seeking admission to the seminary is a legitimate concern. The diocesan bishop is directed by canon law to judge whether the candidates are "capable of dedicating themselves permanently to the sacred ministries in light of their . . . physical and psychological health" (c. 241, §1).

(Note that c. 1051, 1° requires the seminary rector, prior to the candidates' ordination and after a "duly executed inquiry," to furnish to the bishop a testimonial concerning the state of the candidates' physical health. See also c. 1029.)

In practice, the physical health situation of a prospective diocesan seminarian is usually ascertained through a medical questionnaire completed by the candidate and a physical examination administered by a physician, who fills out a form provided by the diocese. Upon receipt of these completed forms, the vocation director transmits a copy to the seminary rector.

In drafting its health forms, the diocese must strike the proper balance between its right to all pertinent medical information about the candidate and the candidate's rights to good reputation and privacy (cc. 220 and 642).

In recent years seminary and vocation personnel have grappled with the question of whether human immunodeficiency virus (HIV) testing should be included as part of a seminary candidate's physical examination. The U.S. bishops have suggested, somewhat tentatively, "It may be appropriate for seminaries and religious communities to screen for the HIV antibody" ("Called to Compassion and Responsibility: A Response to the HIV/AIDS Crisis," *Origins* 19, n. 45 (1989) 430). Some dioceses, religious communities and seminaries have explicit policies regarding HIV testing of candidates. These policies vary widely. Some, like the one in question here specify HIV testing of all applicants. Others exclude such testing. A third approach is to decide whether to require testing on a case by case basis, taking into account the personal history of the candidate.

The question posed does not indicate whether the diocesan policy under discussion specifies how the diocese should respond to a positive HIV finding. Some admissions policies explicitly provide that an HIV-positive result renders the seminary candidate ineligible for admission. The U.S. bishops stress that a positive HIV finding should not mean automatic exclusion of a seminary candidate. Rather, the finding should be a factor carefully considered in discerning the candidate's present health situation, future health prospects, and overall capacity to carry out ministerial responsibilities (ibid.).

Opponents of strict HIV testing policies in the seminary admissions context have emphasized the alleged unreliability of the testing procedures and the undependability of projections of future health prospects for those who test positive. Those who favor testing stress the need for careful stewardship of financial and personnel resources and the possibly tremendous financial and emotional burden that a diocese, religious community, or seminary is unknowingly assuming if there is no required testing. Different concepts of vocation and ministry, concerns about homosexuality, worries about potential liability in the event others are infected by the applicant, and anxiety about charges of

51

discrimination affect the discussion as well.

The diocesan requirement in question here is a legitimate one. The bishop, charged with obligations regarding seminary admissions and promotion to orders, can decide to require testing for this admittedly serious disease. The diocesan policy, however, should insure that the results of any testing are kept confidential and are shared only with those charged with ultimate responsibility for seminary admissions and then only with the explicit written consent of the candidate.

Because of the alleged uncertainty that surrounds HIV testing, the possibilities of medical advances, and the uniqueness of each person's medical situation, the policy should not provide for automatic exclusion of those who test HIV-positive. If there is a positive finding, the final decision regarding the particular candidate's admission should not be made without consultation with a physician expert in this field and, if feasible, with the candidate's primary-care physician, and only after taking into account all components of the candidate's application.

The diocesan policy should make provision for pre-test counseling and, obviously for those who test positive, post-test counseling. As in all cases, the vocation personnel should be prepared to suggest vocational alternatives, if appropriate, to those who are not accepted into the seminary.

(See, generally, National Religious Vocation Conference and National Conference of Diocesan Vocation Directors, *Information Packet on HIV Testing* [Chicago, undated]; Secretariat, Bishops' Committee on Vocations and Bishops' Committee on Priestly Formation, *Handbook for Vocation and Seminary Personnel* [Washington: USCC, 1987]; Bishops' Committee on Vocations, *A Reflection on the Relationship between Seminary and Vocation Personnel* [Washington: USCC, 1988] 31-32.)

Robert C. Gibbons [1991]

CANONS 265; 384; AND 122

OBLIGATION OF THE ORIGINAL DIOCESE TO PRIESTS INCARDINATED IN A NEWLY FORMED DIOCESE

What is the obligation of a diocese with regard to past ministry of a priest who was formerly incardinated in that diocese, but is now incardinated in a newly created diocese formed from a portion of the original diocese?

OPINION

52

Two areas of canon law touch on this question: the incardination of clergy and the division of dioceses.

1. Incardination is the bond in canon law that attaches a cleric to a diocese or other church entity capable of incardinating (c. 265). Incardination determines the exercise of basic canonical obligations and rights of clergy. For example, canon 283, §1 states that a cleric is not to be absent from his diocese (of incardination) for a notable period of time without at least the presumed permission of his bishop. Canon 384 affirms the responsibility of the bishop to see that in his diocese priests "correctly fulfill the obligations proper to their state" and is to "make provision" for the decent support and social assistance of the priests of his diocese.

Obligations regarding the ministry of a priest will therefore be related at least to his diocese of incardination, even though other church entities may also be involved (for example, a parish, school, or even another diocese where he may be serving on loan).

2. When a new diocese is created out of an existing diocese or dioceses, it is a new "public juridic person" in the Church formed out of what had been part of an existing "public juridic person." Canon 122 states that in such cases:

> it is the obligation of the ecclesiastical authority which is competent to make the division, having observed before all else the intention of the founders and donors, acquired rights, and approved statutes, to see to it personally or through an executor:

> 1° that things held in common which are capable of division, both goods and patrimonial rights as well as the debts and other obligations, are divided among the juridic persons concerned with due proportion based on equity and justice, taking into account all the circumstances and the needs of each . . .

3. The Apostolic See is the ecclesiastical authority competent to make the division of dioceses in the United States. The decree of the Apostolic See creating a new diocese may make the determination listed in canon 122, and may also determine the incardination of priests serving there. If so, that decree would be the first place to determine what obligations would remain with the former diocese of incardination, and what obligations would have transferred to the new diocese for priests who are incardinated in it at its creation. It is likely, however, that the decree does not enter into great detail on this question. Frequently it is left up to the bishops of the old and new dioceses to work these matters out. So when new dioceses are formed out of old, there is frequently an agreement entered into by the bishops of the two dioceses with regard to future obligations of each diocese toward priests. For example, pension rights that priests may have built up in the original diocese need to be sorted out with regard to those priests who are now incardinated in the new diocese. Often

there is an adjustment made to assist the new diocese in establishing a pension plan, for example.

These agreements, however, usually look toward fulfillment of the diocese's future obligations towards priests. It is unlikely that they would specify the obligations that may exist for past ministry of the priests.

4. Failing any directive in the decree from the Apostolic See, and failing any understanding already entered into by the two bishops on behalf of their dioceses, canon 122, 1°, gives the basic principle to be applied in resolving individual questions arising out of the division of dioceses: "due proportion based on equity and justice, taking into account all the circumstances and the need of each."

To apply this to a particular case, if a priest were incardinated in diocese "A" and performed his ministry there; and if that same priest were later incardinated in diocese "B"; and if after the change in incardination, questions arose concerning his ministry in diocese "A" which could affect not only the priest but also the liability of diocese "A," what is the "due proportion based on equity and justice" to be applied to the defense of the priest (and eventually diocese "A")?

It would appear on the basis of equity at least, that diocese "A" retains an obligation toward the ministry performed by the priest while incardinated in diocese "A," and diocese "B" has obligations toward the ministry performed by the priest since his move to diocese "B" and eventual incardination there. This would apply whether the priest was moving from one continent to another, or only changed incardination because of the action of the Apostolic See creating a new diocese out of the one in which he has been incardinated.

Diocese "B" did not exist at the time the ministry in question was performed, so it could not have assumed at that time any obligations toward them. The equitable distribution of obligations mentioned in canon 122 should recognize that the obligation to supervise a priest's ministry exists at the time the priest performs the ministry (c. 384), and should remain with the church authorities who are competent at the time the ministry is performed, and not be shifted to some new authorities who could not have exercised any supervision over that ministry at the time it was performed.

It is my opinion, therefore, that if questions are raised about the ministry of a priest while he served in diocese "A," and if diocese "B" (where he is now incardinated) has incurred expenses defending the priest with regard to that past ministry, it is legitimate for diocese "B" to obtain reimbursement from diocese "A" for these expenses.

James H. Provost [1991]

Canon 267

Excardination of a Transient Deacon Prohibited by His Bishop from Promotion to Order of Presbyterate

A man was called to orders by his bishop and then ordained a deacon as a step toward priesthood. Subsequently the bishop for serious reason decided not to ordain him a priest. May this deacon be incardinated into another diocese as a permanent deacon?

Opinion

There seems to be no reason why such a man could not be incardinated in another diocese. Obviously, one way that this could be expedited is for him to obtain a benevolent bishop, and then seek a letter of excardination from his own bishop and a corresponding letter of incardination from the new bishop (c. 267). Realistically, however, given the problems that have motivated the bishop not to advance him to the presbyterate, this may be unlikely at the moment.

Another possibility might be for him to move to another diocese with the presumed permission of his current bishop. Once again this presumes his finding a benevolent bishop to give him an opportunity to serve. Such a move would give the deacon the chance to determine whether he is suited for ministry in the new diocese. Likewise it would give the bishop of that diocese an opportunity to assess the adequacy of the man's ministry. If all goes well, then there might be the possibility of applying the *ipso iure* incardination provisions of canon 268, §1. This means that after five years of service in the new diocese the deacon could make known his desire for incardination in that diocese and the two bishops would have an opportunity within four months to express their opposition in writing. Should neither of them do so, the deacon in question would be incardinated in the new diocese.

Should the deacon in question experience any significant problems regarding permission to move to the new diocese or the application of the *ipso iure* incardination provisions, then it would seem recourse to the Congregation for the Clergy might well be an option.

Thomas J. Green [1988]

Canon 268

Ipso Iure Incardination

Did this canon [on ipso iure *incardination after five years in another diocese, under certain conditions] begin to apply when the new code took effect, or is it retroactive in virtue of* Ecclesiae Sanctae?

The norm of canon 268 is a restatement of the provisions of *Ecclesiae Sanctae,* and therefore, is a continuation of what was already the law of the Church. In that sense it is "retroactive," but really it only continues the law that has been in effect since 1966.

James H. Provost [1984]

CANONS 277, §§2 & 3; 212, §3; AND 221, §§1 & 3

POLICY GOVERNING INTERVENTION AND TREATMENT OF A PRIEST ACCUSED OF SEX ABUSE

The diocese has drafted a policy governing intervention and treatment of a priest accused of sexual abuse of minors and others at risk. The presbyteral council is in the process of reviewing the current policy. What are the essential elements that should be provided for in such a policy?

If the Church is to deal effectively with the issue of sexual misconduct by the clergy, it must first be acknowledged that, unfortunately, incidents of this tragic and destructive behavior have been poorly handled, resulting in further injury to victims of sexual abuse, their families, and the wider Christian community. It has also lessened the Church's credibility and contributed to the greater impairment of those members of the clergy who must be persuaded to confront this serious psychological problem in their lives and deal with it in a realistic and therapeutic manner.

Mishandling of cases of pedophilia and pederasty has included instances in which the offending priest is simply re-assigned in the hope that somehow the problem will just go away. In other instances, dioceses have been advised that in order to lessen the possibility for a civil lawsuit and to create as much "distancing" as possible from a purported incident of sexual abuse, there should be absolutely no contact with either the victim and his or her family or the priest who has been accused of misconduct.

Actions of this sort leave parents and the victim of abuse confused, angry and hurt. The Church, which professes a principal ministry as healer and reconciler, suddenly abandons this role precisely when healing and reconciliation are most urgently needed by persons who have been seriously harmed by the actions of one of its priests. The priest responsible for such conduct, whether or not he is in a state of denial, is left without the support of the Church, moral or otherwise, at a time that is most traumatic in his life. He is in effect ostracized with minimal contact from either the bishop or other forms of diocesan priestly support; and if knowledge of his conduct has become public, he may even have to fend for himself in the face of civil and possibly criminal litigation.

Additionally, attempts of some dioceses to impose canonical remedies or sanctions against a priest guilty of sexual abuse have met with frustration due to the inept handling of the Church's canonical procedures, such as the improper insertion into the canonical forum of evidence gathered through processes conducted in a civil or criminal forum or other actions that have jeopardized and doomed to failure the validity of the canonical process.

Fortunately today, most dioceses are putting into place more enlightened policies and procedures, which are designed to deal sensitively with reported incidents of sexual misconduct and child abuse by the clergy. These policies attempt to address not only the needs of the victims of such assaults and their families, but also the complex questions regarding the treatment of a priest who is guilty of sexual abuse. These questions must include not only determinations regarding therapy and treatment, but also the difficult decisions that need to be made in the canonical forum addressing the possibility, if any, of a priest's being able to return to the exercise of the priestly ministry after therapy.

Thus, a diocesan policy dealing with the sexual abuse of minors by the clergy must carefully address the rights and needs of all parties, both the victim and his or her family, and those of a priest who is guilty of sexual misconduct; and so, as the questioner implies, such policies must be carefully formulated.

The diocesan bishop may elect to consult with the presbyteral council in confronting this task, and it is not uncommon for diocesan civil attorneys and liability insurance carriers to become involved in the process.

While it is also imperative to consider applicable principles of canon law in the formative process, the details of such a policy, which include areas of civil liability and liability insurance coverage, cannot be based on canon law alone. For reasons of space, however, this advisory opinion must limit its examination solely to general questions arising from considerations of canon law in an attempt to suggest to a presbyteral council topics for discussion in reviewing a diocesan policy on sexual abuse by the clergy.

The first consideration is an application of the principle found in canon 212, which provides that the Christian faithful do have a right ''to make known their

needs, especially spiritual ones, and their desires to the pastors of the Church''
(§2).

Clearly, there is no need more pressing than that of a child who has been the
victim of a sexual assault by a member of the clergy. Hence, it is imperative
that any policy provide parents with both the opportunity and the means of
bringing such allegations of abuse to the attention of church authorities
(*Ecclesiae pastores*).

The immediate response of the diocese must attend to the victim and his or her
family. Thus, it is obvious and important that a diocesan policy provide a
means for the victim and family to receive counselling or therapy.

The diocese must also deal with the priest who has been accused of an incident
of sexual abuse. He cannot and must not be presumed guilty simply on the basis
of an allegation; and he must certainly be provided with an appropriate
opportunity and forum in which to respond to the charge that has been made.
But at the same time, the diocese must act in a responsible manner on the basis
of the information it has received.

This leads directly to the second canonical consideration. A priest accused of
sexual misconduct has a right to respond to this charge before a competent
ecclesiastical forum, regardless of any action that may be taking place in a civil
or criminal forum. A cleric also has the right not to be punished with canonical
sanctions or to have his rights curtailed except in accord with the norms of
canon law (c. 221, §§1 and 3).[1]

Thus, while civil law and liability insurance policy may properly require that
a priest — or anyone for that matter — under suspicion of sexual abuse of a
minor be placed on ''administrative leave'' or ''administrative suspension''
while the charge is being investigated, this action cannot be construed as having
canonical impact or significance. Civil determinations alone cannot be the basis
for the imposition of canonical sanctions or remedies, since such determinations
may involve information or evidence not properly included in a canonical
procedure.[2]

Hence, a priest cannot be suspended (that is, the canonical censure of
suspension in c. 1333 cannot be imposed); nor can he be denied his right to
room, board or financial compensation simply because he is being placed on a
civilly required ''administrative leave'' or ''administrative suspension'' while the
allegations of sexual abuse are being investigated. This would constitute a
violation not only of canon 221, §3, in that the censure of suspension or an
expiatory penalty limiting the right of remuneration would have been imposed
without due process in canon law, but also of canon 1350, which provides that
a cleric loses the right of remuneration only following dismissal from the clerical
state.

Canon law does provide the diocesan bishop with the means of dealing with a priest suspected of sexual misconduct. If a spirit of cooperation exists between the priest and the diocesan authorities investigating the situation, no formal canonical action may be necessary. However, if this is not the case, the diocesan bishop by reason of his office has the right on the basis of canon 277, §§2 and 3, to impose specific guidelines that a priest under suspicion of sexual misconduct would be required to follow until the accuracy of the allegations have been resolved. These guidelines, which would parallel the requirements of an "administrative leave" or "administrative suspension," are not penal in nature and do not necessarily imply guilt on the part of the priest.

Once the specific issues of the case become clearer, the diocesan bishop or other local ordinary will then be in a better position to determine whether further canonical action is warranted. Such action might be an investigation into the possibility of declaring the priest impeded from any future exercise of the priestly ministry (see c. 1044, §2, 2°) or a penal investigation to determine whether the application of a canonical penalty is necessary or appropriate (see cc. 1717-1731).

A final consideration must guide any canonical action taken after having established the guilt of the priest. Despite the nature of his actions, care must be exercised that he is afforded every opportunity of undergoing therapy and of dealing with this serious problem in his life in order to determine whether there is any possibility of his returning to some form of active ministry. These considerations can be most difficult, especially if there has been adverse publicity or public outcry has taken on a "lynch mentality."

Canon 1341 serves as a reminder that the Church's first concern must be the repair of scandal, the restoration of justice, and the reform of the accused by all possible means of pastoral care before resorting to the imposition of canonical penalties.

Notes

[1] Note that in the CLSA translation of canon 221, §1, "foro competenti ecclesiastico" is rendered as "competent ecclesiastical court." This is imprecise and possibly misleading. A competent ecclesiastical forum" need not be limited to a court, that is, a tribunal action. The possibility of an administrative action taken by an ordinary outside of a formal trial is an appropriate application of this paragraph. The proper application of §3 would, of course, require the use of the penal process.

[2] For example, a penitent might choose to provide information protected under the seal of confession. While a civil forum might properly utilize such evidence, a canonical procedure cannot consider such information under any circumstances (see c. 1550, §2, 2°).

Gregory Ingels [1992]

I. Basic Principles

It would seem that any policy established by a diocese or a religious institute regarding the situation of priests involved in acts of sexual misconduct with minors or with others at risk should first take the following basic principles into account:

— allegations of sexual misconduct are to be taken seriously;
— there will be compliance with applicable secular and canonical legislation;
— priority shall be given to the protection of children and of others at risk;
— an accused person is presumed innocent until proven otherwise;
— the reputation of persons involved in instances of sexual misconduct is to be protected.

II. The Rights to be Protected

Once these principles are recognized and incorporated into the policy, it would then be a question of determining the rights of all those involved in the situation and providing for their protection.

a. The rights of the Church

The Church itself has the right to its reputation and to its good name. It also has the right to see that its clerics seek holiness in their lives (c. 276, §1) and that they "shun completely everything that is unbecoming of their state" (c. 285, §1).

b. The rights of those who have been abused

It seems obvious that there should be arrangements made for pastoral support, both for the children and their parents.

In no instance should minors or other persons at risk be blamed for causing or encouraging the actions of the priest.

Depending on the availability of such services, it would seem that those who were abused would have the right to receive appropriate counselling, with the costs being assumed by the diocese or religious institute.

c. The rights of the priest who is involved in sexual misconduct

(1) First of all, the priest has a right to his *reputation*, no matter how unacceptable the actions he committed.

(2) Then, *imputability* must be proven, particularly if penalties are to be imposed on him.

(3) He would also have a right to *canonical counsel* — this constitutes part of the natural *right of defense*, especially if there is to be a penal trial (see cc. 1481, §2 and 1723, §1).

(4) The priest has the right to certain material benefits (see c. 1350). In order to avoid serious misunderstandings, however, it would be important that a diocese have a policy prepared beforehand, determining what type of assistance would be given to the priest. I would think that a diocese is not bound for life to provide for a priest who is guilty of serious sexual misconduct, particularly after a warning. Although there might be exceptions to this, it would seem that if a priest is in good health and is reasonably young, he should be able to earn his own living. Therefore, it would seem that a two-year (or some other appropriate) period would be sufficient in which to provide transitional assistance.

In addition to these recognized rights, possibly other ones could be incorporated into the policy of a particular diocese.

(5) The first of these would be the question of *therapy*. This would be essential if there was a question of any eventual return of the priest to ministry after having been found guilty of sexual misconduct with minors or other persons at risk.

(6) It does not seem that the priest has a right to have all his *legal expenses* assumed by the diocese or institute. At times he might have to rely on legal aid. A diocese cannot be expected to be obliged to assume excessive costs for trials and rehabilitation. The priest's lawyer should not be the diocesan counsel.

(7) A priest does not have a right to a *penal trial* to clear his name, because he is presumed innocent until proven otherwise (*Communicationes* 12 [1980] 191).

(8) According to the Latin code, a priest does not have a right to be assigned a *ministry*, although the Eastern code does provide for this right if the priest is found qualified for the task (*CCEO*, c. 371, §1).

(9) Finally, a priest does not have a right to *reside* in a rectory or other church-related institution. A bishop may decide that it is necessary for a priest convicted of sexual abuse to live away from any rectory or institution for some time (see c. 1336). In the case of a religious, however, the norms regarding community living and forced exclaustration would have to be observed.

d. *The rights of the parish*

The code does not spell out in detail the rights of parishioners. However, by looking at the obligations of parish priests and of other priests assigned to parochial ministry, we could find a corresponding right on the part of the faithful.

If the parishioners have been scandalized by the actions of the priest, they would have a right to expect some type of healing process.

The parishioners as a whole would not have a right to know everything about a priest's background, but certain members of the pastoral council might be informed to make certain that they can assist their priest in whatever way possible.

III. Establishing a Procedure

Once the various rights have been recognized and determined, then it is important to make certain that the appropriate procedures are set in place, distinguishing very clearly between rumors, hearsay, allegations, and formal charges.

A key appointment would be that of the bishop's delegate, a priest mandated to hear allegations and to take the appropriate steps to address the issue carefully and according to law.

The diocesan procedures, if they are to be appropriate, would call for an inter-disciplinary diocesan committee to be established to investigate such matters. The committee could comprise, for example, the priest in charge (bishop's delegate), a canonist, a criminal lawyer, a lawyer specialized in civil suits, and a licensed person experienced in the treatment of persons who have been the subject of sexual abuse. If possible, the tribunal personnel should not be assigned to the committee in case a penal trial were to be held against the priest at a later date (c. 1717, §3). However, if there is a serious shortage of available qualified priests, other canonists should be retained for the penal trial and, in this case, the local canonists could be part of the committee.

The responsibilities and duties of the priest in charge would have to be spelled out carefully so as to remove the bishop from direct involvement at the beginning of the procedures.

It would also be important to see that the canonical inquiry (c. 1717) is carried out in accordance with law. This inquiry could even have two phases: the first would be to determine whether there is any foundation to the allegations; the second, to see whether there is a basis to proceed to administrative or judicial action. At times, though, it might be appropriate to suspend all canonical procedures until the secular ones are completed, so as to avoid any potential conflict of interest and similar difficulties.

Only when it appears that there is some substance to the allegations (possibly after the first phase of the preliminary inquiry), should action be taken to give the priest administrative leave from his office.

I believe that it would also be important for the priests to be aware beforehand of the diocesan policy so that they are not surprised if the procedures are invoked against them.

Other points that could be taken into consideration in a diocesan procedure would include: (1) establishing appropriate relations with the media; (2) establishing good relations with the appropriate reporting agency (children's aid societies, etc.); (3) having an accurate knowledge of applicable secular law; (4)

having lawyers on retainer so that they can help when necessary; (5) making suitable arrangements beforehand with treatment centers and other specialists; (6) verifying the coverage of insurance policies; (7) taking particular care of written records in case there is a trial at some later date; (8) noting in writing steps taken to comply with applicable legislation; (9) making certain that those persons involved in the process do not hear the accused priest's confession.

Francis G. Morrisey, O.M.I. [1992]

Canon 281

Obligation of Support to a Priest in Treatment

A priest incardinated in a diocese is now serving a five year sentence on probation from a secular court. The first year of the probation required that he receive treatment at a center in a different state from his diocese, and he has completed this. From the query it is not clear if the terms of the probation required the remaining four years to be spent in a specified place or type of institution.

The priest's bishop has now assigned him to another institution for the care of priests again outside his own diocese. The bishop refuses to pay the expenses of the priest's stay at the Villa, claiming the priest's own inheritance from his parents should cover this. The cost, which is over $4,000 per month, is normally paid by the diocese for other priests at the same facility. The priest fears he will be unable to support himself once his probation is up if he spends the money now while under assignment from his bishop. What advice can be given to the priest?

Opinion

A cleric's right to remuneration, as it has been developed and expressed in canon 281, is an entirely new concept in canon law. Although remuneration was dealt with in the 1917 code, its consideration was associated with the benefice system, which was the subject of detailed legislation throughout the Pio-Benedictine code. In principle, though, legislation contained in the 1917 code determined that clerics, whether they possessed a benefice or not, received their remuneration as a consequence of their exercise of the ministry.

Even with the reform of the benefice system, the emphasis in the early development of the 1983 code concerning the remuneration of clerics continued to focus on the exercise of ministry as the motivating principle for providing for the remuneration of the clergy. (See *Communicationes* 16 [1984] 191, which presents a proposed canon concerning the remuneration of clergy as it was expressed in the 1977 *schema* of the code.)

With the promulgation of the 1983 Code of Canon Law, however, a new principle regarding remuneration emerged. No longer was remuneration of the clergy to be dependant upon the *exercise of ministry*; remuneration was now listed among those rights enjoyed by the clergy, a right which was to be merited "when clerics dedicate themselves to the ecclesiastical ministry" (c. 281, §1).

Hence, in current law a right to remuneration hinges primarily on a cleric's *dedication to ministry*; and questions considering this right and a bishop's responsibility to provide for the remuneration of his clergy must be attentive to this principle.

The code itself presents a number of legislative principles that impact on the remuneration of clerics. These include the following:

1. Remuneration must be "consistent with their condition in accord with the nature of their responsibilities and with the conditions of time and place" (c. 281, §1).
2. Remuneration should enable clerics "to provide for the needs of their own life and for the equitable payment of those whose services they need" (c. 281, §1).
3. Special consideration is to be afforded clerics who remain dedicated to the ministry but who are experiencing personal difficulties in the exercise of their ministry:

    Provision is likewise to be made so that [clerics] possess that social assistance by which their needs are suitably provided for if they suffer from illness, incapacity or old age (c. 281, §2).
4. Should it be necessary for a cleric to be removed from an office which is the source of his financial support, by the decree of the competent authority, provision must be made by this same authority for his support for a suitable time "unless it is provided otherwise" (c. 195).
5. Penal law does provide that a cleric's right to remuneration can be limited by means of an expiatory penalty (c. 1336, §1, 2°); however, the law clearly states that the complete termination of remuneration can only be associated with the penalty of dismissal from the clerical state (c. 1350, §1); but even in the case of dismissal, an obligation in charity remains to see to the care of a person who has been dismissed from the clerical state and who is truly in need due to the penalty (c. 1350, §2).

In applying these considerations to the situation of a priest who has been assigned by his bishop to continued treatment at an institution outside of his own diocese, the first question that must be examined is his dedication to the ministry. Although it is not clear in the present case whether or not the conditions of his probation require him to remain outside of the diocese or at the "second institution," it is clear that he did accept the assignment given him by his bishop to be at this institution; and he accepted this assignment despite the personal financial hardship that this has brought about. This would indicate that he does remain dedicated to the ministry of the priesthood and hopes to return to the active ministry at some time in the future.

Although the nature of his difficulties are not specified, it is apparent that the behavior of this priest — which has resulted in his being sentenced to probation by the secular courts — has raised serious questions posed by his bishop concerning his suitability to exercise the ministry of the priesthood for the present. Under the 1917 Code of Canon Law, this may well have been sufficient to limit or discontinue his remuneration (see 1917 code, cc. 2298 ff.). The current law of the Church, however, directs that there is a responsibility to greater pastoral sensitivity in providing for the assistance of a cleric who is suffering "from illness, incapacity or old age" (c. 281, §2).

The five year probation imposed by the secular courts does not imply that a canonical penalty has likewise been imposed on this priest either administratively or judicially. Thus, there appears to be no basis under the penal law of the Church to limit or to revoke this priest's right to remuneration.

Canon 384 addresses itself to that special concern a bishop is to exercise in protecting the rights of his priests and in seeing that they have the assistance necessary to insure their ability to fulfill the obligations proper to their calling. Thus, there is no question that a bishop has a serious obligation to see to the needs of a priest of his diocese who is laboring under difficulties that require residential treatment or therapy, especially since this priest has demonstrated that he is remaining dedicated to the ministry of the priesthood and in light of the fact that he has been assigned to such treatment by his bishop and considering the fact that he has not been placed under an ecclesiastical sanction.

The manner in which the bishop would fulfill this responsibility might well depend on the health care and insurance programs of the particular diocese. However, if such a program of health or insurance benefits is in place and a particular priest is being denied assistance solely due to the unique circumstances of the difficulties he is experiencing or the probation to which he has been sentenced by the secular courts, it would seem clear that he is being denied rights that are guaranteed by canon law under canons 281 and 384.

Gregory Ingels [1989]

There are two ways in which a priest can be required to live in a place outside his diocese. One is if he voluntarily agrees to go there; the other is if it is imposed as a church penalty. It is not clear from the query whether the priest's present assignment was imposed as a penalty, or is a voluntary one.

An order to live in a particular place, even for a specified length of time, can be imposed as a church penalty (cc. 1336, §1, 1°; and 1337). If it was imposed as a penalty, the bishop would have had to follow a procedure of calling the priest in to a hearing, providing him with a chance to present his side of the case, and assuring him the assistance of counsel in canon law. He would then have had to review the situation with two advisers, before ordering the priest to live in a particular place. As part of that penalty, he could also deprive the priest of financial support from the diocese provided he had assurances that the priest would not be truly destitute. The priest's own inheritance would have given the bishop that assurance.

An order to live in a specified place can also be required during a penal process (c. 1722), but the priest must first have been cited (to start the process — c. 1512), and both the priest and promoter of justice must have been heard before the bishop issued a temporary order to live in a place outside the diocese. The order can be enforced, however, only for the duration of the trial, and the priest's decent support must also be assured.

Yet that does not resolve the cost of the institution where the priest is now assigned; for a bishop to impose living in a certain place as a penalty or as a temporary order in a penal process, the bishop must also make arrangements with the place where the priest is forced to live. In such a situation, it would be up to the institution to be certain the expenses will be paid for before they accept a priest; the burden would seem to be on those running the institution if the priest came as a result of a church penalty.

But if the bishop did not follow the procedure for imposing a penalty, then the priest's acceptance of an assignment to live in an institution in another state is a voluntary thing, something he has agreed to do as an obedient priest of the diocese. But as a priest of the diocese, he is entitled to financial support. Canon 281 says that when a priest is dedicated to ministry he deserves a remuneration that will provide for the needs of his own life and the equitable payment of those whose services he needs. It also requires that the priest be assured suitable health, disability and old age benefits. Canon 384 obliges the bishop to make sure these things are taken care of.

If the priest is living at the institution voluntarily (i.e., the bishop asked him to go there, and the priest agreed — rather than the bishop imposed this after the required procedure), the priest is still "dedicated to ministry" and entitled to the support just mentioned. So the diocese would be obliged to provide the priest with sufficient support to pay for the institution that cares for him.

Regrettably, from the query it is not clear which situation exists in this case, assignment to the institution as a penalty or in the course of a trial, or voluntarily. However, in either situation it seems the bishop has an obligation to provide for the necessary expenses of the institution.

My recommendation is to clarify the conditions under which the priest is at the institution. If it is as a penalty, then those who are running the institution should indicate to the bishop they cannot accept priests under the provisions of canons 1336 and 1337 unless the bishop will agree to pay the costs. If it is voluntarily, then the priest should write to the bishop making claim to the support he is supposed to provide in keeping with canons 281 and 384.

In this latter case, if the bishop refuses the priest, he has ten days from receipt of the bishop's letter of refusal to appeal this decision to Rome. To do this, the priest must write a letter to the bishop, indicating his intention to appeal to Rome, and asking the bishop's assistance in doing this. The priest has fifteen days in which to prepare the letter of appeal and to send it to the Congregation for Clergy. If he decides to take this route, he would be well advised to seek the counsel of a canon lawyer to help prepare the documents.

James H. Provost [1989, revised 1993]

CANON 281

DIOCESAN RESPONSIBILITY FOR A PRIEST SERVING
OUTSIDE THE DIOCESE

Is a diocese responsible for the medical/hospital/surgical insurance of a priest in good standing but who is outside the diocese, e.g., serving as military chaplain, or paying his own way through school? Alternatively, can a priest avail himself of diocesan group insurance plans if he pays the premium himself?

OPINION

The answer to these questions is based upon the fundamental relationship arising out of incardination, by which a priest and diocese are intimately bound together. Canon 281, §1 says that "when clerics dedicate themselves to the ecclesiastical ministry" they deserve to be remunerated appropriately. Canon 281, §2 adds that "provision is likewise to be made so that they possess that social assistance by which their needs are suitably provided for if they suffer from illness, incapacity or old age.''

This does not mean that a priest must automatically be paid and given insurance coverage by the diocese. The diocese is to see that these provisions are made (and that proper remuneration is paid), but it can do this either by taking care of this itself or by seeing that it is cared for by other means. For example, if a priest is serving as a military chaplain the diocese is assured that the priest's remuneration is being provided by his pay as an officer in the military. The same is true for his ''social assistance'' — even if like other officers, the priest must take care of this out of his own military pay.

For a priest who is studying full-time, obviously if the diocese is sponsoring him, then the diocese must make sure he is covered by insurance, usually continuing him on the diocesan plan. If he is studying full-time on his own, although with the agreement of the diocese, the situation is less clear. Again, the diocese has a ''safety net'' obligation to see that the priest is protected, but that does not mean it cannot insist that the priest obtain his own insurance coverage; for example, through the health plan most universities provide for students who are not otherwise covered. An understanding on this should be worked out between the priest and the diocese before the priest receives permission to study on his own.

Whether a priest in good standing but away from the diocese — in the military, or studying — can be covered by the diocesan group policy even if he pays the premium himself, will depend on the terms of the diocese's policy. There is no standard health insurance policy for all U.S. dioceses. Each one contracts for its own. So the priest would have to check with the plan administrator to find out if he can do this.

James H. Provost [1991]

Canon 285

A. The Right of Clergy to Exercise Civil Power of Attorney on Behalf of Their Parents

Priests frequently find themselves in situations of concern and care for elderly parents who are no longer able to take care of their affairs. The priest may feel he needs to assume power of attorney for the parents, administer their property, arrange for health care and even assume ownership of property or act as trustee. Canon 285, §4 forbids certain financial activity for priests without the permission of the ordinary. To what extent does this canon apply to the situation of priests becoming agents for goods belonging to their family of origin or otherwise engaging in activities over property?

OPINION

The norm of canon 285, §4 is not intended to forbid priests who are not prevented from doing so by vows from managing their own affairs. Rather, it is meant to indicate what types of activities should not be included in these affairs because they are not in conformity with the priestly state or carry the danger of conflicting interests or the necessity of being accountable to non-ecclesiastical authorities.

In those situations where a priest finds it necessary to exercise some function of control or supervision over the affairs of parents or other family members, they should observe the same care as they would in their personal affairs. Certainly, justice and charity will require that priests take steps to protect the person and goods of family members who are incapable of self maintenance. The commentators on the former code and on the new law recognize that the restriction on priests acting on behalf of the interests of others does not include such family situations (cf., *The Code of Canon Law: A Text and Commentary,* 225).

It should be pointed out that in accord with the norm of the canon and as stated above, the priest is bound by the same restrictions in the managing of family affairs as in his own. Thus he should not presume to act more speculatively with the goods of those who depend on him than with his own goods. Also, should the goods in question include such things as managing a business or acting on behalf of third parties, then these activities should be entrusted to someone else either directly or as a trustee. As a general rule, canon 285, §4 is not intended to prevent the priest from assuming his responsibilities for family members, but even in doing so he must not act in a way that is inconsistent with his state in life or in which he may be subject to unnecessary civil or corporate control. However, he certainly must be careful to insure that his actions are legal and to fulfill proper civil requirements, e.g., Internal Revenue or probate court regulations.

Finally, it might be pointed out that canon 285, §4 says that such activities are forbidden for clerics, not just priests. Thus, it is important to realize that canon 288 explicitly says that permanent deacons are not bound by these restrictions unless particular law determines otherwise. Nevertheless, permanent deacons should be aware of the necessity that they not appear to be acting in a manner that can result in harm to their ministry or to the Church.

Jerald A. Doyle [1988]

B. The Right of Catholic Clergy to Officiate At the Marriage of Parties Who Are Not Obliged to Canonical Form

See opinions under canons 1109; 1110; and 1117.

Canon 285, §3

Clergy and Public Offices with Civil Power

Canon 285, §3 states: "Clerics are forbidden to assume public offices which entail a participation in the exercise of civil power." Please explain:
1. What do "public offices" and "civil power" mean?
2. Is the Congress a public office?
3. Is a cleric forbidden to be a congressman?
4. What is the spirit of this canon 285, §3?

Opinion

Since the question is presented in four parts, each part will be answered separately.

1. It might be helpful to attempt some definitions. "Public office" is any position which is established by those who make provision for the public order. Such an office could be established in a fundamental document such as a constitution or charter or by the legislator/legislature in a statute or decree or by one who has the appropriate administrative or judicial authority.

Such offices would be those of chief executive officer of a city, state or nation, members of legislatures and judges. Also, appointed members of commissions or boards that regulate some aspect of the public order, such as members of the cabinet, zoning boards or school boards. It would not include private functions for which the public authority gives permission or approval, but for which the individual is not publicly accountable except for abuses or crimes. Some examples might be lawyers, teachers, certified public accountants or a clergyman performing a marriage.

It seems that for purposes of this question it would be appropriate to define "a participation in the exercise of civil power" as being capable of placing acts which have consequences in the public order. Such acts could be legislative, administrative or judicial in nature and there is some accountability for the person acting. To some degree others are empowered or restricted by such acts.

Civil power would be exercised by those public offices mentioned above. It would not necessarily be exercised by those serving on various advisory boards or commissions formed for a particular task such as public school curriculum development. Clearly, it is possible to exercise some civil power without holding a public office, as is the case for all who exercise their right to vote. It is important to note that these definitions refer to the public order and not, necessarily, to the public good, which is an entirely different concept.

2. From the points mentioned in the answer to part 1, it is clear that to be a member of Congress is to hold a public office that entails a participation in the exercise of civil power. This is so because the office is established in the foundational document of the public order of these United States; i.e., the Constitution. Furthermore, to participate in forming the legislation that further defines the public order and binds all those subject to it is to participate in the exercise of civil power.

3. Canon 285, §3 does forbid clerics to hold the office of legislator (congress-man or senator). However, since canon 288 explicitly exempts permanent deacons from the provisions of canon 285, §3, it is clear that the prohibition applies to bishops, priests and transitional deacons. Moreover, canons 672 and 739 extend this prohibition to members of religious institutes and societies of apostolic life, whether they be clerics or not.

In virtue of canon 87, §1 the diocesan bishop can dispense the faithful from this disciplinary law when he judges it will contribute to their spiritual good. There is no corresponding right given to superiors of religious institutes or of societies of apostolic life, even if they are ordinaries, to give such a dispensa-tion.

4. To develop the "spirit" of this canon in a few lines would be most difficult. Perhaps it might be capsulized as follows: the priest, and others to whom this canon applies, are to be completely dedicated to matters of the spiritual realm. Since certain tasks demand a great deal of attention to the worldly realm, they are not consistent with the sense of complete dedication. Even if there is no overt conflict between those concerned for the spiritual and the political spheres, one cannot give full attention to both at the same time.

Thus, one should not conclude that the spirit of the law implies that there is something intrinsically wrong with holding "public offices which entail a participation in the exercise of civil power." The Church sees this as a fitting and proper role for lay members of the faithful. Even though it is possible that in some circumstances there could be ideological conflicts between the Catholic Church and certain governments, this is not the reason for the law. Rather the Church judges such tasks as inconsistent with the acceptance of public ministry and witness in the canonical order. One cannot serve two masters.

On the practical level one need only review the history of this question in ecclesiastical legislation to see that this principle is not new. Certainly the wording of the 1917 code was more detailed and explicit in naming various forbidden functions and identifying the level of authority on which they depended. One only has to recall the recent experience of clerics who were congressmen to see that ecclesiastical authorities are not inclined to lessen the prohibition. A concise overview of this question is presented by John E. Lynch, C.S.P., in *The Code of Canon Law: A Text and Commentary*, ed. James A. Coriden et. al. (New York/Mahwah, NJ: Paulist Press, 1985) 223-225.

Jerald A. Doyle [1989]

ANOTHER OPINION

This canon is part of a series of canons that list the obligations and rights of clergy. It has a long history, more than we need to explore here, but it reflects the long-standing concern that clergy stay out of politics, and leave the governance of secular affairs to lay persons. Down through history there have been exceptions, and even today the diocesan bishop can dispense from this law for individual cases. Aside from such special exceptions, the law is a straightforward prohibition of clergy assuming public offices which entail a participation in the exercise of civil power.

1. Meaning of "public office" and "civil power"

Public office is any office which is part of the public organization of society. It includes positions in civil government; i.e., any office in city, county, state or federal government. These could be positions in the legislative, executive, or judicial branches of government. It could also include membership on a citizens' advisory board, library or school board, improvement district council, etc.

Civil power means the exercise of the power of government in civil society. The member of a city council, for example, holds an office which exercises civil power; the member of a citizens' advisory group does not. Whether the members of a school board exercise civil power depends on the authority vested in the school board; i.e., is it advisory to the superintendent, or does it really have the final say?

Only those public offices which entail a participation in the exercise of civil power are forbidden to clergy.

2. Is the Congress a public office?

Yes, being a member of Congress is holding public office in the United States. This is also a public office which, because of the legislative power exercised as a member of Congress, entails the exercise of civil power.

3. Is a cleric forbidden to be a Congressman?

Yes, the canon prohibits clerics from holding this kind of public office; i.e., one which entails a participation in the exercise of civil power.

The diocesan bishop can dispense the cleric from this prohibition in individual cases and provided there is sufficient reason. For example, in some European countries clergy are named as senators; this is considered to be for the good of the Church, and dispensation is routinely given. However, in the present situation of the Church and of the world, it is generally considered preferable for clergy not to hold such positions, and therefore, the dispensation is rarely given in most countries.

4. What is the spirit of canon 285, §3?

Basically the spirit is one of not involving the clergy in the government of secular society. Canon 672 applies the same prohibition to lay religious.

The canon is a recognition of the proper role of lay persons as living in the world, and carrying the primary responsibility of witnessing to the gospel in worldly affairs. Canon 225 insists on this responsibility for lay persons, and canon 227 affirms the freedom of lay persons in conducting secular affairs and calls on them to do so imbued with the spirit of the gospel.

This does not mean that the clergy have no concern for secular affairs, or for the application of gospel values in civil government. They do, but not as direct participants in the exercise of civil power itself.

James H. Provost [1989]

CANON 290

PENAL DISMISSAL FROM THE CLERICAL STATE

May a compulsive pedophile be dismissed from the clerical state by a judicial penal process?

OPINION

73

I. The State of the Question

1. We are assuming that ordination is valid. Validly ordained clerics may lose the clerical state in two ways:

   a. by a rescript of the Apostolic See;

   b. by the legitimate infliction of the penalty of dismissal.

A rescript of the Apostolic See is granted upon *petition of the cleric* to deacons for serious reasons and to presbyters for the most serious reasons (c. 290). The previous practice of granting dismissal from the clerical state upon *petition of the ordinary* is apparently no longer available. Hence a priest convicted of pederasty who does not voluntarily petition for dismissal can only be dismissed by a penal process.

2. Pederasty is an offense in church law sanctionable by dismissal from the clerical state:

   "If a cleric has committed an offense against the sixth commandment of the Decalogue . . . with a minor below the age of sixteen, the cleric is to be punished with just penalties including dismissal from the clerical state if the case warrants it" (c. 1395, §2).

3. Dismissal from the clerical state is a permanent expiatory penalty (c. 1336, §1, 5°) and may only be inflicted by a tribunal of three judges.

   a. Perpetual penalties cannot be imposed or declared by a decree (c. 1336, §2).

   b. Penal cases concerning offenses which can entail the penalty of dismissal from the clerical state are reserved to a collegiate tribunal of three judges (c. 1425, §1, 2°).

II. One Response

Canon 1324, §1, 10° states that a penalty set by law must be tempered or a penance substituted in its place if the offense was committed by one who acted without full imputability provided there was grave imputability.

Some canonists argue that a cleric who "falls from grace" and *deliberately* sins against the sixth commandment with a minor may be dismissed from the clerical state if the case warrants. However, a pedophile suffers from a disease and an addiction or compulsion that limits free consent, and therefore, diminishes full imputability. Hence a pedophile, if convicted, may be penalized only by a penalty less than dismissal.

Other canonists argue that sins against the sixth commandment of the Decalogue are "sins of the flesh" and should be treated as *crimes passionels* in the continental sense.

A crime of passion is not exempt from a penalty for transgression of a law, but the penalty set by the law must be tempered, unless of course, the passion totally impedes the use of reason (in which case no penalty is applicable) or the passion is voluntarily stirred up or fostered (in which case full imputability is presumed).

Some would argue that the heat of sexual passion at the time of any sin against the sixth commandment excuses from the full rigor of the law though, of course, not from all penalty.

There are three alternatives to dismissal from the clerical state:

1. The judge may impose a penalty somewhat less than dismissal, e.g.:

Deprivation of power, office, function, right, privilege, faculty, favor, title or insignia.

Prohibition (even permanent) against exercising the above.

Prohibition or an order (even permanent) concerning living in a certain place (c. 1336, §1).

2. The ordinary may impose by decree using the administrative penal process, a temporary or indeterminate (but not permanent) prohibition against exercising a power, office, function, right, privilege, faculty, favor, title or insignia.

A temporary or indeterminate (but not permanent) prohibition or order concerning living in a certain place (c. 1342, §2).

3. The ordinary may decree (non-penally and after consultation with experts) that the accused is impeded from the exercise of orders on the basis of a psychic defect that renders him incapable of rightly carrying out the ministry. This impediment may only be lifted by the ordinary after consulting with an expert (c. 1044, §2, 2° and c. 1041, §1).

III. Some Problems

1. When expiatory penalties are inflicted (other than dismissal from the clerical state) the diocese is still responsible for support and maintenance of the cleric:

Canon 1350, §1 states that when penalties are imposed upon a cleric (unless it is a question of dismissal from the clerical state) provision must always be made that he does not lack those things that are necessary for his decent support.

Civil attorneys argue that the obligation to provide support may imply the right and obligation to control behavior. The diocese may still be held vicariously responsible for such a cleric's behavior if failure to supervise and control is demonstrated.

2. Even a perpetual expiatory penalty can be remitted by the ordinary of the place where the offender lives. True, the ordinary should consult with the

ordinary who set in motion the trial to impose the penalty or who imposed the penalty by administrative penal decree (c. 1355).

Extraordinary circumstances, however, permit the remission without consultation. Civil attorneys argue that a perpetual expiatory penalty must therefore be communicated with all ordinaries as well as the reasons for such a decree or sentence. Failure to do so may not limit the diocese of origin from responsibility when a convicted pederast and pedophile is permitted to exercise ministry on the basis of remission of penalty by his ordinary of residence.

Hence the diocese is between the rock and a hard place. On the one hand, the diocese must pay for support and maintenance of a convicted pedophile for the rest of his life. On the other hand, the diocese is constantly subject to the possibility of civil suit for failure to control the cleric or to inform other dioceses in the case of a totally inactive and uncontrollable cleric.

IV. Another Response

The judge must balance two concerns defined in our penal law.

Of course, clemency is a gospel value and must be attended to in church courts. Hence the judge must temper a penalty set by law when the cleric acted without full imputability, provided there was grave imputability (c. 1324, §1, 10°).

On the other hand, a judge can punish more severely than the law states in the following situations.

A. When a person has abused authority of office to commit the offense (c. 1326, §1, 2°). In specific cases priests guilty of this crime have used their influence over children as pastor, confessor or even counselor, catechist, etc., to establish the relationship that eventually leads to the offense. When a shepherd turns against the lambs his offense is aggravated even though the shepherd himself needs pastoral care.

B. When the accused foresaw what was to happen, yet nonetheless did not take the precautions any diligent person would have employed to avoid it (c. 1326, §1, 3 °). The actual act of pederasty is preceded by a long period of "set up" in which the child's trust and friendship are won and more and more intimate relationships are established. A judge, in a particular case, may find that the accused, aware of his own tendencies, had a special obligation to take the precautions of any diligent person. He should not have permitted children to play unsupervised in the rectory nor should he have taken them on camping trips without another adult present. In fact he is obliged to protect innocent victims by avoiding private and unsupervised relationships between himself and a child. Hence in a particular case, the judge may find that reduced imputability by reason of

76

sexual compulsion or pedophilia is balanced by the failure of the accused to take even ordinary precautions against hurting the victim.

Finally, it seems naive to equate sexual abuse of a minor with "sins of the flesh" or *crimes passionels* in the continental sense. Just as rape is more an act of violence and hatred than sexual passion, so a sin against the sixth commandment with minors is more an act of abuse and victimization than a mere "sin of the flesh."

Canon law distinguishes three levels of "passion" and the effect on imputability:

1. The serious heat of passion which precedes and impedes all deliberation of mind and consent of will and which has not been voluntarily stirred up or fostered. A person who acts under such ungovernable passion lacks the use of reason and is, therefore, not subject to canonical penalties when a law is violated (c. 1323, §6 read with c. 1324, §3).

2. The serious heat of passion which does not destroy the use of reason, i.e., which does not precede and impede *all* deliberation of mind and consent of will, as long as the passion had not been voluntarily stirred up or fostered (c. 1324, §12, 3°). A person who violates a law under the influence of such passion is not exempt from a penalty, but the penalty must be tempered.

3. Passion which is deliberately aroused or fostered can never be considered in evaluating either the lack of use of reason in canon 1323 or diminished imputability of canon 1324.

A judge might well find, in a particular case, that the passion under which the act of child sexual abuse was committed was deliberately aroused or fostered during the long period of romantic relationship and "friendship" before the child was alone with the accused in a situation where sexual abuse, from the pedophile's point of view, is compulsive, passionate and uncontrollable.

V. Conclusion

Therapists as *periti* should be examined regarding the legal issues raised above. But the therapist's opinion is not absolutely binding on the judge.

Canon 1579 instructs the judge:

to weigh attentively the conclusion of the experts and also to attend to other circumstances of the case. In giving the reasons for the decision the judge must express what considerations prompted him to admit or reject their conclusions.

Absent an authentic interpretation of the legislator, judges must "bite the bullet" and apply the canons and the legal opinions that best relate to the case at hand. Appeals may clarify the law, particularly if an appeal is accepted by the Holy See after two concordant sentences.

Finally, sentences which imply that pedophiles can never be dismissed from the clerical state by a penal process may well convince the Holy See to revise its position against administrative dismissal or petition of the ordinary.

My conclusion is that convicted pedophiles can be dismissed from the clerical state by a penal process. The mitigation of penalty in canon 1324, §1, 3° (crimes committed in the heat of passion) and canon 1324, §1, 10° (crimes committed with grave but not full imputability) must be balanced with the right to impose especially severe penalties in the case of abuse of authority or office (c. 1326, §1, 2°), failure to take precautions against transgressions (c. 1326, §1, 3°) and the rule to consider fully imputable transgressions committed in the heat of passion deliberately aroused or fostered (c. 1325).

The alternative, it seems, is to put the dioceses at risk for vicarious liability when an uncontrollable "cleric" even though inactive is not controlled!

Mr. Bumble (the Beadle in *Oliver Twist*) was informed that a husband is responsible for his wife's actions since the law presumes that a husband can *control* his wife's actions. Mr Bumble replies, "If that is the law, Sir, then the law is an ass!"

Bertram F. Griffin [1988]

CANONS 292 AND 1333, §1, 3°

ELIGIBILITY FOR CANONICAL OFFICES AFTER BEING LAICIZED

Can a cleric with a licentiate or a doctorate in canon law who has been laicized hold the office of advocate, defender of the bond, etc.? In other words, what offices in the Church can a laicized cleric hold?

OPINION

The question as it is posed implies the laicization to have been granted by a rescript of the Apostolic See rather than as a consequence of a declaration of invalidity of orders or the infliction of the canonical penalty of dismissal from the clerical state (c. 290). This presumption means the Procedural Norms Regarding a Dispensation from Priestly Celibacy (cf., *CLD* 7: 110-117, and *CLD* 9: 92-99), the circular letter of the Congregation for the Doctrine of the Faith on the Reduction to the Lay State (cf., *CLD* 7: 117-121) and the interpretation of the procedural norms by the same Roman congregation (cf.,

CLD 7: 121-124) affect a response.

The consequence of laicization is a loss of the juridical status of cleric so that the individual no longer has a right to exercise lawfully the power of orders. He also forfeits the privileges of clerics and returns to the condition of a lay man. Any exercise of the power of governance then would consist in cooperating in its exercise rather than possessing the habitual capacity to exercise this power (c. 129, §2). Thus, any exercise of jurisdiction would include any limitations appropriate to its exercise by a lay person.

Additionally, specific restrictions established by the Procedural Norms Regarding a Dispensation from Priestly Celibacy (January 13, 1971) regarding holding offices have effect. The norms explicitly prohibit: (1) the exercise of any function of sacred orders; (2) having any liturgical role in celebrations with people where his condition is known and from ever giving a homily; (3) having any pastoral office; (4) functioning as rector or any other administrative office, spiritual director or teacher in seminaries, theological faculties and similar institutions; and (5) discharging the functions of director of a Catholic school or teacher of religion in any kind of school, whether Catholic or not (*CLD* 7: 116). The interpretation of these norms by the same Roman congregation (June 26, 1972) interprets the words "similar institutions" to refer to faculties, institutes, schools, etc., of ecclesiastical or religious sciences (e.g., faculties of canon law, missiology, Church history, philosophy, or pastoral institutes of religion, catechetical, etc., education) and all other centers of higher studies, even those not strictly dependent upon Church authority in which theological or religious disciplines are taught (*CLD* 7: 123).

Only the third exclusion, namely, having any pastoral office, could prohibit a laicized priest from serving as an advocate, defender of the bond, or judge in an ecclesiastical tribunal. The other exclusions are related to the teaching or sanctifying offices of the Church and thus are not germane to this topic.

Richard Hill succinctly summarizes the conciliar teaching on ecclesiastical offices. He notes that *Presbyterorum ordinis* 20 decided that office in the Church was to be understood as any function (*munus*) conferred in a stable manner for a spiritual purpose. This reflected the statement of *Lumen gentium* 33 that lay persons might be deputed by the hierarchy for certain roles (*munera*) to be carried out for a spiritual purpose. In conformity with this conciliar action the revised law suppressed the distinction found in the 1917 code between office in the strict and broad sense (c. 145, §1). Hill concludes: "In the 1917 code only a cleric could hold office in the strict sense; now a lay person can receive an ecclesiastical office in the only sense recognized by the law" (Title IX: Ecclesiastical Office [cc. 145-196], in *The Code of Canon Law: A Text and Commentary*, ed. James A. Coriden et al. [New York/Mahwah: Paulist Press, 1985] 99). Because of this understanding of office, lay persons can be appointed to the office of judge (c. 1421, §2), auditor (c. 1428, §2), the defender of the bond (c. 1435), procurator or advocate (c. 1483).

This understanding of office is reflected in the rescripts of the Congregation for the Doctrine of the Faith and more recently of the Congregation for Divine Worship and the Discipline of the Sacraments, which do not prescribe holding pastoral office but only prohibit holding directive pastoral offices (rescripts, n. 4b: "*nec potest officium gerere directivum in ambitu pastorali*"). Since it is a matter of an exception to laws, that is, the laws that permit lay persons to hold certain judicial offices, a strict interpretation is appropriate (c. 18). This means that a dispensed cleric would be prohibited from holding a directive office in a tribunal such as judicial vicar or assistant judicial vicar (c. 1420, §4 specifically requires that these office holders be priests anyhow), while there is nothing to prevent their appointment to other judicial offices. In the case of the office of judge, the special requirements of canon 1421, §2 need to be observed.

Ronald J. Bowers [1992]

ANOTHER OPINION

The response to the first question is unequivocally in the affirmative. It is based on the principle that a cleric who has returned to the lay state (that is, who has been dispensed from the obligation of celibacy) is a lay person in good standing in the Church. As such, he may hold those offices, exercise those ministries, and be employed in those positions in which lay persons may function. Canons 96; 129, §2; and 228, §1 give expression to this basic principle. This same principle supplies guidance for a response to the second, more general question.

The canons that state the requirements for appointment to the offices of advocate, defender and judge (cc. 1483; 1435; and 1421, §2) explicitly state that lay persons may assume them. Nowhere is any prohibition of laicized clerics expressed or implied.

The norms issued by the Congregation for the Doctrine of the Faith (October 14, 1980; *CLD* 9: 92-99) state no restrictions on the future offices, ministries or church employment of those dispensed.

The rescripts of laicization themselves, both those issued by the CDF (e.g., *CLD* 9: 99-101) and those currently being issued by the Congregation for Divine Worship and Discipline of the Sacraments (as recently as January, 1992) mention no prohibition of tribunal offices. The rescripts do urge the dispensed cleric to avoid certain liturgical, pastoral and educational roles that might cause confusion among the faithful. Tribunal offices are not among them.

The CLSA committee report, published in *Chicago Studies* (J. Provost, K. Lasch, H. Skillin, "Dispensed Priests in Ecclesial Ministry: A Canonical Reflection," *Chicago Studies* 14 [1975] 121-134), contains excellent guidance in this whole matter, as does a later article by J. Provost, "Employing Dispensed Priests for Ministry," *Priest* 34 (October 1978) 29-33.

Finally, it is a well-known fact that dispensed clerics with canonical credentials are actually functioning in matrimonial tribunals in the United States. This writer knows of at least two archdioceses where priests returned to the lay state are currently performing the roles of judge and defender. Their names are routinely submitted to the Signatura in the tribunals' reports.

James A. Coriden [1992]

ANOTHER OPINION

The Procedural Norms Regarding a Dispensation from Priestly Celibacy, (S.C. for the Doctrine of the Faith, October 14, 1980, *AAS* 72 [1980] 1132, henceforth Norms), appear to be framed within the Church's immemorial concern for scandal or the idea that a laicized cleric is an embarrassment to the Church and may cause confusion among the faithful. The measure of scandal arising from an incident bringing with it disgrace differs from community to community. In American culture where it is fashionable to change career and vocational direction it can be said that the faithful are, probably, not as scandalized by the news of a priest or deacon leaving active ministry as they may have been when defections and laicizations began to substantially increase some twenty years ago. In fact, there are many parishes across the country that show remarkable acceptance of married priests and their spouses and have no problems accepting the active participation of these couples.

The standard rescript of laicization makes no explicit mention of the inability of a dispensed cleric to function with any of the offices of the ecclesiastical court beyond n. 4a *et al.* where it states: "the dispensed priest automatically loses the rights proper to the clerical state as well as ecclesiastical dignities and offices. . . ." Thus, if a priest or deacon is functioning as an advocate, defender of the bond or judge, he automatically loses that office with the notification and acceptance of the rescript, if not already by his suspension (c. 1333, §1, 3°) from ordained service by his ordinary upon commencement of the laicization procedure (Norms, art. 4). Given mention of the inability to function in the public sacramental and liturgical ministries and to teach the theological sciences in institutions accredited by the Church as conditions for the rescript, one can easily see a strong implication that the dispensed cleric is not to function in any official capacity.

Canons 194, §1, 1° and 292 would emphasize this point where the law says a cleric who loses the clerical state in accord with the norm of law is deprived of all offices, functions and any delegated power. Given the special character, thorough dedication, and lifetime service implied by ordained service in the Catholic Church, a cleric leaving ministry is seen to be an anomaly, hence the Church's instructions regarding the restricted contexts within which he can move once he forsakes ordained ministry.

No. 5 of the standard rescript explains that a "laicized priest ought to stay away from places where his previous status is known; another ordinary after consultation with the man's original ordinary might allow him to function in lower capacities if scandal is judged not to be apparent." Thus, given that the offices of advocate, defender of the bond and judge are public offices (c. 145) in the Church, a case can be made that a dispensed cleric is forbidden to function in these positions.

The current norms and standard rescript, a revision of the original 1971 procedures, have seen no revision since their publication in 1980.

Concerns about an unwelcome influence on seminarians or students of theology by a dispensed cleric (probably lessened in the instance of a deacon) or confusion on the part of the faithful witnessing the activity of dispensed clerics in the community, seemingly, would not be as grave in the arena of the church courts with the exercise of justice, especially when it comes to the clarification of the validity of the marriage bond. Tribunals are specialized, more restricted departments of diocesan administration involving contact with a limited, although significant, group of the faithful.

An argument can be posed that justice must be a constant current in the Church. Pressing pastoral needs in dioceses around the world, the issue of priestly numbers and the need for adequate numbers of degreed persons in tribunals might be reason enough for a bishop to look at a dispensed cleric-canonist who also needs employment. And, all things being equal, when a tribunal stands to be understaffed by qualified officers, an argument can be brought forth that the Church should employ an available dispensed cleric as an advocate or defender of the bond or judge member of a collegiate panel. Thus the faithful may benefit from the processes of justice and the clarification of rights without interruption. The employment of the former cleric must not render any scandal to the community and especially if the dispensed cleric stands to be employed in a diocese where he did not function as an ordained minister.

The 1917 code left the appointment of tribunal officers with degrees or equivalent experience to the diocesan bishop. While appointments of degreed officers to the church courts is still the responsibility of the bishop, there is the intervention today of the *stylus curiae Romanae*, which takes a different direction. In an effort to secure qualified courts and personnel around the world, the Apostolic Signatura has been carrying on active correspondence with tribunals, especially in English speaking countries, regarding the qualifications of their staffs. Therefore, when it comes to considering laicized clerics for public office in the Church, it would appear that ordinaries are not free to take exceptions with the norms and the canons and the implementation of the rescript in individual cases without consultation with the Holy See.

Yet, a dispensed cleric, canonist or not, is technically a lay person and, theoretically, can therefore, function in any capacity in a tribunal that can be filled by any other lay person. It is, therefore, the opinion of this author that a laicized cleric who is a degreed canonist can function in a tribunal as advocate, defender of the bond or collegiate judge (the office of judge being dependent on the power of orders), but, probably, not without a particular rescript from the Signatura, after specific request made by a diocesan bishop for temporary or for indefinite employment. Enough petitions from ordinaries this way would certainly surface the *mens curiae Romanae* on the subject.

Should a dispensed cleric be found functioning in these capacities without a Roman rescript, such functioning would not affect the validity of acts placed in the tribunal since the issue of the activity of laicized clerics in the Church is purely a disciplinary matter.

Joseph N. Perry [1992]

CANON 293

RETURN TO MINISTRY OF PRIEST WHO LEFT AND MARRIED

A priest left a religious community and attempted marriage. Now after about a dozen years he is seeking to be reinstated. What should the superior general do?

OPINION

It is not clear from your letter if he was even laicized. It is true that there are a number of priests who have returned to the active ministry after an absence such as the case here; for those who had been laicized this seems to be the process being followed.

The priest requests from a bishop (or religious superior in this case) permission to return to the active ministry. If he had been laicized then the request has to be forwarded to the Holy See. If the Holy See agrees, the man normally spends about a year in a monastery or other secluded setting, spending time for spiritual renewal and also learning once again the practices he will need to follow in pastoral life, especially since so many of them have changed in the intervening years. Then, permission is granted by the Holy See for the man to return to active ministry and to be restored to the clerical state (c. 293).

If he was not laicized, his situation is a bit different. First of all, once the new code took effect he is no longer under any excommunication. The old code automatically excommunicated a priest who attempted marriage (1917 code, c. 2388). This penalty no longer appears in the new code. As a result, the provisions that the new code has for cases where the penalty is no longer in effect mean that the excommunication is done away with retroactively, so the priests who were excommunicated under the old code are no longer (c. 1313, §2), even though they may still not be fully reconciled with the Church.

So, the first obstacle is out of the way if the man were not laicized and had attempted marriage. The second obstacle, however, is the fact that he is irregular (c. 1044, §1, 3°). This irregularity is reserved to the Holy See if his situation was not occult (c. 1047, §2, 1°). I suspect that a man who was married for about a dozen years is no longer considered to be in an occult marriage and therefore dispensation from the irregularity would have to be obtained from the Holy See.

Insofar as readmission to active life in the community is concerned, those who attempt marriage are automatically dismissed from their community under the old code (c. 646) and under the new code (c. 694). Therefore, in order to return to the same community he would have to be readmitted to the institute.

James H. Provost [1984]

Canon 298

Canonical Options for CRS

Where does an organization such as Catholic Relief Services (CRS) fit, canonically speaking, in its relations to the Church in other countries?

Opinion

Your inquiry concerns the status of CRS under the code, as a separately incorporated (in civil law) agency of the NCCB. As a separately incorporated agency it carries on important work within the United States, but also in other countries where, unlike many other church agencies, it has its own staff.

Although it is a separate corporation in United States civil law, that does not necessarily constitute it a distinct juridic entity in canon law. I will try to analyze what I see as the various options for CRS.

First, it can be a civil corporation with no status in canon law. That is, the NCCB may have established CRS only as a civil law corporation, without intending to give it any special status in canon law. Under this possibility, CRS would enjoy all the rights and privileges of a civil corporation engaged in international activities, but would not be subject to the specific provisions of canon law concerning property, persons, etc. In effect, dealing with CRS would be no different from dealing with, for example, Oxfam so far as church law is concerned.

Second, it could be set up as an association under canon law. The new code has reorganized the law on associations in the Church and provides some clarity concerning what it would mean, and who could set it up. Church associations can be set up by private persons (c. 299, §1) and are known as private associations. They can also be set up by competent church authorities, and then are known as public associations (c. 301, §§2 and 3). All types of associations are free to run their own activities according to their own "statutes" (constitution and by-laws), but are subject to the vigilance of the Holy See and of the bishops of those places where they are active.

Church associations can be set up to carry out the various works of the Church, including works of charity. Public associations (those set up by competent church authorities) are considered at various levels — in particular, those which are destined to carry on their work throughout an entire nation are to be set up by the conference of bishops; those which are "universal" and international are to be set up by the Holy See.

CRS could be considered to be an association established by the NCCB to carry on relief services by collecting resources throughout the United States, and disbursing them where needed around the world. I do not think that would make it the same as an international association, but this is a new area of church law and I stand open to correction.

I might add that the nature of an association is really a grouping of people. I suspect that CRS is more a bureau or agency than a grouping of people, and so doesn't fit the "association" label fully.

A third alternative is to consider the possibility of a juridic person. This was called a "moral person" under the 1917 code. It is something like a corporation under civil law, although not precisely the same. A group of people, an agency, or an aggregate of material resources can be set up as a juridic person. This provides it with a certain protection and independence within canon law which resembles the protection provided by civil incorporation under civil law. The juridic person can hold title to property, can benefit from various privileges, can enter into contracts, and enjoys various other rights and duties under canon law.

A juridic person can be set up by a competent ecclesiastical authority. The new code does not specify who is competent to set up what kinds of juridic persons, but in parallel with associations it is clear the NCCB is competent to set up a juridic person with a national scope (c. 322, §1, when correlated with c. 312, §1, 2°). The law, however, does not contain the same restrictions on what level of operations a juridic person would engage in as it seems to apply to associations. So it seems clear that the NCCB could erect the CRS into a juridic person under the new code.

Juridic persons can be public (diocese, parish, NCCB itself) or private. There is less red tape connected with being a private juridic person; its property does not become "ecclesiastical goods." It would retain all the benefits of civil incorporation, as well as provide a clear status in canon law. It would enable CRS as a recognized church entity, even though a private one, to enter into contracts with national hierarchies, local bishops, etc., with binding force in canon law as well as in civil law.

With this rather complex background, let me now address some of the specific questions you raised.

First, in regard to the financial and administrative operations of CRS, it seems to me you are adequately protected by civil incorporation from undue outside interference, other than government regulations in the various countries where CRS is operating. If CRS is only a civil law agency, it would not be subject to the kind of supervision and control which canon law entities could encounter from various local church authorities.

On the other land, as an association it would not necessarily "own" material goods in the canon law sense, but could benefit as an association of people from various privileges which local bishops in various parts of the world where you serve might be willing to give the members of the association. In this sense it would be more like the kind of parallel you have suggested with a religious community or the military vicariate, although clearly CRS is neither.

As a juridic person it could hold title in canon law to its resources the same as it holds title in civil law through civil incorporation. It could enter into contracts with various bishops and conferences of bishops for the operations it conducts in their areas, and even for special privileges to be given to those working for CRS in those areas. It would, however, be subject to closer canonical restrictions on the management of its resources.

James H. Provost [1984]

86

CANONS 311 AND 677, §2

ASSOCIATE MEMBERSHIP WITHIN AN
INSTITUTE OF CONSECRATED LIFE

What are the canonical implications of an institute of consecrated life establishing associate membership? In other words, is it necessary for there to be distinctions between the rights and duties of the permanently consecrated members of the institute and those who choose associate affiliation?

OPINION

As phrased above, the term "associate membership" might suggest a form of membership in an institute of consecrated life, when more accurately it denotes a relationship with the institute, more or less structured according to guidelines that the establishing institute and the associate accept. It is with that understanding that this opinion is offered.

The inquiry focuses on the necessity for distinctions between the rights and duties of the permanently consecrated members and those of the associates. Rights and duties derive from the status of persons. Insofar as the status of religious differs from that of those not consecrated as religious, rights and duties differ. The obligations of the religious vows and the commitment to community life, for example, cannot be imposed on those who are not religious. Nor could an institute convey to its associates those rights reserved by the institute's proper law to the members.

Canon 677, §2 addresses a specific duty of the institute of consecrated life vis-à-vis its associates: it must assist them "with special care so that they are imbued with a genuine spirit of their family." The canon is found in the chapter on the apostolate of religious institutes. This recalls canon 311, which provides that the institute which moderates or assists a related association see to it that the association assist in the ministry of the diocese, in cooperation with other associations. For the associates, then, a correlative right/duty is participation in ministry according to the spirit of the institute and the directives of their own statutes.

The rights and duties should be set forth in proper law: that of the institute and that of the association. Distinguishing those proper to each will avoid confusion in expectations, and preserve for the groups their own fruitful identity.

Esther Redmann, O.S.U. [1992]

OBLIGATION OF SUPPORT TO A PRIEST IN TREATMENT

See opinion under 281.

CANON 384

RESPONSIBILITY OF BISHOP TO PRIESTS OUTSIDE THE DIOCESE

There are a number of priests and deacons incardinated in our diocese who are no longer serving here. In light of the discussion in the Clergy Procedural Handbook, *is our diocesan priests' retirement fund liable for them? This seems unfair, as it privileges those who have left the diocese over those who remain and carry the burden of the work here.*

OPINION

The basic law is canon 384, which states that it is part of the responsibilities of the diocesan bishop "to make provision for their [presbyters of the diocese] decent support and social assistance, in accord with the norm of law." The norm of law is stated in canon 281, §2: "Provision is likewise to be made so that they possess that social assistance by which their needs are suitably provided for if they suffer from illness, incapacity, or old age."

The first thing to note is that it is the bishop who has this responsibility, not a diocesan retirement fund. Usually it is through the diocesan retirement fund that these responsibilities are taken care of, but the bishop can see that "provision" is made through other means; for example, if he stays in touch with diocesan clergy who are outside the diocese and knows that they are covered by a retirement plan where they are now working, he is making "provision" without having to provide the money himself.

If it is a question of a priest who has taken a permanent leave of absence, there should be some agreement with the priest that the diocese will not impose the obligations of clerical status on him, and that he will not make claims on the benefits a cleric dedicated to ministry is entitled to. The agreement might also specify that the priest is to assure his retirement through social security and the usual means attached to his secular employment (presuming he is secularly employed). If it is a priest who has gone AWOL, the bishop still has the ultimate responsibility to see that he is provided with a "safety net" if he becomes truly indigent.

The second thing to note is the reason that underlies these responsibilities of the bishop. Through ordination a man has become a sacred minister, and the sacred ministry deserves special care. The 1917 code had a "right" of the clergy that they not be left destitute. While this "right" is no longer expressed in those terms in the 1983 code, the basic concept remains that clergy should not be allowed to languish in the gutter; they deserve at least that "decent support" which puts a roof over their head and that they have adequate food and clothing. The reason for this is the respect due to the sacrament of orders, not some special privilege the man has on his own. It is this respect for the sacrament of orders which the law on incardination is designed to protect, for it identifies the bishop (or religious superior) who is responsible to see that proper care is given to one who has been marked with the sacrament of orders.

If a cleric — deacon or priest — is truly destitute, his bishop of incardination is the one the Church identifies as having the responsibility to see that he is adequately cared for. Sometimes this is done by asking the bishop of the place where the destitute cleric is located to look after him. Sometimes it may require some payment of money. But it is different from providing him with a "pension" in the full sense of the word, if he has left active ministry and is no longer dedicated to the ministry of the Church.

Some dioceses have so structured their retirement plan that priests are "vested" after a number of years of service (e.g., after 10 years). If they leave the active ministry in the diocese prior to that time, they have no claim on payments from the retirement plan (although if they remain clerics, the bishop remains obliged to see they have "decent support" if they are destitute). If they leave the active ministry in the diocese after that time, they are entitled to a pro-rated payment from the retirement plan when they reach retirement age. The pro-rating is usually in terms of a percentage figured on the basis of the number of years they would have served if they had remained in active ministry in the diocese, adjusted by the number of years they actually did serve.

Take, for example, a priest who leaves the diocese at age 35 after serving for 12 years. Presume for the sake of the example that priests in that diocese can begin drawing on the retirement plan when they reach age 65. If the priest in our example would have remained in the diocese for the duration of his ministry, he would have served 42 years. But he only served for 12. So he gets 12/42 x the amount of the pension payment.

Of course, this depends on the pension plan of each diocese. There is no standard for the U.S.A. on this, nor does canon law set such specifics. But it is one way dioceses have adopted of covering this residual obligation of the bishop toward clergy incardinated in the diocese but no longer serving there, and it seems to be a way that meets the basic standards of fairness without breaking the bank.

You may want to take a close look at the provisions of your retirement plan to see whether some similar kind of provision exists. If not, the residual responsibility resides with the diocesan bishop, and it is advisable in any event that the bishop keep some sort of fund to meet emergencies of incardinated clergy who become destitute.

The situation is not so bleak as your inquiry might imply, but it is one that requires the kind of careful attention you are already giving it.

James H. Provost [1993]

CANONS 403; 409; AND 421

APPOINTMENT OF A DIOCESAN ADMINISTRATOR
OR A COADJUTOR

At the time of retirement or resignation, can a diocesan bishop name the diocesan administrator or his own coadjutor?

OPINION

The basic answer is no, the diocesan bishop cannot name the administrator who will take over upon his resignation. However, this is not always reserved to an election by the consultors.

When a bishop reaches 75 — or earlier, if he has personal reasons or due to health considerations — he is invited to submit his resignation to the Holy Father. It is up to the pope to decide whether and when to accept the resignation. When he does, there are several possibilities.

(1) Sometimes the pope appoints an administrator at the same time as he accepts the bishop's resignation. This kind of administrator is called an "apostolic administrator," and is able to do more than an elected "diocesan administrator" (which I will mention in a moment). Often the retiring bishop himself is named as the apostolic administrator until his successor is named. At other times another bishop is named to this position.

(2) The pope can name a coadjutor bishop before he accepts the resignation of the retiring bishop. Sometimes this is done before the retiring bishop submits his letter of resignation, sometimes afterward. The effect, however, is the

same: once the pope accepts the retiring bishop's resignation, the coadjutor automatically takes over as diocesan bishop, with no interregnum and no need for an administrator.

(3) If the pope accepts a bishop's letter of resignation but does not name an apostolic administrator and there is no coadjutor to take over automatically, then the diocese becomes vacant from the time the acceptance is made known. The diocesan consultors have eight days in which to meet and to elect an administrator to run the diocese until a new diocesan bishop takes over. This kind of administrator is a "diocesan administrator."

The situation can be more complicated when a bishop is transferred, but I will not go into that here!

James H. Provost [1991]

Canon 483

The Power of Lay Chancellors to Dispense

Can a lay person appointed to the office of chancellor be delegated to grant marriage dispensations?

Opinion

1. A lay person may be appointed to the office of diocesan chancellor. Under the former code, the chancellor had to be a priest (1917 code, c. 372, §1). There is no such restriction in the qualifications given for chancellor in the new code (c. 483, §2), although only a priest is to be named as notary in a case in which the reputation of a priest may be called into question.

Moreover, the office of chancellor is not one which per se requires the exercise of the power of governance. In the universal law, the chancellor is responsible to see that "the acts of the curia are gathered, arranged and safeguarded in the archive of the curia" (c. 482, §1); the chancellor is automatically a notary and secretary of the diocesan curia (c. 482, §3). These are not an exercise of executive power; they are administrative responsibilities. So the office of chancellor is not one of those which is restricted to clergy in virtue of canon 274, §1 ("only clerics can obtain those offices for whose exercise there is required the power of orders or the power of ecclesiastical governance").

2. The granting of matrimonial dispensations is not part of the office of

91

chancellor per se. In some dioceses the practice has developed of delegating the chancellor to grant marriage dispensations.

The new code grants to local ordinaries the power to dispense from marriage impediments not reserved to the Apostolic See (c. 1078, §1), and from nearly all of these in danger of death (c. 1079, §1) or in situations where everything is ready for the wedding (c. 1080, §§1 and 2). It also authorizes local ordinaries to dispense from canonical form in religiously mixed marriages (c. 1127, §2).

One who has the power to dispense may delegate that power (c. 85). This delegation may be for all cases, or only for certain specified ones (c. 137, §1). The usual practice in places where the chancellor has been delegated to grant marriage dispensations has been to grant the power for all cases.

3. While there is no question that the chancellor can be delegated to grant marriage dispensations, and there is strong historical precedent for it, the fact that lay persons can now be named to this office raises the question of whether a lay chancellor may continue to be delegated to grant marriage dispensations in keeping with past practice.

The crux of the problem seems to be whether lay persons can be delegated the exercise of executive authority, since to dispense is to exercise executive authority. Some hold that only those things that are explicitly stated in the law may be done; thus unless the law explicitly states that a lay person can be authorized to grant dispensations, a lay person may not do so. Others hold that where the law is silent, church authorities have the freedom to act.

The first approach does not permit a lay chancellor to be delegated to grant marriage dispensations because of its interpretation of canon 129. This is part of a much larger theoretical debate about power in the Church, which goes beyond the scope of this opinion. For details on the debate, see especially J. James Cuneo, "The Power of Jurisdiction: Empowerment for Church Functioning and Mission Distinct from the Power of Orders," *The Jurist* 39 (1979) 183-219, and James H. Provost, "The Participation of the Laity in the Governance of the Church," *Studia Canonica* 17 (1983) 417-448. But let me summarize the application of this debate to the question at hand.

The Question of Capacity

Canon 129 states that "in accord with the prescriptions of law, those who have received sacred orders are capable of the power of governance." Lay persons "can cooperate in the exercise of this power in accord with the norm of law." The first approach argues that since clergy are termed "capable" (*habiles*) but the term is not applied to lay persons, lay persons are not "capable" of the power of governance — they are *inhabiles*. So, they cannot be delegated to grant dispensations.

The difficulty with this argument is that it presumes what it sets out to prove. It presumes that since clergy are termed "capable," this is exclusive: only those termed "capable" in the law are capable; all others are not. Yet if this were true, then the law would have to specify in other circumstances that various persons are "capable" before the law could authorize them to do special activities. But this is not the case, even in dealing with lay persons.

Take, for example, the *munus docendi*. The law does not say that lay persons are "capable" of a specialized exercise of this *munus*, even though that specialized role is proper to the ordained (cc. 756-757). Yet the law states that lay persons can be called to cooperate in the specialized exercise of this *munus*, in addition to what they are authorized to do in virtue of baptism and confirmation (c. 759, after the semi-colon). Thus, lay persons are "capable" of this additional specialized role, even though the law does not state this explicitly (that is, does not term them *habiles*).

Moreover, canon 129 on the exercise of the *munus regendi* does not state that *only* those in sacred orders are "capable." It merely affirms that they are indeed capable. Thus the canon does not explicitly exclude lay persons from the exercise of the power of governance. The general norm on interpreting laws of this type is that "only those laws which expressly state that an act is null or that a person is incapable of acting are to be considered to be invalidating or incapacitating" (c. 10).

As explained above, canon 274, §1 does make an exclusive statement that only clerics can obtain *offices* for whose exercise the power of governance is required. Leaving aside the obvious difficulties with this canon, in light of other provisions of the code that explicitly permit lay persons to be named to such offices (e.g., c. 1421, §2), the point here is that what is restricted to clerics is not the power of governance itself, but only those offices for whose exercise this power is required.

The Question of Cooperation

Thus the second approach argues that lay chancellors can be delegated the power to grant marriage dispensations, since this is to cooperate in the power of governance, something which canon 129, §2 specifically authorizes them to do. It is to be done "in accord with the norm of law," and the law specifically permits those with the power to dispense to delegate that power, as indicated above.

Those who hold the first view counter that "to cooperate" does not include the possibility of granting marriage dispensations, since lay persons are not capable of exercising the power of governance. But again, this presumes what it sets out to prove.

The term "cooperate" was deliberately selected by the Code Commission, according to its Secretary Monsignor Julian Herranz, when he discussed this matter in a presentation to the Canadian Canon Law Society in October 1985. It is not intended to exclude possibilities.

"Cooperate" appears twenty-nine times in the new code, in six forms of the word. It is used to describe various relationships.

Some are the cooperation of peers with one another, or of similar kinds of organizations with one another. Thus, clergy are to cooperate with one another (c. 275, §1); bishops within an ecclesiastical region (c. 434); parents and teachers (c. 796, §2); lay people working to improve the public media (c. 822, §2); even married people in their sexual relations (c. 1096, §1). The law also calls for cooperation among associations of the faithful (c. 328), religious institutes and secular clergy (c. 680), conferences of major superiors and of bishops (c. 708), ecclesiastical universities and faculties (c. 820), and dioceses in handling funds for the support of ministers (c. 1274, §4).

Cooperation is also used in reference to persons who help another in works for which that other is the primary responsible agent. Thus, cooperation is applied to the work of bishops who help the pope in the Synod of Bishops, as cardinals, or in the Roman Curia (c. 334), and to the support cardinals provide the pope in a special way (c. 356); to the work of other presbyters and deacons with the pastor (c. 519), and in a special way to the work of parochial vicars with their pastor (c. 545, §1); to the work of assistants to the director of novices (cc. 651, §1 and 652, §1), and to the efforts of all members of the religious institute in general in the formation of novices (c. 652, §4); even to the activities of those who become irregular by cooperating in a completed abortion or homicide (c. 1041, 4°).

Cooperation is used, finally, to describe the relations of persons with special responsibilities which are related, but differ in some way. So, all the Christian faithful cooperate in building up the Body of Christ (c. 208); seminarians are to be co-workers (cooperators) with the bishop (c. 245, §2), as are priests with the bishop (cc. 369 and 757) and pastors with the bishop and the rest of the presbyterate (c. 529, §2). A special form of cooperation is "missionary cooperation" (cc. 787, §1 and 791), which covers a multitude of activities by a variety of persons.

In regard to lay persons cooperating with others, lay persons cooperate organically with a personal prelature (c. 296), with other members of a secular institute in serving the ecclesiastical community (c. 713, §2), with the bishop and presbyters in the specialized exercise of the *munus docendi* (c. 759), and in the exercise of the power of governance (c. 129, §2).

Lay cooperation in the power of governance is clearly more than the mutual cooperation of peers with one another. It belongs to either of the other two categories. Can it include the exercise of delegated power? If the term "cooperate" can be used, as it is, to include even the role of bishops in the Roman Curia, it would seem the term can include the exercise of a delegated power.

Since the law does not specifically prohibit that lay chancellors be delegated to grant marriage dispensations, and since lay people can cooperate in the exercise of the power of governance in accord with the norm of law, then it would be in keeping with the use of the term "cooperate" for lay chancellors to be able to exercise this delegated power.

Delegation by the Law

An argument against the possibility of lay chancellors being delegated to grant marriage dispensations is raised from an example of when the law itself lists those who are authorized to dispense in certain circumstances. These lists do not include lay persons who can otherwise assist at marriages. Let me explain.

The new code permits under restricted conditions that lay persons can be delegated to assist at marriages where priests or deacons are lacking (c. 1112, §1). Yet when the code lists the various persons authorized to dispense in danger of death (c. 1079, §2), or for occult cases when everything is ready for the marriage (c. 1080, §1), it does not include these delegated lay persons in its detailed list. So, it is argued, they cannot be delegated to dispense.

This argument again presumes what it sets out to prove. The fact that the law does not grant the delegation to such lay persons does not necessarily mean they *can* not be delegated; it only means they *are* not delegated *ipso iure*. This could be due to several factors: it might be a *lacuna* in the law, for the possibility of a lay person being delegated to assist at a marriage is new with this code; or, it could be that the matter has been left to the local bishop, who must delegate the lay person to assist at marriages in the first place. So the silence of the code in this matter does not of itself prove that lay persons cannot be delegated to grant marriage dispensations; several explanations for the code's silence are possible.

Rights of the Bishop

An argument in favor of the bishop being able to delegate a lay chancellor to grant marriage dispensations relates to the rights of the bishop. As one with the power to dispense, the bishop has the right to delegate this power. Any restriction on his right to delegate must be interpreted strictly (c. 18).

Yet as discussed above, a strict interpretation of the law does not yield a limitation that would restrict the bishop from being able to delegate a lay chancellor to grant marriage dispensations. Therefore, there is a presumption that the bishop has the right to delegate even in this manner.

Danger of Invalid Dispensations

Those opposed to lay chancellors being delegated to grant marriage dispensations raise the possibility that in the present state of the question, it is not clear that dispensations granted by such a delegated lay chancellor would be valid. The attempt to issue a dispensation by someone who cannot be authorized to do it would result in an invalid dispensation, and so in an invalid marriage. When the validity of a sacrament is at stake, it is important to act in such a way that the validity will be safeguarded.

Even if it is not entirely convincing to argue that lay chancellors cannot be delegated to grant marriage dispensations, it is at least necessary to protect the validity of marriages until the question is given an authentic interpretation by the Commission for the Authentic Interpretation of the Code. In matters of the sacraments, the safest route is always to be preferred.

This concern is a very important one. However, it has already been anticipated in the code itself. Canon 14 declares that "when there is a doubt of law, laws do not bind even if they be nullifying or disqualifying ones." Given the current state of this question, both sides admit that a *dubium iuris* may be said to exist. In such a situation, canon 14 assures the validity of the delegation to lay chancellors, and hence the validity of the dispensations which may be granted by such a delegated lay chancellor.

James H. Provost [1986]

ANOTHER OPINION

The question of empowerment for various ecclesiastical functions has become very important, especially since non-ordained persons are more frequently called to serve in positions of full-time service in the Church that were formerly held by clerics alone. Typical of the questions is this above inquiry concerning the authority that might be given to the diocesan chancellor who is a lay person. It is my opinion that lay chancellors may be given the power to dispense from marriage impediments as well as other functions of executive authority or power of governance. There are several points, however, which need to be considered in this topic.

1. There exist in the Church two sources of empowerment for church functions: the power of orders and the power of jurisdiction. (The full meaning of the distinction of power has been presented in my earlier article on jurisdiction cited by Provost in his opinion above.) The old code was explicit in stating the distinction (c. 109). Since Vatican Council II the intimate theological relationship between the two sources of power and the three

96

ecclesiastical functions (teaching, sanctifying and governing) is more clearly recognized, in particular with those who have been ordained as bishops (*Lumen gentium*, n. 21). Nevertheless, the Fathers of the Council continued to recognize a distinction between power which is conferred by ordination and power which is conferred by canonical mission, hierarchical communion with the pope and bishops (cf. *Nota praevia* added to the document on the Church, *Lumen gentium*). Finally canon 274, §1 of the new code indicates a continued recognition of two powers or distinctions of power.

2. With regard to those who are ordained, the Church recognizes a certain personal, innate right or ability to exercise ecclesiastical power including the function of governance. For example, in the new code canon 129 states that those who are ordained are capable (*habiles sunt*) of governing power. Elsewhere the code has reduced the requirements of priests to receive additional faculties for certain functions such as preaching (c. 764), administering the sacrament of penance (c. 967, §2). Ordination seems to confer an innate or personal capacity for these functions and perhaps carries a presumption of the Church that with the conferral of ordination the cleric stands in hierarchical communion for exercising authority. The distinction between power of orders and power of jurisdiction remains, however, at least logically distinct in clerics and in some situations really distinct (where additional faculties are explicitly needed or can be restricted or suspended).

3. With regard to lay persons it is clear that functions which require the power of orders cannot be conferred upon them. Functions which involve the power of jurisdiction (traditionally functions of teaching and governing) can be shared by lay persons (v.g., c. 129, §2: "Lay members of the Christian faithful can cooperate in the exercise of this power of governance in accord with the norm of law." Also cf., cc. 759; 766; 1112; 1421, §2).

4. The difference between ordained and lay persons in this regard seems to be that the law of the Church does not recognize in lay persons that innate, sacramentally conferred or automatically presumed capacity (*habilitas*), or that right given by orders by divine institution, to exercise the power of governance. Nevertheless lay persons can be named to exercise this power. By ordination clerics are capable of governing power. According to the norm of law (designation? delegation? canonical mission?) lay person may share in the exercise of governing power. It would seem that part of the essential difference between clergy and laity resides in the essentially different mode of conferral of the ecclesiastical function and in the different extent of the stability of the right to exercise power of governance. It seems, however, the Church recognizes lay persons can exercise power of governance dependent on the nature of the individual mandate.

5. According to canon 274, §1 only clerics can obtain those offices for whose

exercise there is required the power of orders or the power of ecclesiastical governance. Again, it seems to me, the issue here is the notion of stability. Ecclesiastical office (c. 145) is any function constituted *in a stable manner* by divine or ecclesiastical law . . . Therefore, in current legislation a lay person cannot be given an *office* involving power of governance.

We note, however, the distinction between power of office and delegated power in canon 131, §1: "The ordinary power of governance is that which is joined to a certain office by the law itself; delegated power is that which is granted to a person, but not by means of an office." Therefore, only clerics may be given an office of governance, but delegated power of governance is precisely not ordinary power; it is power granted to a person but not by means of an office; it is given without the stability of an office. Canon 274, §1 reserves the power of office of governance to clerics. The restriction does not extend to delegated power. Canon 129, §2 permits lay persons to cooperate in the exercise of power of governance according to law. This exercise would seem to follow the norms of law regarding delegated power; it could never enjoy the stability of rights involved with ordinary power or the power of office.

6. The office of chancellor is not reserved to clerics (c. 483). Lay persons may be given this office enjoying all the rights and obligations of that function constituted in the stable fashion of an ecclesiastical office (c. 145). In some dioceses certain additional executive functions such as power to dispense or to grant permission of the ordinary where needed, have been attached to the office of chancellor. These additional functions, however, were not and are not part of the code's job description of the office of chancellor.

If a lay person is given the office of chancellor, it seems the bishop could also delegate to this person some exercise of the power of governance. The power, however, would be precisely only delegated, not ordinary, never attached as such to the office of chancellor, but conferred upon the person without the stability of ecclesiastical office. The delegated power of governance that would be given to a lay person, who happens also to be chancellor, would be subject to the usual limitations and restrictions of delegated power; for example, it could be revoked by the bishop at his discretion (c. 142), even though the lay person could continue to hold the office of chancellor with its proper functions conferred in a stable manner.

In conclusion it seems some power of governance, executive authority, may be given to a person who is a lay person holding the office of chancellor. The power is delegated to the person and not attached to the office of chancellor. In a similar way it seems some participation in the power of governance may be given to other lay persons who hold offices in the Church, such as parochial ministers named to parishes that have no resident priest (c. 517, §2). It seems they could be given some delegated or sub-delegated power of jurisdiction, for example, to preach (other than homily), to officiate at marriages, or to grant permission for mixed marriages according to the norms of canon 1125 and with the faculty of the bishop. It seems these are the possibilities intended by canon 129, §2 for lay persons, whether they be chancellors or in some other position.

J. James Cuneo [1986]

Canon 494

Religious Affiliation of the Diocesan Finance Officer

Does the law require that the diocesan business manager (finance officer), mentioned in canon 494, be a member of the Catholic Church?

Opinion

Canon 494 does not, by its own terms, impose the requirement that the diocesan business manager be a member of the Catholic Church. This canon, which creates the office of diocesan business manager, poses only two requirements, namely that the business manager is to be "truly skilled in financial affairs and absolutely distinguished for honesty" (c. 494, §1). Thus, if the diocesan business manager must, by law, be a member of the Catholic Church, this requirement must come from some other place in the code. It is not found in canon 494.

Canons 129 and 149 have been cited as a possible basis for this requirement. Canon 129, §2 states that "[l]ay members of the Christian faithful can cooperate in the exercise of this power [of jurisdiction] in accord with the norm of law." The immediate question that the citation of this canon raises in regard to the diocesan business manager is whether or not that officer shares in the exercise of the power of jurisdiction. It is not obvious that this officer does. The code describes this person as a budget administrator, a person who acts within the clear confines set forth in a budget established by the diocesan finance council (c. 494, §3). This person is also a bill-payer, but only of bills that the bishop or his delegate has authorized (c. 494, §3). Finally, the diocesan business manager makes yearly reports to the diocesan finance council (c. 494, §4).

What kind of power does the diocesan business manager truly exercise? Clearly it is not legislative or judicial; that would leave only the possibility of executive power. But canon 136 describes executive power as being a power exercised over subjects. What subjects does a budget administrator, payer of bills and report-maker have? It is not apparent that such a person has any true

99

subjects. This officer is a functionary, a skilled one, but nevertheless a functionary. There is a very good argument that this office as defined in the code does not require the exercise of the power of jurisdiction.

Canon 149, §1 states that "[i]n order to be promoted to an ecclesiastical office, a person must be in the communion of the Church. . . ." The first question that must be asked, then, is whether the office of diocesan business manager is an ecclesiastical office. According to canon 145, §1, an ecclesiastical office is "any function constituted in a stable manner by divine or ecclesiastical law to be exercised for a spiritual purpose." The office of diocesan business manager is created by the code (c. 494, §1) and it does exist on a stable basis (five year term, c. 494, §2). Does it have a spiritual purpose? While there may be those who believe that asset management has no spiritual aspect, it is the code's view that property, properly managed, does fulfill a spiritual function (c. 1254, §2). The office of diocesan business manager, then, would qualify as an ecclesiastical office. Note that it is clearly not an office entailing the care of souls.

It follows that the requirement of canon 149, §1, that an office-holder be "in the communion of the Church" applies to the diocesan business manager. This conclusion makes any reliance on canon 129 and any analysis of the question of the diocesan business manager's exercise of the power of jurisdiction unnecessary, since the terminology of canon 129, "a lay member of the Christian faithful" does not add anything to the terminology of canon 149, §1, "in the communion of the Church." The fact of the matter is that any member of the Christian faithful will somehow be in the communion of the Church. The language of canon 129 is no more restrictive than the language of canon 149, and since it is clear that canon 149 does apply to the diocesan business manager, while canon 129 may not, this analysis will proceed using the requirement imposed by canon 149, §1, namely that the diocesan business manager must be "in the communion of the Church."

What does it mean to be "in the communion of the Church"? The code speaks of this concept in two different canons. Canon 204, §1 states that the "Christian faithful are those who, inasmuch as they have been incorporated in Christ through baptism, have been constituted as the people of God; for this reason, since they have become sharers in Christ's priestly, prophetic and royal office in their own manner, they are called to exercise the mission which God has entrusted to the Church to fulfill in the world, in accord with the condition proper to each." Canon 205 states that: "[t]hose baptized are fully in communion with the Catholic Church on this earth who are joined with Christ in its visible structure by the bonds of profession of faith, of the sacraments and of ecclesiastical governance."

The code, therefore, speaks of communion with the Church in two senses.

There is the strict sense of full communion that requires baptism plus the sharing in the common bonds of faith, sacraments and church governance. This is the sense of canon 205. But there is also the sense of canon 204, §1 that admits that there are persons who are members of the Christian faithful by virtue of their incorporation in Christ through baptism. This sense, it would have to be admitted, is not as strict as the sense of canon 205. It would allow that baptism alone somehow puts the baptized person in communion with the Church, albeit not in the full sense of canon 205.

The roots of this distinction are in *Lumen gentium.* As Yves Congar has written:

> [T]he Council did not identify the Mystical Body purely and simply with the Roman Catholic Church or even with the Church of Christ. 'This Church . . . subsists in the Roman Catholic Church, *subsistit in Ecclesia catholica*, although many elements of sanctification and truth can be found outside her visible structures' (*LG* 8, 2). By expressing the matter in this way, the Council established the possibility of recognizing other Christians as truly belonging to the Body of Christ and of speaking of the relation of other Churches and ecclesial communities with the Catholic Church in terms of a real, although imperfect, communion. (Y. Congar, "What Belonging To The Church Has Come To Mean," in J. Hite, ed., *Readings, Cases and Materials in Canon Law* [Collegeville: The Liturgical Press, 1990] 171).

This distinction is important because the qualifying phrase in canon 149, §1 is "in the communion of the Church." The adjective "full" is not used in describing "communion." Yet when he chooses to, the legislator knows how to establish full communion as a prerequisite to holding a particular office. For example, canon 512, §1, speaking of the diocesan pastoral council, states that council members must be "Christian faithful who are in full communion with the Church."

Therefore, in order to exercise the office of diocesan business manager, the candidate must meet the requirement of canon 204, §1, that is, the person must have been incorporated in Christ through baptism. The more restrictive constraint of canon 205 requiring "full" communion does not apply because neither in canon 494 itself, nor in the general law on office-holders, is this more restrictive terminology used.

Therefore, to the question of whether the diocesan business manager must be a member of the Catholic Church, I would answer no. A diocesan business manager must only meet the criterion of canon 204, §1, namely baptism into Christ, thereby allowing any baptized person to fulfill this role. I believe that this result is in accord with the thinking of the council, in whose light the code must always be interpreted. Additionally, given the previous animadversions that the office of diocesan business manager is purely functionary, and probably not a true exercise of jurisdiction, it makes little sense to hold that a baptized member of another Christian community is disqualified from holding this office.

Nicholas P. Cafardi [1992]

CANON 495

AUXILIARY BISHOPS AS MEMBERS OF THE PRESBYTERAL COUNCIL

In larger sees where there are auxiliary bishops the diocesan bishops are determined to have the auxiliaries on councils. Insofar as deacons are not envisioned as members of presbyteral councils, can it be that members of the episcopal college are also not so envisioned? It seems that there must be some other kind of manner of council for them. It can be noted that the code uses "sacerdos" and not "presbyter" in reference to those who are members or have rights (e.g., voting) in regard to the council. Do auxiliary bishops have a right or can they be appointed to a presbyteral council?

OPINION

As you note, canon 495 uses the word "*sacerdos*" rather than "*presbyter*" in describing the members of the presbyteral council. The word "*sacerdos*" is used consistently throughout the code when it means to include both bishops and priests; the word "*presbyter*" is used when specifically priests are intended.

Therefore, it is possible for an auxiliary bishop to be elected to membership on a presbyteral council since he is a "*sacerdos*." Moreover the statutes of the presbyteral council can provide for appointed and *ex officio* members. Auxiliary bishops could satisfy membership under any of those rubrics, in keeping with the statutes of the presbyteral council.

James H. Provost [1985]

CANON 502

MEMBERSHIP OF PRESBYTERAL COUNCIL AND CONSULTORS

In a diocese where the presbyteral council has only eleven members, can the bishop appoint the entire council as the college of consultors?

As far as I can tell the bishop can appoint all eleven members of the senate to be his board of consultors. However, you might want to consider adjusting the term of office to five years so that their term as senators and as consultors would be coterminous.

James H. Provost [1984, revised 1993]

CANON 502

1. COORDINATING TERMS OF OFFICE FOR CONSULTORS, DEANS, PRIEST COUNCIL MEMBERS

In our diocese the deans are nominated through an election by the presbyterate and appointed to the position by the bishop for a term of two years; they automatically become members of the priests' council during their term in office. The council has three other ex officio *members, and three members elected at-large. Our concern is how to correlate the five year term which consultors have, with the various terms as dean and on the priests' council.*

First, it is important to recognize that there are various offices in question here. To be a dean is a distinct office, with the special responsibilities of animating the pastoral and priestly life of the deanery. The selection process you are following is in keeping with the provisions of the new code (c. 554), including the fact that deans are named for a term set by diocesan law (2 years in your case).

Second, that deans serve on the priests' council for the duration of their term as dean means they are *ex officio* members of the council, rather than elected members. It would appear from your description of the council that only the three at-large members are what the code considers elected in terms of canon 497, 1°. However, since their designation as deans follows nomination by election, it would appear the spirit of the law is being observed. Canon 499 requires the statutes of the priests' council to determine how elected members are to be chosen, and if your statutes incorporate the diocesan policy of presbyterate election to nominate deans, this would be taken care of.

103

It should be clear, however, that serving as a member of the priests' council is a different responsibility from being a dean. Members of the priests' council are not representatives of districts, but of the presbyterate as a whole. I can see no problem with the deans serving on the priests' council provided they keep in mind they are performing a different function from that of dean here.

Third, the office of consultor is a distinct position from that of dean or of member of the priests' council. The idea was to provide for a special group the bishop could consult about delicate matters of finance, and which would carry the responsibility for the diocese when the see becomes vacant.

Consultors are not necessarily part of the priests' council. That is, when selected to be a consultor a priest must be a member of the priests' council. But consultors are named for a term of five years, and the intent of the law is that they be named as a body for five years (i.e., without staggered terms). It is conceivable that a priest would complete his term on the priests' council before his term as a consultor expires; he remains one of the consultors until this distinct term is up.

In this country there has been a concern to combine the functions of consultors and priests' council. There are many reasons for this. In a diocese such as yours, with a limited number of priests, it makes good sense to cut down unnecessary duplication and to make the best use possible of the priests available. Some dioceses also argue that given the size of their presbyterate, a relatively small priests' council is appropriate and it is, therefore, convenient to combine the two bodies. Similarly, a number of dioceses desire to maintain continuity in the case of a vacant see, and having the same priests serve on the priests' council and as consultors will assure this. In even a few dioceses there is a concern lest the two bodies be played off against one another, resulting in no effective input from the presbyterate in the governance affairs of the diocese.

For these and other reasons, it was proposed in drafting the new code that consultors be dropped altogether and replaced with the priests' council. One of the reasons this was not done was to provide for those situations where the bishop may not wish to discuss sensitive financial matters with a large priests' council, and may also want to be able to select from among the council's members the more experienced and astute who would advise him on financial matters and be responsible when the see becomes vacant. Keeping the two bodies, the code at least tried to relate them better than previously by requiring the consultors be selected from among the members of the priests' council.

Your specific problem, however, relates to term of office. For deans, it is now two years in your diocese. For consultors, by law it is five years. Thus if the bishop selects the entire twelve member priests' council as consultors, this particular group of twelve will remain as consultors for the next five years even though many if not all of them will rotate off the priests' council in that time.

104

There are several possible solutions. One is to reduce the number of consultors, so the members of the priests' council and consultors never are identically the same. From the outset this would make the point that the consultors are a distinct group selected by the bishop, so it really does not matter if eventually some or all of them go off the priests' council.

Another possible solution is to make a new category on the priests' council among the *ex officio* members. This would make it possible for any members of the priests' council who are also consultors, and whose term on the priests' council expires, to remain on the council for the duration of the time they are a consultor but now as an *ex officio* member in virtue of being a consultor.

A third solution some dioceses have adopted is to bite the bullet, and to name the priests' council for a five year term. Then they can make the council (provided it has only 12 members or less) the consultors, and the two are co-terminous, i.e., their terms as members of the priests' council and as consultors expire at the same time.

In your situation, the combination of dean + member of priests' council + consultor would mean that a group of six priests would occupy all three of these key consultative positions in the diocese for a five year term.

It seems to me you need to make a prudential judgment. If the number of priests is indeed so small, and the available talent so restricted, that it is essential to have the same priests fulfill the two jobs of dean and member of priests' council simultaneously, why should they not serve for a five year term? If, on the other hand, it is more for convenience that the deans are automatically members of the priests' council, why not enlarge the membership of the council by new *ex officio* members to continue on the council those who have been named consultors, even though they are no longer deans? I realize this will result in some members of the priests' council not being consultors at various times, but your system does not seem to provide any relief from this possibility, short of moving to the five year term simultaneously for dean, council member and consultor.

Could there be another option, namely that the bishop dispense from the five year term set for consultors in the code, so that priests serving their two years as dean and member of the priests' council could also serve as consultor for that time, but then be replaced in all three positions? I think not. The law clearly determines a five year term for consultors (c. 502, §1). Indeed, it is the "college" as such that is constituted for five years, not just individuals in it. In effect, canon 502, §1 appears to be a constitutive law, defining what essentially constitutes the juridical institute of the college of consultors, and is therefore not subject to dispensation by the diocesan bishop (c. 86). So, whatever solution is adopted for term of office on the priests' council, it cannot change the term for members of the consultors.

105

The final option available seems to be that of permitting some vacancies to occur on the consultors. The authentic interpretation from the Code Commission in 1984 indicated it is not essential that vacancies be filled in the college of consultors, provided sufficient number remain to carry out their purpose. At least three members would seem to be the ultimate minimum required to function. Thus, if the twelve now serving as members of the priests' council include six who are not deans, and therefore, not subject to the two year term in force for deans, it would be possible for the statutes of the priests's council to provide for a longer term for these six (three *ex officio* and three at-large). If the priests who are elected dean resign from being consultors when they leave the offices of dean and council member, the number of consultors would be diminished, but would remain composed of persons actually serving on the council. Of course, there does not appear to be a way in which a priest could be forced to resign as consultor once his two year term as dean and council member expired. So, if a priest were to decide not to resign, you could be back at the situation of having consultors who are not members of the priests' council. I really think this final option would prove more troublesome in the long run.

James H. Provost [1985]

2. Dispensation from Number of Consultors and from Length of Term of Office in a Small Diocese Formerly an Apostolic Vicariate

The 1917 code allowed small dioceses to function with four consultors rather than six (c. 425) and the term of office was three years. Also in vicariates and prefectures apostolic it was sufficient to establish a council of three missionaries (c. 302). The 1983 code also permits a council of three missionaries in such vicariates (c. 495), but in diocesan structure no longer mentions the reduction to four consultors in small dioceses, and the term is five years (c. 502).

In one particular diocese, which was once an apostolic vicariate, the situation exists that there are only eighteen priests. The diocese (which is not in the United States) operates under three civil corporations: (1) a religious corporation which owns church buildings, land, rectories, convents; (2) a school corporation which owns the school buildings and operates them; (3) a welfare corporation which owns nursery buildings and operates them. Over the years the diocese has maintained five consultors and has named the same five consultors to each of the above civil corporations so that the corporation boards and consultors are identical for the sake of unity and coordination of diocesan business. Furthermore state law requires the corporation members to have three year terms so the diocese names its consultors for three years.

Under the new code, may the bishop of this diocese keep the number of consultors at five and name them for three year terms? This has been the practice since 1973 when the apostolic vicar was made diocesan bishop.

OPINION

The query is 1) whether a small diocese with only few priests can still follow the prescription of the 1917 code in the appointment of consultors; or 2) if the reply to query 1) is in the negative, whether the diocesan bishop can dispense from canon 502, §1 with regard to a) the number of consultors; and b) their term of office.

1. In the present code particular churches are divided into dioceses, territorial prelatures or territorial abbacies, apostolic vicariates or apostolic prefectures, and apostolic administrations. A diocese is a portion of the people of God entrusted for pastoral care to a bishop. A territorial prelature or territorial abbacy is a certain portion of the people of God established within certain territorial boundaries and whose care, due to special circumstances, is entrusted to some prelate or abbot who governs it as its proper pastor, like a diocesan bishop. An apostolic vicariate, an apostolic prefecture, or an apostolic administration is a certain portion of the people of God which is not yet erected into a diocese due to particular circumstances, and whose pastoral care is entrusted to an apostolic vicar, apostolic prefect, or apostolic administrator, who governs it in the name of the Supreme Pontiff.

The code provides that in all these particular churches there be a council of consultors. In dioceses the minimum number of consultors is six and the maximum, twelve. But in mission territories, where the number of Christian faithful is too small to erect a diocese and where the apostolic vicariate, prefecture or administration is established, the code provides for a council of consultors with a minimum of 3 missionary presbyters. Though the 1917 code required a minimum of 4 consultors in dioceses of few priests, in the present code we do not find any privilege for dioceses of few priests with regard to the number of consultors. Even dioceses with few priests are bound to have a college of at least 6 consultors. The assumption is that when a diocese is erected there would be enough priests from whom 6 consultors can be appointed.

The diocese in this query, formerly an apostolic vicariate, was erected into a diocese in 1973. Hence, the provision of canon 495, §2 does not apply to it, whereas it is bound by canon 502, §1, which requires a council of at least 6 consultors.

107

Hence, the reply to query (1) is in the negative.

2. The second query is whether the diocesan bishop can dispense from canon 502, §1 with regard to (a) the number of consultors, (b) their term of office.

According to canon 85 a dispensation from a merely ecclesiastical law in a particular case can be granted by those who enjoy executive power within the limits of their competence. However, to the extent that laws define that which essentially constitutes juridical institutes or acts, they are not subject to dispensation (c. 86).

Now, the bishop certainly has executive power and canon 502 is, no doubt, a merely ecclesiastical law. Hence, the bishop can dispense from canon 502, subject to one condition, viz., that this merely ecclesiastical law does not define that which essentially constitutes the juridical institute, which is the college of consultors. So, the point to be clarified is whether the content of canon 502, §1, with regard to the two elements pertinent to our problem, namely (a) the number of consultors and (b) their term of office, defines that which essentially constitutes the college of consultors.

a. Number of consultors

In the 1917 code the number of consultors in dioceses was to be six, but in dioceses of few priests the minimum number was fixed as four. In the new code the function of the college of consultors in apostolic vicariates and prefectures belongs to a council of at least 3 missionary presbyters. If the number ''6'' belonged to the essence of the college of consultors in the mind of the legislator there would not have been a variation in number in the college of consultors both in the old and in the new codes. Hence, number of consultors is not an essential constituent of the college of consultors. However, the number should be such as to ensure the purpose of the college of consultors, which is to furnish consent or counsel to the bishop before he can place certain acts determined by law (cf., c. 127, §1). The praxis of the Church indicates that their number cannot be less than four in a diocese.

b. Term of office

The 1917 code required that the college of consultors be appointed for a 3 year term and the 1983 code requires a 5 year term. The term of office of the college of consultors in the apostolic vicariates and prefectures, i.e., of the mission council, is not determined by the code. Here again the variations in the term of office of the consultors is an indication of the mind of the legislator, which seems to be that the five year term is not an essential constituent of the college of consultors. However, at least in dioceses the college of consultors should enjoy a certain stability of office, in order to be able to function effectively without fear or favor.

Hence, the reply to queries 2(a) and 2(b) is in the affirmative; i.e., the diocesan bishop can dispense from canon 502, §1 with regard to both the number of the college of consultors as well as its term of office.

In order to arrive at a practical conclusion in the particular case here, we have to take into account another important canon regarding dispensation.

A dispensation from an ecclesiastical law may not be granted without a just and reasonable cause and without taking into consideration the circumstances of the case and the gravity of the law from which the dispensation is to be given; otherwise the dispensation is illicit and unless it is given by the legislator himself or his superior, it is also invalid (c. 90, §1).

When there is a doubt about the sufficiency of the cause, a dispensation is granted validly and licitly (c. 90, §2).

The question is whether in the particular situation and circumstances existing in the said diocese, there is a just and reasonable cause for the dispensation.

It is a fact that the diocese has only 14 active priests, which is indeed too small. However, the diocese has 5 consultors now and there seems to be no problem with it mentioned in the letter, and the vicar general admits that they could add more priests to the college of consultors, without much difficulty, I presume. The real problem with the diocese appears to me as adjusting the consultors to the boards of the three civil corporations through which the diocese operates. I do not understand why the college of consultors and church corporation boards should be identical. What is important, according to me, is that the consultors wield a majority in the church corporation boards, in order to ensure that the decisions of the college of consultors are carried through. Without having to change the statutes of the church corporations or going against civil laws the bishop can distribute the six consultors required by the code into the three corporations, so that there are three consultors on each board, who can manage the majority in the five-member board. They can be appointed to the boards for a three year term, as the civil law requires, and reappointed for another term of three years when the first three-year term expires. If any change is effected in the college of consultors after the five-year term, changes can be made accordingly in the personnel of the corporation boards when their three-year term expires, dropping the retired consultors and filling in the vacancy with the newly appointed consultors.

Hence, my opinion is that considering the circumstances described in the query, the bishop does not have a just and reasonable cause to dispense from the number of diocesan consultors or from their term of office.

Joseph K. Parampath [1985]

CANON 515

SUPPRESSION AND MERGER OF PARISHES:
BRIEF OVERVIEW OF CANONICAL ISSUES

The erection, suppression and merger of parishes each seem to affect the rights of the faithful, the pastors (for example, their tenure of office) and the bishop and religious communities (who may have a parish entrusted to their care). What are some of the canonical issues to which the parties involved should pay attention when proposing or effecting the suppression or merger of parishes?

OPINION

The pastoral care of a diocese is entrusted to the diocesan bishop in cooperation with the presbyterate (c. 369). Each diocese is to be divided into parishes (c. 374).

Canon 515, §1. A parish is a definite community of the Christian faithful established on a stable basis within a particular church; the pastoral care of the parish is entrusted to a pastor as its own shepherd under the authority of the diocesan bishop.

§2. The diocesan bishop alone is competent to erect, suppress or alter parishes; he is not to erect, suppress or notably alter them without hearing the presbyteral council.

§3. A legitimately erected parish has juridic personality by the law itself.

Rights of the Faithful

All of Christ's faithful have the right to receive from the Church's pastors the spiritual goods of the Church, especially the Word of God and the sacraments (c. 213). The faithful have a right, therefore, to expect the opportunity to be nourished by Word and sacrament. That right does not extend to demanding that a particular parish be maintained for them to exercise that right. A bishop must make decisions about parishes taking into account, certainly, the good of the people immediately involved, but also the resources of the diocese and the broader good of the diocese. There is no inherent right for a particular parish to remain in existence.

The faithful do have a right to make their needs and desires known to the bishop and pastor and even to other persons, with due regard for the common good (c. 212, §§2 and 3). It would be appropriate, therefore, for any process leading to the closing or consolidation of parishes to make provision for due consultation with the people involved. Ultimately, the faithful are called to follow what the bishop determines as best for the Church (c. 212, §1).

The pastor has tenure in his office, either unlimited or for a definite period (c. 522). If a parish continues in existence, the pastor's tenure continues. Should the bishop suppress a parish or merge two or more parishes to form a new one, the office in the suppressed parishes would cease. The pastor would not have a continued right to a non-existent office. He retains his right to support from the Church (c. 281). It is appropriate that a new appointment be provided, but, in my opinion, the laws pertaining to the transfer or removal of pastors do not apply after a parish no longer exists.

Religious communities deserve special consideration when they are involved. The written agreement between the diocesan bishop and the competent superior should be consulted. In general, the diocesan bishop's right to suppress or change parishes will prevail, but adequate consultation with the community involved will always be well-advised.

Process of Suppression or Merger

The diocesan bishop establishes, suppresses or changes parishes by means of a canonical decree signed by himself. It is to be signed by the chancellor or another ecclesiastical notary (c. 474).

Before the diocesan bishop may *validly* issue a decree that would suppress or notably change a parish (merge it with another parish, for instance) he must hear the presbyteral council (c. 515, §2 and c. 127). The consent of the council is not required, but they must be consulted or the action would be canonically invalid. Ordinarily the consultation must take place at a meeting, but the statutes of the council could permit consultation by mail or telephone in an instance such as this. If the statutes of the group make no special provision, a meeting to discuss the proposed action is required. The bishop is not required to follow the opinion of a majority of the council, but obviously would act otherwise only with serious overriding reasons (by analogy with c. 127, §2, 2°).

In the case of a merger, the presumption is that the resulting parish will be territorial (c. 518). The new boundaries should be clearly stated in the decree, together with any effect on the boundaries of other parishes. In case of suppression, the effect on the boundaries of other parishes should be made clear.

If a personal parish is to be established, this should be clearly stated as should the basis upon which membership in that parish is established (c. 518).

If a new church building is to be erected, the diocesan bishop is not to give his permission (which must be in writing) without consulting both the presbyteral council and the pastors of neighboring parishes (c. 1215, §2). Again, the bishop is not bound to follow their opinions.

The Canonical Effects of Suppression/Amalgamation

111

Regarding Property and Other Assets

Let it first be said that it will be absolutely necessary for church administrators to attend to civil law provisions in these matters. Much will depend on the form of civil incorporation or other mode of holding assets. The corporate charter or by-laws may contain pertinent provisions about both process and disposition. Ideally, these will have been prepared carefully so that there is no discrepancy with canon law, but such may not always be the case. Conflicts at this level must be carefully dealt with on a case by case basis.

The parishioners do not own the church or any of the parish assets. A parish is a public juridic person in canon law (see cc. 115-116). This is somewhat like a corporation in civil law. The public juridic person has the right of ownership of all goods it has legitimately acquired by donation, bequest, purchase, or which have otherwise come to it (c. 1256). Ownership in canon law is strictly interpreted so that others, including the parishioners, cannot be considered canonically as having any ownership.

At the same time, it is clear canonically as well as civilly that for anything received with specific restrictions or instructions, the intentions of the donor must be respected (c. 1267, §3).

The Code of Canon Law makes specific provisions for instances when public juridic persons are suppressed or merged.

If the decree of establishment or statutes of the parish or diocese make provision for the disposition of property or other goods, their stipulations are to be followed. If no such provisions are contained, all goods pass to the juridic person immediately superior, in this case the diocese (c. 123). Any outstanding obligations also belong to the diocese in such a case. The restrictions or instructions attached to any funds or properties must continue to be honored.

When two or more parishes are merged into one, the new parish owns the goods and patrimony of the pre-existing parishes and assumes their obligations (c. 121). Again the intentions of donors must be respected.

More complex questions can occur. For example, five or six parishes might be reduced to two. It is essential that the decree or decrees effecting this action make clear what is being done. Simple merger might be involved. On the other hand, several parishes might simply be suppressed and the territory assigned to other parishes. The exact canonical disposition of the property and patrimony involved will depend on precisely what canonical action was taken by the diocesan bishop (see cc. 121-123).

Sale of Property

Often the resulting parish or the diocese itself will want to dispose of excess properties. It is important to note that the regulations regarding alienation of church property must be followed (cc. 1292-1298). These requirements will not be specifically detailed in this opinion. Special attention must be given if the property is of historical significance or artistic value (c. 1292, §2).

If it is a church building that is to be sold, the diocesan bishop may provide for the sale for other use, but he must hear the presbyteral council (c. 1222, §2). Other persons, a patron who donated a church in return for specific action by the parish or diocese, for example, may have special rights when sale or destruction is contemplated. Such would not ordinarily be true of persons who contributed at the time of the construction of a church and in return were memorialized by a plaque on some specific furniture or piece of decor or those mentioned on a general memorial plaque in a church.

John J. Myers [1987]

CANONS 515-517

MISSION PARISHES (QUASI-PARISHES) CHANGED TO STATUS OF PARISH

May a mission parish be designated a parish although there would be no resident priest? Furthermore, must the bishop issue a decree designating the change from mission status to parish status?

OPINION

First of all, the revised code emphasizes the parish as a *certa communitas Christifidelium* (c. 515, §1) somewhat comparable to the description of the diocese as a *populi Dei portio* (c. 368). A detailed discussion of the varied elements of the juridic personality of the parish (c. 515, §3) seems inappropriate here. However, it can probably be stated that the key feature of the parish is the community of the faithful for whom pastoral care is exercised on an ongoing basis. This pastoral care is normally undertaken by one individual functioning as the proper pastor of the parish (c. 515, §1). He may be assisted by others in exercising his sanctifying, teaching, and pastoral governance responsibilities (c. 519). Most of the canons in the chapter on parishes, pastors, and parochial vicars (cc. 515-552) deal with such pastors, one of whose principal obligations is residence in the parish (c. 550).

While the ordinary situation envisioned in the code is one resident pastor in each parish, there are some exceptions to this rule since the most basic value to be preserved is not precisely the one resident pastor norm but rather the efficacious pastoral care of a given community of the faithful. Accordingly, canon 517, §1 empowers a group of priests to exercise the pastoral care of a parish or parishes *in solidum* (team ministry) while one priest functions as moderator of the group. Enhanced episcopal discretion in the structuring of parishes is even more evident in canon 517, §2. If there is a shortage of priests, the bishop may entrust a share in the exercise of pastoral care in a parish to a deacon, a lay person, or a group of such persons. A priest who is not technically the pastor is to fulfill a supervisory role in the exercise of such pastoral care. Furthermore, canon 526, §1 states that normally a pastor is to exercise pastoral care in only one parish. However, it also indicates that if there is a shortage of clergy or if other circumstances suggest it, such a pastor may exercise a leadership role in more than one parish.

In short there seems to be a norm and various pastoral exceptions. The norm is a resident pastor in a parish; the exceptions are one priest ministering to a number of neighboring parishes or team ministry, i.e., in the proper sense, a group of priests exercising pastoral care in one or more parishes or, in the improper sense, a deacon or lay person(s) supervised by a priest with the powers of a pastor. Therefore, there seems to be no reason why the mission 'parish' (which is perhaps more properly a quasi-parish in the sense of c. 516) could not be designated a parish in the proper sense of the word although it would not have a resident pastor. If the current pastor of the 'mother parish' remained as pastor of the new parish, a situation comparable to canon 526, §1 would seemingly be verified.

It seems that the bishop would have to issue a decree constituting such a mission 'parish' now as a parish in the proper sense of the word. This is crucial in view of the new legal status of this particular group of the faithful, e.g., legal personality as indicated in canon 515, §3. Changing the status of the mission to a parish in the proper sense of the word seems to reflect a judgment that this group of the faithful enjoys a certain stability — the key characteristic that differentiates the parish (c. 515) from the quasi-parish/other pastoral provisions (c. 516). This would have long-term implications for the ongoing provision of pastoral care.

If the bishop decides to issue such a decree, he must consult the presbyteral council (c. 515, §2) since this is an example of a significant administrative decision for which the bishop needs to be guided by the pastoral wisdom of a representative group of presbyters.

Thomas J. Green [1986]

CANON 517

114

A Catholic campus community has been organized and administered by a priest and a nun. The bishop has designated them "co-pastors," and they equally share in the administrative and (to the extent possible) ministerial functions of the parish. In setting up the community as a parish, is it possible to list both the priest and the sister in the incorporation documents as "co-pastors"?

OPINION

Only a priest can be named a pastor (c. 521, §1). Similarly, only several priests can be named to the care of a community as a team or "co-pastors" (cc. 517, §1 and 542). If a religious sister has been called a "co-pastor" this is not the canonical use of the term "co-pastor" but rather a popularized, non-canonical and non-binding use of the term.

Calling the sister a "co-pastor" does not constitute an ecclesiastical appointment to the office of pastor or co-pastor because as a person who is not a priest she cannot be validly appointed. Canon 149, §2 states that "provision of an ecclesiastical office made in favor of a person who lacks the required qualities is invalid only if the qualities are expressly required for the validity of the provision by universal or particular law . . . ." In this case the quality of being a priest is required by universal law for the validity of the appointment as pastor or co-pastor.

So, in the articles of incorporation, she cannot be designated "co-pastor." However, this does not change the duties which have legitimately been given to her as a lay minister by the bishop when he assigned her to the community, in keeping with canon 517, §2.

James H. Provost [1986]

CANON 517

JURISDICTION FOR LAITY

How much jurisdiction can those members of the non-ordained who are in charge of a parish exercise?

OPINION

Canon 517, §2 provides the canonical basis for the growing phenomenon worldwide and even in this country of placing non-ordained ministers in charge of parishes. The canon provides:

1. This arrangement may be made only in situations where there is a shortage of priests. The situation is "extraordinary" even though it may be the usual experience of the people as in some mission areas or a prolonged situation as is foreseen in parts of the United States and Canada.

2. The judgment as to the advisability and conditions for implementing this canon is left to the diocesan bishop.

3. The bishop has three options under this canon:

    a. He may appoint an ordained minister (deacon).

    b. He may appoint a non-ordained minister (who is of course qualified for the position and granted the necessary deputation and faculties).

    c. He may appoint a team of lay ministers.

    Language for this position is still fluid in the United States, although there are indications that the preferred title is *Parish Minister* (for the deacon or lay minister) and *Parish Ministry Team* (for the team mentioned in the canon).

4. Note that it is the diocesan bishop who entrusts the parish to a parish minister. The appointment would not be made by other local ordinaries without special mandate.

5. The parish minister "participates in the exercise of pastoral care." Full pastoral care, of course, can only be exercised by a priest. It would be advisable for the bishop to define the rights and duties of the parish minister and the limits and extent of their participation in the exercise of pastoral care, either by particular law or in the letter of appointment.

6. The bishop is also to appoint a priest to moderate or supervise the pastoral care. This priest is also known by several titles in the United States, but language seems to be standardizing on the title "(parish) priest moderator."

7. The priest moderator is not technically a *parochus*, but he is endowed with the powers and faculties of a parish priest. Diocesan legislation, or at least the letter of appointment, should define and grant the necessary powers and faculties and hopefully clarify the relationship between the priest moderator and parish minister(s).

The priest moderator ordinarily cares for several parishes in a cluster or pastoral zone. Participation in the exercise of pastoral care in these parishes is conducted by lay people, deacons, or pastoral teams. The parishes remain open and active even though the diocese lacks sufficient priests to appoint a resident parish priest for each. The priest moderator provides supervision and that pastoral care reserved to priests or specified in the letter of appointment.

116

Can the non-ordained parish minister with such an appointment exercise any parochial jurisdiction?

In the strict sense a *parochus* or parish priest has only minimum power of jurisdiction or *potestas regiminis* by reason of his office. The parish priest does not have the legislative, judicial, or executive power of a local ordinary (cc. 129 and 135). However, canon 519 refers to his exercise of the *munus regendi* or governing role, which includes:

a. Certain *habitual faculties* granted by law or the diocesan bishop (c. 132).

b. The *potestas dispensandi* — an extension of executive power, and therefore, the power of jurisdiction (cc. 85 and 137-142). Ordinarily, the parish priest may not dispense unless this power has been expressly granted him. The code and diocesan faculties grant such powers in several cases.

c. Pastoral authority or *commissions*. Several pastoral functions are committed to the authority of the parish priest (c. 530). This authority may be called "jurisdiction" in a wide sense.

The *parish priest moderator* is *also* endowed by law and the diocesan bishop with these faculties.

I. Habitual Faculties

The parish priest and priest moderator possess several faculties.

A. *Confirmation* (cc. 882-883)

In danger of death, the parish priest, the priest moderator, and any presbyter may confirm. The parish priest in this country by mandate baptizes adults and receives already baptized adults into full communion. Hence by office the parish priest and priest moderator may also be granted additional faculties to confirm by the diocesan bishop.

Clearly neither the ordained (deacon) nor non-ordained parish minister may share in these faculties.

B. *Penance*

The parish priest and priest moderator possess the faculty to hear confessions within their jurisdiction by virtue of their office (c. 968, §1). Again, neither the ordained deacon nor the non-ordained parish minister may share in these faculties.

C. *Marriage*

The parish priest and priest moderator by virtue of their office are the canonical witnesses at marriage (c. 1108) and can delegate this faculty to other priests and to deacons within their territory (c. 1111). Ordinarily, the lay parish minister does not share in this faculty.

Canon 144 supplies jurisdiction in cases of common error or positive and probable doubt in the above three faculties.

Marriage: A Special Case

However, in virtue of canon 1112, a non-ordained parish minister could be granted the faculty to assist at marriages by the diocesan bishop. Since the bishop could grant him or her habitual faculties, this seems to be a case where a non-ordained person "cooperates in the exercise of jurisdiction" at least in the wide sense (c. 129, §2).

Note nine juridic steps in providing for a lay minister to witness marriages in the name of the Church.

1. *Enabling Legislation.*

    Under the Gasparri code, neither deacons nor lay persons could be granted the faculty or delegation to witness marriage. The 1983 code has enabling legislation for deacons in canons 1108, §1 and 1111, §1 and for lay persons in canon 1112.

2. Prior *favorable opinion* of the Conference of Bishops.

    The United States Conference of Catholic Bishops has voted in favor of permitting bishops to seek an indult.

3. *Permission* of the Holy See.

    It is my understanding that Alaskan dioceses have obtained such permission.

4. Qualification or *Certification* of the lay minister.

    Canon 1112, §2 states that the lay minister:

    a.   must be suitable;

    b.   must be capable of providing pre-marriage formation;

    c.   must be qualified to celebrate the marriage liturgy correctly.

    Hence the diocese would need to initiate a training program and standards for certification.

5. *Authorization.*

    Even after a person is qualified as suitable, it is the diocesan bishop who designates that lay person as an official minister of the Catholic Church authorized to witness marriages in the name of the Church.

6. *Registration.*

    In some states (as in Oregon) the authorized minister (whether ordained or not) must register with the county before civil law permits him or her to witness marriages. A letter of authorization from the chancery is presented to the county clerk.

7. *Appointment.*

118

In many dioceses even priests and deacons, though authorized by their ordination to perform marriages, are not given general faculties to do so unless they are appointed to a pastoral office (parish priest, parochial vicar, a deacon appointed to a parish as parish minister or to a parish staff as an associate, a university chaplain, etc.). It would seem appropriate to limit the use of lay ministers as official ministers of marriage to those appointed as parish ministers or some similar pastoral office.

8. *Delegation.*

In the situation where a diocese were to receive the indult of canon 1112, the diocesan bishop would grant the delegation (either in single cases or habitually) to the lay parish minister, to be exercised in the absence of the priest moderator. General faculties would presumably be given in the letter of appointment.

Note that the priest moderator does not have the power to delegate the lay minister even if he or she has been authorized as an official witness. The priest moderator may delegate another authorized priest or a deacon (c. 1111, §1); only the diocesan bishop may delegate the non-ordained parish minister.

9. *Permission.*

Since marriage is a function committed to the parish priest (or priest moderator), the parish minister needs at least the presumed permission of the priest moderator for a particular marriage (c. 530, §4). If the parish minister has general faculties from the diocesan bishop, may they be sub-delegated? Since habitual faculties are governed by the prescription for delegated power (c. 132, §1), it seems logical that the parish minister could sub-delegate a priest or deacon for a particular marriage. (In a real life scenario, the priest moderator is absent on vacation and has granted permission to the parish minister with habitual faculties from the bishop to witness a marriage next Saturday. The parish minister falls ill and delegates a permanent deacon visiting in the parish for that marriage.) Since the diocesan bishop but not the pastor delegates a lay person to witness marriage, it would seem illogical for the lay parish minister to be able to sub-delegate another lay minister for this marriage.

D. *Preaching*

All priests and deacons have the faculty to preach everywhere (c. 764). This faculty is a form of teaching jurisdiction. The faculty, like delegated jurisdiction, may be restricted or removed by the competent ordinary. Prior to the present code, dioceses granted faculties to preach to visiting clergy. Pastors could delegate this faculty according to diocesan norms. The faculty to preach was considered the jurisdiction to preach. Now the presumption is in favor of the faculty granted by law. By reason of canon 766, lay persons can be granted the faculty to preach if it is necessary, or even useful, in particular cases. The lay parish minister who leads the Sunday assembly on those days when the priest moderator is celebrating the Eucharist in another parish would likely have the faculty to preach in the diocese from the diocesan bishop. This habitual faculty is a form of jurisdiction or a "cooperating in the exercise of the power of jurisdiction." It should be noted that granting a lay person the faculty to preach does not relieve the parish priest or priest moderator from his obligation to preach a homily when he celebrates the Mass. Lay persons may preach sermons but not the Eucharistic homily (c. 766).

II. The Power to Dispense

The law grants the parish priest (and therefore, also the priest moderator) the power to dispense in several circumstances. This power to dispense is an extension of the *potestas regiminis* and is, therefore, a form of jurisdiction.

A. The parish priest (and priest moderator) may dispense their own subjects as well as travelers from private vows (c. 1196, §1) and from promissory oaths (c. 1203). This power is not granted the parish minister by law.

B. The parish priest and priest moderator can in individual cases dispense from the obligation to observe a feast day or day of penance or can commute the obligation to other pious works (c. 1245). This power is not granted the parish minister by law.

C. As confessor, the parish priest and priest moderator can remit in the internal sacramental forum any undeclared *latae sententiae* excommunication or interdict (c. 1357, §1) when recourse to the competent superior would be hard on the penitent; and in danger of death, any censure can be remitted (c. 976). Such power to remit is analogous to the power to dispense; obviously the lay parish minister cannot exercise this power.

D. The confessor and the priest or deacon with faculties to witness marriage can grant certain dispensations in the area of marriage law. Obviously these powers to dispense apply to the parish priest or priest moderator.

1. In danger of death, the parish priest or priest moderator and the properly delegated *sacred minister* (priest or deacon) can dispense from the canonical form and all impediments of ecclesiastical law except the impediment arising from the sacred order of priesthood when the local ordinary cannot be reached.

2. In danger of death, the confessor can dispense from occult impediments for the internal forum.

3. When wedding preparations are made and there is danger of delay, the above persons can also dispense from occult impediments of ecclesiastical law except the impediment of sacred order or public perpetual vow

of chastity in a religious institute of pontifical right.

Since the lay minister delegated to witness marriage is not mentioned in these canons, he or she lacks such power to dispense even in danger of death or when all preparations for the wedding have been made and there would be danger in delay. This may be a *lacuna* in the law which Rome could remedy by indult for those countries where the episcopal conference has been granted permission to delegate lay persons as official witnesses.

III. Special functions committed to the authority of the parish priest and priest moderator (c. 530)

This pastoral authority is an exercise of the *munus regendi* of the parish priest and is only jurisdiction in the wide sense. The authority is possessed by the parish priest or priest moderator. In some cases the lay parish minister may exercise these functions with at least the presumed permission of the priest moderator. The lay minister does not exercise jurisdiction in these areas of law but performs the functions under the "jurisdiction" of the pastor.

1. The parish minister may be deputed to baptize by the local ordinary (c. 861, §2). He does so under the authority or "jurisdiction" of the priest moderator.
2. The parish minister, deputed as an extraordinary minister of communion, may administer Viaticum with permission of the priest moderator.
3. As stated above, the parish minister with faculties to witness marriages from the diocesan bishop, may do so with permission of the priest moderator.
4. The parish minister with permission of the moderator may celebrate funerals, but obviously not the funeral Mass.

Some committed functions may only be exercised by the priest moderator and not the lay parish minister.

1. Confirmation in danger of death.
2. Anointing of the sick.
3. Blessing of the baptismal font during the Easter season and the imparting of a solemn blessing outside the church (the code does not grant lay people the power to bless: c. 1169).
4. Celebration of the Eucharist on Sundays and holy days. Only a priest may celebrate the Eucharist, of course. The parish priest has special responsibility for the Eucharist on Sundays and holy days. The lay parish minister may be deputed to preside over the Liturgy of the Word on Sundays in the absence of the priest moderator and may administer Holy Communion. The lay minister may also preside over a communion service during the week.

Summary

The parish priest does not exercise the jurisdiction of a local ordinary. Jurisdiction is the power of government and includes legislative, judicial, and executive power. The parish priest governs the local church or parish under the authority of the bishop with pastoral authority and shares in some jurisdiction both by reason of office and by diocesan faculties. The parish priest in consultation with the pastoral council enacts pastoral policies but does not have legislative authority. The parish priest is often involved in conflict resolution but does not have judicial power. The parish priest supervises pastoral care and has pastoral authority in certain areas committed to him but he does not have the executive authority of a local ordinary. However, the parish priest in this country has the mandate to baptize adults and to receive already baptized adults into full communion of the Church. He, therefore, has by law and by reason of his office the faculty to confirm them as well as to confirm those in danger of death. By reason of office, he has the faculty to celebrate the sacrament of reconciliation and to delegate other priests and deacons to assist at marriages in his territory. By reason of his ordination he has the faculty to preach.

The parish priest also has the power to dispense in areas granted him by law. The power to dispense is an extension of executive power and is hence jurisdiction.

Finally, the parish priest governs the parish under the authority of the bishop and certain pastoral functions are committed to his authority. The law states that the priest moderator is endowed with the powers and faculties of the parish priest, and commentators add as well the authority to supervise pastoral functions which are especially committed to the parish priest.

The lay parish minister may cooperate in the exercise of jurisdiction according to the norm of law. He or she may be admitted to preach, thus sharing in this form of jurisdiction. In some countries the lay parish minister may be delegated by the bishop to assist at marriages with permission of the priest moderator, thus receiving the faculty to perform marriages and marriage jurisdiction. The law does not grant to the lay minister the power to dispense in any case.

Finally, the lay minister may be deputed to perform certain pastoral functions under the authority or "jurisdiction" of the parish priest. The bishop may depute the lay minister to baptize, to act as extraordinary minister of communion and even Viaticum, to preside over the Liturgy of the Word and distribute Communion at the Sunday assembly (and during the week) — all under the authority and supervision of the priest moderator.

The 1983 code, therefore, provides three examples where lay people cooperate in the exercise of the power of jurisdiction.

1. They may cooperate in the judicial jurisdiction of the church as a lay judge on a tribunal with two other clerics (c. 1421, §2).

2. They cooperate with the pastoral jurisdiction of the Church by:
   a. being admitted to preach when necessary or even when useful in particular cases. When the priest moderator is present for Mass, however, he is obliged to preach the homily. The lay person may preach a sermon but not the Eucharistic homily.
   b. receiving the faculty to witness marriages under the supervision of the priest moderator and with his permission if Rome, the episcopal conference, and the diocesan bishop so decide. Lay people who have this faculty, however, may not grant dispensations in the area of marriage, at least according to the law.

A Final Question

Many dioceses grant the parish priest and priest moderator (and indeed many other priests and deacons) additional faculties and powers to dispense. In the Portland Archdiocese the parish priest and priest moderator, for example, have the power to dispense from the impediment of disparity of cult under the usual conditions. Moreover, they are authorized to celebrate mixed marriages and several of the pastorally sensitive marriages listed in canon 1071 without the need to obtain permission from the bishop. May the diocesan bishop grant similar faculties to the non-ordained parish minister? May the bishop grant to the lay parish minister the power to dispense in other areas which the law attributes to the parish priest?

A conservative reading of the law implies that the bishop may not do so. Canon 129, §2 states that lay members of the Christian faithful can cooperate in the exercise of the power of jurisdiction *"in accord with the norm of law."* Canon 89 states that the parish priest and other presbyters or deacons cannot dispense from a universal or particular law unless this power has been expressly granted to them; no mention is made of granting this power to lay members of the Christian faithful. The norm of law grants to lay persons the ability to "cooperate in the power of jurisdiction" only in the three areas mentioned above.

A more liberal reading of the law would permit the local ordinary to delegate dispensing power and the granting of permissions to lay persons (e.g., a lay chancellor or lay parish minister). According to this opinion, the *law* does not grant dispensing power, but the Ordinary may grant *delegation* to dispense. The issue is disputed by canonists; the Apostolic Delegate in a private letter recognizes the *dubium juris* and recommends that such delegation not be granted as the safer course.

Bertram F. Griffin [1987]

CANONS 517 AND 526

PRIESTS SERVING AS PASTORS IN MORE THAN ONE PARISH

May a diocesan bishop appoint one priest as the true and full canonical pastor of two or more separate parishes simultaneously?

Those who hold to the affirmative point to the express statement in canon 526, §1, that the "care" of several adjoining parishes may be given to one pastor, under necessity. They add that this express statement is in contrast to the law in the 1917 code, canon 460, §1, with its attendant reference to canon 156, and forbiddance of holding two offices that cannot be discharged at the same time by the same person. This is now, they hold, explicitly endorsed with regard to parishes.

Those who hold to the negative point to the first phrase of canon 526, §1, as expressly forbidding all simultaneous multiple pastorships. They hold that this current law, a) simply repeats the previous law, and b) recognizes what has always been the American practice, under the older as well as the newer law, of a pastor "caring for" adjoining parishes, as "missions," but in no sense as simultaneous full pastorates. The new law, they say, merely canonizes the older American custom, and endorses it.

Which is the more tenable position?

OPINION

There seem to be at least two views on this, some holding that the bishop may do this, and others holding that he may not, and both appeal to canon 526. I do not think there is a clear consensus on which opinion must be followed. However, I hope the following comments will be of some help.

Central to this issue is the new understanding of "parish" in the 1983 code. It is no longer identified primarily in terms of the priest who pastors it (as with a benefice under the 1917 code), but in terms of the definite community of persons who make it up (c. 515, §1). So even if a parish is without a resident pastor, it can remain a parish in virtue of the definite community of persons. It does not have to become a mission, but can retain the status of parish even though it is cared for by a non-resident priest or by resident non-priests.

Normally, the pastoral care of a parish is committed (*committitur*) to a priest as its resident pastor (c. 515, §1). However, by exception it can be cared for in other ways: it can be committed (*committi potest*) to several priests *in solidum* (c. 517, §1), one of whom is to serve as moderator, but all of whom each have the obligations and functions of a pastor (c. 543). Another exception is possible when there is a shortage of priests; namely, a participation in the pastoral care can be entrusted (*concredendam esse*) to non-priests, such as deacons or other persons who are not priests, supervised by a priest (c. 517, §2).

This is the context in which canon 526 is to be understood. Canon 526 sets down the basic principles in light of the usual norm that the pastoral care of a parish is committed to a priest as its resident pastor: one parish per pastor (§1), one pastor per parish (§2). For each of these it also recognizes the exceptions noted above. To the "one pastor per parish" rule in §2 it recognizes the exception of a parish entrusted to several priests *in solidum*. To the "one parish per pastor" rule in §2, it uses the same terminology as canon 517, §2 in permitting non-priests to be "entrusted" with a share in the pastoral care of a parish without a resident pastor.

Both the clause under question in canon 526, §1 and canon 517, §2 begin with a reference to the shortage of priests. Rather than the term used for a pastor or for priests appointed *in solidum* — "commit" (*committere*) — both use the verb "entrust" (*concredere*) to describe the relationship which the bishop establishes for the *cura* (pastoral care) of a parish. In canon 517, §2 clearly the people to whom this *cura* is "entrusted" are *not* pastors, for they are not priests and only a priest can be a pastor (c. 521, §1). Rather, the parish is without a resident pastor. The same seems to be true of the situation in canon 526, §1: the parish remains without a resident pastor, but its pastoral care has been entrusted to a priest who is a resident pastor elsewhere, rather than to one or more people who are not priests (c. 517, §2).

There are some practical considerations that enter into the debate. These include the questions of authorization for various actions as a pastor, vacancy of the office of pastor, appointment and removal of the priest.

The priest who supervises those who are not priests need not be himself a pastor; he could be a chancery official, for example, or seminary teacher, etc. But for the parish in question the law requires that he be given the faculties a pastor would need for such matters as marriage, etc. (c. 517, §2). A pastor who provides pastoral care for a parish of which he is not pastor will also need such faculties; the law does not specify this in his case, however (c. 526, §1). It is not clear whether the canon presumes such faculties will be given, or whether the canon really means for him to be appointed pastor of the several other parishes as well.

If the priest is considered to be appointed as pastor for each of the parishes, certain personnel considerations will have to be attended to carefully by the bishop. For example, the priest will need to be installed canonically in order to act as pastor in each of the parishes; or else, he must be dispensed from this requirement, and the dispensation will have to be communicated to the people

125

of each of the parishes (c. 527). Once he has taken possession, none of the parishes is vacant any longer, and no change can be made in the arrangement without the resignation, transfer, or removal of the pastor from the specific parishes involved. Any attempt to switch who is responsible for any of the several parishes which fails to do this will be invalid, and a subsequent appointment would also be invalid because the office would not be vacant (c. 153). To transfer the priest or remove him, a separate process will be needed for each of the parishes to which he has been assigned as pastor.

On the other hand, if the priest is pastor of only one parish, but is entrusted with the pastoral care of other parishes, these other parishes remain "vacant" and the bishop can change the arrangement at any time. If the bishop wants to change the structuring of their pastoral care the priest would not have to resign, transfer, or be removed; moreover, the priest would not be able to make any claim on remaining in charge of these additional parishes, for "entrusting" the care to him does not give him a *ius in re* on the basis of which he could object to any change.

In light of these theoretical and practical considerations, I am of the opinion that the priest is pastor of only one parish, even though he may be entrusted with the pastoral care of other parishes due to the shortage of priests or for other reasons. But I also recognize that this is a developing area in the law, that the framers of the code did not attempt to set down minute rules governing these extraordinary situations, and that we will learn from practical developments what the real meaning of the law is (for as c. 27 reminds us, "custom is the best interpreter of laws").

James H. Provost [1992]

Canon 518

Parish Membership on other than Territorial Basis

Can the diocesan bishop empower a person to become a member of a parish other than the parish of domicile or quasi-domicile merely by choosing to do so for personal reasons (e.g., children attend school there, geographical or other convenience, good liturgical celebration and preaching)?

Opinion

You place a disclaimer in your case to the effect that there is here no question of a personal parish. I am going to offer a canonical argument which

126

necessarily entails the concept of personal parish, although my concluding remarks do not.

You have a proposal from some source that a diocesan bishop be empowered to permit a person to become a member of a parish other than his or her parish by reason of domicile or quasi-domicile merely by choosing to do so for personal reasons, e.g., children attending school there, geographical or other convenience, good liturgical celebration and preaching.

There is no question here of the person losing his or her parish by reason of residence. The bishop cannot dispense from canon 107, because acquisition of parish is constitutional, not disciplinary, constitutive not precisely of a parochial community, but constitutive of the canonical condition (juridic status) of a Catholic in the Church (cf., the rubric of Chapter I at c. 96). Canon 515, §2 is relevant here, but not because the proposal entails only a minor alteration in an existing parish. The canonical argument implies a dramatic change inasmuch as it calls for the erection of potentially numerous personal parishes in existing territorial parishes. The argument I present would require truly persuasive arguments in the consultation with the presbyteral council, arguments that may not be practically possible.

It is my opinion that it may be possible to interpret the last clause of canon 518 (*alia etiam ratione*) to include the situation suggested in your diocese. In order to do this the "other determining factor" (CLSA translation) or "some other basis" (British-Irish translation) or "other plan," as I prefer to call it, would have to be a matter of clearly articulated and published diocesan policy, including the procedure to be followed and the objective and verifiable criteria for permitting a Catholic to become a member of another parish (which in this case would be personal because the reasons are other than residence). As I have already said, the person does not thereby lose the residential parish; there is cumulative jurisdiction here. Put another way, *alia ratio* cannot include purely personal preference; it necessarily implies objectivity and entails a true permanence or stability of membership in the chosen parish.

There is, however, another argument which I believe is genuinely convincing. Inherent in the pastoral office of the diocesan bishop is the obligation and right to provide appropriate pastoral care for the members of the diocese. If he judges that in some cases he cannot do this by means of the ordinary established parishes, but at the same time judges that there are not a sufficient number of such instances to determine a clear common denominator by reason of which he can erect a personal parish, even in a territorial parish, he must discover effective means of providing pastoral ministry for these individuals or families. The inherent nature of the episcopal office coupled with the true impossibility of observing the law in specific cases excuses him. He can and should assign these exceptional cases to the pastoral care of another pastor. This is not a case of dispensation, but of excuse discerned through a legitimate judgment in epikeia. This course of action would imply an habitual delegation of the parochial power to another pastor, but this would be adequate for the needs of the faithful.

It seems obvious, however, that if there exist truly objective reasons motivating large numbers of Catholics to seek pastoral ministry on a permanent basis (as opposed to shopping around) from pastors other than their proper pastors, the ministry of the pastors of their residences has become ineffective and transfer or removal is indicated.

Richard A. Hill, S.J. [1984]

CANON 522

NON-RETROACTIVITY OF TERM APPOINTMENTS FOR PASTORS

Now that the episcopal conference has decreed that a diocesan bishop can appoint a pastor for a certain period of time (term of appointment), is this retroactive? In other words, if a pastor was legitimately appointed in 1980 for five years, would his term of appointment terminate in 1985? Or was an indult from the Holy See required to implement a limited term of office before this?

OPINION

As of this writing [May, 1984] the episcopal conference's decree has not been promulgated so is not yet in effect. The provision that a bishop may appoint a pastor for a definite period of time (term of appointment) once the authorization of the episcopal conference has been given applies only to pastors appointed after the bishop has implemented the authorization from the episcopal conference. It is not retroactive. This is because it applies to making appointments, and therefore, looks toward the future. Moreover, the new code in canon 4 indicates that acquired rights are not revoked unless expressly stated in the canons of the code, and that is not done in this matter. So, a term of office would apply only to pastors appointed after the bishop receives the permission from the episcopal conference and decides to implement it. Of course, if he had an indult before the code took effect, it would apply to appointments made at that time; but all such indults ceased when the code took effect on November 27, 1983.

James H. Provost [1984]

CANON 522

Limited Tenure of Office for Pastors and Others

After consultation with the priests' council the bishop of a certain diocese established a policy for limited tenure of pastors. The policy states that it is a directive of the Holy Father to have limited tenure for pastors and it goes on to apply a six year term to those currently holding appointment as pastors as well as to future appointments. The policy also establishes limited terms in other positions, including parochial vicars, special ministers, and, to the extent possible, religious.

Does the policy conform with canonical norms?

OPINION

There are several items on which it may be useful to comment.

First, it is not required that a limited tenure be established for pastors. Canon 522 makes this a possible option, but presumes appointment for an indefinite period unless the local diocese decides otherwise. The canon reads as follows:

> The pastor ought to possess stability in office and, therefore, he is to be named for an indefinite period of time; the diocesan bishop can name him for a certain period of time only if a decree of the conference of bishops has permitted this.

The NCCB adopted such a decree in November 1983. Given the complexity of the pastoral situations in the United States, the U.S. bishops decided not to set a specific number of years as the term that would have to be adopted if a particular diocesan bishop decided to adopt limited tenure for pastors in his diocese; they left it up to the local bishops to determine what the terms would be. However, there was some confusion as to whether the NCCB decree permitting limited tenure was the kind of decree which needs prior review by the Apostolic See before it can take effect. After several communications back and forth with various officials at the Vatican, it became apparent that the Congregation for Clergy was insisting on a definite term for all dioceses that would decide to implement it within a given country, and that the term has to be six years. It is reported this was the wish of the Holy Father.

This is now in effect for the United States. What it means is that pastors are appointed for an indefinite term, unless the bishop in an individual diocese decides to appoint pastors for a term of six years. The appointment for six years can be renewed in the same parish, but the term is always six years.

The proposed policy under question here applies this option within that diocese. It states that as of June 1, 1985, all appointments of pastors will be for a term of six years. This is in keeping with the provisions of the code. The code itself does not require the consultation the bishop here reports he has undertaken, and does not strictly require him to consult with the presbyteral council which he proposes to do. So he is going well beyond the letter of the law, and is implementing it in the proper spirit.

There is a second question, however, which is raised by the proposed policy. Can it be imposed retroactively, so that it begins to apply even to those who are now assigned as pastors? The wording of the first two provisions of the policy give the impression this is being done, although at the end of the policy these pastors are "invited" to submit their resignations, so perhaps it is not being imposed retroactively.

If the application of the new policy is being imposed retroactively on those who were appointed pastor before the policy takes effect, the legality of this will depend on whether the diocese had an indult before the new code took effect, which permitted appointments for a limited term. Some dioceses in the United States sought such indults, so that pastors appointed under them were named for a term of six years. If this diocese had such an arrangement, then the proposed policy merely extends that same practice under the new code. The only problematic cases are those of pastors named after November 27, 1983, when the old indults expired, and June 1, 1985 when the new policy will take effect.

Some dioceses in this country had a "gentlemen's agreement" between the priests and the bishop, which in effect established a limited term, but not a canonically binding one. It was an agreement whereby priests expected to be transferred after a definite time had elapsed. If the diocese had one of these, the retroactive effect of the proposed policy has only the force of such a gentlemen's agreement.

If there is no indult, and even if there were a gentlemen's agreement, the policy cannot be retroactive automatically. That is, limitation on the term of pastor only applies to those who will be appointed on June 1, 1985 and thereafter. Those who were appointed before that time remain in office even after six years has expired. To be moved from the parish, the procedure for transfer of pastors must be followed. It is not an automatic vacancy in their cases.

Why? There are several reasons.

1. Laws look to the future, not to the past (c. 9), unless specific provision is made in the laws concerning the past. Even though the policy makes such specific provision, however, it goes beyond the authority of the bishop to do so. That is clear from the next point.

2. Appointment to the office of pastor is for an indefinite time, unless the

special steps described above have been taken (c. 522). Those who were appointed before the proposed policy takes effect were appointed according to this general norm, and have an indefinite term in the office of pastor. To be transferred or removed, the special procedures for pastors must be followed. This is an exceptional situation in the law, but clearly set forth in canons 1740-1752.

3. An office automatically is lost (parish becomes vacant) when the time of a limited tenure appointment runs out, and the priest is so notified by the bishop (c. 186). However, this happens only when the limited term was applied in the appointment to the office. If a pastor is appointed according to the general norm for an indefinite time, there is no "lapse of the determined time" in his case.

4. An additional argument comes from the fact that the new code does not do away with acquired rights unless it expressly says so in the new code (c. 4). A pastor appointed to his parish before the new code took effect has an acquired right to that parish in light of the provisions of the old code, hence on the basis of universal law. The new code does not take away that right.

Moreover, diocesan law cannot go counter to the law of the code in such a matter (c. 135, §2). The diocesan policy, therefore, cannot take away the acquired rights of pastors appointed before the policy takes effect.

What can be done to achieve a proper transition to the new policy? There are several options. One is for the pastors who have been in their present assignments for six years to agree voluntarily to be reassigned effective June 1, 1985, in keeping with the provisions of the policy. Similarly, those who are now pastors but have not been in this assignment for six years could agree to resign voluntarily when six years have passed from the time of appointment.

In those rare cases where a pastor refuses to cooperate, the parish would not be automatically vacant, nor would it be voluntarily vacant. So the bishop would have to observe the usual procedure for transfer in order to reassign the pastor once the six years are up. In doing this he would have to show the proper cause as illustrated in the canons (c. 1748, or even c. 1741).

As for parochial vicars and special ministers, they are appointed at the discretion of the diocesan bishop (c. 547) and he can remove them provided he has a just cause (c. 552), which includes the bishop's own estimation of what is required for the good of souls. The proposed policy appears to be within the provisions of the law, and does attempt to assure some limited stability in service for these persons.

The hope expressed that the limited term provisions would be observed by religious is in keeping with the spirit not only of the policy but also of the code, for religious do not enjoy the same stability in office, even as pastors, which secular clergy enjoy (see c. 682, §2).

Canon 522

Limited Tenure of Office for Pastors

1. First Question:

A bishop received an indult in 1980 which permitted the appointment of pastors for a six year term, renewable for a second term of up to six additional years. Under the new code, the same kind of limited term of six years, renewable for a second six years, has been authorized for dioceses in this country. But what about priests who were appointed pastors prior to the 1980 indult? Are they subject to a limited term, or is their appointment for an "indefinite period of time" (in the terms of c. 522 of the new code)?

Opinion

It is important to keep several matters in mind.

First, the appointment of pastors is the prerogative of the bishop. It is also his responsibility to see to the proper placement of priests in terms of the pastoral needs of the Church. The new code places this in a new perspective: the parish is seen primarily in terms of the community of the faithful. This is a change from the former code, where the parish was described as a "benefice" and understood primarily in terms of the rights and welfare of the pastor.

Second, while pastors are to "possess stability in office" (c. 522), this is not an absolute stability but, as the Magisterium teaches in the documents of Vatican II, it is a stability determined by what "the good of souls demands" (*Christus Dominus* 31). Since the bishop is the one with ultimate responsibility in his diocese to assure what is necessary for the good of souls, he is the one who determines when a change in pastors may be necessary for the good of souls in a parish.

The possibility of appointing pastors for a limited term, rather than for an indefinite period of time, must also be related to the good of souls in the parishes of the diocese. This had to be a primary reason for the Apostolic See to grant the indult to the bishop in 1980, and it remains a primary reason for any bishop to determine whether to institute a limited term for pastors in his diocese.

Third, there are several ways in which a priest may cease being pastor of a particular parish. If he was appointed for a limited term, then when the time of his term runs out and he is notified of this by the bishop, then he is no longer the pastor. No special procedures are required to terminate him; this happens by being notified his term has expired.

If he was not appointed for a limited term, and therefore, was named for an indefinite period of time, he may cease being pastor of the parish by accepting transfer to another parish or church office, or by being removed from the parish. Transfer and removal require specific processes that are designed to respect the good of souls and also the concerns of the individual priest as well as those of the bishop. These procedures are spelled out in the new code: transfer, in canons 1748-1752; removal, in canons 1740-1747.

There is no longer any "irremovable pastor"; even under the old code, an "irremovable" pastor could still be moved, but a more complicated procedure was required to do so. Today, the same procedure applies to any pastor who is being removed, except for those whose term has expired and for which there is no special procedure required to terminate his time in a particular parish.

Now, as to your specific question, the following seem to be the pertinent norms.

Appointments for a limited term are not retroactive. That is, the indult received by the bishop in 1980 was not retroactive. All the indults issued by the Apostolic See for limited terms were for future appointments, not for past ones. Similarly, the possibility in the new code for appointing pastors for a limited term, which has been implemented in this country, is also not retroactive.

So, a priest who was appointed a pastor in the diocese prior to the 1980 rescript, and is still serving in the same parish, is serving for an indefinite period of time and not for a limited six year term.

This would be different for a priest who was a pastor before the 1980 indult, but then accepted a transfer to being pastor in some other parish once the limited term was put into effect in the diocese, either under the indult or under the 1983 code. The new appointment is for a limited term.

In other words, only those appointed a pastor prior to limited term being implemented in the diocese and who remain in that same appointment are exempted from the limited term. Moreover, this does not make them "irremovable," for they can be transferred or removed from being pastor if, in the judgment of the bishop and after following the appropriate procedures, he determines this to be justified.

James H. Provost [1986]

2. Second Question:

133

If a priest was named a pastor before term of office went into effect in his diocese, does he become subject to that term if he accepts a transfer to a new parish?

OPINION

The term of office is not retroactive; so, a priest who is serving as pastor at the time a policy of limited term of office takes effect in his diocese is not subject to the limited term in regard to the appointment he is currently holding. However, if he accepts a transfer to a new parish, then the new appointment is subject to the limited term.

Transfer to a new parish constitutes a new appointment. In effect, the priest agrees to resign his existing appointment and to accept a new one, when he agrees to a transfer. The limited term does not apply to the priest as an individual, but to the specific appointment to a particular parish. That is why, even though he was not subject to a limited term in his former parish, when he accepts a transfer he also becomes subject to the limited term that applies to his new appointment.

In effect, there are not two classes of pastors — those who were appointed a pastor initially without limited term, and those who were subject to a limited term the first time they were appointed a pastor. Instead, there are two classes of appointments — some which were made prior to the policy of a limited term taking effect (and these are, therefore, without a limited term); and appointments which are made under a policy of limited terms once that policy takes effect.

A priest appointed as pastor before a policy of limited term took effect can be removed from office, can agree to a transfer, or can resign; but otherwise he remains in office indefinitely. A priest appointed after a policy of limited term took effect in the diocese serves for the duration of that term; once he is notified that the term has run out, he is automatically no longer pastor of that parish.

It remains possible, of course, for a bishop to appoint a pastor for an indefinite term (i.e., without a limited term) even if a policy of limited term has been adopted in the diocese. The bishop can always make an exception to the policy. Whether it would be advisable for him to do so is another question, one which goes beyond purely canonical considerations.

Another idea which seems to underlay the concerns of this query is that once a priest is appointed a pastor, some think he remains "pastor" for all future appointments. This may have been true under the previous code (although even that is debated), but it is not true under the new code. Canon 1748 on transfer from the office of pastor, for example, explicitly states the bishop may transfer a priest to another parish or to "another office" (e.g., associate, chancellor, chaplain, etc.). Canon 1746 on removal of a pastor from office states the bishop can pension the man, or appoint him to some other office — not necessarily an office of being pastor.

Clearly, then, if the bishop can appoint him to some other office besides being a pastor, the bishop can appoint him to the office of pastor with a limited term. The only limitation is that limited term appointments are not retroactive, so that those who were appointed to their present parish before a policy of limited term took effect are not subject to limited term *in that appointment*, but would be in any future appointments.

James H. Provost [1986]

CANON 522

DIOCESAN POLICIES TOWARD PASTORS WITH LIMITED TERMS OF OFFICE

Please comment from a canon law point of view on our diocesan policy for limited term of pastors and for moving pastors who are currently assigned when this policy took effect.

OPINION

The policy in your diocese is explained in a letter from the bishop which has several numbered sections. My analysis of it comes up with two policies, a conclusion that seems to be confirmed by the concluding paragraph of the bishop's letter where he refers to the "two policies" contained in the letter. However, he does not specifically identify the two policies by name.

So, from my reading of the document, the first policy (no. 1 in the letter) sets a six year term for new appointments of pastors. The second policy (nos. 2-4 in the letter) indicates how this can be extended for three or even six additional years, and also advises (in no. 4) on the procedure which will be followed to adjust the assignments of existing pastors to the new limited term situation.

Here's the crux of the problem. It is possible for a diocese to announce a personnel policy such that priests should expect to be asked to accept a transfer every so often. This can apply even to existing appointments. It is also possible for a diocese to announce a policy of limited term appointments for pastors. This can apply only to those appointments made after the policy is announced.

The difference is this. If the policy is one of limited term appointments, when the term is up the bishop has only to notify the priest of this fact, and the parish becomes vacant; there are no special procedures which have to be used to transfer him to another parish or office, or even to place him on a pension. The priest has no claim on the parish once the canonical term expires and he is notified of this fact.

On the other hand, if the policy is one of announcing that priests should expect a transfer every so often, then when the time comes that the diocese wishes the priest to transfer there are very explicit procedures that must be followed. The pastor has a claim on the parish in which he is serving, and can be moved only if the bishop follows the procedure for transfer of pastors (cc. 1748-1752) or, if need be, the procedure for removal of pastors (cc. 1740-1747). The very fact of having served a specified number of years is not sufficient of itself to justify the transfer or removal, but it can trigger an examination of various pastoral and other factors, which the bishop may eventually judge sufficient to warrant the move.

As I indicated, to my way of reading the letter the first of these policies is the one which establishes a limited term of six years as pastor; the second is the policy which spells out when priests not subject to the limited term can expect to be asked to accept a transfer.

The first policy establishes a limited term of six years. It indicates the priest is asked to make a six year commitment, and by establishing the six year term it indicates the diocese is making a similar commitment. During the course of the six years the pastor can be moved only by using the formal procedures for transfer or removal, unless of course he himself asks for or agrees to the move. Moreover, when the six years are up the priest can remain in the parish as pastor until he is notified that the term is up, and there does not appear to be any time limit for how long the bishop can delay sending the priest this notification.

The second policy clarifies when a priest can expect to be asked to transfer. Here are the two situations: a priest appointed with a limited term, and a priest already appointed as pastor before the limited term policy took effect.

For a priest appointed under the new limited term policy, after the six years are up he can be moved at any time by the bishop, without any special procedures or for any specified reason, since his claim on the parish has expired at the end of the six year term. What your diocesan policy is saying is that if it seems mutually beneficial to the priest and the personnel board, the bishop will not notify him that his term has expired, but will let him continue for to stay on for another three years, the bishop will not notify him that his six year term expired until this additional time is over.

The pastoral intent of the policy is clear: to provide flexibility in pastoral assignments. The canonical justification for it may seem a bit strained, but it would appear to remain within the law. The effect at the bottom line, however, is that under the policy a pastor can be moved against his will only through a formal procedure for the first six years he is in a parish; after that time, he can be moved without any procedural requirements in canon law other than being notified by the bishop that his six year term has expired and he is no longer pastor of the parish.

The second policy applies to another situation, that of a priest who was already serving as a pastor when the new limited term policy took effect. For this priest the second policy indicates when he should expect a change in the next few years. This is only informational. If a pastor in this situation does not want to move when he is asked to do so in keeping with this second policy, he is entitled to the full formal procedure for transfer or removal. All this second policy does for these pastors is state the administrative intent of the bishop and personnel board. Unlike the case of a pastor appointed with a limited term, pastors previously appointed are not automatically terminated when a specified time is up.

James H. Provost [1987]

CANON 524

CONSULTATION FOR THE APPOINTMENT OF PASTORS

What consultations must a bishop undertake prior to making pastoral appointments?

OPINION

Canon 524 of the Code of Canon Law speaks of provisions for the office of pastor by the diocesan bishop. It refers to consultation only; the bishop does not require the consent of those mentioned. It does not refer specifically to appointment of assistant pastors, chaplains or other pastoral personnel. Its requirements apply to the office of pastor and not to these other positions, even though some consultative process might well be advisable. Other canons might sometimes be pertinent, such as canons 146-196 on ecclesiastical offices.

The canon is neither extremely detailed nor exhaustive. The diocesan bishop may further specify and supplement its provisions as he establishes procedures and consultative groups to assist in the personnel process, including the appointment of pastors. It is clearly within his capacity to establish personnel boards, personnel offices and a variety of personnel policies.

The bishop is to weigh all circumstances, such as the special characteristics of the parish and the qualifications of available personnel. Some qualifications are mentioned in canon 521 but others are implicit in the duties of pastors as detailed throughout the code. The eligible priests are to be judged impartially. In making his judgment, the bishop is to consult and investigate. He is to listen to the vicar forane (dean) and may listen to others, either presbyters or lay persons.

The precise nature and order of these investigations and consultations is not established in the general law. Diocesan law may specify such matters. Clearly the diocesan bishop may conduct the investigations and consultations through a representative such as a vicar, a personnel director, or the members of a personnel board.

The vicar forane, if the office exists in a diocese, is to be involved in some way. He might be consulted early about the special needs of a parish awaiting the appointment of a pastor. While the vicar forane is to know the clerics of his district (cc. 553-555), he cannot be presumed to know all the clergy available for pastoral assignment in a diocese, either the diocesan clergy or religious clergy. Some diocesan bishops might want to involve the vicar forane throughout the process of evaluating vacant parishes and selecting a pastor from among the priests available and qualified. Others may prefer to seek the vicar's counsel only on the special needs of the parish without involving him in the evaluation of personnel. The latter consultation satisfies the requirements of the canon.

John J. Myers [1985]

CANON 526

RIGHTS OF PASTOR BEING TRANSFERRED
CONCERNING APPOINTMENT

A priest has agreed to transfer from being pastor of one parish to a new assignment where he will have charge of two parishes. However, he finds he is only appointed administrator, not pastor. What are his rights?

OPINION

So far as I can tell, it is up to the decision of the diocesan bishop whether to appoint a priest pastor or not. Canon 523 indicates that it is up to the diocesan bishop to provide for the office of pastor by means of "free conferral."

138

Basically, a priest does not have a right to be named a pastor. The decision whether to appoint a priest a pastor or to some other office pertains to the bishop. The norms in the new code concerning removal from office and transfer from office make it very clear that the fact that a priest was a pastor at one time does not give him a vested right to be named a pastor in a subsequent assignment. For example, canon 1748 indicates that a pastor can be transferred either to another parish or "to another office."

The position of administrator of a parish is another office. It is a prudential decision by the bishop whether to appoint an administrator to a parish, which is considered a temporary arrangement, or to appoint a pastor.

In the long run, canon law will not be of much help to the priest in this situation. It is a question of the bishop's exercise of his discretion, and he has acted within the provisions of the law. Whatever a person may think of the bishop's prudential judgement, it was within his legal rights to make it.

James H. Provost [1984]

Canons 530-531

Stole Fees

The old code listed the functions especially reserved to pastors (e.g., baptisms, weddings, funerals) and affirmed the pastor's right to stole fees given to him on these occasions (cc. 462-463). If someone other than the pastor performed the function, the stole fee still went to the pastor. The new code lists the same functions especially reserved to the pastor, but is silent on the question of stole fees given him on those occasions (c. 530). If someone other than the pastor performs these functions, the stole fee goes to the parish account, and the diocesan bishop may issue regulations for the allocation of this money and the remuneration of the clerics who perform these functions (c. 531).

What is clear and certain is that the new code revokes the pastor's right to stole fees that are given to another person who performs the tasks especially reserved to the pastor. The money goes to the parish and the bishop may determine how it may be distributed. What does the new code determine about the pastor's right to stole fees given to him when he himself performs the functions especially reserved to him? The new code is silent there. It does not affirm or deny his right; it does not say what is to be done with the stole fee given to him.

It would seem the pastor keeps his right to stole fees when he performs the function (since this is a long-standing right of pastors which has not been explicitly abrogated by the new code). Other clerics would turn the money back to the parish if they perform the pastoral functions, but the bishop could legislate that the fees be returned by the parish to the cleric as remuneration. Therefore, it would seem the pastor could still keep the fee given to him based on his right not being abrogated by the new law; other clerics could be allowed to keep the stole fees as remuneration based on possible local legislation.

OPINION

First, the old code did reserve certain functions to the pastor, but the new code no longer does. Instead, these are specially "committed" (*commissae*) to him. They are not restricted or reserved to him, so the pastor does not have the same rights in their regard as he had under the old code.

Second, stole fees clearly are dealt with in a principal way in Book V, where canon 1264 specifies that the provincial meeting of bishops is to set the amount for stole fees. Moreover, canon 1267, §1 specifies that "unless the contrary is established, the offerings given to superiors or administrators of any ecclesiastical juridic person, even to a private one, are presumed to be given to that juridic person." The parish is a public juridic person (c. 515, §3). The pastor is by law the administrator of that public juridic person (c. 532). There is no contrary provision in law to the norm of canon 1267, §1 with regard to stole fees. So, they go to the parish, not the pastor.

Taking the provisions of these canons together, it is clear that all stole fees go to the parish — those the pastor receives, in light of canon 1267, §1; those which others receive (parochial vicar, pastor emeritus, visiting priest, deacon, or whatever) are to be given to the parish in virtue of canon 531.

Why is canon 531 in the section on parishes rather than in Book V? Probably because it is so closely related to canon 530, which changes the former norm from functions *reserved* to the pastor, to functions *committed* to him. The possibility of others performing these functions is quite real, so the law goes on to specify what happens to stole fees when others do the work.

A third factor in all this is that the legal structuring of clergy support has been changed from the right to support which was based on the "title" of ordination in the old code. Now the cleric, when he dedicates himself to sacred ministry, deserves a remuneration consistent with his responsibilities (c. 281, §1). Compensation for the paper work and preparation for the various functions listed in canon 530 is properly taken into account in determining the pastor's salary. Canon 531 recognizes others may not be remunerated so handsomely as the pastor since their responsibilities are not commensurate with his, but when they provide these functions some consideration needs to be given to their added work.

Finally, the code intends to apply the council. Vatican II emphasized the spiritual dimension of the functions listed in canon 530. The first Instruction for implementing the conciliar decree on the liturgy set down the general principle that "any suggestion of moneymaking is [to be] avoided" in liturgical services (*Inter Oecumenici* 35). As part of the effort to implement this principle the code has adopted the new discipline relative to stole fees.

Does this do away with the right a pastor appointed under the old code may have acquired to stole fees, so that at least these pastors would not be required to turn stole fees over to the parish? It is important to distinguish between the right to stole fees for services actually performed in the past, and a generic right to stole fees.

Clearly any stole fees due for services rendered prior to the new code taking effect are properly due the pastor, unless particular legislation had already changed the norms concerning stole fees locally.

But this does not seem to warrant the claim that the pastor has an acquired right to stole fees generically, a right which would remain under the new code although contrary to it. The pastor's claim on stole fees under the old code were a recognition that certain functions were reserved to him. Once that restriction is taken away and the whole institute of stole fees has been reorganized, as the 1983 code has done, the basis for the pastor's claim no longer exists.

To sum up, the law has changed the system of stole fees. They now pertain to the parish, not the pastor. In determining the remuneration due pastors and other priests, the diocesan bishop is to take into account the conditions of time and place, and therefore, the work they do. Canon 531 is merely a reminder that in determining this remuneration for priests who are not pastors, the work they do in functions which are specially committed to a pastor is to be taken into account.

James H. Provost [1985]

ANOTHER OPINION

The diocesan bishop, having consulted the council of priests, is to determine two things: (1) the allocation (*destinatio*) of the stole fees, and (2) the remuneration of the clergy, including the pastor, who have carried out the functions enumerated in the preceding canon.

The revised code, having determined in accord with Vatican II (*Presbyterorum ordinis* 20) that benefices are to be suppressed or at least phased out and their endowments transferred to a restricted diocesan or interdiocesan fund out of which the support of the clergy is to be provided (c. 1274), does not advert to our system in which support of the clergy is provided by the parish or other work to which they are assigned; the remuneration of substitutes for the pastor, e.g., associates, supply priests, deacon, is provided from the same sources. Neither does it reprobate our system.

I agree that the canon seems to have in mind that stole fees belong to the parish fund or general account, but the bishop, in turn, is to determine that the offering is disposed of in a specific manner and this can be by determining that the stole fee belongs to the priest or deacon who performed the liturgical function, whether it comes to him directly from the donor or through the parish account, especially when it is to be tax-deductible.

The bishop could also decide that the minister, including the pastor, shall receive a determined stipend regardless of whether the actual offering is below or above this amount. In this case the presumption would be that the parish general fund would not ultimately be significantly affected by this. We have to bear in mind that canon 1274 expects that the diocese has a fund which equitably provides for the support of the clergy, which in our system would be a diocesan subsidy in poorer parishes.

I believe that the code is trying to equalize the income of the clergy in such a way that service in a poor parish is as financially rewarding for a priest or deacon as service in an affluent parish. At the same time the will of the donor remains paramount, which sometimes is regrettable.

Richard A. Hill, S.J. [1985]

CANON 531

DISPOSITION OF STOLE FEES

Under the provisions of this canon, should a fund be established into which the priests of the diocese would contribute all stole fees not specifically given to them? The idea is to divide this periodically among the active priests of the diocese.

OPINION

The idea is an interesting one, but it is not specifically what is foreseen in canon 531 or the other canons which concern stole fees.

Canon 1264, §2, leaves it up to the bishops of a province in their regular meetings to set the limit on the stole fees in the dioceses of the province. Canon 848 indicates that a priest cannot ask more than the amount fixed by the bishops of the province. Canon 1267, §1 indicates that stole fees go to the parish. Stole fees are offerings given to the pastor or other priests assigned to the parish, the parish is an ecclesiastical juridic person, and unless the contrary is established in the giving of the money by the individual then the money goes to the parish in keeping with canon 1267, §1.

Canon 531 is designed to cover the case when the sacraments are provided by someone who is not assigned to the parish, and therefore, is not subject to the provisions of canon 1267, §1. For these people the money also does not go to them individually, unless the will of the donor is clearly otherwise, but in virtue of canon 531 the money goes to the parish just as it would if the sacraments or other ceremonies had been provided by the pastor or another priest assigned to the parish.

In effect, therefore, the law is saying that stole fees go to the parish, no matter who provides the services — someone assigned to the parish, or someone not assigned to the parish.

Canon 531 goes on to try to provide some way of giving the priest who is not assigned to the parish some recompense for his service. A number of dioceses have established some form of scale for "supply priests." This would be the kind of thing that canon 531 is considering.

As to the bishop's proposal to set up a special fund into which all stole fees would be deposited and then later divide it among the priests, this would amount to a tax on the parishes since the stole fees now are parish property. The bishop can establish such taxes on parishes provided it is proportionate to their income, is for diocesan needs, and is imposed after he has heard the diocesan financial council and presbyteral council. I think it might be argued that the stole fee fund, established by taxing the parishes for the stole fees which they receive, would be proportionate to their "stole fee" income, would be for a diocesan need (in the sense of supporting the priests of the entire diocese), but could be set up only after the bishop has listened to the diocesan finance council and the presbyteral council.

Even if this is done, it would still be necessary to provide some form of recompense for priests who are not of the diocese and who provide various services in the diocese.

James H. Provost [1984]

Canon 534

The Mass *Pro Populo* and Acceptance of Other Intentions

Is it forbidden to remember other people during the celebration of a stipend Mass or Mass pro populo?

Opinion

In your question concerning the *pro populo* Mass, which you mention arose from a vicariate meeting, there is in its wording an ambiguity that almost has a rhetorical ring to it, whether it is forbidden to remember any other people during the celebration of a stipend Mass. I doubt that any priest, especially when using the first Eucharistic Prayer, fails to remember a lot of people in addition to the principal intention of that Mass. Indeed the texts of the Eucharistic Prayers require this: the pope, the bishop, all bishops, those present in the celebration, all the deceased.

The issue in the *pro populo* is the conscious designation of that particular Mass as fulfilling the pastor's (and bishop's) obligation to offer the Eucharist for his people. For this he may not receive a stipend and could not also offer that Mass for an intention for which a stipend has been given, although he can and sometimes should recall special intentions other than the needs of his parishioners. What he has to do is designate another Mass for the intention for which he has accepted a stipend.

Richard A. Hill, S.J. [1985]

Canon 535

Regulations Concerning the Format of Sacramental Registers

Is there anything in canon law for or against having our sacramental records, such as baptisms, marriages, etc., kept in heavy bound loose leaf binders like they use in county court houses, state offices, for their records, so you can take the sheets out, type the information on them, and re-insert them in the binder? I have been told by the F. J. Remey Company that it is their understanding that loose leaf books are not acceptable for permanent records, especially for baptism, since pages may become detached, lost or changed. As you know, some of the writing in our registers is not legible and, if typed in, it would simplify matters a great deal. If this type of loose leaf binder is good enough for county or state records, I don't see why the Church would not permit it.

OPINION

Canon 535 of the 1983 Code of Canon Law is the chief canon dealing with sacramental registers. Its parallel in the 1917 code was canon 470, which contained substantially the same provisions. Canon 535 mandates that every parish maintain records of baptism, marriage, and deaths, as well as any registers prescribed by the conference of bishops or the local diocesan bishop. It further describes the type of information which must be noted in the baptismal register, requires that the registers be kept in a parish archive, and also requires that older parish books be carefully preserved in accord with the norms of particular law. This canon is located in the context of the code's discussion of parishes and the office of pastor. Thus, it would be the pastor who bears primary responsibility for parish records. Canon 895 stipulates that the record of confirmations is to be kept in a diocesan register, unless the conference of bishops or the diocesan bishop has made provisions for confirmations to be recorded in parish registers. Other canons of the 1983 code also refer to various sacramental registers (cc. 877; 895; 1053; 1054; 1081; 1121; 1122; 1123; 1133; 1182; 1685; 1706), but none of these contain any regulations specifying the forms such registers should take. Thus, there is no universal law which requires only bound books to be used in sacramental records.

There is a role for particular law to specify such matters. Since the promulgation of the 1983 code, however, the National Conference of Catholic Bishops has not issued any regulation governing sacramental registers, their nature, type, or means of preservation. Of course, some individual dioceses may very well have issued diocesan regulations. Consultation with the archivist of the National Conference of Catholic Bishops failed to uncover any legislation of the episcopal conference prior to the new code. It is not impossible that sometime in the past instructions were given to printers regarding the types of registers that would be acceptable. If so, it appears that this was informal guidance rather than any type of legislation. Thus, as far as this author has been able to determine, there is no canon law, universal or particular, that would forbid the kind of record keeping suggested by the inquiry.

However, before adopting another format for sacramental records, it is appropriate to ask: What values does the current legislation, as minimal as it is, strive to foster? Clearly church law values sacramental records and expects that information be accurately and carefully entered. The problem of illegibility raised in the inquiry is real. Yet, that problem seems to be merely one indication of a wider concern with the carelessness with which some sacramental registers are kept. Whatever the problems with legibility that exist currently,

145

replacing the bound parish registers now used with heavy bound loose leaf versions with pages that could be inserted into a typewriter might lead to new and more serious problems. If a different style of sacramental register led to pages being lost or misfiled through carelessness, any advantage gained by better legibility would be more than offset by the problem of missing records. Indeed, county court houses and state offices, many of which are staffed by people with special training in record keeping, do successfully use loose leaf style registers. Whether a similar style of record keeping is appropriate in parishes where many different people (who do not necessarily have special training in record keeping) handle the registers is a question for consideration.

There are also other possibilities for addressing the concern raised in this inquiry. Given the many new technologies for record keeping involving computers, laser discs and the like, it may also be that one of these formats would be the wisest to adopt for the preservation of sacramental information. Some parishes may already be using computer databases for their sacramental records. However, there are legitimate concerns about the safety and longevity of storing information solely in computer memories. The law presently envisions written registers, and for the time being modern information retrieval formats would best be used as supplements for permanent written records.

In conclusion, there seems to be no legal reason that presently requires parishes to use the standard bound sacramental register currently in service. Given the importance of sacramental records, whatever format is chosen should maximize the values of careful preservation and accurate inscription, while minimizing as much as possible the dangers of having records lost or destroyed because of our all too human tendencies to carelessness. There is room for particular legislation to specify approved formats, either on the level of the episcopal conference or in each local diocese. In fact, printers are apt to be very reticent to adopt any different format for sacramental records in the absence of some legislation or other official guidance. Given new possibilities for record keeping that exist today, particular legislation drafted after appropriate research into the various possibilities could do an important service.

Craig A. Cox [1990, revised 1993]

ANOTHER OPINION

First, a preliminary comment on the canonical aspects. The 1983 code, canon 535, §1, gives the general rules: each parish is to possess a set of parish books (including baptismal, marriage and death registers, as well as other registers prescribes by the conference of bishops or the diocesan bishop). The pastor is to see to it that these registers are accurately inscribed and carefully preserved.

By comparison, the 1917 code, canon 470, obligated the pastor to keep the parochial books "with great care and according to the approved custom of the Church or the regulations of the bishop."

The changed language of the canon is perhaps subtle, but it does allow that someone other than the pastor make the entries in a way that is more legible. The obligation in law of the pastor is to oversee this work, and to provide for the preservation of the registers. Regarding the content of these books, various canons regulate the entries, e.g., for baptism, confirmation, orders, perpetual religious profession, marriage, nullity and dissolution.

Secondly, concerning the format of the registers. Following the 1917 code, a survey of the *Canon Law Digest* yields no entry of any determination of a required format for these registers. Subsequent to the 1983 code, and upon inquiry to the Associate General Secretary of the NCCB (April, 1990), no action has been taken, nor is any action anticipated in the near future, concerning the format of these registers.

Commenting on canon 535, J. Janicki [*The Code of Canon Law: A Text and Commentary*, CLSA, 1985] first refers to the purchase of "blank registers which are set up in the *required manner*" (emphasis added), but further on notes that increasingly parishes are using "computer systems for storing and processing sacramental data" (p. 430).

It is this author's opinion that, provided safekeeping and the safeguarding of confidentiality, it is possible for a parish to keep both the usual registers and computer records, the latter making it somewhat easier to retrieve records for the purpose of providing accurate sacramental documentation, etc.

Joseph J. Koury [1990]

CANONS 535 AND 882

CONFIRMATION OF BAPTIZED CATHOLICS IN A SCHISMATIC CHURCH

Recently a number of baptized Roman Catholics, mostly adolescents, were confirmed in a schismatic chapel associated with Archbishop Lefebvre and the Society of St. Pius X. The sacrament was conferred by a schismatic bishop, presumably validly ordained to the episcopacy. A question has arisen over how these confirmations should be recorded.

Is the conferral of confirmation by a schismatic bishop valid? Assuming validity, where and how should these confirmations be recorded? Should a notation be included in the person's baptismal and/or confirmation records, indicating reception from a schismatic bishop? And finally, would reception of confirmation in such a schismatic church constitute a formal renunciation of the Catholic faith?

Confirmation, once validly received, cannot be repeated (c. 845, §1). A validly ordained bishop validly administers the sacrament of confirmation (c. 882). The bishops, presbyters, and deacons who adhere to the schismatic church known as the Society of St. Pius X are validly ordained. The validity of the sacraments in the Church are not in question. However, it is illicit to receive sacraments from a minister in that Church, unless it is a case of emergency baptism, or the conditions of canon 844, §2 are verified. This law permits Catholics to receive the sacraments of penance, Eucharist, and anointing of the sick from non-Catholic ministers in whose churches these sacraments are valid whenever necessity requires or genuine spiritual advantage suggests, provided the danger of error or indifferentism is avoided and when it is physically or morally impossible to approach a Catholic minister.

Canon 844, §1 states that Catholic members of the Christian faithful may licitly receive the sacraments only from Catholic ministers except where the law provides otherwise. The law does not permit a Catholic to receive the sacrament of confirmation in a non-Catholic church. Therefore, such reception, while valid, is gravely illicit, and the recipient may be subject to a canonical penalty (c. 1365). Moreover, parents who hand their children over to be baptized or educated in a non-Catholic religion are subject to a censure or another just penalty (c. 1366).

Having pointed out these provisions of the law, I would add that a penal process would not be appropriate in the case you described. It appears that those who were confirmed either did not intend to join the schismatic church in question, or else they did join it and now they wish to return to the Catholic Church. If they had intended to remain members of the schismatic church, the question of where their confirmation is to be recorded would not even have arisen.

In judging whether they left the Catholic Church by means of a formal act, it is important to discover the intention of the persons. By presenting themselves for confirmation to a schismatic bishop, was their intention to adhere to the schismatic church? Were they consciously leaving the Catholic Church? If so, confirmation in the schismatic church would be one clear indication of their leaving it by means of a formal act. Other indications could include regular participation in the Eucharist and other sacraments in the schismatic church, education in that church, membership in a parish of the church, financial support of the church, and so forth.

There might, however, have been some other motivation for their confirmation. Perhaps they acted out of ignorance or error, presenting themselves to the non-Catholic bishop under the false notion that the Society of St. Pius X is part of the Catholic Church. Perhaps they merely preferred to be confirmed according to the pre-Vatican II liturgical rite with its exotic language and ceremonies, without realizing that they were forbidden from doing so by canon law. If they had no intention of leaving the Catholic Church, then the mere act of being confirmed in a schismatic church would not constitute leaving the Church by means of a formal act.

If the validity of a marriage were at stake (cf., cc. 1086, §1 and 1117), it would be necessary for a church court to determine whether a party had left the Catholic Church by means of a formal act. For present pastoral purposes, however, it would suffice simply to ask the persons what their intention was, whether they had intended to leave the Catholic Church or not. If they had intended to leave the Catholic Church, it should be determined whether they incurred the penalty of *latae sententiae* excommunication, presumably undeclared (cf., cc. 1364; 1323; 1324, §3) and, if so, what is the most fitting way of remitting the penalty (cf., cc. 1355-1357). It is likely that most or all of the persons you described (certainly not those under 18 years of age) did not incur the automatic penalty even if they intentionally choose to join the schismatic church.

Proof of confirmation can be had in accord with canon 894. If it is not prejudicial to anyone, one's confirmation can be proven by the declaration of a single witness who is above suspicion or by the oath of the confirmed person, if the person was at least seven years old and enjoyed the use of reason at the time of the confirmation. A letter or certificate from the minister or parish of confirmation would also be proof.

Although proof of confirmation is easily obtainable in the case you described, the confirmation also should be recorded in the baptismal register in the parish of baptism. Canon 535, §2 states that a person's confirmation is to be recorded in the baptismal register of the parish of baptism; this requirement does not exclude confirmations illicitly conferred. It would be helpful to have a record of confirmation when proof of it is needed in the future, for example, before admission to the seminary, to a novitiate of a religious institute, or to a society of apostolic life (cc. 241, §2; 645, §1; 735, §2), or before marriage (c. 1065, §1).

The law requires the recording of the name of the minister of confirmation in the confirmation register (c. 895), but not in the baptismal register. The confirmation would only be recorded in the confirmation register if performed by a Catholic minister.

When the confirmation is recorded in the baptismal register there should be no notation that it was performed by a schismatic bishop. In receiving confirmation from a schismatic bishop the Catholic persons erred, may have committed a grave sin, or may even have incurred excommunication. Noting the fact of this illicit confirmation in a public, permanent record would violate the rights of those persons, now repentant, to privacy and to a good reputation (c. 220).

John M. Huels, O.S.M. [1993]

Canon 536

Pastor's Right to Dissolve the Parish Council

According to canon 536 the diocesan bishop, after consultation with the presbyteral council, may mandate the establishment of pastoral councils in each of the parishes. These councils, over which the pastor presides, have consultative vote only and are governed by norms to be determined by the diocesan bishop. One hears of disputes arising between the pastor and the council. The question raised in several cases: whether or not the pastor has a right to dissolve the pastoral council in the parish?

Opinion

According to canon 536, the universal law of the Church does not mandate a pastoral council for each parish. The canon, however, does give *the bishop the right* to mandate a parish council in each parish after consultation with the priests' council. The canon also adds that the bishop determines the norms by which the pastoral councils are to be governed. These local norms must recognize the universal constitutive principle that the parish council is consultative and not deliberative.

Canon 536 is silent regarding the right of pastors to dissolve the parish council. That issue would, therefore, be handled by the local diocesan norms. In the concrete cases leading to the above question, it appears that the local norms have also been silent on the issue of possible dissolution of the parish council. It would seem that the pastor does not have a right to refuse to establish a parish council once it has been mandated by the local bishop. On the other hand, it seems in principle there would be a right to dissolve the council for a serious reason.

150

Perhaps canon 501, §3 offers some possible resolution by way of analogy. This canon permits a bishop to dissolve the presbyteral council under certain conditions even though canon 495 mandates that each diocese have a presbyteral council. By analogy it would seem that the diocesan bishop could recognize the right of pastors to dissolve a parish council. It would seem that the right to dissolve a parish council should depend on the diocesan bishop's norms and his interpretation of the norms. It is probably opportune that the norms contain a section to cover this possibility; but if such does not exist at the time of a potential dispute and attempt at dissolution, the bishop could recognize the right of the pastor in principle to dissolve the council. Thereafter some process should be initiated whereby the reason for the dissolution is examined and steps taken for establishment of a new council within a reasonable time.

It would seem that there should exist some serious reason for the dissolution of a parish council by the pastor, for example, the existence of some abuse. It has happened that a new pastor is appointed to a parish where the previous pastor may have been rather permissive in allowing the council to assume quasi-deliberative status; and the new pastor then finds himself under constant pressure to abide by the council's decisions because of their acquired expectations. It may be that the written constitution or by-laws of the council are discovered by a new pastor to be inconsistent with diocesan regulations and for some reason the council cannot come to agreement to correct the discrepancy. This could be reason for dissolution. It may be helpful to insist that the dissolution be made only after consultation with the diocesan bishop and/or after some attempt at reconciliation involving assistance from the bishop's office.

If the pastor has already attempted dissolution of the council without consultation with the bishop and in a diocese in which there are no written guidelines for a dissolution, several reactions are possible: (1) The bishop could recognize the dissolution which took place, but then insist that the reason for the dissolution be made known and discussed by the pastor, the laity and the bishop in a process of reconciliation, whereafter the council would be reinstated or a new council formed. (2) The bishop could refuse in the circumstances to recognize the dissolution of the council and insist that the pastor reinstate the council to its status quo, and only then permit the pastor to express his reason for wanting a dissolution and thereby submit the problem to the bishop's consultation, whereafter the pastor may dissolve the council with the bishop's approval, keeping in mind that the dissolution would only be temporary, that the problem be resolved, and then a new council formed. Therefore, several options are possible either in the way the diocesan norms are written or in the way a concrete situation is resolved.

In conclusion, based on an analogy with canon 501, it is my opinion that a pastor has the right to dissolve a parish council. The right is conditioned by the existence of a legitimate reason, which the bishop could judge, and is conditioned by the norms and interpretations of the bishop in mandating the councils. The bishop could intervene by insisting on reinstatement if no legitimate reason exists. If the council is dissolved, the problem should be resolved and a new council established, since the pastor is not free to avoid having a council on a permanent basis.

J. James Cuneo [1988]

CANON 539

PAROCHIAL ADMINISTRATOR'S LENGTH OF OFFICE AND THE BISHOP'S OBLIGATION TO NAME A PASTOR

A small country parish is currently being cared for by an extern priest appointed to it as administrator. The pastor of another parish applies for transfer to be pastor of the country parish, but his request is denied; he is given as the reason for the denial that the administrator is willing to stay on and therefore, the parish is not canonically vacant. Moreover, it seems to be the bishop's opinion that an administrator enjoys the same tenure rights as a pastor. What is the law on such a situation?

OPINION

First, the country parish is canonically vacant. An administrator is not a pastor. Only if there is a pastor appointed is the ecclesiastical office of *parochus* not vacant. Moreover, if there is no pastor of the parish at the time and the parish is vacant, one way the bishop can provide for the pastoral care of that community is to appoint an administrator — and by definition in this case he serves while the parish is vacant (c. 539).

Second, the provision of an office entailing the care of souls is not to be deferred without serious cause (c. 151). According to the 1917 code, the bishop was to name someone to fill the office within six months. However, the new code does not place any time limit on this, and leaves the decision of when to provide for the office up to the prudent decision of the diocesan bishop, whose prerogative alone it is to name pastors (c. 523).

Third, it is only pastors who are appointed to an indeterminate term (or to a specified term of six years, in the case where the bishop has implemented the option for appointment for a limited term — c. 522). Although canon 540, §1 provides an administrator with the same "rights" as a pastor, this applies to the pastor's rights in pastoral ministry. It does not apply to appointment, as is clear from the conditions under which an administrator is appointed (c. 539) and the very notion of an administrator as supply for a pastor on an interim basis. Administrators of parishes serve at the pleasure of the bishop, and can be removed without the formal process for transfer or removal of a pastor (cc. 1740-1752), and the bishop needs only a cause which he himself considers just (c. 193, §3). So, an administrator does not have the same "tenure" rights as a pastor.

However, some changes have been introduced with the new code which seem to apply in this case, and which weaken the claim a priest may have to be appointed to the office of pastor in such a parish.

First, the law does not require the bishop to appoint a pastor. It permits him to put the parish in the care of a priest who is pastor of some other parish (c. 526, §1), in the care of a team of priests who may be in charge of one or several parishes (c. 517, §1), or even in the care of non-priests under the supervision of a priest who may have the faculties of a pastor but is not the *de iure* pastor of that particular parish (c. 517, §2). While all of these situations are described as taking place when there is a shortage of clergy, it is left to the judgment of the diocesan bishop to decide whether there is a sufficient shortage to justify such arrangements.

The law also allows the appointment of an administrator to care for a vacant parish (c. 539); no time limit is specified for how long an administrator may be left in charge of the parish, and during the time he cares for the parish he is bound by the same duties and enjoys all the rights of a pastor unless the diocesan bishop determines otherwise (c. 540, §1).

So, very clearly the bishop is able to leave a parish in the charge of an administrator. Although the law prefers a pastor be appointed to each parish, the bishop is not strictly obliged by the law to appoint a pastor for a particular parish provided the care of souls is adequately provided for.

Second, the law does not give any priest a right to make a claim on a vacant parish. It is true that the bishop is to appoint the person he judges suited to fulfill the pastoral care of a parish, without any partiality (c. 524); but it is also true that the bishop has the right of free conferral unless someone has the right of presentation or election (c. 523), and free conferral means he freely selects whom to appoint and himself confers the office on the person (c. 157).

Third, although a priest may currently be holding the office of pastor, under the new law he no longer has a claim to continue being a pastor in his subsequent assignments. Transfer may now be to "another parish or *another office*" (c. 1748, emphasis added). The old code's requirement of transfer to another parish of equal or better status for immovable pastors has been dropped.

So, a priest — even a pastor — does not have a canonical right to be appointed pastor of a particular parish. That is left to the free decision of the bishop, and he does not even have to give a reason for denying the request to be appointed to a particular parish.

James H. Provost [1986]

CANON 548

THE GOVERNING POWER OF THE OFFICE OF PAROCHIAL VICAR

Is the position of parochial vicar a canonical office? If it is a canonical office, does a parochial vicar possess ordinary jurisdiction for witnessing marriages? Canon 548, §2 speaks of the "office" of a parochial vicar. Thus, it seems to me that this is an office in the canonical sense. The question in other words is this: Is the ordinary power of jurisdiction or governance attached to this office? On the one hand it would seem that the parochial vicar may have all of the executive authority of the pastor much like a vicar general in relationship to the diocesan bishop (c. 479, §1). On the other hand, the law refers to the local ordinary or pastor delegating a priest or deacon to assist at marriages so that it would seem the law restricts the ordinary jurisdiction for witnessing marriages only to pastors. Might this be analogous to the restriction of certain executive authority to the diocesan bishop as allowed for and stipulated in canon 123, §3?

OPINION

Anytime the question of office and jurisdiction arises the canonist must enter an area of both practical concern and theoretical intrigue. There is really no end to the discussion which is possible. The answer to this question lies in our definitions of office and of ordinary power. The concepts overlap and inter-relate but are not coterminous. All ordinary power is attached to an office, but not all offices enjoy ordinary power.

An ecclesiastical office, according to canon 145, is any ecclesiastical function which is constituted in a stable manner by divine or ecclesiastical law to be exercised for a spiritual purpose. This definition of office does not automatical-ly include power of governance. It represents a major change from the 1917 Code of Canon Law (c. 145) which had distinguished office "in the wide sense" from office "in the strict sense." The definition of office in the present code corresponds to an office in the wide sense of the old code. Ecclesiastical office in the strict sense was defined as a function which was stably constituted by divine or ecclesiastical ordination, conferred according to the norms of the

154

sacred canons and which involved at least some participation in ecclesiastical power of orders or of jurisdiction. The new code has dropped the strict association of ecclesiastical office with participation in power of orders or jurisdiction. Therefore, conferral of office does not automatically mean conferral of power of governance. It would depend on the specific office itself and what the law has attached to it or what the superior has given to the person holding the office.

When the law itself attaches power of governance to an office, the power is called "ordinary power" (c. 131, §1: "The ordinary power of governance is that which is joined to a certain office by the law itself; delegated power is that which is granted to a person, but not by means of an office"). This would mean that ordinary power of governance is always associated by law with a given office; but the reverse is not true, namely not every office is associated with ordinary power of governance.

The parochial vicar has the function of serving in pastoral ministry as co-worker with the pastor and under his authority (c. 545, §1). Certainly the code treats this function as an office, a function that is stably constituted by divine or ecclesiastical law and exercised for a spiritual purpose. Canon 548 explicitly calls the function of parochial vicar an "office" (§2) and it summarizes the rights and obligations. The law itself, however, does not seem to associate to this office any power of governance.

We note that the relationship between pastor and parochial vicar is not the same as the relationship between the bishop and the vicar general. Canon 479, §1 explicitly states that the law attaches to the office of the vicar general executive power (hence ordinary power of governance). On the other hand, canons 545 and 548 describe the office of parochial vicar in terms of assisting the pastor in parochial ministry. The term "*ministerium*" is a more generic one and is not to be equated with "*regimen*" in the strict sense of power of governance. (We could keep in mind here the fact that the *ministerium* of priest who has care of souls frequently involves functions such as preaching the Word of God and sanctifying functions such as sacramental absolution, which traditional canonical opinion considered to be exercises of the power of jurisdiction. It may be possible to interpret that by virtue of the law in canons 757, 764 and 968 any priest with an office of care of souls enjoys power of jurisdiction for the function of preaching and sacramental absolution. The present code, however, seems to restrict the notion of ordinary power to the function of governance — legislative, executive and judicial. For that reason the *ministerium* of a priest, or more specifically of a parochial vicar, does not automatically include *regimen* — power of governance.)

Canon 548 states that the rights and obligations of the parochial vicar, other than those listed in these canons, derive more specifically from the bishop's

155

letter of appointment and in the mandate given by the pastor. Since the law itself does not specifically confer any power of governance on the office of parochial vicar, it appears any power of governance would be delegated and not ordinary.

With regard to the specific function of assisting at marriage, canons 1108 and 1109 confer the jurisdiction upon the office of local ordinary and pastor. Others may assist at marriages by way of delegation. Canon 1111, §1 gives to the office of the local ordinary and the pastor the power to give to other priests and deacons the faculty, even a general one, to assist at marriages. It would seem that this general faculty is one usually to be given to parochial vicars and it would be treated as delegated power (c. 132, §1). The law seems quite clear that it provides the office of local ordinary and pastor the jurisdiction to assist at marriages (ordinary power), but that other ministers (parochial vicars, etc.) assist at marriages with delegated power.

In a similar way canon 1079, §2 extends the bishop's power to dispense from marriage impediments to pastors and to properly delegated sacred ministers. Here again we have an example where the law itself attaches this power of governance to an office (local ordinary and pastor) so that it would be called ordinary power. Other ministers, such as parochial vicar, would exercise this dispensing power only in connection with delegation.

Therefore, it is my opinion that parochial vicar is a canonical office in the strict sense, but any exercise of the power of governance is not ordinary power but delegated. Canon 549, however, may be one exception to consider. In the absence of the pastor, when an administrator has not been named, it becomes the obligation of the parochial vicar to follow the prescriptions of canon 541, §1: "the parochial vicar is to assume the governance (*regimen*) of the parish in the meantime until a parochial administrator is appointed." It would seem in that situation the law itself confers on the office of parochial vicar a limited participation in the power of governance which would be considered ordinary; for the law itself establishes that the office of parochial vicar in that one circumstance enjoys the governance power attached to the office of pastor.

As mentioned at the start, it is impossible to presume any final word has ever been spoken in the matter of the power of jurisdiction. Theories of ecclesiastical power and office, their definitions, nature and source, seem endless. There seems always room for another opinion. For example, Gommarus Michiels held the opinion that the power of jurisdiction could be considered ordinary if it were attached to an office by a particular law. He did not restrict the element of *ipso iure* to universal law or to the code itself. Thus, he said if a bishop by local law attached to the office of vicar forane the power of dispensing from certain impediments, this would be considered ordinary power. (*De potestate ordinaria et delegata*, Tornai. Desclé e [1964] 122-123.) Michiels of course also noted here that other authors disagreed and would call this delegated power.

J. James Cuneo [1987]

Canon 564

"Non-Priests" as Chaplains

What nomenclature can be used for non-priests who provide chaplaincy services in various institutions such as prisons?

Opinion

The 1917 code did not have any specific provisions for chaplaincy services in institutions. It did deal with military chaplains in relationship to pastors, and with chaplains for lay associations and religious houses. The new code, however, has a special section on chaplains — canons 564-572.

Chaplains have been dealt with in documents issued after the 1917 code. For example, in the apostolic constitution on the spiritual care of migrants, *Exsul Familia* (August 1, 1952), Pius XII dealt with chaplains of ships (see *CLD* 3: 92-93). The Consistorial Congregation issued norms and faculties for priests who serve as chaplains of ships (March 19, 1954; *CLD* 4: 111-115) or as chaplains in the Apostolate of the Sea (April 2, 1954; *CLD* 4: 115-120). In both instances, "chaplains" are understood to be priests.

The question of chaplains in prisons witnessing marriages was addressed by the Congregation of the Council in 1926; a distinction was made between full-time and part-time chaplains, but both types were presumed to be priests (see *CLD* 5: 522-523).

These documents, however, must be understood in light of the context in which they were issued. Prior to Vatican II, only clergy were able to hold ecclesiastical office. The position of chaplain, at least on a formal basis, was considered an office. So as a matter of fact, only clergy were chaplains. At Vatican II a couple of major changes were introduced that affect all this. The first was the reinstatement of the diaconate as a proper and permanent order (*LG* 29), with the resulting possibility that deacons would be available for some of the clergy positions for which formerly only priests were available. The second change was that the definition of office was changed (*PO* 20) so that equivalently it was similar to the "broad" definition in the 1917 code (c. 145), resulting in the possibility of lay people holding ecclesiastical offices not specifically

157

reserved to clergy.

Since the law did not specifically reserve the position of chaplain to priests, it seemed that deacons could be appointed chaplains. Since the law did not specify much at all for chaplains, there seemed to be no restriction against naming qualified lay persons as chaplains. In an age of increasing numbers of persons competent and interested in ministry, and decreasing numbers of priests available for various ministries, this seemed to be an acceptable solution.

However, the code takes a slightly different approach to the position of chaplain. It is understood as participating in the care of souls (c. 564) and so is more similar to the role of a pastor than it is dissimilar (although it is not the same as pastor). Moreover, the code gives the chaplain in virtue of his office the faculty to hear confessions (c. 566) and only a priest can do that (c. 965). Accordingly, as for pastors (c. 521) so with chaplains, only a priest can be appointed to the position as it is canonically understood.

This, however, does not solve the problem of shortage of clergy, nor does it address the situation of competent and willing deacons and lay persons who are available to provide chaplaincy services. Really, the code does not address them at all. In this sense, there is a "*lacuna*" or hole in the law. Canon 19 directs us to seek a way of dealing with such a situation by looking to parallels in church law, and such a parallel exists in canon 517, §2. This canon deals with participation in the pastoral care of communities by persons who are not priests, when there is a dearth of priests. Deacons, religious and lay persons may be entrusted with the exercise of pastoral care for those communities; there may be no resident pastor, but a priest is named to supervise the pastoral care they provide, and to supply those elements of pastoral care for which a priest is needed.

This is a new arrangement in the law, and there is only a limited experience in practice to draw on. However, it may provide a way to understand how deacons and lay persons in chaplaincy services may continue to provide the ministry they have been supplying.

The new code in this respect places the responsibility on the local diocese to develop its own policies and procedures for training, screening and placement, particularly of nonordained ministers. There are canons dealing with permanent deacons and the NCCB has further guidelines in this regard. The code, however, has only a few indications as to what should be included in policies and procedures for lay ministers. These include the canons on ecclesiastical office (cc. 145-196, especially cc. 146-156 on provision of office and cc. 192-195 on removal from office), canon 231 (on preparation for an involvement in ministry by lay persons, and a just remuneration for those doing it), and canon 1290 on contracts.

With regard to what to call such persons in chaplaincy service, the new code does pose a problem vis-à-vis prior practice. Since there was no legal description specifically restricting "chaplain" to "priest," many persons in chaplaincy services came to be known as "chaplain" and in some places need to have that title in order to be paid (e.g., in non-Catholic health care facilities, state-funded institutions such as prisons, etc.).

It seems to me that canon 564 specifies that "chaplain" in the canonical sense is a priest; it does not in itself restrict the nomenclature "chaplain" in general usage. However, whatever nomenclature is used needs to respect this canonical provision. There are no norms in the law which specify what terms to use for non-priests in such ministry, any more than there are norms for what to call non-priests involved in parish ministry. In this latter situation, a great variety of terms are used around the country: pastoral associates, pastoral minister, etc. For chaplains, it may be possible to adopt such titles as "deacon chaplain" or "lay chaplain" or, in cases where it applies, "sister chaplain." If this is used, my suggestion would be to have priests in such positions titled "priest chaplain."

My point is this. No matter what titles are used, it should be clear to the people with whom the chaplain is dealing whether the chaplain is or is not a priest. A priest who is a chaplain has, in virtue of the law itself, some very important faculties; but a person in chaplaincy services who does not have presbyteral orders cannot receive such faculties, since they apply to the exercise of priestly orders.

James H. Provost [1985]

CANON 579

ERECTION OF A DIOCESAN INSTITUTE

What is a fair procedure for a diocese to use in establishing a new religious institute?

OPINION

The question about fairness in establishing a new religious institute implies that certain rights are involved. While it is difficult to present an exhaustive listing of the rights here, several can be considered in discussing a reasonable procedure. Three groups are involved in the procedure: the institute and its members, the diocesan bishop and the local church he tends, and the universal Church.

The members of the proposed institute have the right according to canon 215 to form and govern an association for religious purposes. Initially, the association would be a private association as defined in canon 299. The members form a private agreement among themselves to establish the association. The statutes can form the basis of the future constitutions of the group (c. 304, §1). They should include ordinances on the temporal goods of the association.

Associations of the Christian faithful are governed by canons 298-329. The diocesan bishop must review the statutes (c. 299, §3). After the stability of the association has been demonstrated by mutually agreed-upon criteria, the diocesan bishop would consider giving it his approbation as a public association through a formal decree (c. 312, §2).

Actually it is not the diocese but the diocesan bishop who establishes a new religious institute (c. 579). However, the bishop would be wise to involve various parts of the diocese in caring for the association and determining its feasibility as a diocesan religious institute. The bishop probably would involve the episcopal vicar for religious, provided he has one, at the very beginning of the process. Ordinarily the vicar will be directly involved throughout the procedure. The bishop also might approach various consultative bodies within the diocese about establishing the institute. The pertinent canons do not require consultation. However, the groups might be able to offer wisdom about the establishment of the proposed institute. Various councils the bishop might consult are the presbyteral council, the diocesan pastoral council, and, if it exists, the council of religious.

Since the bishop has the obligation of care for associations in the diocese and the right of visiting them (c. 305, §1), he can be in close contact with the proposed institute throughout its development. Ordinarily, the care and visitation will be done by the vicar for religious. It would be helpful to have a mutually established time frame so that the matter is not delayed indefinitely, resulting in difficulties for either the institute or the diocese.

An important question during this time of diminishing resources in the Church is whether the proposed institute shares the spirit of another religious community (c. 303). If it does, it should seek some kind of relationship with the established institute of consecrated life. While the Church is supportive of gifts given by the Spirit (c. 605), it is also cautious about the proliferation of institutes having the same charism and end or mission.

After a given time, the bishop would proceed to establish the group as a diocesan institute of consecrated life. He must consult the Holy See to receive its *nihil obstat*. Several documents must accompany the request. A list of the documents can be found in *CLD* 7: 458.

The Apostolic See has the right to be consulted before the diocesan bishop establishes the group as a diocesan institute of consecrated life (c. 579). Missionary dioceses contact the Apostolic See through the Congregation for the Evangelization of Peoples; for other dioceses the contact is through the Congregation for Institutes of Consecrated Life and Societies of Apostolic Life.

If the association is clerical (c. 302) or has clerical members, the matter of incardination needs to be considered. While the proposed institute remains an association, either private or public, a clerical member remains incardinated to the diocese or religious community to which he originally belonged. After the institute has been formally established, the cleric becomes incardinated when he is admitted perpetually or definitively in the institute (c. 268, §2), unless the constitutions indicate otherwise.

Michael P. Joyce, C.M. [1992, revised 1993]

ANOTHER OPINION

Consecrated life is of divine origin. It is a gift of the Holy Spirit in and for the Church (*Lumen gentium* 44; c. 575). The Church protects a wide variety of institutes of consecrated life by approving them as public juridic persons, providing canonical norms for their stable living, and encouraging the growth and development of these institutes according to the spirit of the founders and their traditions (c. 576).

A person, believing that he or she is prompted by the Spirit to initiate such a charism in the Church, presents the inspiration to the diocesan bishop or his vicar for religious for careful scrutiny. The diocesan bishop or the vicar for religious then studies the gift: its uniqueness and possible development vis-à-vis the already existing institutes of consecrated life, its response to the needs of the people, and its potential contribution to the life and holiness of the Church (c. 605). The present decline in vocations to consecrated life and the escalating costs of these institutes in their apostolates, health care and retirement provisions for sick and aged members raise serious practical reservations regarding the proliferation of institutes of consecrated life closely resembling those already enjoying public juridic status in the Church.

The canonical status of the founder or foundress should be clearly determined at the first interview. Often this precludes future complex problems. The proposals offered by the founder or foundress should include the essential elements of an institute of consecrated life according to the universal law of the Church (cc. 573; 607; and 710). After hearing the proposal, the bishop or his vicar may recognize it to be more in keeping with a society of apostolic life (c. 731) or a new form of consecrated life (c. 605).

If the essential elements of consecrated life are present, the diocesan bishop can permit the person and his/her companions to remain under the supervision of the vicar for religious as a private association in the diocese (c. 299). During this time, which should not be hurried and can extend over a period of years, the stability and vitality of the lifestyle and the ability to attract and maintain members should be monitored by the vicar for religious. The financial security of the private association should be reviewed by the competent officials of the diocese. The diocesan bishop or his vicar should encourage the founder or foundress to write the way of life of the association (cc. 299, §3; and 304). Although in a transitional stage as a private association, the way of life can reflect the proper law or constitutions of an institute of consecrated life to which it aspires. The founder or foundress should receive some canonical assistance regarding essential content of this text (c. 605).

After a significant period of time in which the stability and development of the private association can be seen, the bishop can approve the group as a public association by a written decree. This formal approval by the diocesan bishop gives the association canonical status as a public juridic person in the Church. At this time the way of life or proper law of the public association should be reviewed, refined and presented to the diocesan bishop for formal approval (cc. 301 and 304).

With this step it would be well for the diocesan bishop to advise the Apostolic See (Congregation for Institutes of Consecrated Life and Societies of Apostolic Life, hereafter CICLSAL) of the existence of this public association which aspires to become a diocesan institute of consecrated life. A brief history of the founder or foundress and the association, its development in the diocese, the number, names and status of the members, and a copy of the proper law should be sent to CICLSAL.

This remote preparation for the eventual consultation with CICLSAL precludes any element of surprise and offers helpful background for the eventual consultation. The diocesan bishop can request an opinion or reading from CICLSAL regarding the materials sent to the congregation and his intention of erecting the public association as a diocesan institute of consecrated life.

Before the diocesan bishop erects the public association as a diocesan institute of consecrated life and approves its constitutions, he formally consults CICLSAL. This action is required for validity. The bishop should send an updated report of the materials mentioned in the above paragraph. A briefing on the history, membership, apostolate, and copies of the proper law of the association should be enclosed. If CICLSAL sent any response to the initial communication, the protocol number should be used in this second communication.

When the *nihil obstat* is obtained from the Apostolic See, the diocesan bishop will issue the formal decree of erection and approve the proper law (c. 579). The public association becomes a diocesan institute of consecrated life. Its charism is recognized as an authentic expression of the Gospel, and it is entrusted with a canonical mission which its members perform in the name of the Church (cc. 574, §2 and 577). The institute is an integral part of the life and holiness of the Church. The Church continues to guide and encourage the institute according to the spirit of the founder or foundress and its wholesome traditions (c. 576).

Rose M. McDermott, S.S.J. [1992]

CANON 604

ADMISSION TO THE ORDER OF VIRGINS

Canon 604 is a new canon in the 1983 Code of Canon Law. How would the diocesan bishop judge the suitability of one who petitions to be admitted to the order of virgins? What would be some qualities that this person should possess? What directives can be offered to the diocesan bishop to guide him in his decision to admit or refuse a candidate to the order of virgins?

OPINION

While the consecration of virgins is of ancient tradition in the Church, canon 604 is new and provides for this state of life in the 1983 Code of Canon Law. There are few norms for a bishop in determining the suitability of the person who petitions to be admitted to the order of virgins. It would seem, therefore, that the diocesan bishop or his vicar for religious should be familiar with the canons for preparation, admission and on-going formation in consecrated life. In an analogous way, these canons can provide guidelines for a bishop or his delegate to determine the suitability of a candidate for the order of virgins. Based on these canons and recent commentaries on the order of virgins, the following procedures are recommended.

The candidate for the order of virgins should be a Catholic with the right intention, requisite qualities, free from any impediments, and have suitable preparation before being admitted (c. 597). Certificates of baptism and confirmation, a letter from the pastor of the parish wherein the candidate is registered, as well as diplomas from schools and testimonials from employers, et. al., should be requested (c. 645).

It would seem that the candidate should be at least thirty years of age, having never been married. The candidate should not be held by a sacred bond with an institute of consecrated life nor incorporated in a society of apostolic life. Likewise, one should not conceal incorporation in an institute of consecrated life or a society of apostolic life. The request should be without force, grave fear or fraud (c. 643).

The candidate should have sufficient education in and practice of the faith, good spiritual, psychological and physical health, an integrated sexuality, and have never lived in open violation of chastity. One should be financially independent and self-providing (cc. 642 and 644).

The applicant should petition the diocesan bishop through a formal written petition, and submit to him a plan of life (*sanctum propositum*) that one is determined to live as a consecrated virgin. This proposal should reflect a life rooted in Christ and the practice of the evangelical counsels. It should be open to God's Word through fidelity to the prayer of the Church, daily Eucharist, and spiritual reading. The consecrated virgin should practice frequent penance, seek spiritual direction, make an annual retreat, and attend days of recollection planned by the diocesan bishop or his delegate (cc. 652, §2; 659, §§1-2; 661-664; 666).

The diocesan file should contain a copy of the petition for consecration and admission to the order of virgins, copies of the above mentioned documents, *curriculum vitae*, and plan of life. There should be a statement signed by the diocesan bishop indicating that he consecrated and admitted the petitioner to the order of virgins on a certain date in accord with the Church's approved liturgical rite and canonical requirements. Finally, the file should include a waiver signed by the consecrated virgin stating that neither the Church nor the particular diocese has any financial responsibility towards the person or anyone else.

Associations of consecrated virgins, whether private or public, can provide support for the commitment to follow Christ more closely and dedicate one's life to service to the Church (c. 604, §2). However, these associations are not similar to the forms of life prescribed in the code and the respective proper laws for members of institutes of consecrated life (c. 573, §2).

If a consecrated virgin wishes to move to another diocese, that person should request a recommendation in writing from the diocesan bishop of the first diocese, and petition the new diocesan bishop to be received as a consecrated virgin in his diocese. A consecrated virgin who petitions for a grave reason can be dispensed by the diocesan bishop from the obligations of the state (c. 691, §2). It would seem that the solemn promise of the consecrated virgin does not constitute a diriment impediment to marriage (c. 1078, §2, 1°). For grave delicts, the diocesan bishop can dismiss a person from the order of virgins.

Rose M. McDermott, S.S.J. [1993]

Canon 604

Previously Married Person Becoming a Consecrated Virgin

A question has arisen on whether the status of consecrated virgin in canon 604 is appropriate for someone who has been previously married and either widowed, divorced or received an ecclesiastical annulment. What are some of the historical and theological considerations since the canon does not state any qualifications or limitations?

Opinion

A ritual consecration of women as virgins emerged by the fourth century. That rite applied to both women living in the world and women living in monasteries as cloistered nuns. By the tenth century two distinct rites evolved: the rite for the consecration of virgins who were living in the world and another for virgins who lived in cloistered monasteries. By the middle of the eleventh century there was no longer a distinction between the two types of consecration. There was only one rite, which centered on those virgins who lived in monasteries. The chief reason for this evolution can be traced to the development of religious orders. By the eleventh century almost any woman wishing to live a life of consecrated virginity could do so in a monastery. Between the eleventh and the twentieth centuries, for the few isolated cases of women who wished to be consecrated virgins while living in the world, some bishops adopted the rite for those consecrated virgins who were cloistered nuns.

It was in this historical context that the Congregation for Religious replied to a request from some bishops for faculties to consecrate women living in the world as virgins. In 1927, the Congregation for Religious responded, "In the negative, let no novelties be introduced" (*CLD* 1: 266). Then in 1950, Pope Pius XII decreed that "the ancient formulae for the consecration of virgins, which are in the Roman Pontifical, are reserved to nuns" (*CLD* 3: 234). Twenty years later, on May 31, 1970, the Congregation for Divine Worship issued a decree which reversed this twentieth century prohibition on consecrating women living in the world as virgins. This new rite provides for the consecration of *nuns* as well as *women living in the world*. For both categories the rite requires that candidates for consecration as virgins be women "who have never entered into marriage and have not publicly or openly lived in a state contrary to chastity" (*CLD* 7: 423). It appears as though this restored rite considers *virginity* as a permanent state, open only to the woman who has never been married or is known to have never participated in sexual relations. It seems that the woman who has been married previously, whether widowed or divorced, with or without an ecclesial annulment, is not eligible to be consecrated a virgin according to the rite promulgated in 1970. These requirements are signs that the candidate is, in fact, a virgin. The state of virginity, which is a constitutive element of the requirements for admission to the Rite of Consecration, cannot be dispensed. However, a person who may have been "legally" married but perhaps never cohabitated or can prove non-consummation, may present a compelling case for dispensation from the requirement of non-marriage.

Canon 604 provides for the continued celebration of this 1970 Rite of Consecration. The canon underscores the element of mystical betrothal to Christ. In addition to the traditional marital symbolism of the union of Christ with the Church, there is an additional level of meaning present. Not only does the consecration of a virgin symbolize the union of Christ with the Church, but a sacred union of the virgin with Christ comes into being. Some suggest that the juridic effect of that union invalidates a subsequent attempt to marry.

The canon also highlights the ecclesial relationship that the consecrated virgin assumes. The canon states that the diocesan bishop, the competent authority to admit a woman living in the world to the rite, is the appropriate minister. In addition, the rite's introduction suggests that for persons living in the world, the rite takes place normally in the cathedral. Canon 604, as well as the rite itself, suggests that the celebration of the Rite of Consecration is integrally tied to dedicated service in the Church. A suggested homily contained in the rite ties this service especially to those in need: the poor, the weak, the ignorant, the young, the old, the widowed and to all in adversity. It seems, then, that there is a special relationship between the consecrated virgin and the local church.

The 1983 Code of Canon Law does not modify the provisions of the Rite of Consecration concerning admission to the rite (c. 2). Only those who have never entered marriage and have neither publicly nor openly lived in a state contrary to chastity may be consecrated as virgins. However, the 1983 code also encourages diocesan bishops "to strive to discern new gifts of consecrated life" (c. 605). While church law maintains that the Apostolic See alone can approve new forms of consecrated life, canon 605 suggests that diocesan bishops should be attentive to emerging forms of consecrated life. As previously married persons increasingly state their desire to be more closely united with Christ and dedicated to the service of the Church, diocesan bishops and others serving in pastoral ministry will need to assist these previously married persons as they discern their call. Who knows? We may see the reemergence of the order of widows as well as the rise of other states of consecrated celibacy.

Catherine C. Darcy, R.S.M. [1993]

Canons 607; 623; 625; and 654

Associate Members Holding Office

*May associate members in a religious institute be appointed or elected to office?
May they be listed along with the professed members in the official directory of
the province or the institute?*

Opinion

Unfortunately, there are many misconceptions about the growing phenomenon of having lay men and women, sometimes non-Catholics, minister together with men and women religious or reside with professed religious in their houses and mission residences. These lay people are often designated as associates, affiliates, lay missioners or similar names. However, they are not truly members of the religious community, nor do they have the same rights and obligations of professed members. They do not profess the public vows of chastity, poverty and obedience according to the constitutions of the religious institute. They are not obliged to live the community life which is expected of professed members and determined according to the traditions and proper law of the institute.

The practice of treating associates as full members of the institute manifests the confusion, at times, which some religious have concerning their own identity as religious within the Catholic Church and the implications which flow from that. In the strict sense of the term, the only people who are legally members of a religious institute are those who have completed a valid novitiate and have made profession of vows (c. 654).

The code (cc. 623 and 625) states that the institute's own proper law (constitutions and directory) must specify the qualifications for certain offices in the community. Sometimes there are expectations over and beyond perpetual profession, such as the number of years in profession or the age of the candidate, before a religious may qualify for certain offices. While non-members may not hold these offices because they are not professed religious, they can certainly assist in a variety of ways those religious who are in positions of authority. For example, while the role of a general or provincial treasurer is reserved to a member of the institute, non-members could act as business managers or accountants as long as they are professionally qualified.

In my opinion, the term "member" ought not to be used in speaking of associates. It is both a disservice to the professed members and to the associates to equate them. Professed religious are the only ones who have clear rights and obligations in the institute. Whatever expectations the institute has of its associates and whatever expectations the associates have of the institute should be stated in the appropriate community documents, agreements or contracts.

However, it is both legally indefensible and a terrible inequity to fail to distinguish between true members, the professed religious, and those non-members who are only associated or affiliated with the religious institute. Finally, since associates are not members of the religious institute, it is highly inappropriate to list them in official documents as if they were members.

David F. O'Connor, S.T. [1993]

Canons 617-618 and 698

Having a Neutral Party Present for a Meeting between the Major Superior and a Difficult Member

Does a major superior have a right to include a neutral third party at a meeting with a difficult member of the institute? (Or the reverse, does a member of a religious institute have a right to exclude a neutral person from a meeting when the major superior has requested the presence of such a person?)

Opinion

Canon 698 protects the member's right of defense in matters concerning dismissal from the institute (cc. 695; 696). Presuming the matters relating to the "difficult member" are not those of dismissal, the member's right of defense remains (c. 221) but could be mitigated. The mitigation could be by proper law (c. 617) or by the appropriate exercise of the superior's personal authority (cc. 618-619).

Canon 617 indicates that the proper law of a particular institute could contain stipulations concerning the presence of a neutral party at a meeting between the major superior and a member. If so, proper law would govern the situation.

Recognizing the divine source of the superior's authority through the ministry of the Church, canon 618 clearly states that the superior has the personal authority "to decide and prescribe." Just as clearly, canon 619 emphasizes that the superior be pastoral in exercising personal authority. With pastoral prudence, serious discretion and obvious good will, then, in light of the personal authority of the office, if deemed necessary, the superior could invite a neutral third party to a meeting with a difficult member.

168

Obviously such an invitation would be the exception, not the rule. The value of the third party would need to be weighed with the protection of the difficult member's reputation and right to privacy (c. 220). Admittedly, in this regard, the rights in the Code of Canon Law are on the side of the perpetually professed individual and not the institute as represented by the major superior. However, the rights of the difficult member do have corresponding obligations in the vowed life, including "submission of the will to legitimate superiors" (c. 601).

In the lived experience of religious life, the issue in regard to the difficult member is usually not so much reputation as privacy. Because of prolonged behavioral patterns in community, the difficult member's reputation is usually well-known; however, privacy about the confrontation with the superior might be at stake. To honor such privacy, the major superior could request a councilor to be the third party at the meeting since secrecy could be imposed on the councilor (cc. 627 and 127, §3).

Conceivably, situations could warrant the invitation of a third party to the meeting. One such situation would be the major superior's need to have a councilor-witness verify that the difficult member has been properly informed of the seriousness of his/her transgressions. In the most prudent approach to such a meeting, the superior would inform the difficult member of the identity of the third party who would be present. The presence of a witness could impress upon the difficult member the seriousness of the transgressions. In addition, the presence of a third party might help balance any personality conflicts that could exist between the superior and the difficult member. Should the major superior have to pursue more serious steps in regard to the difficult member's continued transgressions, or if the member denies that the issue had ever been addressed, the witness would be available, as well as the meeting's documentation, for future reference.

However, the difficult member would have the right to exclude a neutral person from a meeting with the major superior if proper law so determines (c. 617), if the superior's use of personal authority is clearly inappropriate (cc. 618-619), or if the member's reputation and privacy would seriously be violated (c. 220).

Mary Conroy, O.S.U. [1992]

ANOTHER OPINION

Interaction with a "difficult" member of a religious institute calls for wisdom, openness and empathy. For such a meeting to be effective, a major superior needs to possess these and other gifts. The code instructs superiors to exercise their authority in a spirit of service and to listen willingly to all members of the institute (c. 618). Superiors are also to meet the personal needs of the members in an appropriate fashion and to be patient (c. 619).

All members of religious institutes, whether they be labeled "difficult" or not, have the same obligations arising from the evangelical counsels (c. 598) and from common life (c. 602).

The inquiry does not determine the type of meeting which is to be taking place between the major superior and the "difficult" member. It could be the meeting during which the superior is making known the accusations and proofs to the member who is about to be dismissed (c. 695, §2). Or, it could be the meeting during an official visitation of the superior (c. 626, §1). Also, it could be a special meeting requested either by the superior or the member to deal with an agenda not clearly known to the other. I will assume we are dealing with this last type of meeting.

The question is about inviting a disinterested person to sit in on a conversation between a member and his/her major superior. Since Vatican II, the use of such a neutral third party has increased in popularity. The basis of this practice is not found in canon law but in communication theory. If the third party is indeed neutral to both principals, that person can facilitate the conversation so that both the member and the superior truly hear each other by conveying their thoughts and feelings clearly. The third party also is a witness. In my experience such a third party is often welcomed and sometimes requested by the superior or the member.

The main problem with such an arrangement has been that the third party is not perceived by one of the principals (usually the member) as being truly neutral or unbiased. If this is the case, the superior and the member negotiate about the acceptability of some other person. I have never been involved in a case where the presence of a third party is seen as a problem because one of the principals did not want a witness to the conversation. The conversation is usually transcribed and given to the member to review and sign, if necessary. The document serves as a witness.

The inquiry asks if the major superior has a *right* to invite this neutral third party and, conversely, does the member have the *right* to exclude such a person. We often use the term "right" very loosely to describe things which deal with fairness, appropriateness or suitability. In the technical sense, a right is an arena of free choice based on fundamental understandings of human persons and of society. Canonically, rights are expressed in the law. I cannot find such a right in the law which would cover our question. From the texts I have quoted above I can argue that a superior could be acting responsibly by wanting such a third party when talking to a member with whom communication in the past has been difficult. The member could be acting responsibly by rejecting the superior's choice because of the reasons cited above. But I do not see these actions as based on rights in the strict sense.

Paul L. Golden, C.M. [1992]

CANON 627

THE TERM OF COUNCILORS CALCULATED ACCORDING TO DATE OF LEGISLATION

In our 1984 Chapter we designated a term of office for general councilors. They may serve two consecutive terms or eight years. We presently have sisters on the council who served one or two terms as councilors prior to the 1984 legislation. Would their term as councilors expire at this time, or would their term be counted from the time of the 1984 legislation, thus leaving them eligible for another term?

OPINION

Regarding your question on the norms for eligibility for election of general councilors, I offer my opinion assuming that no clear determination in the matter was made at the time of the 1984 Chapter. From the code's general norms we have the basic principle that laws come into existence when they are promulgated (c. 7). In this case then, the limit of general councilors to two consecutive terms began to be your proper law in 1984. There is also the canonical norm that: "Laws deal with the future and not the past, unless specific provision be made in the laws concerning the past" (c. 9).

In light of these principles then, it would be my opinion that only terms served from 1984 to 1988 would be counted in computing the eligibility of persons to serve as general councilor in the 1988 election. If the 1984 chapter left no clear understanding that this was intended to be retroactive, I believe this would be the best interpretation for this one-time question. Obviously if the delegates feel that someone has served long enough, they may effect the spirit of the new legislation by how they vote. Similarly, if persons who have been in office for two or more terms feel that they have served long enough, and your constitutions do not require acceptance of office, these sisters would be free to decline even though they are technically eligible.

Sharon L. Holland, I.H.M. [1988]

CANON 631

PARTICIPATION OF NON-DELEGATES IN THE GENERAL CHAPTER

We are attempting to provide for more participation for non-delegates in our chapter. It is our wish that any community member may take part in the discussion and deliberations of the chapter upon approval of the delegates. The right to vote on matters would be the sole right of the elected delegates. Does such an arrangement, in any way, diminish the authority of the elected delegates?

OPINION

Regarding your question on participation for non-delegates in your chapter, I believe you have expressed awareness of the values that need to be kept in balance. Allowing members of the congregation to be present at sessions of the chapter of affairs, to express their opinions at designated times and to witness first-hand the deliberations of the delegates, both enhances their understanding of the decisions that are made and their sense of ownership of those decisions. On the other hand, as you have noted, the delegates cannot lose sight of the fact that they are the final decision makers. They have been elected by the others to exercise that responsibility.

The canons do not precisely address this question. I would make a first preliminary distinction between the chapter's election function and its action on other matters. As you know the "supreme moderator" or general superior must be elected through canonical election (c. 625, §1). Canon 626 speaks further of the uprightness of elections, but the main body of norms are in canons 164 ff. These canons are very clear about the secrecy of ballots and participation in elections only by members of the elective body. The nature of elections, these canons, and the necessary confidentiality that would surround any discernment process which might precede actual balloting preclude the observers or other participants from this part of the chapter's functions.

With regard to the other deliberations of the chapter, the canons leave a fairly broad scope by which proper law may build in provision for how the chapter is "celebrated" (c. 631, §2). Two particular things which should be spelled out are: 1) only the capitulars (elected delegates or *ex officio*) may vote; 2) the chapter members have the right to call for an executive session (i.e., without any observers) when they feel it is needed. Beyond these, depending on the size of the group, the number of non-delegates wishing to participate, the amount of time available for the meetings, etc., norms should be drawn up for when observers may participate (total group sessions and/or small group sessions), how frequently or at what point in deliberations. It seems to be helpful to have members of the congregation make a commitment ahead of chapter for the degree of participation they wish — i.e., if they wish to have a right to speak at designated times, it may be required that they study certain preparatory materials. Others may wish only to come and listen. The person presiding should have the authority, within the norms, to make certain that the capitulars have sufficient time for their deliberations and voting.

The experiences of recent general chapters urges increased prudence in planning for such participation. Capitulars must be clear on their obligations and rights, and on the central duty of having at heart the well-being of the entire institute. They have been elected precisely to form a body representative of the whole (c. 631, §1). Geography, availability and particular interests can result in a presence of observers which skews the representative composition of the group. This in turn can inadvertently exert undue influence on decisions.

Sharon L. Holland, I.H.M. [1988]

Canons 631-633

Allowing Associate Members to Vote at a General Assembly

Are associate members of a religious congregation able to be granted the right to vote in a general assembly?

Opinion

I have studied the provincial chapter constitutions, which I am presuming have been approved by the superior general with the consent of the general council. While some of the language of this document is imprecise and even misleading, it appears that the provincial chapter, which is a standing body and meets at least once every year, is composed of specified *ex officio* members and elected members and is distinct from the general assembly, which comprises all the sisters who are present at the time the provincial chapter is in session, whether they are members of the chapter or not.

It is also clearly stated in the provincial chapter constitutions that the general assembly is a consultative body, even if the members are asked to vote when the expression of their opinion will help to achieve consensus. The provincial chapter is said to be a consultative, deliberative and legislative body. It also appears to be clear that the actions of the assembly do not bind the delegates to the chapter to anything more than that they be willing to listen to what the members of the assembly have to say.

If all of this is so, I see no antecedent bar to giving the right to vote to associate members, provided of course that this amendment of the provincial chapter constitutions is approved by the superior general with the consent of the council. The implication of saying that the members of the assembly may be asked to vote with a view to achieving consensus is that voting is not the usual procedure in discussions in the assembly.

Richard A. Hill, S.J. [1990]

ANOTHER OPINION

The three issues which must be weighed in arriving at a decision on this matter are: (1) the meaning of the term "general assembly"; (2) the prescriptions surrounding the voting privileges of the membership which are contained in the congregational documents; and (3) the meaning of incorporated membership in religious institutes. This canonical opinion is a result of having reviewed the pertinent content of the particular congregation's constitutions and the acts of its general chapter in 1986.

The nature of the associate membership program is crucial to answering the question of extending the right to vote. The following analysis is offered after reviewing the congregation's documents on the program. The documents establish that the associate membership is an affiliation *without canonical vows* and made for *a determined length of time*. In addition, the associate member has *no obligations* to form community or share in the congregation's financial concerns and practices. The nature of the associate membership appears to be a way to offer the laity a forum through which they can make a commitment for a period of time which is free of any canonical responsibilities other than to pray and share, in varying degrees, in the apostolic works of the congregation.

Such an affiliation is the right of the congregation to develop. However, in offering such an affiliation the congregation must remain clear about the distinction between associate membership and incorporated membership. Incorporated membership is defined within several sections of the constitutions of the congregation. The constitutions specify that incorporated membership involves a total consecration by vow to observe the evangelical counsels and to live a communal life. At several points, the constitutions accent the value of a communal lifestyle and the view that the commitment of the apostolate is lifelong. Thus, incorporated members share all aspects of their life together, including financial, since the commitment is perpetual. This is distinctly different from the intent of associate membership.

It is essential to keep the distinctions between associate membership and incorporated membership in mind when considering the origin of and right to voting privileges. The constitutions state that only the delegates, who must be finally professed members of the congregation, can vote in chapter, whether in the general or provincial chapters. There is nothing in the constitutions to allow for the extension of this right to vote, either for delegates or for the chapter itself, to associate members. Such an extension would appear to be beyond the spirit of the universal law of the Church on religious institutes and the congregation's constitutions which were approved in 1985 by the Congregation for Institutes of Consecrated Life and Societies of Apostolic Life.

At the same time, the provincial is to provide opportunities for the sisters to participate in determining and evaluating the goals and policies of the province. Since the term "general assembly" is not defined within the constitutions, it is possible that it means a meeting less formal than a chapter. The extension of voting privileges would appear to be possible within a meeting other than a chapter since the universal law of the Church and the particular law of the congregation address only the formal legal structure of a chapter.

In conclusion, the proposal of extending voting rights in chapter to associate members within the congregation is contrary to the nature and rights of incorporated membership. This conclusion is reached after a review of the congregation's constitutions and in light of the universal law of the Church. The issue remains whether the term "general assembly" is the same as the term "chapter." If there is a difference in these two terms, then the potential for extending the voting rights to associate members within a general assembly exists.

Lynn M. Jarrell, O.S.U. [1990]

CANONS 170; 172; 625; AND 631

DESIGNATING SOME OF THE DELEGATES TO A CHAPTER OF ELECTIONS AS THE DISCERNING BODY

A religious institute with a delegated chapter of elections wishes to make use of a discernment process in electing its next general superior and council. A proposed step is to select some of the delegates to serve as the discerning body. This would mean that this select group of delegates would meet separately with the individuals who have been suggested as leaders for a period of a day or

175

more during the chapter of elections in order to facilitate the discernment. The reason for proposing this step is because the size of the chapter hampers discernment and reaching consensus. The question has arisen as to whether such splitting off of a group of the delegates, once the chapter of elections is convened, unjustly restricts the right of each delegate to active voice. In other words, some of the delegates will have the opportunity to obtain valuable information about the proposed leaders in a manner and way not available to the rest of the delegates. Does this practice have the potential of invalidating the elections?

OPINION

This question focuses on the impact that particular steps of a discernment process within a chapter of elections can have on the right of each delegate to exercise active voice equally and freely. At the core of the question is the reason for desiring to select a few of the delegates as the discerning body instead of understanding that this is the role and authority of all the members of a chapter of elections.

The authority to elect the general superior belongs to the general chapter as stated in canon 631, §1. This is a vested right of the elected members of a chapter of elections. Any type of restriction of this vested right, whether by a formal structure or by some type of pressure or influence put upon all or even one of the delegates, can be serious enough to invalidate the election.

Difficulty arises when trying to balance this right of the delegates with the current variations in election processes which are occurring in many religious institutes. The law, in canon 631, §2, specifies that the order to be observed regarding elections is to be determined in the particular law of the given institute. Concerning the election of the general superior, canon 625 designates that the election is to be conducted according to the institute's constitutions. Thus, universal law allows for variations in general elections as long as the essential elements for a valid election of persons are preserved. These essential elements, as stated in canons 170 and 172, focus on the election and on the electors.

The election by its very nature must be free of all force and undue influence. This would mean that the steps in the election process must not in any way predetermine the ones to be elected. Nor should the process, including schedule and location, restrict the presence of the delegates and their consideration of persons for election. For example, the procedure for balloting and handling a tie, defined in canon 119, 1°, can be modified by the particular law of an institute but cannot be altered to such an extent that balloting is *pro forma* and/or consensus is expected of the delegates. Such an alteration would be beyond the scope of the flexibility allowed for in canons 631, §2, and 625.

The freedom of the electors must be provided for throughout the election process. Canon 172 specifies that for a vote to be valid it must be 1) free, 2) secret, 3) certain, 4) absolute, 5) determinate, and 6) without any conditions placed upon the outcome. For example, in an election of persons it is necessary to use a written ballot in order to ensure that the vote of a particular elector remains secret. These six requirements create an environment and procedure which allow the electors to cast their ballots based on their convictions. Thus, the electors will be able to fulfill their responsibilities which flow from the right of active voice.

In the question at hand, it is the preservation of the freedom of the delegates that is at issue. The use of a discernment process in a chapter of elections is possible and certainly in keeping with the context of canons 631 and 625. Both of these canons direct that the details of the election process in a given institute are to be described within its constitutions and/or any other documents which comprise its particular law.

Yet, while the institute has the authority to establish an election process which reflects the thinking and needs of its membership, it does not have the competency to alter the essential elements of active voice. None of the steps in the election process should unduly restrict and/or favor any one delegate in obtaining the information needed for exercising responsibly the right and duty of active voice. Designating some of the delegates as the discerning body to meet with the suggested leaders certainly alters the understanding of the role and authority of the entire chapter body. In practice, the question arises as to how the information from such a meeting will be shared appropriately with the rest of the delegates. Even if an appropriate format is designed, the exchange of this information will be filtered through the perceptions and verbal skills of the delegates and/or other individuals who were at the session with the suggested leaders.

The law is clear that the right to active voice must remain free of any structure or pressure which restricts a delegate in casting a vote. Once elected, the delegates become the official discerning body of the institute. The size of this discerning body is dependent on the institute's documents. Thus, if the desired discernment process would work more easily with a smaller discerning body, then the present chapter would be free to change the number of delegates for its next general chapter as long as the concept of a delegated chapter is preserved. The institute would need to request approval for any necessary changes in its constitutions. This type of alteration would be part of the flexibility allowed for within canons 631 and 625 and addresses the reason given for wanting to select some of the delegates to serve as the discerning body.

177

CANON 636

QUALIFICATIONS OF A TREASURER OF AN INSTITUTE OF CONSECRATED LIFE

May a person who is not a member of a given institute of consecrated life, either permanently or in any stage of formation, be appointed the canonical treasurer of the institute?

OPINION

Canon 636, §1 states that in each institute of consecrated life and likewise in each province which is governed by a major superior there is to be a finance officer. This officer, distinct from the major superior and constituted according to the norm of proper law, administers the goods of the institute under the direction of the respective superior. Even in local communities there is to be a finance officer distinct from the local superior to the extent that it is possible.

While this canon does not explicitly state that the finance officer or treasurer must be a member of the institute, it is certainly implied from its phraseology that this is what is intended. Moreover, in practice it has always been a rightful assumption that the treasurer is, indeed, a member of the religious institute who is elected or appointed by the proper superior or governing group. After all, the canonical treasurer is an official position within the institute whose role and qualifications are treated in the constitutions of religious institutes. Until relatively recent times, this has always been taken for granted and it has not presented any problems.

However, because of the increased complexity and sophistication of financial matters, especially on the generalate and provincial levels of large or active religious communities, it is recognized that some professional expertise or experience is required. This may not be as necessary for small independent monasteries of religious where the role of the treasurer is not a full-time job. Also, some small groups may not have any member remotely prepared, willing or interested in undertaking the job. It is easy to understand why such religious may be forced into some arrangement not treated in the code.

Some religious communities have hired an experienced lay person, or a religious from another institute, to function as a business manager and to perform some or all of the duties which would ordinarily be a part of the role

178

description of the treasurer. At the same time, the religious community has named a member, for example, one of the provincial councilors, as the canonical treasurer who acts as the liaison with the business manager.

When we consider that a religious treasurer (or a hired business manager) in a large or active community must deal with retirement issues, annuities and investments, make reports to government agencies, safeguard and increase income, practice social responsibility and stewardship, keep and interpret financial books, deal with real estate matters or complicated canonical and legal issues, etc., one realizes that very few people will possess many of these professional competencies. That is why today the professional help of hired consultants will always be necessary for treasurers and business managers.

Those experienced in the role of treasurer suggest that a religious community not rely on the charity of relatives or friends of the community to act as experts or consultors. They also strongly advise that external audits or reviews be an annual practice for each legal entity. Likewise, the professional performances of hired experts should be periodically evaluated by other experts. Indeed, written reports from investment counselors should be presented to the proper religious superiors to justify proposals for investments.

The treasurer and a business manager have the responsibility to function under the proper religious authorities and make reports to them (c. 636, §2). Under no condition should anyone who is not a member of the religious community be given discretionary control over the assets of the community. This is the exclusive right and duty of the proper religious superiors within the community. The treasurer has a fiduciary role within the community to protect the assets of the community and this should not be abdicated to others outside the community.

Therefore, the canonical title of treasurer ought to be reserved to a member of the institute. However, the actual role and complex duties involving the technical aspects of accounting and financial planning, which are associated with the role of a treasurer, can be performed by one or more people, within or outside of the membership of the community, always doing so with the expert advice and counsel of competent professional consultants.

I would suggest those interested consult NATRI Monograph 1, "The Role of the Treasurer," by Sr. Clare Lorenzatti, S.S.J., D.B.A. (National Association of Treasurers of Religious Institutes, 8824 Cameron Street, Silver Spring, MD 20910).

David F. O'Connor, S.T. [1992]

ANOTHER OPINION

In my opinion only a member of the religious institute may hold the canonical office of treasurer of the institute. Non-members may be employed in various capacities to assist the religious treasurer in managing the business affairs of the institute, but they are not qualified to serve in the canonical office of treasurer of the institute.

According to canon 636 every religious institute, as well as every province or unit equivalent to a province, is to have a finance officer distinct from the major superior. The term finance officer is not so much a title as a description of function. The 1917 code used the term "bursar." In religious institutes in the United States the title "treasurer" is the term usually employed.

Canon 636, which speaks of the finance officer, and other canons which speak of specific offices, structures, and responsibilities within a religious institute presume membership in the institute in order to be eligible to hold certain offices and to fulfill their responsibilities. The presumption is grounded in canon 607, which deals with the character of religious life and the public witness to which religious are called.

Canon 634 makes clear the capacity of religious institutes to possess and administer temporal goods. Canon 635 states that temporal goods of religious institutes are ecclesiastical goods and are to be administered and used by an institute in ways that foster and give witness to the poverty appropriate to the institute. Canons 635 and 636 leave to proper law the establishment of norms to accomplish these ends. Canon 636, §2 specifically demands that an institute's proper law require financial officers and other administrators to make reports of their administration to the competent superior.

The office and responsibilities of the institute's treasurer have a distinct bearing upon the internal life of the institute in a manner analogous to other offices such as those of chapter members, superiors, and council members. To be eligible to be named superior at every level, the code requires membership in the institute for a period of time after perpetual profession. Though the government structure requires a general chapter (cc. 631-633), general council (c. 627), and finance officer (c. 636), the code leaves to proper law the specification of eligibility requirements. There can be no doubt concerning the requirement of membership in the institute for eligibility to be a chapter member or councilor, given the context and function of these offices. Why should there be any doubt concerning the requirement of membership for the institute's treasurer? In constitutions approved by the Holy See, the treasurer ordinarily is an *ex officio* member of the general chapter. Whether the treasurer should be a councilor has been a debated point. Practice has varied.

The office of treasurer is, in a certain sense, an extension of the office of the major superior in relation to the management of business affairs of the institute. The code provides that at least two persons at the highest level of government be involved in business affairs, since it both prohibits the major superior to be treasurer and requires that the treasurer carry out the administration of temporal goods under the direction of the major superior. A treasurer who is imbued with the spirit of the institute can be of invaluable assistance to the major superior in respect to decisions concerning temporal goods.

In the governance of religious institutes, officers regularly utilize the assistance of other persons in carrying out their responsibilities. Such persons may be paid employees or volunteers, members or non-members of the institute, clerics or lay persons or members of other religious institutes. Depending on the size and complexity of the institute, the treasurer, in order to fulfill his or her responsibilities, may assign many duties to competent and trusted persons with varied expertise. While respecting and utilizing the competence of others, the member of the religious institute named as treasurer retains full responsibility. There is need, therefore, for the treasurer to define the parameters and expectations of each position and to establish appropriate and timely accountability mechanisms. Ultimately, at least at the highest level of governance, it is the member of the religious institute designated as treasurer who has the responsibility, under the major superior, for the financial administration of the institute.

Rosemary Smith, S.C. [1992]

Canons 647-649

Certain Questions on the Validity of Novitiate

1. How long can a novice be out of novitiate, and for what reasons?

Opinion

Canon 648, §1 states that, in order for the novitiate to be valid, it must include twelve months spent in the community of the novitiate itself. Since the novitiate admits of interruption, the twelve months of novitiate are to be reckoned as having thirty days each in accord with canons 201 and 202 that is, a total of 360 days.

Absence from the novitiate house which lasts more than three months renders the novitiate invalid (c. 649, §1). Thus, a novice who has had various absences that total more than ninety days must begin the novitiate anew.

An absence of more than fifteen days must be made up (c. 649, §1). For example, if a novice were absent twenty days, it would be necessary to add five days to the twelve months of novitiate before profession. This is required for the validity of the novitiate, and consequently also for the validity of profession.

In speaking of time spent in the novitiate, the code speaks of "novitiate community" in canon 648, §1 and "novitiate house" in canon 649, §1. It does not seem that a technical distinction is being made here, and so the terms can be considered as equivalent. The novitiate house or community should be understood as that residence, whether permanent or temporary, which has been duly established by the competent major superior in accord with canon 647.

The permanent novitiate house is erected through a written decree of the supreme moderator of the institute with the consent of his or her council (c. 647, §1). In particular cases and by exception, the supreme moderator, with the consent of the council, can allow a candidate to make the novitiate in another house of the institute under the guidance of an approved religious who assumes the role of director of novices (c. 647, §2). Any competent major superior can permit a group of novices to live for a stated period of time in another house of the institute, designated by the same superior (c. 647, §3). In the latter two instances where a novice or a group of novices are outside the permanent novitiate house, that residence is still to be considered the novitiate for as long a time as the competent major superior has approved it as such, and the time spent there would not count as an absence from the novitiate.

An absence from the novitiate is an absence from the lawfully approved novitiate residence, whether it be that of paragraphs 1, 2, or 3 of canon 647. The constitutions and other sources of proper law of the institute should also be consulted for further regulations governing absence from the novitiate and its effects.

Canonically, the nature of the reason for the absence from novitiate is of no consequence. It makes no difference whether the absence is legitimate or not. For example, hospitalization, attendance at a funeral, performance of a civic duty, etc., are absences. Even if the days of absence are considered an integral part of the novitiate year, such as for retreats, conferences, attendance at provincial chapter, apostolic work, and travel to and from the novitiate, they count against the canonical days that must be validly spent in the duly established novitiate community.

A standard opinion holds that days of absence from the novitiate should be computed from midnight to midnight (cf., c. 202, §1), such that if the novice were absent for the total of that 24 hour period, he or she would have missed a day of novitiate.[1] For example, if the novice left at 1:00 a.m. on Monday, and returned at 11:00 p.m. on Tuesday, this forty-six hour absence would not be computed as a missed canonical day since the novice would have been present for some time on both days, albeit only one hour.[2]

Over and above the fifteen days of absence permitted, the law also allows profession to be anticipated by the competent major superior. Some common reasons for granting the anticipation include the desire to have profession on a special day, the convenience of novices or others, the request of the novice director to have a vacation, etc.

In sum, novitiate must last twelve months for validity. Absences from the duly established place of novitiate for any reason whatsoever, which are over fifteen days, must be made up for the validity of novitiate and profession. Over and above the absences, a fifteen day anticipation of profession can always be granted by the competent major superior. Absences (exclusive of legitimate anticipation) that total more than three months invalidate the novitiate, and the novice so absent must begin the novitiate over.

2. Does canon law specify who can make decisions for absences from the novitiate? Must it be our provincial, or can it be our mission superior who, according to our mission statutes, is a major superior for the missions operated by our province? In a mission with only one established house, can a novice be in a village where a professed member lives, but the residence is not an officially established house or novitiate?

OPINION

Since the mission superior in your institute, like the provincial, is a major superior with all the powers of a major superior, except where restricted by your proper law, both the provincial and the mission superior have competence to allow a group of novices in their jurisdiction (or a single novice if there is only one novice that year) to live for a stated period of time in another house of the institute designated by the same major superior (c. 647, §3). This permission must be explicit. It can validly be given orally, but it is always preferable to put it in writing because it is dealing with a matter that affects the validity of the novitiate.

The stated period can be any length of time determined by the major superior. It should not be an indefinite period — there must be a terminus to it. However, the major superior could say in the grant of permission that the novices may live in that house "for up to two months," for example, which would mean that there would be the flexibility to return to the novitiate before the two months elapsed.

The term "religious house" has both a strict technical meaning and also a broad meaning in canon law and the *praxis* of religious life. In the strict sense, it is a place established as a juridic person in accord with the formalities of canons 607ff. Such a house is one that has been legitimately established under the authority of the superior designated according to the norm of law, with the previous written consent of the diocesan bishop and having an oratory or church in which the Eucharist is celebrated and reserved. Any such house of the institute could validly be designated for the temporary place of novitiate spoken of in canon 647, §3.

The broad meaning of "religious house" refers to the place where members of a religious institute live together in common, even if it has not been erected with all the legal formalities. In fact, the majority of religious in the United States in this century have not lived in a formally erected *domus religiosa*, but in rectories and convents attached to apostolates.[3]

In keeping with the principle that "favors should be multiplied and burdens restricted," I believe that religious are correct in interpreting the meaning of "house" in canon 647, §3 also in its broad sense, namely, as any approved, stable residence of the institute to which members of the institute are regularly assigned to live as a community. This would include a small mission house, convent, rectory or the like. Unless it were a formally erected juridical person, it would exclude the residences of members of the institute who live by themselves. Since common life is an essential element of religious life, even in a broad sense one could hardly classify as a religious house a residence where a religious does not live the *vita fraterna in communi* (c. 607, §2).

Common life implies at least two members of the institute living together. It is not necessary to have three members in accord with canon 115, §2, because a religious house in the broad sense does not have to be a formally established juridic person. Even if the house had been established as a juridic person and originally had three or more members, it would not lose juridic personality simply because there are presently only one or two members there (cf. c. 120, §2).

In sum, novices can be permitted to live for a stated period of time outside the novitiate house by the competent major superior, which house can be any stable residence of the religious institute to which members are assigned, and their stay in this house counts as part of their twelve canonical months of novitiate. Days spent travelling to and from the novitiate house as computed above under question 1 would count as absences.

3. If through error or negligence on the part of the superior or novice director, the laws on the novitiate year and house have not been followed, can a situation be regularized?

OPINION

184

Error or ignorance does not excuse from invalidating laws (c. 15, §1). Thus, even if in good faith the novice director and major superior approved a novice for profession who did not complete twelve months in the novitiate (minus fifteen days for permissible absence and up to a fifteen day anticipation if there was one), the novitiate and subsequent professions would be invalid.

If someone has made an invalid profession because some juridical technicality for the validity of novitiate was not observed, it may be possible to obtain a *sanatio in radice* from the Apostolic See. A sanation of religious profession is parallel to that for marriage. It can be given without the knowledge of the one who is invalidly professed, and the effects are retroactive, that is, the person is legally considered to be professed from the date he or she first professed invalidly. The pertinent facts of the case should be given in writing, including indications that the person in question is happy and wants to continue in religious life. This should be sent to the Congregation for Religious and Secular Institutes. The nuncio or apostolic delegate in a country can often facilitate the transmission of such a request.

Notes

[1] A. Tabera, G. M. de Antonana, G. Escudero, *Il diritto dei religiosi* (Rome: Commentarium pro Religiosis, 1961) 278.

[2] It should be noted, however, that this law does not affect the period between the Instruction *Renovationis causam* and the revised code, that is, between January 6, 1969 and November 27, 1983. If a novitiate year ended after the former date, or concluded before the latter date, the pertinent law in question did not require for validity that absences over fifteen days be made up. Only absences of more than three months were invalidating. See Congregation for Religious and Secular Institutes, Instruction on the renewal and adaptation of formation for living religious life, *Renovationis causam*, January 6, 1989, *AAS* 61 (1969) 103, no. 22, II.

[3] Elizabeth McDonough, O.P., *Religious in the 1983 Code* (Chicago: Franciscan Herald Press, 1984) 60. See also *idem*, "Religious Houses — Acquisition of Rights," *Proceedings of the Forty-Sixth Annual Convention of the Canon Law Society of America* (Washington, DC: CLSA, 1985) 149-160.

John M. Huels, O.S.M. [1988]

CANONS 647-649

PERMITTED ABSENCES FROM THE NOVITIATE

What is the scope of activities which count as absences from the canonical year of the novitiate? Does this scope of activities vary between the canonical novitiate year and a second year of novitiate?

The reply to this question depends upon one's interpretation of the words used in the inquiry. The question stated above refers primarily to canon 649, §1, and secondarily to canons 647, §3 and 648, §2. Canon 649, §1, determines that a novitiate is invalidated by an absence from the novitiate house of more than three months, continuous or broken, and that any absence of more than fifteen days must be made good.

There are two other canons that pertain to this discussion. Canon 647, §3 allows for a group of novices to reside, for a certain period of time, in another specified house of the institute with the permission of the major superior. Canon 648, §2 authorizes the constitutions of the institute to prescribe, in addition to the time mentioned in §1, one or more periods of apostolic activity, to be performed outside the novitiate community.

What needs to be determined before making any reply is what constitutes the "novitiate." In other words, what is the definition of a novitiate? Is it a place (as we read in c. 647) or does it have a broader meaning than a physical location? For a previous discussion on this topic, consult the article by Richard Hill, S.J. (in *Review for Religious* 85 [1985] 600-603).

It is my interpretation that the term "novitiate" refers more to a "moral body" than a "physical body." Contrary to some commentators, the novitiate is to be identified, first of all, as a program and, secondarily, as a physical location. This re-definition is implied in canon 648, §2, when it speaks of the "novitiate community." Hence, the inquiry needs to be restated: What is the scope of activities which count as absences from the canonical year of the novitiate program?

The reason for raising the issue of the novitiate as a program as well as a place is the growing awareness that many of the present canons are rapidly becoming obsolete. The canons reflect the previous experience of religious institutes who had many candidates in a well structured canonical year, located at a novitiate building or "wing," and who were supervised by formation personnel who were freed of all apostolic obligations so as to devote their energies to their novices.

As time and experience have demonstrated, the novices are fewer in number and hence need fewer personnel other than a director. The intended goal of the intense interaction between novices within the space of a canonical year is now lacking. Given the hesitation to have formation take place solely within one location, there is a desire to see the novices have other experiences within the houses or ministries of the institute. But this means that they must leave the novitiate site.

With the two previous questions in mind, we can turn to the inquiry and make the following responses.

The absences listed in canon 649, §1, in the mind of this author, are absences not just from the location determined by law for the novitiate but from the actual program itself. An absence means a separation from contact with the novice director and the other novices in the program so designed for that year. If the novitiate as a group (or class) travels to a ministry location for a period of time, then the program is not interrupted. But, if a novice exits for medical, physical, psychological leave, or goes home to care for a sick parent, the rules governing absences apply.

The questions being raised today about absences from the novitiate's canonical year go much further than activities or ministries. Novice directors are being faced with illnesses, physical and psychological, which call for the novice to exit the program and novitiate house for surgery, therapy, or psychological counselling away from the novitiate itself. Novice directors are asking whether or not the canonical year can be "suspended" while the novice undergoes therapy outside the novitiate community. The answer is obviously a negative one to any suggestion of suspension. After an absence of three months, the canons call for termination of the novitiate with the possibility of later reentry.

Since *Renovationis causam*, it has been customary for the novices to divide up during the final summer months and have individual experiences in various ministry locations. This is foreseen in canon 648, §2, but with the understanding that the time spent in apostolic work will be added to the canonical year. If it is not added to the year, then this time away represents a separation from the program and the necessary interaction with each other. Interaction with professed members of the institute in various ministry settings can be accomplished in other ways, namely, before or after the canonical year.

There are other secondary questions that institutes should consider carefully. For example, is the novice entitled to a home vacation before profession? Some express the opinion that such a break away from the program gives the novice an opportunity to reflect on the novitiate experience away from the novitiate itself. They will return better equipped to make profession. This author is of the opinion that, in order to be consistent, such an absence is a separation from the program and the institute. An absence of more than fifteen days must be made up, but, in fact, if we are considering a home visit, it should essentially be discouraged.

David M. Hynous, O.P. [1992]

ANOTHER OPINION

Canon 648 mandates that for a novitiate to be valid it must include a twelve month period of residence "in the community of the novitiate itself." This twelve month residency period need not be continuous (continuity was required by the 1917 Code of Canon Law in c. 555, §1, 2°). Also, according to canon 652, §5, the time must be directed solely to the formative process. "[T]he novices are not to be occupied with studies and duties which do not directly serve this formation."

Canon 649 stipulates that absences from the novitiate house of more than fifteen days must be made up, and that absence from the novitiate house for more than three months, either continuous or interrupted, invalidates the novitiate. The one exception to this is found in canon 647, §3, which permits the major superior to designate another house of the institute as the residence for the novices.

Canon 648, §2 recognizes that the constitutions of an institute can require periods of apostolic activity which take the novices away from the novitiate house, but it is clear in the canon that these periods, if they occur, take place during that part of the novitiate experience regulated by particular law and outside the twelve month residency regulated by the code.

In other words, the concern of the code is the twelve month long novitiate experience during which the novice must reside in the appointed house of the institute and give full attention to the formative process. Thus, canon 649 legislates on absences during this period of residency, which might or might not be broken up by periods of apostolic activity required by particular law.

In determining the scope of activities which constitute absence from the novitiate, it might seem overly legalistic to define "absence" as simply a lack of physical presence under the specified roof. After all, the residency requirement of the law is only a means to an end; that end being the assurance of a stable period of time during which the novice and the formation personnel of the institute can mutually discern the reality of the novice's vocation to the institute.

However, since the law is very specific about the number of days a novice may be absent, and since an absence of more than three months invalidates the novitiate, it is necessary to have clarity in the matter of what constitutes absence. Without clarity, neither the rights of the individual novice nor the rights of the institute can be adequately safeguarded. In addition to the need for clarity, there is a need to respect the canonical principle of giving narrow interpretation to those elements in the law which are "odious," or in this case, invalidating.

Consequently, my response to the first question posed is: There is no "scope of activities" which constitutes absence. Activities do not constitute it. Literal physical absence of the novice from the appointed house of the institute constitutes absence, regardless of what activity might have caused the absence. (Note that absence is calculated according to cc. 200-203.)

The second question posed can be answered in two ways; with reference to the code, and then with reference to the particular law of an institute. First, with reference to the code, there are no attendance/residence requirements for the novitiate beyond what is stipulated for the "canonical year." Thus, absence is not an issue if there is a second year of novitiate. The second response is with reference to the particular law of a given institute. That law's requirements for a valid novitiate within the institute must be carefully identified. What might or might not constitute absence in the second year of novitiate must then be determined within the framework of that law.

Elissa A. Rinere, C.P. [1992]

Canon 656

Legitimate Superior for Admitting and Receiving Religious Vows

The 1983 Code of Canon Law specifies that the competent superior with the vote of the council is to admit the candidate to vows. Is it this same competent superior who receives the individual's vows in the name of the congregation?

Opinion

Canon 656 states: For the validity of temporary profession it is required that:

3° admission has been freely given by a competent superior with the vote of the council in accord with the norm of law;

5° the profession be received by the legitimate superior personally or through another.

Canon 658 incorporates by reference 3° and 5° of canon 656 with respect to the validity of perpetual profession.

In referring to "the norm of law" canon 656, 3° alerts religious institutes that they must identify the admitting superior and the receiving superior in their own legislation. The validity of temporary profession, renewal of temporary profession, and perpetual profession itself is at stake here.

The Latin word *votum*, translated here as "vote," can mean either the consent or only the advice of the council of the admitting superior, and this too must be clear in the institute's own law.

189

In 5° of canon 656 the expression "personally or through someone else" implies that the superior designated in the institute's own legislation to receive the profession of vows can delegate someone else to receive the profession on behalf of the superior if this is judged to be appropriate.

The question that is asked is whether the superior of 5° is the same as the superior in 3°. Rose McDermott, S.S.J., is correct when she states that the superior receiving a temporary profession or a perpetual profession "may or may not be the same superior" (*The Code of Canon Law: A Text and Commentary*, ed. James Coriden et al. [New York/Mahwah: Paulist Press, 1985] 497). The internal legislation of a religious institute may designate the superior general as the person who admits to temporary and perpetual profession or only to perpetual profession, while designating some other superior as the person who actually receives the profession, for example, a provincial superior.

In stating that the superior who is designated to receive a profession of vows can do so "through someone else," the canon does not specify that this must be another member of the same religious community. Unless legislation of the institute itself requires that the person who receives the profession must be one of its own members, the superior could, in unusual circumstances, delegate someone who is not a member or not even a religious. It could be a bishop or a priest or a lay person. What must be clearly stated, however, is that the person so delegated is acting as the agent of the superior and is acting in the name of the Church and of the religious institute. This requires a mandate which is simply a written designation of an individual to receive this profession.

Richard A. Hill, S.J. [1991]

ANOTHER OPINION

First, it is important to see what the law says.

Canon 656: For the validity of temporary profession, it is required that:

1° the person who is about to make the profession shall have completed at least the eighteenth year of age;

2° the novitiate has been validly completed;

3° admission has been freely given by the competent superior with the vote of the council in accord with the norm of law;

4° the profession be expressed and made without force, grave fear or fraud;

5° the profession be received by the legitimate superior personally or through another.

The law states "competent superior" in 3° and "legitimate superior" in 5° without any qualification or restriction. The superior receiving the profession of the person could certainly be the same superior who admits to profession. Likewise, since there is no restriction or qualification, the "legitimate superior" receiving the profession could be a different superior than the "competent superior" admitting to profession. This determination is left to the proper law of the institute.

Rose M. McDermott, S.S.J. [1991]

CANON 657

EXTENSION OF TEMPORARY VOWS AND
ANTICIPATION OF PERPETUAL VOWS

What is to be done in the case of a certain sister, a member of an institute of consecrated life, whose temporary vows are expiring on April 21. She wishes to make her perpetual profession, but on a date in May of the same year. How does the superior arrange the extension of the temporary vows and/or the anticipation of perpetual vows, if the temporary vows are renewed?

OPINION

The guiding legislation is canon 657, §2, which states that a period of temporary profession can be extended by the competent superior, if this is provided for by the proper law of the institute, and with the provision that these extensions not exceed nine years.

In the question under consideration here, a certain Sister *X* has had temporary vows which expire on April 21st. She wishes to make her perpetual profession a few weeks later in May, the exact date not yet determined, but around May 15th. Can the temporary profession be extended for a period of time so that the religious would not be living without vows during that short period of less than a month?

It is my belief that such a situation can be suitably arranged. The intent of such extensions in the law is for reason of further probation of the candidate. The legislation also provides a protection for the individual religious in that the probation period cannot be extended beyond nine years: at that time the community must make a decision one way or the other regarding their religious.

191

In *A Handbook on Canons 573-746* published by The Liturgical Press, Father Hite states "the whole purpose of the time of temporary vows is to bring the person to that level of spiritual maturity so that a perpetual commitment can be made."

Canon 657, §3 allows perpetual profession to be *anticipated* for a just cause but not by more than three months. In answer to your question I think that we have to use the legislation regarding anticipation, rather than delay or postponement.

The solution I would offer for your consideration is to ask the competent superior, acting in accordance with proper law, which is found in the constitutions hopefully, to extend the temporary vows by a period of three months. In the case at issue the vows with the temporary profession would be extended from April 21st to July 21st. Then because of a just cause which would be present, which unfortunately has not been made known to me, the perpetual profession could be *anticipated* within three months of July 21st, thereby making May 15th a possible date of choice.

William A. Varvaro [1987]

Canon 669

Changing Regulations on Clothing in a Religious Congregation

A congregation of religious women is interested in changing the current provisions of their proper law regarding clothing. What authority does the general chapter have?

Opinion

As you are aware, the primary concern reflected in the canon on religious clothing is that it be a sign of public consecration and a witness to poverty. Your use of the terminology of *Perfectae Caritatis* gives expression to this in your constitutions.

Since your constitutions have received approbation from the Apostolic See, any future changes in them must also be approved by the same authority (c. 587, §2). The normal procedure is that a desired change is introduced and discussed at general chapter. If the proposed revision receives two thirds approval from the chapter it is then submitted to the Congregation for Religious and Secular Institutes (CRIS) for approval.

192

Thus, for example, if the chapter wished to remove explicit reference to the veil from the constitutions, the above process would be observed. When submitting the matter to CRIS, it is helpful to include some of the rationale for the change which emerged during the chapter discussion, and to give a report of the vote on the matter. While the veil is an ancient symbol of consecration, not all religious congregations have had or retain its use. Therefore, it is a change which is not contrary to universal law, and which could be granted, given reasonable causes.

The directory of your congregation, as an important part of your proper law, is fully subject to your general chapter. Although it had to be submitted for review to the Apostolic See along with the constitutions at the time of their approbation, subsequent changes in it do not require confirmation from ecclesiastical authority (c. 587, §4). Consequently, for example, if your chapter wished to change the provisions of the directory by adding other appropriate colors, this could be done by a two-thirds vote of the chapter. Obviously, just as changes in the constitutions must be in conformity with universal church law, so changes in your directory must be in harmony with your constitutions.

Sharon L. Holland, I.H.M. [1987]

Canons 671-672

Lay Religious Serving as Power of Attorney and/or Guardian

What canonical considerations govern a lay religious assuming power of attorney and/or guardianship?

Opinion

Canon 671 and 672 are pertinent to this question, especially the reference to canon 285, §4. Further considerations are the canons related to the vow of poverty: canons 600 and 668.

Basically these canons state or imply that a religious must have permission from the superior to be a guardian or to assume the power of attorney. The issue, then, is not the possibility of guardianship or power of attorney. The issue is the religious member's need to discuss with the superior the reasons for requesting permission to accept the role of guardian or to assume the power of attorney. Moreover, the superior needs to have a thorough understanding of the situation before granting or denying the permission. Both parties might find the following principles helpful for the discussion.

Canon 671 is premised on the primary commitment a religious has to the life and works of the institute. Thus, in the discussion of assuming either guardianship or power of attorney, the superior and the religious need to determine:

1. if the role being considered is consistent with religious commitment;
2. if the time commitment required in either guardianship or power of attorney is realistic and in conformity to the religious' ministry in the Church.

The reference in canon 672 to canon 285, §4 concerns religious assuming obligations in which financial accounts are required and financial liability is undertaken. Probably this reference is more clearly directed to power of attorney than to guardianship. The guardianship, however, might well include financial responsibilities. In discussion, the superior and the religious should:

1. review the expected responsibilities, financial and moral;
2. determine the manner in which financial and moral responsibilities will be met;
3. clarify:
    a. that the individual religious, not the institute, is assuming the moral responsibilities incumbent with the role;
    b. that the religious is administering, not assuming, the financial aspects of the role;
    c. that the religious institute is not liable for potential financial obligations, unless in charity and justice the institute undertakes such obligations.

It would be important for the superior and the religious to recall the obligation of the vow of poverty (c. 600) in relation to assuming either guardianship or power of attorney. One reason that a religious cedes the power of administration over personal property (c. 668) is to be free from financial responsibilities in order to be more fully committed to his/her calling. Assuming financial obligations for others without sound reason would not be in accord with the spirit of the vow.

There is nothing in canon law requiring a written record of the conclusions drawn from the discussion of the superior and the religious who requests to assume either guardianship or power of attorney. However, such a record is clearly in order for the protection of the religious, the superior and the institute.

Mary Conroy, O.S.U. [1992]

194

Canon 672

Religious as Members of Labor Unions

What are the canonical ramifications of men or women religious being members of labor unions when employed by agencies under the direction of the diocesan bishop?

Opinion

The right and even obligation of religious to seek membership in labor unions was addressed at a *plenaria* of the Sacred Congregation of Religious and Secular Institutes in April of 1978 in a document entitled "Religious and Human Promotion," which was not made public until 1980.[1] In this document, the Congregation stressed that "involvement in trade union activities demands a clear awareness of pastoral objectives as well as of the limitations and risks of exploitation that could result in the lives and activities of religious" (n. 10); and it established specific principles which must guide the consideration of such membership.

These principles expressly state that "there does not seem to be any intrinsic incompatibility between religious life and social involvement even at trade union level," and it recognizes that "involvement in trade union activity might be a necessary part of participation in the world of labor . . . prompted by solidarity in the legitimate defence of human rights" (ibid).

The Code of Canon Law does not specifically prohibit the participation of religious in labor unions, although canon 672 does bind religious to the prescription of canon 287, 2° which, in paragraph 2, prohibits an active role in the direction of labor unions "unless the need to protect the rights of the Church or to promote the common good requires it in the judgment of the competent ecclesiastical authority."

The specific focus of this inquiry, however, directs the question of union membership to agencies under the direction of the diocesan bishop.

Within the United States, religious who are serving in Catholic institutions of education and health care do join labor unions. This practice has not met much opposition provided that it does not violate the constitutions of a particular religious institute. However, since colleges, universities and hospitals are generally not under the direct supervision or governance of the diocesan bishop, these institutions fall outside of the parameters of this inquiry, which is concerned solely with "agencies under the direction of the diocesan bishop."

In regulating the apostolate of religious engaged in work within diocesan agencies, several canons address the relationship between the diocesan bishop

195

and the religious institute. Canon 678 speaks of the obligation of religious to respect the authority of the bishop in those matters "which involve the care of souls, the public exercise of divine worship and other works of the apostolate" (§1). This canon also calls for consultation between the diocesan bishop and religious superiors in organizing the works of the apostolate (§3).

Under certain circumstances, a diocesan bishop can prohibit a member of a religious institute from exercising the apostolate within his diocese and even from living in his diocese (c. 679). Likewise, it is the diocesan bishop who directs the "orderly cooperation as well as a coordination of all apostolic works and activities" between religious and secular clergy within his diocese "with due regard for the character and purpose of the individual institutes" (c. 680).

And finally, canon 681 directs that works entrusted to religious by the diocesan bishop "are subject to the authority and direction of this same bishop" (§1). In such cases, a written agreement is to be drawn up between the religious superior and the diocesan bishop clearly defining "what pertains to the work to be carried out, the members to be devoted to this, and economic matters" (§2).

Thus, canon law appears to envision a special relationship between the diocesan bishop, the religious superior and the individual members of the institute who are involved in works of the apostolate subject to the direct governance of the diocesan bishop; and it can be asked whether membership in a labor union would possibly compromise or intrude into this working relationship in an inappropriate manner.

If, for example, a dispute were to arise involving a religious employee of a diocesan agency over a financial matter or the termination of that particular person's employment, there could be serious ramifications if an individual religious employee were to seek a resolution of the dispute through the intervention of the labor union, especially if this resulted in a determination that did not correspond to the written agreement of the diocesan bishop and the religious superior spoken of in canon 681, §2.

Although individual cases should be considered on their own merit and it might be argued that the diocesan bishop and the religious superior can agree to permit union membership to individual religious employees without necessarily violating the principle found in canon 681, §2, it would be wise in making such determinations to give serious consideration to canons 22 and 1290, which present the principles by which the Church defers to civil law except in situations which would be contrary to divine law or in which canon law has made some other provision. Clearly, the working relationship between the individual religious employee and the diocesan bishop who is the employer in the case of diocesan agencies is specifically provided for in canon law.

Note

[1] This document was originally published in a supplement of *L'Osservatore Romano*, n. 262, 12 November 1980. It can also be found in Ochoa, *Leges Ecclesiae*, VI, n. 4789; and an English translation is found in *CLD* 9: 379-410.

Gregory Ingels [1992]

CANON 686

THE RIGHT OF RELIGIOUS TO EXCLAUSTRATION

Canon 686, §1, allows the supreme moderator with the consent of the council to grant exclaustration to a perpetually professed member for a grave reason. If a grave reason is said to be lacking, does the member nevertheless have a right to be exclaustrated?

OPINION

In the time period following the close of Vatican II, religious institutes had been given permission to expand the previously restricted privileges to grant its members either a leave of absence or to petition the Holy See for a decree of exclaustration for its professed members. Both means of separation were valuable for those testing out their vocation.

When the 1983 Code of Canon Law was promulgated, these two forms of departure were carefully distinguished. In canon 665, §1, a leave of absence is not a form of separation from the institute but rather a permission to live apart from the communities of the institute. This permission is found in the canons on the prerogatives of the professed members, i.e., the right to live in community. Individuals on a leave retain active and passive voice in elections, have full rights to membership and are expected to live according to the three evangelical counsels.

However, an exclaustration is a true form of separation, temporary but not permanent, which imposes certain restrictions upon those requesting it. It is now within the authority of the major superior and council to grant an indult of exclaustration up to three years (cf. cc. 686, §1 and 687). The right to exercise active and passive voice is suspended during the time of exclaustration.

The supposition is that the member will live and exercise ministry outside of the normal channels of the institute. It is not merely a permission to live outside of community while retaining full membership but an indult to depart from community-living to determine whether to remain a religious or not. In some rare instances, the indult is granted for those who wish to remain religious but

197

who cannot exercise their ministry within the original community.

This ministry may be related to the Church at large or even be secular. Again, the primary motive seems to be the testing of one's vocation but done outside of the confines and restrictions of community life and legal structures. Members of clerical institutes may temporarily minister in a diocese or seek admission to a new religious institute. In most instances, the religious seeks the freedom to exercise whatever ministry or lifestyle he or she finds appropriate.

It is at this point that the question of rights occurs. The individual religious has a "right to request" this form of separation, but does the institute have the "right to refuse"? My answer is yes and for the following reasons.

Not only does the individual lose the right to exercise active and passive voice and to live in community, but the individual is asking to be freed from *some* of the obligations of the three vows that would impede independent living. Immediately every commentator on the canons will repeat the obvious fact that no faculty can be granted to test out the vow of chastity. That vow remains intact. If the individual wants to begin a search for an appropriate partner in marriage, then a dispensation from the vowed life is called for.

The normal practice is to relieve the religious from some of the obligations of the vows of obedience and poverty. They are not subject to assignments nor are they expected to contribute to the community the income from their ministry. Herein lies the major area of difficulty. The determination of how far these obligations are relaxed is to be defined by the leadership, given the individual's particular situations. The final decision is that of the major superior and council. If the lifestyle to be assumed by the individual is contrary to the nature of either religious life in general or the institute itself, then the leadership has the right to refuse the request.

For example, the religious petitions for exclaustration to return to the family so as to assist a widowed mother in running the family business. However, the company is an international one and the religious will become the C.E.O., draw a large salary, and live a corporate executive's lifestyle. While this may benefit the family, it causes embarrassment to the institute since the individual is still a religious with a vow of poverty.

In regard to the vow of obedience, the religious is seeking employment in a secular position that militates against the teachings of the Church and the community. The religious is a counsellor and proposes working for an agency that counsels pregnant women contemplating having an abortion. While the religious may not directly be involved in abortions, the agency is in fact an abortion clinic. Again, the institute may refuse an indult with this employment in mind.

Both examples, of course, describe the extreme possibilities. There are many lesser cases that can be brought forward which would not militate against granting exclaustration. The decision, however, rests with the major superior and council. It is the leadership who has the common good of the institute in mind and heart. The individual's good is also important, but, when it comes to a conflict, the common good of the institute and religious life is to prevail.

What recourse is there for the individual? There remains the "right to appeal" to the Congregation for Institutes of Consecrated Life and Societies of Apostolic Life.

David M. Hynous, O.P. [1993]

ANOTHER OPINION

This canon has reference to voluntary exclaustration, so it is to be supposed that the member believes there is a grave reason for the request. To re-phrase the question, then, does that member have a right to an indult to depart temporarily from the institute in which perpetual vows were made, despite the supreme moderator's perception that no grave reason exists for doing so?

The question raises a number of pastoral questions, but the law is clear. The member's right is to ask for a remedy for a perceived need. The supreme moderator's corresponding duty is to provide for the need. To say that the reason given for exclaustration is inadequate is to say equivalently that the remedy proposed is inappropriate to the need.

Further, while the law does not describe indults, it is evident that they are of the nature of favors. If the granting of a favor is conditioned, as in this case it is by a "grave reason," there cannot be a duty for the grantor to concede it despite a conviction that the condition has not been met.

Since the granting or withholding of the indult is an administrative decision, the member has the further right of appeal to the next higher authority. This authority is the diocesan bishop if the institute is of diocesan right, and CICLSAL if the institute is of pontifical right.

Esther A. Redmann, O.S.U. [1993]

CANONS 693-694

INCARDINATION OF A PRIEST RELIGIOUS WHO HAS BEEN DISMISSED FROM HIS INSTITUTE

A priest who was on leave from his religious institute entered a civil marriage and was later divorced. He was subsequently dismissed from the institute under canon 694, §2.

Later the priest applied to a diocesan bishop to help him become active again in the ministry. The rescript removing the irregularity for attempted marriage instructed the bishop that in incardinating the man into the diocese, he should respect canon 693.

The religious superior says that an indult is not necessary because the man is no longer a member of the institute; however, the bishop is reluctant to make a declaration of incardination because of the specific mention of canon 693 in the rescript.

OPINION

It is important to note the distinction found in the Code of Canon Law between Article 2, "Departure from an Institute" (cc. 686-693), and Article 3, "Dismissal of Members from an Institute" (cc. 694-704). The decision whether or not to incardinate this priest must take into consideration the fact that he has been dismissed from his institute in accord with the norm of law and has not departed the institute.

Canon 694, §1, 2° states that:

A member is to be held *ipso facto* dismissed from the institute who: . . . has contracted marriage or has attempted it, even only civilly.

Since there is no question that this priest did attempt civil marriage and since this canon determines that a member of an institute is dismissed by the very fact that marriage has been attempted, this priest is clearly dismissed from his institute by force of the law itself.

The second paragraph of canon 694 provides for the formalities that should be followed in order to establish the dismissal juridically.

In these instances the major superior with the council without any delay and after having collected proofs should issue a declaration of the fact so that the dismissal is established juridically.

Since dismissal is provided for by the law itself, the only responsibility of the major superior is to provide for the formalities of this fact, not by issuing a decree of dismissal, but by issuing a declaration of the fact that the dismissal provided for by law has in fact taken place. A failure to provide for these formalities would not alter the fact that the member is *ipso facto* dismissed.

While the requirement of canon 700, which addresses itself only to a decree of dismissal, is mute, the requirement of canon 701 certainly remains effective. This canon provides that a cleric who has been legitimately dismissed from an institute

. . . cannot exercise sacred orders until he finds a bishop who receives him after a suitable probationary period in the diocese according to can. 693 or at least allows him to exercise sacred orders.

The reference to canon 693 in canon 701 must be taken in context. Canon 693 is not found in the article dealing with dismissal of members from an institute; rather, it is located in the article which deals with departure from an institute. A cleric who wishes to depart his institute is informed by canon 693 that

. . . the indult [of exclaustration] is not granted before he first finds a bishop who will incardinate him into a diocese or at least receive him experimentally. If he is received experimentally, he is incardinated into the diocese by the law itself after five years have passed, unless the bishop has refused him.

It must be remembered that the priest under consideration in this question has not departed his institute; he has been dismissed by the law itself.

Since "ecclesiastical laws are to be understood in accord with the proper meaning of the words considered in their text and context" (c. 17), two points must direct an understanding of the reference to canon 693 found in canon 701:

1. The words "*ad normam can. 693*" are set off by commas in the Latin text indicating a parenthetical usage.

2. The requirements of canon 693 address themselves to the situation of a cleric who is departing from an institute and not the case of a cleric who has been dismissed from an institute under canon 694.

It must be concluded, therefore, that the reference "*ad normam can. 693*" is intended only to clarify what is meant by the "probationary period" spoken of in canon 701 during which a cleric would be received into a diocese experimentally. Since a dismissed cleric would neither seek nor be granted an indult of exclaustration, there is no reason to expect him to have such an indult prior to incardination into a diocese.

The irregularity which this priest has incurred is reserved (c. 1047, §2, 1°) and, thus, is dispensed only by the Holy See. In instructing the bishop to respect canon 693, the only requirement the Congregation could be calling for, in light of the considerations which have preceded, is that of "at least receiv[ing the priest] experimentally" and of being attentive to the fact that "he is incardinated into the diocese by the law itself after five years have passed, unless the bishop has refused him."

Once the bishop has determined to receive this priest into his diocese experimentally, he can himself remit the *latae sententiae* suspension that is attached to a cleric's attempt to marry civilly (c. 1394, §1) by virtue of canon

201

1355, §2. This penalty can also be remitted by any priest to whom the proper faculty has been granted by the diocesan bishop.

The religious superior who has maintained that an indult of exclaustration is not necessary in the situation of this priest is correct. Thus, should the bishop choose to incardinate the priest, no other requirement is necessary other than respecting what canon 693 states concerning receiving the priest experimentally and the fact of his incardination by the law itself after a five year period unless he has refused the request for incardination within this period of time. Should the bishop choose not to incardinate the priest, his dismissal from the institute would remain in force, although he would no longer be subject to the irregularity of canon 1047, §2, 1°, since it has been dispensed by the Holy See. The priest would also not be subject to the suspension spoken of in canon 1394, §1, if it has been remitted by the diocesan bishop or a priest with the proper faculty.

Gregory Ingels [1989]

ANOTHER OPINION

(a) Background to the Opinion

In order to arrive at an opinion on this inquiry it is essential to start by considering the obligation of a priest to observe "perfect and perpetual continence." The seriousness of this obligation of priesthood as currently defined within the 1983 code is a foundational responsibility for both secular and religious order priests (cc. 277 and 599).

It is this obligation of celibacy which is the basis for the penalty of *latae sententiae* suspension from priestly duties and rights for attempting marriage (c. 1394, §1). The suspension can lead to more penalties, eventually resulting in dismissal from the clerical state. This penalty can be lifted at the discretion of the bishop involved if the offense and any ill-effects have ceased.

Such an attempted marriage by a priest is automatically invalid. The 1983 code is painstakingly clear on this matter by specifying the invalidity of a marriage attempted by a priest (cc. 1087-1088).

In addition, the intended spouse is also subject to penalties (*latae sententiae* or *ferendae sententiae*, depending on the circumstances) for being an accomplice in the offense (c. 1329). The law leaves it to the competent authority to determine and impose the appropriate penalty. However, in practice it is vague how all this is to be handled. What is clear in the text of the 1983 code is that any canonical office should be lost (c. 194, §1, 3°). The law is referring to canonical offices defined within the code, meaning offices to which jurisdiction is attached. The primary reason behind imposing the loss of office as a result

202

of attempting marriage by a priest is because of the harm to the common good such an act can cause (c. 223). Thus, it follows that the loss of office should be extended to any public position in the Church in which either party involved would be carrying out the work of teaching, governing, or sanctifying.

(b) Response to the Inquiry

The above information serves as background for addressing the inquiry. The inquiry presents the situation of a religious order priest who attempted marriage without first seeking dispensation from his religious vows and laicization from the clerical state. These are two separate acts and two separate sets of rights and obligations. The 1983 code indicates the separateness of these acts and the variation in impact of the attempted marriage on the religious priest's status as a member of his institute and his status as an ordained cleric.

First, consider the impact of the attempted marriage on the rights and obligations of the religious priest which result from the profession of final vows. His status as a religious is *ipso iure* lost by the act of attempting marriage (c. 694). To attempt to reverse this dismissal from the religious state, the former religious would have to leave the marriage, first taking care of any responsibilities stemming from the attempted marriage. Then he would need to petition his general superior for re-admission to the institute. Taking into consideration any scandal and obligations related to the marriage, the general superior can decide whether the process for readmission could be initiated according to the institute's particular law. Determination of a period of probation and/or on-going sanctions are within the realm of the general superior's authority based on the norms in the particular law. The point is that the religious state is lost automatically by the very act of attempting marriage. However, the *ipso iure* loss of the religious state does not address the impact of the attempted marriage on the individual's clerical status.

The second consideration is that of the religious priest's loss of the clerical state by the act of attempting marriage. Recall the earlier discussion of the *latae sententiae* suspension from the priesthood incurred for attempting marriage (c. 1394, §1). The religious priest is no different in the law from the secular priest in this matter. Even though the individual has lost his religious state by the *ipso iure* dismissal, he is still bound to the priesthood despite the suspension. Technically, he is lacking incardination since he was incardinated into the congregation at the time of ordination to the diaconate (c. 266, §2); however, he is no longer a member of the congregation. In this inquiry, the religious is seeking incardination into a diocese where he has found a benevolent bishop. Thus, the required steps for a valid incardination as prescribed in canons 265-272 would apply.

The essential point is that by the act of *ipso iure* losing the religious state, a religious priest does not lose his clerical state. He is suspended and could eventually be dismissed if he persists in the offense. Reinstatement to the active ministry requires that he first be incardinated. The rights and obligations of priestly ministry, as the 1983 code perceives them, are carefully framed by the basic premise that the individual is tied by incardination to a competent authority, meaning either a general superior or a bishop. Otherwise, the individual is not free to practice his priestly rights and duties. To change incardination requires that the *a quo* competent authority be involved in the process. Certainly within the case at point, the benevolent bishop who is the *ad quem* competent authority would be well advised to communicate with the general superior before allowing the former religious to incardinate in his diocese. However, an indult is not necessary since the priest is no longer a religious. Rather, the former religious is in need of incardination and having the *latae sententiae* suspension lifted, which the benevolent bishop has the jurisdiction to do.

Lynn Jarrell, O.S.U. [1989]

ANOTHER OPINION

As I understand the situation, a priest who was a member of a religious community took a leave of absence. While on leave, he attempted a civil marriage. By the fact of attempting the civil marriage, he was *ipso facto* dismissed from the religious institute (c. 694, §1, 2°).

Later, he divorced his wife, and has sought to return to active ministry by applying to a diocesan bishop. When the diocesan bishop approached the Holy See, they instructed him to follow canon 693 in incardinating the priest.

The bishop has interpreted canon 693 as requiring an indult of dismissal from the religious superior before the bishop can proceed to incardinate the priest. The religious superior holds that the indult is not necessary, since the man is no longer a member of the community.

It seems to me another interpretation of the Roman directive is possible. Canon 694, §2 calls for the major superior with his council to issue a declaration of the fact that the dismissal incurred by attempting marriage has been incurred. The bishop may legitimately ask the religious superior to follow through on this requirement if he has not already done so or if he has done so, to provide the bishop with a copy of this declaration.

James H. Provost [1989]

CANON 701

GRANTING DIOCESAN FACULTIES TO A
DISMISSED RELIGIOUS PRIEST

A religious priest has been dismissed from his religious community. It is maintained that the priest in question may be dismissed as a religious but remains incardinated in the institute as a priest until taken into a diocese. May a bishop grant faculties to a dismissed religious priest even though the priest is not incardinated in the diocese?

OPINION

Two questions are posed in this inquiry. The first question is the continuing incardination of a religious priest in his institute after dismissal. The second question is the discretion of the diocesan bishop to grant him diocesan faculties even without incardination. Let us deal with each question briefly and in order.

A professed member of a religious institute in perpetual vows or a definitively incorporated member of a clerical society of apostolic life is incardinated as a cleric to the institute or society through the reception of the diaconate unless in the case of societies their constitutions establish otherwise (c. 266, §2). A member of a secular institute is incardinated into a particular church for whose service he has been advanced through the reception of the diaconate unless he is incardinated into the institute itself by virtue of a grant of the Apostolic See (c. 266, §3). The above question of incardination concerns all the aforementioned clerics except the members of the secular institute incardinated into a particular church.

Such a religious incardination perdures until the cleric obtains a voluntary indult of departure (c. 692) or is involuntarily dismissed from the institute (c. 701). The former canon states that the indult of departure brings with it, by the law itself, a dispensation from vows and from all obligations arising from profession. The latter canon, more pertinent to our case, states somewhat more comprehensively that vows, rights and obligations derived from profession cease *ipso facto* by legitimate dismissal. "Legitimate dismissal" means that the formalities of canons 694-700 have been carefully followed and especially that after any possible recourse the dismissal action of the institute has been sustained. In both instances there is a complete severing of the juridic bond to the institute.

One should differentiate here between the religious priest who voluntarily seeks an indult of departure and the one who is involuntarily dismissed for serious cause. Canon 693 indicates that the departing religious cleric does not receive the indult until he finds a benevolent bishop who will incardinate him or at least accept him experimentally. In the latter case the practice of the Holy See seems to be to grant him only an indult of exclaustration for the time of his conditional acceptance in the diocese. One sees reflected here the concern of canon 265 that there not be unattached or transient clerics for their sake and for the good of the diocese and the institute.

On the contrary, there seems to be somewhat of an anomalous situation in the case of the dismissed religious priest according to canon 701. His penal indult of dismissal takes effect *ipso facto* when the legal formalities are expedited whether he finds a benevolent bishop or not although he is obliged to find such a bishop if he is to function ministerially. There is no basis for affirming that the legitimately dismissed cleric remains incardinated in the institute until he is taken into a diocese, and hence this does seem to be a case of an unattached or transient cleric contrary to the intent of canon 265.

Let us proceed to the second question on the bishop's discretion to grant faculties to the dismissed religious priest. The latter must seek some type of insertion in a diocese if he is to function ministerially, since he is otherwise prohibited from exercising sacred orders as a result of the dismissal (c. 701).

As regards reception in a diocese, there is a rather significant difference between the religious priest voluntarily seeking an indult of departure (c. 693) and the one involuntarily dismissed from the institute (c. 701). According to the former canon, the bishop can either immediately incardinate the priest legitimately departing the institute without a probationary period, or at least receive him experimentally for a probationary period. The episcopal options here, especially the possibility of immediate incardination, seem to mean that there may be no significant problems leading to the departure that would preclude the bishop's making a permanent commitment to the former religious and enabling him to serve in the diocese. However, the bishop is not to incardinate such a cleric unless, among other things, it is necessary or advantageous for the diocese, the priest has declared in writing his commitment to diocesan service, and the bishop has information from the institute regarding the priest's life, morals and studies (c. 269). Prudence may well dictate receiving such a religious priest only experimentally so that the bishop can get to know the priest in question and the latter can familiarize himself with the diocese and its ministerial needs. Bishops and their advisors should note, however, that the religious cleric admitted experimentally to the diocese is automatically incardinated after five years unless the bishop refuses such incardination. Presumably this provision is for the protection of the cleric lest he be left indefinitely without a definitive ministerial commitment. It is analogous to the provision for *ipso iure* incardination of diocesan clerics in canon 268 §1.

The situation is somewhat different for the dismissed religious priest in canon 701, the subject of our inquiry. Immediate incardination is not an option. If the ex-religious finds a benevolent bishop, the latter may either accept the former experimentally or the priest may simply be permitted to exercise sacred orders without any more substantial diocesan commitment to him. After a suitable probationary period, which entails a certain diocesan commitment to the individual, the bishop may conceivably decide to incardinate him in the diocese. On the contrary, merely permitting the priest to exercise sacred orders without any intent to incardinate him does not entail any specific diocesan commitment to him.

In speaking of the "probationary period" for the dismissed cleric, canon 701 refers to the aforementioned canon 693. The latter canon is technically situated in the article on departure from the institute rather than in the one on dismissal from it. However, canon 693 is also relevant to the situation of the dismissed cleric because it clarifies what is meant by that probationary period during which the dismissed cleric is received into the diocese. Bishops and their advisors should also be aware that the provision for *ipso iure* incardination of the departed cleric in canon 693 seems applicable analogously to the dismissed cleric in canon 701.

The difference between the departure and dismissal situations is based upon the fact that in the latter instance a significant breach of ecclesiastical faith or order has led to the dismissal of the priest from the institute. And hence there are presumably serious questions about the appropriateness of the bishop's assigning him to a diocesan or parish ministry experimentally or even permitting him to exercise such orders without a formal assignment. Furthermore, depending on the nature of the offense that led to dismissal, the priest may have incurred an irregularity barring him from the exercise of orders (cc. 1041 and 1044). Accordingly, the practical issue of the bishop's granting faculties to the dismissed religious (e.g., to reconcile penitents — c. 969, §1) raises various questions. Among other things they concern the grounds for dismissal, the possible delict(s) involved and the possible incurring of an irregularity, to say nothing of the prudential question of the bishop's obligation to foster the pastoral welfare of his diocese with due regard for the welfare of the religious priest in question.

The aforementioned issues can hardly be treated in detail. However, a few general observations may suffice. First of all, since we are dealing here with the restriction of the free exercise of rights, a strict interpretation of the law is warranted (c. 18). Secondly, in dealing with the dismissed ex-religious priest, the bishop and his advisors need to clarify the reasons for the dismissal action of the institute. The same provisions for the confidential sharing of information that apply to transfers of diocesan clerics should be operative here.

The 1983 code has three categories for dismissal of religious: 1) *automatic* dismissal for notoriously abandoning the faith or attempting to contract marriage (c. 694); 2) instances in which dismissal is not automatic but *ought to be initiated* by competent authority for the delicts specified in canons 1397 (homicide and other violations of persons), 1398 (abortion) and 1395 (various sexual violations including those with minors) although some qualifications are made for violations of canon 1395, §2 (c. 695); 3) instances in which dismissal is not automatic but *may be initiated*, e.g., habitual neglect of the obligations of consecrated life, grave scandal arising from the culpable behavior of the member, etc. (c. 696).

In some instances the reasons for dismissal may be factors that create an irregularity for the exercise of orders, e.g., attempting to contract marriage (cc. 1044, §1, 2° and 1041, 3°) or positive cooperation in a completed abortion (cc. 1044, §1, 3° and 1041, 4°). Obviously this issue needs to be addressed on a case-by-case basis. Furthermore, in some instances the dispensation from the irregularity is reserved to the Apostolic See, e.g., the irregularity mentioned in canon 1041, 3° (attempted marriage), yet only in public cases and the irregularity mentioned in canon 1041, 4° even in occult cases. Otherwise the ordinary can dispense from all such irregularities unless the issue has been brought to the judicial forum (c. 1047).

If after a careful inquiry all is in order and the dismissed religious priest is judged suitable for some diocesan or parish ministry, then the bishop may give him appropriate faculties. Whether the priest is received experimentally for a probationary period that may lead to incardination or whether he is simply permitted to exercise orders on an *ad hoc* basis, arrangements should be made regularly to monitor the exercise of his ministry. The bishop does not have the same relationship to such a priest and commensurate responsibilities to him as he does to those priests incardinated in the diocese. However canon 384 on the bishop's concern for priests should be analogously operative in the case of such an ex-religious priest. In the final analysis, however, it is the bishop's prudent assessment of the dismissed priest's ability to serve the people of God in the diocese well and on a sustained basis that should ground any judgment regarding possible incardination.

The code does not explicitly state what happens if the dismissed religious priest cannot find a benevolent bishop to take him experimentally or at least permit him to exercise orders. A similar situation would be true if after a probationary period the bishop chooses not to incardinate him. As noted above, this situation is an anomalous one and contrary to the thrust of canon 265 against unattached or transient clerics. Presumably the priest could take recourse to the Congregation for Institutes of Consecrated Life and Societies of Apostolic Life and await its directives. Should the priest not take such an initiative, perhaps the bishop of the diocese in which the priest is living and to whose care he is subject could also contact the congregation.

For further discussion see Elizabeth McDonough, "Separation of Members from the Institute: Canons 684-709," in Jordan Hite et al., eds., *A Handbook on Canons 573-746*, published under the auspices of the Canon Law Society of America (Collegeville, Minnesota: The Liturgical Press, 1985) 247-262. See also James H. Provost, "Process of Incardination," in Randolph R. Calvo and Nevin J. Klinger, eds., *Clergy Procedural Handbook* (Washington: CLSA, 1992) 73-74.

Thomas J. Green [1993]

ANOTHER OPINION

It is disputed whether such a priest remains incardinated in the religious institute or is not incardinated anywhere, but there does seem to be more weight to the proposition that the religious is not incardinated anywhere. Since the question assumes that the religious is nowhere incardinated, this opinion will assume this fact. It must be noted that an unincardinated priest is an anomaly in the law, which provides that all priests are to be incardinated (c. 265). This means that the priest would have no ecclesiastical superior unless perhaps that superior might be the Holy See.

Canon 701 allows a bishop who does not wish to grant a trial period for incardination to a dismissed religious priest to allow the priest to exercise sacred orders within the diocese. The priest may not function in a diocese without this permission. The law does not state whether this permission has to be in the form of a grant of faculties or in some other form. Certainly whatever form this permission takes must be carefully drafted, setting forth necessary conditions, time limits, and other matters.

The only necessary faculty seems to be that for hearing confessions (c. 966, §1); others are granted by the law itself. Even though the priest is not incardinated, it would seem that the bishop can grant him this faculty, since canon 969, §1 provides that the local ordinary can confer upon *any* presbyter *whatsoever* the faculty of hearing confessions. Once such a priest is granted faculties under canon 966, §1, it may be that he has that faculty everywhere. Since this is a significant faculty, the bishop could withdraw it, but he must have serious reason to do so (c. 974, §1). It may be advisable to grant the faculty only for a limited period of time (c. 972).

There are also a number of other faculties regularly granted by bishops to the priests of a diocese. Therefore, it seems that a dismissed religious priest could exercise some significant functions of sacred orders without faculties, but with permission. It would seem that the permission is broader than the grant of faculties, but less specific.

In this case there may be more than merely granting faculties to allowing such a priest to exercise sacred orders within a diocese. Some more explicit permission or document may also be advisable, depending on the circumstances.

One must also raise the issue as to what end are these faculties being granted. Is the bishop giving the priest an office? What will be the role of this priest and his relationship to the bishop? Dismissal of a religious is not lightly requested or granted. Dismissal must be based on serious misconduct or some other type of problem. It would be prudent for the bishop to obtain a release from the priest and find out the basis for the dismissal, perhaps reviewing some of the acts or conferring with his superiors. If there are problems but the bishop wishes to allow the priest to exercise sacred orders within the diocese, then the relationship with the priest must be very carefully structured.

In this litigious age, bishops must also consider civil law ramifications of their actions. Granting faculties could arguably be a basis for attorneys to argue that a priest with faculties, although not incardinated, is an agent of the bishop. While most diocesan attorneys would argue that this is not the law, there is a case in California that might support the position that such a priest could in certain circumstances be considered in civil law to be an agent of the bishop.

Ralph E. Wiatrowski [1993]

BOOK III

THE TEACHING OFFICE OF THE CHURCH

CANONS 751; 1364; AND 1382

UNAPPROVED EPISCOPAL ORDINATIONS

Several questions have been raised regarding the ecclesiastical status of the Chinese Catholic Patriotic Association, established in 1957, which since 1958 has consecrated numerous bishops without the appropriate mandate or confirmation. Contained in the questions are inquiries about the penal situation of these bishops and whether or not the faithful may receive sacraments by validly ordained ministers of that church. The questions have been placed with reference to the excommunication of Archbishop Marcel Lefebvre who on his own authority similarly consecrated bishops and asked if there are different norms applicable to the Church in communist countries, especially concerning the clergy, since there does not seem to be any formal decree of excommunication or suspension pertaining to the participating bishops and their followers.

OPINION

The questions posed are particularly sensitive in view of the fact that the Chinese Catholic Patriotic Association has the appearance of being a schismatic church. It is clearly an agency of the state and does not share any formal communion with the Holy See. In the eyes of the government this is the officially recognized ''Catholic'' church and it has about fifty bishops. In addition to canon 2229, §3, 3° of the 1917 Code of Canon Law which was the *ius vigens* at the time of these original illicit episcopal consecrations, a decree of the Congregation of the Holy Office, dated April 9, 1951, was in effect which stated that the pressure of grave fear did not excuse bishops who illicitly consecrated or illicitly received consecration from the *latae sententiae* penalty of excommunication (*AAS* 43 [1951] 217-218). No special declaratory sentence seems to have been imposed on the Chinese bishops. One must note that a lengthy process preceded the declaratory sentence imposed on Archbishop Lefebvre, encouraging him into full communion and giving advice concerning the consequences if he pursued his intention to consecrate bishops illicitly. There was a certain flagrancy on his part. His circumstances and that of the Chinese bishops are considerably different.

Chinese Catholics have been living in a pastorally very compromising situation since 1957. Some have opted simply to go along with the state recognized Church. A second group has quietly and secretly practiced their faith in full communion with the Holy See, refusing any form of religious contact with those who joined the patriotic church. A third group, among those who are publicly associated with the patriotic church, privately remain steadfastly united to the Holy See, recognizing their situation of compromise. Hence the situation is quite complex, not only canonically, but also at the emotional level.

Whatever harsh attitudes one might hold towards the bishops who participated in the illicit consecrations, the 1983 Code of Canon Law somewhat changes their situation. Book VI, *Sanctions in the Church*, states in canon 1313 that if a law is changed after an offense has been committed, the law which is more favorable to the accused is to be applied. Canon 2229 of the 1917 code, cited by the Congregation of the Holy Office in 1951, has no parallel in the 1983 code. Hence it would seem that the new code offers some possible relief from the harsh and automatic application of the penalty of excommunication attached to the participating bishops if they acted out of grave fear. However, even the 1983 code in canon 1323, §4 does not consider grave fear as an excusing factor from the penalty if the act is intrinsically evil or verges on the harm of souls.

Canon 1382 clearly states that an automatic (*latae sententiae*) excommunication reserved to the Holy See is incurred by consecrator and bishop consecrated who are involved in an unauthorized episcopal consecration. Hence a special declaratory sentence to incur the excommunication is not necessary. Such an additional declaration has other public consequences, e.g., canon 194 regarding the loss of ecclesiastical office, or canon 1352 and the observance of *latae sententiae* penalties. Canon 1323 indicates various and multiple circumstances when a violation of a law or precept excuses from the penalty, and connects this to the prescription of canon 1324, §1, 2°, excusing a person with only an imperfect use of reason. Canon 1324, in general, moderates penalties when the forbidden act is performed under mitigating circumstances. Canon 1324, §1, 8° moderates the penalty even if the person acted culpably, if that person thought that the excusing factor in canon 1323, 4° was verified.

Hence, without all facts at hand, it is difficult to ascertain whether or not the automatic excommunication was incurred by the participating bishops. One would be hard pressed to suggest that a brain-washed or partially drugged consecrating bishop would be found sufficiently culpable to incur the automatic excommunication. One might suggest that canon 1324, §3 applies to at least some of the bishops in question and thus for these eliminates the question of the stated automatic ecclesiastical penalty. The circumstances are quite different from those relative to the case of Archbishop Lefebvre. Furthermore, absent a declaration of penalty, the faithful may still legitimately request sacraments and other ecclesiastical services from those excommunicated *latae sententiae* and these may licitly fulfill the requests, according to canon 1335. These complicated factors may partially explain why no specific declaration of excommunication from the Holy See has been reported.

By virtue of its own constitutive documents, it would appear that the government approved church is a schismatic church. Certainly we can observe that it is not in any form of communion with the Holy See. Were we operating under the terms of canon 1325, §2 of the 1917 code, one would see all members of this schismatic church as being schismatic. However, the term "schismatic" is a technical term described in canon 751 of the 1983 code. It seems to be a bit more sharply described and more restrictive than its 1917 counterpart, partially by the use of the words *communionis . . . detrectatio* as compared to the 1917 terms, *subiectis communicare recusat*. I entertain a warm suspicion that many Chinese Catholics who ended up in the government approved church found themselves in a state of compromise rather than being adamantly unwilling to be in full communion with the Holy See, stubbornly refusing to communicate with its subjects. I would be inclined to call their situation irregular rather than schismatic. Hence, I would hazard the awkward opinion that the patriotic church is a schismatic church, but not all of its members are schismatic.

Canon 12 states that universal laws bind everywhere those for whom they were made unless some exemption is made. This applies to all Catholics everywhere, clergy and lay, in China and in other communist countries. Some special provisions have been made in the past for places under duress. There are in fact some special pastoral provisions made for Catholics in China who do not have easy access to priests in full communion with the Holy See. These are not much different from the traditional and common teachings of moral theology regarding the reception of sacraments from schismatic clergy under certain circumstances.

The code itself provides ample norms to assist Catholics living under these extraordinary circumstances, as mentioned above. The mitigating and softer elements of the code apply in these places under communist control as well as the forces behind the last sentence in the code expressed in canon 1752 "with due regard for canonical equity and having before one's eyes the salvation of souls, which is always the supreme law of the Church." Pastoral ministry in these places is a very complicated reality, as we are reminded by the December 1, 1989, conversation between Pope John Paul II and President Mikhael Gorbachev, when the Holy Father diplomatically stated that we are in a compromise situation as the pope was attempting to improve the lot of Ukrainian Catholics living behind the iron curtain. The faithful receive the sacraments and are guided by shepherds, not always under ideal circumstances and are invited to do the best they can, realizing that no one is held to the impossible. A realistic application of the canons of the Church must take these factors into consideration.

213

CANON 766

PARISH MISSION BY LAY PERSON

Can a qualified lay person be allowed to conduct a parish mission in church?

OPINION

You are correct in identifying canons 766 and 767 of the 1983 code as normative. There the distinction is made between the homily, which is reserved to the deacon or the priest, and a sermon given by a qualified lay person.

You ask certain questions and I would like to answer them in the reverse order in which you ask them. What kind of restrictions must be imposed upon a lay person speaking/preaching in church? None, if she or he is qualified in the subject of the preaching; Dr. P. seems eminently qualified. Must he lead a parish mission in a building other than the parish church? Canon 766 specifically deals with preaching in a church or chapel (oratory).

May he do so at the time of the homily, understanding that he is not giving the homily? Here we need some canonical precision, which I think a pastor who is willing even to entertain the thought of a lay person giving a parish mission should have no difficulty in handling in a responsible manner. On Sundays and holy days there must be a homily unless there is a grave reason for omitting it; on weekdays it is strongly recommended when there are enough people present. If "at the time of the homily" means before the universal petitions, the answer is yes. If it means in place of the homily, my answer is negative, except in a case of grave need. But I take it for granted that, if your parish mission begins or concludes on a Sunday or on a Saturday afternoon, you, as an experienced pastor, should have no difficulty in giving a fine three-minute, authentic homily by way of tying in the mission with the liturgy of the week; I presume you would have to say something. This would be, in my opinion, necessary, entirely apart from any law, to exercise your leadership of the parish, to authenticate Dr. P.'s appearance in your church, and to link the mission to the liturgy.

Canon 766 speaks of permitting lay persons to preach in accord with the prescriptions of the episcopal conference. We are not going to have policies from the NCCB on this matter by the time you propose to have the parish mission; it is a relatively low priority item on their immediate agenda. In that case the diocesan bishop decides on his own, and it would be my hope that your bishop would warmly approve what you are proposing and thus provide an experienced affirmative vote when the bishops eventually take up this matter. The Germans have been doing this by indult for years — another example of successful indults becoming part of the law.

Richard A. Hill, S.J. [1984]

CANON 766

PREACHING BY A LAY PERSON AND A NON-CATHOLIC

1. Is it permitted for non-ordained, lay men and women, to preach in the context of a Mass immediately following the proclamation of the Gospel?

2. Is it permissible for a non-Catholic, either lay or ordained minister, to preach at such a time?

OPINION

Let me begin with the second question first. The 1967 *Ecumenical Directory*, n. 56, stated that a non-Catholic "is not to act as a Scripture reader or to preach during the celebration of the Eucharist." However, in practice the diocesan bishop, in virtue of *Christus Dominus* 8b, and in virtue of the motu proprio *De episcoporum muneribus*, could dispense from this disciplinary law of the Church in individual cases, and so could permit a non-Catholic to preach at Mass. This is often termed "pulpit sharing" and is usually permitted on special occasions of some importance for ecumenical awareness, for example during the Week of Prayer for Christian Unity.

The new code has not changed the restriction in the 1967 *Directory*, nor has the new code restricted the power of the bishop to dispense in this case. So, the practice which developed prior to the new code may continue under it, with the same safeguards and requirements as before.

In regard to whether a lay person may preach in the context of a Mass, and immediately following the proclamation of the Gospel, there seem to be two schools of thought.

Both schools of thought recognize that canon 766 reverses the former discipline, which forbade lay persons to preach in church buildings. The new code now explicitly permits this, under appropriate safeguards, including any prescriptions the conference of bishops may set down as well as any norms the

215

diocesan bishop may issue for his diocese (c. 772, §1). They differ, however, in interpreting the restriction in canon 766: "salvo canon 767, §1."

Canon 767 is about the homily. In section 1 it describes what the homily is: "it is a part of the liturgy itself and is reserved to a priest or to a deacon; in the homily the mysteries of faith and the norms of Christian living are to be expounded from the sacred text throughout the course of the liturgical year."

The homily is also described there as preeminent "among the forms of preaching." This means it must also conform to the norms concerning preaching, such as canon 768 (preachers are to propose "those things which one ought to believe and do for the glory of God and for the salvation of human-kind" and in particular "to impart to the faithful the teaching which the magisterium of the Church proposes concerning the dignity and freedom of the human person," etc.). Moreover, as a form of preaching it is an element in the ministry of the divine word, which is governed by canon 760: "The mystery of Christ is to be expounded completely and faithfully in the ministry of the word, which ought to be based upon sacred scripture, tradition, liturgy, the magisterium and the life of the Church."

The substance of the homily, therefore, in keeping with the other norms about the ministry of the word and preaching itself, might not always be materially different from other forms of preaching, given the rich concept of preaching contained in the code.

The difference in the two schools of thought seems to boil down to whether canon 767, §1 differentiates a "homily" from other forms of preaching by the place in the celebration where it takes place, or by the person who is authorized to do it.

One school of thought sees the homily as a preaching which is done at a particular place in the liturgical celebration, after the Gospel, and so the restriction of the homily to a priest or deacon means only an ordained person may preach at that time. Thus a lay person is not permitted to replace the homily with a lay preaching after the Gospel, and if the lay person is to be admitted to preach during Mass it must be at some other place. Most frequently this seems to be indicated for after Communion.

The other school of thought sees the homily as a part of the liturgy reserved to a priest or deacon, rather than as a particular place in the liturgical celebration. If someone else were to preach at that same place in the liturgical celebration it would by definition not be a homily. Thus, in pulpit exchange for ecumenical reasons, the non-Catholic could preach after the Gospel instead of a homily being given by a Catholic priest or deacon. Similarly, the *Directory for Masses with Children* indicates that if the priest celebrant is not able to address the children in words they can understand, another person (lay persons included) may address a few words to the children about the meaning of the

Gospel at the time when the priest would normally give the homily; but the Directory carefully does not refer to the lay person's words as a "homily," since this is restricted to what a priest or deacon does as part of the liturgy.

The NCCB has not issued any prescriptions concerning lay preaching. The diocesan bishop is, therefore, free to issue norms of his own concerning lay preaching in his diocese. It would be up to his prudential pastoral judgment which school of thought to follow in regard to whether lay persons could be permitted to preach during Mass after the Gospel. If he were to permit this, he might wish to explain the precedents for it in the practice relative to non-Catholics who on occasion may be permitted to preach as part of a pulpit exchange during the Week of Prayer for Christian Unity, and in the *Directory for Masses with Children.*

James H. Provost [1986]

CANON 766

LAY PREACHING

When is it permissible for laity to be given the faculties to preach in liturgical functions?

OPINION

Under the 1917 code the laity were categorically forbidden to preach in churches (c. 1342, §2). The 1983 code permits lay preaching in churches and oratories when necessary and even when useful in special cases (c. 766). Norms on lay preaching should be established by the conference of bishops. When such norms are absent or delayed, the particular church is not paralyzed but may implement the code in accordance with prudent decisions of pastors and rectors of churches and particular legislation of the diocesan bishop, if any. The code asks for legislation by the conference of bishops in many canons. When the conference decides not to act or delays in enacting legislation and the diocese has no particular legislation, the code may be followed by pastors. Some examples:

1. Radio and television preaching may continue even if the conference of bishops does not enact legislation (c. 772, §2).

2. Clerical garb is regulated by legitimate local customs in the absence of conference norms (c. 284).

3. Confessionals are still used even when the conference passes no regulations (c. 964, §2).

4. Ordinaries can dispense from canonical form even when the conference fails to act (c. 1127, §2).

5. Matrimonial engagements are regulated by custom and civil law, which must also be recognized by norms of the conference of bishops if enacted (c. 1062, §1).

6. Mixed marriage permissions are granted and the required promises and declarations continue to be made even without conference norms (c. 1126).

7. Pastors conduct pre-marriage examinations regarding freedom to marry even though the conference has established no norms (c. 1067).

Hence, particular churches can permit lay preaching in churches and oratories in accordance with canon law, diocesan legislation and prudent decisions of pastors, even without conference norms.

It should be noted that neither the 1917 code nor the 1983 code regulate lay preaching outside of churches. Such preaching occurs at summer camps and retreat centers, youth conventions, bible study and prayer groups, base communities and meetings of associations of the faithful, as well as street preaching and televangelism (which can be regulated by conference norms because of the public nature of such preaching).

Further differences between the 1917 and the 1983 codes should be noted. In the 1917 code the bishop had the serious obligation to preach (c. 1327, §2). Secular clerics and non-exempt religious clerics needed faculties from the local ordinary before they were permitted to preach (c. 1337). Such faculties were granted only after examination and could be revoked if the preacher lacked the necessary qualifications (c. 1340).

In the 1983 code bishops, presbyters and deacons are authorized to preach by the code itself and do not need faculties (cc. 763 & 764). The presumed consent of the rector of the church (or the religious superior in religious churches or oratories) is all that is required.

Although the system of faculties is not mentioned in the new code, some version of faculties may well be the matter of conference or diocesan norms in the case of lay preachers. The homily is a special case, and must be preached by an ordained minister. This is the nature of a homily (c. 767, §1). Besides the requirement of competent and orthodox preaching, the Church prefers apostolic preaching by the bishops and those with whom they share the powers of ordination. The Church is created by apostolic preaching and assembles as the Body of Christ to hear the Word preached by the apostles and to share the Body of Christ celebrated with the apostles and those who share their priesthood. Hence, ordained preaching is required at Sunday and holy day Masses and can only be omitted for serious reasons. However, instruction could be given by a lay person in place of the homily.

Similarly, liturgical norms state that a homily be preached by the ordained presider of funerals and weddings. When a lay person presides (with approval of the conference of bishops) then that same lay person preaches a sermon or instruction in place of the homily.

Lay persons may be admitted to the preaching office in churches and oratories in circumstances when their preaching is necessary because an ordained minister is absent or impeded. This would include:

1. Liturgy of the Hours or Liturgy of the Word with or without Communion at daily services as well as Sunday services in the absence of a priest or deacon;

2. Liturgical services, including Mass, presided over by a priest who is not fluent enough in the language to preach;

3. Marriages and funerals presided over by a cleric who may be competent enough to read the service in a foreign language but not fluent enough to preach.

Diocesan norms might well require faculties for such preaching. Such faculties could be granted to catechists and pastoral associates who are qualified to preach by reason of education and experience.

Lay preaching is useful in special circumstances such as:

1. Pulpit exchanges for ecumenical services;

2. Preaching on stewardship, Catholic education, Campaign for Human Development and other annual occasions;

3. Seminarians preaching as part of a pastoral in-service program.

In such cases faculties seem like excessive ''micro-managing.'' Perhaps diocesan guidelines would be preferable, leaving the decision as to competence up to the local pastor.

Finally, there are many parishes where the pastor is the only ordained preacher available, Sunday after Sunday. The pastor may feel he has serious reasons to omit the homily and ask a lay preacher to substitute a sermon or instruction so the congregation can hear another voice. Diocesan legislation may require faculties for such preachers, particularly if they regularly replace the ordained preacher. And diocesan legislation may provide guidelines to pastors in evaluating those serious reasons which permit the substitution of a lay sermon for the homily and to balance the usefulness of a lay sermon in particular cases against the general obligation of a pastor to provide ordained preaching on Sundays.

Summary Recommendations

1. The pastor or rector of the church may designate a lay preacher for an occasional sermon even on Sundays or holy days.

2. Faculties should be required for lay preachers who preach on a regular basis.

3. Diocesan guidelines should establish training and other requirements before granting faculties.

4. When faculties are requested by the pastor, missionary, or a rector of a church for a lay preacher who will preach on a regular basis, the ordinary should be informed of the reason for the request as well as the qualifications of the lay person.

5. Pastors also need some in-service training on the use of lay preachers:

a. supervisory obligation;

b. examples of necessary or useful reasons for lay preachers;

c. examples of serious reasons for replacing the homily on Sundays, holy days, funerals and weddings with a sermon by a lay person with faculties to preach.

Bertram F. Griffin [1992]

CANON 767, §1

PULPIT SHARING DURING EUCHARIST

Does this canon (and the new code elsewhere) prohibit an ordained minister from another Christian Church from preaching during the eucharistic liturgy? Or may a diocese continue to follow directives developed under the 1967 Ecumenical Directory?

OPINION

Except in those areas where the new code entirely reorganizes the provisions of the 1967 *Ecumenical Directory*, that document remains in force. For example, the provisions on *communicatio in sacris* have been reorganized by canon 844, which now replace all previous regulations in this regard.

So far as I can determine, the code has not reorganized the provisions on pulpit exchange contained in the 1967 *Directory* and any subsequent norms, whether from the Vatican or other Catholic authorities.

No. 56 of the *Directory* ruled out Scripture reading or preaching by a "separated brother" during the celebration of the Eucharist in the Catholic Church, or by a Catholic during the celebration of the Lord's Supper or at the

220

principal liturgical service of the Word held by Christians separated from us. The previous permission of the local ordinary and of the appropriate official of the other church were required for exercising such functions in other services, even liturgical ones.

There is a distinction between permissions which a bishop can give under the law, and a dispensation from the law. In the former situation, the law is being observed; the intervention of the bishop is required in order to be observing the law, but any actions which take place with his permission are not an exception to the law, but according to it. When a dispensation is granted, it relaxes the law in an individual case. An exception is made; what is done is not according to the law normally applicable, but it is legal since it is done with a dispensation (if the one who gave the dispensation was authorized to do so).

Vatican II, in *Christus Dominus* 8b, authorized the diocesan bishop to dispense from disciplinary laws of the Church except in cases reserved to the Apostolic See. In the motu proprio *De episcoporum muneribus* this was not one of the disciplinary norms reserved to the Apostolic See. So, the diocesan bishop could dispense from it if he had sufficient cause, which could be the spiritual welfare of the people. Many bishops did exercise this power to dispense in order to permit pulpit sharing on certain more suitable occasions, such as the Week of Prayer for Christian Unity. Your own guidelines (no. 22) make this application for whatever occasions may seem desirable for this to happen.

The new code does not change any of this. Indeed, the dispensing power of the diocesan bishop is explicitly affirmed in canon 87, §1. The problem you have raised is whether canon 767, §1, which characterizes the "homily" as being preeminent among the forms of preaching and defines it as "a part of the liturgy itself" which "is reserved to a priest or to a deacon," now excludes the possibility of preaching by a non-Catholic in a Catholic liturgical service.

Again, some distinctions must be made. The law itself distinguishes between "preaching" and the "homily," which is one form of preaching. The new code reverses the 1917 code and permits lay persons to "preach" in church (c. 766). It indicates they cannot give a homily, but that is because by definition a homily is a portion of the liturgy which is done by a priest or deacon.

This same distinction has been made before. In the directions for Masses for children, if the celebrant (a priest, obviously) is not able to adapt himself to the mentality of the children, then instead of a "homily" a lay person may explain the Gospel to the children after the Gospel has been read. This is a "preaching" which replaces a homily for a serious pastoral reason (namely, to be able to communicate effectively with those for whom the celebration is intended).

This same distinction can be applied in other settings, where for one reason or another there is "serious reason" to replace the homily (which only a priest or deacon are able to provide) with a preaching, which others who are not ordained are able to provide. Such lay preaching must be done in keeping with the prescriptions of the conference of bishops (if there are any — there are none currently in the United States) and under the norms issued by the diocesan bishop concerning the exercise of preaching (c. 772, §1).

Canon 767 in subsequent sections requires a homily on Sundays and holy days of obligation. However, it also permits the homily to be omitted for "serious reason." Since a serious reason is already required for the bishop or his delegate to dispense from the provisions of the *Ecumenical Directory* in order to permit non-Catholics to read Scripture or to preach during the Eucharist, it would seem the same serious reason could also be used by the bishop to determine that the exception provided for in canon 767, §2 would apply on this occasion, and therefore, the homily could be replaced by the pulpit sharing in question.

James H. Provost [1984]

CANON 788, §3

HABITUAL FACULTY TO USE ABBREVIATED CATECHUMENATE

Does the Rite of Christian Initiation of Adults *favor the granting of a general diocesan faculty to parish priests to use the abbreviated catechumenate, or the simple rite of initiation in whole or in part?*

OPINION

The *Rite of Christian Initiation of Adults* (*RCIA*, 1988 U.S. version, n. 331) states that the local bishop can allow the use of the abbreviated form of the rite of initiation in "extraordinary circumstances," that is, "either events that prevent the candidate from completing all the steps of the catechumenate or a depth of Christian conversion and a degree of religious maturity that lead the local bishop to decide that the candidate may receive baptism without delay." Examples of extraordinary events are given: "sickness, old age, change of residence, long absence for travel" (*RCIA*, n. 332). The National Statutes for the Catechumenate, n. 20, say that the diocesan bishop may permit the abbreviated catechumenate "only in individual and exceptional cases" and it "should always be as limited as possible."

These statutes emanate from a higher authority than the diocesan bishop, namely the Holy See and the National Conference of Catholic Bishops. The bishop cannot act contrary to them. Their intent is clearly to limit the abbreviated form of adult initiation to extraordinary circumstances. For that reason, the faculty to permit the abbreviated catechumenate is restricted to the diocesan bishop himself who must judge the adequacy of the reasons for granting the permission on a case by case basis.

The diocesan bishop may delegate the faculty to permit the abbreviated rite in accord with the usual rules for delegating the executive power of governance. Delegation of the faculty to all parish priests in the diocese would be valid, but it would be contrary to the purpose of the *RCIA*. The statutes clearly manifest the aim of limiting the use of the abbreviated rite to extraordinary circumstan ces, and for that reason it restricts the faculty to permit its use to the diocesan bishop who must assess the circumstances of each case. If all parish priests could grant this permission, there would be a danger of the law being ignored and the abbreviated rite being used routinely and unjustifiably.

It would be more in keeping with the spirit and purpose of the national statutes if the bishop were to delegate the faculty to grant this permission to other officials of the diocese, such as the head of the diocesan liturgical commission and/or the other local ordinaries. In so doing he could be better assured that there would be an adequate assessment of each individual case before the permission were granted.

John M. Huels, O.S.M. [1992]

CANON 791

DIOCESAN DIRECTOR OF PROPAGATION OF THE FAITH

May lay persons be appointed to administer the development funds and other administrative elements of the missionary works in a diocese? Could a non-priest be named director for the Propagation of the Faith in a diocese, or even associate director?

OPINION

The canon distinguishes various ways in which missionary cooperation is to be promoted in a diocese, and who may be placed in charge of each.

Missionary vocations are to be encouraged (c. 791, 1°). The responsibility for promoting vocations pertains to all the Christian faithful, especially Christian families, educators, and parish priests, together with the bishop (c. 233, §1).

The promotion work is to stir up interest and involvement in the various missionary works of the Church. This is to be placed in the hands of a priest (c. 791, 2°).

The celebration of an annual day for the missions is to be organized (c. 791, 3°). The canon does not say by whom. Canon 1244, §2 indicates the diocesan bishop may mandate this for the diocese on individual occasions. The preparation of materials and other elements needed for a successful diocesan observance of such a day is left to the bishop, and to those who assist him as part of the diocesan curia (c. 469). These latter may be priests, religious or lay persons selected by the bishop (c. 470). Provided they do not by office exercise authority (the ecclesiastical power of regimen — c. 129, §2), lay persons may be appointed to various posts in the diocesan curia (including chancellor [c. 483, §2] and fiscal manager [c. 494]).

A collection is to be taken up each year for the missions, and is to be forwarded to the Holy See (c. 791, 4°). The diocesan bishop is responsible to see that this is done (cc. 1266 & 1271), and is to see that the funds are properly administered (c. 1276 — i.e., sent to the Holy See). He can be aided in this by others, including the diocesan fiscal manager (c. 1278), who may appoint others to assist in the work.

So, it appears legitimate to make the following distinctions:

1. A priest is to be appointed to see that "promotion" of the missions takes place. That is, he is to see that talks are given on the missions, the consciousness of the people is raised as to the missionary work of the Church, etc. This is an educational and "public relations" type of position. The law requires that a priest be placed in charge of it, although it does not restrict him from permitting or arranging for others to do the actual speaking, etc. (such as, for example, religious and lay missionaries; indeed, lay persons can even be authorized to preach in church under the revised code — c. 766).

2. Lay persons are directly involved in recruiting missionary vocations, as part of their overall responsibility for promoting vocations in the Church. This task is distinct from that of promoting the missions as such, and is not restricted as a task which only a priest may be authorized to do.

3. Lay persons may assist the bishop in the responsibility for preparing the annual celebrations of "mission day" in the diocese, and may assist the bishop in taking up and administering collections for the missions. They may be appointed to offices in the diocesan curia for administering these activities on behalf of the missions.

In response to your question, therefore, let me state the following:

1. Lay persons may be named to administer the development funds and other administrative elements of the missionary works in a diocese.

2. Depending on how the office of "Director of the Propagation of the

Faith" or "Assistant Director" of that office is defined, a non-priest could be assigned to such an office. That is, if the definition of the office in a particular diocese did not include the primary responsibility for promotion, but assigned that to a priest who is placed in charge of "promotion work" for the missions, then a non-priest could have the position of director or assistant director, handling the administrative responsibilities of the office.

Even if a priest is named director, a non-priest could be named assistant (or associate) director, with the various responsibilities distributed appropriately in keeping with the talents, time and qualifications of the director and assistant.

The law places greater emphasis on the fact of promoting the missions than on the priestly character of the one who is in charge of it. So, it should be noted in a time of growing shortage of clergy that, as the classical canonical adage observes, "no one is held to the impossible." If in a given diocese a priest is not available to direct the work of promotion, the bishop would have to assure the promotion work through others.

James H. Provost [1984, revised 1993]

CANONS 810; 812; AND 833

RELATIONSHIP OF BISHOP TO UNIVERSITY AUTHORITIES

The bishop of the diocese is an ex officio *member of the board of trustees of a diocesan university. The university's by-laws state that the powers of the trustees include "ultimate authority over regulations concerning . . . professorships, assistantships and internships and the qualifications therefore." The board has delegated and continues to delegate the authority to appoint faculty to its official representative, the president of the university, in consultation with members of the department the faculty member will join.*

Pursuant to this responsibility, the president or provost (often both) and the dean, as well as members of the department, interview all faculty applicants and make a special determination as to their compatibility with the mission and goals of this Roman Catholic university. If the applicant is a member of the clergy, the university also arranges that he be interviewed by the bishop or his delegate, since if appointed to the faculty he would doubtless seek authorization for the exercise of priestly faculties within the diocese.

The university's board-approved academic freedom document, published in the faculty handbook and binding on all members of the faculty, states that "since

225

this is an independent Catholic university, faculty members are expected to refrain from inculcating doctrines opposed to the essentials of the Catholic faith and from disseminating doctrines and views which are inimical to the aims and purposes of the university as a Catholic institution committed to the upholding of Christian faith and morality. The 'freedom' to teach and act in a fashion incompatible with the purposes of the university would be destructive of the basic right and freedom of the university to fulfill the very reasons for its foundation and continued operation. " Removal of faculty can be accomplished for the reasons and through the procedures specified in its board-approved policy of appointment, reappointment, rank and tenure under the section "Dismissal for Serious Cause. " Does this satisfy the requirements of canon 810?

Since the board of trustees, with the bishop as an ex officio *member, has delegated and continues to delegate the president to appoint faculty, including faculty teaching theological disciplines, does this satisfy the requirements of canon 812 concerning the "mandate"?*

At the official Mass of the Holy Spirit which opens each academic year, the university proposes to arrange to have the profession of faith printed in the program and recited by the congregation following the Gospel and the homily. Does this satisfy the requirement of canon 833, 7°?

OPINION

Let me begin by reviewing the law, and then apply it to this particular situation. The law makes a clear distinction between canon 810, §1 and canon 812.

Canon 810, §1 refers to the hiring and dismissal of faculty members, an institutional responsibility which must be carried out with full respect for the provisions of the statutes of the institution itself. Unlike the provisions for schools (i.e., primary, middle and secondary schools), where the diocesan bishop may have a direct role in the naming or approving of religion teachers and likewise in removing them or demanding that they be removed (c. 805), the appointment and removal of faculty even in the field of religious studies in an institution of higher learning (a college or university, for example) is the responsibility of the authorities of the institution.

Canon 812, on the other hand, refers to the individuals who teach theological disciplines in universities and similar institutions. They are held personally to have the "mandate to teach." This is to come from a "competent ecclesiastical authority." Neither the canons nor canonical tradition specify the meaning of the "mandate" or what ecclesiastical authorities are "competent" to grant it. This is a new canon, not contained in the former code, and what precedents do

226

exist do not seem to provide a clear legal history to guide in its interpretation.

However, some things are clear from the discussion of the canon in the Code Commission sessions where it was drafted and revised. The earlier formulation of "canonical mission" was changed, lest the impression be given that an ecclesiastical office is being conferred. The mandate is, therefore, not an empowerment, the way canonical mission may be understood. On the other hand the phrase "*licentia docendi*" was not used even though there is a long tradition in concordat law to recommend it. So it has been argued by some that the mandate is more than just a permission to teach.

Another important element to consider in interpreting the "mandate" is the fact that the diocesan bishop in his responsibility for vigilance over doctrine within the diocese is instructed to acknowledge "a rightful freedom in the further investigations" of the truths of faith (c. 386, §2). It seems the mandate does not make the teacher of theological disciplines a proxy for the bishop or other competent ecclesiastical authority; it does not make the teacher a delegate of such authorities. Indeed, the law specifically guarantees teachers in the sacred disciplines "a lawful freedom of inquiry and of prudently expressing their opinions on matters in which they have expertise, while observing a due respect for the magisterium of the Church" (c. 218).

Since no procedure for granting the mandate to teach has been specified by general law, no determination has been made in the code as to what ecclesiastical authorities are "competent" in the matter. Since, as indicated above, the mandate is not the conferring of an ecclesiastical office, it would not of itself require the same kind of authority as is needed to confer an office. The mandate, moreover, applies not to institutions but to individuals. Various approaches have developed for implementing this canon. For example, in one European country the mandate is granted to those who are completing their academic training, prior to employment by any particular institution. In other situations, it appears the mandate is being considered to have been granted implicitly to those who have obtained degrees in the sacred sciences, whether these be ecclesiastical degrees or their civil equivalents.

In the United States there are further complications due to possible repercussions in civil law and for accreditation. The various committees of the NCCB and USCC, which have considered this issue, have encouraged the bishops not to take any public actions at this time while these implications are reviewed. For example, because of the unique character of higher education in this country where the worth of a degree is measured by the report of private accrediting agencies, the very future of our extensive system of Catholic higher education depends on how carefully the provisions of the code are handled in regard to the academic integrity of these institutions. If the accrediting agencies judge that the way in which canons 810, §1 and 812 are implemented amounts to an infringement on the academic integrity of the institutions, they have already indicated serious concern as to whether our colleges and institutions can be accredited. If they were to lose accreditation, the degrees of their graduates would not be recognized by other institutions, with serious repercussions to the future of Catholic higher education.

To date the conferences have not recommended a specific approach other than to ask that the bishops consult with the appropriate officers and committees of the NCCB/USCC before taking any specific action. Further clarification on this point might be sought from the USCC Education Department, or from the Association of Catholic Colleges and Universities, which has worked closely with the NCCB and USCC on this issue.

I mention all of this as prelude, for the issues raised in the inquiry are indeed quite serious not only for the diocese and the institution, but also for other Catholic institutions of higher learning in this country. Let me now turn to the specific points of the query.

Canon 810, §1 requires that the provisions of the statutes be followed in the appointment and removal of faculty. The query indicates the provisions of the statutes of the institution in question provide for the president to be the delegate of the board of trustees for finalizing appointments, and provide for clearly defined procedures for removal. Thus in keeping with civil law and canon law, the appointment and removal of faculty is provided for in the statutes. So far as I can tell, the query's interpretation of the application of canon 810, §1 in this situation is correct.

The second issue concerns the mandate to teach. While the law does not specify what ecclesiastical authorities are competent to grant the mandate, it is reasonable to conclude that at least the diocesan bishop may do so within his own diocese. Moreover, the diocesan bishop is not restricted in terms of to whom he may delegate this responsibility. So from a canon law point of view, if the bishop of the diocese determines to interpret canon 812 as requiring a specific mandate (as distinct from the degree qualifications which others have used to interpret the canon, or even the special credentialling being used in Europe, as I explained above), then he is also free to delegate to others the granting of the mandate. The arrangement discussed by the query would, therefore, be consonant with the canon law on this point.

The civil law issue, and the concern for academic integrity raised by the accrediting agencies, must also be considered. I am not the most competent person to comment on this, since my expertise lies in the field of canon law. However, from my reading of the situation, the arrangement discussed in the query would also appear to be within the limits imposed by these concerns. Since the bishop is a member of the board of trustees, his delegating the president (whether explicitly, or implicitly through the institution's statutes) would still be an action within the authorities of the academic institution itself. It would not represent an intrusion by an outside authority, which would breach the academic integrity of the institution.

The third point concerns the manner in which the profession of faith is administered to the president or rector of the institution and to teachers of disciplines which deal with faith and morals. The profession of faith approved by the Apostolic See is fundamentally the Nicene-Constantinopolitan Creed which is used in the Mass, with three concluding paragraphs of additional elements. While canon 833 requires the profession of faith to be made personally, it is to be done "in the presence of" various officials, not necessarily in a one-to-one setting. That it take place in a liturgical setting is certainly in keeping with the traditional liturgical purpose of credal statements. The only additional formality which is observed in some institutions is to have professors sign a written copy of the profession of faith (at some time other than the liturgical ceremony) and this is kept on file so there is a record of the profession having been made.

These, then, are my comments. I would encourage consultation with the appropriate authorities at the national level, however, so that there is a common understanding not only of the arrangement locally but also of its national ramifications.

James H. Provost [1985]

CANON 823

IMPRIMATUR

Is the imprimatur *needed on a book which is primarily a detailed resource book for adults to use in planning and executing children's Liturgy of the Word? It is not a textbook as such, but is like a series of lesson plans based on the Scriptures of the Lectionary.*

OPINION

As you know, the question of the meaning of the *imprimatur* has become somewhat confused by recent events. Under the 1917 code, permission to publish was needed for any books of the type described above (1917 code, c. 1385, §1, 2°). This was changed under Paul VI, and the norms as they now appear in the new code permit such books to be published without an *imprimatur*, although the law does affirm that the bishops can demand that the writings

229

to be published by the Christian faithful which touch upon faith or morals be submitted to their judgment (c. 823, §1).

However, only certain types of materials must be submitted for prior approval; encouragement is given that other writings which deal with religious disciplines be submitted, but these do not require an *imprimatur* (c. 827, §3). It now appears that they may not be given an *imprimatur* unless they exactly present official church doctrine.

Those books which must have an *imprimatur* fit into these categories:

1. Books of Scripture, which are to receive approval from the Apostolic See or the conference of bishops (c. 825, §1);

2. Prayer books for the public or private use of the faithful, for whom the local ordinary gives the permission (c. 826, §3);

3. Catechisms and other writings dealing with catechetical formation need the local ordinary's permission (c. 827, §1) — however, this appears to mean books which contain the content to be taught, not books of method or lesson plans which are to be used with other, primary sources;

4. Books which are going to be used as textbooks at any level of education in the fields of sacred scripture, theology, canon law, church history, or dealing with religious or moral disciplines (c. 827, §2) — but these are textbooks strictly speaking, which propose the official teaching of the Church, not outside reading, background information for teachers, lesson plans, or the like.

Books which reprint in whole or in part material from the liturgical books of the Church must have an attestation that they correspond with the approved edition; this is to be given by the local ordinary of the place of publication (c. 826, §2).

So far as I can tell from the above, the book under consideration may have some texts reprinted from the liturgical books. For these texts, an attestation should be given that they do correspond with the approved edition.

It is not absolutely clear from the question that the book is intended solely to *prepare* for celebrations of the Word and will not be used as a book of service during such celebrations. If it is intended as a book of service, it would become a prayer book which needs an *imprimatur* (c. 826, §3) which the local ordinary could give. If the book is not intended as a prayer book for the public or private use of the faithful, it would not need an *imprimatur*.

The proposed work is not a catechism, and is not intended as a text book which would present official church doctrine. It, therefore, does not require an *imprimatur* on this score. Indeed, if recent events do reflect the proper understanding of the *imprimatur* (i.e., a guarantee that the book does indeed

230

present official church doctrine as the Church understands it, and not private opinion), then I doubt if the book should be given an *imprimatur* unless it really is a book of service.

On the other hand, the book is proposed as one which would deal with Sacred Scripture (Liturgy of the Word) and would be of special concern to religion for children. Canon 827, §3 encourages that it be submitted to the judgment of the local ordinary, even though current events seem to imply that the local ordinary's judgment should be expressed in some manner other than the *imprimatur*. There is no indication in the law that I can find, however, which would specify how the judgment is to be expressed.

In the old code secular clergy were required to obtain permission from their local ordinary (and religious from their superior) in order to publish anything even of a profane nature (c. 1386, §1). This was not an *imprimatur* as such, and was sometimes expressed by an *"imprimi potest"* and at other times by a letter from the bishop or superior. In keeping with this previous practice, which is no longer called for under the new code, it might be possible to implement the encouragement of canon 827, §3 by a letter of introduction. The letter could indicate that the bishop has reviewed the book and is pleased to present it for the use for which it is intended, namely to prepare celebrations of the Liturgy of the Word for children.

James H. Provost [1984]

BOOK IV

THE OFFICE OF SANCTIFYING IN THE CHURCH

CANONS 835 AND 838

BLESSING OF OILS BY THE BISHOP IN A PARISH CHURCH

May I invite the bishop to come for the blessing of the renovated parish church, and on that occasion bless oils — including chrism? There is a special new setting for the oils in the renovated church. This would take place during November (i.e., outside the usual time for blessing oils).

OPINION

The bishop is to be concerned with promoting the whole liturgical life of the diocese (c. 835, §1), and is himself bound to the liturgical norms adopted by the Apostolic See and the conference of bishops (c. 838). The liturgical norms — in the Ceremonial for Bishops, the Roman Pontifical, and the Roman Missal — specify that the blessing of oils is to be done on Holy Thursday at the Chrism Mass, or some date close to Holy Thursday selected for the convenience of the presbyterate and the diocese. The rubrics for the Chrism Mass itself make it very clear that the celebration is a diocesan celebration, not a private celebration or one which is for a limited group such as an individual parish.

While there is no direct prohibition which would keep a bishop from blessing the oils, and particularly chrism, at some other time (especially in a case of emergency), the mind of the legislator is quite clear: the blessing is to be in the context of Lent, and preferably of the Sacred Triduum; and it is to be diocesan-wide in intent.

The blessing of oils at some other time is intended as part of the liturgical action of a sacrament, such as oil of catechumens being blessed by a priest as part of a baptism, or the oil of the sick being blessed by a priest as part of the anointing of the sick. The blessing of oils in these contexts is presented as having significance as part of the liturgical action itself, and does not focus on the oils as such.

It is my canonical opinion, therefore, that it would be inappropriate for the bishop to bless oils on the occasion of visiting a parish, or on the occasion of the restoration of the interior of a church and its arrangements for the preservation of the oils. Rather, this might be classified as an abuse, since the blessing would be neither diocesan-wide and (in November) during the proper liturgical season, nor related to a specific sacramental celebration.

What the bishop could do is bless the receptacles for the oils, and even preside at a somewhat formal pouring of new oils into the receptacles. If you do not have enough blessed oils on hand for the sign value of the action, you may want to mix blessed oils with new oil in advance, or even in the process, similar to the practice for increasing the water in a holy water font which had run low, and there was no one available to bless new holy water.

James H. Provost [1993]

CANONS 838, §4 AND 899

RIGHT OF A BISHOP TO OVERSEE THE LITURGY

A question has arisen concerning the right of the diocesan bishop to oversee the celebration of the Eucharist in his diocese. A local association of the faithful, lacking ecclesiastical approbation, has invited a priest from outside the diocese to celebrate Mass for them. This association, however, refuses to identify the priest. The bishop is concerned over who this priest is and whether he is abiding by diocesan policies regarding the liturgy. What is the right of the bishop to insist on learning the identity of the priest?

OPINION

The question to be looked at concerning this matter is that of the unknown celebrant. What are the rights of the bishop in this matter? Does he have a right to insist on knowing who the celebrant is, where he comes from, etc.?

A number of Roman documents, as well as the Code of Canon Law, are pertinent.

The Congregation for Bishops, in the *Directory on the Pastoral Ministry of Bishops* (February 22, 1973) spoke of the role of the bishop in the sacramental life of the faith community. Article 87 is especially applicable. It reads:

Whenever the sacraments are celebrated, the bishop, as the one responsible for regulating their administration according to the norms established by competent authority, sees to it that the ministers and faithful understand and express the religious meaning of the sacraments for both the individual and the community . . .

a) The bishop exercises vigilance that preaching and pastoral practice relating to the sacraments, especially baptism, penance, the Eucharist, and marriage, are in complete harmony with the Church's teaching.

233

b) He sees to it that these sacraments are celebrated by all rightly, carefully, and with the greatest reverence, in keeping with the rites recently restored by the Apostolic See. . . .

Clearly this statement can be seen as resting on conciliar statements. Again for example, *Lumen gentium*, article 26:

Every lawful celebration of the Eucharist is regulated by the bishop, to whom is committed the office of offering to the divine majesty the worship of Christian religion and of administering it in accordance with the Lord's commandments and the Church's law, as further specified by his particular judgment for his diocese.

Finally the decree *Cum Missale Romanum*, from the Congregation for Divine Worship (March 27, 1975), concerning the revised Roman Missal, stated in article 59:

Every authentic celebration of the Eucharist is directed by the bishop, either in person or through the presbyters, who are his helpers. . . .

Canon 838 of the revised Code of Canon Law reflects this teaching. The canon states that the ordering and guidance of the sacred liturgy depends solely upon the authority of the Church, namely the Apostolic See and, as provided by law, that of the diocesan bishop. This same canon later states that within the limits of his competence, it belongs to the diocesan bishop to lay down for the church entrusted to his care liturgical regulations which are binding on all.

The premise underlying this norm is that of *Christus Dominus* 8, where there is a presumption that the bishop has all the power over the governance of the liturgy that is required for the exercise of his pastoral office, always excepting cases reserved to the supreme authority or other ecclesiastical authority. Further, this canon, in section 4, sees it as belonging to the diocesan bishop to enact liturgical norms within his competence. The regulation of the liturgy is no longer exclusively or uniquely the responsibility of the Apostolic See (as provided in the 1917 code, c. 1257). Note also that the final clause of canon 838, §4, holds all bound by diocesan liturgical law. It avoids the possibility of exceptions to or exemptions from the binding force of such laws. This is in harmony with the conciliar decree that religious exemption from diocesan authority is not applicable to the public exercise of divine worship.

Canon 899, §2 is also applicable. It reads:

In the Eucharistic assembly the people of God are called together under the presidency of the bishop or a *priest authorized by him* (emphasis added) . . .

This canon, based on the magisterial teaching as exampled above, clearly places on the bishop the responsibility of overseeing the administration of the sacraments in the local church entrusted to his care. This responsibility would be limited only by universal church law which reserves something to the Apostolic See or the conference of bishops. Basically, then, it pertains to the local diocesan bishop to see to the proper celebration of the sacraments, especially the Eucharist. This is not so much a matter of law as it is a responsibility merely reflected by the law.

It must also be kept in mind that there is no such thing as a private celebration of the Eucharist. By its very nature the Eucharist is a public act of prayer and worship. Note canon 899, §1:

> The celebration of the Eucharist is an action of Christ and of the Church. . . .

Thus, while an association of the faithful may arrange for a priest to offer Mass for them, it still remains a public act of worship. "Public" need not refer to a celebration open to the general public such as would be the case in a Sunday liturgy offered in a parish church. It is much broader than that. Essentially there is no such thing as a "private" Mass. Indeed there may be a celebration of Mass without a congregation or with a very limited group, such as we are dealing with here. Yet it remains public. It is an action of the Church and not merely of that select group present. Therefore, it necessarily remains under the jurisdiction of the local bishop, exercising his responsibility to oversee the administration of the sacraments. All celebrations of the Eucharist remain under the care of the diocesan bishop; there are no exemptions.

Given all this, I cannot see how one could possibly expect the bishop to fulfill this responsibility, as stated in canon law and founded on magisterial teaching, and at the same time not be allowed to know the name of the celebrant. Obviously it remains the right of the bishop to know the celebrant so as to be able to ascertain that he is a priest in good standing, with the requisite faculties. Canon 903 states that a priest is to be permitted to celebrate the Eucharist, even if unknown to the rector of the church, provided he presents commendatory letters (not more than a year old) or if it can be prudently judged he is not debarred from celebrating. How can this possibly be done if he remains a mystery — not revealing his name or whence he comes?

Concerning preaching the Word of God, a few canons are applicable here. Canon 764 states that priests and deacons, by the fact of ordination, possess the faculty to preach everywhere *unless* that faculty has been restricted or taken away by competent authority, or unless express permission is required by particular law. Thus, any priest or deacon in good standing would enjoy the faculty of preaching the Word. He has this by the very fact of his ordination.

Canon 772 goes on to state that the diocesan bishop may still regulate preaching in his territory by issuing suitable norms. While he does not grant faculties to preach any longer, the bishop does retain the authority to regulate the preaching in the diocese entrusted to his care. Canon 756, §2 points out that the diocesan bishops "exercise this responsibility [in their local dioceses] since within it they are the moderators of the entire ministry of the word."

Again, these canons highlight the responsibility of the bishop. This is seen now not only in the sacramental life of the community but also in proclaiming the Word. And thus again I must ask, how can one expect the diocesan bishop to fulfill this responsibility when denied the right to know the name and credentials of an individual coming into the diocese? Obviously he cannot.

Bottom line: Clearly it is the right of the bishop to insist on knowing who the celebrant is in the situation presented here, and what are his credentials. This right can certainly be seen as flowing from the canons cited here, which in turn are rooted in the responsibility given the bishop to oversee the sacramental life of the local church. The code does not explicitly state that the bishop has a right to know who the celebrant is. Why, one might ask? I think it is more than safe to say the legislator would not even imagine such a situation arising. It is just a "given" that if the bishop is to oversee the sacramental life of the local church entrusted to him then he would have a right to know who was functioning within his diocese. While the law may grant certain rights to a priest to celebrate the Eucharist and to preach, as discussed above, this certainly would still have to be seen within the context of the bishop's role of overseeing the local church entrusted to his care.

James I. Donlon [1992]

CANON 843

DENIAL OF A SACRAMENT WITHOUT DUE PROCESS

Can an individual be denied the sacraments without first having gone through a due process proceeding?

OPINION

The answer to this question depends on the case. If the denial of the sacraments in question is an *ad hoc* decision of a single minister, then no formal process has to be observed. If, however, the denial of a sacrament is a penal measure which is intended to be enforced by all ministers, then most certainly a judicial or administrative procedure must be observed.

Canon 843, §1 permits an ordained minister to refuse a sacrament in three cases: if the faithful ask for it at an inappropriate time, if they are not properly disposed, or if they are prohibited by law from receiving it. Any one of these three reasons is sufficient for a minister in a particular case to refuse a sacrament to a person without a canonical process. Some examples may be helpful.

1. *Inappropriate time:* A person, not in danger of death, asks to receive confirmation at a time that is not convenient for the bishop. The bishop could lawfully refuse on the grounds that the time is inappropriate.

2. *Lack of proper disposition:* A confessor determines that a penitent has no sorrow for sin, or lacks a firm purpose of amendment. The confessor should deny absolution due to a lack of proper disposition on the part of the penitent (cc. 959; 980; 987).

3. *Prohibited by law:* A person asks to receive Holy Communion outside Mass, but has no just reason for the request. The request should be denied because the law requires a just cause to receive Communion outside the Eucharistic celebration (c. 918).

In all these cases the refusal of the sacrament is really only intended to be a delay in administering it. The person in question does not lose the right to the sacrament, but is delayed from receiving it until he or she requests it at an appropriate time, or attains the proper disposition, or meets the requirements of law.

With particular reference to the Eucharist and the anointing of the sick, the code calls for the denial of these sacraments to a person who "obstinately persists in manifest sin" (cc. 915 and 1007). These canons may in a particular case be applied by a minister without a process. In effect, the minister is judging here that the person lacks the proper disposition because he or she is in a state of grave sin. Moreover, because the serious sin is manifest, the giving of the sacraments would likely cause scandal. However, a process would be necessary if the bishop or other competent ecclesiastical authority were to ban all ministers in his jurisdiction from administering these sacraments to that person. Such a ban would be tantamount to the imposition of a penalty.

For example, in a certain country the president is a military dictator who is hated by the populace because he rules by virtue of force, kidnapping, torture, and murder. At a public liturgy the president approaches the bishop to receive Holy Communion. The bishop refuses because he has serious doubts whether the president is properly disposed and he judges that, due to the probability of scandal, the common good outweighs the right of the individual to the sacrament in this particular situation (c. 223, §2).

On the other hand, if the ordinary of the dictator wanted all Catholic ministers to deny him Communion until he reforms, a penal process would be necessary. A general ban on the reception of the sacraments is a penalty. Indeed, it is a principal effect of interdict and excommunication. No penalty can be imposed without legitimately observing a canonical penal process. If the process is not observed, there is no penalty. All ministers could continue licitly to administer the sacraments to that person.

Canon 213 establishes the right of the faithful to the sacraments. If this right is to be denied, it can only be done in accord with the law. Canon 221, §1 states that the faithful are entitled to vindicate and defend their rights before a competent tribunal. If this procedural right is to have any meaning at all, it simply must apply in the case of the denial of one or more sacraments as a penal measure. Moreover, even before the competent ordinary initiates an administrative or judicial penal process, he must first observe the requirements of canon 1341 on the steps to be taken to avoid a penal process.

If a person believes that the sacraments are unjustly being denied by a minister, he or she should go to another minister to receive them, or write a complaint to the minister's ecclesiastical superior. If the case warrants it, the person might even initiate a penal process against the minister himself for abuse of ecclesiastical power or function (c. 1389).

John M. Huels, O.S.M. [1991]

ANOTHER OPINION

Canon 843, using double negatives, spells out three conditions which would have to be fulfilled before the sacraments are to be administered to a person: 1) that person must ask for the sacraments at an appropriate time; 2) be properly disposed; and 3) not be prohibited by law from receiving them. The sacraments are not to be denied otherwise. Since their denial is an odious matter — restricting rights, the absence of any one or more of these conditions would have to be interpreted strictly (c. 18) and, indeed, unless there was proof that one of them was missing, the person requesting could not be denied the sacraments. It would also seem that, because of the fundamental dignity of the human person (cf., c. 208), there is a general presumption to the effect that those who approach the sacraments would do so for the right reasons.

The Conditions

Each of these three conditions could be examined briefly.

(1) The "appropriate time" could refer to the liturgical season, the time of day, or the actual moment (for instance, just before the celebration of Mass). It could also refer to a mandatory preparation period prescribed by particular

law.

(2) It should be noted that the code uses the expression "properly disposed." It does not speak of being "in the state of grace," because in certain instances pertaining to the sacraments of penance and the anointing of the sick, the celebration of the sacrament would lead to the restoration of this state. In other words, the person approaching the sacraments must do so for the right reasons. The question of "disposition" would not refer, it seems, to a person's political or social opinions. At least it would not directly do so. It might, however, be applicable to external actions which have a direct negative influence upon the faith community (cf., c. 1399).

(3) The third condition, "not prohibited by law" could refer to a number of elements either of universal law or of particular law or proper law. Such prohibitions could take the form of impediments, incapacities of various types, or prohibitions imposed as a consequence of penalty duly inflicted or arising from other sources.

Admission to the Eucharist

When it comes to admission to the Eucharist, canon 912 states that "any baptized person who is not prohibited by law can and must be admitted to Holy Communion." Consequently, the minister of the Eucharist would have to be certain that the person who is being turned away is indeed prohibited by law from receiving Communion.

Canon 915 spells out four conditions which must be applied simultaneously before a person can be refused the Eucharist. That person must "(1) obstinately (2) persist in (3) manifest (4) grave sin." A person would not be considered to be "obstinately" persisting in grave sin without having previously been admonished to cease the behavior. On occasion, the law even calls for two admonitions before penalties can be imposed (see, for instance, c. 697, 2° and c. 1347, §1). The question of "grave sin" could be considered in two ways: objectively, certain actions are considered to be gravely sinful in themselves; or, subjectively, the person who performed the action does not consider that it is sinful, let alone gravely sinful. Unless the element of public scandal enters into play, it would seem that the subjective evaluation of the situation would apply.

Absolution in Confession

As regards the sacrament of penance, canon 980 provides that the confessor is not to refuse or delay absolution if he has no doubt about the disposition of a penitent. Again, it would seem that the presumption is in favor of the penitent.

General Rights of the Faithful

Looking at other parts of the code, we note that canon 221, §3 provides that the "faithful have the right not to be punished with canonical penalties except in accord with the norm of law." The question to be asked, then, when a person is to be denied the sacraments, is whether such an action is indeed a "penalty" in the strict sense of the term, or rather some other type of "medicinal" action whose primary purpose is to help that person become properly disposed.

The term "due process" is often used to refer to "the norm of law." However, it does not appear as such in the Code of Canon Law. Rather, it is a concept that arises from other sources, particularly from secular law. It usually implies a right to be present, to be heard, and to controvert statements made against oneself. It would not of itself, however, imply the right to a full canonical trial since restrictions may also be imposed by an administrative act (cf., c. 1342).

Even though a full canonical process (either penal or administrative) is not required by law before a person is denied admission to the sacraments, someone whose rights are restricted or denied would at least have the basic natural right to be heard before a decision is made. Such a right is referred to generally in the code as the "right of defense" (cf., cc. 1598; 1620; etc.).

Two examples would help to illustrate the principle: 1) If, for instance, there are diocesan regulations prohibiting the celebration of marriage during the Sunday liturgy, then a person who asked to have a wedding celebrated at that time would not be asking for it at an opportune time, and would not be able to be married at that particular moment. Certainly, no process would be necessary in such a case to refuse the celebration of the sacrament. 2) Nor would a process be required if a person who wished to be married was bound by an impediment of divine law.

Public and private denial of the sacraments

One additional factor to be kept in mind is whether the person in question is being denied the sacraments in a public or in a private manner. If the denial is public, the prescriptions of canon 220 would have to be observed: protecting that person's reputation and right to privacy.

Because of the reluctance of the law to impose penalties and to restrict rights, it would seem that the denial of the sacraments should be a rather rare occurrence, unless the situation is public and calls for remedial action for the good of the community. Thus, for instance, on January 7, 1991, Bishop M. Hesayne, Bishop of Viedma in Argentina, proclaimed that in accordance with the norms of canon 1332, those who during the military regime and the antisubversive campaign in Argentina (on either side of the issue) have seriously and notoriously violated human rights and have not yet publicly manifested a

240

sufficient degree of repentance, are not to be admitted to the sacraments (in *La Documentation Catholique* 88 [1991] 361-362).

If a person had been notified privately about the risk of being denied the sacraments and did nothing to remedy the situation, as could be the case with persons continuing to live in public concubinage in a small parish where everyone is known and who nevertheless have been receiving Communion publicly, then, if these private admonitions were to no avail and the couple came forward to receive Communion, they could be turned away since the situation is of public knowledge.

However, in every case, it would seem not only appropriate, but even necessary, to contact the person in question beforehand to give a right of response. Otherwise, the person should be admitted to the sacraments, at least on that occasion.

Francis G. Morrisey, O.M.I. [1991]

Canon 844

Diocesan Bishop's Authority on Eucharistic Sharing

What is the authority of the diocesan bishop to permit access to the Eucharist by baptized non-Catholics on certain occasions? Can this be considered on a case-by-case basis?

Opinion

1. *Situation.* Two situations are foreseen in the canon.

a. Danger of Death. In this situation, it is not necessary for the Catholic minister (priest or other authorized minister of the Eucharist) to consult the bishop; the law itself provides that if the other conditions are met, the baptized non-Catholic may receive the Eucharist (as well as penance and anointing).

b. Other grave necessity. What constitutes such "grave necessity" was originally given as prison and during persecution (1967 *Ecumenical Directory*, n. 55). This understanding can be taken to be a material interpretation (i.e., these material conditions must be present for "grave necessity" to exist). A more spiritual interpretation was provided by the June 1, 1972 "Instruction Concerning Cases When Other Christians May Be Admitted to Eucharistic Communion in the Catholic Church." In this document grave necessity could be considered to be present when such Christians "experience a serious spiritual need for the eucharistic sustenance'' (n. 4, b).

The 1972 Instruction clarified that the 1967 *Directory* had allowed ''fairly wide discretionary power to the episcopal authority in judging whether the necessary conditions are present for these exceptional cases'' (n. 6). While the conference of bishops could set some general guidelines for recurring cases, it was left to the diocesan bishop to make the determination in practical cases.

The 1983 code continues this position; it even makes it clearer that determining when ''grave necessity'' is present is up to the diocesan bishop and the conference of bishops. Both are competent to determine ''grave necessity,'' so that it is possible for a diocesan bishop to act even if the conference has not done so. The conference may also act even if individual diocesan bishops have not done so in their own dioceses, although it is possible for a diocesan bishop to dispense from such norms of the conference (c. 88). ''Grave necessity'' can be interpreted, in keeping with the precedents set in the postconciliar documents, in either a material or a spiritual sense; the code does not specify further, so it would be up to the free determination of the respective authority (diocesan bishop or conference of bishops) to do so.

2. *Access to own minister.* The canon repeats a provision of the previous documents, namely that the other Christian does not have access to his or her own minister when approaching the Catholic minister.

There is a significant difference between the 1983 code and its predecessors on this point, however. The 1967 *Directory* and 1972 Instruction both required that the lack of access to the person's own minister must be *''diu''* — for a notable period of time. There was considerable debate as to whether this was chronological time, and what would constitute it (a day, a week, etc.), or whether it was to be considered spiritually, in the same way ''time'' has been interpreted in relation to absolution of censures by a confessor when it would be a spiritual hardship for a penitent to wait until the confessor had recourse to an authority with the faculty to remit the censure (1917 code, c. 2254). The debate about *diu*, however, is moot because canon 844 of the 1983 code does not contain the word. It only says *''qui ad suae communitatis ministerium accedere nequeant,''* with no indication as to how long this condition must exist in order to receive Eucharist in the Catholic Church.

3. *Faith requirement.* To receive the Eucharist in the Catholic Church another Christian must ''manifest Catholic faith'' in the sacrament. For the Orthodox, the 1967 *Directory* indicated some sharing was permissible and the 1972 Instruction clarified that Orthodox Christians are to be presumed to have the same faith in the Eucharist as Catholics. For other Christians, the 1972 Instruction directed that ''the person concerned is asked to manifest a faith in the Eucharist in conformity with that of the Church, i.e., in the Eucharist as Christ instituted it and as the Catholic Church hands it on'' (n. 5). This would

not seem to require an ability to give a detailed theological explanation of the Eucharist (i.e., to explain or even understand transubstantiation as a theologian might), but at least the same faith in the Eucharist as would be required of a Catholic (cf., 1983 code, c. 913 concerning the minimum understanding required for first reception of Eucharist by children).

How this faith is to be manifested is not specified in the law. This is something the bishop could specify, whether by requiring an explicit statement of faith in advance of reception, or by the same standard of an attitude of reverence and devotion as is normally used at every celebration of the Eucharist in admitting persons presumed to be baptized Catholics.

4. *Properly disposed.* This may be the most difficult element to determine in specific cases. The proper disposition of a Catholic is very difficult to determine objectively. The code requires that if one is conscious of grave sin, the person is not to approach the Eucharist without first seeking absolution, unless "a grave cause is present" and there is no opportunity of confessing (c. 916). However, such a person can approach the Eucharist (and therefore, by law be considered to be "properly disposed") even under this exceptional case (i.e., not able to receive absolution) if the person makes an act of perfect contrition. So there is no precise way to judge externally whether a person is properly disposed for the Eucharist, for making an act of perfect contrition is always considered a possibility by the law.

To determine the proper disposition of Catholics, generally that person is considered to be properly disposed who is living a life in conformity with the usual standards of Catholic morality in the area. The question of divorced and remarried persons, or those who are married outside Church, is a complicating factor here, for the new code does not impose any canonical sanction on them and their situation must be judged according to pastoral-moral considerations rather than canonical ones when it comes to receiving the Eucharist.

The canonical norms which do determine the outer limits of disposition are found in canon 915. To be refused the Eucharist, even at the Communion station, are those who are excommunicated or interdicted — but only if the censure has been declared or imposed, not if it has been incurred automatically (*latae sententiae*) and is occult. Also to be refused are those who obstinately persist in manifest grave sin. Since the canon is a restriction on a right (the right being expressed in c. 912; see c. 18 on interpretation of canons which restrict the free exercise of rights), each of these qualifiers must be present: "obstinate," which requires an advance warning to differentiate the person from a recidivist; "grave sin," which requires serious matter, sufficient reflection and full consent of the will; "manifest," which means the grave sin is evident to others as a grave sin.

It seems to me that a non-Catholic Christian who is living a life in keeping with the standards of morality observed among Catholics who are admitted to the Eucharist in the same locality would be "properly disposed." Whether the marital status of the individual constitutes obstinate perseverance in manifest grave sin would have to be judged according to the case.

There is one other point which may be of some interest from this canon. It indicates that admission to the sacraments of Eucharist, penance and anointing is possible not only on an individual, case-by-case basis but also according to general norms which may be applied for recurring cases. However, such general norms (as differentiated from a case-by-case approach) require advance consultation with the local competent authority of the respective churches involved.

Finally, to answer your questions, these are my comments.

1. Is it permissible for the local ordinary to grant the baptized non-Catholic permission to receive the Eucharist? My answer is yes, in keeping with the above understanding of the canon.

Would this apply to such occasions as a Cursillo (or similar spiritual renewal event), or reception of Eucharist by a baptized non-Catholic parent on the occasion of the baptism or First Communion of a child in the Catholic Church, or reception of the Eucharist by a non-Catholic spouse on the occasion of a wedding? Yes, provided the non-Catholic is baptized, and that the other conditions indicated above are verified. If the bishop adopts the spiritual interpretation of the "grave necessity" in keeping with the 1972 Instruction, these cases would seem to be possibilities, all other things being equal.

In your letter, you indicated the case of a non-baptized non-Catholic spouse seeking to receive Eucharist on the occasion of a wedding. Clearly this is not permissible, since one must be baptized in order to be admitted to any of the other sacraments (c. 842, §1).

2. Can the diocesan bishop do this, not as a general permission, but in a particular case? Again, the answer is yes. He can certainly do it in particular cases. If he wishes to publish norms on this for the diocese, however, he must first engage in the proper advance consultation with the competent authorities of the other churches which would be affected.

He can also establish norms (with the proviso of the same advance consultation) for recurring cases in the diocese. This was done some years ago in some dioceses in this country.

James H. Provost [1984]

CANON 844

RECEPTION OF THE SACRAMENTS BY CATHOLICS IN
EASTERN ORTHODOX CHURCHES

There are locations and times when no canonically approved Catholic priest is available to minister to members of the Armed Forces. The same could be said of other cases, such as in prisons, hospitals, nursing homes, and on cruise ships. In such instances can a Catholic receive the sacraments validly and licitly from a priest of the Eastern Orthodox Churches?

OPINION

The pre-Vatican II legislation forbade the administration of the sacraments to non-Catholics, even though they were in good faith and requested the sacraments, unless they had previously renounced their errors and obtained reconciliation with the Catholic Church.

This norm, however, excepted the Eastern Christians in danger of death and the Orthodox students attending Catholic schools (cf., *Responsa Congregationis pro Fidei Doctrina*: November 15, 1941 and March 27, 1957).

Since Vatican II this matter of *communicatio in sacris* has been increasingly a subject of paramount importance (cf., *Unitatis redintegratio*, in *Enchiridion Vaticanum* (=EV) nn. 528 & 549; *Orientalium Ecclesiarum*, EV nn. 487-490; *Ad Totam Ecclesiam*, EV 3, nn. 2800-2845; *In Quibus Rerum*, EV 4, nn. 1634-1640).

With the promulgation of the Code of Canon Law (*CIC*) in 1983 and the Code of Canons of the Eastern Churches (*CCEO*) in 1990, the norms regulating this sacramental sharing are embodied in *CIC* canon 844 and *CCEO* canon 671.

The *communicatio in sacris* consists of the sharing of liturgical worship or the participation in the sacramental mysteries of another Church. The active *communicatio* is the acceptance/admission of non-Catholics to a Catholic act of worship, while the passive one is the acceptance/admission of Catholics to a non-Catholic act of worship.

The above two canons — *CIC* canon 844 and *CCEO* canon 671 — refer to the possibility of *communicatio* in the sacraments of penance, Eucharist and anointing of the sick. These sacraments concern the Catholic faithful who are physically or morally impeded from approaching a Catholic minister (bishop or presbyter).

The physical impossibility is clear. Moral theologians have offered us several cases where it is morally difficult to contact a Catholic minister for the sacrament of penance. One could add some hypotheses for the Eucharist and the anointing of the sick. For instance, during a persecution, to contact a Catholic priest would be dangerous for both the faithful and the minister. A

245

necessity or a genuine spiritual advantage is called for in order that the Catholic faithful can licitly ask for the said sacraments. We can affirm that the sacrament of penance is necessary for the faithful in the state of serious sin, and the anointing of the sick could be said necessary in the case of a serious illness. As for the Eucharist, it seems difficult to offer some conclusions: perhaps, when the faithful have been kept away from the sacrament for a long time, or because of sickness or in some particular circumstance.

On the other hand, it seems easier to offer cases of genuine spiritual advantage. The word "genuine" connotes here a restrictive value, while the concept of spiritual advantage is always wide and subjective.

It is not enough for the Catholic faithful to be in particular circumstances and moved by an adequate motive. It is also necessary that any danger of error and indifferentism is avoided and this not only by the Catholic faithful who asks for the sacraments, but even by the community to which the individual belongs.

After having presented one's circumstances, the motives and conditions, the Catholic faithful is required to approach a specific minister. The two canons — Latin and Eastern — specify the lawful ministers to approach as "those in whose Churches these sacraments are valid."

The Vatican II fathers have given us the distinction of Eastern Churches and western ecclesial communities. The ecclesial communities that have valid priesthood, and therefore, celebrate validly the Eucharist, are considered Churches. All the other organized groups should be considered as ecclesial communities — without valid priesthood.

The present norms then exclude the ecclesial communities, and restrict *communicatio* of the Catholic faithful to the Churches whose sacraments — penance, Eucharist and anointing of the sick — are valid.

The Churches in question consist of: the Assyrian Church which rejected the decisions of the Council of Ephesus in 431; the Ancient Oriental Churches — Coptic, Ethiopian, Syriac, Malankarese and Armenian — which objected to the decisions of the Council of Chalcedon in 451; and the Churches of Byzantine tradition.

To conclude, the reception of the sacraments by the Catholic faithful in Eastern Orthodox Churches is permitted for the sacraments of penance, Eucharist and anointing of the sick, under determined conditions and in well-restricted circumstances. The conditions and the circumstances ought to be evaluated by the recipient himself/herself.

George D. Gallaro [1991]

ANOTHER OPINION

The conciliar decree *Orientalium Ecclesiarum* shows the special place of the Orthodox Churches in Christian life as an obvious fact of life. From a Catholic perspective, these Churches are regarded as sister Churches almost in full communion with the Catholic Church. Special provisions are made regarding Catholics receiving the sacraments of penance, the Eucharist, and the anointing of the sick from Orthodox ministers (*OE* 27). These issues are directly included in the *Ecumenical Directory* (*AAS* 59 [1967] 574-592). The above cited documents provide the background for canon 844, which leaves virtually intact the teaching and legislation of Vatican II on these points. The proposed canon 797 of the 1980 *Schema* appears with some modifications in the 1983 code as canon 844. Efforts were made in the discussion of this proposed canon 797 to impose more severe restrictions in sharing the sacraments under discussion with Orthodox Christians.

The suggested restrictions were rejected because they were contrary to the already *ius vigens* stated in *OE* and *ED*. Thus the more liberally stated text of canon 844 was adopted (*Communicationes* 15, n. 2, 175-176).

Similarly, the council made special provisions regarding inter-ecclesial marriages, i.e., Catholics who marry an Orthodox Christian in an Orthodox Church can do so validly without a dispensation from the requirement of form (*OE* 18).

The code recognizes the reception of certain spiritual goods, including the sacraments and word of God, as stemming from divine right, by divine ordinance (c. 213). These Christian rights are not easily restricted and can only be limited by duly authorized ecclesiastical authority within their competence, which restrictions are to be interpreted strictly (cc. 18 and 841). Mere disciplinary predispositions cannot interfere with the exercise of a divine right. An overriding serious reason is required for such ecclesiastical interference in a constitutive right. Ecclesial communion is one such overriding consideration. The question of full ecclesial communion is described in canon 205, thus suggesting that some of the Christian faithful might be in communion, but not in full communion. One easily sees the inconsistent use of these terms throughout different books of the code, leading to ambiguity and very different possible interpretations, some perhaps bordering on canonical nominalism and/or legalism.

For the purpose of this brief study, I will cut through these distinctions and simply say that the primary intent of the code is to be involved with Christians in full communion even though the phrase "in communion" is used perhaps as a short cut version for "in full communion," and that ministers, rites, rights and obligations, etc., are meant to mean of the fully and only Catholic sort although this is not consistently, explicitly and persuasively stated. Let context suggest proper interpretation!

Hence at the practical level, when giving pastoral advice to a Catholic about rights and obligations relative to the reception of the Eucharist and Sunday Mass observance, I would keep in mind the last canon of the code and recall that one does not easily limit rights or impose obligations when dealing with the salvation of souls, "which is always the supreme law of the Church" (c. 1752).

Simply put, canon 844, §2 states that a Catholic may receive penance, Eucharist and anointing of the sick from a validly ordained non-Catholic minister whenever necessity requires or genuine spiritual advantage suggests provided that religious error or indifference is not involved. At this point the canon does not distinguish between the Orthodox and other non-Catholic Christians, although as the text of the canon moves from point to point it clearly distinguishes between the Orthodox and other non-Catholic Christians, allowing a Catholic minister to provide these sacraments to an Orthodox Christian upon request, whereas the parallel provision for other non-Catholic Christians is more restrictive. The point I make here is that sacramental sharing with the Orthodox is more open than with others from the canonical perspective.

The *coetus* which formulated canon 1248 regarding fulfillment of the precept to participate in Mass in a Catholic rite on Sundays and Holy Days discussed making reference to Orthodox liturgies in the canon. The *coetus* was satisfied by simply referring to *ED* I, n. 47, which states that a Catholic who occasionally is present at an Orthodox liturgy on a day of precept is held to no further obligation (*Communicationes* 12, n. 2, 362). This section of *ED* I also includes the recommendations that in the absence of a Catholic liturgy, a Catholic might worship in an Orthodox liturgy, without imposing the obligation to do so. *ED* I, n. 50, points out a number of justifying causes which connect with the above references, i.e., the exercise of a public office or duty, relationship, friendship, a desire for greater understanding, etc. The inclusion of the "etc." into the text gives this a very broad interpretation indeed! However, *ED* I, n. 44, is considerably more restrictive when it comes to receiving the above mentioned sacraments from the Orthodox. Apart from necessity it requires a just cause and provides the following as just causes: moral and material impossibility from receiving these sacraments from a Catholic minister, thus depriving a Catholic of these spiritual fruits without a justification for a longer period of time.

Is a Catholic obliged to attend and participate in an Orthodox liturgy on a Sunday in order to fulfill the Sunday obligation, absent a Catholic priest? In view of the above mentioned predispositions of the code, I would say no, since this specific obligation is not stated. However, the recommendation of *ED* I, n. 47, remains intact. I would say that a Catholic who actually lives in a place where a Catholic Mass is regularly impossible or difficult to participate in would be remiss if he or she did not avail himself/herself of the Orthodox Eucharistic Liturgy where possible, at least occasionally.

However, even though the *coetus* which drew up canon 844, §2 cites *ED* as its source, it seems to depart from the language of *ED* I, n. 44, by replacing the words "just cause" with the phrase "genuine spiritual advantage." Perhaps to some readers the two phrases have the same meaning, but it seems to me that the earlier term "just cause" is more restrictive than the more pastoral and newer phrase "genuine spiritual advantage." Thus perhaps other less urgent situations might recommend receiving the Eucharist at an Orthodox liturgy, but ecclesiastical documents do not list them while appearing to allude to the possibility. Parallel circumstances relative to participating in the administration of other sacraments, i.e., sacramental godparents, marriage ceremonies, and provisions for interritual households, which could also be inter-ecclesial, regarding fasting and calendar customs, seem to indicate a broad and friendly perspective.

This area is an awkward body of law, filled with occasional tension, some-times with merit and sometimes without, so legal negative responses are often stated while eyes are winked when the contrary is done in practice. One is reminded that on September 5, 1978, Metropolitan Nikodim of Leningrad and Novogrod, in the company of Orthodox clergy as part of his entourage, came to greet the newly elected Pope John Paul I. While in audience the metropolitan suffered a fatal heart attack and was ministered to by the pope. It seems that the pope himself administered the last sacraments in the presence of available Orthodox clergy (cf., V. Rusnack, "Funeral of Metropolitan Nikodim," *Journal of the Moscow Patriarchate*, English edition [November, 1978], 13). This example of sacramental hospitality went beyond the stated norms of *ED* I, apparently with considerable justification in the mind of the then reigning pope who saw other spiritual values as overriding.

James C. Gurzynski [1991]

ANOTHER OPINION

The inquirer posed the question from the perspective of the law of the Latin rite of the Catholic Church. However, a complete answer cannot be given to the query without some consideration of the practice of the Orthodox Churches.

The pertinent law of the Latin rite of the Catholic Church is found in the Code of Canon Law, canon 844. In canon 844, §1 it is noted that Catholics "may licitly receive the sacraments only from Catholic ministers with due regard for §§2, 3, and 4 of this canon and canon 861, §2." Sections 3 and 4 of canon 844 are concerned with Catholic ministers admitting non-Catholics to the sacraments. Canon 861 is concerned with the administration of baptism.

Thus, canons 861 and 844, §§3 and 4 are not germane to this discussion.

The answer to the query is found in canon 844, §2 wherein it is noted:

> Whenever necessity requires or genuine spiritual advantage suggests, and provided that the danger of error or indifferentism is avoided, it is lawful for the faithful for whom it is physically or morally impossible to approach a Catholic minister, to receive the sacraments from non-Catholic ministers in whose Churches these sacraments are valid.

It should be noted that this section of canon 844 delineates five prerequisites to be determined as existent prior to making use of this variance from the norm, i.e., that Catholics receive the sacraments only from Catholic ministers. First, there must be necessity or genuine spiritual advantage which recommends such action. Second, the reception of the sacraments cannot result in error or indifferentism. One can presume that the legislator is concerned for both the recipient and those who are aware of his/her reception. Third, physical or moral impossibility of approaching a Catholic minister must be present. Fourth, the Catholic must seek to receive only those sacraments which are permitted (penance, Eucharist, and anointing of the sick). Finally, the sacraments must be administered by a minister in whose Church these sacraments are considered valid by the Catholic Church.

The inquirer has posed this question in such a fashion that it is apparent that there is a genuine necessity and such reception would be of spiritual advantage to the recipient. The issue of avoiding error or indifferentism cannot be answered in general, but must be addressed *in specie* by the person who desires to receive the sacraments and the community which might administer them. It is equally apparent that, as asked, the question envisions the impossibility of a Catholic receiving any sacraments from a minister of the Catholic Church. Presumedly, the Catholic would request reception of one of these three sacraments which he/she is allowed to receive from a minister in whose Church these sacraments would be considered valid by the Catholic Church, namely, the Orthodox Churches. Therefore, under the conditions presented in the inquiry and according to the law of the Latin rite of the Catholic Church, a Catholic of the Latin rite can licitly receive penance, Eucharist and anointing of the sick from a priest of an Orthodox Church.

One must not, however, ignore the practice of the Eastern and Oriental Orthodox Churches in attempting to respond to the inquiry. Among these Churches, *communicatio in sacris* is regarded as the right and privilege of those who are united not only in faith but with the visible structures of the Church. Based upon this position, only members of Orthodox Churches are permitted to receive the sacraments (mysteries) from priests of these Churches. Thus, Catholics of the Latin rite attempting to make use of canon 844, §2 would probably not be allowed, despite their requests or obvious need, to receive the sacraments in the Eastern and Oriental Orthodox Churches. Moreover, canon 844, §5 states, "Neither the diocesan bishop nor the conference of bishops is to enact general norms except after consultation with at least the local competent authority of the interested non-Catholic Church or community." While section 5 is concerned with "general norms," by way of analogy, one deduces that no individual Catholic should presume to receive any sacraments in an Orthodox Church without first having consulted the local Eastern or Oriental Orthodox minister.

In conclusion, one can answer the inquiry by noting that members of the Latin rite of the Catholic Church are permitted, under special circumstances, by canon 844, §2, to receive the sacraments of penance, Eucharist and anointing of the sick from ministers of the Eastern and Oriental Orthodox Churches and such reception would be both valid and licit. However, any attempt to receive these sacraments in those Churches would probably be met by refusal on the part of the ministers of those Churches.

Herbert J. May [1991]

CANONS 847 AND 785

ANOINTING PARISH LEADERS AND CATECHISTS WITH OIL

What is to be thought of the practice which has developed in some parishes of anointing with oil parish leaders, catechists, etc., when they begin their term of office or at the beginning of the school year?

OPINION

The anointing of teachers, parish council members, parish ministers, etc., at the beginning of their term has become a practice in some places, just as the anointing of sick persons is done in some charismatic groups, without any intention in any of these cases of performing a sacrament. These anointings are not liturgical anointings, but are done for a pastoral purpose.

For such situations it would seem more appropriate to bless the oil which is to be used with a prayer accommodated to the celebration, similar to the provision in the liturgical books for the blessing of oils to be used in baptism and anointing of the sick. This would incorporate the pastoral and catechetical insights contained in the liturgy, and would not be a confusion regarding the oil being used (those blessed by the bishop, such as chrism, and other oils blessed in the actual celebration of a sacrament, being intended for the purposes specified in the liturgical rites themselves).

James H. Provost [1993]

CANON 849

DEFECT OF FORM IN BAPTISM

At the Easter Vigil the celebrant in a particular parish spoke the Trinitarian formula of baptism from the pulpit while the deacon immersed the candidates in the baptismal pool. This was clearly illicit. Was it also invalid? Elsewhere I heard of a priest baptizing using the formula, "You are baptized in the name of the Father, and the Son, and the Holy Spirit." Finally although this case is only hypothetical as far as I know, would it be valid to baptize "in the name of the Creator, the Sustainer, and the Holy Spirit" to avoid using masculine language for God?

OPINION

All the baptisms would be invalid as you have described them. For validity, the minister of baptism must have the intention of doing what the Church does when it baptizes, and must pronounce the Trinitarian formula while pouring true water on the candidate or immersing the candidate in the water. Sprinkling with water is valid but illicit. The formula for validity must express the one baptizing, the one being baptized, the present act of baptizing, and the three divine persons and their unity. (See Eduardo Regatillo, *Ius Sacramentarium*, 3rd ed., Santander: Sal Terrae, 1960, 33, n. 38.)

Regarding the first case, the Trinitarian formula was correct but it did not express the identity of the one baptizing. The minister who pours the water or immerses must be the one who simultaneously pronounces the words. If perchance the deacon who was immersing said the Trinitarian formula and had the intention of baptizing, then the baptisms were validly performed by the deacon. The priest would have been merely announcing the words being said by the deacon for the benefit of the congregation.

Regarding the second case, there are two defects in saying "You are baptized." First, it does not verify who is the one baptizing. Second, because it uses the passive tense, it does not verify that the baptism is an action taking place in the present.

252

Regarding the third case, to change the names of the blessed Trinity would constitute a substantial alteration in the form of baptism. The form pertains to the essence of the rite and is considered to be of divine law. No one but the supreme authority in the Church can alter the requirements for the validity of sacraments (c. 841). "Creator" and "Sustainer" may not be validly substituted for "Father" and "Son" because, despite the intention of the minister (which may be to invoke the persons of the Trinity under different names), he would have no authority to change a sacramental form.

Regarding the identity of the one being baptized (which was not a defect in the case you mentioned), it is not necessary for validity to identify the one being baptized by proper name. It would be valid simply to say, "I baptize you," or "I baptize this person" in the name of the Father, and of the Son, and of the Holy Spirit.

John M. Huels, O.S.M. [1990]

CANONS 850 AND 1117

HOW VARIATIONS IN THE BAPTISMAL FORMULA IMPACT THE VALIDITY OF MARRIAGE

A local Lutheran bishop indicated in the news media that it was not appropriate for Lutheran ministers to be baptizing infants using the formula, "In the name of the Creator, the Redeemer, and the Comforter," rather than the classic Trinitarian formula. The report does suggest that this has been the practice for at least a few Lutheran pastors in the area.

If in the future one of these people (that is an individual who has been baptized with this alternative formula rather than the traditional Trinitarian formula) wishes to enter into a marriage with a Catholic would that person's baptism be considered valid? Is this alternative formula the equivalent of the Trinitarian formula, or would we need to consider the person as non-baptized and obtain a dispensation from disparity of cult?

OPINION

The question has been previously raised about the use of the terms, Creator, Redeemer, and Comforter, in place of the ordinary Trinitarian formula in the rite of baptism. John Huels wrote in the 1990 edition of *Advisory Opinions* (reprinted above) that this mutated formula of baptism is a substantial change in

253

the sacramental form of baptism contrary to the provision of canon 841, and therefore, such baptisms are invalid. The present question relates to a person so baptized and his/her possible marriage to a Catholic in terms of canonical requirements and effect.

On the surface, the response to the present inquiry seems quite simple. Canon 1073 states that a diriment impediment renders a person incapable of contracting marriage validly and canon 1086 establishes what is commonly understood as the impediment of disparity of cult. Hence, one who is bound to the form of marriage simply cannot enter marriage with a non-baptized person unless the impediment of disparity of cult is first dispensed. Thus, a person whose baptism is invalid because the substantially mutated Trinitarian formula was used is simply not sacramentally baptized and the disparity of cult impediment comes into play when marriage with a Catholic is contemplated.

However, the situation is quite complicated because it raises the question of the possibility of the existence of a doubtful impediment resulting from a baptism, the validity of which is in question. Canon 869, §2 implies that baptisms in non-Catholic ecclesial communions are considered valid unless the contrary is established. The *Ecumenical Directory* (*DOL*, 966-967) makes provision to assist in resolving doubts about non-Catholic baptism. The question as posed speaks of a Lutheran who was baptized with the mutated form. The Catholic Church respects valid Lutheran baptisms. But doubts can be raised about the validity of a baptism conferred by anyone if circumstances warrant it. Since canon 1058 speaks of the right to marry, taking into consideration matters which might restrict that right, canon 18 would suggest that some rigor be employed before a Catholic be prevented from marrying a presumably validly baptized non-Catholic Christian, even though a just and reasonable cause is required to permit such marriage as stipulated in canon 1125. Lack of clarity about the non-Catholic's baptismal status touches upon the exercise of the right to marry in the face of a possible diriment impediment.

What if there is a doubt about the existence of the impediment of disparity of cult because the validity of a baptism is questioned? The code itself gives special treatment when it comes to doubtful impediments. Canon 14 states that when there is simply a doubt of fact concerning the existence of an impediment, ordinaries can dispense. Canon 1084, §2 addresses the special question about doubtful impotence, stating that in case of doubt, the marriage should not be impeded. Canon 1091, §4 addresses doubts about certain questions related to the impediment deriving from consanguinity and in these cases states that the marriages are not permitted. These two canons take opposite approaches regarding one's freedom to marry under the specified circumstances involving doubtful impediments to marriage. It should be mentioned that both of these canons speak to matters held to be of divine law and not subject to the ordinary canonical provisions for dispensation.

Canon 1066 states that it must be evident that nothing stands in the way of the valid and licit celebration of a marriage. Hence, in the marriage preparation a non-Catholic's baptismal status needs to be ascertained so that the required permission or dispensation can be obtained in order to marry a Catholic. Canons 1069; 1070; 1111; and 1113 lead to the strong suggestion that it is the pastor of the place where the marriage is to be celebrated who has the ordinary obligation to make sure that canon 1066 is observed. While ordinary care might be required when dealing with non-Catholics baptized in ecclesial communions whose baptism we commonly accept, special circumstances might require more detailed inquiry about the form employed at the non-Catholic's baptism. If it is clear that the mutated Trinitarian formula was used, then the ordinary procedures used for disparity of cult marriages should be engaged. If the situation is doubtful, then canon 14 should be employed. I do not believe that canon 18 could be used as an excuse not to seek out the dispensation mentioned in canon 14, since explicit canonical provision is made to cover the circumstance — a provision which does not limit the rights contemplated by canon 18, but rather indicates how the exercise of the right mentioned in canon 1058 might be facilitated.

Canon 1060 states that marriage enjoys the favor of the law. Canon 1086, which establishes the disparity of cult impediment, refers to canon 1060 when it comes to marriages already celebrated with a non-Catholic whose baptism has doubts attached to it. These marriages also hold the favor of the law "until it is proven with certainty that one party was baptized and the other was not." Should it be discovered after the celebration of the marriage that the non-Catholic party was not validly baptized, i.e., perhaps with the mutated Trinitarian formula, then I suggest that the canons on radical sanation be considered (cc. 1161-1165).

For the record, I found parallel canons in the Code of Canons of the Eastern Churches for all the above cited canons of the 1983 *CIC*, except two. The discussion herein presented could also have been accomplished by referring to the *CCEO* instead of the 1983 *CIC*.

James C. Gurzynski [1992]

CANON 851, 1°

RECEPTION OF BAPTIZED NON-CATHOLICS
WHO ARE DIVORCED AND REMARRIED

1. May baptized non-Catholics who have been divorced and remarried be permitted to be "welcomed into the catechumenate" when their marriage case has not yet been decided by the tribunal?

OPINION

Irrespective of their marital status, baptized non-Catholics may never be "welcomed into the catechumenate" in the technical sense. The *Rite for the Christian Initiation of Adults*, n. 477, states quite explicitly: "Anything that would equate candidates for reception with those who are catechumens is to be absolutely avoided." The "National Statutes for the Catechumenate" of the NCCB emphasize: "Those who have already been baptized in another Church or ecclesial community should not be treated as catechumens or so designated" (30).

However, *RCIA*, n. 478, does permit the use of one or several of the special rites developed for the preparation of baptized but uncatechized (Catholic) adults for Confirmation and Eucharist. Even here, the *RCIA* adds this note: "In all cases, however, discernment should be made regarding the length of catechetical formation required for each individual candidate for reception into the full communion of the Catholic Church." In other words, the process must be individualized, and not made into some pre-packaged program.

Among the rites which can be used during the preparation of such baptized non-Catholics for reception into full communion is the "Rite of Welcoming the Candidates."

So far as I can find, there is nothing in the *RCIA* or in the "National Statutes for the Catechumenate" which prohibits welcoming divorced and remarried baptized non-Catholics as candidates for reception into full communion, even before their marital situation has received a definitive decision from the tribunal. In practice it has often proved beneficial to include as part of the conversion process a careful review of one's life such as is conducted in the process of gathering evidence in a marriage case.

2. If a negative decision is given by the tribunal in the case involving a baptized non-Catholic entering into full communion with the Catholic Church, could the "internal forum solution" be utilized and, if so, on what grounds?

OPINION

This is a very delicate question. It involves two distinct but closely related issues, that of the advisability of admitting persons to full communion in the

256

Catholic Church who will be in an irregular situation insofar as their marital status is concerned, and the possibility of admitting to the Eucharist divorced and remarried persons whose present union is not recognized in the Church.

Let me begin by clarifying that the so-called "internal forum solution," if it is truly internal forum, is not a question for external forum policy. If it is appropriate matter for a policy, it is no longer in the internal forum but has become an external forum activity.

Baptized non-Catholics who enter into full communion with the Catholic Church would be in no different condition in these situations from Catholics who have received a negative decision from the tribunal. However, in preparing such non-Catholics for reception into full ecclesial communion, it would be important to explain to them the pastoral practice of the Church for Catholics in such a situation.

James H. Provost [1989]

CANON 868

QUESTION OF CATHOLIC BAPTISM

A Catholic priest-chaplain in a Catholic hospital in Germany during an air raid baptized all the infants in the nursery. Among these infants was a baby of parents who were not Catholic. He was not raised a Catholic, and he has been married successively twice in the Lutheran church. His current marriage is to a Catholic, who would like to validate their union in the Church. Was the man bound by the Catholic form for marriage in his previous two Lutheran unions? The question arises because of a doubt on the part of the diocesan tribunal on whether the man's baptism by a Catholic priest constituted incorporation into the Catholic Church.

OPINION

For an adult under the law at that time (1917 code c. 752), and under the present code (c. 865), there must be some intention on the part of the recipient in order for the baptism to be licit — and therefore, to incorporate the person into the Catholic Church with all the legal effects of baptism. A baptism illicit because it is done against the will of the adult would not produce those juridic effects, even though the baptism may arguably be considered valid.

Adult baptism constitutes the norm for our law on the intention to join the

257

Church. The norms concerning licit infant baptism are analogous, and consider the parents, guardians, etc., as supplying the intention to join the Catholic Church for the infant. For an adult, even in danger of death there must be at least the presumed intention to be baptized (and baptized a Catholic) for the legal effects to follow.

But for an infant, the law does not seem to be the same. Under both the old and new codes, an infant may be validly and licitly baptized by a Catholic priest in danger of death, even though the parents are unwilling. The 1917 code (c. 750) stated the children of infidels (i.e., non-baptized persons) could licitly be baptized against the wishes of the parents only in real danger of death, from which it was not foreseen they would recover.

It is not clear from your description whether the parents were "infidels" — i.e., not baptized. If they were baptized, then even though they were "*acatholici*" the baptism of their child against their wishes would still be valid; canon 750 only applied when the parents were not baptized. The new code (c. 868, §2) is even more explicit, in that a child in danger of death may be baptized against the wishes of the parents, whether they are Catholic or not, baptized or not; also, it does not retain the condition that it is foreseen the infant will not recover from the danger of death.

Does an air raid during World War II constitute being "*in . . . vitae discrimine*" (1917 code, c. 750, §1)? Apparently it did to the priest on the scene; he baptized all the infants in the nursery indiscriminately. At least in the judgment of a person qualified to make that judgment (the priest on the scene), the conditions for baptism in danger of death were present.

Moreover, given the kind of bombing that did take place during that war, it was not unreasonable to fear that civilian targets, even hospitals, might be hit, placing all in the area in the proximate danger of loss of life. Under the circumstances of the times, this was a generally understood "danger of death" situation.

It would seem, then, that the man was licitly as well as validly baptized a Roman Catholic. The fact that the nuns told his mother about it and that he himself was so informed (to the extent that he has professed this fact throughout his life) reaffirms this opinion.

There is an added factor in this case. It relates to the intention of the ecclesiastical legislator in terms of who was bound by the form. As of January 1, 1949, anyone who had been baptized a Roman Catholic, even though of non-Catholic parents and raised non-Catholic, was bound by the Catholic form of marriage. Your case would appear to be a classic example of the situation which the legislator intended to cover in abrogating the final clause of canon 1099, §2, in the 1917 code.

Therefore, it is my opinion that the man was definitely bound by the Catholic form of marriage when he attempted marriage in the Lutheran church.

James H. Provost [1988]

Canon 869

Intention of Baptist Ministers

Of all major faith groups, the Baptists do not have a common creed or set of doctrines. As they deny infant baptism on the grounds that salvation is by faith, I have heard that some Baptist ministers perceive baptism as only an initiation or affiliation with the local faith groups. A person's relationship with God was established the moment he or she "believed." Other Baptist ministers hold to our belief in the sacrament. As a result, in the reception of Baptists into full communion with the Catholic Church, I always investigate the minister's intention or else give conditional baptism. Is this correct?

Opinion

I read your question to a professor at a Baptist theological seminary. He agreed that the Baptists do not have a common creed of beliefs, but he disagreed with the statement that some Baptist ministers "perceive baptism as only an initiation or affiliation with the local faith groups." Only ordained ministers can baptize in the Baptist faith, and he assured me that no minister would be ordained who did not accept the sacramental efficacy of water baptism with the Trinitarian formula. Confusion on this issue may have arisen, he stated, because a small minority of conservative Baptists rebaptize converts, who had been baptized in infancy in another faith, in order to maintain the connection between adult faith and baptism. However, even this minority of ministers would not consider baptism *in the Baptist faith*, which is the issue at hand, as being anything less than what Christ commanded in the Gospel and which Christians commonly believe about baptism. In other words, Baptist ministers intend "to do what the Church does" when it baptizes.

The 1967 *Ecumenical Directory*, no. 13b, states: "Insufficient faith on the part of the minister never, of itself, makes baptism invalid. Sufficient intention in the baptizing minister is to be presumed, unless there is serious ground for doubting that he intends to do what Christians do."

In my opinion, there is not a serious reason for doubting that Baptist ministers of baptism have sufficient intention. Sufficient intention in the Baptist minister should be presumed unless there is evidence of invalidity in a particular case. If such evidence has not been presented, there is no basis for doubt and no need to investigate the minister's intention.

As for conditional baptism, this should only be done as a last resort. In a case of doubtfully valid baptism, the provisions of canon 869 are to be followed. There must be a serious investigation of the facts of the case, namely, an examination of (1) the matter and the form of words used; (2) the intention of the baptized person, if baptized as an adult; and (3) the intention of the minister of baptism. If a doubt remains after this investigation, baptism is administered conditionally, but not until the Church's teaching about baptism is explained to the person, if an adult, and the reasons for the doubtful validity of the baptism have been explained to the adult recipient or to the parents of an infant.

John M. Huels, O.S.M. [1988]

Canon 871

The Baptism of Fetuses

In the Catholic hospital where I am a chaplain, the policy of the pastoral care department is to baptize all fetuses, whether alive or dead. Is this in accord with canon law?

Opinion

Canon 871 of the Code of Canon Law states: "If aborted fetuses are alive, they are to be baptized if this is possible."

If there is a doubt whether the fetus or other person is dead, baptism can be conferred conditionally. If there is no doubt that the person is dead, then the minister may not baptize.

The practice of baptizing dead fetuses in your hospital is doubtless followed for what is believed to be a pastorally sensitive reason, namely, to comfort the grieving parents. However, a truly pastoral response cannot be one which deceives people by pretending to administer a sacrament, which is a grave abuse of the sacrament as instituted by Christ, and which is a serious violation of church law.

The best practice in this case is indicated in *Pastoral Care of the Sick: Rites of Anointing and Viaticum*, no. 224, which states: "It may be necessary to explain to the family of the person who is dead that sacraments are celebrated for the living, not for the dead, and that the dead are effectively helped by the

260

prayers of the living." Chapter seven of this liturgical book gives prayers which can be used by a minister who has been called to attend a person who is already dead. The book has been mandated for use in the dioceses of the United States from November 27, 1983, and its norms have the force of law.

John M. Huels, O.S.M. [1988]

CANON 874

A. MEMBERS OF GREEK ORTHODOX CHURCH AS SPONSORS AT CATHOLIC BAPTISM

The following question provides its own opinion and asks for further comment: Can a Greek Orthodox person function as a sponsor at a Catholic baptism together with a baptized non-Catholic, a Protestant, who would function as a Christian witness?

Paragraph 48 of the Ecumenical Directory, *issued by the Secretariat for Promoting Christian Unity in 1967 (translated in* Canon Law Digest 6: *716-734), states this: "It is permissible for a just cause for a member of the Oriental churches to act as godparent together with a Catholic godparent at the baptism of a Catholic infant or adult. . ." It would appear that the 1983 code does not deal with this matter. Canon 874, §2 speaks of a baptized person who belongs to a non-Catholic ecclesial community being admitted as a witness together with a Catholic sponsor. The code, as well as the* Ecumenical Directory, *consistently distinguishes between non-Catholics in whose churches the sacraments are not accepted as valid (e.g. c. 844). Thus, it may well be the case that there is a lacuna in the 1983 code and that paragraph 2 of canon 874 does not rule out the possibility of a member of one of the Orthodox churches functioning as a sponsor or godparent and not simply as a Christian witness.*

Be that as it may, it would seem that the wording of the Ecumenical Directory, *if in fact that is still the* ius vigens, *requires that the member of the non-Catholic Oriental church be admitted as a godparent together with a Catholic godparent. Thus, while in the case mentioned above, the Orthodox person could be admitted as a godparent, the Orthodox could not function as godparent together with a Lutheran as a Christian witness. An Orthodox person could only function as a godparent at a Catholic baptism together with a Catholic godparent.*

OPINION

261

In this case the conclusion of the above inquirer seems to be the correct one. The *Ecumenical Directory* in 1967 had treated the situation of non-Catholic sponsors in two separate sections: Paragraph 48 permits members of the Oriental Churches which are separated from the Roman Catholic Church to serve as one of the godparents together with a Catholic godparent. The obligation of securing the Christian education of the baptized person rests in the first place with the godparent of the Church in which the child was baptized. Paragraph 57 explicitly states that a member of a non-Catholic community (with the exception of the Oriental communities mentioned in paragraph 48) is not permitted to act as a godparent in the liturgical and canonical sense at baptism or confirmation; but the non-Catholic may be permitted to act as a Christian witness along with a Catholic godparent.

The *Ecumenical Directory* made a "liturgical and canonical" distinction between the role of godparent and Christian witness: "The reason is that a godparent is not merely undertaking his responsibility for the Christian education of the person baptized or confirmed, as a relative or friend; he is also, as a representative of a community of faith, standing as a sponsor for the faith of the candidate." When a non-Catholic, as a friend or relative of the family, serves as the Christian witness at baptism, it is understood that the responsibility for Christian education belongs of itself to the godparent who is Catholic. Therefore, the *Ecumenical Directory* gives recognition to the closer sacramental ties between the Roman and Orthodox churches and permits the function of "godparent" to be shared as an ecclesial function. On the other hand the function of "Christian witness," which is permitted to members of other Christian churches not in communion with the Roman Church, is interpreted as a familial function and not ecclesial, although the sharing in faith in Christ is recognized.

In the cases of both the non-Catholic Christian witness and the non-Catholic Oriental godparent, each could be named only with a Catholic godparent. Therefore, the *Ecumenical Directory* would not seem to anticipate permission for a Greek Orthodox godparent to serve together with a Protestant Christian witness at a Catholic baptism. Either one or the other would be permitted to function only with the Catholic sponsor. This is the same discipline contained in canon 874, §2, which states that "a baptized person who belongs to a non-Catholic ecclesial community may not be admitted except as a witness to baptism and together with a Catholic sponsor."

It is interesting that canon 874 does not contain the distinctions made in the *Ecumenical Directory* between Oriental non-Catholics as godparents and other non-Catholics as Christian witnesses. This raises the second aspect of the present inquiry, namely, what is the *ius vigens* concerning the capacity of Oriental non-Catholics to serve not just as Christian witnesses, but as godparents with a Catholic sponsor. Should the fact that the 1983 Code of Canon Law ignores the distinction of the 1967 *Ecumenical Directory* be interpreted as an abrogation of the distinction, according to the general norms? Canon 6 states that when this code goes into effect, the following are abrogated: ". . . 2° other universal or particular laws contrary to the prescriptions of this code, unless particular laws are other wise expressly provided for; . . . 4° other universal disciplinary laws dealing with a matter which is regulated *ex integro* by this code . . ."

The Pontifical Commission on the Revision of the Code was conscious of the fact that the draft of the canon did not make the distinction for non-Catholic Orientals to serve as a godparent with a Catholic sponsor. A resolution to introduce the distinction was defeated in a vote. No reason for the decision was given; but clearly the distinction was rejected (cf., *Communicationes* 13 [1981] 230-231). In a later session of the Commission the same question was raised again: "*Iuxta Directorium Oecumenicum orientales non catholici possunt una cum catholico ad munus patrini admitti, quod non amplius in schemate invenitur.*" The Commission determined it was not necessary to make the distinction in the Latin code: "*Non videtur necessarium in Codice pro Ecclesia latina hoc exprimendum*" (cf., *Communicationes* 15 [1983] 185). No further explanation is given. It would seem that the Latin code has abrogated the distinction for a Latin Rite baptism and intends that any non-Catholic is prohibited from the role of godparent in the strict sense.

The General Introduction to Rites of Christian Initiation, n. 10 was amended in 1984 by the Congregation for Divine Worship for the purpose of bringing liturgical law into conformity with the new code. The emendation on this matter states that baptized, non-Catholic Christians may not serve as sponsors but may be admitted as Christian witnesses along with a sponsor who is Catholic. The emendation adds that the practice of the Oriental Churches in this matter is to be respected. The draft of the new Code of Canon Law for the Oriental Church states that an Eastern non-Catholic can serve as a sponsor for a good cause, but always along with a Catholic sponsor, and provided that the Catholic education of the child is guaranteed (c. 682, §2).

Therefore, it is my opinion that the Latin code has dropped the earlier distinction for non-Catholic Oriental Christians as sponsors in Catholic baptism which will take place in the Latin rite. They may serve as Christian witnesses. The Latin code leaves to the liturgical books and Code of the Oriental Churches what is to be decided in baptism rituals for the Eastern Rites.

J. James Cuneo [1988]

I concur with the opinion provided by J. James Cuneo that a member of a Protestant communion or Orthodox Church can participate in a Catholic baptism only if there is a Catholic sponsor. However, it is my opinion that the 1983 Code of Canon Law does not abrogate the provisions of the *Ecumenical Directory*, which makes a distinction between a member of a Protestant community and an Orthodox Church. According to the *Ecumenical Directory*, a Protestant can function as a witness (*testis*) and an Orthodox can function as a sponsor (*patrinus*) in a Catholic baptism. I hold that this distinction is still valid in canon law.

It seems that the 1983 *CIC* canon 874 does not treat the question of a member of an Orthodox church participating in a Catholic baptism. The terminology of canon 874 indicates that it is referring only to the Protestants: the term employed is *communitas ecclesialis*. When the 1983 *CIC* refers to the Orthodox churches, it employs the term *Ecclesia* or *Ecclesia orientalis* (See c. 844, §§2-3).

CCEO canon 685, §3 indicates that a member of an Orthodox church can be admitted to serve as a sponsor (*patrinus*) in a Catholic baptism along with a Catholic sponsor:

> *Iusta de causa licet admittere christifidelem alicuius Ecclesiae orientalis acatholicae ad munus patrini, sed semper simul cum patrino catholico.*

One notes that no mention is made of a member of a *communitas ecclesialis*. Thus, the *CCEO* does not in any way provide for the possibility of the admission of a Protestant even as a witness in a Catholic baptism; rather, this matter is left to the code of the Latin church.

The two canons are complementary expressions of the provisions of the *Ecumenical Directory*: one treats non-Catholics who are members of communities which originated in the Latin Church; the other treats non-Catholics who are members of communities which originated in one of the Eastern Catholic churches.

The question arises: Can an Orthodox serve as a sponsor in a Latin Catholic baptism? My response is affirmative. Canon 874, §2 does not restrict itself to the celebration of Latin Catholic baptisms. It simply states that a member of a non-Catholic ecclesial community can serve as a witness in a baptism. Further, *CCEO* canon 685, §3 permits the admission of a member of an Eastern non-Catholic church as a sponsor. No restriction is made with reference to an Eastern Catholic baptism. Therefore, it is my opinion that an Eastern non-Catholic can serve as a sponsor in a Latin Catholic baptism.

John D. Faris [1988]

B. Ex-Catholic as Christian Witness at Baptism

Can an ex-Catholic who has joined a Protestant religion serve as a Christian witness to baptism in virtue of canon 874, §2?

Opinion

In the canonical system, a person who is baptized Catholic or received into the Catholic Church is always a Catholic and is bound to ecclesiastical law (c. 11). In marriage law, however, ex-Catholics in some respects are treated like non-Catholics. One who has left the Catholic Church by a formal act (such as formally joining another religion) is not bound to the canonical form (c. 1117), and if such a person were to marry a Catholic a dispensation from canonical form would be possible. Such a marriage would require permission from the local ordinary (c. 1071, 4°), who is not to give the permission unless the norms of canon 1125 are observed regarding the declaration and promise of the Catholic party to a mixed marriage (c. 1071, §2).

Since a person who formally leaves the Catholic faith is nevertheless still a Catholic in the law, such a person could not serve as a Christian witness in virtue of canon 874, §2.

A Catholic who joins a Protestant religion is considered a heretic in the law. Heretics, schismatics, and apostates are automatically excommunicated (c. 1364, §1). Such "ex-Catholics" would not be barred from being godparents in virtue of canon 874, 4° unless the penalty were legitimately imposed or declared. However, since they are excommunicated, they would be barred from being godparents in virtue of canon 874, 3° which requires that they "lead a life in harmony with the faith and the role to be undertaken."

On the other hand, an ex-Catholic is not legally prohibited from serving as a witness to a marriage. Anyone with the use of reason can function as a witness to marriage. Such witness is not an ecclesiastical function, office, or ministry, but simply a passive presence that can testify to the exchange of consent and other relevant facts.

Similarly, in a case of necessity when there is no godparent available, anyone with the use of reason (including an ex-Catholic) is qualified to serve as a witness to the conferral of the baptism (see c. 875). But this is not the kind of witness envisioned in canon 874, §2.

John M. Huels, O.S.M. [1988]

Canons 874 and 1247

Ecumenical Permissions with Orthodox

Are the permissions in the 1967 Ecumenical Directory *still in effect under the 1983 code whereby a member of the Oriental Churches could be a godparent at a Catholic baptism (*Directory, *no. 48) and whereby a Catholic who attended the Divine Liturgy in a non-Catholic Oriental church could thereby satisfy the obligation of attending Sunday Mass (*Directory, *no. 47)?*

Opinion

First, let me offer a general observation about the focus of the 1983 code. It is specifically directed to Roman Catholics of the Latin Church (cc. 1 and 11). There has been some concern expressed about its lack of sensitivity in certain issues involved in interritual relations within the Catholic communion. See, for example, the articles by Meletius M. Wojnar, O.S.B.M., in *The Jurist* 43 (1983) 191-198, and by John A. Faris in *Studia Canonica* 17 (1983) 239-259. Whatever one may think of such criticism, in light of it I do not find it surprising that the 1983 Latin code has not attended more thoroughly to issues involved in Catholic-Orthodox relationships.

Second, there is the question as to the force of the 1967 *Ecumenical Directory* under the 1983 code. The *Directory* was issued with the confirmation of the Holy Father and on his order. It was intended for all ritual churches in the Catholic communion, Latin as well as Eastern (see especially the note to no. 7). It was a document containing supraritual norms, not norms only for the Latin Church. In my opinion, it remains in force for Latin as well as Eastern Catholics, except in those matters where specific provisions of the *Directory* are contrary to the 1983 code (c. 6, §1, 2°) even though many of the provisions of the *Directory* are dealt with in the 1983 code (such as some forms of *communicatio in sacris*, c. 844). For the *Directory* is more than "universal law," that term being one which applies to the law for all of a ritual church *sui iuris*, but not to supraritual norms; for a fuller discussion of the meaning of "universal law," see Wilhelm Onclin, "Ordinatio Ecclesiae Universae in Specie ad Ecclesias Rituales Sui Iuris Quod Attinet," *Revue de droit canonique* 30 (1980) 304-317. Even insofar as it establishes universal law for the Latin Church, it has not been replaced by an *ex integro* treatment of its contents, since these are dealt with only partially and piecemeal in the new code.

Third, the failure of the 1983 code to include the two specific permissions under question (Orthodox as godparents, and satisfaction of Sunday obligation

266

at Divine Liturgy in non-Catholic Oriental Churches) is understandable in light of the fact that even prior to the new code, the Latin code did not establish the norms for Latin-Eastern relations; these were contained, even for Latin Church Catholics, in the Eastern code. For example, norms to determine the rite in which children should be baptized are contained in *Cleri sanctitati* (c. 15); similarly, the revised Eastern code will contain norms binding on Latin Catholics as well as Eastern Catholics. So it seems one should normally expect that the permissions in question will more aptly be dealt with in the Eastern code when it is revised. Their absence from the Latin code does not, therefore, necessarily constitute an abrogation of those permissions.

Fourth, with reference to an Orthodox serving as a godparent in the Catholic Church, the rationale given in the 1967 *Directory* remains in effect: "because of the close communion between the Catholic Church and the separated Eastern Churches, as described above (*Directory*, n. 40). . . ." Moreover, the 1983 code is carefully nuanced in regard to this question. It indicates that "a baptized person who belongs to a *non-Catholic ecclesial community* may not be admitted except as a witness to baptism . . ." (c. 874, §2; emphasis added); yet it is silent about baptized persons who belong to a church which is not in full Catholic communion. The documents of Vatican II and subsequent documents of the magisterium have been careful to respect the distinction between churches (a term which is clearly used in reference to the Orthodox) and ecclesial communities (a term which is never used in reference to the Churches of the East which are not in the Catholic communion). The 1983 code itself repeats the distinction in the special attention given in canon 844, §3 to Oriental Churches not in full communion with the Catholic Church, separate from the treatment given to other Christians in canon 844, §4.

In effect, the 1983 code is silent about Orthodox serving as godparents, even though canon 874, §2 repeats the provisions of the 1967 *Directory* relative to other Christians (*Directory*, n. 57). There seems to be a *lacuna*, or hole in the law, which is to be filled in keeping with the principles of canons 19 and 21. Therefore, the permission for Orthodox to serve as godparents does remain in effect.

Fifth, the permission to satisfy the Sunday obligation also appears to remain in effect. There are two reasons for this statement.

Canon 844, §2 addresses the reception of the sacraments of penance, Eucharist and anointing by Catholics in other churches where these sacraments are valid. Traditionally this has specifically included the Orthodox (the 1967 *Directory* is ample testimony to this, as is the Decree on Ecumenism itself). If the Eucharist itself can be received there, the lesser juridic reality of satisfying the Sunday obligation should also be able to be satisfied there.

A second reason is based on an interpretation of canon 1248, §1, which states that "the precept of participating in the Mass is satisfied by assistance at a Mass which is celebrated anywhere in a Catholic rite. . . ." A broad interpretation of this canon has been circulated by private letters from officials of the Apostolic See, although it is not an authentic interpretation. This interpretation considers participation at celebrations according to the Tridentine Missal to satisfy the obligation, even if these celebrations do not take place with the local bishop's permission and may even be done by priests or in groups which are clearly opposed to the Church's current teaching — for example, the followers of Archbishop Lefebvre and other similar groups. This is a "Catholic rite" in the sense of liturgical ritual, not in the sense of ritual church *sui iuris*. The liturgical ritual in question is one which is not authorized, unless special permission has been given by the local bishop. So the interpretation being circulated privately by officials of the Apostolic See could lead to the conclusion that any liturgical rite which was previously accepted in the Catholic communion would satisfy the Sunday obligation, even though not currently celebrated in full communion.

I admit that this last argument may seem to be stretching things a bit, and I do not think it is the strongest reason for holding that the permissions in the *Directory* are still in effect. Yet even this tenuous position is based on an interpretation being circulated by officials of the Apostolic See which they have been asked to reconsider, and which they continue to propose as valid.

In summary, it is my opinion that the permissions in the 1967 *Directory* are still in effect, and may be used under the same conditions and with the same qualifications as given in that *Directory*.

James H. Provost [1985]

CANON 883, 2°

ADMITTING BAPTIZED CHRISTIANS TO FULL COMMUNION

What jurisdiction is needed to receive a baptized Christian into full communion with the Catholic Church? For example, could the profession of faith be received by a lay person, such as a Director of Religious Education, who would ask the local pastor to record it after the reception? Another example is this: if someone wishes to be received into the Catholic Church but does not wish to enter the RCIA process in the local parish, but instead prefers to receive private instructions from a friend involved in campus ministry at a nearby college, may this be done? Does it make a difference if the campus minister is a lay person or cleric? If the campus minister is able to receive the person into full communion with the Catholic Church, would the minister have the reception recorded in the baptismal records of the person's proper parish, or of the parish in whose territory the profession of faith was made?

OPINION

The query has two major issues: (1) who is the minister authorized to receive baptized Christians into full communion with the Catholic Church; (2) no matter who the authorized minister is, must a baptized Christian be received into full communion in their proper parish, or can this be done in some other place?

In answer to the first question, the norms governing the reception of baptized Christians into full communion with the Catholic Church are found in the 1988 revised version of the *Rite of Christian Initiation of Adults*. This has been normative for the Catholic Church in the United States since September 1, 1988. Specifically, Part II, Rites for Particular Circumstances, number 5, Reception of Baptized Christians into the Full Communion of the Catholic Church, sets the norms which are to be observed.

Number 481 states: "It is the office of the bishop to receive baptized Christians into the full communion of the Catholic Church." Thus, as to what jurisdiction is needed to receive a baptized Christian into full communion, the answer is quite simply, the jurisdiction of the diocesan bishop.

But this does not mean the diocesan bishop must perform this rite personally for all such persons being received into full communion with the Catholic Church. The ritual continues, "a priest to whom the bishop entrusts the celebration of the rite has the faculty of confirming the candidate within the rite of reception, unless the person received has already been validly confirmed." Thus, a priest may clearly be delegated by the bishop to receive a baptized Christian into full communion.

The ritual describes two ceremonies for receiving the profession of faith, one within the celebration of the Eucharist and the other outside such a celebration. In each case, the celebrant is clearly a priest (nn. 490, 502). Moreover, only a priest can receive the faculty, either from the law or by delegation from the bishop, to confirm, and confirmation normally is administered at the same time as the person is admitted to full communion as part of the full initiation of the person.

So in regard to the question, could the profession of faith be received by a lay person, the answer is generally no. However, it may be argued that under special circumstances a lay person could be authorized to receive a baptized Christian into full communion. The basis for this is canon 861, §2 concerning the minister of baptism: "If the ordinary minister is absent or impeded, a catechist or other person deputed for this function by the local ordinary confers baptism licitly." This is in addition to a "case of necessity" when "any person with the right intention" licitly confers baptism. If the bishop can depute a catechist or other lay person to administer baptism when the ordinary minister (bishop, priest or deacon) is absent or impeded, by analogy it would be possible for the bishop to depute a catechist, director of religious education, or other lay person to receive the profession of faith and admit a baptized Christian into full communion with the Catholic Church.

The possibility would exist if the ordinary minister (bishop, or priest delegated by the bishop) were absent or impeded from carrying out this function. It could not be simply presumed by the lay person that they are authorized to perform this rite, however, for the deputation of the bishop is needed, as it is for a priest to receive such a person into full communion. For priests this is often given in the diocesan faculties issued to each priest individually, which are habitual faculties (c. 132, §1). For catechists, directors of religious education, or the like, it could be granted in an habitual manner, as an habitual faculty, or it could be delegated for a specific case or cases. In either event, the lay person would not be able to confirm the newly received Catholic, although in a celebration of reception it would be possible for a properly authorized extraordinary minister of the Eucharist to administer Communion to the newly received Catholic.

The second question in the query relates to the place where reception into full communion takes place. It should first be clarified that a baptized Christian is not a catechumen, and should not be confused with one (see *Rite of Christian Initiation of Adults*, n. 477: "Anything that would equate candidates for reception with those who are catechumens is to be absolutely avoided"). While they are not permitted to be regarded as catechumens, they are "to receive both doctrinal and spiritual preparation, adapted to individual pastoral requirements" (n. 477). Instead of the liturgical rites of the catechumenate, they may benefit from the rites included in "Preparation of Uncatechized Adults for Confirmation and Eucharist" which are given in Part II, 4, of the *Rite of Christian Initiation of Adults* (see n. 478).

It would seem that baptized Christians are not restricted to their proper parish in becoming prepared for full communion in the Catholic Church. Neither the *Rite of Christian Initiation of Adults* nor the Code of Canon Law restricts this preparation to the person's proper parish.

Instruction prior to reception into full communion is not limited to clergy. Indeed, the *Rite of Christian Initiation of Adults* encourages that someone who has "had the principal part in guiding or preparing the candidate . . . should be the sponsor" at the rite of reception (n. 483). It is the competence of a person to prepare a candidate, rather than status as cleric or lay person, which determines who prepares the person for reception into full communion.

Whether the preparation has been done in or apart from the candidate's proper parish, the rite of reception does not seem limited to that parish. It pertains first to the diocesan bishop to perform the rite. He can designate another priest or, as argued above, under special circumstances another person, to receive the candidate into full communion. The bishop is not limited to parish boundaries in doing this. So it would be possible for a campus minister, properly delegated by the bishop in light of the above, to receive the candidate into full communion even outside a parish church.

The *Rite of Christian Initiation of Adults* calls for reception to be recorded "in a special book" (n. 486). Unless the bishops' conference specifies otherwise, this book would appear to be the baptismal register (c. 535, §1); so far as I know, the NCCB has not made any specification in this regard. If confirmation has also been administered as part of reception, it is also to be noted (c. 895). Such registers are to be kept in parishes. If the campus ministry has been established as a parish (c. 813) it would have such a register of its own, and the event would be recorded there. If it is not erected as a parish, it would be recorded in the book of the parish in which the campus is located. The principle is that the event should be recorded in the book of the place where the rite took place, wherever that may be.

James H. Provost [1989]

CANON 884, §1

CONFIRMATION BY A PRESBYTER

In virtue of canon 884, §1, a parochial vicar has applied to the bishop for the faculty to confirm three merely lapsed and unconfirmed adult Catholics who are preparing to return to full active participation in the life of the Church by a renewal of their profession of faith during the forthcoming Easter Vigil liturgy. Similar requests are expected from other quarters.

OPINION

Legal Aspects

Canons 883 and 884, new to the *ius vigens*, enhance the role of the presbyter as a minister of the sacrament of Confirmation. Canon 884, §1 enables the diocesan bishop to give the faculty to confirm to a specified presbyter if necessity so requires (*"si necessitas id requirat"*). Since the legislator has not limited the scope of the diocesan bishop in this regard concerning the requirement of necessity, I do not see that this faculty has to be otherwise limited. I believe that the parallel drawn with the notion of marriage delegation is valid in this instance (cf., cc. 17 and 19).

Within the parameter of necessity I do not believe that the faculty should be restricted at the lower level to pastors because the legislator has not imposed any such limitation. Based on the *Ordo Confirmationis*, n. 8, Frederick McManus in his commentary in the CLSA commentary on the revised Code of Canon Law on canon 884, §1 states that it may be appropriate to choose a vicar general, an episcopal vicar, a pastor, etc., in the selection of presbyters as extraordinary ministers of confirmation. Within the same context McManus also points out that no restriction is placed on the diocesan bishop in this regard.

With regard to an emergency situation (presumedly this refers to danger of death) the legislator has already covered that contingency in canon 883, 3° and canon 885, §2. In this situation the pastor or indeed any presbyter has the faculty by the law to confirm.

One basic question facing a diocesan bishop in this *RCIA* type situation is *not*, can the presbyter be given the faculty *but rather* does necessity require it? One could answer YES because (in accordance with good sacramental theology) the interrelationship and sequence between confirmation and Eucharist should be maintained (cf., c. 842, §2). On the other hand, one could answer NO because the situation is one neither of danger of death nor of the sequence of initiation in the strict sense.

The case of the catechumen, the previously baptized Christian or the Catholic who is returning to full communion from a state of apostasy, heresy or schism differs from that of the merely lapsed Catholic. The latter while dormant never cut himself or herself off canonically from the Church and has already been initiated into the Catholic Church. Those who were never Catholic were never fully members of the Church even if in the case of non-Catholic Christians there was already a bonding because of valid baptism. Those returning from a state of apostasy, heresy or schism were formally severed from full communion with the Church and are being fully reintegrated through the remaining sacraments of initiation.

Further, because in the Latin Church the bishop is the ordinary minister of confirmation (c. 882), then from a pastoral perspective it is fitting that the sacrament should be administered by him in normal circumstances. The revision process for the formulation of the 1983 code was quite clear in this regard. It did not extend the confirmation faculty to presbyters in the case of reactivating merely lapsed Catholics because the Pontifical Commission for the Interpretation of the Decrees of Vatican II had already settled the question by a refusal to do so. The revision fathers were anxious lest the bishop should seem to be put in a position of isolation or of losing contact with the people committed to his pastoral care.

In his commentary on canons 882 and 883, McManus points out that when a presbyter confirms he does so in virtue of a faculty conceded especially to him either by the law or by the diocesan bishop. Even then, for validity, the presbyter's faculty is a restricted one (either territorially or in virtue of circumstances [i.e., initiation or danger of death]) whereas a bishop can confirm validly anywhere even though not always licitly (c. 886, §2).

Pastoral Aspects

In the Latin Church the preference is for the bishop to confirm the Catholic mentioned in this situation unless necessity or danger of death dictates otherwise. The law already gives the faculty to confirm to any presbyter when there is danger of death (c. 883, 3°). In a case of necessity the diocesan bishop can give the faculty to one or more specified presbyters (c. 884, §1).

The diocesan bishop can reserve to himself the baptism of adults, at least those who have completed their fourteenth year (c. 863) and thus in effect reserve their confirmation to himself. The same would hold true for the rite of reception of non-Catholic Christians into full communion, of which confirmation is an integral part unless the person has already been validly confirmed (cf., *RCIA* n. 481 [NCCB edition]).

When a presbyter, however, receives a catechumen or previously baptized person into full communion with the Church, the law not only gives that presbyter the faculty to confirm the person at the same time but also states that this faculty should ordinarily be exercised immediately without deferring the confirmation to a bishop at a later time unless some serious reason stands in the way (*RCIA*, n. 215 [NCCB edition]).

With regard to this situation, the *mens ecclesiae* is that in the normal course of events (apart from *RCIA* type situations) the confirmation of Latin Catholics should be administered by a bishop unless church law provides otherwise. Since some adult Catholics can understandably feel uncomfortable as prominent participants in a liturgy with a predominance of younger people, perhaps an adult confirmation liturgy could be scheduled by the bishop on a regular basis.

Finally, if in a particular case a reactivating Catholic is unable to avail himself or herself of the opportunity to be confirmed by the bishop and if at the same time necessity so requires, I believe that the bishop is empowered to give the faculty to confirm to whatever presbyter he considers most suitable in the particular circumstances prevailing (c. 884, §1).

Louis Naughton [1990, revised 1993]

Canon 890

Right of Parents to Withdraw Children from Sacramental Preparation Classes which Contain Elements of Sex Education

(Editor's note: This question is similar to the one developed above under canon 226. The source of the question is different. Furthermore, this question does not simply refer to programs in Catholic schools or religious education programs in general, but specifically concerns a claimed right to withdraw from sacramental preparation classes.)

In Social Justice Review (March/April 1988, 50-55), Mary K. Smith of the National Coalition of Clergy and Laity, presents an article entitled "Textbooks, Good and Bad," in which she prints a "Petition for Exemption From Certain Compulsory Instruction by Reason of Conscience." The petition is intended for signature and presentation to pastors or diocesan authorities by parents who feel that the contents of religious education classes, sacramental preparation classes, etc., are offensive to their conscience in regard to matters of education in sexuality. The petition claims the right to freedom of conscience and the obligation that the pastoral authority respect it. The petition also claims the same right for persons over the age of 18 years who may have moral or religious objections regarding attendance at marriage preparation programs.

In response to the above petition, the question has been asked: whether parents have the right to exempt their children from religious education classes and sacramental preparation classes on the basis that the mandated programs contain materials contrary to their conscience?

Opinion

(See also the opinion under canon 226.)

I would agree with the opinion of James Coriden in this matter, namely that parents do not have a right to withdraw students from religious education courses legitimately mandated by proper ecclesiastical authorities. The question raised here is basically the same, except for the specific additional claim of a right to exempt a child from sacramental preparation programs, which is not addressed explicitly by Coriden.

In this regard, it is my opinion that the Church determines what is appropriate for sacramental preparation. It would seem that the law of the Church (for example, cc. 890 and 1063) places the obligation on the pastors (ultimately the bishop and magisterium of the Church) to judge the requirements of the preparation and the suitability of the contents. The claim for right of exemption is based on right of freedom of conscience, for example, in canon 748, and right of freedom of choice in regard to education of children, canon 793. Freedom of conscience in this regard is always a complicated topic. One's right to be free of coercion by civil authority in matters of religious choice does not mean that a member of the Church can claim freedom from the magisterium of the Church in accepting what is mandated in sacramental preparation classes.

In individual situations, however, there may be room for a local due process whereby a conflict is resolved. Persons may have a legitimate right to request an investigation to determine if a certain program is indeed teaching false or unfair material or materials of dubious value, so that adjustments can be made. But the law seems to imply that catechetical material and sacramental preparation is subject to the magisterium, although respect for the parents may involve legitimate hearing, due process and perhaps even a dispensation in an individual case. This latter process is not the same as claiming a basic right to withdraw children from the program or an exemption from mandated preparation, if the conscience of the individual differs from the decision of the legitimate magisterial authority of the Church.

J. James Cuneo [1988]

Canon 902

Restrictions on Concelebration

Does canon 902 grant priests a legal right to concelebrate? Can liturgy planners decide not to have concelebration? Can restrictions be placed on the number of concelebrants?

Opinion

Canon 902 does not give priests a right to concelebrate Mass. On the contrary, it states the right of priests to celebrate individually, "though not during the time when there is a concelebration in the same church or oratory," and provided there is "the participation of at least some member of the faithful, except for a just and reasonable cause" (c. 906). Clearly, there cannot be a right to concelebrate when there also is a right to celebrate individually, because the two rights would conflict whenever different priests wanted to exercise both rights at the same Mass. The intent of canon 902 is not to grant priests an unlimited right to concelebrate Mass, but for the first time since concelebration was restored at Vatican II, to allow them to concelebrate *without the permission of their ordinary.*

It was for this reason, when liturgical law was revised following the promulgation of the 1983 code, that the following sentence was deleted from n. 155 of the General Instruction of the Roman Missal: "The right to decide on the advisability of concelebration and to permit it in his churches and oratories belongs to every ordinary and even to every major superior of nonexempt clerical religious institutes and of societies of clerics living in community without vows." Thus, in accord with canon 902, priests may concelebrate without the permission of their ordinary, but this does not mean they may concelebrate whenever they wish. Not all Masses are concelebrated Masses. Indeed, the law requires concelebration only on two occasions — the ordinations of presbyters and bishops, and the Chrism Mass[1] — but even then not all the priests present are required to concelebrate, nor is there a right for them to do so.

Even at Masses which are concelebrated, the number of concelebrants can be restricted for purposes of good order, aesthetics, or other reasons. This was clear from the beginning of the restored practice as seen in the 1965 *Rite of Concelebration,* which said that the ordinary "may limit the number of concelebrants . . . if, all circumstances being considered, he decides that the dignity of the rite requires this."[2]

When concelebration was first restored, it was a novelty which could be done only with the ordinary's permission, but it soon became a regular practice not only in the cathedral churches and large religious houses, but in parishes and small religious communities as well. Clearly, it was impossible for the typical bishop or major superior to determine how many concelebrants could be admitted for every concelebrated Mass everywhere in his jurisdiction. These decisions had to be made by local officials entrusted by the ordinary with the worship and pastoral care of the local Christian communities — the pastors, local superiors, presiders, and liturgy planners. Those in charge of preparing the liturgy on the local level were best able to determine whether Mass was to be concelebrated, and if so, how many concelebrants were to be admitted. Canon 902 in no way changes this practice.

Nothing in universal law prevents liturgy planners, be they clerical, religious, or lay, from determining, with the agreement of the presider, that a given Eucharistic celebration will not be concelebrated (outside of the two cases mentioned above) or that the number of concelebrants will be restricted. Can a diocesan bishop, however, establish a right *in particular law* for priests to concelebrate?

The revised n. 155 of the General Instruction of the Roman Missal states: "The right to regulate, in accord with the law, the discipline for concelebration in his diocese, even in churches and oratories of exempt religious, belongs to the bishop." An indication of what it means to regulate concelebration can be seen in a 1966 particular decree of the Sacred Congregation of Rites. Regarding the bishop's authority, the decree stated: "It belongs to the bishop . . . to regulate the practice of concelebration in his own diocese (see SC art. 57, §2), e.g., to forbid concelebration in other churches at the time of a concelebration in the cathedral; to prevent abuses; to ensure individual celebration of Masses for the benefit of the faithful; to give rules on the observance of the rite and its practice, on the prayer of the faithful, and on other like matters."[3] The bishop can issue norms or guidelines on concelebration in keeping with his general authority over the liturgy in the diocese, to which even members of pontifical religious institutes are subject.[4] However, the bishop could not impose concelebration, or give priests the right to concelebrate whenever they wish, because this would be contrary to the right of priests to celebrate individually, a right given in canon 902. At most, it seems the bishop could establish a right to concelebrate only at Masses at which he himself is the presider, but even then the right would be limited by available space. The 1965 *Rite of Concelebration*, n. 4, reinforces this latter point: "In each case the number of concelebrants is to be settled by considering how many the church and the altar of concelebration can accommodate, even if all the concelebrants are not right next to the table of the altar. The faithful's clear view of the rite must be ensured. . . ."

Notes

[1] General Instruction of the Roman Missal, n. 153.
[2] *Ritus servandus in concelebratione Missae et Ritus Communionis sub utraque specie* (Typis Polyglottis Vaticanis, 1965), n. 3; translation in *Documents on the Liturgy 1963-1979: Conciliar, Papal and Curial Tests* (DOL) (Collegeville: Liturgical Press, 1982) n. 1796.
[3] *Notitiae* 2 (1966) 266. Translation in DOL, n. 1354.
[4] See canons 392, §2; 835, §1; 838, §§1 & 4; and 678, §1.

John M. Huels, O.S.M. [1987]

Canon 902

Some Distinctions on Concelebration

Does canon 902 grant priests a legal right to concelebrate?

ANOTHER OPINION

(Editor's Note: This opinion is a reply to the above opinion.)

Huels indicates that canon 902 does not grant priests the *right* to concelebrate, but rather assures the right of priests to celebrate individually. The rationale is that if it granted both rights, they could be in conflict. Some additional nuance may be in order. The canon itself forbids the exercise of the right to celebrate individually at the time a concelebration is going on, so it already resolves one aspect of the potential conflict in favor of concelebration.

It is up to the rector of a church to see that good order is observed in the church (c. 561). This applies to admitting priests to celebrate there (c. 903), as well as preaching in the church building (c. 767, §4). It would seem that it is the responsibility of the rector (or of another legitimate superior — also mentioned in c. 561) to determine when concelebrated Masses are to take place in the building, and therefore, to limit the right of other priests to celebrate individually at that time and in that place.

But by the same token, the rector or other legitimate superior would also be the person responsible for determining the appropriate number of concelebrants for the church and altar of concelebration — of course, within the norms of the liturgical books and any particular regulations set down by the diocesan bishop. But if a priest wished to concelebrate at a Mass of concelebration, and his participation would be within the number admissible for that concelebration, then the canon says he "can" (*possunt*) concelebrate and it would seem hard to deny him admission to concelebrate (provided the prescriptions of c. 903 are met, which presume he is to be admitted if he at least has a *celebret*).

In light of this, the following distinctions are proposed:

1. Every priest has the right to celebrate individually, provided it is at a time when a concelebration is not being held in the church, provided that if possible at least some of the faithful participate, and provided that the welfare of the Christian faithful does not require or urge otherwise.

2. Every priest is at liberty (*possunt*) to concelebrate, provided it is within the directives of the rector of the church, in keeping with liturgical norms and diocesan norms, and provided that the welfare of the Christian faithful does not require or urge otherwise.

3. A priest who wishes to concelebrate at a concelebration Mass cannot be denied this, unless he is not to be admitted to celebrate in that church, or unless his participation would go beyond the number of concelebrants to be admitted to that concelebration. So in this sense, he does seem to have a right to concelebrate — a limited right, but

his right to celebrate individually is also a limited right.

Finally, the role of the rector of the church raises questions about the role of the presider, and of a liturgy planning group.

With regard to the presider, he must operate within the norms for the church building where he is presiding at a celebration. These norms come from general liturgical law, from the particular law the diocesan bishop may have set down, but also from the rector of the church (or other legitimate superior). Within those parameters, the presider is responsible for the good ordering of the particular celebration at which he presides, and therefore, over the conduct of the concelebrants as well as the others who exercise their legitimate roles in the celebration.

With regard to a liturgy planning group, they too must operate within the norms for the church building where the celebration is to take place. The presider should be a part of the liturgy planning group itself, so as to assure the unity of the celebration. But if he is not, how is a potential conflict between the liturgy planning group's work and the responsibilities of the presider to be worked out? Obviously it should be handled prior to the celebration, ideally through dialogue. But when the "buck stops," it is supposed to stop with the presider, rather than with the planning group; in one sense they are acting in his name, since he is the one who at the celebration itself has the responsibility to see that all takes place in good order.

James H. Provost [1988]

CANON 910

A. Non-Functioning of Extraordinary Eucharistic Ministers When Clergy are Present

See opinion under canon 230

B. Authentic or Private Interpretation

See opinion under canon 16.

CANON 913

ADMITTING DISABLED PERSONS TO EUCHARIST

What is the situation under the new code for admitting persons with physical and developmental disabilities to the Eucharist?

OPINION

Let me start by saying that I am somewhat puzzled by your reference to canon 866. While canon 866 does refer to Holy Communion immediately after baptism and confirmation, it directly concerns the sacraments of initiation for adults. In the context of the developmentally handicapped, I think that canon 866 is clear when taken in the light of canon 913, to which you do not allude. I will deal here with canon 913, which in turn governs canon 914, to which you refer.

It happens to be relatively easy to offer you a canonical opinion about the norms for the Eucharist for developmentally handicapped persons, leaving you to judge for yourselves whether it is more pastoral. I doubt that any canonist could handle this matter in a more accurate, clear and suasive manner than was done by Sister Mary Therese Harrington, S.M., in *SPRED* (Chicago), vol. 30, no. 3, March 1983. She correctly identifies the four points to be considered and her treatment of each is canonically, as well as pastorally, flawless in my opinion.

I would add only one observation to Sr. Harrington's remarks about distinguishing the eucharistic bread from ordinary bread. This is a reference to canon 913, §2, which repeats the former canon 854, §2, and derives from Pope Pius X. The provision of this canon is directly applicable to a child who is in danger of death — not necessarily actually dying — and Sr. Harrington treats it that way. I would go a bit further and say that, in the case of a person who is developmentally impaired in such a way that this is all that can be expected for the whole of his or her life, this person is "sufficiently disposed," and there would be no need to speak only of Viaticum.

In brief, it is my opinion that this article in *SPRED* more than adequately serves as a correct application of canon 913, which is then easily extended, as it should be, to canons 914 and 866, in the event that the disabled person is to be confirmed.

Richard A. Hill, S.J. [1984]

Canon 914

Diocesan Guidelines for First Eucharist and Penance

*Does the 1983 code require any change in existing diocesan guidelines for first penance which leave open the option of receiving first Eucharist before first penance? This inquiry is caused by the phrase "*praemissa sacramentali confessione*" in canon 914 of the 1983 code.*

Opinion

The proper interpretation of a canon must be done in light of the text and context of the canon. In the case of canon 914, it must first be placed in its proper context. There are two key canons which help to interpret it. The first is the canon on the preparation for first reception of the sacrament of the Eucharist, indicating what is required before one can be admitted to it (c. 913); the second concerns who is obliged to confess their sins (c. 989).

Canon 913, §1 establishes the prerequisites for admission of children to first Eucharist under normal circumstances:

a. Sufficient knowledge;

b. Careful preparation so as to understand the mystery of Christ according to their capacity;

c. Ability to receive the Eucharist with faith and devotion.

Canon 913, §2 provides for emergency situations. Here, all that is required in danger of death is that the child be able to distinguish the Body of Christ from ordinary food and be able to receive Communion reverently.

In neither situation does the canon itself require confession of sins. Obviously, the canon about those in serious sin applies: canon 916 states that those who are *conscious* (my emphasis) of grave sin are not to receive the Eucharist without prior sacramental confession — unless a grave reason is present and there is no opportunity of confessing. In this latter situation, the person is to make an act of perfect contrition (which includes the intention to confess as soon as possible) and may then receive the Eucharist.

The requirements for admission to first Eucharist, therefore, do not of themselves include sacramental confession. That is a requirement of law only for those who are conscious of grave sin, and would apply to those approaching first Eucharist who are conscious of grave sin.

This is confirmed by canon 989. Reaffirming the position of the Council of Trent (Sess. XIV, "*De paenitentiae*" [DS 1683] and c. 8 [DS 1708]), which itself was a reaffirmation of the position of the IV Lateran Council (Cap. 12, "*De confessione facienda. . .* " [DS 812]), the canon makes clear what had been the common understanding of the position of those councils, namely that the obligation to confess only applies to those who are conscious of grave (or "mortal") sin.

Several other canons may also help to understand the situation. The reception of the Eucharist is a right which pertains to all the faithful (c. 213), and clergy cannot refuse the sacrament when it is asked for at an appropriate time, the person is properly disposed, and there is no prohibition of law to keep the person from receiving it (c. 843, §1). Penance is not listed as a prerequisite for Eucharist except for those who are conscious of grave sin, as mentioned above.

Baptism, confirmation and Eucharist are given in the law as the sacraments of initiation, required for full Christian initiation (c. 842, §2). Penance is not listed as part of the sacraments of initiation, such that it would have to be received in order to be fully initiated, whereas Eucharist is so listed.

What, then, is to be made of the phrase, inserted at the last minute into canon 914, "*praemissa sacramentali confessione*" ("preceded by sacramental confession")? Legally, it is not a condition *sine qua non*, without which admission to the sacrament would be invalid or illicit. It is a descriptive ablative absolute, describing what is in some areas of the world a standard pastoral practice; it is not a universally mandated action. If it were to be interpreted otherwise, then it would be going counter to the Church's tradition from Lateran Council IV and the Council of Trent, and counter to the legal requirements both for reception of Eucharist and for mandatory sacramental confession. Law of its nature is conservative, and would not break with such a long tradition without explicitly stating so (cc. 20 and 21).

Confirmation of this position has been circulated informally in light of a discussion in the summer or fall of 1983 between a group of American bishops and officials of the Congregation for the Clergy, which has the responsibility for catechesis and so for norms on admission to first Eucharist and first penance. It is reported that officials of the Congregation did admit, after the above considerations about the teachings of Lateran IV, Trent, and the new code were brought to their attention, that first penance before first Eucharist was what the members of the Congregation prefer, but not something which is absolutely mandated by law for the universal Church.

The inclusion of the phrase at the last minute in canon 914 has a certain dissonance with the rest of the canons. This is not atypical of such last minute insertions; the changes in other canons leave equal confusion. For example, canon 277 was considerably rewritten at the last minute; it now requires married men who become deacons (and hence clerics) to be continent, even with their wives! (Canonists have been quick to point out, I might add, that such married men have an acquired right in virtue of their marriage covenant, so are not bound in their relations with their wives by the restriction of c. 277.) There are other instances where last minute insertions were not carefully integrated with the rest of the system in the code.

So, the phrase is a bit out of step with the rest of the canons on the requirements for first reception of Eucharist, but it is not unknown in the code for such dissonance to be present. To resolve the situation, recourse is to be had to parallel places and the general doctrine of the law. This clearly indicates that first reception of penance is mandatory prior to first reception of Eucharist only for those who are conscious of grave sin.

In keeping with the approved authors in moral theology, the judgment whether someone is conscious of grave sin is a judgment of conscience, not one of pastors or diocesan policies. Diocesan policy, however, can require that the option be made available of first reception of penance prior to first reception of Eucharist, even while admitting exceptions in individual cases for pastoral reasons. This appears to be consonant both with church tradition on penance and the present wording of canon 914 (For a more detailed discussion see James H. Provost, "The Reception of First Penance," *The Jurist* 47 [1987] 294-340).

James H. Provost [1984]

CANON 915

RECEPTION/INITIATION OF NON-CATHOLICS IN IRREGULAR MARRIAGES

Non-Catholics in irregular marriages are routinely restricted from reception/ initiation into the Catholic Church until the irregularity is remedied through an external forum procedure. Does a canonical presumption exist that such non-Catholics are guilty of the sin referred to in canon 915? Is this restriction canonically justified? Is an external forum procedure the required and only available remedy?

OPINION

You are correct in stating that non-Catholics in irregular marriages are barred from reception/initiation into the Catholic Church until the irregularity is remedied through an external forum procedure. Persons in irregular marriages may be accepted into the catechumenate, but they are unable to receive the sacraments of initiation. This practice was affirmed by the Congregation for the Doctrine of the Faith in a July 11, 1983 reply. (See *CLD* 10: 139-40; *Roman Replies 1983*, 2-3.)

The basis for this practice lies in the Church's moral teaching and theology rather than in canon 915. Those who are in irregular unions are excluded from the reception of the sacraments because, according to the traditional way of thinking, they are said to be committing the sin of adultery since one or both partners had entered into a previous union with another spouse. The theology of Christian marriage is also relevant. Pope John Paul II, on the denial of the Eucharist to those in irregular marriages, stated that, "They are unable to be admitted thereto from the fact that their state and condition of life objectively contradict that union of love between Christ and the Church which is signified and effected by the Eucharist." The pope also alluded to the traditional argument that to go against this practice would cause scandal to the faithful and would confuse them and lead them into error about the Church's teaching. (See apostolic exhortation *Familiaris consortio*, November 22, 1980, *AAS* 74, n. 84 [1982] 81-191.)

The pope was not speaking here of catechumens in irregular marriages who desire sacramental initiation, but the reasons are applicable to their situation. Through the sacraments of initiation, persons make a public commitment to undertake the obligations of the Christian life. However, if they are in an irregular marriage they are unable to commit themselves to the teaching of Christ and the Church on marital indissolubility. Their marital irregularity is seen as objectively contradicting this teaching.

No internal forum solution is possible in such a situation. The internal forum or good conscience solution is applicable only for the private, spiritual welfare of the individual. A condition for its application is the avoidance of publicity and scandal. The internal forum solution could never be used to "convalidate" a union which remains invalid in the external forum. Likewise, it cannot be used by a catechumen in an irregular marriage as a basis for legitimizing the reception of the sacraments of initiation. The sacraments of initiation are public acts, just as marriage is a public act.

When there are persons in irregular marriages in the catechumenate, it is desirable fairly early in their formation to explain the Church's teaching on marriage and to speak in a positive way about processes of annulment and dissolution. It is also necessary for those who direct the *RCIA* not to take a programmatic view of the catechumenate, as if it were only a catechism course which ends with "graduation" at the Easter Vigil. Rather, the catechumenate is a process which must be geared to the individual needs, faith, and readiness of each person, and which must include sufficient time — as long as it takes — to obtain an external forum solution to a marital irregularity.

In danger of death catechumens could receive the sacraments of initiation if they promise to observe the requirements of the Christian religion. Presumedly they would already have "some knowledge of the principle truths of the faith" and by their entry into the catechumenate would have "in some way manifested the intention of receiving baptism" (c. 865, §2). The baptism of desire suffices for the salvation of catechumens who were not able to be baptized before they died (c. 849; cf., cc. 1183, §1 and 206).

I do not believe canon 915 is directly relevant to this issue. The canon addresses those who administer Holy Communion, not the recipients of it. It gives the conditions under which a minister may refuse to give Communion to someone, namely, those inflicted with or declared to have incurred the penalty of excommunication or interdict, and others who obstinately persist in manifest serious sin. The canon is not referring to the situation of catechumens. They cannot in any case receive Communion because they are not baptized.

Although not directly relevant to catechumens, I would like to make a comment on canon 915 anyway. Since it creates a restriction on the right of the faithful to be given Communion, it is subject to strict interpretation (c. 18). If a minister is doubtful whether someone truly is obstinately persisting in manifest serious sin, then Communion should not be denied to the person who requests it. Indeed, it could often happen that a minister may doubt whether a baptized person in an irregular marriage who comes to Communion is *obstinately* persisting in *manifest, serious sin*. The mere fact that a person is in an irregular marriage does not in itself demonstrate persistent obstinateness, or the public nature of the sin, or even its gravity in the internal forum.

John M. Huels, O.S.M. [1990]

CANON 918

WEEKDAY COMMUNION SERVICES BY EXTRAORDINARY MINISTERS OF THE EUCHARIST

For the past few months a Communion service presided over by extraordinary ministers of the Eucharist has been conducted on weekdays at a parish church. Three priests — a pastor and two associates — are assigned full-time to the parish. A fourth priest is in residence. The normal parish schedule of three daily masses has been maintained in addition to this Communion service, which was initiated in response to the request of an office worker in the area for a Mass to be scheduled circa noon to facilitate people in that situation. Is this an acceptable practice?

OPINION

Holy Communion can be received licitly outside the context of Mass (c. 918; cf., c. 213). The approved ritual to which the *ius vigens* is related was published in 1973. However, canon 918 qualifies this lawful practice by stating clearly that there should be a just cause for Holy Communion to be administered apart from Mass ("*tamen iusta de causa. . . extra Missam ministretur . . .* ").

Huels' interpretation in the CLSA commentary of this canon is based on the *mens ecclesiae*, which is that Communion should be given primarily during Mass. Because of this, Huels maintains that the requirement of a just cause outside Mass should be strictly observed.

Turning to parallel places (cf. cc. 17 and 19), n. 21 of the *Directory for Sunday Celebrations in the Absence of a Priest* clearly states that such celebrations, being substitutional, can never be held in places where Mass has already been celebrated or is to be celebrated or was celebrated on the vigil, even if the Mass in question is celebrated in a different language. Nor is it right to have more than one celebration of this kind on any given Sunday. It is difficult to set aside the tenor of such unambiguous language.

In a recent address to a group of U.S. bishops, Pope John Paul II stated that there may be some need to revise diocesan policies with regard to the use of extraordinary ministers of the Eucharist in order "to foster the true notion and genuine character of the participation of the laity in the life and mission of the Church" (cf., *Origins* 18:29 [December 29, 1988] 477).

With regard to Communion services outside Mass, a NCCB-BCL official, in a private communication, has stated that Communion should be distributed outside of Mass only when there is a specific need and should not be done merely for convenience.

From the pastor's letter it would appear that what this parish is offering is being availed of on the basis of convenience. The pastor's considered assessment is that the "people face the choice between convenient and inconvenient times, not between Mass and a Communion service." The critical question is: does such convenience fall within the category of *iusta de causa*?

Liturgical Aspects

Liturgically, the reception of Communion apart from Mass should be the exception. At the present time, three scheduled daily Masses are available in this parish. In such circumstances can one either canonically or liturgically justify a Communion service in addition to three daily Masses, especially when the *mens ecclesiae* strives to impress upon the faithful at large an understanding of the reception of Communion as an integral part of active participation in the Mass? Mass is the normal setting in which the reception of Communion should take place.

Further, can such a practice be justified merely on the basis of convenience?

On the basis of Huels' interpretation of canon 918 that the requirement of *iusta de causa* be strictly observed, it would appear that the circumstances prevailing in this parish run counter to both the spirit and the letter of good liturgical and canonical practice.

Pastoral Aspects

Attendance at the Communion services has varied from 17 to 2 persons. Considering that these services were introduced to accomodate office workers in the area, how many of those who requested the noon-time Mass are willing to avail themselves of either such a Mass or the Communion service which has been offered as an alternative? A response of 2 persons is small by any count.

Perhaps a solution would be to vary the daily Mass schedule somewhat on a trial basis so as to determine what kind of response a Mass in the middle of the day would elicit (cf., c. 213). This parish is blessed with being able to offer three daily Masses. It is further blessed with the generally very impressive response which the current Mass schedule realizes. The pastor is in the best position to determine if and how any alteration of the present Mass schedule would elicit an even greater response than that already prevailing.

A further pastoral concern would be the risk of inculcating or reinforcing in the minds of some the false notion that the reception of Communion is all that matters, e.g., the notion that "If I can get to Communion at noon I need not consider getting to an earlier or later Mass." Such would certainly be *contra mentem ecclesiae*.

In a separate but related context an important pastoral concern has been expressed as follows: "While it is certainly true that being deprived of the Eucharist is undesirable, it is equally true that Catholics should never become accustomed to the reception of the Eucharist apart from the priestly ministry or apart from the celebration of Mass. Otherwise we are moving toward an ecclesiology and sacramentology which fails to link Eucharist and priesthood which is, of course, precisely what Our Lord did on Holy Thursday by instituting both sacraments together" (cf. P. Stravinskas, "Lay People," *The Catholic Answer* 3:1 [1989] 18).

Louis Naughton [1990]

CANON 924

BREAD WITHOUT GLUTEN FOR EUCHARIST

A person in our diocese medically cannot tolerate the gluten in wheat flour, and this to the degree that he is unable to receive Holy Communion in the form of bread. Wheat flour with the gluten removed is available. Is such wheat flour with the gluten removed valid matter for consecration at Holy Mass?

OPINION

To be valid matter for the Eucharist, bread must be made substantially of wheat flour. If there are any additives, they cannot be such that they would change the wheat bread into some other substance. The determination of whether anything is wheat bread or something else is made by the common estimation of persons.

I have not been able to find any positive prohibitions by the Holy See on using wheat flour without gluten for the Eucharist. Additives are forbidden, especially those that would change the substance of the bread into something other than bread, but I find nothing in standard commentaries and canonical collections that indicate that the issue of the removal of gluten has been addressed.

My opinion is that it would be valid matter. Presumably nothing has been added to this wheat flour to change its nature. The gluten has been removed, but the underlying substance appears to be made exclusively from wheat and no other grain. The criterion for validity is whether the bread is made from wheat, and the bread you describe clearly is such.

Another solution would be to administer Holy Communion under the form of wine alone in accord with canon 925.

John M. Huels, O.S.M. [1989]

CANONS 934-935 AND 1205

THE PLACE OF EUCHARISTIC RESERVATION

[Editor's Note: The following questions came from various persons but they are handled together by the author since they all deal with the same issue.]

1. In addition to the Masses in the parish church, we also have two Sunday Masses in our multi-purpose hall. The bishop, after the parish visitation, directed us to put a tabernacle in the hall. I find this directive strange and unsuitable. Does canon law say anything about it?

2. Our archbishop has written to all the priests encouraging them to reserve the Blessed Sacrament in the rectory so that they can more readily pray before it. Is this proper?

3. Two women religious living in an apartment wish to have the reserved Eucharist in a spare bedroom that they use for their prayer. They claim that their constitutions require that they have an oratory in the religious house with the Blessed Sacrament reserved. It seems this is against canon law. What takes precedence, the law, or their constitutions?

4. May a hermit (c. 603) have the Blessed Sacrament reserved in a small tabernacle in her hermitage for private adoration?

OPINION

Canon 934, §1 speaks of reservation, both mandatory and optional, in *sacred places*. The sacred places in question are churches, oratories, bishops' chapels, and other private chapels with the permission of the local ordinary. Sacred places are only those places which have been dedicated or blessed by the appropriate liturgical rite and set apart exclusively for divine worship (cf., cc. 1205-1234). None of the places described above is a sacred place. Furthermore, wherever the Eucharist is reserved, Mass must be celebrated there at least twice a month insofar as possible (c. 934, §2). Except for the first place, the Eucharist is not being celebrated in the places described.

The multi-purpose hall is not a sacred place, even though Mass is celebrated there (cf. c. 932, §1). Since the bishop has required a tabernacle in the hall, there is only one possible interpretation of this directive that is in accord with the law: the regular, permanent place of reservation is in the church (ideally, in a Blessed Sacrament chapel adjacent to the church). The tabernacle in the multi-purpose hall should be used only for reserving the consecrated hosts not used for Communion. These remaining hosts are to be transferred to the church immediately after Mass. If a eucharistic minister transfers the Blessed Sacrament immediately after Communion, there would be no need at all for a tabernacle in the hall.

Questions 2-4 deal with reservation by private persons in their own homes. This is regulated by canon 935, which forbids personal retention of the Eucharist "unless there is an urgent pastoral need and the precepts of the diocesan bishop are observed." Urgent pastoral need does not include the desire of private individuals for prayer before the Blessed Sacrament. Such individuals, even though they be priests, religious, or hermits, are expected to go to their parish church or other sacred place when they wish to pray before the Blessed Sacrament (cf. c. 937).

Concerning the third question, there is no true conflict between the constitutions of religious institutes and canon law on this point. If the constitutions of the institute require each religious house to have a tabernacle with the reserved Eucharist, this could only be understood in the canonical sense of a religious house. A canonical religious *domus* must: 1) be legitimately constituted by the competent authority of the institute with the previous written consent of the diocesan bishop; 2) be under the authority of the competent superior; 3) have a church or oratory in which the Eucharist is celebrated (cc. 608-609). If these three requirements are not observed, there is no true religious house and no right to have the reserved Eucharist.

Before the ordinary can permit an oratory to be established, he must visit the place, either personally or through another, to see if it is suitably constructed (c. 1224, §1). Before granting permission for Eucharistic reservation, he should also be assured that the Eucharist will be celebrated in that sacred place at least twice a month.

John M. Huels, O.S.M. [1993]

Canons 937-938 and 392

Prohibition of a Blessed Sacrament Chapel

We are in the final stages of planning for the remodeling of our parish church. We wanted to build a new Blessed Sacrament chapel for private adoration, but the bishop insisted that the tabernacle be in the sanctuary so that everyone can be at all times in the presence of the Blessed Sacrament. Does the bishop have the authority to do this?

Opinion

The bishop appears to be motivated by the desire that all the faithful have access to the Blessed Sacrament for private prayer and adoration. This value is directly supported in canon 937: "Unless a grave reason prevents it, the church in which the Most Holy Eucharist is reserved should be open to the faithful for at least some hours each day so that they are able to spend time in prayer before the Most Blessed Sacrament."

However, the bishop does not seem to be aware that the law favors reservation in a chapel, set apart from the main body of the church, precisely for the purpose of visitation and private prayer by the faithful.

290

1) *The General Instruction of the Roman Missal*, n. 276, states: "Every encouragement should be given to the practice of Eucharistic reservation in a chapel suited to the faithful's private adoration and prayer."

2) *The Rite of Holy Communion and Worship of the Eucharist Outside Mass*, n. 9, states: "The place for the reservation of the Eucharist should be truly preeminent. It is highly recommended that the place be suitable also for private adoration and prayer so that the faithful may readily and fruitfully continue to honor the Lord, present in the sacrament, through personal worship. This will be achieved more readily if the chapel is separate from the body of the church . . . "

3) *The Ceremonial of Bishops*, n. 49, states: "It is recommended that the *tabernacle*, in accordance with a very ancient tradition in cathedral churches, should be located in a chapel separate from the main body of the church." The ceremonial, n. 46, says the arrangement and decoration of the cathedral is to serve as "a model for the other churches of the diocese in its conformity to the directives laid down in the liturgical documents and books."

These laws have the literary form of a "recommendation." They do not mandate that every church remove its tabernacle from the sanctuary and erect a separate Blessed Sacrament chapel for it. However, there can be no doubt about the preference of the law. All things being equal, a Blessed Sacrament chapel, adjacent to the church and easily accessible by the faithful, is the optimal place for reserving the Eucharist.

One reason for the law's preference for a Blessed Sacrament chapel is so that the faithful may have a quiet place for private prayer and adoration. Another reason is given in the document of the Bishops' Committee on the Liturgy, *Environment and Art in Catholic Worship*, n. 78: "A room or chapel specifically designed and separate from the major space is important so that no confusion can take place between the celebration of the Eucharist and reservation. Active and static aspects of the same reality cannot claim the same human attention at the same time." Christ is actively present during the liturgy: in the assembly, the Word, the ministers, and the consecrated bread and wine. During Mass the focus of the faithful's prayerful participation should be on Christ's active presence here and now, not on the sacrament reserved from a previous celebration.

I believe that your bishop's viewpoint on this issue is not in keeping with the universal law. Canon 392, §1 states: "Since he must protect the unity of the universal Church, the bishop is bound to promote the common discipline of the whole Church, and therefore, to urge the observance of all ecclesiastical laws."

Nor can the bishop validly establish his own particular law contrary to the universal discipline (c. 135, §2).

John M. Huels, O.S.M. [1993]

Canons 945-946

Mass Stipends and Offerings for Special Intentions

What is the legitimacy of certain practices of pastors who leave a book in church inviting people to list special intentions for Masses and also place an offering box alongside the book for free-will donations?

Opinion

You describe a system for handling Mass intentions and the free-will offerings (stipends) accompanying them, which preserves anonymity for the donor (at least usually). I call to your attention a response of the Congregation for the Clergy to the vicar general of the Diocese of Baton Rouge and published in *CLD* 9: 590. The inquiry from Baton Rouge described a system similar to that in the above question. The response of the Congregation was as follows (issued August 21, 1981):

> On the premise that the canonical principle of "as many Masses as there are stipends" (*tot Missae . . . quot stipendia*) canon 828 *CIC* [1917 code], the pastor who receives offerings in the manner set forth in your Reverence's letter must celebrate (or have celebrated) as many Masses as could be celebrated with the amount received, determining the number of Masses according to the current diocesan stipend.

In my opinion certain principles have to be rather carefully safeguarded in any method of receiving offerings of the faithful given on the occasion of a request for the application of Mass for a specific intention.

First, the people are commonly accustomed to requesting the application of a Mass for a stated intention with a sense of special guarantee that a Mass will be celebrated for that intention when an offering is given and accepted. It is only the positive law of the Church, undoubtedly first enacted centuries ago because of abuses, that limits the acceptance of a stipend for any individual Mass. In and of itself a priest could apply the Mass equally for several intentions for which several stipends were received.

292

While the people cannot obligate a priest to offer the Eucharist principally for such a special intention unless he undertakes to do so, people do have a right to receive assistance from the sacred pastors of the Church, especially the word of God and the sacraments (c. 213), and to "thereby contribute to the good of the Church and by their offering share the concern of the Church for the support of its ministers and works" (c. 946).

Any policy which altogether precludes the right of the faithful to request the application of a Mass for their individual intentions renders canon 946 meaningless, and if it is such that it renders their sharing in the support of the ministers and the works of the Church morally impossible or excessively difficult, e.g., due to embarrassment or to a stated policy inhibiting their free choice, it has in my opinion the same effect.

Secondly, the principle that as many Masses must be offered as there are stipends received has to be preserved. At the very least this means that the total amount of stipends received must be divided by the amount established in the diocese as usual for a stipend and the resulting number of Masses must be celebrated for those intentions. This is the issue addressed in the reply of the Congregation for Clergy to Baton Rouge. It reflects the concern of the Church that there not be even the appearance of any trafficking or greed with respect to stipends.

Thirdly, the right of every priest, modified, of course, in the case of religious priests, to receive stipends has also to be respected. There could not, therefore, be a parish or diocesan policy which would prevent a priest from exercising his right which is stated in canon 945. While an individual priest or a group of priests may voluntarily agree to forego the exercise of this canonical right, an individual can change his mind and withdraw from the plan and a newcomer could not be compelled to surrender the exercise of his right.

The irreducible minimum, in my opinion, requires that the parishioners and even visitors to the parish church be unequivocally informed, e.g., by a clearly worded sign, that the offerings which are in fact given do not mean that an individual's intention written in the book will be the principal intention remembered at a single Mass. In other words, the offering is not really a Mass stipend.

If, however, as I suspect would at least occasionally happen, the pastor finds in the offering box an amount of money, e.g., in an envelope, with a stated intention, he would have to treat that as a true stipend and either celebrate Mass for that intention or have another priest do so, having been given the entire amount of the offering, or return the money to the donor.

When you think about it I believe there is a sort of anomaly in what these widespread systems are attempting to do. By having a book in which the people can enter their special intentions with the assurance that these will be specially remembered at Masses celebrated in the parish or elsewhere, any suspicion is avoided that their intentions will not be remembered, that they are buying a Mass, and that those who can afford a monetary offering receive a little more attention than those who cannot. By having an offering box alongside the book, however, an effort is being made to maintain the level of stipend income received in the traditional way. Whether both of these purposes can be realized without violating canon law remains to be seen.

Richard A. Hill, S.J. [1985]

Canons 949-952

Offerings for Novena of Masses

A newly appointed pastor in this diocese dislikes intensely the notion of Mass stipends and as a result finds particularly repelling the considerable sum of money involved in the offering for the All Souls Novena of Masses. "Because I dislike the whole notion of Mass offerings," says the new pastor, "I am going to attach a five dollar stipend to each novena Mass and I am putting the rest of the money involved into the parish funds." One of his associates objects to this arbitrary decision. The bishops of the province in which this diocese is located have not given any directive in accordance with canon 952, §1 and the custom in effect in the diocese is observed (cf., c. 952, §2).

Opinion

In accordance with canon 949, one who has the obligation of celebrating Mass and applying it for the intention of those who made the offering is bound by the same obligation even if the offerings received have been lost. Hence it follows that the priests who fulfill the intentions of the donors of the stipends are entitled to the full amount of the offerings in question. The offerings given by the faithful for a definite purpose can be applied only for that same purpose (c. 1267, §3). The object of offerings given for a novena of Masses is clearly and unambiguously for the purpose of the offering of the Masses in question. While it is NOT licit for a priest to ASK a donor to offer a larger sum than is customary for the celebration and application of a Mass, it IS lawful for a priest to accept for the application of a Mass a voluntary offering that is larger or smaller than that which is customary (cf., c. 952, §1). It is not lawful for someone else to decide arbitrarily (even with goodwill) *praeter/contra legem* to withhold from a priest any portion of the offering which has been made for the application of the Mass which he celebrates.

All Souls (and similar) offerings made for the purpose of an All Souls (or similar) novena are to be given to the priests who fulfill this intention. The priests who accept such offerings are seriously obliged to fulfill this intention. The offerings belong by right to the priests who honor the Mass stipends in question because the intentions of the donors are that the offerings are given in connection with the Masses so offered.

Unless particular law dictates otherwise (as perhaps in religious or secular institutes or societies of apostolic life), nobody is entitled to withhold from a priest his fair share of the offerings given for the specific purpose of a novena of Masses. Otherwise, whoever would presume to direct any portion of the novena Mass offerings elsewhere would thereby take on the obligation of fulfilling *pro rata* the number of Masses involved.

In some parishes in this diocese it is customary for the total sum of the novena Mass offerings to be evenly divided among the various priests of the rectory irrespective of the actual number of the novena Masses offered by the individual priests concerned. Of course there should be unanimous agreement in this regard. Otherwise the offerings should be distributed strictly *pro rata* on the basis of the actual number of Masses offered by each individual priest. Such an agreement could contribute not only to rectory morale but could also assist in meeting other personal needs. However, in order to offset any appearance of trafficking or commerce in this regard (cc. 947 and 951), I would suggest that each priest who wished to avail himself of an even share of the novena offerings would be asked to agree personally to offer a total of nine Masses (including the particular Masses of the novena proper for which he might happen to scheduled). If this could be arranged, the wishes of those who made the offerings would be more than minimally honored. Not only would the actual number of Masses exceed the minimum of nine obliged by the acceptance of the novena Mass offerings, but also every priest involved would bear his fair share of the obligation. The most important consideration of all would be the increase beyond minimalism of the prayerful concern expressed by the increased number of Masses in this regard. As in other areas of his life, the priest could then determine how he wished to dispose of the finances thus accrued (whether to a charitable cause of his own choice or otherwise).

Apart from the kind of exception mentioned above (with regard to particular law or c. 952, §2), because this is a matter of (distributive) justice, it would seem to be a violation of the law regarding Mass stipends to direct any portion of novena Mass offerings to other causes apart from the priests who participate in the fulfillment of the particular obligations involved.

Louis Naughton [1990]

Canon 951

Stipend for Second Mass after *Missa pro populo*

May a pastor who offers the Missa pro populo *and celebrates again on the same day retain a stipend for himself for the Mass other than the* pro populo?

Opinion

I am of the opinion that the law has been significantly changed with respect to the pastor receiving a stipend for himself for the Mass other than the *pro populo*.

The 1917 code, canon 824, §2, prohibits a binating pastor from accepting a stipend for himself if one of the Masses is offered *ex titulo iustitiae*. Since the application of the Mass *pro populo* is from a title of justice, this precluded receiving a stipend for himself for the other Mass.

The 1983 code, canon 951, §1, is obviously parallel to the former canon 824, §2, which it amends principally by omitting the reference to the title of justice. The former §1 is now canon 945, §1, and the new §2 derives from a declaration of the S.C. for Divine Worship, 8/7/72, no. 3b.

Communicationes does not report why the reference to the title of justice was omitted (cf., *Communicationes* 4 [1972] 57-59; 7 [1975] 33-34; 8 [1981] 433). The 1975 schema, canon 111, which was referenced to former canon 824, omitted it and it never reappeared.

Were a generous parishioner to give the pastor an "offering" for the *pro populo* Mass this would be by way of personal gift because the obligation arises not from this offering, but from canon law. A stipend for a third Mass is governed by canon 951, §1 as well.

I think this change makes good sense. It permits the pastor to celebrate the Mass for the people when it is prescribed and at the same time to accept this special kind of contribution to his own support. It also cuts away the rationale commonly given for the fact that the pastor receives a slightly higher monthly salary because of his obligation to apply the *Missa pro populo*.

Richard A. Hill, S.J. [1984]

Canon 983

INTERPRETERS FOR SACRAMENT OF PENANCE

Can interpreters be used for the sacrament of penance, and could this include sign language as well as interpreters of various spoken tongues?

OPINION

Interpreters are permitted for the sacrament of penance. The only canonical norm in their regard is that they observe the seal of the confessional (c. 983, §2); failure to do so is punishable as a crime in the Church (c. 1388, §2).

There is a statement of qualifications for interpreters in the canons on marriage — canon 1106, which permits marriage to be contracted through interpreters (presumably, although not exclusively, because the parties don't understand one another!). The qualification is that the pastor who assists at such a marriage is to be convinced of the interpreter's trustworthiness. A similar caution would appear to be obvious in regard to an interpreter who assists in the celebration of the sacrament of penance. The canons I noted earlier would add to the quality of trustworthiness as an interpreter, the quality of being able to keep the confessional secret. This applies as well to interpreters using sign language.

James H. Provost [1985]

CANONS 983 AND 984

CONFIDENTIALITY OF THE SEAL OF CONFESSION IN CONNECTION WITH POST-ABORTION COUNSELING

The question is two-fold: (1) If a woman comes to a priest in a confessional situation and the priest determines there is a need to refer her to a counseling service and if it would be of help to the counselor to have some kind of professional report from the priest about this case, what are the different "Seals of Confession," and can that priest say anything . . . even with the patient's permission? (2) Secondly, if a woman should enter counseling and is then referred to a spiritual advisor/confessor because there seems to be work that needs to be done on both the counselor's and the spiritual advisor's levels then what kind of collaboration can be carried out without involving a violation of the seal of confession?

OPINION

The confidentiality of confession is treated in canons 983 and 984.

Canon 983, §1: The sacramental seal is inviolable; therefore, it is a crime for a confessor in any way to betray a penitent by word or in any other manner or for any reason. §2: An interpreter, if there is one present, is also obliged to observe the secret, and also all others to whom knowledge of sins from confession shall come in any way.

Canon 984, §1: Even if every danger of revelation is excluded, a confessor is absolutely forbidden to use knowledge acquired from confession when it might harm the penitent. §2: One who is placed in authority can in no way use for external governance knowledge about sins which he has received in confession at any time.

It is seen from the reading of these two canons that the Church enjoins strict confidentiality on the confessor (and interpreter, etc.), preventing any disclosure whatsoever of information received in the confessional. The canons also prohibit *use* of confessional matter, even if the penitent's identity is not to be disclosed, when it might harm the penitent. Even if it seems potentially helpful to the penitent, direct disclosure of confessional matter is strictly forbidden, given the sacred nature of the seal and the importance the Church attaches to its protection for the good of this sacrament. Some indirect use of knowledge from the confessional may be permitted if the nature of the sin and the identity of the person were not revealed and if the penitent were not harmed by it.

Two other canons also seem pertinent in response to the questions: a) Canon 1388, §1: A confessor who directly violates the seal of confession incurs an automatic excommunication reserved to the Apostolic See; if he does so only indirectly, he is to be punished in accord with the seriousness of the offense. §2: An interpreter and any other persons mentioned in canon 983, §2 who violate the secrecy are to be punished with a just penalty not excluding excommunication. b) Canon 1550 lists persons who are incapable of acting as witnesses in ecclesiastical trials. "The following are considered incapable . . . . §2 Priests as regards everything which has become known to them by reason of sacramental confession, even if the penitent requests the manifestation. Moreover, whatever has been heard by anyone or in any way on the occasion of confession cannot be accepted as even an indication of the truth."

It is clear from these canons and commentaries written on them that these prescriptions of law are treating the confidentiality of confession as a grave obligation. Commentators consider protection of the seal of confession as a matter of both divine and ecclesiastical law. Commentators indicate there is no such thing as a minor violation of the seal of confession. Even the most minor disclosure is considered an offense against God and sacrilegious violation of the virtue of religion. Commentators indicate that if there is the slightest doubt that some action or speech might reveal what is confidential in this area, then the person is to treat the matter in the safest way and avoid what could even appear to be disclosure. On June 9, 1915, the "Holy Office" issued an instruction on confession and secrecy of the seal that counselled confessors against making impersonal references in preaching to matters learned in confession. They indicated that, although all danger of disclosure or injury might be absent, the broad confidence of penitents in the inviolability of the sacramental secrecy might be lessened (cf., Frederick R. McManus, "Title IV: The Sacrament of Penance," in *The Code of Canon Law: A Text and Commentary*, J. Coriden et al., eds., New York/Mahwah: Paulist Press [1985] 691-692.).

The question is asked whether or not, for the good of the penitent confessing the sin of abortion, the confessor could become involved in open counseling sessions. The question posed here presupposes that the penitent is going to give permission for the confessor to discuss confessional matter in a counseling situation (perhaps group sessions) whose purpose is to assist the penitent's adjustment after abortion. From the strictness of the interpretation of the confidentiality of the seal of confession, it would seem that such use of confessional matter would be prohibited. We note that confessors are not permitted to testify in ecclesiastical trials even if the penitent were to grant them a release. Therefore, the Church does not seem to recognize in the penitent a right to release the confessor from the seal. The secrecy of the confessional transcends even the will of the penitent in order to protect the good of the Church and the sacrament on behalf of all the faithful. It is also possible that someone in emotional turmoil could momentarily ask the confessor to participate in counseling sessions, and then, at a later date, regret such a release from confidentiality because the disclosure or use of the material becomes embarrassing, at which point the penitent could take an adverse reaction against the Church for use of the information. A penitent could forget that she or he released the priest or could resent the release. Also there could be danger that other parties, hearing the disclosure or use of confessional matter but not knowing of the so-called release, could be scandalized to think that a priest confessor became involved in open discussion of someone's confession. Therefore, even if the penitent should presume to offer a release to the confessor, it does not seem the law permits the confessor to act on the release and discuss the material in a counseling session involving persons other than the penitent.

In the situation addressed in these questions it would seem that the confessor could suggest that the penitent undertake the counseling therapy available; but the confessor is not free to become involved in the counseling sessions lest secrecy of confession be jeopardized. Also, in the second scenario mentioned in the question, if a woman already involved in post-abortion counseling demonstrates to the counselor a need and readiness for spiritual direction and sacramental absolution, the counselor may suggest that the woman return to her confessor or spiritual director for further assistance on the spiritual/sacramental level. The confessor, however, cannot then become involved in subsequent counseling sessions which would involve discussion or use of confessional information when other priests are present. We realize that counseling sessions and group therapy mean a great deal of disclosure of very personal, confidential, occult material. If a person chooses to undertake such sessions with the counselor, that is considered his or her right and privilege. The matter disclosed and discussed in confession, however, remains religiously sealed with the confessor in the name of the Church and cannot be used in any other forum. Therefore, it does not seem permissible for confessor and counselor to be involved in sharing information even though both are operating for the good of the penitent.

J. James Cuneo [1987]

CANON 1006

HOSPITAL EMERGENCY ROOM POLICY ON ANOINTING

What is the legality under the new code of the policy in a Catholic hospital which requires that everyone admitted to its emergency room unconscious and in critical condition, and whose religious background is unknown, must be anointed?

OPINION

I find it almost unbelievable that a Catholic hospital has a policy requiring that everyone who is admitted to its emergency room unconscious and in critical condition and whose religious background is unknown must be anointed (and presumably absolved, not to say conditionally baptized). This is the well-known case of the unknown, unconscious, probably dying person. Such a policy is clearly contrary to canon law and at odds with the *Rite of Anointing of the Sick*.

This is by no means something new in the law of the Church. The 1917 Code of Canon Law stated:

> Canon 943: This sacrament [Extreme Unction], however, should nevertheless be absolutely extended to infirm persons who, when in possession of their faculties, had at least implicitly requested it, even though thereafter they have lost consciousness or the use of reason.

> Canon 752, §3: If, however, an adult is not even able to request

300

baptism, but either beforehand or in his or her present state has made known in some probable way the intention of receiving it, he or she is to be conditionally baptized.

The revised Code of Canon Law substantially repeats the 1917 code, simplifying it:

Canon 1006: This sacrament is to be conferred upon sick persons who requested it at least implicitly when they were in control of their faculties.

Canon 865, §2: An adult in danger of death may be baptized if, having some knowledge of the principal truths of faith, the person has in any way manifested an intention of receiving baptism and promises to observe the commandments of the Christian religion.

I allude to baptism because a certain percentage of unconscious, critical patients admitted to your emergency room are certainly not baptized, e.g., Jews or people whose families have for generations been unchurched. Yet you do not mention conditional baptism as a matter of policy.

I would like also to call your attention to *Ethical and Religious Directives for Catholic Health Facilities* (USCC, 1977), art. 41:

Normally the sacrament (Anointing of the Sick) is celebrated when the sick person is fully conscious. It may be conferred upon the sick who have lost consciousness or the use of reason, if, as Christian believers, they would have asked for it if they were in control of their faculties.

In the 1930s and 1940s some American moralists developed a pastoral position, which at best had some plausibility, according to which a presumption was asserted that the vast majority of Americans are either in fact baptized Christians or so imbued with Christian values that, if they were given the chance in danger of death, they would want to receive the appropriate sacraments. At best this argument asserted the permissibility of conferring conditional baptism, absolution and anointing. No one, as far as I know, ever had the audacity to claim that this presumption created an obligation so to act.

Today this presumption is patently implausible. The Second Vatican Council was conspicuously careful to avoid any hint that all people of good will are really Christians because they have received the grace of baptism by reason of their desire (*in voto*) to do good as they perceive it. The concept of anonymous Christians had already been discredited. Instead, the council asserted that the unbaptized who consistently try to follow the light of their consciences are saved by God's grace which is not restricted to a sacramental system.

I have no hesitation in saying that the policy you describe is clearly at odds with correct pastoral practice, canon law and a healthy theology of sacraments and grace. It violates the chaplain's right to integrity, is ecumenically untenable and is scandalous, even if scandal has not yet occurred. Eventually it will. Were this policy to become a condition of appointment or of continued employment it would be manifestly unjust.

Richard A. Hill, S.J. [1984]

Canon 1031, §2

Unmarried Permanent Deacon Candidate

An unmarried candidate for ordination as a permanent deacon will only be 33¼ years old at the time he is scheduled to be ordained. Although the 1983 code, canon 1031, §2 specified the minimum age for such a candidate as 25, in §3 of that same canon the bishops' conference is authorized to set an older age. This has been done by the NCCB, which established 35 as the minimum age for any candidate for the permanent diaconate, married or unmarried. What authority is competent to dispense from the age requirement in this particular case?

Opinion

First, it is clear the Apostolic See can dispense from the age requirement. As the authority which established the code, it can dispense from requirements in the code; as the superior of the episcopal conference, it can dispense from laws made by the episcopal conference. This does not violate the legislative authority of the episcopal conference, since we are dealing here only with a dispensation, which is the relaxation of a law in a particular case and does not touch the law itself (c. 85).

Second, is it possible for the diocesan bishop to dispense? This requires a more careful analysis of the source of the law, and the specific provisions of canon 1031.

a. The source of the age limit of 35 for all candidates for the permanent diaconate is *Permanent Deacons in the United States: Guidelines on Their Formation and Ministry, 1984 Revision*. The legal character of a "guidelines" document is not clear: is it a general decree (and thus a law — c. 29), a general executory decree (which further specifies and enforces a law — c. 31), or an instruction (which gives directions to those responsible for implementing a law — c. 34)? To avoid any uncertainty about the effectiveness of the "guidelines," the NCCB took the special step of obtaining the *recognitio* from the Apostolic See for the whole document, and not just those portions which contain a legal decree (cc. 455, §2 and 456). Thus it is safe to say that whatever the general legal character of the "Guidelines," whatever decrees they contain do have the force of law.

b. The Guidelines contain the following provision with regard to dispensation from the age of 35: "The diocesan bishop may dispense up to one year from this age requirement" (page 29). The text then footnotes a reference to canon 1031, §4.

However, canon 1031, §4 states: "The Apostolic See reserves to itself the dispensation from the age required in §§1 and 2 when it is a question of more than one year." This includes the minimum ages set in the canon for permanent deacons (§2). Thus if an unmarried candidate were under 24 years old, he would definitely have to be dispensed by the Apostolic See before he could be ordained.

What if the candidate is over 24, but more than one year younger then the age set by the conference of bishops in light of the authorization given them in canon 1031, §3? Is this also restricted to the Apostolic See?

In my opinion, it is not. There are two reasons for this.

First, the wording of canon 1031, §4 is clear: only the ages set in §§1 and 2 of canon 1031 are under this limitation. While the bishops' conference can set an older age for presbyters and diaconate, the Apostolic See has not reserved to itself dispensation from more than a year younger then the age a bishops' conference may set but only from more than a year younger than the age the Apostolic See itself has set in §§1 and 2 of the canon. The canon does not set a limit on the power of the diocesan bishop to dispense from a higher age which his bishops' conference may have set. To determine the dispensing power of the bishop in this kind of situation, we must look elsewhere in the code.

This brings me to my second reason. Canon 88 authorizes the local ordinary (thus, the vicar general and episcopal vicars within their competence, as well as the diocesan bishop) to dispense "from laws passed by a plenary or provincial council or by the conference of bishops" "as often as he judges that a dispensation will contribute to the good of the faithful." Thus the bishop has the authority, clearly stated in law, to dispense from a law which is passed by the conference of bishops, provided he judges the dispensation will contribute to the good of the faithful. This could be the good of the individual being ordained or could be the good of the people he will serve as a deacon, etc.

Of course, he can dispense only insofar as the law is a law passed by the conference; if the conference were merely to repeat a law issued by the Apostolic See (repeat a canon in the code, for example), he would be bound by the more stringent norms concerning dispensing from those types of laws. But this does not seem to be the case in this situation, even though the Guidelines cite canon 1031, §4. As I have already pointed out, that citation applies only to §§1 and 2 of the canon, and not to a higher age which might be set in virtue of §3. Moreover, the conference does not have the power to restrict the power of the local ordinary to dispense from one of its laws, so it does not have the power to restrict the power of the diocesan bishop to dispense more than one year from the conference's higher age requirement.

In my opinion, the restriction stated on page 29 of the Guidelines is without legal force because it is contrary to canon 88, which specifically gives the bishop broader dispensing power than the one year limit stated in the Guidelines. Moreover, even though the Guidelines received the *recognitio* from the Apostolic See, this did not make them laws of the Apostolic See; they retain their character as passed by the bishops' conference, and hence subject to canon 88.

So, in addition to the Apostolic See, the following can dispense from the 35 age limit set by the NCCB for unmarried candidates to the permanent diaconate. First, the diocesan bishop can dispense for candidates at least 24 years old. This is because he can dispense from universal disciplinary laws except for those reserved to the Apostolic See or another authority (c. 87, §1), and dispensing below the age of 24 is reserved to the Apostolic See (c. 1031, §4). Second, other local ordinaries can dispense for candidates at least 25 years old. They are included among those who can dispense from a law issued by the conference of bishops (c. 88), but not among those who under usual circumstances can dispense from universal laws (c. 87, §1). Under the conditions set down in canon 87, §2, these other local ordinaries could also dispense for candidates at least 24 years old.

James H. Provost [1989]

CANONS 1032 AND 1035

DISPENSATION FROM INTERVAL OF TIME BEFORE DIACONATE ORDINATION

A candidate for the permanent diaconate in the second year of the formation program has been diagnosed as having a terminal illness. According to his doctor's report he will become progressively weaker. His doctor believes that his ordination, if it could be accelerated, would greatly benefit him emotionally. Are there any canonical obstacles to an earlier ordination?

OPINION

The response to this question is first governed by the following canons: a)

304

canon 1032, §3: An aspirant to the permanent diaconate is not to be promoted to that order unless he has completed the time of formation; b) canon 1035, §1: Before anyone is promoted to either the permanent or the transitional diaconate he is required to have received the ministries of lector and acolyte and to have exercised them for a stable period of time — §2 Between the conferral of acolyte and diaconate there is to be an interval of at least six months.

Several points should be noted in applying these canons to the case in question:

1. The formation program for permanent deacons is left to the discretion of the diocese. Therefore, it would seem to be the right of the bishop to determine if and when a particular candidate had fulfilled the requirements of formation. The bishop for good reasons could dispense from the locally legislated formation requirements.

2. The code does not specify any interval between conferral of lector and acolyte.

3. The code, while requiring a six month interval between acolyte and diaconate ordination as a universal norm, does not, however, reserve the dispensation from this norm to the Apostolic See. Therefore, it would seem that the general dispensing authority of the bishop given in canon 87 applies: "As often as he judges that a dispensation will contribute to the spiritual good of the faithful, the diocesan bishop can dispense from both universal and particular disciplinary laws established for his territory or for his subjects by the supreme authority of the Church. He cannot dispense, however, from procedural or penal laws or from those laws whose dispensation is especially reserved to the Apostolic See or to another authority."

4. In deciding whether or not there is sufficient good reason to dispense from the interval, the bishop should keep in mind the norm of canon 1025, §2: "It is further required that, in the judgment of the same legitimate superior he (the candidate) is considered to be useful for the ministry of the Church." Sacred orders is not to be conferred as a strictly private, spiritual benefit for the person ordained. The purpose of ordination is public service to the Church. The fact that a candidate will be personally uplifted by the grace of ordination may not be sufficient reason in itself to dispense from the full formation program and normal intervals for exercise of ministries of lector and acolyte. The criterion of benefit to the Church should enter the decision about dispensation, although it certainly does not seem necessary to place a minimal time limit on the anticipated length of period of the future service and benefit to the Church. The benefit to the Church need not and perhaps cannot be measured in terms of time of service.

Therefore, it would seem that the code permits the bishop to dispense from the six month interval in order to ordain the deacon at an earlier time, all things being considered for the spiritual good of the faithful and benefit of the Church.

J. James Cuneo [1987]

CANONS 1034 AND 1035

A. CANDIDACY AND INSTALLATION IN MINISTRIES

In many American seminaries installation in the lay ministries of lector and acolyte takes place prior to admission to candidacy for orders. Various reasons are given for this, including the desire to relate candidacy more directly to sacred orders themselves.

However, a seminary which serves a number of American dioceses outside the country is located in a diocese where the custom prevails of requiring students be admitted to candidacy before they are installed in the lay ministries of lector and acolyte. Are there any decisions of the U.S. bishops bearing on this which might assist the seminary in discussing the situation with officials of the local diocese?

OPINION

There is nothing I can find in the general norms of the Church which requires the reception of candidacy prior to installation in the ministries. However, there does not seem to be anything which prohibits this, either.

1. The liturgical books refer to installation as a distinct rite, whereas the admission to candidacy is dealt within the context of the sacrament of orders. This is true, for example, in the recent *Caeremoniale Episcoporum* (Vatican City: Typis Polyglottis Vaticanis, 1985) as well as in the pontifical and other rituals on which it is based.

Liturgically the two are not joined, but there is no prohibition against a local determination to have candidacy precede or follow installation — or for that matter, take place between the two installations. From a liturgical perspective, they are distinct concerns, not necessarily joined, since installation is to lay ministries which have meaning in themselves and need not lead to sacred orders.

2. The motu proprio *Ministeria quaedam*, which did away with tonsure and the minor orders, established two universally applicable lay ministries, lector and acolyte, for the Latin Church. It does indicate that candidates for sacred orders are to be installed in the ministries if this has not already been done (cf., no. 11) — hence, does not specify any priority between candidacy and

306

installation in the ministries.

Similarly, the motu proprio *Ad pascendum* (no. 2), which established the requirement of candidacy as a rite, also mentioned that candidates for sacred orders must be installed in the two lay ministries if this has not already been done. Again, no priority is specified.

3. I do not have any documents which would indicate that the United States bishops as a body have taken any decision on the relative order between candidacy and installation.

Normally such a decision would appear in the introduction to the ritual relative to candidacy, installation, or both. I have not been able to find any reference to such a decision in the rituals available to me.

Regrettably, the American bishops have failed to adopt a systematic manner of reporting decisions of their episcopal conference, and their decisions remain closed in minutes of their meetings that are restricted to NCCB members — hence, not available for non-bishop scholars. No decision is reported in *Complementary Norms* (Washington: NCCB, 1991), which does report decisions implementing the 1983 code.

What seems to be happening in the local diocese where the seminary is located is that the pattern established prior to the changes mandated by Pope Paul VI has been retained; namely, tonsure has been replaced by candidacy in the practice of the local diocese, hence has been made mandatory prior to the lay ministries of lector and acolyte, which continue to be treated as "minor orders" of the old dispensation.

There is nothing in general law against this custom; there is nothing in general law requiring this custom. However, the seminary officials will probably have to make their case to the local diocese without being able to rely on a mandated practice of the American bishops, since there is no record I can find of such a mandate.

James H. Provost [1988, revised 1993]

B. Intervals Between Ministries and Diaconate

The chancery in our diocese has notified me that, as a major superior of a clerical religious institute, I may dispense my subjects from the requirement of the six-month interval between the institution to the ministry of acolyte and ordination to the diaconate. Is this correct?

OPINION

It is not correct. The dispensation in question can be given by the diocesan bishop, but not by the major superior. Before the 1983 code went into effect, it was possible in the United States to obtain a dispensation from the law of the interval from the ordinary, namely, the competent local ordinary or clerical major superior.

The previously existing universal law permitted the episcopal conferences to specify a determined length of time for the interval that must be observed between institution to the two ministries of lector and acolyte. Regarding the interval between institution to the ministries and ordination to the diaconate, the universal law only stated that the two ministries be exercised for an "appropriate period of time" (*Ministeriam quaedam*, no. X).

The National Conference of Catholic Bishops issued regulations governing the ministries of lector and acolyte in 1972. One of its norms stated that candidates for the diaconate are to have served in their second ministry (either acolyte or lector, depending on which was received first) for at least six months before ordination to the diaconate. The NCCB law also provided that the ordinary may dispense from the six-month interval in particular cases (*CLD* 8: 629-630).

This provision of the 1972 NCCB legislation was revoked when the revised code went into effect. The 1983 code specified an interval of at least six months between acolyte and diaconate (c. 1035, §2). The minimal six-month interval is now universal law, not particular law. Since the new code does not mention that the ordinary may dispense, one must presume that only the diocesan bishop may do so (c. 87, §1).

The 1972 legislation of the NCCB on lector and acolyte is particular law, not universal law. Its provision allowing the ordinary to dispense from the six-month interval between institution to the second ministry (lector or acolyte) and ordination to the diaconate is abrogated because it is contrary to the code, which does not permit this (c. 6, §1, 2°).

Those parts of this 1972 legislation of the NCCB which are not contrary to the new code are still in effect. Among the regulations that are still binding particular law in the United States are the following:

1. The minimum age for institution in the ministries of lector or acolyte is eighteen; the ordinary may dispense from this norm in individual cases.

2. There must be a six-month interval between institution as a lector and institution as an acolyte (or between acolyte and lector if institution to the ministry of acolyte occurred first). The ordinary may dispense without detriment to the distinction of the two ministries and the authenticity of their exercise.

John M. Huels, O.S.M. [1988]

Canon 1041

A. Irregularity for Reception of Orders Following Attempted Marriage and Following Ecclesiastical Declaration of Nullity of Marriage

A man, after being admitted to candidacy for the permanent diaconate, was thought to be irregular for ordination (c. 1041, §3) because he had attempted marriage after a civil divorce. At the time he was divorced from the civil union also. If the first union is declared null by the Church, will the man become eligible for orders?

Opinion

I would agree with the opinion that the irregularity would not apply if the first marriage were annulled since the basis of the irregularity seems to be the combination of the attempted marriage and the valid prior bond, be it on the part of the man or the woman with whom he attempted the union. Once the prior marriage is annulled, there seems to be no basis then for the irregularity.

This may not be the place to discuss the issue, but one should also note that this case raises the question of the appropriateness of a serious inquiry by seminary admissions boards before accepting candidates who have been married and divorced. Perhaps some of the reasons that may have led to the break-up of the marriage may be pertinent to a judgment regarding the candidate's suitability for admission to orders.

Thomas J. Green [1988]

B. Irregularity for Receiving Order of Diaconate (Permanent) Following Vasectomy

A candidate for the permanent diaconate has confided to this director of the program that several years prior to this he underwent a vasectomy. At the time, his wife was medically advised not to bear any other children for reasons of health. There is no public awareness of this fact and the candidate had treated this moral matter in the internal forum. Is the candidate now under the irregularity listed in canon 1041, §5? What is the director of the permanent diaconate program obliged to do regarding this candidate?

Opinion

1. The 1983 Code of Canon Law (c. 1041, §5) states as an irregularity to receiving (or exercising) orders *"qui seipsum graviter et dolose mutilaverit."*

2. Canon 1047, §4 of the same Code of Canon Law states that the ordinary can dispense from those irregularities which are not reserved to the Holy See. The case at issue of possible mutilation is not among the reserved cases.

3. Several years ago the Congregation for the Doctrine of the Faith issued a declaration permitting vasectomized males to enter valid marriage and forbade church courts to declare a marriage entered into by a vasectomized man to be invalid.

4. *Commento al Codice di Diritto Canonico* by Pio Vito Pinto (Urbaniana Univ. Press, 1985) comments on page 611: "le irregolarità *ex delicto*, si producono soltanto se l'atto compiuto dall'individuo e peccato grave, esterno (pubblico od occulto poco importa) e commesso dopo il battesimo. Quindi, se uno non ha peccato gravemente, sia che fosse in buona fede, sia che si trattesse di cosa poco importante non incorre l'irregolaritae *ex delicto*." Further: "Al n. 5 [c. 1041, §5] si tratta di azione peccaminosa e per mutalazione deve considerarsi un organo che svolga una sua specifica funzione: mano, occhio, piede, ecc."

5. The well-known text book of Bouscaren-Ellis, one of the older commentators on the 1917 code, says this about the former canon 985, §5: "Those who have mutilated themselves or others. . . In order to induce the irregularity, the mutilation must be notable, that is, a part of the body which has its own function distinct from that of other members must be cut off; for instance, a hand, a foot, an eye, complete castration. If the member is not cut off, but merely rendered useless, no irregularity is incurred though the act may be grievously sinful" (3rd edition, page 428.).

6. It would appear, therefore, that a vasectomy in a male does not constitute a canonical irregularity of mutilation. There is no mutilation of an *external* organ, which seems to be a key element in the traditional understanding of this irregularity.

7. But there is another consideration to be made regarding the *reputation* of diaconal candidates and their *right to privacy*. This is protected by canon 220 of the 1983 Code of Canon Law: "no one is permitted to damage unlawfully the good reputation which another person enjoys nor to violate the right of another person to protect his or her privacy." This is based on the Vatican II teaching found in *Gaudium et spes* 26.

It would seem, therefore, in the case at issue that the irregularity itself does not exist canonically; that the candidate has a right to his reputation in this matter; that as long as the director of the diaconate program is assured that whatever moral guilt was involved has been presented in the internal forum of the sacrament of reconciliation; that as long as the matter is not public or notorious — the candidate could be accepted for ordination to the diaconate.

The Wanderer reported a similar situation on June 2, 1988 regarding a candidate denied diaconal ordination for the past six years "because of 'public knowledge' that he had a vasectomy in 1971." We can learn from this experience that the notion of "public knowledge" is a relative one. It makes a difference if the knowledge is known in a small town or a large city, in the place where a person grew up and continues to reside or in a distant place, in a situation where the vasectomized person has told others himself, or where the information would hardly become known, etc. In short, the decision to admit or not admit a candidate to orders becomes a practical judgment in a pastoral situation where the ultimate and best interests of the Catholic Church must have precedence over the particular interests and private hopes of the individual.

William A. Varvaro [1988]

Canon 1041, 2° & 3°

Dispensations from the Irregularities of Schism and Attempted Marriage

John, a candidate for the diaconate, was previously married, and also became affiliated with an anti-Catholic evangelical group for a period of time. For the past five years he has been reconciled with the Church. Is it necessary to seek dispensation from the irregularities of canon 1041, 2° and 3°?

Opinion

Since the man is presently married in the Church, I am presuming that he is a candidate for the permanent diaconate (c. 1042, 1°), and that his present marriage was celebrated with the appropriate determination of his freedom to marry with regard to his first attempt at marriage, and according to proper canonical form.

1. Irregularity of Canon 1041, 2°

The canon declares irregular "a person who has committed the delict of apostasy, heresy or schism." Whether he is exempted from the penalties attached to this delict is not the question here. It is whether he committed the delict since "ignorance of the irregularities . . . does not exempt from them" (c. 1045).

311

The original query indicates some hesitation in characterizing John's actions as leaving the Catholic Church by a formal act, but it describes his activities as affiliating with an evangelical Protestant group and writing anti-Catholic polemic for one or more of their periodicals.

It is not necessary that a person leave the Catholic Church by a formal act for that person to commit the delict of schism. "Schism is the refusal of submission to the Roman Pontiff or of communion with the members of the Church subject to him" (c. 751). This can be done by persons who have not made a "formal act" to leave the Catholic Church, but who do refuse submission and communion.

It could be argued that some Catholics participate in prayer services of Protestant evangelical groups without intending to leave the Catholic Church by a formal act, or to refuse submission to the pope or communion with the members of the Catholic Church. Rather, for them it is a type of devotional practice rather than a change in ecclesial communion.

However, in light of your description, and lacking any further details, it would appear that John went well beyond even this marginal possibility. He actively participated in anti-Catholic polemic by writing for the publications of the Protestant evangelical group. On the face of it, this would appear to be at least schism.

So, in light of the facts as described, it is my opinion that he has incurred this irregularity.

2. Irregularity of Canon 1041, 3°

The canon declares irregular "a person who has attempted marriage, even a civil one only, . . . with a woman bound by a valid marriage . . . ."

John, a baptized Catholic bound by the form, attempted civil marriage with Jane, a non-baptized woman who was herself previously married. The marriage was invalid due to lack of form, the impediment of disparity of worship, and the impediment of prior bond. However, since no tribunal formalities were required for the determination of John's freedom to marry after the breakup of his attempted union with Jane, I suspect there is no judicial evidence as to the validity of her previous union(s).

In such a situation, however, the presumption of canon 1060 comes into play and her first marriage must be presumed to be valid until proven otherwise. If it were proven that none of her previous marriages were valid canonically, the irregularity of canon 1041, 3° would not exist, for the canon requires that she be "bound by a valid marriage."

Even though the marriage was invalid due to lack of form and at least the impediment of disparity of worship, it would still establish the irregularity since

312

the canon is quite clear: "attempted marriage, even a civil one only."

It is my opinion that unless the previous marriages of Jane can be proven not to be valid, the presumption of canon 1060 establishes the presumed validity of her previous marriage and the irregularity was incurred.

3. Dispensation from These Irregularities

If the delict of schism is public, the dispensation from the irregularity of canon 1041, 2° is reserved to the Apostolic See (c. 1047, §2, 1°). Since John engaged in writing anti-Catholic materials for the publications of a Protestant evangelical group, his actions would seem to be "public" in the sense intended by the canon, and the dispensation from this irregularity is reserved to the Apostolic See.

The dispensation of the irregularity from an attempted civil marriage with a woman bound by a valid marriage is also reserved to the Apostolic See if it is public (c. 1047, §2, 1°), or if it has been brought to the judicial forum (c. 1047, §1). Some authors hold that the "judicial forum" here is only an ecclesiastical court. Others hold it includes secular as well (and so a divorce would qualify as "judicial forum"). The question is probably moot, unless John's marriage with Jane was so unknown that it could be classified as occult. Moreover, since a dispensation has to be requested from the Apostolic See for the irregularity of canon 1041, 2°, all irregularities have to be indicated in the petition (c. 1049, §1).

It will be important for the bishop to provide serious reasons for seeking a dispensation from these irregularities in this case, particularly since John's return to full Catholic communion took place only five years ago.

James H. Provost [1991]

CANON 1058

PROHIBITION AGAINST MARRIAGE OF AIDS VICTIMS

The case of an AIDS victim wishing to enter marriage in the Catholic Church was given attention in the news media. The subsequent decision of the parish and Archdiocese involved leads to a consideration of the question in general: Can an AIDS victim be permitted to marry in the Church?

OPINION

313

The New York Times reported on January 9, 1987: "A Victim of AIDS is Denied A Wedding at St. Patrick's."

David Hefner, a 38 year old Protestant, wanted to validate a three year civil marriage with Maria Ribeiro, a 33 year old Catholic. This couple had lived together for a year, and then married at City Hall in February of 1984. Although a date, February 14, 1987 at 9:00 a.m., had been set for the validation ceremony, the rector of the cathedral, Msgr. James Rigney, reversed this decision on the grounds that it was his "own personal judgment" that people in a "life-threatening situation" such as AIDS would receive better pre-marriage counselling in their local parish rather than the cathedral. (The couple's own parish was Our Lady of the Scapular on East 28th Street in Manhattan.)

In May-June of 1986 Mr. Hefner was diagnosed as having AIDS, the disease that destroys the body's immune system thereby leaving the person vulnerable to a fatal disease. *The Times* article states that at the previous meeting at the cathedral "they made it clear that Mr. Hefner was a homosexual before their marriage and that he was suffering from AIDS."

Another reason offered by the cathedral for not performing the ceremony was that "Mr. Hefner's disease was transmittable." Mr. Hefner rightly asserted that it was "transmissible only through sexual contact." Evidence has been offered that Maria's blood was not infected by the AIDS virus, by three negative tests. It was also reported that Mr. Hefner was admitted to New York University Hospital on January 5th.

On Monday, January 12th both *The Times* and *The Daily News* reported that the Cardinal Archbishop of New York would review this ruling given by the rector of the cathedral. He stated: "If they would meet the requirements of the Church for a church wedding, I would see no problem, and if that's determined and the appropriate instructions are given, perhaps best by a parish priest, then I would imagine the rector of the cathedral would welcome them to the cathedral."

On January 13th *The Times* reported that "John Cardinal O'Connor yesterday reversed the decision of the rector of the cathedral, Msgr. James F. Rigney." A compromise was reached whereby "the couple will be prepared for marriage by their local parish priest, but will take their vows at St. Patrick's."

Within three months Mr. Hefner died on May 3, 1987, having succumbed to an illness he was not able to combat due to the AIDS virus depriving him of immunity to disease.

What are the "requirements of the Church" in this case and similar situations? And what should be done in these cases?

A related NC News release, in *The Tablet* on January 17, 1987, reports an opinion expressed by Msgr. William B. Smith regarding this case. "'AIDS itself is not an impediment to marriage,' Msgr. Smith said. But the impossibility of physically consummating a union — presumably the case for an AIDS patient trying to avoid transmitting the disease to a spouse or child — would be an impediment, he said. If the couple intended to prevent the birth of children, it would be impossible for a priest to witness the marriage, he said. And if they planned to prevent transmission of disease through the use of contraceptives, an 'intrinsically wrong act,' the Church could not approve the marriage, he said.''

The Times article of 1/9/87 also quotes a spokesman for the Archdiocese of New York, Joseph Zwilling, as saying: ''Obviously, this is a new area that will have to be addressed by the Church.'' True as this may be, I believe that there are enough principles of moral theology and canon law available to shed considerable light on this situation, and perhaps help to reach a satisfactory decision on this case, or other similar ones.

1. First of all, let us look at the *rights of persons to enter marriage* in the Catholic Tradition. This is one of the very basic and fundamental human rights which has always been protected by the Church throughout her history. This principle of freedom is stated very clearly in the contemporary law: "All persons who are not prohibited by law can contract marriage" (c. 1058).

This however does mean that *some* persons *are indeed* prohibited by law from entering marriage: who might they be? The *Commentary on the Code of Canon Law* tells us that sometimes prohibitions are placed on marriages in view of the effect this would have on "the spouses, the children, and the community" (page 743, col. 2). It goes on to say that such prohibitions "are not an unjust denial of individual freedom but a limitation placed on the right to marry for the good of all concerned" (page 743, col. 2). The *Commentary* notes that throughout history customary or legal structures have been provided "which in certain instances restrict the exercise of the right to marry."

These restrictions may arise from divine law or ecclesiastical law. As examples we may cite the case of marriages between natural brothers and sisters, which are incestuous and forbidden by divine law, or adulterous unions, which are again forbidden by divine law. We may also cite the prohibition of all clerics in sacred orders to marry, which is prohibition of ecclesiastical law.

It is clear that a person would be forbidden to marry if free marital consent cannot be given. So for example, the mentally insane, the intoxicated person, the abducted person, cannot validly marry. Also people who cannot fulfill marital obligations cannot validly marry, e.g., two females, two males, a certainly impotent person (e.g., completely lacking sexual organs). But there are also cases like the AIDS situation, which I believe fall into the category of a divine law prohibition to marriage.

Why? Because the natural law forbids a human being to place him/herself in a situation which is extremely dangerous to life and health. This is clearly expressed in the fifth commandment of the Decalogue: "Thou shalt not kill," since the moral theology which applies here demands that we have to have care and concern for our own physical bodies.

2. *What is AIDS?*

While the present medical stage of understanding this disease grows with each passing day there are still many unanswered questions. One of the things we do know for certain is that this disease is transferred by sexual intercourse with an infected person (vaginal or anal intercourse, homosexual and also heterosexual relations) and by exchanges of blood through intravenous injections with needles that have been used by others whose blood has been infected with AIDS (drug addicts), or by transfusions with infected blood. AIDS is transmitted through invisible breaks in the surface inside the vagina or on the penis; the virus may also enter through mucous membranes in the genital areas.

Another thing we know for sure is that AIDS can be harbored as a debilitating virus for a long time, for many years in fact, without the immune deficiency syndrome erupting or becoming visibly apparent.

We, therefore, must distinguish two segments of people affected by this disease: 1) the AIDS *Victim*, who is in an actual state of immune deficiency, liable to many diseases especially Karposi's sarcoma (a form of cancer), pulmonary difficulties, etc.; and 2) the AIDS *Carrier* who harbors the virus and is a possible transmitter of the disease while he/she may not directly be visibly affected by it.

I believe the question of possible marriage for each of these classes of persons must also be distinguished.

3. *There is no known cure for an AIDS Victim.*

The AIDS *Victim* is affected by a certainly fatal disease. There is no known way at the present time to control or eliminate the disease. As Msgr. Eugene V. Clark states in "The Deadly Silence" (*Crisis*, May 1987, 35): "AIDS is 100 percent lethal." Present statistics show us that over 50% of AIDS *Victims* have already died, and the other *Victims* will eventually die also. Msgr. Clark states this dramatically: "Every AIDS victim diagnosed in 1982 and 1983 is now dead. Soon those of 1984 will be dead — all of them."

On January 30, 1987 *The New York Times* quoted Dr. Otis R. Bowen, Secretary of Health and Human Services, to the effect that 50 to 100 million people will be affected worldwide over the next two decades, and that about 270,000 cases are expected in the U.S. within the next five years.

There is no known cure for AIDS. On January 17, 1987, New York City's Health Commissioner reported that "there are 500,000 people in this city who are infected with the virus," equal to one in every ten adults (*The New York Times*, January 17, 1987).

As of April 14, 1987, there were 33,000 confirmed AIDS cases in the U.S.;

this refers to AIDS *Victims*. The *New York Times* reported on March 4, 1987 that "more than a million Americans will have developed the disease [AIDS] by the year 2000." The Federal Center for Disease Control estimate that 20-30% of carriers will develop AIDS within five years of initial infection.

I believe it is true to say that from the viewpoint of canon law *all* AIDS *Victims* are in *danger of death* situations. The disease progresses to a stage where hospitalization usually becomes necessary. In some cases hospice care may prove to be adequate. But the end result is that the AIDS *Victim* is not able to care for him/herself, and will eventually get a disease that proves fatal. This is certainly living in *danger of death*. I would say in the case under study that Mr. Hefner was in such a danger of death situation, and all the accepted moral and canonical principles should have been applied.

In these circumstances the Church *could* have allowed a death-bed marriage as is done in other cases involving serious danger or imminence of death. This would follow accepted principles.

However, we can also say that an AIDS *Victim* should generally not be allowed to marry because the disease is so debilitating and fatal that the choice of an AIDS *Victim* as a *suitable* marriage partner would be seriously questioned. We are here considering the intention of the partner who is not affected with the AIDS virus.

An AIDS *Victim* would be acting morally wrong and irresponsibly to choose to have sexual relations with a spouse. Natural law would forbid such a union. As Msgr. Smith noted above, it would be wrong for a couple in this situation to engage in sexual intercourse for fear of infecting the other party and further spreading the disease, and also for fear of infecting a child who may possibly be conceived, and certainly the Catholic Church does not condone the use of condoms as many health officers are still promoting so strongly. For a Catholic AIDS *Victim*, or a Catholic married to an AIDS *Victim*, the only possible moral choice is full abstinence from sexual relations, which raises difficulties when marriage is at issue.

Msgr. Clark has recently stated the question:

> Since AIDS kills 100 percent of its victims, does a known HIV carrier have a right to marry? A right to sexual acts with another person, knowing it is more than probable that he or she will transmit the lethal virus? We forbid marriage of first cousins for the safety and health of progeny. But we have yet even to ask the question: May a known AIDS carrier be allowed to acquire a right to sexual intercourse with a non-infected person or sire an infected baby? Will the AIDS carrier enjoy the protection of civil rights in bringing about the death of the spouse and child? Perhaps of contributing to genocide? (In *Crisis*, May 1987, 38).

While Monsignor Clark's remarks may be very pessimistic, he at least is asking the question few seem willing to propose, even in view of the serious situation we face.

(In some cases an AIDS *Victim* could certainly be allowed to receive the Eucharist based upon the accepted moral principles governing the so-called brother-sister relationship, i.e., the man and woman would be permitted to cohabit and to approach the Eucharist, *provided* there is no sexual intercourse occurring between them. Obviously this has always been seen as an heroic situation for human beings, and requires great spiritual assistance.)

4. What about the AIDS *Carrier*? Can the AIDS *Carrier* be permitted to marry in the Catholic Church?

It is my opinion that an AIDS *Carrier* is generally forbidden to marry, and that this prohibition rests upon a natural law understanding of the requirements of marriage.

A marriage between a man and a woman is intended to be a union of support, psychic and physical, as well as moral and spiritual, with the possibility of the raising of a human family from the relationship itself. In the case of an AIDS *Carrier* this becomes almost impossible.

The possibility of the AIDS virus erupting at some future time in the marital relationship is a clear possibility, and this would render the intimate marital relationship practically impossible. Sexual intercourse would become an impossibility because of the moral demand to avoid such activity; the transmission of AIDS to a fetus would be a morally reprehensible, imprudent, humanly irrational action; non-genital sexual intimacy could also become problematical since it would often arouse human passion to the level that intercourse would be desired. Once again we must remember that the Catholic Church does not accept the possibility of engaging in sexual intercourse with a condom, and therefore this practice, endorsed strongly by health officials, remains unacceptable; complete abstinence from sexual relations remains the only choice for a Catholic conscience in an AIDS situation.

The consequences that would fall upon a married couple who, after marriage, discern the presence of AIDS, would bring about tremendous psychological, physical, and economic strain to the extent that such a relationship would require the greatest of Christian charity to effectively survive.

5. What about the knowledge of the AIDS virus infection?

This would be a critical aspect of the canonical implications when faced with a desire to marry on the part of people infected by AIDS.

a. For the AIDS *Victim* the knowledge of the AIDS infection would be clearly evident. Knowledge of the situation would be available to the parties wishing to marry and their intentions would take this information into account.

b. For the AIDS *Carrier* the situation is much more complicated. Sometimes the AIDS *Carrier* is not even aware of the presence of the virus; testing is not obligatory in most cases, but it might be considered obligatory if a person has lived a lifestyle which makes it possible that he/she is infected with the AIDS virus and might be a carrier. The AIDS virus can lurk in the body without causing disease, and among those who develop AIDS, the average time between infection and diagnosis of AIDS may be five years or more.

If an AIDS *Carrier* is in fact aware of the presence of the virus, then an obligation exists to make this condition known to any future spouse. In the contemporary scene many prospective spouses are more concerned with learning of the previous "sexual history" of a partner, in the hope of avoiding an infected spousal relationship.

This was stated very succinctly by Dr. Bowen in an article in *The New York Times* of January 30, 1987: "So remember when a person has sex, they're not just having it with that partner, they're having it with everybody that partner had it with for the past 10 years."

The still undeveloped canonical doctrine on fraud may be applicable if an AIDS *Carrier* is aware of the presence of the virus and withholds such information from a prospective spouse.

6. What about a civil marriage for AIDS related cases?

The civil law obviously must make its own determinations on this matter. It is the opinion of the undersigned that the common good demands that AIDS related persons not be permitted to marry. The State does not permit everyone to marry; it also can impose restrictions for the common good of the populace.

In the past, persons infected with venereal disease were not allowed to obtain a civil license to marry. While this restriction was done away in New York City within recent years, it should be re-imposed for AIDS related situations to protect the common good.

7. What kind of counselling would be given to couples wanting to marry when a partner has AIDS?

The AIDS *Victim* is always to be considered to be in a danger of death situation. Counselling which is appropriate here would be identical to anyone preparing to meet death. For a Catholic, reconciliation with the Church is a necessary aspect of counselling. Certainly the spirit of resignation of God's will and the acceptance of suffering can be underscored in a counselling situation.

A critical aspect of this counselling would involve the need for complete abstinence from sexual relations. If the AIDS *Victim* is so debilitated as to require hospitalization, sexual intercourse would not usually be possible due to the physical separation which would be imposed.

On January 10th *The Daily News* quoted Monsignor Rigney as saying: "If one party is suffering from an illness that may threaten the life of a spouse, or of a child who may later be conceived . . . compassion must be accompanied by a most serious effort to see that the problem is met in a manner harmonious with the church's teaching. This may require time, prayer and discussion, and even lengthy counselling.''

This is the crux of the problem. This counselling which must treat of the aspects of abstinence from sexual relations for the physical good of the couple themselves, which at first sight would be seen by many to be so much at variance with the Church's own teaching about the goodness of sexual activity in marriage, and also at variance with contemporary secular mores where sexual activity has not often been restricted by personal intent. This is where couples must be helped in developing good attitudes. Educational programs about AIDS can be of great help in this.

The question can be raised if a true marriage can be entered when the couple agrees to abstain perpetually from sexual relations. Diverse answers have been given, but there is no question that the Church has accepted the validity of such a marriage when such an agreement has been made freely by the couple intending to marry. A full discussion of this controversial issue can be found in Eduardus Regatillo's work *Ius Sacramentarium* (Santander [1960] 807-808).

It is on this precise point that I believe Monsignor Smith errs, or at least demonstrates confusion. The NC News article states: "Msgr. William B. Smith, dean and professor of moral theology at the archdiocesan St. Joseph's Seminary, in an interview questioned whether an AIDS victim would consummate the marriage because of the possibility of transmitting the disease. Under church law an inability to consummate the marriage is an impediment to marriage." This is misleading. I agree with the position that an AIDS *Victim* should not consummate a marriage on the moral grounds established in this presentation. But the impediment to marriage that is mentioned here is a physical or psychological reason for being unable to have sexual intercourse, e.g., inability to have an erection, phobia of sexual intimacy, etc. The impediment does not apply when two people voluntarily agree not to engage in sexual intercourse for proper motives. The doctrine noted above in E. Regatillo's work clearly supports this view of mine.

Again the NC News article causes confusion: "the impossibility of physically consummating a union — presumably the case for an AIDS patient trying to avoid transmitting the disease to a spouse or child — would be an impediment [Msgr. Smith] said. If the couple intended to prevent the birth of children, it would be impossible for a priest to witness the marriage, he said." I must point out the lack of clarity of thought here. It is not impossible for an AIDS *Victim* to consummate a marriage; it is irresponsible and immoral to do so, but not impossible; hence the impediment of impotency cannot be applied specifically to AIDS situations. A couple can intend to prevent the birth of children and still be married by a priest (and/or deacon to be exact): the point here is the means the couple choose for such prevention; there are moral means and there are immoral means, e.g., there is abstinence or natural family planning, and there is contraceptive intercourse — the distinction concerning the means chosen is crucial here and does not deserve confusion or misunderstanding.

In a recent issue of *Ethics and Medics*, Rev. Msgr. Orville N. Griese, S.T.D., J.C.D., takes up this issue and seemingly comes to a very simplified conclusion:

> Since the AIDS infection can lie dormant for years without any detectable symptoms, any adult who is contemplating marriage and who has a positive reason for being "at risk" or "AIDS-exposed" . . . should feel obligated to submit voluntarily to an AIDS antibody test and to share the results of such a test with his or her prospective spouse. If after informed and prudent counselling, the other party agrees to the marriage despite the revelation of an AIDS infection (or disease) the couple should be motivated to have recourse to Natural Family Planning so as to avoid the risk of transmitting the infection to at least some of the children born of that marriage, since the risk of transmission is apparently high, although not inevitable.

I believe such an opinion is much too lenient considering the dangers that AIDS presents in the present situations.

It would be my opinion that it would be totally irresponsible for a minister of the Church to permit an AIDS Victim to marry someone, if the couple plans or intends to engage in sexual intercourse.

It is likewise my opinion that it would be even more irresponsible to allow an AIDS Carrier to marry and to encourage him/her to engage in sexual intercourse, along with the possible generation of AIDS afflicted children.

It appears to be irrefutable according to Catholic doctrine that a person infected with the AIDS virus cannot morally engage in sexual intercourse.

8. Does *classical moral theology* offer any help?

Marcellinus Zalba, S.J. (*Theologia Moralis Compendium*, Madrid, 1958) treats of "indirect suicide and its proximate danger" (Vol. I, 854). He says that the "obligation for a single determined person to face certain death occurs more rarely" but that "it is licit to face certain and proximate death, always for the *public good*, e.g., when a priest or religious or nurse or doctor continue to assist the sick infected with a contagious disease" (I, 855, n. 1573, 2).

Another classical text, H. Noldin-A. Schmitt-G. Heinzel (*Summa Theologiae Moralis*, Innsbruck, 1959) teaches that the person who "without cause exposes him/herself to proximate danger of life, sins gravely. The greater the danger of death which flows from the action, so much greater ought the reason to be, by which it can become licit" (Vol. III, 295-296). If a person has no hope of escaping death, he says, then "vitam non periculo exponere, sed perimere dicitur"; in other words, when there is no hope we do not speak of exposing ourselves to danger, but really we are destroying life.

Bernard Häring (*The Law of Christ*, The Newman Press, Westminster, Maryland, 1966) teaches "we are not permitted to place either our own life or that of others in danger without good reason" (Vol. III, 214). "Whoever unnecessarily exposes his own life or the life of his neighbor to danger commits a sin which is by its nature (*ex natura sua*) grave" (Vol. III, 215-217).

Father Häring offers further material for consideration. "Health is both an individual and social good. . . . Today indeed the most dangerous contagious diseases, the pests and plagues, have been wiped out or at least held in check and kept under control" (Vol. III, 227). Certainly this was true when he wrote these words, but the AIDS situation has changed our world situation again.

He supports state intervention: "Civil legislation in these matters which affect the social order basically binds strictly in conscience to the degree and measure in which it is concerned with a real and important service for the health of the people . . . . hygienic measures for the prevention of communicable disease, extensive powers by boards of health to safeguard public health, etc." (Vol. III, 227).

His most appropriate remarks, however, come when he discusses the moral implications of making a responsible decision for marriage: "The very choice of a partner in marriage must have in view the natural and supernatural good of the children who are hoped for" (Vol. III, 336). "The responsibility to service in life assumed in marriage totally excludes the right to choose a partner and enter a union from which — as far as can at all be foreseen — there will spring children laboring under a severe handicap in life. . . ." (Vol. III, 337). How much truer would these words be as applied to children born and infected with AIDS who face certain death. He continues, "in more serious cases of this kind [i.e. marriages producing defective and sick children] those who contemplate such a union must be urgently advised to shun it" (Vol. 111. 337).

In a very strong opinion he says: "It is desirable that couples contemplating marriage should be well informed regarding all points of health which can affect their marriage and their future offspring . . . . unless it is quite apparent from other sources that the status of their health (including the hereditary strains) favors a happy marriage and healthy offspring, they should exchange health certificates before engagement. Such certificates of health testifying to freedom from communicable and hereditary disease are to be provided by a physician who is expert in psychology and eugenics" (Vol. III, 337-338). If this opinion were to be followed in situations involving AIDS we would certainly have a clearer view of the human situation.

9. It is, therefore, the opinion of the undersigned that:

a. an AIDS *victim* can marry in the Church, provided suitable and adequate counselling is given, since he/she is always in a danger of death situation;

b. an AIDS *carrier* should be persuaded not to marry in the Church, because of the catastrophic consequences that are foreseen for the spouse, the children, and the community. If such a person were to persevere in his/her intention, the canonical possibility to forbid a marriage for a time and for a serious reason (c. 1077) should be invoked by ecclesiastical authority, and since AIDS has no cure at the present time, this prohibition could be renewed in a particular case more than once.

William A. Varvaro [1987]

(Editorial Note: Unlike other changes made to preserve anonymity, those names included in this question are a matter of public record and have not been changed here.)

ANOTHER OPINION

[At the 1986 Annual Conference of the Canon Law Society of Great Britain and Ireland, in response to a paper on the medical aspects of the AIDS epidemic, Father Pius Smart, O.F.M. Cap. was asked to look at some of the canonical problems posed by this new disease. The part of his paper dealing with the same question is reproduced here with the permission of the Canon Law Society of Great Britain and Ireland.]

I would like first of all to make a few general comments. The first is that the fact that a person has contracted AIDS has no direct canonical or moral significance. As we have heard the disease can be contracted through the transfusion of blood or blood products unbeknown to anyone until symptoms appear or tests are carried out. The existence of the disease may suggest the likelihood of a particular life-style, since the incidence of AIDS is much higher among homosexuals and drug abusers than among the general population. The existence of AIDS may thus indicate a deeper investigation into a person's suitability for marriage.

As we have already heard, one effect of AIDS is a considerably reduced life expectancy. The situation is too new for reliable statistics to be available, and it is highly probably that treatment will be developed which will enable people with AIDS to live longer than they are doing at present. In marriage there is a very high probability that the disease will be spread to the other partner through normal sexual intercourse. Finally there is the fact that any children born to a woman suffering from AIDS will be born with the same syndrome and with a very short life expectancy.

Having made those general comments I would like to move on to examine the situation when Nigel and Prunella ring the doorbell of the presbytery and say that they want to get married. They want the ceremony as soon as possible because they know that Nigel has AIDS and therefore their time together is going to be short. Obviously the situation demands more than the usual amount of caution. But it must be remembered that the couple have a basic natural right to marry; as canon 1058 expresses the matter, "All can contract marriage who are not prohibited by law." If the couple insists on exercising that right, then it is difficult to see how they can be prevented from marrying.

What has first of all to be done is that Nigel and Prunella should be asked to accept counselling about their situation. Such counselling will make clear to them the likely results of their marrying, both to themselves and also the effects of the disease on any children born to them. If the couple refuses to accept counselling and the opportunity to discuss their situation then I think the prudent course is to seek advice of the local Ordinary.

Let us presume that they agree to discuss their situation and look at the advice they are likely to be given and their possible reactions to that advice. They will be told that, if they lead a normal married life, then Prunella will almost certainly contract AIDS, with the resultant shortening of her life. She could well be told that she does not have the moral right to run such a great risk of shortening her own life. But Prunella might well reply (though perhaps not in quite such theological terms) that the value and importance of sharing the sacrament and their value to each other in growing in love of God and each other was such that it outweighs, in their view, the value of preserving Prunella's life to a ripe old age.

The next step in counselling will presumably be to point out the fact that, if Prunella contracts AIDS, as she is most likely to do through normal sexual intercourse, then any children born to her will be born with the disease and with a very limited expectancy of life. Their reply to this information could be that they have already discussed the problem and decided that they will not have a family.

It would then appear that Nigel and Prunella could not be allowed to marry for, as canon 1101, §2 states, "If, however, either or both the parties should by a positive act of the will exclude marriage itself or any essential element of marriage or any essential property, such party contracts invalidly." Openness to the procreation and upbringing of children is of the very nature of marriage (cf. c. 1055, §1). But let us presume that the counselling has revealed that Nigel and Prunella are both committed to the Catholic Faith and sound in their practice of it, and that marriage would seem to be a genuine and important step in their Christian progress. Must they be refused permission to marry? I would suggest not. If they regard their intention as delaying a family in the hope (maybe a forlorn one, but still not outside the realms of possibility) that one day Nigel will be cured and they could then have a family, then I think that the marriage could be allowed to go ahead.

I would base my argument on the premise that the procreation and upbringing of children, while essential to the nature of marriage in general, is not an essential element in every individual marriage. I would suggest that canon 1085, §3 supports my point when it says, "Sterility neither forbids nor invalidates marriage." Sterility means that children are physically impossible. I would argue that, in the case of Nigel and Prunella, children are morally impossible. In their situation there is a moral imperative not to have children. It would be wrong for them to have children, knowing that every child would be born diseased and with a very short life expectancy. I would therefore allow their marriage.

So far I have been considering the hypothetical case of Nigel and Prunella, obviously both intelligent and sensible about their relationship. But what of those who wish to marry but who are clearly not taking the fact that one of them has AIDS seriously? (In fact it is unlikely that people with such an attitude and with the sort of back ground most likely to give rise to AIDS would appear at the presbytery - but you never know.) If a person does not appreciate that AIDS will have a dramatic effect on any marriage, then I would suggest that there is a *prima facie* case for the lack of discretionary judgement which is described in canon 1095. There will obviously be a need for further investigation and, if this confirms the first impressions, then it would be reasonable for the local Ordinary to forbid that particular marriage.

Pius Smart, O.F.M. Cap. [1987]

CANON 1059

RECOGNITION OF COMMON LAW MARRIAGES
BY CIVIL JURISDICTIONS

Which civil jurisdictions in the United States recognize the validity of common law marriage? In those jurisdictions which recognize common law marriage, what criteria are used to determine the validity of such a marriage? Does the

Catholic Church recognize the validity of a common law marriage where such is recognized as valid by a civil law jurisdiction?

OPINION

Canon law establishes the principle in canon 11 that "merely ecclesiastical laws bind those baptized in the Catholic Church or received into it and who enjoy the sufficient use of reason and, unless the law expressly provides otherwise, have completed seven years of age." This principle is extended to the sacrament of Matrimony in canon 1059, which states that "even if only one party is Catholic, the marriage of Catholics is regulated not only by divine law but also by canon law, with due regard for the competence of civil authority concerning the merely civil effects of such a marriage." The extension of the principle of canon 11 is what is left unsaid, namely, that if neither party is Catholic, marriage is regulated only by the divine and natural law, with due regard for the competence of civil authority.

The presumption of the validity of common law marriages involving unbaptized persons or baptized non-Catholics is clearly established in the Church's history and jurisprudence; and this history and jurisprudence has been well presented in the dissertation of Robert E. Dillon, *Common Law Marriage* (Catholic University of America, 1942, no. 153) and need not be repeated here. Although the conclusions which he presented took into consideration the legislation of the 1917 code, the principles are equally applicable to the current Code of Canon law. Among these are:

1. Those exempted from observing the Catholic form of marriage, namely, unbaptized persons and baptized non-Catholics, may validly enter a common law marriage.
2. The civil authority is competent to establish impediments and invalidating laws which would regulate common law marriage.

Since marriage in the United States is regulated by the individual states, the first criterion which a tribunal must use in examining the validity of a common law marriage must be an investigation of the principles of law governing common law marriage in the particular state in which the parties live. Since these vary from state to state, it is not practical to make an exhaustive presentation here.

By way of example, however, this author's own state of California presents the following basic principles regulating common law marriage:

A common law marriage may be defined as a non-ceremonial or informal marriage by agreement entered into by a man and woman having capacity to marry, ordinarily without compliance with such statutory formalities as those pertaining to marriage licenses.

According to most courts, however, common law marriage cannot be contracted by agreement alone, but only by an agreement plus consummation, which includes at least cohabitation as husband and wife. Though under the present law in the state, it is necessary, as a rule, that a marriage be licensed, and that it be solemnized as authorized by the statutes, it has been stated that common law marriages, if valid according to the law of the jurisdiction in which they were entered into, will be recognized as valid in this state (32 *Cal Jur*, 3rd ed., §51).

There then follows a detailed presentation concerning the application of these principles.

In principle, however, couples in the state of California may not establish a common law bond here at this time. However, if they have established such a union in a jurisdiction which accepts common law marriage as valid, it will be recognized as valid within this state.

A tribunal's investigation of a common law marriage in California would first have to determine the status of the couple within the jurisdiction in which the common law marriage was entered in order to determine the status of a couple within the state of California. This determination would then guide the tribunal's decision concerning the validity of the bond.

Proofs associated with a common law marriage under investigation by a tribunal would follow the usual principles of law found in the code regarding the introduction of private documents (since public documentation would probably not exist), the declaration of the parties themselves and the use of witness testimony.

Gregory Ingels [1990]

ANOTHER OPINION

The most recent state-by-state compilation known to this author is the *Martindale-Hubbell Law Digest*, 1993. It covers the fifty U.S. states, District of Columbia, Puerto Rico and the U.S. Virgin Islands.

Common law marriage is the mutual agreement by two persons (not of the same sex) to cohabit for a substantial period of time with the intention of acting as husband and wife, but without benefit of a wedding ceremony or other compliance with legal formalities (such as license to marry, blood tests, etc.). Common law marriage was widely practiced and recognized in England before the 18th century, and later in some of the English colonies in America and elsewhere. In other countries whose legal system is derived from the Anglo common law tradition, such marriages are known as *de facto* marriage.

The legal trend in the 20th century has been to discontinue legal recognition of common law marriage. Thus statutory enactments in many state jurisdictions established dates *after* which common law marriage is "not recognized" or "not valid ": Florida, January 1, 1968; Illinois, June 30, 1905; Indiana, January 1, 1958; Michigan, January 1, 1957; Minnesota, April 26, 1941; Mississippi, April 5, 1956; Missouri, March 31, 1921; Nebraska, 1923; Nevada, March 29, 1943; New Jersey, December 1, 1939; New York, April 29, 1933; South Dakota, July 1, 1959.

Those jurisdictions which currently recognize the validity of common law marriage generally do so by virtue of statutory law, or court decision where there is no statute (e.g., Oklahoma). Common law marriages are valid in Alabama, Colorado, District of Columbia, Georgia, Idaho, Iowa, Kansas, Montana, Ohio, Oklahoma, Pennsylvania, Rhode Island, South Carolina, and Texas. For Utah,

> "unsolemnized marriage arising out of contract is valid if a court or administrative order finds two parties (1) capable of consent, (2) legally capable of a solemnized marriage, (3) have cohabited, (4) mutually assume marital rights, duties or obligations, and (5) contend and are believed to be husband and wife."

Some jurisdictions which ordinarily do not permit common law marriage, however, extend recognition to common law marriage if it is entered into in another state that recognizes such marriages as valid; thus, Arizona (except for residents of Arizona who contract common law marriage in another state to evade Arizona law), Arkansas, California, Delaware, Illinois, Kentucky, Louisiana, Maine ("common law marriage probably not recognized . . . out of state common law marriage would probably be recognized"), Maryland, Michigan, Mississippi, Nebraska, New Hampshire (if parties become permanent residents of New Hampshire), New Mexico, New York, North Carolina ("common law marriage consummated in this state are not recognized in this state . . . but such marriages consummated in another state which validates same are recognized by this state"), Oregon, South Dakota, Tennessee, Virgin Islands, Virginia (not, however, if Virginia residents contract common law marriage in another state and return to Virginia), Washington, West Virginia, and Wyoming.

In the other states common law marriage is not valid, nor is recognition extended to such marriages contracted out of state.

Caution, however, is urged, since even in those states which recognize common law marriage as valid, there is no standard set of criteria of facts, conditions or intentions. Most states require some or all of the following elements, beyond mere cohabitation: the legal capacity to enter a legal marriage, e.g., minimum age; freedom to marry; intent and/or consent, i.e., an actual or present agreement to be husband and wife; good faith cohabitation for an extended period of time and/or consummation; and holding themselves out to others as husband and wife.

For a time, commentators (see C.B. Alford, *The Jurist* 2 [1942] 248-262; R. Dillon, *Common Law Marriage*, Catholic University: Canon Law Series, n. 143) distinguished the marriage of non-baptized persons, which marriage civil law could regulate (thus, including civil law recognition of common law marriage), from the marriages of baptized non-Catholics, who, as baptized persons, were subject to the exclusive jurisdiction of ecclesiastical authority.

Such a distinction need no longer be maintained, since by its current law (see cc. 1059; 1108; 1117) the Catholic Church requires no particular form for the validity of the marriage of non-baptized persons or for baptized non-Catholic persons (with the *exception* of those who are baptized in the Orthodox churches, for whom Orthodox form is required for the validity of their marriage).

Thus, for those persons who are not bound by an obligation of form for contracting a valid marriage, and whose civil law jurisdictions recognize common law as valid, the Catholic Church would likewise recognize the validity of such a marriage.

Again, caution is urged: mere cohabitation even over an extended period of time, in most jurisdictions, is not sufficient to establish the validity in civil law of alleged common law marriage. Other requirements of civil law must be fulfilled. The burden of proof falls upon the one making the claim of a valid common law marriage.

Certitude, however, could be had if an administrative tribunal or court of the civil authority had declared the legality and/or effects in civil law of the common law marriage in question, provided that the persons are not otherwise bound by ecclesiastical law to a form for validly contracting marriage, and who would otherwise be free to marry.

Joseph J. Koury [1990, revised 1993]

CANON 1059

INVALID CIVIL MARRIAGE

Would a marriage between non-baptized persons be invalid if the two parties failed to observe the civil law requirements for the wedding ceremony? The problem in the specific marriage being questioned is that the couple's marriage certificate indicates that there was only one witness and the state law requires two.

OPINION

First, some comments on civil law requirements for witnesses at the marriage ceremony. Marriage in civil law in the U.S. is governed by state law; it would require a careful examination of the constitutions, codes, or other collections of state domestic or family law to know in which states the requirement of one or two witnesses has effect on the legal standing of marriage.

A digest of current civil law (see *Martindale-Hubbell Law Digest*, 1993), in what is perhaps contrary to general impressions, reveals that relatively few civil law jurisdictions in the U.S. (the *Law Digest* includes Washington, D.C., Virgin Islands, Puerto Rico) specifically require that there must be two or "at least two witnesses" to a marriage ceremony. Those listed in the *Digest* which do so are Delaware, Kentucky, Louisiana, Maine, Michigan, Minnesota, Nebraska, New Jersey, North Carolina, Oklahoma ("at least two *adult* witnesses"), Oregon, Puerto Rico ("signature of witnesses"), Washington, Wisconsin ("two *competent* adult witnesses"), and Wyoming. One state requires only one witness: Nevada. For New York, the *Digest* reports "attending witness or witnesses." The *Law Digest* entries for other civil jurisdictions are either silent about such requirements or state "No provisions as to witnesses" (e.g., entry for Maryland).

Where the law specifies "adult" witnesses, then the state's rule on age of majority must be considered (this ranges from age 18 to 21); similarly, the requirement of "competency."

Secondly, the problem as described does not provide sufficient information about the requirement(s) of the civil law and its effects. Is it a requirement *for validity* of the marriage in civil law that the signature of both witnesses appear on the marriage certificate? For even those who do require signatures of the witnesses, is it clear that failure to do so resulted in a null marriage? Are we to understand that this marriage was not properly registered with the competent civil authority at the time of the wedding ceremony? It should be noted that many states require only the signature of the one who officiates or solemnizes the marriage.

Thirdly, even where the law requires the signature of one or two witnesses and this is certainly lacking, can the invalidity of the marriage in civil law be presumed, or must it be declared by competent authority? Unless civil law specifically penalizes as *void ab initio* or *voidable* a marriage which lacks a witness or witness' signature, then it cannot be presumed that this marriage lacks validity in civil law. Civil law distinguishes, a) that marriage which is *void*, meaning, null *ab initio*, because it seriously offends law or public policy, a marriage not good from its very inception for any legal purpose, i.e., a marriage from which the parties may separate without need of a court order such as divorce or annulment (does lack of a signature constitute such a cause?), from, b) that marriage which is *voidable*, one which is valid when entered into, but which suffers from an imperfection and requires a proceeding to obtain a judgment (e.g., of divorce or annulment, declaring it void). Has either of these occurred in the marriage in question?

Fourthly, even if such provision (by statute or by case decision) existed in civil law, declaring or rendering the marriage invalid, still, according to the canons the marriage of two non-baptized persons requires no particular form for validity. Many might be the marriages which civil law forbids, restricts, regulates or penalizes, but violation of such provisions do not constitute invalidity of the marriage in canon law; all the more so in the case of marriage of two non-baptized persons, who are not bound to any particular form for marrying.

If the doubt is whether this marriage lacked publicity according to canon law (i.e., is tantamount to a clandestine marriage), it seems to me that such is not the case, there being a certificate of marriage in this instance, and, presumably other, if not signatory, witnesses.

It seems to me that this marriage must be presumed to be valid in canon law.

Joseph J. Koury [1992, revised 1993]

CANON 1060

COMMON LAW MARRIAGE REQUIRES CANONICAL INVESTIGATION

A baptized non-Catholic and a non-baptized person entered a "common law" union in Iowa. The marriage broke up and, on the advice of civil attorneys in Nebraska, a civil divorce was obtained. The baptized non-Catholic wants to know if he is free to marry a Catholic in the Church. Does his prior union enjoy the favor of the law, so that a formal canonical examination of the marriage case is necessary?

OPINION

It is my opinion in the query which you submitted regarding baptized Protestant James and unbaptized Mary, and their Iowa "common law" union, that this union did in fact bring them under the necessity of a formal, canonical examination, should James wish to marry again and in the Catholic Church.

I say this for many reasons.

Central is the concept that a baptized non-Roman Catholic is, according to the Roman Catholic concept of the sacrament of matrimony, bound for validity to *no* specified "form" for that commitment. This would obviously hold as well if both parties had been baptized Protestants. In the case of this present interfaith union, I feel that this does not alter the principle, or the commitment. While *un*baptized parties are required in natural law to follow the civil requirements and "form" which affects them, it is my opinion that a solid opinion would exempt this interfaith couple from that requirement of civil form.

The questioner's observation that in the event of both having been unbaptized a "Pauline Privilege" might be obtainable is, of course, correct. In the present interfaith conjunction a dissolution by the Pontiff in favor of the faith might also be available, under the appropriate conditions. And in any case the nature of the bond might be examined in a canonical procedure, with a charge of possible invalidity upon some psychological or other grounds.

More central to the present case, however, is a two-fold question. Was this a true marital commitment, even if only one of "common law?" And secondly, is the response really strengthened by the Iowa civil acceptance of such unions?

With regard to the first, it is my opinion that the usual jurisprudence connected with "common law" allegations would be followed: *did* they consider themselves as "married"; *did* they use "Mr. and Mrs."; *did* they have joint bank accounts and other accoutrements of many marriages; *did* they sign themselves as spouses in legal instruments; *did* they file joint forms 1040, etc.? Affirmative answers in judicial evidence to these questions would enforce the contention of a true commitment, in terms of consent having been exchanged. Other evidence might enforce the claim of the *lack* of a true commitment upon, for example, "psychological" grounds.

The asserted Iowa acceptance, secondly, of such givings of consent in an informal manner, to constitute true marriage, leaves me a little skeptical. At least in the past, it has been stated that the vast majority of American civil jurisdictions did not in fact recognize the authenticity of a "common law" consent.

But this may well be changing, to respond to the second question raised above. The assertion of the questioner regarding Iowa legislation, and the observation regarding Nebraska acquiescence, would seem to endorse the position of there having been here a true, civil, marital commitment (and therefore, the necessity of a canonical trial of its asserted invalidity).

Further, recent civil law attitudes speak eloquently of a kind of common law recognition of common law arrangements: the so-called "palimony cases" of recent fame, where a couple, merely and explicitly living together, were recognized as having acquired by that fact certain property rights which normally accompany a more conventional marriage. If *their* union is recognized civilly as effective, and if Iowa recognizes a commitment even more explicitly conjugal, even if still without a civil "form" and informal in nature (maybe even completely clandestine), by so much the more it would seem that the union deseribed by the questioner has a presumption of civil and natural validity.

This reaffirms the position of canon 1060. While it might be argued superficially that a Protestant and an unbaptized person are outside the directive of this law, it would be responded that canon 1060 seems a principle of natural law, whose contrary would be unthinkable (i.e., marriages are presumed invalid), and John and Mary hence must, in my opinion, be at least presumed to be validly married.

Ellsworth Kneal [1984]

CANON 1066

PRE-NUPTIAL CONTRACT DISCOVERED DURING MARRIAGE PREPARATION

In the course of marriage preparation, it is learned that a couple have signed a pre-nuptial contract which would settle any property questions if the tragedy of a divorce should ever befall their marriage. Do such agreements invalidate marriages entered in the Catholic Church after the agreement has been signed?

OPINION

There are several canonical problems involved here.

The first is whether the agreement is evidence of a mentality that excludes the permanence of marriage. If it does, then that mentality would be either a partial simulation (i.e., "I marry you but intend a divorceable marriage, one that is not by nature permanent") or an error about the nature of marriage which enters into the act of commitment itself (i.e., "I fail to include indissolubility in the commitment I make because I just don't understand it as essential to marriage"). Either case would invalidate the marriage. However, it is not the pre-nuptial agreement itself which would invalidate, but rather the defect in the person's consent which is expressed in various ways, including such a pre-nuptial agreement.

333

The second is whether the agreement constitutes a condition *sine qua non* for entering the marriage. Not all conditions are so serious; that is, people can enter marriage with various understandings which are incorrect, or even with what they might consider to be a "condition," but actually they would marry whether the condition were verified or not. It is not an essential condition, without which they would not marry.

Other conditions are that essential. The 1983 code makes any marriage entered with a future condition invalid; i.e., "I will marry you if you will agree that in the event of a divorce [a future situation] the property will be divided in such and such a way." The condition is about the future, not about the present, and the marriage would be invalid (c. 1102, §1).

On the other hand, a person might enter a marriage with a condition about the present; i.e., "I will marry you only if you will agree now [present] to this pre-nuptial agreement." It is entering the pre-nuptial agreement itself, not the possible implementation of it in the future, that is the necessary condition before entering the marriage. The 1983 code states that such marriages are valid, but may not be entered lawfully unless the written permission of the local ordinary has been obtained (c. 1102, §§2 and 3).

Finally, it could be that the pre-nuptial agreement does not reflect a simulation or failure to include indissolubility, nor is it a condition for the entering of the marriage. It is an agreement which the couple make, not as a condition, but as part of the personal circumstances and arrangements they make in preparing for marriage. It could be similar to an agreement to open a joint banking account once they are married, or to make various provisions in their wills in the event of the death of one of the parties before the death of the other. Such agreements in themselves do not invalidate marriage but would if they were made a condition *sine qua non*.

In my opinion, therefore, pre-marital agreements do not in themselves, by their very nature, invalidate marriage; but they could, if they amounted to simulation or its equivalent, or to an invalidating future condition. They would render the marriage illicit if they were a present condition which was not permitted by the local ordinary. Or they may have no effect on the marriage at all. The only way to determine what the effect of a particular pre-nuptial agreement might be is to examine each case in itself.

The pastorally prudent course is obviously to work with the couple so they understand the indissolubility and permanence of marriage, and truly give genuine consent to a lasting Christian union. If they indicate they are entering a pre-nuptial agreement such as you described, it would be important to discuss with them what they intend by such an agreement and to determine whether it constituted an invalidating factor in their preparation for marriage.

You might also want to check with a civil lawyer to see if such prenuptial agreements are recognized in law. I have not done a study on this myself, but have heard from others that there can be some civil law questions about their effectiveness in various jurisdictions.

James H. Provost [1984]

Canon 1066

Pre-Nuptial Agreements

A couple preparing for marriage has signed a pre-nuptial agreement stating that in the event of the civil dissolution of their marriage, one party will not sue the other except for monies and property which have been acquired during the time of their common life. The motivation of this pre-nuptial agreement is the fact that one party will become the beneficiary of a $500 million trust fund and this party's family wants to protect this trust from any future claim or litigation by a former spouse that might result from a civil dissolution of the marriage. What are the canonical implications of such a pre-nuptial agreement?

Opinion

The question of pre-nuptial agreements has been treated in an earlier advisory opinion in which the author suggests that:

> pre-marital agreements do not in themselves, by their very nature, invalidate marriage; but they could, if they amounted to simulation or its equivalent, or to an invalidating future condition. They would render the marriage illicit if they were a present condition not permitted by the local ordinary. Or they may have no effect on the marriage at all. The only way to determine what the effect of a particular pre-nuptial agreement might be is to examine each case in itself (James H. Provost, JCD, *Roman Replies and CLSA Advisory Opinions 1984*, 54-55).

The author concludes that the pastorally prudent course is to work with the couple to ascertain their understanding of Christian marriage in light of the pre-nuptial agreement which they are entering.

I would offer the following observations only as a corollary to this opinion.

Canon 1059 establishes that the Church not only recognizes but also accepts the competence of the civil authority to regulate the civil effects of marriage. Based upon this principle, and that of canon 22, the Church acknowledges that

335

parties whose marriages have ended will have to seek certain civil remedies in order to protect personal rights. Thus, we have traditionally permitted civil divorce as a means of settling questions such as spousal and child support or other purely civil matters.

Permitting persons to seek such civil remedies is not seen as a compromise of our belief in the indissolubility of marriage, but rather as a means of protecting in the civil forum the rights of parties associated with the marriage, especially those of the children born of the union.

In our increasingly litigious society, circumstances such as those presented in the present question have given rise to the necessity of innovative civil formalities such as pre-nuptial agreements in order to provide additional protection in the civil forum, extending not only to the rights of the couple themselves and their children but also to the families of each of the parties in the event that the marriage should end.

From this perspective, a pre-nuptial agreement need not be seen as a present or future condition affecting the consent the couple is placing, which would render the marriage either null or illicit (c. 1102), or even as a presumption that the marriage will fail. Rather, a pre-nuptial agreement can be viewed as a civilly acceptable means by which the parties and their families are accorded necessary protection in civil law which they may deem necessary.

This canonical perspective, of course, does not diminish the need for proper pastoral care during the period of marriage preparation; it may well intensify special concern. The couple should certainly be counselled to seek competent legal advice from a civil attorney to ascertain that any agreement they intend to execute is in conformity with the laws of their particular state or jurisdiction; and it may be well to seek a canonical assessment of the agreement to ascertain that it does not contain conditions which would be contrary to divine or canon law.

Gregory Ingels [1990]

CANONS 1066-1067

PROOF OF FREEDOM TO MARRY AFTER NON-CANONICAL MARRIAGE

In a memorandum dated October 21, 1984, the Office of the National Conference of Catholic Bishops reported the following question and answer from the Pontifical Commission for the Authentic Interpretation of the Code of Canon Law:

Q. To prove the state of freedom of those who although bound to canonical form attempted marriage before a civil official or a non-Catholic minister, is the documentary process mentioned in canon 1686 necessarily required or does the pre-nuptial investigation dealt with in canons 1066-1067 suffice?

R: Negative to the first; affirmative to the second.

Has there been any further commentary in this regard? Have we effectively done away with the requirement that a declaration of nullity be issued by competent authority for defect of form cases?

OPINION

To understand the Commission's response you may find it helpful to review the comments by Edward Dillon in "Administrative Process in Canonical Form Cases," *The Jurist* 43 (1983) 233-237. He distinguishes between lack of form cases in which there was no species of form (i.e., people married without any canonical form or without any dispensation from it), and defect of form cases in which there was at least some semblance of form but it was defective. These would be cases in which the person who assisted at the marriage (e.g., the priest) lacked proper delegation.

The authentic interpretation relates to the first type of case, those in which there is a lack of any canonical form whatsoever. Prior to the new code this type of case was taken care of according to the procedure in *Provida Mater*, in which the bishop or the parish priest in consultation with the bishop was to declare the lack of any form prior to admitting the person to a new marriage. Basically this was part of the proof of freedom to marry, a pastoral procedure rather than a judicial procedure of the tribunal.

In some dioceses in the U.S.A. the tribunal was delegated by the bishop to handle such situations. There was a case of one U.S. diocese reported not long ago in which the Signatura was asked to intervene, and did, and in which it was clarified that it was improper for the *officialis* to handle such cases without a special mandate from the bishop since the procedure was administrative or pastoral rather than judicial.

The Commission has indicated that the procedures required prior to the new code remain in effect for lack of form cases. The documentary process, involving citation of parties and intervention of the defender of the bond, is required only for defect of form cases.

While the Commission did not comment further on their interpretation, it should be noted that canon 1071, §1, 3°, requires that the local ordinary grant permission prior to anyone assisting at the marriage of a person who is bound by natural obligations toward another party or toward children arising from a prior union. In effect, therefore, before witnessing the marriage of someone involved in a lack of form case the priest or other delegated person who is to assist at the marriage must contact the local ordinary.

In some dioceses the priests assigned to parishes have been delegated by the local ordinary to handle these cases. Other places still require them to be submitted to the chancery before a new marriage is permitted.

There is an added problem under the new code which does not seem to have been addressed either by the Commission or by many of these practices which continue from before the new code. This is the question of what it means to leave the Church by a formal act, and how to determine who really was bound by the canonical form at the time the marriage outside the Church took place.

James H. Provost [1985]

Canon 1071

Restrictions on Marriage Following Prior Union with Continuing Obligations

What are the natural obligations arising from a prior union and how extensive is the requirement for the ordinary's permission to assist at the marriage of a party with such obligations from a prior union?

Opinion

1. Natural obligations toward one's children and former spouse of a prior union would seem to include at least and primarily those mentioned in canon 1689: [After a sentence of nullity of marriage] "parties are to be advised of the moral and even civil obligations which they may have to each other and to their children as regards the support and education of the latter."

The report of the Code Commission (*Communicationes* 9 [1977] 143) briefly explains the origin and purpose of canon 1071, §1, 3°:

> Some proposed that the canon consider the cases of those parties who had contracted a civil marriage and were divorced, perhaps several times, and now want a religious matrimony, or those divorced who do not take care of the obligations to children; it should be examined if they have children but do not provide support.

Therefore, the primary concerns seem to be financial support for the former

338

spouse and children and the education of the children (the latter would most likely include emotional support, visitation, etc.). The canons indicate that the obligations are binding regardless of what any civil court has stipulated and regardless of which party has been given legal custody of the children. The canons also seem to imply that civil law or decrees of the civil court (in the divorce agreement) may specify other obligations that would be binding. We could also presume that general obligations of Christians toward others also apply toward former spouses and children: for example, respect for good name and reputation, respect for privacy (c. 220). However, these latter are not unique to situations of parties coming from a prior union.

Local legislation could develop a more specific set of guidelines on the types of obligations and conflicts which could be anticipated and examined in such cases.

2. Canon 1071, §1, 3° states that except in necessity, without permission of the ordinary, no one is to assist at the marriage of a party who is held to the above obligations from a prior union. The extent of this norm's binding force is a serious pastoral question.

a. First, we know that canon 1071 does not bind under penalty of invalidity; but would failure to obtain permission (except in cases of necessity) render any such a marriage *illicit*? And what is understood by *illicit*?

Canon 1071 is a collection of situations for prematrimonial investigation. Some of these situations were covered in the 1917 code (c. 1065 — notorious defection from the faith; c. 1066 — public sin or censure) which were called "impeding" impediments prohibiting marriage under penalty of illiceity (c. 1036). Other situations in the list were treated in separate canons of the old code in the chapter on prematrimonial investigation and banns (c. 1032 — transients c. 1034 — minors). The new code drops the old concept of an impeding impediment but still retains the concept of illicit celebration of marriage (c. 1066: "Before marriage is celebrated it must be evident that nothing stands in the way of its valid and licit celebration."). Canon 1071 is a collection of situations involving permission for licit celebration of marriage.

The concept of liceity is somewhat vague. Even when the Code Commission discussed the elimination of the impeding impediments, they noted the difficulty in identifying the effect of illiceity. Those consultors in favor of suppressing prohibiting impediments "said that impeding impediments have no effect except in the moral order because the matrimony would be only illicit. The only juridical effect would consist in this, that the pastor is able legitimately to refuse to assist at the matrimony" (*Communicationes* 9 [1977] 134).

Therefore, my opinion is that the binding force of canon 1071 impacts directly not so much on the parties but on the bishop and those in pastoral office. The law mandates special pastoral investigation and care in those cases where there are natural obligations arising from prior unions. Indirectly, the law impacts on the parties implying their fulfillment of these natural obligations as a condition for the licit celebration of marriage.

b. Secondly, regarding the extent of the requirement of the bishop's permission, canon 1071 appears to apply to all cases where parties are bound by natural obligations. For example, there is no indication that permission is required only if the parties are not faithful to their obligations. According to the wording of the canon, this permission is required whether or not the individuals are fulfilling the obligations.

Canon 1071 is a universal mandate to all who have the authority to assist at marriages. The exact execution of the requirement is left to the local exercise of pastoral authority under the direction of the ordinary. The local bishop can determine how the canon is implemented in the diocese and in individual cases.

For example, local legislation can determine: 1) how each case should be investigated and what criteria and how many questions should be considered before permission is given; 2) who should conduct the investigation — the bishop personally, or a diocesan agency, or the parish minister conducting the prematrimonial investigation; 3) what kind of counseling should be available to help parties face responsibilities and resolve problems in this situation. The local bishop can also determine how the permission will be granted: will he grant it personally in all cases, or delegate certain persons to review the investigation and grant permission, or delegate the local minister to grant permission, reserving directly to the bishop's office only those cases where serious problems are discovered?

Since canon 1071 appears in the code under the chapter on prematrimonial investigations, provisions for the implementation of the norm could also be established by the National Conference of Catholic Bishops (c. 1067).

As it reads, canon 1071, §1, 3° applies to all cases: namely, some exercise of the ordinary's pastoral office (either personally or by delegation or through vicars) is mandated any time a party wishes to enter marriage still bound by these natural obligations. If local bishops have not issued any guidelines, then no one is to assist at the marriage without approaching the ordinary for permission in each such case. The pastoral obligation from the canon pertains to all cases, unless or until the local bishop specifies how and when permission is to be obtained or presumed.

J. James Cuneo [1985]

CANON 1071

There is a Catholic man who used to attend our parish, but in the past several years has frequented a "Traditionalist" (Tridentine) Catholic chapel. He wishes now to enter marriage with a Catholic girl in a Catholic ceremony in our parish. The woman practices her faith in our parish. As the pastor, what must I do to permit this marriage? Are there any pastoral procedures to be followed?

OPINION

1. It would be our understanding that at no time has the Traditionalist movement been declared schismatic. It would appear that the Holy See has followed a cautious policy seeking reconciliation to the extent possible and dealing with individual situations as they develop. Since the Traditionalist movement transcends the boundaries of the diocese, it would seem that the local bishop should likewise refrain from any general statement on the status of the Traditionalist congregation.

2. It would seem that the local bishop with the parish clergy should respond then to individual cases as they arise, in particular to determine the canonical and sacramental implications of each situation in regard to practicing Roman Catholics. For example, in Bridgeport, the bishop has made statements to the effect that Roman Catholics do not fulfill their Sunday Mass obligations in a Traditionalist chapel. Also, in certain individual cases, the tribunal has declared null the marriages of Roman Catholics which have taken place in a Traditionalist chapel because of lack of canonical form, i.e., defect of jurisdiction on the part of the officiant.

3. Therefore, with regard to a Traditionalist approaching a Roman Catholic parish for marriage with a practicing Roman Catholic, the individual case should be evaluated separately by the parish clergy and the bishop. It would seem that canon 1071 should govern the procedure:

Canon 1071, §1: Except in cases of necessity, no one is to assist at the following marriages without the permission of the local ordinary: . . . 4°: a marriage of a person who has notoriously rejected the Catholic faith.

Canon 1071, §2: The local ordinary is not to grant permission for assisting at the marriage of a person who has notoriously rejected the Catholic faith unless the norms of canon 1125 have been observed. (Canon 1125 deals with the premises that are made in mixed marriages regarding Catholic upbringing of children, etc.)

According to the Reverend Thomas Doyle, O.P. in the CLSA's *Code of Canon Law: A Text and Commentary,* one who notoriously rejects the faith does not merely neglect its practice, but professes openly that he or she is no longer a Catholic and refuses obedience to the Church and its laws. This differs from those who have simply abandoned the faith without positively rejecting it or those who are temporarily non-practicing. The law presumes that those who have notoriously rejected the faith are hostile to it, pose a danger to the believing party and/or to the Catholic education of children or may be a scandal to the community or source of friction in the marital relationship.

It does not seem, therefore, that we should presume that every Traditionalist Catholic would fit that description of the hostile, defecting Catholic. Yet it does seem that each case requires special pastoral evaluation that would involve a procedure established by the local ordinary.

A Suggested Procedure

When a practicing Roman Catholic wishes to enter marriage with a "Traditionalist" Catholic, the parish priest or deacon should not permit the marriage or assist at it without following these procedures:

1. The parish priest or deacon should initiate a pastoral dialogue with the "Traditionalist" Catholic in order to ascertain the person's attitude toward his or her affiliation with the Catholic Church. Does the person formally reject the law of the Catholic Church, reject ecclesial communion with the present pope and bishops of the Church? Does the person consider his or her participation in the "Traditionalist" congregations to be a rejection of the Roman Catholic Church as it exists in the diocese? Or, on the other hand, is the person merely stating discomfort with some of the practices of the Church since Vatican II, with a feeling of spiritual consolation with the Tridentine rite? In the latter case the person may be considered a Catholic who is weak or confused or disenchanted in the practice of the faith, but not notoriously rejecting it.

2. The parish priest or deacon should then ask the "Traditionalist" Catholic if he or she understands that in the proposed marriage the Roman Catholic must promise to continue the practice of the Catholic faith and baptize and raise the children in the rites of the Roman Catholic Church. The response of the Traditionalist Catholic to this question would be important, for it would probably reveal the true state of the person's mind regarding affiliation with the Roman Catholic Church. The response would also affect the decision of the ordinary regarding permission for the marriage.

3. The practicing Roman Catholic party should then be asked to make the usual promise to continue the practice of the faith in the Roman Catholic Church. The format of these promises would be the same as with cases of mixed religion.

4. The parish priest or deacon should document the results of this investigation, including signatures by the parties and the priest or deacon. A separate form could be provided for this purpose by the chancery office. This form

would also provide space for the priest or deacon to give an opinion in the case: whether or not the marriage should be permitted. (The chancery of the Diocese of Bridgeport has in fact produced such a form. If anyone is interested in a copy, contact the undersigned.)

5. The parish priest or deacon should submit the case to the chancery office with the above documentation showing the results of the pastoral investigation. The local ordinary would make the decision whether or not to permit the marriage.

6. The documentation of this pastoral procedure as well as the rescript of the permission should be kept in the prematrimonial investigation records of the parish, as is done in other types of cases involving dispensations or special permission.

7. This suggested procedure need not be restricted to cases of "Traditionalist" Catholics, but could be adapted to any case where a problem is suspected of possible rejection of the Catholic faith by one of the parties to marriage.

J. James Cuneo [1987]

CANONS 1077 AND 1116

THE RIGHT TO MARRY AND DIOCESAN POLICIES
REQUIRING MINIMAL TIME OF PREPARATION

Please comment on the view published recently ("The Wait to Get Married," by Rodney Crewse, in Homiletic and Pastoral Review *[June 1985] 65-67) that diocesan policies which require a four to six month waiting period before a couple can be married are really imposing a new impediment, and the couple would be justified in using the extraordinary form of marriage.*

OPINION

This view has been circulating for the past year. It is based on two arguments, which are sort of an "either-or" arrangement. The first argument is that marriage preparation policies which require a fixed period of preparation before marriage have instituted a temporary impediment — during the "waiting period" the couple are impeded from marrying. Yet, the argument points out, no one besides the supreme authority of the Church can establish an invalidating impediment to marriage. Since diocesan policies seem to want to do just that, they are illegal and the couple are not bound by them. The second argument is that even if marriage preparation policies do not constitute an impediment for the couple, they do prohibit the priest from witnessing a marriage during the waiting period,'' so a couple who desire to marry and who are delayed for at least a month by the diocesan policy are able to make use of the extraordinary form of canon 1116. Thus, the couple still are not bound by these policies.

I will address each argument in turn.

To the first argument, I know of no diocesan policy which pretends to establish a diriment impediment. A policy might be interpreted as simply impeding marriage, however, if it were to establish a fixed waiting period rather than a time for preparation. The difference is subtle but important.

If the policy says the couple must be adequately prepared before they marry (in keeping with cc. 1063 and 1066), and that adequate preparation requires various activities, and in order to complete these preparations for marriage advance notice must be given to the pastor in plenty of time to assure this can be done — then such a policy, it seems to me, has not established any kind of impediment. It has made a prudent statement in keeping with the bishop's responsibility in canon 1064. On the other hand, if the policy were only to require a certain waiting period and did not provide for preparation activities during that time, it could be construed as if the diocese were establishing a new requirement which might be viewed as a temporary impediment. But even in this situation, it would not be an invalidating impediment — the only kind of ''impediment'' which exists under the new code.

If the content of the policy is directed toward marriage preparation (and not just a waiting period), is it legal? Such a policy is an ''instruction'' or even a general executory decree, according to the new code, something which the bishop is clearly authorized to issue (cc. 31-34). The purpose for the policy is to implement the provisions of canons 1063-1064. To claim such policies are contrary to law would be to ignore the provisions of Book One of the new code.

Furthermore, the policies I have studied provide for cases in which the priest comes to the conclusion that the couple are not ready for marriage. In such cases the decision is not to deny them access to marriage in the Church, but to postpone such access until they are ready. This is a legitimate application of canon 1077, §1: ''In a particular case the local ordinary can prohibit the marriage of his own subjects wherever they are staying and of all persons actually present in his own territory, but only for a time, for a serious cause and as long as that cause exists.'' Clearly, lack of readiness for marriage is a very serious cause as attested to not only by canon 1066, but also by the cases which regularly come before the ecclesiastical courts.

In some dioceses the decision to postpone must be made by an authority higher than the local parish priest; in others, the priest on the scene has been delegated to make the decision. In either case, the determination to postpone is not contrary to canon law, and may even be required by it.

The second argument is that a couple who must wait beyond one month for a priest to assist at their marriage are in the same situation as those for whom a priest is not morally available, and they may, therefore, use the extraordinary form of canon 1116. But what does that canon require?

First, it requires that "the presence of or access to a person who is competent to assist at marriage" is "impossible without serious inconvenience." A diocesan marriage policy does not make the presence or access to a person competent to assist at a marriage impossible; indeed, such access is a key to the whole policy. The purpose for the policy is to provide for access in an orderly, fruitful fashion.

Second, the marriage preparation policies I have studied do not pose such a serious inconvenience to the couple as to warrant application of this canon. They do require the couple to address the preparation for their marriage seriously, and call on the whole Church to assist them. But this is in keeping with canon law (c. 1063). To claim that something in keeping with canon law establishes a situation of moral impossibility is to claim the law itself is impossible. While there are extreme situations where this has been argued even by the classical commentators, to claim such in this case does not seem warranted.

This is because the code calls on the bishop to establish norms for marriage preparation. It leaves it to the bishop's discretion to determine what is appropriate in those norms. The law does not limit the bishop to a one month period. Couples who refuse to obey the norms set down legitimately by the bishop are not in a situation of moral impossibility, but of moral failure to obey their legitimate pastor (c. 212, §1).

If, as some claim, the fact of having to wait more than one month is sufficient to use the extraordinary form, does the same hold true when the wait is due to material reasons rather than because a diocesan policy requires adequate preparation for marriage? For example, what if the church or chapel they want to use is unavailable for over a month? Or more commonly, what if the reception hall they desire is unavailable for six months? Does this mean the wait they must endure places them in the situation of those persons the law understands to be in a state of impossibility without serious inconvenience? No one seems to be claiming this. If couples can wait for the physical arrangements for the wedding celebration, why is it wrong to ask them to spend adequate time preparing for a sacrament they are to share the rest of their lives?

It is true that diocesan marriage policies are binding not only on the couple, but also on priests. For a pastor to fail to obey diocesan policy could be an abuse of his function, a crime punishable according to canon 1389. Just because a particular priest does not like a diocesan policy does not set him up as a new

345

legislator in the Church, nor does it provide him with the authorization to ignore a policy established in keeping with the law and implementing the clear intention of the law.

On the other hand, it would also be an abuse of the pastor's function to treat the preparation of marriage lightly, or too mechanically. Marriage preparation policies are not a question of a "waiting period," or of a mathematical formula that must be observed in order to marry. They call for serious pastoral work, and the effort to involve the community in this important work.

The Church's law includes a necessary flexibility, contains provisions for exceptions and dispensations, and is to be administered in keeping with a Christian spirit and the principles of canonical equity. This situation is a good reminder of these things, lest we slip into a kind of automatism rather than an active pastoral effort at effective marriage preparation.

James H. Provost [1986]

Canon 1084

Impotence Resulting from Prostate Cancer

If a man is not married and has had prostate surgery which has made him impotent, is he impeded from marriage in light of canon 1084? Is age any factor in the question of impotence resulting from prostate surgery?

Opinion

Prostate surgery itself does not render a man impotent according to medical science. In this sense, impotency is an inability to sustain an erection of the penis in the presence of sexual desire. The condition often results from psychological (e.g., stress), physical (e.g., fatigue), or physiological (e.g., hormonal imbalance) factors, but not from surgical removal of the prostate unless certain nerves are cut or some other accident occurs during the procedure.

Whether prostate surgery renders a man impotent according to the Church's definition of this condition demands further discussion. Such a condition may be defined as an inability to have sexual intercourse *per se* apt for the generation of children by failure to achieve erection, penetration, or ejaculation. Particularly relevant is the matter of ejaculation.

While it does not lower a man's sexual desire, removal of the prostate does

346

change the quality of the seminal fluid, which receives its characteristic odor and milky color from components provided by this particular gland. The removal also reduces the amount of fluid ejaculated at orgasm by approximately twenty percent. If the vasa deferentia are tied during the operation, the ejaculate is reduced further but by a minuscule amount. Also the man becomes infertile, since the vasa deferentia convey the sperm from the testes to be mixed with the rest of the seminal fluid.

Infertility, of course, is not an impediment to marriage (c. 1084, §3). However, for years the Rota, following *Cum frequenter* of Sixtus V (1585-1590) and Gasparri (1852-1934), annulled marriages on the grounds of impotence if it was proven that the ejaculate did not contain *verum semem*, that is, if it did not contain fluid provided by the testes (cf., *CLD* 3: 411-420). At the same time the Holy Office held that such marriages were not to be impeded (cf., *CLD* 3: 410-411). A decree issued by the Congregation for the Doctrine of the Faith on May 13, 1977 (*AAS* 69 [1977] 426, and *CLD* 8: 676-677) seems to have ended this debate. The current prevailing view of the Rota, according to commentators such as Urbano Navarette, is now that of the Congregation for the Doctrine of the Faith.

Thus it seems that one cannot now argue that prostate surgery renders a man impotent simply because the vasa deferentia were tied during the procedure. Whether or not they were tied (and sometimes they are not), the man might not be impotent in the eyes of the Church, since other glands (e.g., the epididymis, seminal vesicles, and the Cowper's glands) secrete fluid in the process of ejaculation. The answer turns on whether the fluid provided by these other glands — despite the change of color, odor, and volume — seems to the ordinary person, without a microscope or other modern equipment, apt for the generation of children. If there is any doubt, the marriage is not to be impeded according to canon 1084, §2.

The possibility of retrograde ejaculation complicates the discussion slightly. About eighty percent of men who have undergone prostate surgery appear not to seminate although the sensation of orgasm remains normal. The semen is discharged into the bladder rather than through the penis. While the absence of semination constitutes impotence as understood by the Church, one would have to know whether the man experiences retrograde ejaculation *semper* and *pro semper* or whether he experiences it only sometimes. Again, if there is any doubt, the marriage is not to be impeded.

Retrograde ejaculation, moreover, is curable by minor surgery. Since this procedure can be considered an ordinary means in developed countries, the marriage of one who intends to correct a persistent problem of this type is likewise not to be impeded. Impotence must be perpetual to impede or invalidate marriage (c. 1084, §1).

347

Age would not seem to be a factor in this case. With or without the prostate gland, a man remains capable of sexual intercourse well into old age.

John R. Amos [1992]

CANONS 1086 AND 1160

VALIDATION OF A CATECHUMEN'S MARRIAGE AFTER AN ANNULMENT

A catechumen has received an annulment of 2 previous marriages and wishes to validate the present civil marriage with a Catholic. Should the marriage be validated before or after the catechumen has been received into the Church? If before, does there need to be a dispensation from mixed religion since the person is still a catechumen?

OPINION

The catechumen in question is currently living in a canonically irregular union, which would pose problems relative to full initiation into the Church at the end of the catechumenate process. This is true even given the contemporary discussion about whether persons living in irregular unions may be admitted into eucharistic communion (cf., for example L. Örsy, "Problem Areas and Disputed Questions," in *Marriage in Canon Law* [Wilmington: Michael Glazier, 1985] 288-294.). Accordingly, the soundest legal pastoral approach seems to be first to validate the current civil marriage and then subsequently receive him into full communion.

Catechumens in the code are understood to be non-baptized persons who seek admission to the Church through baptism. They technically have a special relationship with the Church (c. 206), into whose mystery they are gradually being initiated (cf., for example cc. 788-789; 851, §1; 865, §1; 866). The integrity of the various stages of the process of initiation should be carefully respected, and legitimate concerns about validating the marriage should not lead to a premature closure of the process in this instance (cf., for example L. Gaupin, "*RCIA*: Canonical Issues, a Liturgical Response," *CLSA Proceedings* 46 [1984] 130-140). Despite the special relationship with the Church, however, the catechumen's non-baptized status still makes it necessary for a dispensation from disparity of cult under the usual conditions (cc. 1086; 1125-1126) to be obtained by the minister preparing for the validation. After the catechumen has been received into the Church, the validated union would then be considered

348

technically a sacramental bond (c. 1061, §1).

Thomas J. Green [1989]

Another Opinion

A catechumen in an invalid marriage cannot be admitted to the sacraments of initiation.[1] Therefore, after obtaining an annulment or a dissolution of the prior marriage, the catechumen and his or her Catholic spouse should have their marriage convalidated as soon as possible. A dispensation from the impediment of disparity of cult is necessary, since the catechumen is unbaptized. However, the usual requirement of the declaration and promise to be made by the Catholic party to a mixed marriage (cc. 1125; 1086, §2) should not be observed, since this would be meaningless in light of the catechumen's desire to become a Catholic. The convalidation occurs through the observance of the canonical form (c. 1160), that is, the exchange of consent before two witnesses and a priest or deacon who has the faculty and who assists actively by asking for and receiving the consent of the parties (c. 1108). Unsuitable solemnity should be avoided; and the celebration of the Eucharist is prohibited, as it is for all nonsacramental marriages.[2]

If the catechumen were in an irregular second marriage with a *non-Catholic* and then received an annulment or a dissolution of the first marriage, a convalidation would not be necessary since it is a requirement of the ecclesiastical law and does not bind non-Catholics (cc. 1156, §2; 11). The consent given at the beginning of the second marriage and not later revoked is still effective and presumed to be valid (c. 1107).

A commentary treating canonical issues related to the status of catechumens is soon to be published by the Bishops' Committee on the Liturgy in a volume entitled *Pastoral Companion to the Rite of Christian Initiation of Adults*.

Notes

[1] See Congregation for the Doctrine of the Faith, reply, July 11, 1983, *Canon Law Digest* 10: 139-140: *Roman Replies 1983*, ed. William Schumacher (Washington, D.C.: Canon Law Society of America, 1983) 2-3.

[2] Roman Ritual, *Rite of Marriage*, n. 8.

John M. Huels, O.S.M. [1989]

Canons 1091 and 1059

Civil Recognition of Marriages between First Cousins

In which states in the United States is a marriage between first cousins legal? Can residents from a state that prohibits such marriages contract marriage in another state that permits first cousins to marry?

Opinion

These questions lend themselves to deceptively simple and quick responses, which might prove to be incorrect for several reasons: there are degrees of prohibition, celebration and/or recognition of such marriages, as applied to residents or non-residents. Some states have not enacted statutes regarding prohibited kinship marriages (some may have only case rulings); others prohibit certain such marriages from being contracted or celebrated in the state but recognize such a marriage if celebrated in another state which permits them; other jurisdictions do not recognize them regardless of where the marriage was contracted; and yet still other jurisdictions penalize residents who go to another state with the intent to violate the laws of their own state. Hence a second question arises: what (if any) legal consequences might be incurred if resident(s) from one state go to another state in order to get married in that state which allows first cousin marriage, and return to their own state?

A survey of current civil law on prohibited kinship marriage (see *Martin-dale-Hubbell Digest*, 1993) lists the following civil jurisdictions in the United States which permit first cousin marriage: Alabama (the *Digest* entry does not list any prohibited kinship marriage), Colorado, Connecticut, Florida, Hawaii, Maine (but only after filing a certificate of genetic counselling signed by a physician), Maryland, Massachusetts, New Jersey, New Mexico, New York, North Carolina (excluding double first cousins), Rhode Island, South Carolina, Tennessee, Texas, Vermont, Virgin Islands, Virginia, and Washington, DC. (The "statutes . . . decrees" for Georgia were not summarized in the *Digest*, and the "Domestic Relations" volume of Georgia law was unavailable at the time of this writing.)

A number of jurisdictions make special provision to allow first cousins who are of older age or sterile to intermarry: Arizona, if both over 65 or if unable to reproduce; Illinois, 50 years or older; Indiana, as of September, 1977, 65 years or older; Wisconsin, 55 or older, or affidavit of sterility.

In one instance there is apparently no provision at all regarding prohibited degree of kinship marriage (Alabama). The other entries differ in format and content. Some provide a list of blood relatives of the male, another list directed at the female. Others simply list as prohibited any marriage within and/or (not) including "4th degree consanguinity" or employ language such as "nearer of kin than second cousin." Fourth degree of consanguinity is popularly referred to as "first cousins." In common law it may be referred to as "kindred in the fourth degree, being the issue, male or female, of the brother or sister of one's mother or father" (this is also called "cousins german"; see *Black's Law Dictionary*, 6th ed. [West Publishing, 1990], entry "Cousin").

Some jurisdictions specify "first cousin by whole or half blood" (Nebraska: prohibits first cousin marriage "by whole or half blood"; Nevada law states that "persons nearer of kin than second cousins, or cousins of the half blood, may not intermarry"). Oregon prohibits first cousin marriage except when the parties are first cousins by adoption.

Jurisdictions which prohibit first cousin marriages (or those of nearer kinship) for the most part consider them void *ab initio* (i.e., null from their inception, void, "declared void," "absolutely void," or voidable by judgment, including in some states, annulment). A number of these protect the legitimacy of any children born even to such marriages.

A major precaution must be taken, however, since some states specifically provide that resident(s) who intend to contravene the laws of their own state and contract a marriage which is prohibited in their state, by getting married in another state which permits and/or recognizes such marriages, and then return to their home state, are subject to prosecution (e.g., West Virginia: they are punishable as if the prohibited marriage had been made in state), but others may recognize such marriages performed in another state authorizing such marriages (e.g., Oklahoma).

Caution is urged. When even well-meaning Christian faithful, knowing that it might be possible to obtain a dispensation from the canonical impediment (c. 1091, §2), approach a minister of the Church and explain that they are crossing state boundaries in order to enter a first cousin marriage not permitted in their own state, then a simple response, even one motivated by pastoral care, may be misleading and might provide the soil for an illegal act according to the requirements of civil law.

Joseph J. Koury [1993]

CANONS 1098; 1066; AND 128

CONCEALING HIV STATUS FROM INTENDED SPOUSE

A couple in their mid-twenties has begun pre-marriage counselling with Fr. X. In his third session with the couple, he interviews each party separately. In the course of the interview with the bride, it is revealed to Fr. X by the bride that she is HIV+, and cannot bring herself to tell the groom, nor is she willing to have Fr. X inform the groom. She is adamantly opposed to anyone being told of her HIV+ status.

Also, in the state there is a law prohibiting the disclosure of a person's HIV status to anyone for any reason, under threat of one year in jail and a $50,000 fine. This civil law has been proven constitutional, and the chancery of the diocese has warned priests concerning its provisions.

What is Fr. X to do?

OPINION

Infection by the human immunodeficiency virus (HIV) can develop into AIDS, a collapse of the immune system rendering the body vulnerable to a variety of opportunistic diseases. AIDS is fatal and, to date, there is no proven cure for it or vaccine to inoculate against it. Sexual intercourse is one of the few ways HIV is transmitted. Seropositive women can infect men through cervical or vaginal secretions during intercourse. These facts indicate that one partner's HIV+ condition can seriously disrupt a conjugal relationship.

In the situation described above, the priest confronts the moral question of whether he can allow, through the Church's ministerial sanction, one person knowingly to expose another unwittingly to a life-threatening virus through the very act which consummates marriage. Besides this moral issue, there are canonical considerations which significantly narrow the range of the priest's possible responses.

Canon 1098 states that a person contracts marriage invalidly when "deceived by fraud, perpetrated to obtain consent, concerning some quality of the other party which of its very nature can seriously disturb the partnership of conjugal life." In the case at hand, the groom is not aware of the bride's HIV+ status which, as already indicated, can seriously disturb marital life. The bride cannot bring herself to inform the groom of this fact nor will she allow anyone else to reveal this to him. Since the situation presented above gives few details about the bride's interview with the priest, her motivation can only be inferred. In another context, her reluctance to share this information may be generally motivated by issues of privacy and the need to protect against potential social and economic damage. In this context, however, it is reasonable to assume that fear of ending her relationship with her fiancé motivates her concealment. If the groom knew, would he give consent to this marriage? Without discussing it with him, the bride would never know and so her fear is not abated. It is not difficult to conclude that the bride is hiding her HIV + status so as to secure his consent.

Is it evident that concealment of HIV + status constitutes deception? Unless the groom knows or suspects that his fiancée is somehow at risk of being infected with HIV, it is highly probable that he never seriously contemplated whether she was HIV negative or positive. It is equally probable that he would want and intend to marry a person who was free of this deadly virus. Unlike the situation of error in canon 1097, §2, for there to be deceit, the groom does not have to intend consciously, directly or principally, that his bride be HIV negative. But the fact that she knows about her status and chooses to conceal it from him does constitute a misrepresentation. There is deception because this information is grave enough to raise a question in the minds of prudent and reasonable people whether this marriage is advisable and desirable.

Can the groom, however, be said to be "deceived by fraud" in this instance? Fraud or *dolus* is a strong word. Fraud is a premeditated or deliberate intention to deceive. In this case, the bride appears caught in unresolved conflict about informing her fiancé of her HIV infection. Nonetheless, she is adamant in her opposition to disclosure. That she is troubled about this matter, even to the point of revealing her condition to the priest, indicates she is aware of the serious consequences of both disclosure and concealment. This awareness and her continuing concealment amount to deliberation, even though she may feel conflict and fear. In the case of marital consent, to deceive by fraud does not require cold-blooded scheming or calculated intention to do harm. It is sufficient that the intention to deceive be deliberate, as opposed to negligence or careless omission to inform the other party.

Whether the groom's consent would be defective because of *dolus* can only be determined after the fact. However, the factors that could vitiate his consent are present in this case.

The question in this case concerns the priest's response to this situation. Canon 1066 places an obligation on the priest to establish that nothing stands in the way of the valid and lawful celebration of marriage. This obligation is reinforced in canon 1114. Since it is likely the groom's consent would be defective according to canon 1098, the priest in this case cannot lawfully proceed with the wedding.

In this regard, canon 128 raises the question of the priest's liability should he proceed with the wedding under these circumstances. This canon states that anyone who unlawfully inflicts damage upon someone by a juridic act is obliged to compensate for the damage inflicted. As noted above, it would be unlawful for the priest to proceed with this marriage. Presuming that he is to assist at the wedding, his ministerial role is necessary for canonical form and, for this reason, the validity of the marriage as a juridic act. Should the parties marry and the groom become infected with HIV, could one argue a case establishing the priest's canonical liability for this grave injury?

This case is complicated by the state's prohibition of disclosure of another person's HIV status. Regard for privacy and protection against potential damage would motivate this legislation. But in the question of a proposed marriage, the other party has a legitimate interest in this information since the HIV status of his partner directly impinges upon his health and well-being. Would it be a violation of the state's law if the priest in this case merely stated that he could not proceed with this wedding because of information given to him in confidence? He does not reveal the information but only the fact that it is grave enough for him to be constrained by canon law from witnessing this marriage. This is not disclosure of a specific fact. It would more than likely provoke consternation; perhaps the bride would feel coerced to disclose her status to the groom; and should the groom reject his bride, she may sue the priest for forcing her into disclosure. Sensitively and effectively navigating through this morass of conflicting rights, legal constraints, moral obligations, human passion and nuptial expectations require a fine skill in the art of pastoral care. But the priest cannot do otherwise, for the moral and canonical considerations are too compelling.

Randolph R. Calvo [1993]

Canon 1104, §2

External Actions Necessary for Valid Consent

During an interview with a couple preparing for marriage, it is discovered that both parties had been previously married. The woman, a Catholic, had been married by a justice of the peace and thus had a lack of canonical form case. The man, a baptized Baptist, had also been married by a justice of the peace. It was assumed that he had a formal case, given that neither he nor his first former wife had been previously married. In passing, the man remarked that the "ceremony" conducted by the civil official was simply the signature of the official on a piece of paper. No expression of consent was asked for or given by either party.

What act of consent between non-Catholic parties is required in order to satisfy the demands of natural and divine law? Is the simple willingness to stand before an official sufficient in itself for marriage to be contracted? Is the requirement of canon 1104, §2 that "those to be married are to express their matrimonial consent in words" or other equivalent signs merely ecclesiastical law, applicable only to Catholics?

The Church has made it clear that the consent of the parties is necessary in order for a marriage to be constituted. The Church has even recognized that no form is necessary, but that some expression of consent by the parties must be manifested. Thus even so-called clandestine marriages have been recognized by the Church. The imposition of form by the Council of Trent requiring the marriage to be performed in the presence of the pastor and two witnesses applies only to Catholics. However, the fathers at the council were touching the circumstances in which consent is made; they were not changing the essential element of consent itself.

Nevertheless, consent is not something presumed to exist between two people living together as husband and wife. This is true even if the state were to recognize the parties as married because of the condition of their life, e.g., they live together, represent themselves as husband and wife, hold joint accounts, etc. Consent must be constituted by an act of the will of the parties. It cannot simply be presumed to exist because actions normally associated with married life are present. The legal presumption, in the absence of any public ceremony declaring matrimonial consent, must be that the parties are not married. The presumption can fall to contrary evidence, but the simple presence of aspects of married life do not in themselves constitute marriage.

The above applies directly to marriage recognized by the state as common law marriages, but which the parties involved never recognized between themselves as a marriage. This applied even when a divorce decree is obtained by parties who have lived together. A divorce decree can be sought simply as a way to protect the parties' custody and property rights. Extending this to the case at hand, it means that some expression of consent is necessary to constitute marriage. A couple that goes to a county courthouse to obtain a marriage license is expressing a will to be married, but the act of willing to be married is not the same as the act of marrying. "I will marry you" is not the same as "I marry you." The future is only realized in a present and the present must be concrete. Thus it cannot be argued that because a couple obtained a marriage license that all the other formalities are incidental.

Does the fact that the couple went to the courthouse to be married in itself constitute marriage? Once again the answer must be no. It is true that the parties had the intention to marry, but their intention to marry was not satisfied by the actions of the agent. In the particular case, the couple went into the judge's chambers to recite their vows but without any ceremony whatsoever, the judge signed the papers and said, "Congratulations." No expression of consent was made. In fact, the man said to the judge, "When did I say, 'I do'?" Consent makes a marriage, not the signature of a judge which is supposed to attest to the act of the parties. Thus even though the parties willed to be married, they were not given the forum in which to be married. While it may be true that internally they consented to marriage, this cannot be considered legitimate for the external forum.

Canonical Application

It seems clear that the expression of consent in some public way or some verifiable expression of consent is essential to marriage. It is even enough for the parties to say to each other, "I consent to marriage with you." But this must be done. There can be no substitution for this act.

All tribunals are faced with numerous marriages other than Catholic marriages which guarantee that the natural elements of expression are followed. It seems a fair question for tribunals to ask whether or not any expression of consent was made when these non-Catholic ceremonies were conducted. It seems clear that when the expression of marital consent is completely lacking, even when the parties wanted to make some expression of it but were frustrated, then a lack of natural expression can be alleged and the marriage declared invalid. In such cases, the tribunal would only have to establish these facts with moral certitude by following a summary process.

D. Timothy Thompson [1992]

ANOTHER OPINION

In the western canonical tradition it is the exchange of matrimonial consent manifested by persons capable in the law that brings marriage into existence. Canon 1057, §2, which defines matrimonial consent, is one of very few exact definitions in the Code of Canon Law. As an articulation of Christian belief based on revelation and natural law, it not only identifies the way in which marriage comes about for Catholics but also states unequivocally the manner in which marriage comes into being in all cases.

Persons obliged by the law to observe the canonical form of marriage (c. 1117) are subject to purely ecclesiastical laws to be observed for the valid exchange of consent in addition to being bound by the prescripts of divine and natural law. Therefore, the juridic standard for judging who is capable in the law and for identifying the manner in which consent is legally manifested differs according to whether one is bound to the canonical form of marriage. The object of marital consent for those obliged to the canonical form and for those free to exchange consent outside the prescribed canonical form remains the same; that is, in both cases a man and a woman will freely give themselves in a spousal relationship that is faithful, permanent, and open to children.

"Capable in the law" has a substantially different significance for those bound to the canonical form as opposed to those who are not obliged to the juridic requirements of a purely ecclesiastical nature. The same may be said for "the manner in which consent is manifested." Those bound to the canonical form of marriage must manifest consent in an appropriate way through words or signs (c. 1104, §2).

Canon 1104, §2 is unquestionably an ecclesiastical law. An examination of the deliberations of the *coetus* for marriage of the Pontifical Commission for the Revision of the Code of Canon Law reveals that the discussion regarding canon 1104, §2 concentrated primarily on liturgical issues. A primary concern of the *coetus* for canon 1104, §2 was the principle that the liturgical rite of the sacrament of marriage should fit the particular culture both in words and in ritual actions (*Communicationes* 3 [1971] 78-81). The original placement of canon 1104, §2 within a canon of the schema which identified the official witness in the canonical form of marriage also testifies strongly to the canon's purely ecclesiastical nature (*Communicationes* 8 [1976] 36-37).

A proposal was also made to move the provisions of canon 1104, §2 to the chapter on canonical form. It was argued that the canons in the chapter on the canonical form of the celebration of marriage dealt with the extrinsic way in which consent is given. It was affirmed by members of the *coetus* that it was better to leave canon 1104, §2 in the chapter dealing with marital consent (*Communicationes* 9 [1977] 376).

For those bound by the canonical form of marriage and for those not, it is consent itself that is the essential element in the creation of the marriage bond. Nothing may substitute for it. Consent in itself does not exist in the words used to express it. Ecclesiastical law only insists that there be some external sign of the internal act of the will. (Note that in the liturgical books and in the Code of Canon Law there are no exact prescribed words for the valid exchange of consent.)

Those not bound by the canonical form of marriage are free to exchange marital consent in a number of ways. It is the authority to which the parties are subject, ecclesiastical or civil, which indicates the manner in which marital consent is to be manifested. The external act of consent must be observable and may be manifested by simply standing before a legally competent civil official or by signing an appropriate document if that is the manner prescribed by civil law. Even the implicit exchange of consent, which may civilly constitute a common law marriage, at times suffices.

More important than the manner in which consent is exchanged for two non-Catholics is that the demands of natural law be met by the parties. There must be some understanding, if only minimally, of the nature of marriage. The consent exchanged must be free, deliberate and mutual. It must be elicited in regard to a specified person who is the partner.

Gary D. Yanus [1992]

CANON 1108

PRIEST ACTING SOLELY AS CIVIL WITNESS TO MARRIAGE

Can a priest act solely as a civil witness to a marriage? Has the Holy See made any observations on this matter?

OPINION

This is a question debated periodically around the country. As far as I know the Holy See has not issued any statement in this regard. Much, therefore, depends upon the local civil law. My own opinion is that priests cannot serve as civil witnesses to a marriage unless they are also a civil official. In most state jurisdictions they are licensed as a religious official, not as a civil official, and their religious activities have civil effects. So a priest could not act *solely* as a civil witness to a marriage unless the state had so licensed him, and for that you would have to check each individual jurisdiction.

James H. Provost [1984]

CANONS 1109; 1110; AND 1117

THE RIGHT OF CATHOLIC CLERGY TO OFFICIATE AT THE MARRIAGE OF PARTIES WHO ARE NOT OBLIGED TO CANONICAL FORM

We have found two repeating issues concerning priests officiating at non-sacramental marriages in our work in the tribunal. These two issues deal with the right of the priest to officiate as a civil official in a wedding ceremony. The issues are as follows: (1) What is the canonical interpretation for a priest officiating as "civil official only" at a marriage involving at least one person who, in the eyes of the Catholic Church, is not free to marry? (2) What is the canonical interpretation for a priest officiating as civil official at a marriage involving two persons who are free to marry but are not bound to follow Catholic form?

OPINION

This inquiry is not as simple as it may first appear. It becomes clear that the question involves several areas of consideration, basically: a) the issue of canonical form; b) ecumenical considerations or *communicatio in sacris*; and c) penal law prohibiting simulation of a sacrament. For the sake of commentary on this question, we shall not limit ourselves to "non-sacramental" marriages; for it is possible that the hypothetical situations outlined in the above questions would include parties who are baptized but not bound by canonical form. In this latter case a valid matrimonial consent would also be a sacrament (c. 1055, §2). Our opinion will begin by addressing the second part of the question, namely the right of Catholic clergy to officiate at a marriage of parties who are free to marry but not bound by canonical form. Several points must be considered:

1. Canons 1109 and 1110 seem to restrict the right of the clergy to officiate only at the marriage of their subjects or persons of Latin rite. Canon 1109 deals with the territorial ordinary and pastor who, in virtue of their office, "validly assist at the marriages of their subjects as well as of non-subjects provided one of the contractants is of the Latin rite." Canon 1110 deals with personal ordinaries and pastors who "validly assist only at marriages involving at least one of their subjects." These canons are based on the fact that officiating at marriages is a jurisdictional act. The Church defines the limits of the jurisdiction in order to protect the rights and obligations of parties, ministers, personal and territorial pastoral relationships and ritual communities. Lack of jurisdiction of the minister invalidates the canonical form of the marriage. A Catholic bishop, priest or deacon would not have jurisdiction over the marriage of two non-Catholics. The required jurisdiction for valid canonical form of marriage would be lacking. The issue of the inquiry, however, is precisely the situation of parties who are not bound by the canonical form. If they are not bound by the canonical form, then the minister's lack of canonical jurisdiction would not affect the validity of their marriage. It seems that the restrictions of canons 1109 and 1110 affect only the validity of canonical marriage and those who are bound to canonical form.

2. According to canon 1117 the canonical form is to be observed whenever at least one of the contracting parties was baptized in the Catholic Church or was received into it and has not left it by a formal act. If the parties are not bound by canonical form it would seem they are still bound to some public form

359

of celebration for validity (similar to the situation of parties who have been dispensed from the form according to c. 1127, §2). Therefore, even if the priest as minister in this situation would not need canonical jurisdiction to officiate, it is clear that he would need civil jurisdiction and must follow a public form for the marriage to be valid. Each state has its own rules for recognizing a person's jurisdiction to officiate. Some states may not recognize the capacity of a religious minister to act outside the jurisdiction of his or her church, while other states (such as Connecticut) recognize that anyone who is a legitimate minister of a church automatically is empowered to join a couple in matrimony anywhere in the state. Thus a priest who is asked to officiate at the marriage of parties not obliged to canonical form does not seem restricted by canon law from doing so validly, but the civil law may restrict it. The priest would have to follow the civil law in this regard.

3. While it does not seem that the code prohibits a priest from validly officiating at a non-canonical marriage, there are several factors which seem to prevent a priest from licitly doing this, at least without permission of the ordinary. The ecumenical considerations of canon 844 and the practical, matrimonial considerations of canon 1071 need to be addressed in these questions.

Canon 844 states that Catholic ministers "may licitly administer the sacraments to Catholic members of the Christian faithful only and, likewise, the latter may licitly receive the sacraments only from Catholic ministers with due regard for paragraphs 2, 3 and 4 of this canon and canon 861, §2." The canon establishes the general prohibition against *communicatio in sacris,* which would be involved certainly in those cases where two baptized persons, not bound by canonical form, approach the Catholic minister to officiate at the marriage. Their marriage would be a sacrament even if not celebrated with canonical form.

The various paragraphs of this canon then proceed to describe certain situations which would allow exceptions or dispensations from the general rule. We note that the canons deal with exceptions with regard to penance, Eucharist, and anointing of the sick. Marriage is not listed explicitly in the exceptions. This no doubt is related to the fact that the Latin Church recognizes the parties as the ministers of the sacrament of matrimony. If the canon permits exceptions with regard to penance, Eucharist and anointing of the sick, it would seem exceptions could be permitted with regard to a Catholic minister officially witnessing a sacramental marriage of non-Catholics. Nevertheless, it would seem that the same type of canonical reasons and conditions justifying the exception would have to be verified. It would seem the local ordinary would need to legislate the norms or at least be involved in granting the exception in individual cases. Furthermore, norms should be enacted only after consultation with the authorities of the interested non-Catholic church or community. Even if the parties are not bound by the canonical form, the Catholic minister should not presume to officiate at the marriage of parties who are affiliated with other churches. This would be ecumenically offensive.

What if the marriage in question would not be a sacramental marriage? If the persons, who are not obliged to canonical form, are likewise non-baptized (at least one of them), the marriage would not be a sacrament and the prohibitions against *communicatio in sacris* do not seem strictly to apply. Nevertheless, there may be serious issues of interfaith affairs which could affect the liceity (and perhaps even validity) of the marriage before a Catholic minister. Members of non-Catholic or non-Christian communities would be subjects of the authorities and norms of those communities. Those communities may have their own obligations or restrictions regarding valid or licit matrimony of their subjects, so that the Catholic minister should not quickly presume the right to officiate. It is interesting to note that canon 776 of the *1986 Schema Codicis Iuris Canonici Orientalis* states: "If the Church must judge the validity of a marriage entered between persons who are not bound by merely ecclesiastical matrimonial laws the following norms are to be observed: 1) With regard to impediments which are not of divine law, then the law by which the parties are bound is to be observed; 2) with regard to the form of the celebration of marriage the Church recognizes any form prescribed or admitted by the law to which the parties are subject at the time of the celebration of matrimony, provided consent be expressed in a public form and, if at least one of the parties is a Christian of any non-Catholic oriental church, the matrimony be celebrated with sacred rite." The proposed canon would recognize the right of other communities to oblige their members to laws of impediments and celebration. Thus if two persons, not bound by canonical form of marriage, approach a Catholic minister to officiate in non-canonical form, the priest, as a representative of the Catholic Church, must join with the Catholic Church in recognizing the juridical effects of the non-Catholic communities' regulations on their own subjects. The priest should not presume to officiate at the marriage of parties who are not free to marry according to the law of their communities or who are obliged to a form of marriage mandated by their communities. Canon 1071 of the Code of Canon Law (Latin) shows similar respect with regard to purely civil law: "Except in cases of necessity no one is to assist at the following marriages without permission of the local ordinary . . . 2. a marriage which cannot be recognized or celebrated in accord with the norm of civil law; . . ."

Therefore, in summary, a Catholic minister should not officiate at the marriage of two persons who are not held to the form without permission of the ordinary, and without discovering and respecting the ecumenical, interreligious, and even civil norms that would affect the legitimate (and perhaps even valid) celebration of marriage. Even if the marriage would not be sacramental, the right of the Catholic minister to officiate should not be presumed automatically. It would seem permission of the ordinary should be sought.

In addition to the ecumenical, interreligious and civil considerations, there are also other practical, matrimonial considerations such as those listed in canon 1071. Certain circumstances require the intervention of the ordinary. Even if the parties are not obliged to canonical form, nevertheless the Catholic minister does not cease to be a representative of the Church and must be attentive to situations that could have negative effects on the couple, society or Church: for example, a marriage of a person who is bound by natural obligations toward another party or toward children arising from a prior union; or a marriage of a minor child when the parents are unaware of it or are reasonably opposed to it; or a marriage, as mentioned above, that would be restricted by civil law. And what of the situation where one or both parties is a person who has notoriously rejected the Catholic faith? They are not bound by the form, but should they conceivably ask a priest, who is a personal friend, to officiate at their marriage ceremony outside the Church, it seems that the possibility of scandal would be such to prevent the Catholic minister from doing so legitimately, at least without permission of the ordinary.

Finally we address the question of a Catholic minister who officiates at the marriage involving at least one person who, "in the eyes of the Catholic Church," is not free to marry. May the priest, for example, act as a civil official only? It would seem that two canons would address this question and lead to a negative response: 1) Canon 1066 states that before marriage is celebrated, it must be evident that nothing stands in the way of its valid and licit celebration. This imposes upon the Catholic minister a grave obligation to determine the freedom to marry of the parties. Certain impediments such as *ligamen* apply to all parties. The Catholic minister continues to represent the Church even if he acts here in a function which is merely "civil." The state may not be recognizing any jurisdiction of the minister over matrimony unless the minister were a legitimate representative of a church. Therefore, even if the parties themselves do not recognize themselves as impeded (such as by a previous marriage ended in divorce), the Catholic minister would not be free to ignore that element. To function in that case would be scandalous. 2) Canon 1379 of the penal book of the code would impose a just penalty upon anyone who simulates the administration of a sacrament. If the Catholic minister knowingly officiated at the wedding ceremony of parties, who, by Catholic doctrine, are impeded from marriage, he would be simulating the administration of the marriage. Of course, one could make the distinction that a marriage between parties who were not both baptized is not a sacrament; and so strictly speaking the penalty would not apply (penal law must be interpreted strictly). Canon 1384, however, which is more general in its implication, would seem to apply: "Outside the cases mentioned in canons 1379-1383, one who illegitimately carries out a priestly function or another sacred ministry can be punished with a just penalty." To officiate at the marriage of parties who are not free to marry either by ecclesiastical law, or divine law, or civil law, or by the law of the communities to which the parties may be subject, would amount to a violation of the prescription of canon 1066, which requires the minister to be sure of the freedom of the parties to enter marriage before officiating. The fact that the parties are non-Catholic and/or baptized does not dispense the Catholic ministers from their obligations. It may happen that non-Catholics, even lapsed Catholics, feel they are in good conscience attempting a marriage from which they are impeded. This would not, however, permit the Catholic minister to suspend his role as representative of the Church before these parties and their community.

In summary, it would be my opinion that the Catholic minister never has the right to officiate (even as a "civil official only") at the marriage of parties who are not free to marry "in the eyes of the Church," if the impediment is one to which the Church recognizes the parties to be subject, even if the parties themselves do not recognize this. It is my opinion that the Catholic ministers may officiate at the marriage of persons not obliged to canonical form who are free to marry. This role should not be presumed as an automatic right, given the civil, ecumenical, and interreligious complications. It would seem best in this latter situation that the ordinary be consulted in each case, and that local legislation establish guidelines for granting permission.

J. James Cuneo [1987]

CANONS 1109; 1110; AND 1117

THE RIGHT OF CATHOLIC CLERGY TO OFFICIATE AT THE MARRIAGE OF PARTIES WHO ARE NOT OBLIGED TO CANONICAL FORM

What is the canonical interpretation for a priest officiating as a civil official at a marriage involving two persons who are free to marry but are not bound to follow Catholic form? Must the ordinary give the dispensation from the prohibition of canon 285 forbidding civil office to clerics?

(Editor's Note: The following opinion was submitted in response to the above opinion.)

ANOTHER OPINION

363

I read with much interest your opinion on "The right of Catholic clergy to officiate at the marriage of parties who are not obliged to canonical form" as published in the *Roman Replies and CLSA Advisory Opinions 1987*. I would very much appreciate your observations on the following opinion.

Canon 139 of the 1917 Code of Canon Law states that clerics may not, without an apostolic indult, accept public offices which involve the exercise of lay jurisdiction or administration. In a declaration dated July 25, 1917, the Holy Office reasoned that this restriction applied to acting as civil magistrates in marriage (cf., *CLD* 2: 333).

De Episcoporum Muneribus, IX, 3b reserved to the Holy See the power to dispense from the prohibition against clerics assuming public offices which carry with them the exercise of lay jurisdiction or administration. Presumably this includes acting as a civil magistrate in marriage.

The 1983 code rules definitively and without qualification that "clerics are forbidden to assume public offices which entail a participation in the exercise of civil power" (c. 285, §3). Again, it would seem that this prohibition extends to acting as a civil magistrate in marriage. The law makes no provision for the ordinary to grant permission for a cleric to participate in the exercise of civil power. It may be argued that the diocesan bishop has the power to dispense from this disciplinary law by virtue of the power attributed to him in canon 87, §1, and the abrogation of the reservation of *De Episcoporum Muneribus*, IX, 3b by virtue of canon 6, §4.

The Holy See seems to be constant in its frowning on priests exercising lay jurisdiction. In our own country, priests have been asked to abandon public offices to which they were elected. Pope Paul VI and Pope John Paul II have been adamant on the point that lay jurisdiction should be left in the hands of the laity. The present code is, likewise, very firm on the matter.

In your article you state, "It is my opinion that the Catholic ministers may officiate at the marriage of persons not obliged to canonical form who are free to marry. This role should not be presumed as an automatic right, given the civil, ecumenical, and interreligious complications. It would seem best in this latter situation that the ordinary be consulted in each case, and that local legislation establish guidelines for granting permission."

It is my opinion that we are talking about "dispensation" and not "consultation." No Catholic minister, therefore, can take it upon himself to officiate at the marriages of persons not obliged to canonical form when at least one is not baptized. As the history of the matter makes no distinction between natural and sacramental bond marriages, this prohibition probably extends to cases where both parties are baptized but not obliged to the form. Furthermore, if we are talking "dispensation," the issue of diocesan guidelines becomes a non-issue. Each case would have to be examined on its own merits, leading to a specific decision on the part of the diocesan bishop that a relaxation of the law in this instance would redound to the spiritual good of the faithful.

Francis T. Wallace [1988]

EARLIER OPINION CONTINUED

The opinion of Monsignor Francis T. Wallace in this matter has introduced canon 285, §3 into the discussion. This is very much appreciated, inasmuch as I had overlooked that element in my opinion last year. Certainly this canon reinforces my basic opinion that Catholic clergy should not presume the right to act in this capacity.

Regarding the 1917 declaration of the Holy Office which interpreted the prohibition against clerical participation in civil jurisdiction to apply to civil officiating at weddings, I would wonder if that declaration still necessarily implies a universal equation of civil office with every act of officiating civilly at marriage. My own concept of office as a *stable* function leads me to presume that isolated acts of officiating at marriage should not be interpreted as a civil office. On the other hand, if a cleric were to assume the civil office of justice of the peace, for example, without permission, there would be a violation of canon 285.

I do not see individual acts of officiating at marriage as the equivalent to the forbidden assumption of a civil office. Also, I think it should be kept in mind that anytime a cleric performs a wedding (at least in the State of Connecticut), the state recognizes the civil effects of the ceremony without regard to the religious affiliation of the minister or the wedding parties. In such a case we would have to presume: a) either the state considers all ministers to hold civil office whenever they officiate at marriages — in which case even if a Catholic priest officiated at the sacramental marriage of two Catholics it would be a civil office according to the code; or b) the state never considers officiating at marriages by clerics to be a civil office — in which case the cleric who does so, whether for a Catholic ceremony or otherwise, is not exercising civil office as such and not violating canon 285.

J. James Cuneo [1988]

CANONS 1109; 1118; AND 1127, §2

PROPER OFFICIANT IN A MIXED MARRIAGE CELEBRATED IN

A Non-Catholic Church

Who officiates at a wedding (mixed religion) in a non-Catholic church? If it is a question of a dispensation from canonical form, the Catholic party's ordinary grants the dispensation, with consultation if the non-Catholic church is outside the diocese. But what of a couple, neither of whom are residents of the diocese, being married at a Catholic ceremony in a Methodist church in the diocese with a Catholic priest who is also not from the diocese assisting? The local pastor provided delegation, but exactly who is authorized by canon law to grant permission to use the Methodist church?

Opinion

As to who can officiate, clearly it is the bishop in his own diocese, the pastor in his own parish, or a bishop, priest, or deacon delegated by either for their respective territory, provided at least one of the parties is a Catholic of the Latin rite (c. 1109). So in the case you mentioned, so long as at least one of the parties was a Latin rite Catholic (even though not from the area), the local pastor could delegate the priest to assist at the marriage.

Since this question affects the validity of the marriage, it is more clearly spelled out in the law than the other question you have, and is also more enforceable (i.e., the priest must observe the law or else the marriage is invalid). Aside from extraordinary situations or in danger of death, any exceptions to this norm require a dispensation from the law, which is to be given by a local ordinary of the Catholic party (c. 1127, §2).

If the couple intend to marry outside the jurisdiction of that ordinary, before he grants the dispensation he is to consult the ordinary of the place where the couple propose to marry.

The conference of bishops is supposed to set up an orderly way to assure how all this is done, but the NCCB has not taken any action on this issue so far. Its previous norms (effective January 1, 1971) merely called for the ordinary to inform the ordinary of the place where the couple proposed to marry, but did not require that he be asked about it in advance. This has been replaced by the provision of canon 1127, §2, which requires advance consultation. Yet even if the ordinary objects when he is consulted, the one who proposes to grant the dispensation may do so validly and licitly after hearing from the objecting ordinary.

Note that the rules on dispensing from the form of marriage are more restrictive than dispensing from the impediment of disparity of worship, or the norms on granting permission for a Catholic to marry a baptized non Catholic. The ordinary can grant these for his own subjects, even if they are outside his territory. He can also grant it for travellers inside his territory (c. 91). He is not required to consult with any other ordinary in granting the dispensation from the impediment or the permission for a marriage with a baptized non-Catholic.

The question of the place where the wedding takes place is on a different level. It affects the liceity but not the validity of the marriage. It is thus more difficult to enforce. But it is also more complex.

First of all, the law itself contains several exceptions to the norm that weddings should take place in a parish church. The marriage between a Catholic and a non-baptized person, for example, can take place in a church or some other suitable place (c. 1118, §3) and the law does not require any dispensation or permission to use "some other suitable place" in these cases.

Second, the law authorizes the local ordinary or the pastor to permit "another church or oratory" to be used instead of the parish church when a Catholic marries another Catholic or a baptized non-Catholic (c. 1118, §1). From the context, it would seem that "church or oratory" refer to Catholic churches or oratories. See also canons 1214-1222, where clearly the word "church" applies to buildings belonging to the Catholic Church, and not just a generic "church" of whatever type.

Third, when a Catholic marries another Catholic or a baptized non-Catholic the law authorizes the local ordinary to "permit marriage to be celebrated in some other suitable place" (c. 1118, §2). This would include a non-Catholic church building. As to who is the "local ordinary" here, it appears from the wording of the canon to mean the ordinary with jurisdiction in the territory where the "other suitable place" is located. It could be that this is not the local ordinary of the Catholic party.

Note that this latter case is more restrictive, for the pastor is not authorized by the law to do this, only the local ordinary. Of course, the pastor could be delegated to give this permission in the diocesan faculties, but otherwise it is restricted to the local ordinary (bishop, vicar general, episcopal vicar, c. 134, §§1-2).

So, while the pastor can delegate another priest to witness a mixed marriage in the confines of his parish, he cannot give permission for a Catholic to marry a baptized non-Catholic outside of a Catholic church building of some sort (parish church, other church, oratory). It takes a local ordinary or someone delegated by him to give this permission. But note that the permission is not required when a Catholic marries a non-baptized person. Then only the pastor's delegation is needed for another priest to witness the marriage in "some other suitable place."

What is the effect of a wedding of a Catholic and a baptized non-Catholic taking place in "some other suitable place" without the bishop's permission? The marriage is valid, but the ceremony took place illicitly. There does not seem to be any effects for the couple in this situation. Canon 1384 states that a "just penalty" can be used to punish "one who illegitimately carries out a priestly function or another sacred ministry." But this is not a censure, is not incurred automatically, and would require a penal process to be instituted in order to judge the priest (or other sacred minister) guilty and to impose the penalty. In this sense, the requirement of permission here is more difficult to enforce.

To sum up, the bottom line seems to be the following:

1. The local ordinary (bishop, vicar general, episcopal vicar in his jurisdiction) can grant the permission for a mixed marriage with a baptized non-Catholic. The diocesan bishop can grant the dispensation for a Catholic to marry a non-baptized person. He can do this for his own subjects wherever they are, and for visitors who are actually in his territory. He can also delegate others to give the dispensation for him.

Failure to observe these norms can result in an invalid marriage if the other party is non-baptized. In other cases, the marriage is valid, but it was entered illicitly. There are no penalties on the couple resulting from this, but the priest can be penalized by a "just penalty."

2. The local ordinary of the Catholic party can dispense from canonical form for a mixed marriage, but if the couple plan to marry outside his jurisdiction he must first consult with the local ordinary where the couple plan to marry. The ordinary who grants the dispensation can place restrictions on where it can be used. If he does not, however, then all the couple need do is observe some public form of celebration (c. 1127, §2). The ordinary could also delegate someone else to grant the dispensation for him.

Failure to observe these norms could result in an invalid marriage due to defective form. A "just penalty" can be imposed on the one granting the dispensation if the person neglected to consult (c. 1389, §2).

3. The local ordinary and a pastor can witness marriages within their respective jurisdictions, provided at least one of the parties is a Latin rite Catholic. They can also delegate another sacred minister to do this within their respective territories.

Failure to observe these norms may result in an invalid marriage due to defective form, unless it was a case where the Church supplied jurisdiction (c. 144). Unless jurisdiction was supplied, the sacred minister who failed to obtain jurisdiction can be penalized with a "just penalty" (c. 1384).

4. Marriages involving Catholics are supposed to take place in the parish church. But Catholics who marry non-baptized persons may marry in any church, or in some other suitable place, and do not require permission to do so. Catholics who marry other Catholics or baptized non-Catholics need the permission of a local ordinary or of the pastor in order to marry in some other Catholic church building or oratory. Only a local ordinary can give permission for them to marry in some other suitable place.

Failure to observe these norms does not affect the validity of the marriage. The sacred minister who failed to observe the norms, however, can be penalized with a "just penalty" (c. 1384).

After all this legal talk, perhaps it would be well to consider a practical, pastoral approach to the situation.

First, the purpose for the broader provisions of the revised code is to give greater flexibility to the couple in planning their marriage. Any norms the diocese may adopt locally should respect this purpose in the general law of the Church.

Second, it seems to me it would be helpful to determine if there really are places which should be considered "off limits" in the diocese for marriages. These would be places which would not be considered "suitable." This, of course, will vary depending on the pastoral situation. In heavily non-Catholic areas, I know of some dioceses which permit marriages in rose gardens rather than letting the Mormons, for example, have the wedding in their church building! I suspect this determination will be more effective if the people in parish ministry are involved in making the determination.

Third, there are several ways to see to the observance of these "other limits." They should be included in the diocesan marriage preparation policies and communicated to the community at large. They could be sent to other ordinaries who may be consulting before granting a dispensation from canonical form for marriages planned for the diocese. They should be kept in mind by pastors in granting delegation to visiting priests to witness marriages.

On the other hand, the diocese may find it useful to follow the pattern established in a number of American dioceses, where the diocesan faculties give to pastors the delegation to grant the permission to use "some other suitable place" in the case of Catholics marrying baptized non-Catholics, provided the place is considered "suitable" in line with the diocese's policies. This would put the decision more at the local level. But if all in parish ministry were involved in coming to the determination of what is "suitable," it would more likely be followed in practice.

James H. Provost [1991, revised 1993]

Canons 1110 and 1115

Proper Parish for Celebration of Marriage

What is the place of marriage for people of a particular ethnic background who do not relate effectively to their territorial parish, but have been attending elsewhere in view of the accommodation made there to their language and culture? Is it still acceptable to use the concept of "reasonably presumed permission" when a priest deals with a person in this category, and simply performs the marriage; or, does the parish priest need to seek this permission directly from the territorial pastor? The CLSA commentary does not deal with this point, although the commentaries of the former code normally spoke of "presumed permission or delegation."

Opinion

The norm of the new code differs from the old code in that the wedding may licitly take place in the parish in which *either* the bride or the groom has a domicile, quasi-domicile, or habitual residence of at least one month. Thus, it is not restricted to the parish of the bride.

Otherwise, the norm is much as before. To be valid, a marriage must take place with the assistance of the bishop or pastor acting in their territory, or a properly delegated witness also acting within their territory, or by the use of the extraordinary form. The extraordinary form would not seem to apply in the situation you described, so whoever assisted at the wedding would have to do so within his territory for the validity of the marriage. At least one of the parties must be of the Latin rite. In the case of a personal parish (which can be set up for persons on the basis of culture, etc.), at least one of the persons must be a member of the parish (c. 1110).

A priest licitly assists at the weddings of those pertaining to his parish; with the permission of their pastor (territorial or personal) he may assist at the wedding of persons who do not belong to the parish. It would seem that the previous interpretations you mentioned would still be a safe guide to the observance of the law on such permissions. For example, Regatillo (*Ius Sacramentarium* (Santander: Sal Terrae, 4th ed. [1964] 844-845) held that the permission by one pastor to another could be given orally, in writing, or by signs; it could be given expressly or tacitly. Reasonably presumed permission was sufficient, but in this case he held it was necessary later to inform the proper pastor. A general permission would be sufficient, i.e., the permission a pastor might give to the other pastors in town generally.

Regatillo (and others) also discussed what might excuse from seeking the permission. Regatillo indicated grave necessity was needed, such as notable inconvenience to the pastor or prospective spouses, arising for example from a long or difficult journey, or danger of a civil marriage. He held such necessity could excuse the requirement of seeking permission even in situations where it could be foreseen the proper pastor would probably deny the permission.

The only penalty for a priest who validly but illicitly witnessed a marriage under the old code was the requirement to return the stole fee to the proper pastor. Stole fees under the new code pertain to the parish, not to the priest; but it would seem the same norm would apply — namely, if a fee is obtained illicitly, it must be turned over to the parish to which it should have been given.

Finally, the question of weddings should not be isolated from broader pastoral considerations. It would appear advisable to seek some sort of determination for the effective pastoral care for such couples beyond the personal attention of an individual priest. Some dioceses have structured an apostolate for certain ethnic or cultural groups — Hispanic ministry, for example — in such a way that they are permitted to utilize a specific territorial parish as a personal parish in their area, so that even if they live outside the parish which is more sensitive to their needs, they may still belong to it. This might be a better solution than just addressing the wedding question.

James H. Provost [1986]

Canons 1113; 1114; 1684; and 1085, §2

Validity of Marriage Performed prior to Decision of Second Instance

Is a marriage valid which is celebrated according to canonical form and with proper delegation, when the celebration took place after a tribunal of first instance had declared a previous marriage null but before the tribunal of second instance had confirmed that decision (confirmation which was subsequently given)?

Opinion

It is commonly held that the rules in the canons involved touch only liceity (cf., cc. 1085, §2; 1113; 1114; 1684) and not validity (cf., general principle in c. 10). Violation of these rules do not, then, touch the validity of the marriage.

In his *Marriage in Canon Law* (Michael Glazier [1986] 112), Ladislas Örsy comments on canon 1085, §2, succinctly:

The second marriage, however, would not be invalid if the first was indeed null and void but as yet no official document has been issued to the effect. The impediment is in the existence of a previous bond, not in the lack of a document. The wording of the paragraph is consistent with this interpretation, since it speaks of 'not permitted,' *non licet*, a technical term that is not used lightly, and when it is used, it never implies invalidity.

An invalid bond cannot create an impediment. The celebration of the marriage prior to the confirming decision of the second instance tribunal violates only the rule of liceity of establishing the freedom of the parties to marry. There is no reason at all to resort to either a convalidation or sanation, the second marriage being valid.

Joseph J. Koury [1993]

Canon 1117

Formal Defection and Release from the Obligation of Canonical Form

Lucy, a baptized and practicing Catholic, is engaged to Donald, a baptized Baptist with strong anti-Catholic sentiments. He refused to marry Lucy in the Catholic Church. Lucy agreed to marry Donald in the Baptist Church, fearing that he would abandon her. Prior to the wedding in 1991, Lucy reluctantly submitted to "rebaptism" in the Baptist Church as a prerequisite to the wedding. No dispensation from canonical form was received. The couple separated three months after the wedding and Lucy returned to the practice of her Catholic faith. They were eventually divorced. Is this marriage valid because Lucy formally defected from the Catholic Church and hence enjoyed the release from canonical form as provided in canon 1117, or was this action simulation of formal defection?

Opinion

The formal act of defection is the declaration of the intention to disaffiliate oneself from full communion with the Roman Catholic Church. This act may be either explicit ("I hereby separate myself from the Catholic Church") or tacit (official inscription with another religious tradition). Canon 1117 provides that formal defection is accompanied by a release from the obligation of the canonical form for marriage. Formal defection places the individual in a unique category: a "non-Catholic" for the purpose of marriage. The rationale for this release from canonical form in the revised legislation was the avoidance of the multiplication of invalid marriages. The allied questions of degrees of communion and jurisdiction over non-Catholics were not resolved with this provision. The formal act of defection is not performed to gain a release from the obligation of canonical form, but to disaffiliate from the society of the Catholic Church.

In the case of the marriage of Lucy and Donald, the central issue is whether Lucy defected from the Church by a formal act, and thus enjoyed the release from the obligation of canonical form as provided in canon 1117. Since the intention of the individual is the critical element in an act of formal defection, several factors in this case must be examined carefully.

First, the case indicates that Lucy "reluctantly submitted" to the requirement of rebaptism in the Baptist Church. This signals a lack of integrity of intention to freely disaffiliate from the Roman Catholic Church. During the courtship Donald repeatedly rejected Lucy's pleas to be married in the Catholic Church. Furthermore, it is uncertain whether this rebaptism is understood to be an official enrollment in the Baptist Church. Second, Lucy's actions were motivated by her fear of abandonment by Donald. Third, the lack of intention to formally defect is further substantiated by the fact that three months after the wedding, Lucy separated from Donald and resumed practice of the Catholic faith. Her non-practice of the Catholic faith for three months is not evidence that she no longer considered herself to be Catholic. Lucy's practice of the Catholic faith may have been temporarily frustrated, but her personal ecclesial identity appears to have remained Catholic throughout the courtship and the marriage.

There is absent any verified indication that Lucy desired to withdraw from full communion. Her primary intention was the protection of her opportunity to marry Donald. Her actions were a simulation of a formal defection because the requisite intention is not displayed. Thus the release from the obligation of canonical form is not enjoyed. The marriage of Lucy and Donald is invalid on the basis of the lack of observance of the canonical form.

Patrick J. Cogan, S.A. [1993]

CANON 1121

373

*Given the prescriptions of canon 1121, when a Catholic obtains a dispensation
from canonical form from his/her local ordinary but prepares for and celebrates
marriage outside his/her proper diocese:*

*1) Is it the responsibility of the pastor of the parish in whose territory the
marriage actually occurs to make the proper entries in the marriage
register and to retain the marriage papers whether or not the pre-marriage
investigation took place there?*

*2) It would seem that the ordinary who grants the dispensation is responsible
to see that the dispensation and the marriage are inscribed in the archives
of the Catholic party's proper diocese. Is it that ordinary's responsibility
to see that the same are also inscribed in the marriage register of the
Catholic party's proper parish ?*

OPINION

Ours is a tremendously mobile society, and this inquiry reflects that reality.
It discusses a situation that is more and more common, and which can also be
very complicated. First of all, a response to these questions also demands that
canon 1127, §2, on the granting of a dispensation from form, be taken into
consideration. This canon requires that the local ordinary of the Catholic party
"consult" with the ordinary of the place where the marriage is to be celebrated.
Both canons 1127, §2 and 1121, §1, make mention of possible prescriptions of
the episcopal conference that are able to govern these matters. At present, the
National Conference of Catholic Bishops has issued no such regulations.

The law does not require that the pastor of the parish in whose territory the
marriage actually occurs make any notification or keep any records. The law
specifically requires that the ordinary of the place of celebration be consulted.
Possibly, that ordinary may inform the pastor of the place of celebration. But
the law does not specifically require that the pastor of the place of celebration
be informed or consulted by anyone. That pastor may have had no contact at
all with the parties, and can hardly be expected to record the marriage. The law
requires that the marriage be recorded in a register at the diocesan curia that
granted the dispensation. It also requires that the marriage be recorded "at the
parish of the Catholic party whose pastor made the investigation concerning the
free state." According to canon 1121, it is the Catholic spouse who bears the
primary responsibility for informing both his or her pastor and the local ordinary
who granted the dispensation. But the law does indeed expect that the local
ordinary will make sure that the proper registration has been accomplished.

Thus, the law envisions the record of the marriage existing in two separate marriage registers (in addition to being recorded also in the Catholic party's baptismal register).

However, it is true that as a result of these provisions, there may well be no record of the marriage in the parish or the diocese in which the celebration actually took place. Years later, might this create difficulties for people seeking ecclesiastical records? For instance, a civil marriage certificate might indicate that the marriage took place in city "A," which can easily be determined to be located in diocese "N." But the ecclesiastical records of that union may only exist in city "J" and diocese "Z," perhaps hundreds or even thousands of miles away. It is not difficult to conceive a scenario where a person who has legitimate need for an ecclesiastical record may not know enough information to discover easily where those records are located. Although this should not be a common problem, it certainly may occur.

Given this fact, it might be wise for the episcopal conference to issue policies or regulations also mandating that some type of notice be maintained either in the parish or the diocese where the marriage was actually celebrated. Such notifications would include the name of the diocese and the parish where the full records are kept, which would solve the problem described above. If the episcopal conference were to enact such a particular law, the conference would also be able to define the procedures for implementing it. If the conference does not legislate in this area, it would still leave each diocesan bishop free to do so, although a wide divergence in practice might simply muddy the waters even further. Certainly, if a diocese enacted some such particular law, then the ordinary of the place of celebration would have to make arrangements with the local ordinary granting the dispensation at the time of the required consultation to ensure that adequate notifications are made.

Craig A. Cox [1990]

ANOTHER OPINION

Following upon Pope Paul VI's *Matrimonia mixta* (1970), the NCCB issued its "Statement on the Implementation of *Matrimonia mixta*" (effective January 1, 1971). Two specific norms established for the dioceses of the United States, nos. 12 and 13, apply in this instance (see text in *CLD* 7: 730-741).

No. 12 provided that in a mixed marriage for which there has been granted a dispensation from canonical form, an ecclesiastical record of the marriage shall be kept in the chancery of the diocese which granted the dispensation *and* (emphasis added) in the marriage records of the parish from which application

375

for the dispensation was made.

No. 13 provided that it is the responsibility of the priest who submits the request for dispensation to see that, after the public form of marriage ceremony is performed, notices of the marriage are sent in the usual form to: a) the parish and chancery noted above [no. 12]; and b) the place of baptism of the Catholic party.

Canon 1221, §3 of the 1983 code embodies these norms, with the further note that the Catholic spouse is bound to inform the above-named ordinary and pastor of the celebration of the marriage, the place of celebration and the public form that was observed.

Since the promulgation of the 1983 code, there has been no change initiated by the NCCB regarding the recording of such marriages, and, as far as can be determined, this question does not appear on the bishops' agenda of issues to be decided in the near future.

The provision of canon 1121, §1 notwithstanding, it seems that in the case outlined in the question, the 1970 norms and canon 1121, §3 are in effect: records of the marriage are to be kept by the diocese granting the dispensation from canonical form and the parish requesting the dispensation.

Joseph J. Koury [1990]

Canon 1127

Necessity of Consultation with the Ordinary of the Place of Marriage for the Sake of Validity of Dispensation from Canonical Form

In the view of canon 127, §2, 2°, would the local ordinary invalidly dispense his subject from the canonical form in a mixed marriage if he does not even consult the ordinary of the place where the marriage is to be celebrated (c. 1127, §2)?

Opinion

According to canon 1127, §2 the local ordinary of a Catholic party may grant a dispensation from the obligation to observe the canonical form of marriage when that party is contracting marriage with a non-Catholic. However, the canon mentions that the local ordinary where the marriage is to be celebrated is to be consulted. In light of canon 127, §2, 2° is this consultation required for the validity of the dispensation?

376

Canon 127, §2 deals with the situation where the law requires a superior to have the consent or the counsel of certain persons before placing a juridical act. In §2, 2° of this canon it states that when counsel is required the superior acts invalidly if he does not listen to such persons before placing the act. The canon does not say that every time the law makes reference to some form of advice or counsel that the superior is required to receive such. As a general norm, canon 127 should be applied only to those canons which fulfill the general definition, i.e., those which say that consent or counsel is required.

There are a number of canons which require that the superior receive counsel prior to placing an act. These canons contain some expression which indicates that this counsel is required, e.g., a subjunctive verb or a negative or one of the participles indicating a requirement for validity. So, for example, the wording of canons 567, §1 and 579 would seem to require consultation before a local ordinary appoints a chaplain for a religious house or a diocesan bishop erects a religious institute. There are instances where the general principle of canon 127 would indicate that the consultation is for validity.

There are other canons which make reference to some form of consultation without requiring it for validity. For example, the right of the bishop of the principal seat to act relative to the governance of diocesan religious institutes after consulting other bishops (c. 595); the task of judging the existence of irregularities for receiving or exercising orders, after consulting experts (cc. 1041 and 1044); the right of a local ordinary to remit penalties, having consulted the ordinary who imposed them (c. 1355). These canons, usually, deal with some area in which the particular superior is competent to act without the advice of another. But, in some circumstances, the superior should take advantage of the expertise of others or provide for someone else's legitimate interest in the matter. This would appear to be the situation with canon 1127 and the dispensation from canonical form.

The competence to grant a dispensation for his subjects belongs to the one who has the necessary executive power and does not depend on another. This seems obvious on the basis of canon 91, which says that one who possesses the power to dispense can exercise this power for his subjects even if they are outside his territory. Canon 1127 makes it clear that it is the local ordinary of the Catholic party who has the right to grant the dispensation. The dispensed person is only obligated to have some form of public ceremony, but is not limited as to the nature or place of that ceremony, unless this is added as a condition by the one dispensing. Thus, the dispensation could actually be granted without the local ordinary knowing where the public ceremony was to take place or the actual place could be changed after the issuing of the rescript. In neither case would there be any effect on the validity of the dispensation.

However, to say that the consultation mentioned in this canon is not a requirement for validity does not mean that it is of no importance and should be disregarded. It certainly should be seen as a norm of law governing the public order and the proper exercise of authority with respect for the rights of others. However, it does not seem that the absence of such consultation could give rise to an action for the nullity of the marriage in a summary process according to canon 1686.

On a practical level, the question of such consultation is probably seen most often in situations which involve the ordinaries of neighboring, or at least similar, dioceses within the same country. But it is possible that some situations or circumstances may involve important differences in local practice, custom, or even civil law. This is brought out by the statement in canon 1127 that the conference of bishops is to issue norms for the granting of such dispensations in an orderly manner. Such norms might include restrictions on the manner of celebrating marriage outside of the approved canonical form. It is possible that, in accord with canon 13, §2, 2°, such restrictions could bind persons coming from another territory since marriage certainly pertains to the public order and the manner of its celebration is a question of the solemnity of an act. Thus, when the two ordinaries are from different countries and episcopal conferences, this type of consultation may take on a more important role, not so much for the validity of the dispensation, but relative to the Catholic party's ability to fulfill the requirement of having a public ceremony.

On the other hand, since the canon refers to the power of a local ordinary, it does not seem reasonable that it would require the episcopal vicar of one area of a diocese to consult either the bishop, the vicar general or another episcopal vicar within the same diocese when dispensing his subjects who intend to have a public ceremony in some other part of that diocese.

Jerald A. Doyle [1987]

CANON 1136

RIGHT OF PARENTS TO WITHDRAW CHILDREN FROM SEX EDUCATION CLASSES IN CATHOLIC SCHOOLS OR RELIGIOUS EDUCATION PROGRAMS

See questions and opinions under canons 226 and 890.

Canon 1161

Radical Sanation of a Marriage

A man petitioned the Holy See for a Petrine Privilege. The privilege has now been granted but the petitioner is so upset by the length of the procedure that he now refuses to go through a marriage ceremony. Can his present, second marriage be sanated and if so, by whom? Would the marriage be retroactively validated by a sanation and if so, to what point in time? Is this what is called an "imperfect" sanation?

Opinion

Perhaps the most useful way to begin a response to these questions is by the following brief outline of this century's history of the institute.

1. 1904:   On March 2, the Holy Office declared that a marriage contracted with an impediment of natural or divine law cannot be sanated (*Fontes* IV, n. 1270). Gasparri, incidentally, who had been consulted by the Congregation on this question, did not agree that the Church could not sanate such a marriage (*De Matrimonio*, n. 1217).

2. 1917:   Canon 1139, §2 of the code said simply that the Church does not sanate such a marriage, even if the impediment has ceased, not even from the moment of the cessation.

3. 1957:   The Congregation for the Sacraments under Pope Pius XII did, in fact, grant a sanation in such a case, namely a case involving *ligamen* where the previous spouse died, with the sanation being effective from the date of death. The following year Pope John XXIII, through faculties granted to the Holy Office, did the same (*CLD* 5: 551-552).

4. 1982:   The Congregation for the Doctrine of the Faith, in a similar case, decreed "let the marriage be declared convalidated" (*CLD* 10: 188).

5. 1983:   Canon 1165, §2 of the 1983 code says that the diocesan bishop cannot grant a sanation where there was an impediment of the natural or divine positive law. Clearly, however, Rome can grant and does grant such sanations.

6. 1987:   *Pastor bonus*, article 63, would make the Congregation for the Sacraments the proper dicastery to approach (*Communicationes* 20 [1988] 32).The case of the questioner is somewhat different from the cases mentioned above since in this particular case the previous spouse has not died. If granted, therefore, there would be no retroactivity of canonical effects since the impediment of *ligamen* would not cease until the sanation, which takes the place of the new marriage, is granted (cf., Wrenn, *Proce*

379

dures, 115-116).

Furthermore, there is never real retroactivity as regards the marriage itself.

In a sanation, as canon 1161, §2 says in effect, the marriage becomes valid *ex nunc*, never *ex tunc*. It is only the canonical effects that are granted *ex tunc*. The difference between a perfect and an imperfect sanation is that, in a perfect sanation, the *tunc* goes back to the celebration of the marriage whereas in an imperfect sanation, the *tunc* is some later time, like, for example, the time of the cessation of the impediment (Gasparri, n. 1212).

Lawrence G. Wrenn [1992]

Canons 1161-1165

Radical Sanation of Marriage and Pauline Privilege

There exist two methods for the ecclesiastical validation of a civil marriage: ceremonial convalidation and radical sanation. When a formerly unbaptized, civilly remarried person is granted a Pauline Privilege, does the execution of the privilege require ceremonial convalidation alone, or may radical sanation also be employed?

Opinion

It is my opinion that a radical sanation may be employed in the above stated case. At the same time, there needs to be a clarification of the nature of this particular sanation, and who is the competent authority to grant it.

The canons of the 1983 Code of Canon Law which govern the use of the radical sanation are canons 1161-1165. (As a point of information, the corresponding canons of the 1917 code are cc. 1183-1141.) Particular attention must be given to canons 1163 and 1165 of the 1983 code for this sanation. What is seen here is the existence of a prior bond and, therefore, an impediment which must be dealt with before any convalidation or sanation. The nature of this particular impediment is that of a previously valid marriage and, therefore, an impediment of the natural law or of divine positive law. This impediment would cease only upon death or a dissolution such as with the Pauline Privilege. Note well that this is different from a previous bond which has been declared null and void from the beginning due to a defect of consent. Thus, the civil marriage in place would be healed only back to the moment that the impediment ceases to exist, and not to the time of the consent of the civil marriage. Healing back to

380

the moment of the time of consent would result in the impossible situation of being bound to two marriages. Healing back to the time of consent would not occur, since the previous marriage is presumed valid. The nature of this sanation could be said to be that of an imperfect sanation, such as is spoken of in the CLSA *Commentary* (826-827).

Secondly, the competent authority to grant this radical sanation would not be the diocesan bishop, but the Apostolic See, since canon 1165, §2 notes, "The diocesan bishop cannot grant radical sanation, however, if there is present an impediment whose dispensation is reserved to the Apostolic See in accord with canon 1078, §2, or if it is a question of an impediment of the natural law or of divine positive law which has ceased to exist." As I noted earlier, a previously valid marriage which is dissolved by a Pauline Privilege is this type of impediment, and thus the diocesan bishop is not able to grant the sanation. For further clarification, and actual examples, I would refer those interested to *CLD* 10: 185-189.

Kevin W. Vann [1993]

Canon 1176

Right to a Funeral Mass

Is it necessary to have a funeral Mass? So often it is readily apparent that the family has no knowledge of or interest in what is happening. They do not know the responses, when to sit or stand, etc. Can the funeral Mass be omitted in such cases?

Opinion

Canon 1176, §1 says that "the Christian faithful are to be given ecclesiastical funeral rites according to the norm of law." The liturgical law specifies the three stations that comprise these funeral rites: the vigil, the funeral liturgy, and the rite of committal. Catholics have a right to these three services and their parish is obliged to offer them, unless a person is barred according to the norm of canon 1184.

Ordinarily, the funeral liturgy is to be a Mass. On days when funeral Masses are not permitted, or when no priest is available, the funeral liturgy outside Mass is to be used (in accord with the 1989 *Order of Christian Funerals* for use in the United States, nn. 177ff). Moreover, the funeral liturgy outside Mass may be used "when for pastoral reasons the parish priest (pastor) and the family judge that the funeral liturgy outside Mass is a more suitable form of celebration" (ibid., n. 178, §3).

In view of the law's preference for a funeral Mass and the right of the faithful to the Church's funeral rites, I believe that you may not omit the funeral Mass unless the family of the deceased agrees to it. If they want a Mass, you should provide it whether or not they are practicing Catholics. If they completely lack the faith, they would be unlikely to object to the omission of the funeral Mass.

Catholic families should be encouraged to have a funeral Mass. In the case where the Catholic departed person is survived by a non-Catholic family, you might well advise the next of kin to choose the non-Eucharistic option.

Some parishes have drawn upon retired persons to form a choir and to perform the other lay ministries needed at the funeral Mass. Their ministry has greatly enhanced the participation at funeral Masses where the mourners, even when they are practicing Catholics, frequently are not disposed to sing and respond. Moreover, the homily at a funeral Mass is a good opportunity gently to remind all present of their Christian obligations in preparation for the day when they too will join with the faithful departed.

John M. Huels, O.S.M. [1991]

CANONS 1176, §1 AND 1184, §1, 3°

DENIAL OF ECCLESIASTICAL FUNERAL IN THE CASE OF AN ABORTION

Can someone who has incurred the undeclared latae sententiae *excommunication for the offense of abortion be denied ecclesiastical funeral rites on that account alone?*

OPINION

Canon 1184 specifies those who are to be deprived of ecclesiastical funeral rites. Someone who had incurred a *latae sententiae* excommunication for abortion is not included in the listing of excluded persons in canon 1184. Whether or not we interpret strictly the canon on denial will depend upon our answer to the question: is Christian burial a right or a privilege? And again to the question, Is denial of ecclesiastical funeral rights a penalty? If access to ecclesiastical funeral rites is to be viewed as a right rather than a privilege, then the law restricting the right to a Christian funeral must be strictly interpreted in accord with the norms of canon 18. In the same manner, if canon 1184 is a law establishing a penalty, then a strict interpretation must be applied.

The denial of ecclesiastical funeral rites appears both as a restriction of the exercise of a right and as a penalty for certain crimes. Canon 1176 states an overriding presumption and makes a declaration of a right: the Christian faithful departed are to be given ecclesiastical funeral rites. Even though the denial in canon 1184 is not found in Book VI, "Sanctions," it has to be interpreted in the light of a sanction, a penalty for a stated offense. Therefore, on both accounts, a strict interpretation must be given.

Strict interpretation requires that we not extend the meaning of the law beyond the words used or the applications made. For several reasons, based on a strict interpretation of canon 1184, it does not seem that the individual mentioned could be denied ecclesiastical funeral rites. If there has been a connection with the Church since the abortion, that should be interpreted as a sign of repentance, in which case funeral rites are not to be denied. Furthermore, the only category under which the denial could be applied would be a "manifest sinner" (c. 1184, §1, 3°). Manifest sinners must truly be "manifest." The offense must clearly have been public, not merely "known" by the individual or a small group. Such is unlikely in the case cited. Even if the offense were manifest, funeral rites are to be denied only if public scandal would arise were they granted. In most cases in our Church today greater scandal would arise from the denial of ecclesiastical funeral rites than from their being granted. The broadest scope of the Church as an agent of God's mercy and its image as a "refuge of sinners" would be most applicable at the time of death and burial even of a person who might be considered one of the "lost ones."

Barbara Anne Cusack [1992]

ANOTHER OPINION

No. The law is clear.

"The Christian faithful departed are to be given ecclesiastical funeral rites according to the norm of law" (c. 1176, §1). The law states that funeral rites are to be denied in three specific cases. Since this law restricts the freedom and rights of the Christian faithful, it is to be interpreted strictly. One of the three cases for denying Christian funeral rites (and burial) is that of someone who:

1. is a manifest sinner;

2. has given no sign of repentance before death;

3. and whose church funeral would cause public scandal to the faithful (c.

383

1184, §1, 3°).

All of the above elements must concur before a decision to deprive a church member of funeral rites can be made. In the case given, the excommunication was known but not declared, the incident was well in the past and there is no other evidence of the person being a manifest sinner.

The reason for this position is also clear. Denial of Christian funeral rites is a public act with public repercussions. *Latae sententiae* excommunications are enforced in the internal forum by the offender. If the excommunication is not declared, the pastor or rector of the church has no right to judge the conscience decisions of the person who procured an abortion. Canon 1324 lists many reasons why a person is not bound by a *latae sententiae* penalty and, therefore, is not required to abstain from the sacraments even if he or she has procured an abortion. Among the more applicable reasons are:

1. grave fear, even if only relatively grave;

2. necessity;

3. serious inconvenience;

4. ignorance of the penalty at the time the offense was committed;

5. any other circumstance which reduces full imputability even if the imputability is still grave.

Such defenses can be brought to court if the Church seeks to declare a censure. In the absence of a church procedure, the pastor or the rector of the church may not act as judge and deny funeral rites.

Moreover, the pastor or the rector is unaware that the excommunication, even if incurred, may have been absolved. Any confessor can remit in the internal forum an automatic (*latae sententiae*) censure of excommunication which has not been declared if it would be hard on the penitent to remain in a state of serious sin (c. 1357, §1). Any priest can absolve from any censure a penitent in danger of death (c. 976). The pastor or rector of a church has no means of knowing whether the censure may have been absolved. Lacking external forum proof of declaration of the censure, the benefit of the doubt must be given to the offender.

One final and conclusive argument: canon 1331 lists the juridic effects of excommunication. Denial of ecclesiastical funeral rites is not included, even if the censure is declared. Hence even those *declared* excommunicated from the Catholic Church may not be denied ecclesiastical funeral rites unless:

1. they are notorious apostates, heretics and schismatics who have given no signs of repentance before death;

2. they have chosen cremation for reasons opposed to the Christian faith;

3. they are manifest sinners who have given no signs of repentance before their death and for whom ecclesiastical funeral rites cannot be granted without

public scandal to the faithful (c. 1184, §1).

The 1917 code deprived of ecclesiastical burial persons who were excommunicated or interdicted by a declaration or condemnatory sentence and who had manifested no sign of repentance before death (1917 code, c. 1240, §1, 2°). They were also denied ecclesiastical funeral services (1917 code, c. 1241; see also, 1917 code, c. 2260, §2).

This penalty was dropped in the 1983 code. Neither code contains a provision for denying ecclesiastical funeral rites or burial to someone who in the past was subject to a *latae sententiae* censure of excommunication which had not been declared and where there is no other evidence of the person being a "manifest sinner."

Bertram F. Griffin [1992]

Canon 1183

Permission for Catholic Burial of Non-baptized Infant Extended to Celebration of Mass for the Repose of Soul

Is it pastorally appropriate and legal to have Masses celebrated for the repose of the soul of a stillborn child? The Church is so emphatic about its teaching that life begins at conception that it would seem appropriate.

Opinion

The answer is yes, it is both pastorally appropriate and legal to have Masses celebrated for the repose of the soul of a stillborn child.

From the point of view of canon law, the local ordinary can permit children to be buried from the Church if their parents intended to baptize them but the children died before their baptism (c. 1183, §2). Stillborn children are exactly in this category; namely, children who have died prior to baptism. It is not necessary that they be buried from the Church, but it is possible.

So, if Catholic burial is possible, then certainly celebrating Mass for the repose of their soul is possible.

The pastoral point of view also is important. As you point out, the Church's teaching is that life begins with conception. A human being has died when a child is stillborn. As a community of faith, we have solidarity with the child's believing parents; as a human community, we have solidarity with the child who

385

has died.   Requesting Masses to be offered for the repose of the soul of a deceased person is a venerable Catholic expression of such solidarity with both the deceased and those who survive.

It is important, however, not to become maudlin in this matter, or to dwell upon the loss to such an extent or for such a period of time that the parents are unable to experience Christian hope under the circumstances.   Here is where the usual pastoral prudence is required in aiding grieving parents and their friends, while at the same time providing a suitable means for expressing the solidarity of the community.   Thus, Christian hope and trust in God's love and mercy for the stillborn child would seem to indicate that Masses should not continue to be offered publicly too long after the event.

James H. Provost [1987]

CANONS 1183-1184

OFFERING MASS FOR A DECEASED NON-BAPTIZED PERSON

A leading community figure who is a Buddhist has died, and has been buried with Buddhist funeral rites.   Catholic friends ask whether a Mass may be celebrated for the deceased, and whether the person's widow, members of his family, and other members of the civic community may attend.   Is this permitted? The only directive I can find is from the Congregation for the Doctrine of the Faith (June 11, 1976), but it applies to non-Catholics who were baptized.   This case involves a non-baptized person.

OPINION

The decree of the CDF of June 11, 1976, to which you refer contains the clause, "until the promulgation of the new code."   This makes it evident that the June 11, 1976, decree itself is no longer in effect, since the new code was promulgated in 1983.   It is necessary to turn to the new code for guidance.

Canon 2 affirms that the liturgical norms retain their force even with the promulgation of the new code.   The *Ordo Exsequiarum* is clearly intended for the burial of Christians.   Revised in 1983, it conforms to the provisions of the 1983 code concerning the use of the *ordo* for other persons.

Turning to the code itself, the canons on ecclesiastical funeral rites have a chapter on "those to whom ecclesiastical funeral rites are to be granted or to be denied" (cc. 1183-1185).   Canon 1184 contains a list of those who are to be denied ecclesiastical funeral rites, and canon 1185 states that any funeral Mass is also to be denied these persons. However, the list does not include non-Catholic Christians, nor does it include non-baptized persons.

It would seem that the Mass which is requested in the present case is a memorial Mass, not actually a funeral Mass (*Missa exsequialis*). Note that strictly speaking, only this latter type of Mass is prohibited by canon 1185 for those who must be denied ecclesiastical funeral rites.

Canon 1183 contains various provisions permitting Catholic ecclesiastical funeral rites for persons who are not Catholics — catechumens, and with the permission of the local ordinary, Catholic parents' children not yet baptized and baptized non-Catholics. The *Ordo Exsequiarum* now incorporates this provision (General Introduction, n. 14bis). Since a funeral Mass is considered a central element to ecclesiastical funeral rites (although strictly speaking it is not mandatory — *Ordo Exsequiarum*, General Introduction, nn. 6-8), it would seem that a *Missa exsequialis* may be celebrated for these persons even though they were not baptized, or if baptized, were not in full communion with the Catholic Church.

The canons are silent concerning other non-baptized persons. These canons do not consider whether such persons must be denied Catholic funeral rites, or can be granted such rites with the local ordinary's permission. They do not address the issue of a memorial Mass at all.

The obvious presumption is that Catholic funeral rites are restricted to Catholics or at least Christians, so there was no need to mention burial for the non-baptized except in the two circumstances of catechumens and the non-baptized children of Catholics. But what about a memorial Mass? This is not the same as an ecclesiastical funeral rite itself, and may be more in the nature of an intention for which Mass is requested by one of the faithful.

The canons on Mass intentions and stipends (cc. 945-958) contain no restrictions on the intentions for which the faithful may request Masses to be offered. Mass may be requested for various intentions, and not just for the repose of the soul of a deceased Catholic. For example, it is not uncommon for the request to include even physical matters, such as good weather for crops, relief from war, etc. There is no restriction in these canons on requesting that Mass be celebrated for God's mercy even on the non-baptized.

The canons do not need to state the obvious, namely that Mass should not be offered for frivolous, evil, or other intentions which would be disrespectful of the sacrament or cause scandal in the community. If there is any question, the diocesan bishop is the proper judge of the matter, as in other liturgical questions within the diocese (c. 838, §4).

To apply all this to your case will require more detail than is currently available to me. But initially, it would appear that the situation does not involve ecclesiastical funeral rites. The person is already buried according to his own religion. Rather, it seems to be a question of celebrating a memorial Mass.

There does not seem to be any explicit prohibition against celebrating Mass requested by one of the faithful for the consolation of friends and family, and asking God's mercy on a non-baptized person. While normally one does not need to consult the diocesan bishop before accepting to offer Mass for an intention, in this case — given the importance of the deceased in public life — it would seem appropriate for the celebrant to consult the diocesan bishop before offering the Mass.

One of the difficulties which this case raises is that the CDF was considering cases involving other Christians, and did not directly address the situation of the non-baptized. Moreover, its decree is no longer in effect now that the new code is in force. Therefore, the appropriate determination should be made locally in light of all the local conditions. My own recommendation is that the diocesan bishop be consulted, although strictly speaking this may not always be necessary since it is not called for in the law concerning Mass intentions.

James H. Provost [1991]

CANON 1242

"INURNMENT" IN CHAPEL

A parish has recently created a chapel within the parish church building, and has installed there a columbarium for the inurnment of parishioners' ashes. The columbarium is on the inside of the chapel, i.e., the inurnment takes place interior to the church building. There are at present no diocesan policies or guidelines in the diocese in reference to the inurnment of ashes.

In determining whether to construct the chapel and columbarium, in the absence of any specific directives from the diocese, the parish looked to the norms adopted by other dioceses for assistance in determining the legality of including the columbarium in the chapel. Now, however, the bishop of the diocese has objected to the legality of including the columbarium in the chapel; he has also indicated the need to consult appropriately with the presbyteral council in order to develop diocesan policy on this matter (in keeping with c. 495, §1).

Prescinding from the prudence of the decision to include the columbarium within the chapel and from the advisability of any particular diocesan policy, what is the legality of what the parish did in light of universal canon law?

The question is not a simple one to answer. The law applicable to cremation was changed by the Holy Office instruction *Piam et constantem*, May 8, 1963 (*AAS* 56 [1963] 822-823; *CLD* 6: 666-668). The focus of this instruction was to relax the previously universally binding force of canons 1203, §2 (not to carry out a mandate of cremation) and 1240, §1, 5° (denying ecclesiastical burial to persons who ordered that their bodies be cremated); those prohibitions continued to apply only to those who sought cremation as a denial of Christian dogmas, or in a sectarian spirit, or due to hatred of the Christian religion or Catholic Church.

There were restrictions in this instruction, however, with regard to the presence of a priest at the actual place of cremation — even if it were only to accompany the transfer of the remains. Moreover, the instruction clearly favors the traditional practice of burial.

The instruction also called for bishops to issue instructions and exhortations so people would properly understand this new position of the Church. John F. McDonald, commenting on the Holy Office's instruction in *The Jurist* (26 [1966] 204-213), reports on two sets of diocesan instructions, one for the Archdiocese of Vienna and the other for the Archdiocese of Munich and Freising. A survey conducted by the Canon Law Society of America in 1967 found that at least 30 dioceses in the United States had adopted a policy in light of the Holy Office's 1963 instruction, but that at least 47 had not (see *The Jurist* 28 [1968] 257-261). A survey conducted in 1971 by Monsignor Nunzio DeFoe of Vancouver, Canada, found that none of the fourteen American and twelve Canadian dioceses he contacted in the West of both countries had adopted any kind of a policy to implement the Holy Office's 1963 instruction (see *The Jurist* 31 [1971] 638-646).

Even in those policies which were adopted at that time, there does not seem to have been much attention given to the question of a columbarium in a chapel attached to a parish church.

The attitude of the Church toward burial rites and cremation underwent a further evolution with the promulgation of the *Ordo Exsequiarum* on August 15, 1969. In the *Praenotanda* to the rite, at no. 15, the question of Christian funeral rites for those who choose to have their bodies cremated is discussed. The provisions of the Holy Office's instruction of 1963 are recalled, which determined who may receive such funeral rites. The preference for burial is also retained. However, the restriction on where specific rites may be carried out was dropped, and those usually performed at the cemetery chapel or grave-side may now be performed at the crematorium, and even in the crematory hall itself.

The new code reaffirms the preference for burial, but does not forbid Christian burial rites for those who choose cremation, provided cremation has not been chosen for reasons contrary to Christian teaching (c. 1176, §3). This somewhat negative statement, however, needs to be placed in the context of the new code's more explicit concern to respect the will of the deceased in matters relating to ecclesiastical funeral rites. The new code is more explicit than the former one in terms of permitting persons or those responsible for their burial to select whatever place of burial they wish — including the church in which to have the funeral rites, with the permission of its rector (c. 1177, §2) and the cemetery for burial (c. 1180, §2). In other words, the emphasis has shifted from the ecclesiastical institutions ("proper parish" and cemetery) to the persons who are making the decision. It would seem to follow that proper respect must also be shown to those who select cremation, and concern for existing institutions (including Catholic cemeteries) should not be the overriding concern.

The new code does not have specific norms for inurnment of ashes; it only has norms concerning cemeteries and the burial of corpses. Canon 1242 indicates corpses are not to be buried inside church buildings, but does make exceptions for popes, cardinals and diocesan bishops. Canon 1240 asserts the right of the Church, where it is possible, to have its own cemeteries, and canon 1243 calls for particular law (diocesan law, policy, guidelines, etc.) to determine appropriate norms for the discipline to be observed in cemeteries.

Technically, ashes are not a corpse. It is normally not permitted, for example, to treat the ashes as a corpse during a funeral liturgy; the Second Rite (i.e., without the body present) is to be used if the body has already been cremated. So, it can be questioned whether the norm of canon 1242 on not burying corpses in a church building is directly applicable .

In a situation where there is no express prescription of universal or particular law or a custom, the case is to be resolved in light of laws passed in similar circumstances, the general principles of law observed with canonical equity, etc. (c. 19). The new code no longer requires that the parallel laws be those contained in the code, and it is permissible to look to particular laws passed elsewhere in similar circumstances to gain some insight into what might be done. Since there does not seem to be a specific provision in the code governing where a columbarium may be constructed, it was appropriate to consult the guidelines of those places where this question was directly addressed. On the other hand, it is also possible to consider canon 1242 as establishing a general principle that the remains of deceased persons are not to find their final resting place in churches.

So, as indicated earlier, the question does not admit of a simple answer. The arguments advanced by the bishop are serious and are based on a proper reading of the law and the intent expressed in the various documents which have addressed the question of cremation. On the other hand, there are no specific directives of universal law which directly forbid the creation of a distinct chapel in which a columbarium is located. Particular law could make provision for this. So, it would seem that the decision to include a columbarium within the chapel may have been within the law, but that in coming to a decision for diocesan policy, the bishop is free to adopt a policy in either direction.

James H. Provost [1986]

Canon 1245

Right of the Pastor to Dispense from Holy Days of Obligation

What is the extent of the pastor's authority to dispense his people from the obligation to observe a feast day or day of penance? In other words, what does "individual cases" mean, presuming that the bishop has not issued any norms? Could the pastor dispense the entire parish? Could the pastor dispense routinely and frequently, e.g., assuming his poor parishioners live lives of suffering and do not need more penance, or some group of them often find it hard to get to Mass on Sundays?

Opinion

According to canon 1245 the pastor is able to dispense from the obligation of observing a feast day or day of penance for a just cause. In addressing the pastor's ability to dispense, this action must be examined in light of the proper understanding of the meaning of a dispensation.

A dispensation, by which an ecclesiastical law is relaxed, is an individual administrative act. Its interpretation should be understood strictly (cc. 92 and 36). The law explicitly gives the pastor the power to dispense from the obligations attached to feast days and to days of penance (cc. 1245 and 89). In order to avoid any confusion about its valid and lawful concession, however, there ought to be a just reason and due consideration given for the particular circumstances (c. 90, §1).

In the case at hand, it is presumed that the bishop has not established any norms. Therefore, the pastor himself becomes the judge concerning the sufficiency of the reasons advanced for the dispensation, e.g., sickness, physical disability, weather, living conditions, the nature of a person's work, etc., and he must carefully examine them.

This canon attributes the power of dispensing to the pastor only "in individual cases." This would not allow for an habitual dispensation. For this reason each case must stand on its own and cannot establish a precedent. There is a distinction to be made between individual cases and the recurrence of individual instances. The pastor's power may be employed to grant a dispensation which will be protracted over a period of time of considerable duration for as long as the justifying reason exists. Moreover, the pastor ought to imitate the higher authority (c. 87, §1), and as often as he sees that a dispensation will contribute to the spiritual welfare of the faithful he should act accordingly. Yet he must continue to consider each case separately and not allow the concession to become a routine course of action, because this would call into question the necessity of the law itself.

No distinction is made concerning the subject of the dispensation. The pastor may dispense an individual person or persons or an individual group of persons because one dispensation is morally equivalent to as many dispensations as there are persons who belong to the same group and share the same reason which will justify the concession (Abbo-Hannan, *The Sacred Canons*, II, 499). However, this should not include the entire parish since within the community there always will be people who do not possess the cause that will justify the granting of the dispensation (Vermeersch-Creusen, *Epitome*, I, n. 174).

Robert F. Coleman [1992]

ANOTHER OPINION

Pastors, unlike diocesan bishops, do not enjoy a general power to dispense from universal and particular disciplinary laws. They may dispense from such laws only when this power has been expressly granted to them (cf., cc. 87, §1; 89). One express grant of such power to pastors is canon 1245, authorizing them to dispense for a just cause and in individual cases (*singulis in casibus*) from the obligation to observe a feast day (i.e., Sunday or holy day of obligation) or day of penance.

The provision's history is instructive. The 1917 code had authorized pastors for a just cause and in individual cases (*in casibus singularibus*) to dispense from these feast day and penitential day obligations, but it specifically limited the objects of the dispensation to individual persons or individual families (*singulos fideles singulasve familias*, 1917 *CIC*, c. 1245). A standard commentary concluded that "pastors can never dispense their whole parish either from the observance of feast days or of fast and abstinence" (Bouscaren-Ellis, 676).

The revision commission's 1977 schema likewise specified that the pastor could dispense individuals or individual families (*singulis fidelibus . . . singulis familiis*) from these same obligations. It deleted, however, the first code's phrase "in individual cases" (Pontifical Commission for the Revision of the Code, *Schema Canonum Libri IV: De Ecclesiae Munere Sanctificandi, Pars II* [Vatican City: Typis Polyglottis, 1977] c. 43). The consultation process generated criticism of the continuing constraint that only individual persons and individual families could be dispensed. Such critics argued that, in appropriate circumstances, the pastor should be able to dispense the entire parish (e.g., CLSA, "Report of Task Force Committee on the Draft of the Canons of Book Four: The Church's Office to Sanctify, Part Two, Sacred Places and Times and also Divine Cult" [1978], 20).

The Code Commission apparently listened, for the 1980 schema proposed as the only restrictions on this dispensing power of the pastor a "just cause" and "the prescriptions of the local ordinary." Cardinal Bafile objected, arguing that the schema's canon would give the pastor the authority to dispense "the whole parish" (*pro tota paroecia*) rather than individual persons or individual families, and not only once or twice, but for an indeterminate time. Such an expanded power, he sensed, would undermine the Sunday Mass precept. The secretariat responded that future widespread abuse of the dispensing power should not be presumed; that potential abuse is checked by the law's in-built conditions (e.g., dispensations are to be granted in a particular case, for the spiritual good of the faithful, and according to the prescriptions of the local ordinary). The cardinal's argument, the secretariat reasoned, would render impossible any application of the principle of subsidiarity (*Relatio*, 276-277). The 1980 schema's version of this aspect of the canon was not amended by the 1982 schema.

In the 1983 code, the 1982 *schema*'s version had been amended to include the phrase "in individual cases" (*singulis in casibus*). This insertion into the present canon 1245 was apparently made during the final papal review. No reference to "individual persons or individual families" was reinserted, however.

This legislative history, revealing how the phrase "individual faithful or individual families" of the 1917 code was dropped during the revision process, despite specific objection, indicates an intent to allow pastors, where appropriate, the authority to dispense the entire parish.

Other considerations support this interpretation. Canon 138 provides that ordinary executive power (e.g., the power to dispense attached to the pastor's office) "is to be broadly interpreted." The notion of dispensing the entire parish is consistent with Paul VI's definition of a "particular case" (cf., c. 85) in the matter of dispensation: "a particular case concerns not only individual persons but also a number of physical persons constituting a community in the strict sense" (motu proprio *De episcoporum muneribus*, CLD 6: 397).

The phrase in canon 1245, "in individual cases" refers not to the objects of dispensation in the sense of individual persons but rather to the particular fact situation, the circumstances of the case (cf., c. 91), or the motivating cause (cf., c. 93) giving rise to the dispensation. In other words, the limitation "in individual cases" prevents the pastor from giving a permanent dispensation; rather, he must issue the dispensation only when prompted by an identifiable motivating cause, with the dispensation to cease when he specifies or when the motivating cause ceases (cf., c. 93). Compare canon 1700, §1, which contrasts "permanently" with "in individual cases" (*stabiliter vel in singulis casibus*). Examples of "individual cases" given by commentators on the 1917 code's version of canon 1245 include: the rainy season, an illness, a particular trip, the season of Lent (Abbo-Hannan, 2, 499; Dominguez, et al., *Código de Derecho Canónico* (Madrid: BAC [1978] 483).

Could the pastor dispense routinely and frequently? Canon 90 requires that the pastor have a "just and reasonable cause" before granting a dispensation. It also obliges him to "take into consideration . . . the gravity of the law from which the dispensation is to be given." Since participation with the community in the Eucharist on Sundays and holy days of obligation, for example, is surely a crucial aspect of the Christian life, no dispensation should be given lightly, especially to the entire parish. The pastor needs to consider "the circumstances of the case" (cf., c. 90, §1), which would militate against a "routine" issuance of dispensations. The frequency of the dispensation would depend upon the recurrence of circumstances and causes reasonably justifying the dispensation. These are significant matters, since failure to taken them into account invalidates the dispensation (c. 90, §1).

Canon law contemplates situations in which celebration of the Eucharist is impossible for individuals or the parish community (cf., c. 1248, §2). In such cases, no dispensation would be necessary.

Robert C. Gibbons [1992]

CANON 1247

MASS OBLIGATION

Does the obligation to participate at Mass bind on a weekly basis, and if so, must the law be observed under pain of sin?

OPINION

As you will note from canon 1247 the obligation is to participate in Mass on Sundays and other days of precept. It is not, however, an obligation to participate in Mass once a week.

You might also notice the way of satisfying the obligation has been expanded in canon 1248, and in the second section of that canon there are provisions made for situations where Mass is not available.

In the 1983 code there is no indication that failure to participate in Mass on the required days is under "pain of sin." There has been an effort made to distinguish canonical penalties from moral ones, and the code attempts to deal specifically only with canonical penalties — and there does not seem to be a specific one set for failure to observe these canons.

James H. Provost [1984]

CANON 1247

ECUMENICAL PERMISSIONS WITH ORTHODOX

Are the permissions in the 1967 Ecumenical Directory *still in effect under the 1983 code, whereby . . . a Catholic who attended the Divine Liturgy in an Oriental church could thereby satisfy the obligation of attending Sunday Mass (Directory, no. 47)?*

OPINION

See opinion under canon 874.

CANON 1248

SUBSTITUTION OF PRIESTLESS SERVICES
FOR THE SUNDAY OBLIGATION

In our diocese there are priestless parishes and we frequently experience the situation of "Sunday Celebrations in the Absence of a Priest." The question often arises whether such celebrations conducted by deacons or lay leaders fulfill the Sunday obligation.

OPINION

The law of the Church on the Sunday and holy day obligation is found in canons 1247 and 1248 of the Code of Canon Law.

Canon 1247: "On Sundays and other holy days of obligation the faithful are bound to participate in the Mass; they are also to abstain from those labors and business concerns which impede the worship to be rendered to God, the joy which is proper to the Lord's Day, or the proper relaxation of mind and body."

Canon 1248, §1: "The precept of participating in the Mass is satisfied by assistance at a Mass which is celebrated anywhere in a Catholic rite either on the holy day or on the evening of the preceding day."

The obligation to participate in the celebration of the Eucharist on Sundays and holy days is fulfilled by attendance at any Catholic Mass, whether of the Latin rite or an Eastern rite Catholic church, on the Sunday or holy day itself or on the evening before. The obligation can be fulfilled at any Mass, including a ritual Mass such as a wedding Mass. An anticipated Mass should not begin before 4:00 in the afternoon.

Physical attendance at Mass, both the Liturgy of the Word and the Liturgy of the Eucharist, is the minimum form of participation. Optimally, all in attendance should participate fully, by their inner devotion and attentiveness, by their gestures, by their vocal participation in prayer and song, by their gift at the offertory, and by their reception of Holy Communion.

At times it may be impossible to fulfill the Sunday obligation. Some examples include: when there is no Mass being celebrated in the area, when a person is prevented from getting to church due to illness, old age, or another reason; on a trip when someone through no fault of his or her own is unable to locate a Catholic church. Impossibility to observe the law is an excusing cause; there is no sin, venial or mortal, when it is impossible to attend Mass on a day of precept.

When it is impossible to fulfill the precept to attend Mass on a Sunday or holy day, canon law recommends the following alternatives:

Canon 1248, §2: "If because of a lack of an ordained minister or for other grave cause participation in the celebration of the Eucharist is impossible, it is specifically recommended that the faithful take part in the liturgy of the word if it is celebrated in the parish church or in another sacred place according to the prescriptions of the diocesan bishop, or engage in prayer for an appropriate amount of time personally or in a family or, as occasion offers, in groups of families."

The Church recognizes that in many areas of the world the faithful are not able to attend Mass every Sunday and holy day due to the shortage of priests. As a result, it recommends alternate ways for the Catholic people to keep holy the Lord's Day and the other holy days. When it is not possible to attend Mass on a day of precept, faithful Catholics can maintain the special character of these days by attending an alternate service at their parish church, or engaging in prayer personally, in families, and/or in groups.

These latter practices are not required by law; they are recommendations. One cannot say that they technically fulfill the legal obligation to attend Mass; rather, they are praiseworthy ways of observing the sacred character of Sundays and holy days when it is impossible for any reason to participate in the Eucharistic celebration.

John M. Huels, O.S.M. [1989]

Canon 1248

Double Precept Fulfilled at One Mass

We are a small diocese with a shortage of priests. This year Christmas and New Year's Eve fall on a Monday. Due to the difficulties our pastors have in providing a full schedule of Masses for back to back feast days, some are asking whether in certain churches Masses might be offered only on the two Sunday evenings, Christmas Eve and New Year's Eve. Would attendance at one Mass on Sunday evening simultaneously satisfy the obligation to attend Mass both for the Sunday and for the holy day?

Opinion

The faithful are bound to participate in the Mass on Sundays and holy days of obligation (c. 1247), both of which are called "feast days" in canon law. The precept obliges all Catholics who have completed seven years of age and have sufficient use of reason (c. 11). The precept of participating in the Mass can be satisfied by attendance at a Mass celebrated anywhere in a Catholic rite either on the day of precept or on the evening of the preceding day (c. 1248, §1). The obligation is satisfied by attendance at *any* Mass, not only at a Mass using the proper texts of the Sunday or holy day.[1]

In a 1969 article, Aidan Carr claimed that the Congregation for the Clergy responded negatively to the question you posed, that a double obligation could not be fulfilled by attendance at only one Mass.[2] Carr did not give a citation for this, and I have not found any such reply in standard canonical sources, including the *Acta Apostolicae Sedis, Canon Law Digest,* and *Documents on the Liturgy 1963-1979.* Even if the Congregation had issued this reply, it would not have been authentic without express authorization of the legislator (c. 16).

I also made inquiries of the Office for Divine Worship in Chicago, and the secretaries of the Bishops' Committee on the Liturgy in Washington, and neither had any documentation from the Holy See which precisely addresses this issue.

In 1974 the Congregation for Divine Worship considered the question of holy days falling on Saturdays or Mondays, but it was concerned only with the determination of which Mass to celebrate in the evening of the first day, whether the Mass of that day or the anticipated Mass of the next day. Regarding the precept to attend Mass, the Congregation merely observed: "Also at the same celebration some of the people are there to fulfill the precept for the actual day; others, to fulfill the precept for the following day."[3] This statement does not resolve the question posed here.

There are two possible ways of interpreting the law. One could argue that since there are two separate feast days, the Sunday and the holy day, each has a separate obligation. Therefore, a person must attend two Masses to fulfill these obligations, either in the evening before the Sunday or holy day, or on the day itself.

On the other hand, one could argue that the literal meaning of the law is fulfilled even if a person attended only one Mass on the evening of the first day of precept. In this view, if a person attended any evening Mass before midnight on December 24th, he or she would fulfill the obligation for both the Fourth Sunday of Advent and Christmas, and the same would be true for New Year's Eve. This interpretation would not be contrary to the literal wording of canon 1248, §1, that the precept is fulfilled "at a Mass" that *is celebrated on the holy day or on the evening of the preceding day;* the one Mass would satisfy the obligation for the Sunday and the holy day, provided it was celebrated before midnight.

Since both positions are reasonable, I believe there may be a doubt of law here, in which case the more restrictive interpretation would not be binding (c. 14) and one could safely follow the second opinion. The second opinion, moreover, is in keeping with the canonical axiom that "favors are to be multiplied; burdens are to be restricted."

If this reasoning is unconvincing, or seems too legalistic in its approach, you might consider a pastoral solution to the problem. Perhaps the diocesan bishop could dispense from the feast day precept for one of the two days. Or the provision of canon 1248, §2 might be helpful. This is a recommendation to the faithful on how they should observe a feast day when it is impossible to participate in the Eucharist. If a pastor finds that it is physically or morally impossible to prepare adequately and celebrate fittingly many Masses on these two weekends, and therefore, schedules them only on the two Sunday evenings (Christmas Eve and New Year's Eve), the faithful would not be culpable if they only attended Mass that evening. No one is bound to the impossible.

Notes

1   S.C. for the Clergy, reply, April 3, 1971, *CLD* 10: 190.
2   "Questions Answered," *Homiletic and Pastoral Review* 70 (December, 1969) 230-232.
3   Note, *Instructio "Eucharisticum mysterium,"* May, 1974, *Notitiae* 11 (1974) 222-223. *Documents on the Liturgy 1963-1979* (Collegeville: Liturgical Press, 1982) n. 3837.

John M. Huels, O.S.M. [1989, revised 1993]

Canon 1248

Time of Anticipated Masses

Canon 1248 says that the precept to attend Mass on a Sunday or holy day can be satisfied by attendance at Mass on the day itself or on the evening before. How soon can an evening Mass be scheduled? I know of some parishes that have Sunday Mass as early as noon on Saturday. Does attendance at a wedding on Saturday afternoon fulfill the Sunday Mass obligation?

Opinion

In the 1960s and 1970s, indults were granted by the Holy See for various regions permitting anticipated Masses of Sundays and holy days on the previous afternoon or evening. The indult for the United States expired in 1984,[1] and since then the law of canon 1248 must be observed. Anticipated Masses, to fulfill the precept, must be evening Masses.

When evening Masses were first permitted in 1953, Pope Pius XII established the rule that they could not begin before 4:00 pm.[2] Although this law was intended for Masses of the day, not anticipated Masses, the time of 4:00 as the beginning of evening is, nevertheless, directly applicable to the question at hand.

Liturgically, the time for the anticipated Mass should not begin before the liturgical day commences with the celebration of First Vespers of the Sunday or the solemnity. Vespers is the evening prayer of the Church, celebrated at some time in the evening. Liturgical law speaks of evening as the time when "the day is already far spent;"[3] a dominant theme of evening prayer is the setting sun and the approaching nightfall. The beginning of evening is associated with sunset, with the end of the day, with the approach of darkness. Recall that the Church also celebrates the Liturgy of the Hours in the afternoon, at mid-day and mid-afternoon, typically around noon and 3:00. Vespers is not an afternoon prayer; nor is an afternoon Mass an evening Mass.

399

Even in the darkest days of winter, "evening," as understood here, does not begin before 4:00 in the continental United States. Although the daylight hours are considerably longer in the spring and summer, it is still proper in common discourse to speak of evening as the late afternoon hours when "the day is already far spent." Thus, an anticipated Mass could be celebrated at 4:00 or later throughout the year, and it would still be an evening Mass though the sun may be shining brightly.

Regarding your second question, the precept to participate at Mass is satisfied by attendance at *any* Mass celebrated in a Catholic rite, not just a Mass using the proper texts of the Sunday or holy day.[4] One could, therefore, satisfy the precept at a wedding Mass on Saturday evening, provided the Mass began at 4:00 or later. Participation in an afternoon Mass would not fulfill the precept.

This is not empty legalism, for the law upholds an important theological value, namely, the sacredness and centrality of Sunday. Canon 1246 says that "Sunday is the day on which the paschal mystery is celebrated in light of the apostolic tradition and is to be observed as the foremost holy day of obligation in the universal Church." Saturday afternoon is not Sunday; attendance at a Mass on a Saturday afternoon does not fulfill the Sunday obligation unless there is a particular indult permitting this.

Notes

[1] *CLD* 9: 722.
[2] Pius XII, apostolic constitution *Christus Dominus*, January 6, 1953, *AAS* 45, n. VI (1953) 15-24.
[3] General Instruction of the Liturgy of the Hours, n. 39.
[4] S.C. for the Clergy, reply, April 3, 1971, *CLD* 10: 190.

John M. Huels, O.S.M. [1989]

Canon 1248

Fulfilling the Sunday Mass Obligation in a Traditionalist Church

Can Catholics attending the Eucharist in a Traditionalist church fulfill their Sunday obligation?

Opinion

According to canon 1248: "The precept of participating in the Mass is satisfied by assistance at a Mass which is celebrated anywhere in a Catholic rite either on the holy day or on the evening of the preceding day." Under the law of the 1917 code, the place of fulfillment of this obligation was stated more explicitly: "One satisfies the law of hearing Holy Mass who is present at Mass celebrated in any Catholic rite, in the open air or in any church, or public or semi-public oratory and in private cemetery chapels, but not in other private oratories unless this privilege has been granted by the Apostolic See."

Under the 1917 code, it would seem that the Mass obligation would not be fulfilled in a Traditionalist Catholic church, since they are not churches or public oratories or semi-public oratories. They are not sacred places erected for worship with the expressed permission of the ordinary (cf., 1917 code, cc. 1161; 1162; 1191; 1192). The 1983 code likewise defines churches and oratories as places designated for worship which have been established with consent of the diocesan bishops (cc. 1214; 1215; 1223). Therefore, Traditionalist Catholic churches, inasmuch as they are erected without permission of the local bishop, would not be places to fulfill the Mass obligation according to the 1917 code.

The present code, however, allows for fulfillment of the Mass obligation: 1) anywhere; 2) in a Catholic rite. Since the place can be anywhere, there is no necessity that it be in a church or oratory erected with permission of the bishop. The only specified condition for fulfillment is that the Mass itself be celebrated in a Catholic rite.

The question is then reduced to identification of the "Tridentine rite" that is celebrated in Traditionalist churches. We know that Pope John Paul II established the Pontifical Commission *Ecclesia Dei* with authority to encourage bishops to permit certain priests to celebrate the Tridentine Mass according to the Revised Roman Missal of 1962. The purpose of the indult has been to facilitate reconciliation with "Traditionalist Catholics." Obviously when the Tridentine Mass is thus celebrated with the permission of the bishop it constitutes a legitimate Catholic rite and fulfills the Mass obligation of the faithful.

On the other hand, when the Tridentine Mass is celebrated in churches that are erected without permission of the bishop and celebrated by priests who do not have an indult from the pope or bishop or who may even be suspended and/or excommunicated, does the celebration of Mass constitute a Catholic rite? It is certainly not a legitimate celebration of Mass, but is it a Catholic rite, which would fulfill the obligation of Mass attendance?

An answer to this question can be found in the action of the Pontifical Commission for the Revision of the Code. The proposed text of canon 1248 had read: the obligation of Mass attendance is satisfied "anywhere that a

401

Catholic rite is celebrated legitimately." In their discussion members of the commission suggested dropping the word "legitimately." They argued that more often than not the cause of illegitimacy rests with the sacred minister and that the faithful should not be punished for the fault of the minister. The commission voted to accept the change, with the result that the actual law does not explicitly require that a Catholic rite be legitimately celebrated to be normative here (cf., *Communicationes* 12 [1980] 361).

Therefore, in order to fulfill one's obligation to attend Mass on Sunday and holy days it suffices that the Mass be in a Catholic rite, even if not legitimately celebrated, and anywhere, even if the place be not a legitimately erected church or oratory. The Tridentine rite is certainly a Catholic rite, even if it is illegitimate to celebrate it without explicit permission of the Apostolic See or local bishop.

This raises the interesting concept that one can fulfill one's obligation illicitly or that one can worship God in an illicit manner. In these cases there is no indication that the Mass celebrated illegitimately in the Tridentine rite, in Traditional Catholic chapels, is invalid. The priest is acting illicitly in celebrating against the norms of the supreme authority of the Church (c. 841). Nonetheless the Eucharist is being celebrated. The illiceity involves the unauthorized celebration by a priest who may be in doubtful hierarchical communion. The illiceity may also consist in the fact that the faithful themselves, who attend Mass in the Traditional Catholic churches, are not fulfilling their obligation to maintain communion with the pope and bishops (c. 209). Therefore, by attendance at Mass in such circumstances, the faithful may be violating their duties to the Catholic Church and its legitimate authorities. The sacred ministers in such circumstances are violating their obligation to fulfill the norms of sacred liturgy. On the other hand, the specific obligation to attend Mass on Sunday and holy days is being fulfilled.

The situation is analogous to the Roman Catholic who enters marriage in a ceremony taking place according to the Orthodox rite. The marriage is treated as valid. The spouses are truly married, their matrimonial bond is effected as sacramental and their conjugal union will be *ratum et consummatum*. On the other hand, the unauthorized celebration of the marriage by a Roman Catholic in a form other than the Catholic rite is certainly illegitimate (c. 1127, §1: ". . . if a Catholic party contracts marriage with a non-Catholic of an oriental rite, the canonical form of celebration is to be observed *only for liceity; for validity, however, the presence of a sacred minister is required . . .*").

On July 2, 1987, the NC News Service carried a notice entitled: "Illicit Mass Satisfies Sunday Obligation, But Gravely Disobedient." According to the news item, on February 16, 1985, the Congregation for Divine Worship had issued a one page guideline (the original text is not available to the undersigned author) that determined that those who attend Masses in the Tridentine rite can validly satisfy the Sunday obligation, because one considers it as a celebration of the Catholic rite. The news item also reports that this document furthermore states that those who attend a Tridentine rite Mass knowing it to be illicit may be guilty of insubordination and disobedience.

In this situation we, therefore, face the problematic overlapping of the ontological, moral and juridical orders in the sacramental theology of the Church. It would appear that the unauthorized celebration of the Tridentine Mass is valid and that the participation at such a Mass "validly" fulfills one's obligation to attend Mass in a Catholic rite (ecclesiastical law) and to keep holy the sabbath (divine law). This would seem to imply that the Church accepts this attendance as true worship, to which the grace of the sacrament is applied to the person. At the same time the attendance at an unauthorized Tridentine Mass is illicit, raising the confusing situation of an acceptable act of worship being at the same time an illicit act. The illiceity is, therefore, in the juridical order (a transgression of ecclesiastical law and a violation of ecclesial and/or hierarchical communion). The Code of Canon Law itself does not indicate what is the effect of this juridical illiceity on the person in the moral order (sin?). It would seem the Church lets the situation stand thus with its inherent complexity. (Can the humble canon lawyer decode this?)

In my opinion, therefore, the Catholic who goes to Mass in the Tridentine rite of a Traditionalist Catholic church does fulfill the obligation to attend Mass on Sunday and holy days. However, the person is violating his or her obligation to act within ecclesial and hierarchical communion, which is a separately stated obligation.

J. James Cuneo [1991]

ANOTHER OPINION

Canon 1248, §1 states: "The precept of participating in the Mass is satisfied by assistance at a Mass which is celebrated anywhere in a Catholic rite either on the holy day or on the evening of the preceding day."

The meaning of "Catholic rite" (*ritu catholico*) is the crux of the answer to this question. The term "rite" can mean the ritual used for the celebration, or it can refer to the ritual church (the "Latin rite," one of the "Eastern Catholic rites"). To answer this inquiry, it will be necessary to examine both meanings of "rite" in this context.

1. *Rite as a Ritual Church*

403

The most obvious meaning of "a Mass which is celebrated anywhere in a Catholic rite" is that Latin rite Catholics may satisfy the obligation to participate in Mass by assisting at Mass in the Latin rite, or at Mass in one of the Eastern Catholic rites. This is the fundamental meaning of being in communion as Catholics. The Catholic Church itself is a communion of several "rites" or self-governing churches, called "churches *sui iuris*" in the law. The self-governing churches celebrate Mass in various approved Catholic rites, whether Latin or Eastern.

Would it be possible to fulfill the obligation by attending Mass in another Church, one which is not in the Catholic communion?

In preparing the canon, the consultors who worked on it discussed whether to include mention of the provisions in the 1967 *Ecumenical Directory* concerning Catholics who attend Mass in an Orthodox Church.[1] While the consultors decided it was not appropriate to include mention of this in the canon, the *Directory* remained in force even after the 1983 Code of Canon Law took effect. The *Directory*, n. 47, stated that a Catholic who attends Mass in an Orthodox Church on a Sunday or holy day of obligation "is not then bound to assist at Mass in a Catholic Church."[2]

The *Directory*'s statement was based on the fact that the Catholic Church recognizes the validity of holy orders in the Orthodox Church, and also recognizes that there is a closer relationship of communion with the Orthodox than with other Christians.

The statement in the *Directory* could be read in either of two ways. The *Directory* did not state directly that the Orthodox Liturgy satisfied the Catholic obligation, but the practical result of not being bound to assist at Catholic Mass that day can be interpreted to mean that the Orthodox Liturgy did satisfy the Catholic's obligation. But the *Directory* could also be read as saying that the law itself was, in effect, dispensing the Catholic from the obligation, for it said the Catholic "is not then bound" — i.e., the obligation does not bind for that day. This may be closer to the intent of the *Directory*, for it went on to say that it is "a good thing if on such days Catholics, who for just reasons cannot go to Mass in their own Church, attend the Holy Liturgy of their separated Oriental brethren, if this is possible." It did not state that the Catholic was bound to do this. Yet if the Orthodox Liturgy satisfied the Catholic's obligation, it would be reasonable to say that the Catholic would be obliged to attend Orthodox Mass.

It is interesting to note that the new Code of Canons of the Eastern Churches does not address the issue directly. Canon 17 affirms the right of the Christian faithful to divine worship in keeping with the prescriptions of their own self-governing Church. Canon 670, §1 permits Catholics to attend the divine worship of other Christians if they have a just cause, and to participate to the extent this is permitted by their own bishop or by a higher authority. But in dealing with the obligation to attend Mass on days of precept, canon 881 does not contain the same provision of the Latin code, canon 1248, §1, concerning "a Mass which is celebrated anywhere in a Catholic rite."

Nevertheless, it is clear that a Catholic of whatever Catholic rite (i.e., Latin or Eastern) may satisfy the obligation of participating in Mass in any Catholic Mass, and if they participate in the Divine Liturgy (Mass) celebrated in an Orthodox Church, until recently they were not bound to attend Mass that day also in a Catholic Church.

In light of this background, is it possible for a Catholic to satisfy the Sunday obligation by attending Eucharist in a Traditionalist church? By "Traditionalist church" here seems to be meant one which is not in full communion with the Catholic Church. It is possible for the diocesan bishop to permit Mass to be celebrated according to the 1962 Missal as an exception to the general norm. Sometimes this is called a "traditionalist" Mass. But such celebrations are in the Catholic Church, not in a "Traditionalist church," and take place in full communion with the diocesan bishop and the pope.[3]

When Archbishop Lefebvre ordained bishops without the mandate of the Holy Father and contrary to his direct order, he was automatically excommunicated and was declared to be in schism. Those who adhere to his cause are also in schism. Often churches which adhere to Archbishop Lefebvre's movement are termed "Traditionalist churches." Such churches are schismatic, not unlike the Polish National Churches, the Old Catholic Churches, or even the Orthodox Churches. The Catholic Church does recognize the validity of the ministry in these churches even though they are not in communion with the Catholic Church, and, at least for the Orthodox Churches, has admitted the validity of the other sacraments (including Eucharist) that they celebrate.

The only exception the law made for Catholics who attend Mass in other than a Catholic Church is when they do so in an Orthodox Church. There is no exception mentioned in the law for Catholics who attend Mass elsewhere. Consider, for example, the Mass celebrated in the Episcopal Church by a validly ordained but suspended (and excommunicated) Roman Catholic priest who has been accepted into the Episcopal Church. The orders of the priest are certainly valid. The Mass may be celebrated according to the ancient Sarum Use, which was the Catholic rite in England until the Reformation and is sometimes still used in the Anglican Church. In this sense it is (or at least was) a Catholic rite. But the *Ecumenical Directory* did not make an exception for something like this the way it did for Orthodox liturgy, and the discussion by the consultors in drafting the 1983 code did not seem to have included this possibility in their understanding of the canon.

2. *Rite as Ritual*

But could canon 1248, §1 also be interpreted to mean that "a Mass which is celebrated anywhere in a Catholic rite" would mean any Mass celebrated in what is, or at least at one time was, an approved Catholic ritual?

Some years ago private letters to individuals in the United States from officials of the Congregation for Sacraments and Divine Worship were widely circulated among persons attending "Traditionalist Masses," stating that their participation there on Sunday did indeed satisfy the Sunday obligation. The argument in the letters was that the "Traditionalist Mass" is a Mass in a Catholic rite (in the sense of "ritual"), even though that ritual is no longer authorized or at least the particular celebration in that ritual was not authorized by the diocesan bishop.

When scholars in Rome were asked about this matter privately they gave the following explanation. The wording of canon 1248, §1 originally included the provision that the Mass had to be celebrated "legitimately." These scholars interpreted this to mean that Mass which was not celebrated legitimately would include Traditionalist Masses, and they argued that this was done for the sake of Catholics in China. Since only the Mass according to the so-called Tridentine form is permitted there by the government, dropping the requirement that the Mass be celebrated "legitimately" would permit Chinese Catholics to satisfy their Sunday obligation in the only form of Mass available to them.

While this interpretation is laudable, it is not supported by the report of the consultors' discussion on this point. They dropped the word "legitimately" because "most often the illegitimacy resides in the sacred minister and the Christian faithful ought not to be punished for such a fault of the sacred minister."[4]

Moreover, Catholics in China are in an extraordinary situation in which the obligation of Sunday Mass may not even bind, since no one is held to the impossible and it is frequently impossible for them to participate in Mass celebrated in communion with the Catholic Church. The same is not true of persons who attend a Mass at a Traditionalist church when Mass in a Catholic rite celebrated in communion with the bishops and the pope is readily available to them.

Participation at Mass is an external expression of communion with the community represented there. It is in the context of that communion that Catholics exercise their rights and fulfill their obligations. Catholics have the obligation to preserve their communion with the Church (c. 209), something which always binds even when it is not possible to attend Mass on a Sunday. It does not make sense to speak of Catholics fulfilling an obligation they have within the Catholic communion by participating at Mass outside that communion. The revised *Ecumenical Directory* emphasizes this point.

406

Since no exception has been made for Catholics who participate at Mass in a "Traditionalist church," it is my opinion that they do not satisfy their Sunday obligation there. If they did, this would be equivalent to saying that a Catholic who participates at Mass celebrated by a validly ordained Catholic priest, but one who is excommunicated and ministering in some other church (Anglican, Lutheran, or his own creation, such as some of the new churches in Africa), would satisfy the Sunday Mass obligation. This does not seem to be the position of the Church, particularly because of the careful distinctions made in the former *Ecumenical Directory* between participation with Orthodox and with other Christians, and the more restrictive position adopted in the revised *Directory*.

Notes

[1] See discussion of the *coetus* in *Communicationes* 12 (1980) 362.

[2] Secretariat for Promoting Christian Unity, *Directory for the Application of the Decisions of the Second Ecumenical Council of the Vatican Concerning Ecumenical Matters*, May 14, 1967 (Washington: USCC, 1967) 18. This has been dropped in the revised *Directory for the Application of Principles and Norms on Ecumenism* (March 25, 1993) n. 115.

[3] John Paul II, motu proprio *Ecclesia Dei*, July 2, 1988: *AAS* 80 (1980) 1495-1498.

[4] *Communicationes* 12 (1980) 361.

James H. Provost [1991, revised 1993]

BOOK V

THE TEMPORAL GOODS OF THE CHURCH

Canon 1263

Right of the Diocesan Bishop to Levy a Tax
on a Juridic Person Subject to Him

A number of questions have been raised as to the right of the diocesan bishop to levy a tax on a juridic person subject to his authority.

1. Can the diocesan bishop decide once and for all to levy a tax on public juridic persons subject to his authority, or must he consult the bodies mentioned in canon 1263 every time he levies such a tax?

2. How often can he levy the tax? Is it only as an "extraordinary" means?

3. What is to be understood as "the needs of the diocese" for which such a tax can be levied?

Opinion

It will help to understand the present canon if we consider the developments which took place during its drafting. In 1977 the code revision commission proposed that the bishop could impose a tax on ecclesiastical persons, physical as well as juridic, whenever this was necessary for the good of the diocese. He did have to consult the presbyteral council, but did not need to obtain their consent.

Responses to the 1977 *schema* objected that this seemed to give the bishop too much power to tax too many people (clergy individually, as well as any juridic persons, even private ones). The text was revised in the 1980 *schema* to permit the bishop to impose an extraordinary and moderate tax in cases of grave necessity (i.e., more serious need than the 1977 text would require). This tax could be imposed on the Christian faithful (not just the clergy), and on private as well as public juridic persons. The bishop needed to consult the finance council as well as the presbyteral council, but again he did not need to obtain their consent.

Responses to this 1980 *schema* were rather critical. These may be found in *Communicationes* 15 (1984) 28-30, which is a reprinting of the 1981 *Relatio*. Note that these were comments submitted by members of the commission, to which the secretariat responded with the help of consultants. It is clear that the secretariat resisted several efforts to change the canon.

However, at the 1981 plenary meeting of the commission the issue was raised on the floor and debated there. Eventually a compromise was reached, which is reflected in the 1982 text sent to the Holy Father. As with the promulgated version, this permits the bishop to impose a moderate tax proportionate to their income on the public juridic persons subject to his governance. He can also impose an extraordinary and moderate tax on other physical and juridic persons in cases of grave necessity. Again, in either case he must consult the finance council and the presbyteral council, although he is not required to obtain their consent.

The final, promulgated version of the canon deletes mention of no taxes on Mass stipends (contained in the earlier versions of the canon), and adds that in addition to the authority to tax, which this canon gives the bishop, he may have other, even stronger bases for imposing taxes. I think this may be a reflection of the discussion by Cardinal Ratzinger in the 1981 *Relatio* concerning the "church tax" (*Kirchensteuer*) in Germany.

Now, in light of all that, how is this canon to be interpreted in practice? Here we come to your three questions.

1. The diocesan bishop is authorized to impose two types of taxes according to canon 1263. The two are separated by the semi-colon in the canon.

One tax is proportionate to income, may be imposed only on public juridic persons (such as parishes, diocesan religious institutes) subject to his governance, and would appear to be ordinary (or usual) tax. He may impose this tax after proper consultation. He does not need to consult every year to impose this tax. Once he has consulted and then imposed the tax, he may continue to collect it year after year.

This tax is to be proportionate to income. It would seem, provided the proportion does not change, he need not consult further. But if the proportion changes (i.e., increases from one percentage figure to another), he would be imposing a new tax and would need to consult anew.

The other tax is an extraordinary tax. It is not something which continues, but as the *Relatio* explained, by the very nature of being "extraordinary" it is imposed for a limited time. Each time the bishop wishes to impose this kind of tax, he has to consult. Even if he imposed it before and now wants to renew it, the canon requires him to consult anew.

2. How often can the bishop levy these taxes? The first type of tax can be collected on an on-going basis, provided it remains proportionate to the public juridic person's income. The second type of tax can be levied whenever there is a grave need. There is no limitation on the number of times a bishop may impose this second type of tax, other than the requirement that he consult.

3. The purpose of these two taxes may be somewhat different.

The first tax — the ordinary or usual tax — is to meet the needs of the diocese. These could be the needs of diocesan administration (i.e., to run the bishop's office and other diocesan programs), or to subsidize needy parishes or other apostolates in the diocese, etc. The canon does not specify the parameters for such "needs," so you have to look to other places in the code where these may be described — for example, the diocese's responsibilities for the teaching, sanctifying, and pastoral functions within its territory. Schools, catechetics, etc., might be such needs. The support of priests and others involved in sacramental ministry could be such a need, and so on.

The second tax is to be levied only in cases of grave necessity. Although these may also be the needs of the diocese, they are not limited to this. They could relate to famine, refugee relief, etc., if these are judged to be of "grave necessity."

Since the imposition of a tax is always something odious, the law requires that the bishop consult with the presbyteral council (not just the college of consultors), and the finance council. The former should reflect the pastoral sensitivities in the diocese. The latter should be sensitive to the fiscal condition not only of the diocese, but also of the public juridic persons subject to the bishop's governance (since this council reviews their annual financial reports, c. 1287).

This consultation is required for the validity of the tax (c. 127, §1). Moreover, commentators argue that the provision of canon 127, §2, 2° also applies to consultation with a group: "the superior should not act contrary [to the advice received], especially when there is a consensus, unless there be a reason which, in the superior's judgment, is overriding."

The proper application of this canon was clearly a concern throughout the process of revising the code. As the secretariat pointed out in its 1981 *Relatio*, the primary means for supporting the Church are voluntary offerings. Taxation is a last resort and should be used carefully so that it does not weaken the effectiveness of various public juridic persons such as parishes, and so that the leaders of the Church remain close to the people.

James H. Provost [1991]

Canon 1263

The Bishop's Power to Tax All Parish Funds

The diocese is hard pressed financially and considerable discussion has surfaced about the new assessments, which simply had to be increased. Pastors with building funds and projects are complaining that these are restricted funds and should not be subject to taxation.

Does canon 1263 allow for the bishop to tax all the funds of a parish?

OPINION

Canonical scholars have available, through the excellent research of Robert L. Kealy, a very complete legislative history of canon 1263 (R. L. Kealy, *Diocesan Financial Support: Its History and Canonical Status*, Gregorian University, Rome [1986] 312-330). This canon went through various permutations prior to its promulgation in its present form. The primary focus of the drafters and the consultors, however, was not 'what' funds the diocesan bishop could tax, but rather 'whom' he could tax.

The 1973 *schema* initially described those able to be taxed as "ecclesiastical persons, both physical and moral." This was certainly a curious usage since no one knows who or what an "ecclesiastical person" is. By the 1980 *schema*, those able to be taxed were described as "the Christian faithful and public and private juridic persons." By the time the code was promulgated, the object of taxation had changed yet another time to become "public juridic persons subject to [the bishop's] authority" and, in cases of grave necessity, "physical persons and other juridic persons."

There was some discussion in the drafting stages concerning the taxability of Mass funds, and a prohibition against this type of tax appeared in both the 1973 and 1980 *schemata*. This was the only discussion of what kinds of funds could be taxed, however, and when the code was finally promulgated, this prohibition was not made a part of canon 1263, nor does it appear elsewhere in the 1983 code as such. The former code did contain such a prohibition in canon 1506, and Kealy thinks its omission from the present code is an editorial oversight (Kealy, 339). The legislative intent that can be derived from this ambiguous history of the prohibition on taxing Mass funds is not very helpful in the present case, however.

Canon 1263 has also occasioned an authentic interpretation, the only canon in Book V with this distinction to date. In response to the *dubium* of whether the works of religious institutes of pontifical right within a diocese were "public juridic persons subject to the bishop's authority" and thus able to be taxed, the Pontifical Council for the Interpretation of Legislative Texts responded that they were not (*Roman Replies and CLSA Advisory Opinions 1990*, 115). Even this interpretation, however, goes only to the question of who can be taxed, and does not tell us what funds can be taxed.

To the present time, then, the only authoritative information that we have on

411

canon 1263 through legislative history and authentic interpretation deals with who can be taxed and not "what funds" can be taxed. But the question before us involves exactly that issue: what kinds of funds of a subject public juridic person can be taxed? There is no doubt that a parish within a diocese is a public juridic person subject to the bishop's authority, and therefore, is itself a proper object of taxation. But, can all of its property be taxed? What, if any, property of a parish is exempt from the diocesan bishop's taxing authority?

As an initial answer to this question, one would have to say that certainly the stable patrimony of a parish cannot be taken, even in part, by the diocesan bishop under the guise of taxation. It has always been canonical jurisprudence that stable patrimony is not freely movable from one public juridic person to another (cf., Doheny, *Practical Problems In Church Finance* [Milwaukee: Bruce, 1941] 39, and the extensive list of authorities therein cited).

It should also be noted that, in an American civil law context, a diocese should insist on this non-fungibility of parish and diocesan patrimony. To act otherwise, i.e., to treat them interchangeably, would mean that civilly the assets of one would be available to the creditors of another. This would be an unfortunate result in an age of increasing litigation, and we are wise to follow the code and treat the patrimony of a juridic person as the property of that juridic person only.

Are restricted funds such as those described in the inquiry protected from diocesan taxation as the stable patrimony of a parish? They could be, if the proper steps had been taken by the pastor to immobilize them. This would require a formal act of designation by the pastor, and inasmuch as such a stabilization of parish funds is also an act of extraordinary administration, the written approval of the bishop is required by canon 1282, §1. Nonetheless, if these steps have been taken to immobilize certain parish funds, they have become the stable patrimony of the parish and are not subject to taxation.

What if these funds have not been so protected? What if they are simply placed in a bank account that is designated "Parish Building Fund," but no other formalities of the law have been observed? The answer lies in how the funds got there. If these funds had been the free, unrestricted funds of the parish, placed in this account by the pastor, then simply placing these funds in such an account does not immobilize them and does not protect them from taxation. On the other hand, if these funds were placed into such an account "at the designation of donors," then they are protected from taxation.

There is a long canonical history for the proposition that the intent of the donor of a gift to the Church is to be scrupulously observed. This proposition appears in Gratian (cc. 4, 9-11, C. XIII, q. 2; c. 4, C. XVII, q. 4); in the Decretals (cc. 3, 4, 6, 17, 19, X, *de testamentis et ultimis voluntatibus*, III, 26; c. 3, X, *de successionibus ab intestatio*, III, 27; c. un., *de testamentis et ultimis voluntatibus*, III, 6, in Clem.; c. 2, *de religiosis domibus*, III, 11, in Clem.); in the decrees of the Council of Trent (sess. VII, *de ref.*, c. 15); in the 1917 code, canon 1514 and in the 1983 code, canon 1267, §3 and canon 1300. Thus, if a person has responded to a parish solicitation for funds to build a parish structure or has made such a gift spontaneously, and as a result of that act of the donor, the pastor has placed that donor's gift into a parish account designated for that purpose, then a donative intent attaches to such gift funds that prevents their use for another purpose, e.g., the support of the diocese through taxation.

Quite simply, the bishop's right to tax, as established by canon 1263, is limited by the provisions of canons 1267, §3 and 1300, that the intent of the donor controls the use of the donor's gift. This is perhaps why no specific prohibition was placed in the 1983 code against taxing Mass stipends. It was not necessary because canons 1267, §3 and 1300 cover the situation. One would be hard pressed to think of an instance in which money was given to the Church with a clearer donative intent than in gifts to the Church for Masses, and as such they are already protected from taxation by canons 1267, §3 and 1300.

In the final analysis, then, the answer to the inquiry will depend on the facts. If the money in a restricted parish fund came from the free capital of the parish, without formal steps having been taken to immobilize it, then it is subject to diocesan taxation. But if the source of the funds was a donor or donors responding to a parish solicitation, or if the funds were spontaneously given by a donor for a specific purpose, and those funds are on deposit in a fund limited to use for that donative purpose, then such funds may not be taxed because to do so would divert them from the use specified by the donor and would be violative of canons 1267, §3 and 1300.

Nicholas Cafardi [1992]

ANOTHER OPINION

The question of whether or not a diocesan bishop can tax building funds is rooted in the general question of the bishop's right to tax at all. In a very significant departure from the previous law, the 1983 code does give the diocesan bishop "the right to impose a moderate tax on public juridic persons subject to his authority" (c. 1263).[1] In most instances, this tax is imposed on parishes, the most familiar form of public juridic persons.[2] Canon 1263 states simply that this tax, levied for diocesan needs, is to be "moderate" and "proportionate to their income." These words obviously admit of an elastic interpretation.

What is a moderate tax? No tax will seem moderate to the entity being taxed. The right to tax, by its very nature, is the right to take away someone's property. On the other hand, from the view of the one imposing the tax, a diocesan levy of fifteen percent might seem moderate in the United States where many individuals pay a federal income tax of twenty-eight percent of adjusted gross income.

An argument can be made that a moderate tax means one that is "relatively" moderate, not "absolutely" moderate. A moderate tax would mean one which is reasonable in relation to the economic situation of the parish and would take into account such factors as the debt situation of the parish.[3] The test of moderation would be the parish's ability to pay.

The tax is to be proportionate to the income of the parish. This could mean a fixed portion of the income of the parish, such as ten percent for all. But it could also mean a graduated proportion or sliding scale. Whatever, the tax becomes a slice of the income pie of the parish. The proportionate norm would rule out a per capita tax or a flat tax of the same amount on all parishes. The tax must be related to the income.

How one defines and interprets a tax that is to be moderate and proportionate, in the end, depends on whether one is imposing the tax or one is paying the tax.

Canon 17 provides tools for interpreting ecclesiastical laws. One of these is to look to the mind of the legislator. Canon 1263 reflects last-minute interventions of members of the Commission for the Revision of the Code of Canon Law (hereafter, Code Commission), in particular, members from the United States. If one concedes that the Code Commission was the legislator, then it is clear that an interpretation reflective of the legislator would be from the prospective of the one imposing the tax, not from the one paying the tax.[4] If the tax is on the income of the parish, one has to ask what is actually income. Here canon law and accounting principles begin to overlap. The popular idea that a parish derives all of its income from Sunday and holy day collections is too facile. Routinely parishes have income from school tuition, CCD fees, interest and dividend income, sales of candles and religious articles, sales of cemetery lots, bequests, oil royalties, festivals, bake sales, etc. But are loan proceeds a form of income? Is a $50,000 check from an insurer for damages to the roof of the church income?

Canon 1263 gives the diocesan bishop the right to tax the income of a parish. Since this is a very generic right and since the law makes no further distinctions, one could say that *any* income could be taxed. Equity would seem to demand that affluent parishes pay more, but the law does not specify a tax in relation to the parish's ability to pay.

It has been argued that in the name of fairness, the tax should not be a tax on *gross income* but on *net income*, after all expenses are paid.[5] Such a position

414

does not consider taxes as a "cost of doing business" in much the way as are salaries, utilities, repairs, lawn service, etc. Here a tax would be levied on that portion of income that is residual and would hardly serve the original purpose of the levy, that is, "for diocesan needs." It would not generate any significant income.

The inquiry asks if the diocesan bishop can tax building funds. A facile reply would be in the affirmative since the law does not specifically exempt them. But, at the same time, one envisions a parish having a special pledge drive, apart from the Sunday offertory collection, in order to build a new sanctuary. One can also envision someone making a pledge of $1,000 toward the project. At canon 1267, §3 we read: "The offerings given by the faithful for a definite purpose can be applied only for that same purpose." Thus, to impose a tax on this $1,000 would be to violate the wishes of the donor.

On the other hand, the contrary view would hold that the diocesan tax, as a percentage of *all* revenues, is an *expense* of the parish and is to be paid out of an operating account, the same as all other expenses of the parish. Thus, the $1,000 gift is not being invaded to pay the tax.

Further, on a very practical level, when building funds are exempt from taxation, there is the temptation to call all parish revenue contributions to the building fund, sheltering all income from taxation. Parishes have been known to accrue substantial building funds when no building was on the horizon.

The more balanced reply to the inquiry may rest on an examination of the condition attached to the bishop's taxing authority. Canon 1263 states that the levy "may be imposed only after hearing the diocesan finance council and the presbyteral council." Their consent is not required; consultation is required.

This moves the discussion into the area of canon 127 and a detailed study of this canon is not possible here. However, if this consultative process is taken with utmost seriousness, by the one doing the consulting and those being consulted, if there is a frank and honest exchange between the one imposing the tax and those paying the tax, there should emerge a consensus policy or set of guidelines that would delineate which revenues are to be included in the taxable income base. It matters little whether one calls them guidelines or norms. These are euphemisms for particular law, for "negotiated" particular law, formulated in much the same process as the present code. This was a give-and-take process in which many compromises were made.

Particular law to "flesh out" canon 1263 might have some of these features:

—interest on parish debt might be deducted from gross income or only debt reduction;

—parishes with schools might be allowed to deduct the subsidy paid by the parish to cover the school's deficit;

—parishes planning to have a fund drive for a building program might be given a one-year exemption during which any money raised would be exempt from taxes. If the building is not erected in the following year, all of the funds would be taxed;

—new parishes might be granted an exemption from all taxes for three years;

—the diocesan bishop could always use his dispensing power to make special exceptions.

The inquiry speaks of the diocese being hard pressed financially. This suggests a kind of emergency. It might be noted that the second part of canon 1263 also allows the diocesan bishop to impose an "extraordinary" tax but only "in case of grave necessity." Thus, canon 1263 gives a right to the diocesan bishop to impose two kinds of taxes, both moderate and both subject to the same conditions. But the first kind of tax, although not called ordinary, was clearly intended by the Code Commission to be a basic source of diocesan revenue, a regular tax. The second tax, because it is called extraordinary, does appear as a non-recurring kind of tax, imposed in grave necessity and imposed only as a one-time situation or until the grave situation is ended. This may match up with the situation described in the inquiry.

Notes

[1] For a brief history of the evolution of this canon, see Donald J. Frugé, "Taxes in the Proposed Law," *CLSA Proceedings* 44 (1982) 274-288.

[2] C. 515, §3: "A legitimately erected parish has juridic personality by the law itself."

[3] Robert L. Kealy, *Diocesan Financial Support: Its History and Canonical Status* (Rome: Gregorian University, 1986) 334.

[4] For a detailed glimpse into the minds of the legislators in this area, see Donald J. Frugé, *The Taxation Practices of United States Bishops in Relation to the Authority of Bishops to Tax According to the Code of Canon Law and Proposed Revisions*, Canon Law Studies No. 506 (Washington, D.C.: The Catholic University of America, 1982) 204-215. This makes very clear what the tax issues were at the plenary meetings of the Code Commission beginning October 20, 1981. For more insight, especially regarding interventions made by United States members of the Code Commission, see also Kealy, *op. cit.*, 325-330, but especially footnote 79 at 323 and Appendix B.

[5] See Kealy, *op. cit.*, 335.

Donald J. Frugé [1992]

CANON 1274, §2

CIVIL AND CANONICAL REQUIREMENTS
FOR A CLERGY RETIREMENT FUND

A question has arisen concerning the obligation of a diocese to provide for the retirement of its clergy. Is a diocese bound by civil and/or canon law to provide a retirement fund? If so, what is the best way to erect such a fund to ensure its stability?

OPINION

You have asked our opinion on the requirements that civil and canon law place on a clergy retirement fund. The existence of a fund to provide for the social security of the clergy is mandated by canon 1274, §2. This fund is meant to supplement the already existing social security system in the United States.

This canon is almost a direct quotation of *Presbyterorum ordinis*, n. 21, which states:

> Moreover, in countries where social security has not yet been adequately organized for benefit of clergy, episcopal conferences are to make provision, in harmony with the ecclesiastical and civil law, for the setting up of diocesan organizations (even federated with one another), or organizations for different dioceses grouped together, or an association catering for the whole territory: the purpose of these being that under the supervision of the hierarchy satisfactory provision should be made for suitable insurance and what is called health assistance, and for the proper support of priests who suffer from sickness, ill health or old age. (A. P. Flannery, ed. *The Documents of Vatican II*)

Clearly both the council and the code have recognized the responsibility of the Church to establish a means, civilly and canonically effective, to care for priests in their old age, in their illness and their incapacity. Where these systems or means are not pre-existing, it is the responsibility of the episcopal conference to call them into existence.

Canon 1274, §2 imposes an obligation on the episcopal conference and not directly on the diocese. It can even be said that inasmuch as many American dioceses have such funds already, they are not within the coverage of canon 1274 because it speaks only of situations where such funds do not exist.

Where dioceses have created these funds, however, it is our opinion that these funds are subject to a canonical requirement that they be civilly and canonically effective. We reach this conclusion because in situations such as this, where there is a gap in the law, recourse must be had to laws enacted in similar matters (c. 19). Canon 1274 is exactly such a parallel law, and therefore, canonical jurisprudence would apply its requirements to similar situations on a diocesan level.

How then is a diocese to structure a priests' retirement fund so that it is

417

canonically and civilly effective? We will deal with the canonical issues first. Under this heading, the critical concerns are 1) juridic status of the fund; 2) stable patrimony or free capital; and 3) regulations.

What is the juridic status of a diocesan fund established for priests' retirement? One European commentary offers the opinion that such funds should be established as public juridic persons (P. Lombardia, J. I. Arrieta, *Código de Derecho Canónico*, University of Navarra commentary). It is our opinion that public juridic personality, while an option for such funds, is not a requirement. There may be an advantage to public juridic personality in European countries operating under concordats with the Holy See that give civil recognition to public juridic persons, but such is not the case in the United States. It has also not been canonical practice in the United States to erect these funds as public juridic persons by executory decree.

If these funds are not their own public juridic persons, what are they? Canonically they are the property of the juridic person that is holding them, in this case the diocese. This brings us to our second issue: is the fund the stable patrimony or the free capital of the diocese?

For funds to become stable patrimony, something must happen to stabilize them. The code requires that this occur *ex legitima assignatione*, by lawful designation (c. 1291). Although the argument could be made that the retirement fund is already stable patrimony because it has been set aside in perpetuity for this purpose, the best way to allay any doubt is to expressly, canonically, in a written instrument, designate this fund as stable patrimony. Until that occurs, a case could be made that it is not stable patrimony. This act of stabilization is not an alienation.

Should priests' retirement funds be stable patrimony? Again, a case could be made that stabilizing these funds meets the requirement that it be canonically effective. It should be noted that the primary effect of stabilizing a fund is that amounts in excess of the established amount cannot be transferred from the fund without the permission of the Holy See. If this process is understood as a desirable protection, for example, against the actions of a future administrator, then the fund can be designated as stable patrimony.

This brings us to our third issue: What regulations should such a fund have? Canon 94 specifies that aggregations of property, whether they enjoy juridic personality or not, can have statutes that govern their purpose, constitution, government and operations. Certainly a written document that 1) establishes the fund, 2) specifies the statutes, and 3) determines whether the fund is stable patrimony, would be the best way to make the fund one that was "canonically effective" as the law requires.

We will now turn to the civil law issues involved in such a fund. Specifically, these are 1) civil law structure, and 2) civil law regulation.

418

What civil law structures should such a priests' retirement fund have? The civil law presents many possibilities here. However, in our experience, the civil law device that many dioceses and religious institutes have been using for this purpose is the irrevocable trust. This device has been used because it dedicates the funds irrevocably, it insulates the funds from liability, and it provides an ease of administration not present in other legal structures.

A separate word must be said about the protection from civil liability. We believe that this is especially what the law is speaking of when it says that priests' retirement funds are to be civilly effective. No fund is civilly effective if it is so intermingled with other diocesan funds as to be subject to diocesan creditors.

In terms of civil law regulation, it is our opinion that this trust, as a clergy support trust, would qualify as that type of church organization that is exempt from IRS filing, such as Form 990. In terms of ERISA, while some church plans that include lay employees may have to meet some ERISA requirements, a plan that is limited to ordained clergy only would, we believe, be entitled to a constitutional exemption from this type of governmental financial oversight. In effect, a church is free to do with its clergy retirement what it chooses, without governmental interference or governmental regulation.

Nicholas P. Cafardi [1991]
Jordan Hite, T.O.R. [1991]

CANON 1297

LEASING OF GOODS

Is the permission of the Holy See still required for the leasing of ecclesiastical property owned by religious institutes in the United States, particularly in the case of long-term leases?

OPINION

According to canon 1297, it is the duty of the conference of bishops to determine norms for the leasing of ecclesiastical goods, and more particularly to legislate a process for obtaining prior permission from competent ecclesiastical authority in such instances.

The 1917 code, in canon 1541, had prescribed that in certain cases the permission of the Holy See was required: if the value of the goods to be leased

419

exceeded a determined sum and if the duration of the lease was for more than nine years. The 1983 code makes no explicit reference to the mandatory intervention of the Holy See in such cases.

The Canadian bishops, in their decree on leasing of ecclesiastical property (n. 16, CCCB Official Document, n. 575) prescribed that, in addition to the regular permissions to be obtained at the local level, if the total amount of rent to be paid (and not the value of the goods to be leased) exceeds the maximum amount determined for the region for acts of alienation of ecclesiastical goods, and if the lease has a duration of more than nine years, then the permission of the Holy See is also required.

The Australian bishops took a simpler approach: "leases for periods in excess of nine years require the consent of the competent authority mentioned in canon 1292, §1," that is, if the goods belong to a juridic person subject to the diocesan bishop's authority, the consent of the finance committee, of the college of consultors, and of the interested parties is required. Leases of lesser duration do not require these formalities. In the case of goods not belonging to or subject to the diocesan bishop, the statutes of the group are to be followed. Thus, the Australian bishops have decreed that, in the case of long-term leases, the same permissions are required as for acts of alienation of stable patrimony, but without the necessity of having recourse to the Holy See if the value of the goods to be leased exceeds the maximum amount approved for acts of alienation.

The bishops of France in their decree implementing canon 1297 made no reference to the Holy See's intervention (*La Documentation catholique*, 86 [1989] 78). In the case of leases extending over nine years, the provisions of the concordat are to be applied, if the diocese in question is subject to the concordat.

Generally speaking, other conferences have not entered into such details (cf., J. T. Martin De Agar, *Legislazione delle Conferenze Episcopali Complementare al CIC* [Milano: Guiffrè, 1990] passim).

It can be reasonably concluded that the Holy See no longer requires its intervention for the leasing of ecclesiastical property. What it does seem to require, however, is a recognized decree of the conference of bishops determining what permissions are required.

The United States National Conference of Catholic Bishops has not yet issued a formal decree relative to leasing. It did, however, refer to leasing in the provisions it made to apply canon 1277 on extraordinary administration. The bishops consider it an act of extraordinary administration "to lease church property when the annual lease income exceeds the minimum limit" (cf., *Implementation of the 1983 Code of Canon Law. Complementary Norms* [Washington: NCCB, 1991, Publication No. 433-3] 21). This means that local permissions are required. No reference was made to the duration of the lease.

There are, however, a few problems with this U.S. decision. First of all, it does not appear to have obtained the recognition of the Holy See, and thus its validity can be questioned. Secondly, it does not address to which formalities the temporal goods of religious institutes are subject. It could reasonably be concluded that the matter is left to the proper law of the institutes. Indeed, canon 638, §1 provides that "it is for the proper law, within the scope of universal law, to determine acts which exceed the limit and manner of ordinary administration and to determine those things which are necessary to place an act of extraordinary administration validly."

However, the reference in canon 638 to the universal law remains problematic, in the sense that the bishops' decree is generally considered to be a complement to the universal law, and not simply an additional piece of legislation. In other words, it seems that the proper law of an institute should take into account existing particular legislation.

In spite of these possible ambiguities, I believe it is appropriate to state that if the proper law of the religious institute provides for certain required internal permissions, and if these are obtained, it is no longer necessary to have recourse to the Holy See for any additional permission to lease the temporal goods of religious institutes.

One final issue remains: the preparation of particular law in the United States. Until the National Conference of Catholic Bishops issues a formal decree (subsequently recognized by the Holy See), the various canons calling for complementary legislation remain somewhat in abeyance. This gives rise to the impression that it is not important to have such legislation. Hopefully, this will be resolved in due time before attitudes contrary to law are firmly established in the minds of the faithful.

Francis G. Morrisey, O.M.I. [1993]

Canons 1308 - 1309

Canonical Rights to Reduce and to Transfer Mass Obligations

Does a diocesan bishop have any canonical rights regarding Mass obligations arising from Mass offerings?

Opinion

Regarding the administration of obligations arising from Mass offerings, diocesan bishops enjoy two canonical rights — the right to reduce and the right to transfer the obligations, provided the offerings are of a particular type and certain conditions exist.

Donations, intended to form a trust or to be assigned to an endowment, which are made to and validly accepted (cf., c. 1304) by a public juridic person to ensure from their income that Masses are offered for a long time for certain intentions canonically are called *non-autonomous pious foundations* (c. 1303, §2). Other donations, not intended to form a trust, made to and accepted by a priest or an ecclesiastical institution for Masses to be offered for a specified intention are not called *foundations* but merely *offerings* (cf., cc. 945, §1 and 946). A diocesan bishop cannot reduce or transfer obligations arising from simple Mass *offerings*. However, he does enjoy these two rights regarding obligations arising from *foundations*. The exercise of these rights is restricted by law.

CASE 1: The right to reduce Mass obligations arising from a foundation is validly exercised when the income from the foundation becomes *diminished* and if reduction is *expressly provided for in the articles of the foundation* (c. 1308, §2).

CASE 2: Even if not provided for in the articles of the foundation, this right may be exercised validly to bring the number of Masses into conformity with the level of offerings legitimately established in the diocese. The reduction should continue only as long as the income remains diminished. Further, the reduction is to be avoided or terminated if some person competent to increase the income from the foundation can be persuaded to do so (c. 1308, §3).

CASE 3: The law also envisions as a just and necessary reason justifying the reduction of Mass obligations instances when the foundation income proves insufficient to pursue successfully the proper goal of an ecclesiastical institute (e.g., school, hospital, diocese, parish, etc.) bound to foundation obligations for Masses (c. 1308, §4).

The right to reduce Mass obligations is not general but restricted to the circumstances noted above. Final judgment regarding the existence of these circumstances belongs to the bishop. Additionally, all *ordinaries* enjoy this right regarding Case 1. All supreme moderators of clerical institutes of pontifical right enjoy the right regarding Cases 2 and 3.

A second right enjoyed by all three authorities noted above is the right to transfer Mass obligations to days, churches or altars different from those determined in the articles of a foundation (c. 1309). The law restricts the exercise of this right to instances in which the competent authority judges the existence of a suitable reason. The law provides no specification regarding "suitability." However, common canonical tradition holds that a "suitable" reason need not be as weighty as the "just and necessary" reason mentioned in canon 1308.

David R. Perkin [1990]

BOOK VI

SANCTIONS IN THE CHURCH

CANONS 1314; 1369; AND 1374

ECCLESIASTICAL SANCTIONS AGAINST
MEMBERS OF RACIST ASSOCIATIONS

What should a bishop do about Catholics who are openly members or officers of racist or hate groups such as the Ku Klux Klan? Are such Catholics automatically excommunicated? What happens if they make statements to the effect that the principles of their associations are not opposed to their Christian heritage? People voice concern that the Church has automatic penalties against such crimes as abortion but does not have clear penalties for membership in such associations or even organized crime. What can or should be done?

OPINION

The question represents a serious pastoral situation. Occasionally there may be a case of some notoriety in a local area with requests for official reaction. Sometimes we hear of the Catholic burial of persons who are considered members of crime organizations; this is followed by anger among families in which there has been a history of some sanction by the Church, for example, brought on by an irregular marriage. People ask for clarifications feeling there is a justice issue involved. The pastoral authority of the Church is asked to respond. The task is quite complicated, inasmuch as several aspects of ecclesiastical ministry seem to collide: teaching, sanctioning, reconciling. Regarding the type of cases raised in the above question, there are some canonical points that may be helpful, without, however, making the final decisions easy.

1. It seems clear that the bishop cannot automatically excommunicate a person if there has been no promulgated penal law already legislated which explicitly lists membership or activity in such organizations as punishable *ipso facto latae sententiae* (c. 1314). There does not seem to exist in the code any universal legislation which states that such membership incurs automatic penalty.

2. The code does contain generalized descriptions of crimes for which penal action may be taken: a) Canon 1369 states that "a person who uses a public show or speech, published writings, or other media of social communication to blaspheme, seriously damage good morals, express wrongs against religion or against the Church or stir up hatred or contempt against religion or the Church

is to be punished with a just penalty."; b) Canon 1374 states that "one who joins an association which plots against the Church is to be punished with a just penalty. One who promotes or moderates such an association however, is to be punished with an interdict." If examining the concrete situation one suspects that canons 1369 or 1374 are involved, then a penal process could be initiated.

The situation outlined in the question at hand, especially if the persons are public and active members and officers of such a racist group, especially if they have been openly advocating the principles of the group as compatible with Christian heritage, and especially if the local bishop has publicly responded by teaching that such racist groups are not compatible with Christian morality, all suggest the application of canon 1369. There would seem to be a use of public spectacle and speech to undermine the good morality and reputation of Church teaching.

3. Since canon 1369 (and 1374) do not specify an automatic penalty, it would be necessary to conduct a penal process according to law. The following aspects should be noted:

a) According to canon 1341 it would be necessary to initiate some process to ascertain that scandal cannot be sufficiently repaired by means of fraternal correction, rebuke, or other pastoral care. Only then may the ordinary provide a judicial or administrative procedure to impose or declare a penalty. It would, therefore, be presumed that some dialogue would have been initiated between the ordinary and the persons involved to see if they are willing and ready to take the measures needed to overcome the scandal (resigning membership, back off their public position, and/or retract statements). We also note from canon 1347 that a censure cannot be imposed validly unless the accused persons have been warned at least once in advance that they should withdraw from contempt and be given suitable time for repentance. Therefore, some procedure of dialogue is necessary to establish indeed there is no possibility of removing a scandal and no possibility of eliminating the contempt.

b) According to canon 1342 it may be possible after the above process of warning and dialogue that the ordinary issue a decree of penalty by means of an administrative decision (extra-judicial), that is, without a formal trial. The decree would have to show that the persons were in contempt and were in fact violating the canons on public morality in their activity. The decree needs to be accompanied by necessary documents which would record evidence as well as the previous process of warning, dialogue, attempt at fraternal correction, etc.

c) It would seem that the appropriate penalty would be interdict. The notorious, scandalous role of the persons so involved in such associations causes precisely incompatibility with their reception of Holy Communion. The persons should be advised they are not admitted to the Eucharist until the penalty is lifted and their local pastors should be advised not to permit the persons to receive

Holy Communion.

Since the persons involved most probably are not holding ecclesiastical office, it does not seem necessary to impose excommunication as the penalty, since it seems the main problem is the incongruity of their reception of the Eucharist, which the penalty of interdict would resolve until they are reconciled.

4. Another remedy would be that the bishop legislate a local diocesan penal law according to canon 1315, which could involve an automatic penalty of excommunication or interdict *latae sententiae* (c. 1318). This legislation would require a local restatement of church teaching followed by penal legislation, for example: "Anyone who joins or continues to belong to such and such racist or similar organizations which teach hatred, promote bias, teach against equality of persons, and anyone who holds office in such organizations is automatically excommunicated . . . /or/ under interdict . . . and/or absolution reserved to the ordinary." This type of penal legislation, however, would require the usual promulgation of law with one month *vacatio legis* (c. 8). The advantage of the legislation is the elimination of the necessity of initiating a penal process or trial against certain individuals. The disadvantage is the fact that the legislative act involves the bishop making a penal statement that binds the entire diocese, but which, although it may serve as a teaching tool, may still be difficult to enforce on the individuals actually violating the norm.

5. Another pastoral option for the bishop is to delay any penal response to the problem, and to initiate action of his teaching office, issuing a public statement that membership and activity in such racist groups is contrary to Catholic morality and that Catholics in fact are morally obliged to work for justice and an end to prejudice in society. (Such a statement, for example, was recently issued by the bishop of Bridgeport.) The bishop could then maintain magisterial and pastoral vigilance and continue to contradict publicly any statement of those organizations which are contrary to the moral teaching and action of the Church. Then, if the scandal continues or worsens either at the parochial level or in the diocese, the various penal options mentioned above could be initiated. The essence of declared penalties against individuals is precisely notoriety, which unfortunately can serve both the Church's need to clarify and the alleged criminal's need for fame which would exceed the merits of his or her hurtful cause. That, however, may be more a pastoral dilemma than a canonical question.

J. James Cuneo [1987]

CANONS 1336-1337

426

Opinion

See opinion under canon 281.

Canon 1342, §2

Involuntary Dismissal from the Clerical State

In the 1983 Code of Canon Law, canon 1342, §2 does not allow permanent sanctions to be applied in an administrative way against clerics. Can a cleric be dismissed involuntarily from the clerical state without due process proceedings?

Opinion

Canon 290 indicates various ways by which a cleric may lose the clerical state. (For a thoughtful commentary on cc. 290-293, see J. Lynch in *The Code of Canon Law: A Text and Commentary*, ed. James Coriden et al. [New York/Mahwah: Paulist Press, 1985] 229-239.) One way is by voluntarily seeking a rescript from the Apostolic See (n. 3; cf., CDF, instruction and norms, October 14, 1980, *AAS* 72 [1980] 1132-1137; *CLD* 9: 92-101; these norms make no mention of an *ex officio* involuntary laicization as provided for in article VII of the January 13, 1971 CDF laicization norms). The only involuntary way of losing the clerical state today is by incurring the penalty of dismissal from the clerical state (n. 2) (hereafter dismissal).

Dismissal is one of the expiatory penalties mentioned in canon 1336, §1, 5°. As differentiated from censures (cc. 1331-1335), the primary but not exclusive focus of such penalties is remedying damage done to ecclesial values by a given offense and deterring other members of the Church from similar behavior. Such penalties may be inflicted for a given time, indefinitely or forever, as is true for dismissal.

The seriousness of such a penalty prompts the legislator to indicate certain restraints both in its establishment and its infliction. First of all, dismissal is warranted only for eight offenses taxatively listed in the code. (See table 6 in *The Code of Canon Law: A Text and Commentary*, 934. To be added to the list there is canon 1397 on homicide, abduction and mutilation, which explicitly calls for certain expiatory penalties and provides implicitly for possible dismissal in

427

truly serious cases.) Furthermore, a concern to protect the rights of clerics underlies the prohibition on dismissal being established by particular law (c. 1317) or by a penal precept (c. 1319).

The seriousness of most expiatory penalties including dismissal accounts for the prohibition on their being automatic or *latae sententiae* penalties (c. 1336, §2). Hence they must be inflicted through either an administrative (see especially c. 1720) or judicial (see especially cc. 1721-1728) process. This *ferendae sententiae* approach reflects a main thrust of contemporary penal law reform (c. 1314; principle 9 for the revision of the code). A service-oriented exercise of authority requires that authority figures normally deal directly with the concrete circumstances of every alleged offense.

Another key characteristic of the code is a preference for judicial procedure in the inflicting of penalties (c. 1342, §1). Presumably such a procedure better protects the rights of all involved, e.g., the right to reputation (c. 220). However, this judicial emphasis is somewhat qualified since unspecified "just causes" may at times justify proceeding administratively.

Nevertheless, the seriousness of so-called perpetual or irrevocable penalties such as dismissal requires that they be inflicted only after a judicial procedure (c. 1342, §2). There is a certain proportion between the seriousness of the alleged offense and its corresponding penalty and the seriousness of the procedure used to inflict it.

The alleged offenses warranting such a penalty represent notable violations of significant ecclesial values, and hence, must be addressed seriously by church authorities. Yet when the consequences of a given penalty are so weighty (see c. 292 on effects of loss of clerical state), maximal legal protection is to be provided the accused. The right of defense so forcefully emphasized in marriage nullity proceedings is especially pertinent here.

As in formal marriage nullity proceedings, the basic rules on the ordinary contentious process govern penal procedures (c. 1728, §1). However, as in marriage nullity procedures, some special provisions also regulate the penal process (cc. 1717-1731). It is impossible and in fact unnecessary here to examine the penal process in detail. (See Thomas Green, "Part IV Penal Procedure [cc. 1717-1731]," in *The Code of Canon Law: A Text and Commentary*, 1023-1028.) However, certain points pertinent to a dismissal process might be noted briefly.

The seriousness of dismissal, as differentiated from other perpetual penalties, is further emphasized by the requirement that such a penalty normally be inflicted by a collegiate court of three judges (c. 1425, §1, 2°). In fact, the bishop might choose to entrust such a significant process to a tribunal of five judges (c. 1425, §2; see also c. 1718 on the ordinary's decision to initiate a penal process).

The burden of proof in such a process falls primarily on the promoter of justice (c. 1721), who is to prepare the pertinent accusatory *libellus* (cc. 1502 and 1504) and argue the case for the infliction of the penalty. In accepting such a *libellus*, the court should indicate that the statute of limitation has not run out for the prosecution of the offense (c. 1362) and that every effort has been made to resolve the crisis without recourse to a penal process, which is clearly a last resort (c. 1341). The last resort character that characterizes any penal action is especially true for a dismissal process since such a penalty is never indicated as the first or only penalty for the aforementioned taxative listing of offenses. Rather, such a process is justified only when the accused demonstrates notable and abiding contumacy or the scandal and ecclesial damage is particularly serious.

The code's effort to safeguard the rights of the accused especially in such a process is clear from several provisions. (For some insightful reflections on penal procedure especially from the viewpoint of safeguarding the rights of the defendant, see J. Huels, "The Correction and Punishment of a Diocesan Bishop," *The Jurist* 49 [1989] 535-540). For example, canon 1723 requires the appointment of an advocate for the accused if he has not chosen one (see also c. 1481, §2). Canon 1725 accords such an advocate the right to have the last word in the process. Canon 1726 requires the court to declare the innocence of the accused if this is warranted. Finally, canon 1727, §1 reaffirms ordinary appellate options for the accused, and such an appeal has a suspensive effect (c. 1353).

No one can he punished unless there is a seriously imputable violation of a law or precept (c. 1321, §1). A fairly lengthy Title III of Book VI (cc. 1321-1330) clarifies various factors that may mitigate (c. 1324) or even exempt (c. 1323) one from penal imputability. Canon 1324, §2 indicates that such mitigating circumstances exempt one from incurring a *latae sententiae* penalty presumably because of its seriousness. Analogously such an approach should also be true in the case of dismissal. The principle of penal proportionality seems to require maximal imputability for the infliction of an especially serious penalty such as dismissal. Such a principle also underlies the various provisions for judicial discretion in Title VI of Book VI on the applying of penalties (cc. 1341-1353).

Unlike marriage nullity procedures, which require a review of the first affirmative decision (c. 1682, §1), there is no necessary review of an affirmative decision in a dismissal case, yet an appeal would probably be likely. Furthermore, since this is a status of persons case (like a marriage nullity case, c. 1643), the matter technically never becomes definitively adjudicated (*res iudicata*, cc. 1641-1642), and hence the decision is theoretically open to future challenge for due cause (c. 1644).

Only after the sentence of dismissal is executed does the cleric lose the clerical state and become subject to the various provisions of canon 292, i.e., the loss of clerical rights and obligations, the prohibition of the exercise of orders and the privation of all offices, functions and delegated powers. By way of exception the obligation of celibacy remains and can be dispensed only by the pope (c. 291).

Among the clerical rights that are lost is the right to appropriate support (c. 281), which is operative even while the cleric is subject to every other kind of penalty (c. 1350, §1). However, pastoral charity may oblige the ordinary to provide as best he can for the dismissed cleric who is truly in need because of the penalty (c. 1350, §2).

In short the canons on the dismissal process attempt to provide for the welfare of the People of God, who may be harmed seriously by certain clerical offenses. Yet they attempt also to ensure due process for the accused cleric, who for a certain time at least has committed himself to the service of the People of God.

Thomas J. Green [1991]

ANOTHER OPINION

This question is one that is coming to the fore more and more frequently as dioceses face the problem of what to do in cases of serious clerical misconduct in which the cleric can never be returned to the active ministry.

In dealing, for example, with the situation of a fixated pedophile in which successful treatment is highly unlikely, the circumstances are tragic not only for the victims of the sexual abuse, they are equally tragic for the cleric who may or may not be able to deal with the fact of his illness. The local church or religious institute must deal with the scandal, the anger and the pain that always accompanies such cases; and there are serious questions in the areas of liability and responsibility which must be faced in providing treatment for the young victims and their families, to assist them in re-building lives which have been shattered by this experience.

In the midst of the intense emotions surrounding cases of this sort, the Church must also deal with the fact that the offending cleric in all likelihood will never be reassigned to pastoral ministry because of the clear danger of recidivism and the risk and liability which reassignment would entail. If the cleric is in a serious state of denial, even in the face of convincing proof to the contrary, and yet continues adamantly to refuse to seek laicization, the local church is presented with significant difficulties.

In direct response to the question which has been presented, a cleric cannot be dismissed involuntarily from the clerical state by means of an administrative application of the penalty of dismissal from the clerical state or without due process. This would not only be a violation of the principle in canon 1342, §2, which does not permit the imposition or declaration by administrative decree of perpetual penalties, it would also be a violation of canon 231, §3, which provides that "the Christian faithful have the right not to be punished with canonical penalties except in accord with the norm of law."

At the present time, there are only three ways in which a cleric is deprived of the clerical state.

1. Laicization

This dispensation, which is granted only by the Holy Father, is sought by means of the special procedures governed by the Congregation for Divine Worship and the Discipline of the Sacraments. The process is initiated through the cleric's own petition.

Unlike earlier processes, which were regulated in part by the 1917 Code of Canon Law and did allow an ordinary to petition for a cleric's "reduction to the lay state" even in cases in which the cleric was unwilling to participate or was opposed to the process, the current procedure requires that the cleric himself present a petition to the Holy Father. Thus, without the cooperation and participation of the cleric, this dispensation cannot be sought and will not be granted.

2. The Penalty of Dismissal from the Clerical State

The means most readily available to an ordinary seeking the removal of a cleric from the clerical state is the judicial application of the expiatory penalty of dismissal from the clerical state (c. 1336, §1, 5°). Since this penalty is by its very nature perpetual, it cannot be imposed by administrative decree; it must be imposed by means of a definitive sentence pronounced by a collegiate tribunal of at least three judges (c. 1425, §1, 2°).

As a penal case, this action is governed also by canons 1717-1728. Thus, it is necessary to examine related issues such as imputability (cc. 1717; 1321-1330) and the expediency of applying such a penalty (c. 1341).

Reverend Bertram F. Griffin, J.C.D., has presented a thorough examination of the canonical questions related to the dismissal of a cleric convicted of pedophilia by means of the judicial process. This examination can be found below under canon 1722.

Canon 1395, §2, provides for the penalty of dismissal in offenses involving the sexual molestation of minors. Father Griffin presents the difficulties inherent in the judicial imposition of this penalty, especially the lack of full imputability on the part of the offending cleric. However, he does conclude that a civilly convicted pedophile can be dismissed from the clerical state.

This conclusion is based on a consideration that the *grave* if not *full* imputability of a fixated pedophile must be balanced against the cleric's abuse of authority or office. He likewise cites the cleric's failure to exercise foresight by taking necessary precautions assuming the cleric's personal advertence to the seriousness of his problem (see cc. 1324, §1, 10°, and 1326, §1, 2° and 3°).

At the present time, a number of cases seeking the dismissal of clerics are before diocesan tribunals. Some have met with success, others are on appeal.

3. The Nullity of Sacred Ordination

A third but largely untested way in which the clerical state can be lost is through the process which declares null a cleric's sacred ordination (cc. 1708-1712). In this process, the cleric himself or his ordinary presents to the proper Congregation a petition impugning the validity of sacred ordination. Again it is the Congregation for Divine Worship and the Discipline of the Sacraments which is competent to handle these cases (*Pastor Bonus*, art. 68); and this dicastery can choose to remand the matter to a local tribunal for investigation and judgment (c. 1710).

A significant constraint in the presentation of these cases is the Congregation's apparent reluctance to examine cases for nullity on grounds such as the incapacity of the cleric. Hence, this procedure remains largely unused.

It is a matter of interest that the 1917 code did contain a process which distinguished between the question of the invalidity of sacred ordination itself and the invalidity of obligations arising from sacred ordination (1917 code cc. 1993-2002). Although the current code does not make this distinction, the earlier procedure provided for the proposal of a question in which a cleric who was demonstrably incapable of specific obligations associated with the clerical state might be "reduced to the lay state" solely on the basis of the radical incapacity. The issue of the nullity of the sacred ordination of the cleric was not addressed.

Although the possibility of using such a procedure and the related jurisprudence is better considered a subject for research, it certainly is not without merit as a matter of speculation to consider the proposal of a model case alleging that a cleric should be removed from the clerical state on the basis that he is a fixated pedophile and completely incapable of "perfect and perpetual continence" (c. 277, §1). Due to this complete and radical incapacity either to assume the obligation or to honor it, such a clerical obligation could be determined personally "invalid" for the cleric with a resulting decision that he be removed from the clerical state.

Gregory Ingels [1991]

432

Canon 1374

Catholics and Masonic Lodges

In the local press it was reported that a Catholic would not be excommunicated for being a member of a Masonic lodge under the new code. Is that correct?

Opinion

Under the 1917 Code of Canon Law, persons who joined Masonic Lodges or similar associations prohibited by the Church incurred an automatic excommunication reserved to the Holy See (c. 2335). In the new Code of Canon Law, canon 1374 says the following:

One who joins an association which plots against the Church is to be punished with a just penalty; one who promotes or moderates such an association, however, is to be punished with an interdict.

There are two things to be noted about this canon. It does not mention Masonic Lodges by name, as the old code did; it does not impose an automatic penalty such as an automatic excommunication. The penalties it does mention can only be imposed by the proper church authorities after following appropriate church procedures.

Therefore, persons who join Masonic Lodges are not automatically excommunicated in virtue of the law contained in the code. Moreover, canon 1313 indicates that if a later law such as the new code abolishes an earlier law or at least its penalty, such as the excommunication in the 1917 code, the penalty immediately ceases. So, any Catholics who were excommunicated for joining a Masonic Lodge under the 1917 code are no longer excommunicated by law.

This does not necessarily mean that the Church approves of people joining Masonic Lodges. There is a general effort in the new code to reduce the number of penalties, especially automatic ones, and to leave the handling of local situations up to local authorities.

However, just before the new code took effect in November, 1983, the Congregation for the Doctrine of the Faith issued a statement in which it held that Catholics who belong to Masonic Lodges cannot go to Communion. Basically this office of the Vatican was making a statement about the morality of belonging to the Masons, not about whether it was prohibited by canon law. The position of the Congregation is that Masonic Lodges, even those which seem to be neutral or even favorable to the Church, still promote activities contrary to the interests of the Church in other parts of the world. Therefore, to participate in such an organization is considered to be gravely sinful.

I think you will find different interpretations among pastors and even moral theologians as to the meaning of the statement by the Congregation. It certainly does not establish a new law, for the Congregation does not have that power. It is making a statement about the objective moral seriousness of belonging to Masonic Lodges. A person would have to take into consideration the statement of the Congregation to determine more clearly whether they are in grave sin by remaining a member of a Masonic Lodge, or even joining one.

I realize the situation seems complicated. That is because in the Catholic Church we are governed not only by canon law, but also by the moral law and the moral teachings of the Church. I suggest that you talk to your local confessor or the local bishop concerning these matters for moral guidance; all I can tell you is that in the new code it is not an automatic excommunication for a Catholic to join a Masonic Lodge.

James H. Provost [1984]

CANON 1378

EXTENT OF PENALTY FOR INVALID ABSOLUTION

Does this canon refer only to lay persons or does it also apply to clergy who would attempt to impart absolution invalidly? Does "valid" here refer only to lack of orders and jurisdiction, or would it also include lack of sufficient sorrow on the part of the penitent? That is, if a priest knowingly gives absolution to those whom he knows are indisposed, does he fall under this punishment?

OPINION

Canon 1378, §2, 2° applies to both lay persons and clergy who may attempt to impart sacramental absolution when it cannot be given validly. It clearly refers to both lack of ordination and lack of jurisdiction. As to whether it also applies to a situation when a priest knowingly gives absolution to those whom he knows are indisposed, I think the situation is not so clear.

From a canon law point of view, canon 987 does not mention that the disposition is necessary for the canonical validity of the sacrament. Canon 10 indicates that a law must expressly state that an act is null or that the person is incapable of acting in order for the law to be invalidating or incapacitating. My opinion is that even if the person lacks sufficient sorrow the absolution is given validly. It may not be efficacious, but that does not affect the validity of the sacrament, nor does it affect the priest. Rather, it affects only the penitent.

James H. Provost [1984]

CANON 1398

CANONICAL PENALTY FOR ABORTION AS APPLICABLE TO ADMINISTRATORS OF CLINICS AND HOSPITALS

Do Catholics employed as directors of clinics or administrators of hospitals in which abortions are performed incur the latae sententiae *excommunication provided by canon 1398 of the 1983 Code of Canon Law?*

OPINION

"A person who procures a completed abortion incurs an automatic (*latae sententiae*) excommunication" (c. 1398).

"Accomplices who are not named in the law . . . incur an automatic penalty (*latae sententiae*) attached to an offense if it would not have been committed without their efforts and the penalty is of such a nature that it can punish them . . ." (c. 1329, §2).

The Meaning of the Canons

A recent explanation of canon 1398 correctly states: "To procure an abortion means to cause directly and intentionally, by means of physical or moral action, the expulsion of the fetus from the mother's womb. . . . In order for the delict to be verified it is required . . . that it be imputable to the extent that they have been the efficient cause of it, either physically or immorally."[1]

Wernz-Vidal accurately represent the canonical tradition behind the present canon: "*Procurers* are those who *directly, deliberately* and *purposefully* take part in the abortion, either by *physical* or *moral* action, e.g., by command, order or threat."[2]

The canon applies only to those who directly participate in the abortive act; it does not apply to those who are removed from such direct participation.

The law recognizes several ways in which a person can directly participate in an act such as an abortion. The first considers the participants to be co-authors of the delict, co-principals along with those who actually bring about or perform the abortion. This "partner in crime" category was described in the 1917 code (c. 2209, §1) as including those who contribute to the criminal act both intentionally and physically.[3] In the 1983 code this formulation is not

435

explicitly retained in reference to *latae sententiae* censures, but such persons could be considered full cooperators and included within the definition of "procurers."

A second category are accomplices. Accomplices are those "principal or necessary collaborators . . . without whose help the offense could not have been committed."[4] Canon 1329, §2 gives a clear description of the application of *latae sententiae* penalties to accomplices in the commission of delicts: "Accomplices who are not named in the law or in a precept incur a *latae sententiae* penalty attached to an offense *if it would not have been committed without their efforts* and the penalty is of such a nature that it can punish them . . ." (emphasis mine).

In the 1917 code, canon 2209, §3 named the principal accomplices as those who order the action (*mandans*), who persuade others to go through it (*inducens*), or are necessary cooperators (*si delictum sine eorum opera commissum non fuisset*). The 1983 code (c. 1329, §2) simplifies the matter by coalescing the categories into one. The meaning is basically the same, but the present canon is even clearer: accomplices who incur the same *latae sententiae* penalty as the principal actors are only those without whose efforts the delict would not have been carried out.

One further matter about the canon on abortion must be noted. Canon 1398 is in the book of the code on sanctions; it is a penal law and, as such, must be strictly construed. "Laws which establish a penalty . . . are subject to strict interpretation" (c. 18). This means that the terms used in the canon are to be narrowly interpreted, understood in a restrictive sense, and not extended, extrapolated, or applied by analogy.

The Application of the Canons

The law, as understood in light of the above distinctions, must now be applied to the question at hand. Do Catholics employed as directors of clinics or administrators of hospitals in which abortions are performed incur the penalty of canon 1398? (The question concerns institutions wherein other medical procedures in addition to abortions are also performed.)

Administrative personnel do not "procure abortions" in the sense employed in the canon. That is, they do not perform the act of abortion themselves.

Could these officers of administration be considered co-authors of the delict, co-principals along with those who actually perform the abortion? As noted above, this would require both intentionally and physically cooperating in the act. However, it is obvious that hospital and clinic administrators do not physically take part in the actual performance of abortions. They are not *co-delinquentes*.

Might they incur the penalty as accomplices? Administrators manage clinics or hospitals, carry out their policies, oversee their activities, including the hiring and firing of personnel; but they cannot be described as "necessary collaborators" in the medical procedures which take place in their institutions. The operations take place whether or not a given administrator is at work on a given day, or is removed from that office and replaced by someone else. The directors of an agency or clinic are not related to the abortions performed on the premises in such a way that the procedures could not or would not have been done without their efforts. Administrators of medical facilities are not necessary in the way "accomplices" must be in order to incur a *latae sententiae* penalty.

Since they do not fall within the scope of those who "procure abortions" in the meaning of the canon, Catholics who administer hospitals or direct clinics where abortions are performed do not incur the *latae sententiae* excommunication provided by canon 1398 of the 1983 code.

The foregoing argument is based on the first and obvious meaning of the text of the canons, which is the fundamental norm of canonical interpretation (c. 17). The conclusion is not contradicted or qualified by the context of the canons, namely the appropriate parts and titles of the book on sanctions in the Church.

If any doubt or obscurity remains, however, in keeping with the canon on interpretation (c. 17) some further clarity is supplied by reference to a parallel place, namely canon 1041, 4°.

This canon concerns *irregularities* for the reception of orders, and number 4 relates to having procured an abortion. "A person is irregular for the reception of orders . . . who has procured an effective abortion and *all persons who positively cooperated in it" (omnesque positive cooperates*; emphasis mine). In sharp contrast to the language of the penal canon, this provision extends the irregularity to all positive cooperators. The contrast in language illustrates even more clearly that the *latae sententiae* excommunication applies only to the strictly necessary cooperators, and not to any other categories or kinds of cooperators.

The answer to the present question prescinds entirely from all of the possible excusing causes (c. 1323) and mitigating circumstances (c. 1324) which are frequently applicable in individual situations. And it also does not consider the very real possibility of an erroneous conscience or a sincere, good faith conviction on the part of a Catholic administrator that abortion is permissible in certain circumstances.[5] It also prescinds from whether the penalty is occult or whether the *latae sententiae* penalty has been declared either by judicial process or by extra-judicial decree (c. 1342, §1). These secondary considerations do not come into play because the prior issue is the applicability of the penal canon. The canon does not apply, hence there is no need to search for excusing causes or mitigating circumstances — as is otherwise necessary before determining the applicability of a canon to an individual case.

The commentators on the 1983 code support this restrictive interpretation of the abortion canon.[6] They outline the categories of cooperation with delicts (e.g., total/partial, formal/material, principal/accessory, objective/subjective, physical/moral) and describe the automatic penalty for abortion as falling on the principal agents (co-authors, total and formal cooperators) or truly necessary accomplices. "If the delict would not have been committed without their cooperation, then they incur the penalty."[7]

Since the 1983 canon on the abortion penalty is substantially the same as that in the 1917 code, the views of respected commentators on the earlier discipline are relevant (c. 6, §2). These authors all describe procurers as those directly participating in the abortive act, either physically or morally (e.g., by command or threat), and effecting the expulsion of the fetus from the womb. Accomplices are those whose act is necessary to the commission of the delict.[8] The commentators do not consider the involvement of administrative personnel who are removed from the scene of the abortion procedures.

Moral theologians, too, when treating of the canonical penalty for abortion, seem to envision procurers and necessary cooperators as those directly implicated in the abortive act.[9] And, whatever might be said concerning the moral implications of any other species of cooperation, close or remote, slight or grave, the penal canon is inapplicable to the case in question.

Those who have studied the historical background of the present canons[10] indicate how respected authors debated the extension of the penalty to those not directly performing abortions. The more probable opinion before the 1917 code held that even the mother was not included under the censure[11] (c. 2350, §1 of the 1917 code expressly included the mother with the addition of the words *matre non excepta.*). Huser carefully delineates the extent to which the canonical penalty reaches co-agents and necessary cooperators:

> Co-agents in the procuring of abortion are all those who conspire by common intention and at the same time physically participate in the specific action or procedure which effects the abortion. Such participants place executive acts, acts which precisely effect the ejection of the fetus, and not those acts which are only preparatory or facilitating to the abortion itself . . . .

> Persons who prepare or sell drugs, sterilize the instruments, counsel the abortion, etc., perform acts that are in themselves indifferent insofar as the execution of abortion is concerned. Such actions do not constitute the specific physical procedure which effects the abortion, but are rather preparatory and facilitating acts . . . .

> Effective cooperators in abortion may be those who by counsel,

material assistance, or by any other means induce or concur in the commission of the crime, provided, however, that their cooperation was *necessary* for the commission of the *abortion in question*. The *abortion in question*: the condition expressed in canon 2209, §3 — "*si delictum sine eorum opera commissum non fuisset*" — must be referred to a specific instance of abortion, not to the crime of abortion in general.[12]

The canonical tradition of sanctions for abortion goes back many centuries.[13] Even its more modern pre-code enactments occurred in the late sixteenth and nineteenth centuries. They envisioned abortions as individual, isolated events involving very few persons. They were certainly not aimed at routinized, institutionalized abortion procedures which take place in complex facilities with many levels of participating personnel. Serious *moral* responsibility exists at all of these levels (e.g., support staff, counsellors, medical assistants, managers, executives, trustees, donors, licensing agents, lawmakers, etc.), but none of them fall under the canonical sanction of canon 1398.

Notes

[1] "Procurare l'aborto significa causare direttamente ed intenzionalmente, mediante azione fisica o morale, l'espulsione del feto dal seno materno . . . . Perché si verifichi il delitto si richiede . . . deve essere imputabile a quanti ne siano stati causa efficiente o fisicamente o moralmente." F. Nigro, in *Commento al Codice di Diritto Canonico*, ed. P. V. Pinto (Rome: Urbaniana University, 1985) 822, c. 1398.

[2] "*Procurantes* habentur qui *directe* et *studiose* et *ex industria*, sive actione *physica* sive *morali*, v.gr., mandato, iussione, minis, in abortum concurrunt." Wernz-Vidal, *Ius Canonicum* (Rome: Gregorian University, 1951) vol. 7, n. 472. Emphasis is that of the original authors.

[3] "Qui communi delinquendi consilio simul physice concurrunt in delictum, omnes eodem modo rei habentur, nisi adiuncta alicuius culpabilitatem augeant vel minuant."

[4] T. Green, in *The Code of Canon Law: A Text and Commentary*, ed. J. Coriden, T. Green, and D. Heintschel (New York/Mahwah: Paulist, 1985) 906, c. 1329, §2.

[5] On following an erroneous conscience, cf., B. Häring, *Free and Faithful in Christ* (New York: Seabury, 1978) vol. 1, 239-242.

[6] F. Nigro, *Commento*, 769-770, c. 1329, §2, and 821-822, c. 1398; F. Aznar, in *Código de Derecho Canónico*, ed. L. de Echeverria (Madrid: B.A.C., 1985) 641-642, c. 1329, §2 and 682, c. 1398; J. Arias, *Código de Derecho Canónico*, ed. P. Lombardia and J. Arrieta (Pamplona: EUNSA, 1983) 802-803, c. 1329, §2, and 835, c. 1398; T. Green, 905-906, c. 1329, §2, and 930, c. 1398. Green's language on the excommunication is ambiguous and sweeping: "All involved . . . incur. . . ." It must be understood to mean all *directly* involved as principal agents or necessary co-operators.

[7] F. Nigro, 770, c. 1329, §2.

[8] F. Cappello, *Summa Iuris Canonici* (Rome: Gregorian University, 1955) nn. 777-778. Cappello excludes from the censure those who permit abortion: "Quare procurantes non sunt neque ideo subsunt censurae qui abortum permittunt, etiam praevidentes ex propria actione illicita indirecte secuturum" (n. 777).

See also: Conte a Coronata, *Institutiones Iuris Canonici* (Turin: Marietti, 1955) vol. 4, nn. 2014-2017; E. Regatillo, *Institutiones Iuris Canonici* (Santander: Sal Terrae, 1956) vol. 1,

n. 1005; Vermeersch-Creusen, *Epitome Iuris Canonici* (Mechlin: Dessain, 1956) vol. 3, n. 551; S. Sipos, *Enchiridion Iuris Canonici* (Rome: Herder, 1954) 394-395; *Código de Derecho Canónico*, eds. Dominguez, Moran, De Anta (Madrid: B.A.C., 1957) cc. 2350 and 2209; U. Beste, *Introductio In Codicem* (Naples: D Auria, 1956), 1048-1050; G. Michiels, *De Delictis et Poenis* (Paris: Desclée, 1961) vol. 1, 326-363. Also see R. J. Huser, *The Crime of Abortion in Canon Law*, Canon Law Studies, 162 (Washington: Catholic University of America, 1942). Beste uses language of intermediate agency, but this too should be understood in reference to the specific act of expelling the fetus: "sive per se sive per interpositam personam; . . . sive mediate sive immediate, ex directa intentione efficiunt. . (1049).

Michiels and others describe necessary physical cooperation as that without which the abortion *could* not have been committed (rather than would not have been committed). Huser states that this interpretation establishes a *dubium iuris* and concludes: "In any event, as long as there is a positive doubt about the necessity of co-operation in a particular case of abortion, the censure of excommunication cannot be attributed to the person thus co-operating" (146).

9   Vermeersch, *Theologia Moralis* (Rome: Gregorian University, 1945) vol. 2, n. 584; Aertnys-Damen, *Theologia Moralis* (Turin: Marietti, 1947) vol. 2, n. 1073; Regatillo-Zalba, *Theologia Moralis Summa* (Madrid: B.A.C., 1954) vol. 3, n. 1120.

10   Huser, 138-148; A. Delmaille, s.v. "Avortement," *Dictionnaire de Droit Canonique* (Paris: Letouzey et Ané, 1935) vol. 1, cols. 1536-1561.

11   Huser, 142.

12   Ibid., 143-146. Emphasis is that of the original author.

13   For a brief summary, see J. Coriden, "Church Law and Abortion," *The Jurist* 33 (1973) 184-198.

James A. Coriden [1986]

Canon 1398

Absolution from Censure of Abortion

May a priest, in the act of hearing sacramental confession, absolve a penitent of the sin of having incurred a successful abortion, and from the censure attached to this sin, or must he contact the chancery before doing so?

Opinion

The serious nature of this sin is evident from the censure or penalty attached to it. "A person who procures a successful abortion incurs an automatic (*latae sententiae*) excommunication" (c. 1398).

Whenever the sin of abortion is confessed, the priest needs to question the penitent to discover whether he or she has incurred the penalty. If the penalty has been incurred, the confessor needs to provide for absolution from the censure as well as the sin.

The need to absolve from the censure may be rare. Any of the following conditions prevent a person from incurring the penalty of automatic excommunication attached to the sin of abortion: habitual lack of the use of reason (c. 1322); age less than sixteen years; non-culpable ignorance, inadvertence, or error without violating the law; relatively grave fear; legitimate self-defense or the legitimate defense of another (c. 1323). In general, since the censure is attached to the sin, any condition which eliminates the sinfulness of the act eliminates the censure. Moreover, the abortion has to be completed for the penalty to be incurred; merely intending to get an abortion does not cause a person to incur the penalty. In most cases, when the sin of procuring an abortion is confessed, the priest counsels the penitent, gives penance, and absolves the person from the sin.

This way of handling abortion makes a departure from the past. Not only did the 1917 code reserve absolution of the censure, but canons 893 and 895 enabled the local ordinary to reserve absolution of the sin as well. Since absolving the sin was so reserved in the many dioceses, the confessor ordinarily had to call the chancery for the faculty to do so. Absolution was usually given sometime after the sin was confessed. The confessor could absolve from the sin of abortion as soon as it was confessed only when the party was homebound or preparing for marriage or when the confessor judged that the faculty could not be obtained from the local ordinary without great inconvenience to the penitent or without violation of the seal (1917 code c. 900).

Canonical provision for reserving the absolution of sins was abrogated by the 1983 Code of Canon Law. The Apostolic Penitentiary, a division of the Roman Curia, judged this provision pastorally obsolescent.

The net effect of this change is that a confessor does not need to call the chancery or in some other way obtain the faculty to absolve from the sin of abortion. Moreover, the faculties of the diocese may also enable the priest to absolve from the censure. He need not call the chancery for that either.

When absolving a properly disposed penitent from the censure of excommunication attached to the sin of abortion, the confessor need not change the formula of absolution. It suffices that he intend to absolve from the censure as well as the sin. Before absolving from the sin, however, the confessor may separately and distinctly absolve from the censure with this formula: "By the power granted to me, I absolve you from the bond of excommunication. In the name of the Father, and of the Son, and of the Holy Spirit." The penitent responds: "Amen."

John R. Amos [1993]

BOOK VII

PROCESSES

Canon 1421

Roles for Lay Judges

What roles are open to lay judges in a tribunal? Specifically, can a lay judge be the presiding judge in a collegiate tribunal? Can a lay judge be delegated for documentary cases? What other specific responsibilities can be given lay judges?

Opinion

Canon 1421 indicates the bishop appoints diocesan judges in the diocese. These are normally clerics (c. 1421, §1). However, the conference of bishops can permit lay persons to be appointed judges (c. 1421, §2).

The qualifications for lay persons to serve as judges are the same as for clerics; namely, they are to be of "unimpaired reputation and possess doctorates, or at least licentiates, in canon law" (c. 1421, §3). No distinction is made on the basis of sex, so properly qualified women as well as men may be appointed by the diocesan bishop to serve as judges. The openness to women as judges is new with the 1983 code.

1. Collegiate tribunal

Canon 1421 states one opportunity for the service of lay judges. One of them can be named to serve on a collegiate tribunal (c. 1421, §2). When serving on a collegiate tribunal, a lay judge can be named *ponens* by the president of the collegiate tribunal; if another has been named *ponens*, for a just cause the lay judge can be designated *relator* (c. 1429). When the collegiate tribunal meets to come to its decision, the lay judge along with the other judges individually submits in writing his or her conclusions on the merits of the case and the reasons, both in law and in fact, for arriving at these conclusions (c. 1609, §2). If the lay judge dissents, that is, "does not wish to accede to the decision of the others," the lay judge "can demand that his or her conclusions be transmitted to the higher tribunal if there is an appeal" (c. 1609, §4).

In addition to these rights common to all on a collegiate tribunal, is a lay judge able to be named president of the collegiate tribunal? Under the 1917 code, this position was reserved to the officialis or vice-officialis (1917 code, c. 1577, §2). The 1983 code has mitigated this requirement. Although the

1983 code states the judicial vicar or his adjutant "must preside" (*praeesse debet*) at a collegiate tribunal, it qualifies this with the phrase "insofar as this is possible" (*quatenus fieri potest*) (1983 code, c. 1426, §2). If it is not possible, some other judge can be named as president of the collegiate tribunal.

What kind of impossibility is involved here? Clearly if the judicial vicar or his adjutant are physically unable to assume the presidency of the collegiate tribunal, someone else must. But the impossibility could also be due to the size of the case load they are carrying, the specific elements (cultural, linguistic, etc.) of a particular case, or other forms of "moral impossibility" which make it necessary to name someone else to preside.

Who would name such a presiding officer? The judicial vicar is responsible for assigning cases to judges. Normally he would name himself or his adjutant to be part of the collegiate tribunal. But in cases where he is not able to be, the law does not state explicitly that he names the president of the college. Could the members of the collegiate tribunal elect their own president? The law states they are to proceed "as a collegial body" (c. 1426, §1), but this has to do with its conduct of the case, not with the constitution of the collegiate tribunal itself. Since the judicial vicar is responsible for the constitution of the collegiate tribunal, subject to further determinations by the bishop (c. 1425, §3), and since the judicial vicar would normally name himself or his adjutant to preside, it remains the responsibility of the judicial vicar to appoint a substitute president from among the other judges.

Could this other judge be a lay person? There is no specific qualification in the canon limiting this position to a cleric. The diocesan bishop could restrict the position, however, in virtue of his overall supervision of the tribunal and in light of the specific possibility of his intervention with regard to the assignment of judges to individual cases (c. 1425, §3). If the bishop has not intervened, and if it is not possible for the judicial vicar or adjutant judicial vicar to preside in a specific collegiate tribunal, it appears the judicial vicar is free to appoint a lay judge to this position.

The objection could be raised that only clergy can obtain offices for whose exercise is required the power of governance (c. 274, §1). Yet the objection is not so much to a lay judge presiding over a collegiate tribunal hearing a specific case. Rather it addresses the fundamental issue of a lay person holding the ecclesiastical office of tribunal judge as such. That lay persons can be appointed to this ecclesiastical office is evident from the specific provisions of the code (c. 1421, §2). Once appointed to the office, the lay judge is equivalent to any of the other judges beneath the judicial vicar and adjutant judicial vicar, and can perform on a collegiate tribunal any of the functions which other judges can perform.

2. *Documentary process*

Could a lay judge be designated by the judicial vicar to decide a marriage case according to the documentary process of canons 1686-1688? This is a complex question and there are two opinions on whether a lay judge could be designated for the documentary process.

It is important at the outset to recognize the nature of the documentary process. It is a judicial, not an administrative, process. It requires a *libellus*, citation of the parties, and the intervention of the defender of the bond. It is based on documentary evidence, which is subject to no contradiction or exception. It is used for cases of nullity based on the existence of a diriment impediment, defect of legitimate form, and defect of a valid mandate of a proxy.

Therefore, the designated judge in a documentary process is indeed judging the case. The judge does not act as a delegated administrator, but as a designated judge, properly exercising judicial authority. If a single lay judge could be named to do this, it would mean that without the participation of two clerics, the lay judge would be exercising a fully judicial office. There are a number of theoretical questions raised by this possibility since the new code does provide for the laity to cooperate in the exercise of governing power in the Church. For a discussion of some of these theoretical questions, see James H. Provost, "The Participation of the Laity in the Governance of the Church," *Studia Canonica* 17 (1983) 417-448.

The specific issue here is when can a lay judge be involved in the judicial process. Canon 1421, §2 indicates that when necessary a lay judge can be employed to form a collegiate tribunal. Canon 1425, §4 permits a single judge to replace a collegiate tribunal "if it happens that a collegiate tribunal cannot be established for a trial of first instance" and specifies such a single judge is "clerical." Does this mean a lay judge may serve only on a collegiate tribunal, and that only a cleric can serve as a single judge? Here is where there are two opinions.

a. First Opinion

The motu proprio *Causas matrimoniales* (March 28, 1971) is the first document in recent times to permit lay persons (and then, only men) to be named as judges (V, §1). It was only in reference to a collegiate tribunal that the conferences of bishops were given the faculty to set up "a college composed of two clerics and one lay man." The restriction of a lay judge to serving on a collegiate tribunal would also appear to be the presupposition underlying the drafting of the current canons (see discussion of *coetus* drafting the canons in *Communicationes* 10 [1978] 231). Prior to the code it is clear that lay persons could be appointed only to serve on collegiate tribunals, which would exclude the possibility of a lay judge being designated to process documentary cases as judge.

Moreover, in the formulation of canon 1425 lay judges are presented as a secondary option — "when it is necessary" they can be employed to form a collegiate tribunal: but otherwise, this first opinion holds that judging pertains to clerics. This is the presupposition underlying commentaries on the 1983 code which have appeared to date. Most do not address the issue directly, but appear to presuppose the limitation of lay judges to serving on a collegiate tribunal; see Acebal in *Código de Derecho Canónico, Edición bilingue comentada* (Madrid: BAC, 1983) 698; del Amo in *Código de Derecho Canónico, Edición anotada* (Pamplona: EUNSA, 1983) 851-852; Ochoa in *La nuova legislazione canonica* (Rome: Urbaniana University, 1983) 387-389; Valsecchi in *La normativa del nuovo Codice* (Brescia: Queriniana, 1983) 338-339; Wrenn, in *The Code of Canon Law: A Text and Commentary* (New York/Mahwah: Paulist Press, 1985) 955. Ochoa in *Il nuovo codice di diritto canonico* (Rome: Lateran University, 1983) 448 and 450, makes an explicit distinction between the possibility of having lay judges and the possibility of a single clerical judge replacing a collegiate tribunal in first instance, but his point is that the single judge is permissible only in first instance; lay judges can be utilized in second instance as well. Finally, Flatten in *Handbuch des katholischen Kirchenrechts* (Regensburg: Pustet, 1983) 986, objects to the very possibility of lay judges in the true sense, claims there is a mistake in the code, and reduces lay judges to serving as assessors or auditors only.

b. Second Opinion

A second opinion, admittedly a tentative one, proposes that the foregoing is not an absolute position, and that an alternative interpretation is possible. This alternative interpretation is based on the following reasoning.

First, canon 1421, §2 is not expressed as a limitation. Rather, it is an empowerment: when necessary, a lay judge may serve on a collegiate tribunal. In itself it does not restrict a lay judge to serving in this manner. For example, even though not a member of the collegiate tribunal itself, a lay judge could be named auditor in a particular case (c. 1428, §1).

Second, canon 1425, §4 directly concerns only cases in which a collegiate tribunal is required. The law requires a collegiate tribunal to be established in cases concerning the bond of marriage, but treats the documentary process as a separate matter ("with due regard for the prescriptions of cc. 1686 and 1688" — c. 1425, §1, 1°, b). Clearly a lay judge is not to be named as a single judge to hear a marriage case according to the ordinary procedure. But since canon 1425 explicitly respects the provision of canon 1686 that a single judge might hear documentary eases, and since the restriction of single judge to clerics applies specifically to situations where a collegiate tribunal would normally be required, this second opinion proposes it would appear that the judicial vicar is not restricted as to whom he may delegate in determining the judge for a documentary process.

Further confirmation of this opinion may be contained in the provision of canon 1686: "omitting the formalities of the ordinary process." If the requirement for a collegiate tribunal in marriage cases contained in canon 1425, §1 is considered to be a formality of the ordinary process, then the restriction to clerics when there is an exception to the collegiate tribunal, as provided for in canon 1425, §4, is also a formality of the ordinary process and does not apply to the documentary process.

Moreover, canon 1686 states the documentary procedure is conducted by the judicial vicar "or a judge designated by him." It does not restrict the designation to a "clerical judge" as canon 1425, §4 does when a single judge is to be used in the ordinary procedure. Since the canon states the freedom of the judicial vicar to make this determination, and since the procedure in canon 1686 is clearly an exception to the ordinary procedure, limiting his free designation to clerical judges does not appear warranted by a strict reading of the text of the law, even though it may be the common presupposition of the commentators.

To sum up, according to this second opinion (which is admittedly tentative, and a minority view), the code does not prohibit a judicial vicar from appointing a lay judge to a documentary process, even though it does require that for the ordinary process a cleric be named if the case is to be heard by a single judge rather than by a collegiate tribunal.

c. Personal Comment

In my opinion, while this second approach is not common and does not represent the understanding prior to the new code, it is based on an analysis of the canons and merits serious consideration. Since no restriction is given which would make the condition of being a cleric necessary for valid appointment as a judge in documentary cases, the appointment of a lay judge would at least be valid (see c. 149, §2). If one accepts the second opinion above, the appointment would also be licit. From the point of view of the first opinion, however, it would be illicit.

3. Other Functions

In addition to the functions explicitly mentioned outside collegiate tribunals (e.g., auditor — c. 1428), if the second opinion above is adopted there appear to be other functions lay judges might perform for a tribunal.

Canon 1425, §1 restricts certain cases to collegiate tribunals: contentious cases which concern ordination or the nullity of marriage, and penal cases in which the penalties of dismissal from the clerical state or excommunication are at risk. In other contentious and penal cases there is no restriction by the code to use a collegiate tribunal, although the bishop may determine that a collegiate tribunal is to be used if the case is more difficult or of greater importance (c. 1425, §2). In all other cases a single judge may be designated. According to the second opinion above, there does not appear to be a restriction to clerical judges for these other cases.

To repeat the argument made earlier, canon 1425, §4 limits entrusting a case to a single clerical judge in those situations where "it happens that a collegiate tribunal cannot be established for a trial of first instance." That is, the restriction limiting appointment as a single judge to *clerics* exists in those situations where a collegiate tribunal should have been appointed, but as an *exception* a single judge is being used instead. It can be argued that it is only when an exception is being made that the code (c. 1425, §4) limits appointment to a cleric as judge; otherwise, the judicial vicar assigns judges to cases in turn, whether it be a lay judge or a clerical judge who comes next in turn (c. 1425, §3). So, if a collegiate tribunal is not required for a trial of first instance, and if the bishop does not specifically intervene to require a collegiate tribunal (c. 1425, §2), the use of a single judge is not an exception, and therefore, does not entail the limitation to a clerical judge.

On the basis of the same argument it would appear that lay judges could serve in cases relating to arbitration (c. 1716).

Following either opinion as to the appointment of a lay judge as sole judge in a case, there are other activities commonly committed to tribunals in the United States which are properly the responsibility of the local ordinary personally. In these cases any official of the tribunal, even the judicial vicar, acts as a delegate of the local ordinary. It would appear that where there are no restrictions limiting the ordinary to delegate only clerics in such situations, lay persons could be delegated. They are capable of cooperating in the exercise of the executive power of governance (c. 127, §2), which would include this kind of delegation. Here are some possibilities.

Cases of lack of form (i.e., where there was no species of form at all) are not subject to the ordinary or documentary processes, but in virtue of an authentic interpretation of the Code Commission (June 26, 1984) these cases are to be resolved as part of the investigation of freedom to marry. The code requires the permission of the local ordinary before assisting at "a marriage of a person who is bound by natural obligations toward another party or toward children, arising from a prior union" (c. 1071, §1, 3°). In some dioceses the diocesan bishop has delegated the diocesan tribunal to review these cases in his stead and to issue a declaration of freedom. Since this is not properly a tribunal function, but is a pastoral administrative function which in those dioceses has been delegated to the tribunal by the bishop, a lay judge could be assigned to carry out this responsibility provided the bishop did not place any restriction against this when he delegated the tribunal to handle these cases.

The diocesan bishop can commit the instruction of processes for the dispensation of ratified and non-consummated marriages to his own tribunal or to another tribunal (c. 1700, §1). He can also decide not to rely on the tribunal, but to commit the matter to a suitable priest (c. 1700, §1). A lay judge, therefore, could be designated in the tribunal to instruct such cases, but only if the bishop committed the instruction of the case to the tribunal. It should be noted that the judge does have the authority to carry out various acts in instructing these cases, but the decision is restricted to the Apostolic See. In this sense the judge who is conducting the investigation is similar to an auditor or *iudex instructor*, although the investigation is not a formal judicial process. Lay judges can clearly act as auditors (c. 1428, §2).

A lay judge could also be delegated in other matters where the decision is to be made by the bishop, unless there is a limitation on to whom the bishop may choose to delegate such responsibilities. Thus, the bishop could delegate a lay judge in presumed death procedures (c. 1707) and in pauline privilege and other cases of dissolution of the bond (cc. 1143-1150). The "judge" in such cases is acting as a delegate of the local ordinary, not in a strictly judicial capacity.

Norms for the preparation of privilege of the faith cases indicate the process is drawn up by the local ordinary personally or "through another ecclesiastic delegated by him" (Article 1, Procedural Norms of December 6, 1973; *CLD* 8: 1179). Petitions for dispensation from priestly celibacy can only be prepared by the bishop or a priest delegated by him (Article 4, Procedural Norms of October 14, 1980; *The Jurist* 41 [1981] 226). The code restricts serving as a notary to a priest in cases where a priest's reputation may be called into question (c. 483, §2); all the more, it would seem, must it be a priest who is delegated in cases for dispensation from priestly celibacy, or as judge in other cases where a priest's reputation is at stake.

James H. Provost [1985]

CANONS 1421; 1432; 1435; AND 1469

APPOINTMENT OF JUDGES AND DEFENDERS OF THE BOND FROM OUTSIDE THE DIOCESE AND THE PLACE OF THEIR EXERCISE OF JURISDICTION

An archdiocese does not have sufficient qualified personnel to provide adequate judges and defenders of the bond to process, within the time limits established in the law, the cases sent to it on appeal by the suffragan dioceses. Is it possible for the archbishop to appoint as judges and defenders on his metropolitan tribunal, qualified persons who live outside the territory of the archdiocese, and who may even be impeded from coming within that territory to exercise their office on the metropolitan tribunal?

OPINION

There are two issues here. The first concerns who can be named to be a judge or defender on a metropolitan tribunal; the second is the place where the judge or defender acts.

Canon 1421 covers the naming of judges, and canons 1430-1435 concerns the naming of defenders of the bond. They are to be appointed "in the diocese" and are to be persons who possess certain qualities (unimpaired reputation, degree in canon law, and for defenders, of proven prudence and zeal for justice). The canons do not require, however, that the person be incardinated in the diocese (if he is a cleric) or have a domicile or quasi-domicile in that diocese.

The responsibility for naming judges and defenders of the bond lies with the bishop (cc. 1421, 1435). It is his duty, and so his right in keeping with that duty, to name these officials. In the exercise of this duty and right, the bishop is limited by those limitations expressly stated in the law, or by specific actions of higher authorities such as the Apostolic See or the conference of bishops. This is the meaning of canon 18, which requires a strict interpretation to be placed on laws that restrict the free exercise of rights; canon 157 on the competence of the diocesan bishop to provide for ecclesiastical offices in his own particular church by free conferral; and canon 149 on the competence required for appointment to an office.

Since the law does not restrict the bishop to selecting persons who are incardinated in the diocese or have a domicile or quasi-domicile in the diocese, the bishop is free to select persons even from outside his diocese to serve on the tribunal. In other words, it is possible to name someone to a metropolitan tribunal who lives outside the territory of the archdiocese.

The second issue concerns where judges and defenders of the bond may perform their duties. Since the exercise of the power of governance resides directly with the judge, and not with the defender of the bond, this issue concerns only the judge.

The general principle of law is that the power of governance, or jurisdiction, is usually limited to the territory of the one exercising it. The law does make some explicit exceptions. For example, canon 91 permits dispensations to be given outside the territory of the one granting them and canon 136 provides

449

several exceptions for the exercise of executive power.

The general principle limiting jurisdiction to one's territory has been applied to judges from medieval times. It was stated explicitly in the 1917 code (c. 201, §2). The new code seems to presume this principle, but has not repeated the explicit statement of the 1917 code, thus somewhat mitigating the restriction of a judge acting only within his own territory. Why this mitigation was made is not altogether clear; hopefully a fuller investigation of the history of the revision process will clarify this. Moreover, canon 1469 provides three specific exceptions.

The first two of these repeat exceptions known in medieval canon law, and specifically stated in the 1917 code (c. 1637). The first exception is that the judge has been forcibly expelled from his territory (c. 1469, §1). The second exception is that he is impeded from the exercise of jurisdiction in his territory (c. 1469, §1). The third exception, something new with the 1983 code, is that under certain restrictions the judge may go outside his own territory to acquire proofs in a case. For any of these exceptions, the bishop of the place where the judge is acting has a role. In the first two situations, he is to be informed by the judge that the judge is acting in his territory. In the third situation, the local bishop must give permission, and is to designate a site for the judge to gather the proofs.

The situation involved in this query does not pertain directly to the gathering of proofs, for it relates to hearing in second instance cases, which presumably have been adequately instructed already. It also does not pertain to the situation of a judge who has been forcibly expelled from his own territory. But could the condition of a judge who is impeded from exercising jurisdiction within the territory of his tribunal apply to this situation?

The circumstances involved in the query do not seem to be those envisioned by the legislator or in the traditional interpretation of the similar provisions found in the 1917 code. For example, Roberti (*De Processibus*, 4th ed., 1: 461) is of the opinion that the "impediment" to exercising jurisdiction in one's own territory could be of any kind: detention, force and fear, etc.; it could come from public or private authority, provided it is at least relatively grave and unjust. However, his examples would not seem to include an impediment arising out of a shortage of personnel and the physical difficulties of going to the diocese itself where an extern has been named a judge.

But does the law exclude this latter possibility? Some have argued that in keeping with the strict interpretation of law discussed above, this option is not forbidden to the archbishop. They also note that only second instance courts are being considered, not first instance. They argue the judge in first instance should ordinarily be available to the parties, hence normally in the same territory (although even this may not always be required, as in cases heard on the basis of place of contract rather than domicile or other bases). Second instance cases usually rely on the acts gathered in first instance, so it is argued there is not the same urgency of being accessible.

Another consideration which some raise is the role of a metropolitan court of appeals within a province. If, for example, the extern personnel who might be named to a metropolitan court of second instance all came from within the province, those who propose this opinion suggest it would at least be a fitting participation in the archbishop's responsibilities as metropolitan. However, this argument must be viewed with caution, since the authority of metropolitans has become quite restricted in modern times.

In effect, persons of this opinion hold that an archbishop could name qualified persons living in a nearby diocese to serve as judges on the metropolitan tribunal. It may be impossible for these persons to come physically into the territory of the archdiocese to exercise their role as judges on the metropolitan tribunal. But the metropolitan tribunal could constitute them a *turnus*, and forward to them the appropriate acts of cases which have been submitted to it as court of second instance; they could perform their responsibilities on behalf of the metropolitan tribunal by meeting in the place where they live — even though it is outside the physical territory of the archdiocese.

Even those who propose such an arrangement acknowledge there are some restrictions which the law imposes. For example, if any of the judges have been involved in the case in any manner during first instance, they are *ipso iure* excluded from serving as a judge in second instance (c. 1447). However, the office of judge on the metropolitan tribunal is not necessarily incompatible with some other office the person may hold in the diocese where he or she is living, provided the person is able to do the work of both offices properly (c. 152).

It is true that the law no longer requires a bishop to consult the ordinary of a person being named to an office; this was required by canon 149 of the 1917 code. However, it would be normal courtesy to consult with the bishop of the diocese where the prospective judges (or defenders) are living prior to naming them to the metropolitan tribunal. Moreover, the judges themselves are bound by canon 1469 to inform the diocesan bishop of what they are doing.

It should be noted, of course, that the arrangement under discussion here differs from regional or interdiocesan tribunals. In these latter tribunals, the bishops of the participating dioceses form a board, and after receiving the proper authorization from the Apostolic Signatura (or, from the Conference of bishops which itself would seek the Signatura's authorization — see c. 1439, §2) they collegially name the judges, defenders and other officers of the court. In the metropolitan tribunal which recruits additional personnel outside the territory of the archdiocese, it is still only the archbishop who appoints the judges and other personnel of the court; the suffragan bishops do not have a role in this by law, although the archbishop could always consult with them in the process.

The judicial vicar of the metropolitan court retains the responsibility to oversee the activities of judges and defenders of that court, even those residing outside the archdiocese. However, the judicial vicar or adjutant judicial vicar are no longer required to preside in collegiate tribunals; while this was mandated by the 1917 code (c. 1577, §2), the new code permits exceptions to this rule, which binds only "insofar as this is possible" (c. 1426, §2).

Finally, judges of a court who act outside the territory of that court do not thereby gain any jurisdiction over the place in which they are located. Insofar as they are members of the metropolitan court, therefore, judges who might act outside the territory of the archdiocese may act only in cases pending before the metropolitan tribunal.

So in response to your query, it does appear that if an archbishop is unable to provide adequate judges and defenders of the bond to process within the time limits specified in the law those cases submitted to his metropolitan tribunal on appeal, he may name as judges and defenders of the bond qualified persons who live outside the territory of the archdiocese; according to at least some canonists, these persons may be constituted as a *turnus* and issue judgments even outside the territory of the archdiocese if they are impeded from entering that territory to carry out their assigned functions.

Given the limitations of personnel in many other dioceses, this may not prove to be a feasible solution for every archdiocese which suffers such a shortage of personnel. But according to some, it appears to be a legally possible solution for those archdioceses able to obtain the services of additional personnel in this way; such an opinion is not the traditional interpretation of "impediment," but neither does it seem to be altogether excluded by the provisions of the 1983 code.

James H. Provost [1986]

CANONS 1432 AND 1452, §1

DUTY OF THE DEFENDER OF THE BOND

In the observations may the defender of the bond for a marriage nullity case state: "The proofs are sufficient and convincing for me; the marriage is null"?

On the basis of such a statement, may the judge abstain from further instruction of the case, even when the same judge holds that it would be useful or even necessary, and feel obliged to pronounce in favor of nullity?

452

Response to the first question: The defender of the bond can never legitimately declare in the process, "in my opinion, the marriage is null." In fact it does not pertain to this official to judge whether or not the marriage is null.

In marriage nullity cases, "the defender of the bond is bound by office" — as canon 1432 clearly and wisely prescribes — only "to propose and clarify everything which can be reasonably adduced against nullity" of the marriage.

Every word of this legislative prescription is important:

—"bound by office": This is a true duty (the defender not only may, but must) that constitutes the essence of the office of defender of the bond; therefore, the defender cannot dispense him/herself from this, all the more so since this is an office established for the public good;

—"propose and clarify": That is, the defender must not only advance arguments and objections, but also explain them. Therefore, if the defender of the bond sees that these interventions are not duly taken into consideration, he must strive, just as the parties do, to make them count. In fact the defender of the bond, just as the promoter of justice, has practically the same rights that the parties have (cf., cc. 1433-1434, as well as cc. 1451, §1; 1533; 1561 [together with c. 1534]; 1603, §3; 1606; 1626, §1; 1628; 1636, §2; 1678, §1; and 1682, §2).

—"everything which can be . . . adduced": Even when there is but little to adduce reasonably against the nullity of the bond and this little does not seem to be sufficient to prevent the declaration of the nullity of the bond, the defender still must propose and clarify this little (that is, all that there is). These observations can (must) regard not only the considerations *in iure* and the arguments *in facto* adduced during the trial by the parties (their procurators/advocates), or by the judge in the decision rendered in the previous instance, but also the due observance of the procedure, e.g., the way in which the parties and the witnesses were interrogated or the manner in which the reports of the experts were prepared (which might render weak or scarcely credible the testimonies or the reports), the possibility of defense given to the party who is opposed to the declaration of nullity, etc. Furthermore, it must be noted — as can be seen from canon 1432 — that the defender of the bond, being obliged to propose and expound "everything which can be . . . adduced against nullity," can, and often must, *actively demand something*, e.g., propose another witness to be interrogated; propose the items about which the parties or the witnesses proposed by them should be interrogated; request expert reports (*peritiae*); demand the verification of something, etc. Finally, wishing to remain faithful to the mission entrusted to this office in the Church, the defender of the bond will sometimes feel constrained to challenge the decision of the judge.

—"reasonably": The defender of the bond must not, therefore, have recourse to false or artificial arguments; such intervention in fact must contribute to the discovery of the objective truth.

—"against nullity": And not that which can be adduced in favor of the nullity of the bond. The defender of the bond must present to the judge all that can be adduced against nullity (sometimes the respondent joins in doing this); on the other hand, the petitioner proposes and expounds all that can be adduced in favor of nullity (at other times the other spouse joins in this); it pertains to the judge then to weigh the arguments adduced *pro* and *contra* in order to decide whether or not the nullity of the marriage has been proven. This is the dialectic of the process. Its nature becomes perverted — to the harm of the truth — if the defender confuses his/her role with that of the judge or the assessor (the consultant of the judge mentioned in canons 1424 and 1425, §4).

Still one cannot exclude the possibility of a case which is so clear that, even in regard to the observance of the procedural law, there is nothing to take exception to, so that the defender of the bond, after a careful examination of all the acts — remaining within the bounds of his/her responsibility — can and must say that there is nothing to observe or to propose against nullity. In reality, it is difficult to have such a case in which the defender of the bond, who is both diligent and prepared, will not have anything to propose. In the cases examined by the Apostolic Signatura — in which the defender of the bond has declared that there is nothing to object (or worse, acting against the office of the defender of the bond, has expressed an opinion in favor of nullity) — the Supreme Tribunal generally has had to certify that there was gross ignorance or negligence on the part of the defender of the bond.

In regard to the responsibility of the defender of the bond, I would like to mention two important papal addresses to the Roman Rota: one of Pius XII, given on 4 October 1944 (*AAS* 36 [1944] 281-290, esp. 283-285; English version in *CLD* 3: 612-622, esp. 614-616), and one of John Paul II, given on 25 January 1988 (*AAS* 80 [1988] 1178-1185; English version in *L'Osservatore Romano*, English Edition, [15 February 1988] 6-7).

In response to the second question: On the basis of such a statement by the defender of the bond, the judge cannot abstain from asking for — according to canon 1452, §1 ("once a case has been legitimately introduced, however, a judge can and must proceed, even *ex officio*, in . . . cases which involve the public good of the Church or the salvation of souls") — additional proofs that are considered necessary or useful, and much less can the judge feel obliged to pronounce in favor of nullity in violation of the prescription of canon 1608.

In the case described the judge should, instead, urge the defender of the bond to stay within the limits of his/her proper office and to carry it out with diligence.

Zenon Grocholewski [1992, revised 1993]

CANON 1439

LOCATION OF JUDGES IN INTERDIOCESAN APPEAL COURTS

May an interdiocesan tribunal adopt a system whereby a case tried in first instance is reviewed by personnel of the second instance court who happen to be in the same diocese as the first instance court?

OPINION

1. A judge may act only within the territory of the tribunal, except under very limited circumstances (c. 1469). However, a judge may act anywhere within this jurisdiction, and not just in the place where the tribunal has an office with posted hours of operation. In the case of an interdiocesan tribunal, the judges may act within the entire territory included in the interdiocesan tribunal. Thus a judge of an interdiocesan tribunal may act in the diocese in which the judge resides, or in any other territory of the interdiocesan tribunal.

2. A judge who has served in any capacity on a case in first instance may not act as judge in the same case in second instance (c. 1447). Thus a judge on an interdiocesan tribunal may not review or adjudicate a case on appeal if he or she was involved in any manner in the first instance with that case, whether as judge, promoter of justice, defender of the bond, procurator, advocate, witness or expert.

3. When a case is appealed from first instance, it is to be sent to the court of second instance. The canons indicate that the case is to be sent to the appellate court within twenty days of publication of the sentence (c. 1682, §1) for a marriage case, and that if the judge fails to forward the acts the appellate judge is to compel compliance with this requirement (c. 1634, §2). The acts are to be sent to the appellate court with the authentication of a notary, and in a language intelligible to that court (c. 1474).

Although a tribunal is to have a "seat" which, insofar as possible, is stable and has fixed hours during which it is open (c. 1468), there is nothing in the canons concerning appeals which specify that the acts must be forwarded to that seat. Rather, it is to the tribunal as a juridical entity that the appeal is made, not to a given geographic location.

4. In the case of an interdiocesan second instance court, the appeal is made to the appellate court according to the statutes (by-laws) of that interdiocesan court. The canons require that the judicial vicar appoint judges to hear cases according to a designated order, unless the bishop who moderates the tribunal determines otherwise in particular cases (c. 1425, §3). The statutes could determine how the order of rotation is to be set within the interdiocesan tribunal, and may also contain delegation to the judicial vicar by the bishop moderator of the tribunal which would empower the judicial vicar to make exceptions to that order in particular cases.

Thus the statutes (by-laws) of the interdiocesan court may specify:

a. Where cases on appeal are to be sent, whether to the central "seat" of the tribunal or to those judges who are designated by the judicial vicar to hear the case;

b. The order to be followed in taking turns as judges on cases;

c. Delegation to the judicial vicar by the moderator of the court, empowering him to designate judges out of turn for individual cases.

It is, therefore, within the possibilities of the canons for an interdiocesan tribunal to specify that some or all cases heard in first instance in a given tribunal may be appealed to members of the interdiocesan tribunal resident in that same diocese, provided none of the judges acting in second instance has been involved in any way with the case in first instance and that the time limit of twenty days from publication of sentence is observed. This may be done either according to a rotation set up for the interdiocesan court, or by special designation from the judicial vicar, with proper delegation, for individual cases out of turn.

5. Several factors may be considered in determining whether such a system might be opportune.

a. Certainly in cases in which there is no suspicion of the judges as determined according to canons 1447-1451, there is no legal obstacle to this being done.

b. In cases in which the issue has been disputed openly and thoroughly by the petitioner, respondent, defender of the bond and, if called for, the promoter of justice, the case would seem to have been adequately examined from all sides. There would be little likelihood that review in second instance would surface new material. In such cases, hearing within the same geographic location would not seem to pose a problem.

c. Cases in which the issue has not been disputed either because the petitioner and respondent are in agreement, or because the respondent has failed to cooperate, are still to be disputed openly and thoroughly by the defender of the bond. There would seem to be no legal reason requiring such cases to be sent necessarily to a different geographic location for review, unless this were for the convenience of the parties.

d. It may be argued that those working within the same diocese may have a bias in favor of other members of that same diocese. If the experience of the Sacred Roman Rota is any precedent, this is not necessarily the case; such persons may actually prove to be more critical of the work done within their own diocese.

e. In some special circumstances where those who use a language not common in this country are involved, it may be that the persons most qualified to deal with the specific language of the case live within the same geographic area as that which was able to hear the case in first instance. It would facilitate the observance of the requirement of canon 1474, §2 concerning the language of the acts if the review were handled within that same area.

In light of the above observations, it is our opinion that there do not appear to be canonical or practical reasons standing in the way if the bishops of an interdiocesan tribunal determine to establish the statutes with a system such that a case tried in first instance might be reviewed by personnel of the second instance court who happen to be in the same diocese as the first instance court.

Thomas J. Green [1984]
James H. Provost [1984]

Canon 1481, §3

Right of Defense for a Missing Respondent

What obligation does the judge have to appoint an advocate when the respondent is missing?

Opinion

In a contentious trial, such as that of nullity of marriage, the advocate serves to advise the litigant in matters of law with particular attention paid to the observance of the right of defense. Thus, the special responsibility of the advocate is to defend the litigant before the court by invoking the law in favor of the litigant's legal assertion and by means of deductions inferred from the law

457

and the facts of the case.

The canonical principle of the right of defense is of preeminent importance and of great consequence in a contentious trial. The court is bound by natural law to uphold and protect that right which is substantive to the pursuit of truth in the legal process. The right of defense enjoys such a degree of respect in canonical tradition that when it is alleged that it has been denied or in any way overlooked, the sentence of the presiding judge may be challenged with irremediable nullity (c. 1620, 7°).

To promote the right of defense in a canonical trial, the law provides that both principals may name a personal advocate and procurator (c. 1481, §1). By his or her expertise in the law, the advocate is to help the litigant advance the request made before the court. Since normally the litigant does not have sufficient knowledge of the law and the rights accorded him or her under the law, the advocate's participation assures the integrity of the court and the security of the right of defense.

However, paragraph three of canon 1481 excludes marriage cases from contentious trials involving the public good in which a defender is to be appointed for a litigant who is lacking representation before the court. It appears that the legislator wished to exclude from this norm cases of nullity of marriage for the rather pragmatic reason that the Church does not have the means to carry it out. (For the discussion of this issue, see *Communicationes* 10 [1978] 268; 16 [1984] 61.)

The law establishes certain measures to protect the rights of those who come before the court in litigation. Canon 1490 directs that, as far as possible, permanent advocates are to be appointed in every tribunal. Their major responsibility is to serve those who seek their assistance in marriage cases. In cases where the respondent is missing and an advocate from the tribunal staff has been appointed by the presiding judge, it is clear from the law that the advocate is extremely limited in what he or she may do before the court in favor of the client. The absence of an authentic mandate from the respondent requesting the service of an advocate and permitting the advocate to argue for him or her before the court severely restricts the actions of such an advocate (c. 1481, §1; cf. also, c. 1485).

In cases of nullity of marriage, the law presumes the validity of the bond itself (c. 1060). The defender of the bond serves to uphold the validity of the marital bond (c. 1432) and therefore, indirectly yet concretely, protects and maintains the right of defense of the missing respondent. The defender of the bond is charged with the pursuit of the truth in the matter and, when necessary, is obligated to challenge the allegations made by the petitioner. Through the defender of the bond's conscientious observance of the responsibilities proper to the office he or she holds, the missing respondent's right to defend the validity of his or her marriage is upheld.

It is, therefore, concluded that the presiding judge is not obligated under the law to appoint an advocate for a missing respondent since such an advocate would lack an authentic mandate to act before the court, and thus would not be empowered sufficiently to protect his or her client's rights. The right of defense of the missing respondent is provided for and protected by the defender of the bond who is bound by that office to guard the validity of the marriage, which is favored by the law itself.

Gary D. Yanus [1991]

CANONS 1505 AND 1529

THE GATHERING OF PROOFS BEFORE THE JOINDER OF THE ISSUE

Is it permitted in the beginning of the process to collect certain proofs in order to see whether to accept or reject the libellus?

OPINION

Keeping in mind canon 1505, one must distinguish between:

a. the proofs concerning the competence of the tribunal and the petitioner's legitimate personal standing in court; and

b. the proofs concerning the merits of the case.

According to canon 1505, §1, before being able to accept or reject the *libellus* the judge must verify whether or not the tribunal is competent (in regard to matrimonial cases, cf., c. 1673) and whether the petitioner has legitimate personal standing in court (cf., cc. 1476-1480, and, specifically in regard to marriage nullity cases, cc. 1674-1675). Therefore, the judge must gather adequate proofs concerning these elements before the acceptance of the *libellus*. For example, if the petitioner affirms that the tribunal is competent to treat the marriage case by reason of the quasi-domicile of the respondent (cf., c. 1673, 2°), the tribunal may and must collect adequate proofs in this regard. Similarly, whenever one wishes to introduce a matrimonial case before a tribunal, claiming that it is the forum of most of the proofs, the tribunal must verify whether in reality it is "the tribunal of the place in which *de facto* most of the proofs are to be collected" and whether the other conditions required by canon 1673, §4 in order to consider itself competent are verified (in this regard, see the Declaration of the Apostolic Signatura of 27 April 1989, in *AAS* 81 [1989] 892-894; an

English translation, together with a commentary by F. Daneels, Promotor of Justice of the Apostolic Signatura, is found in *The Jurist* 50 [1990] 289-309; another translation is found in *Roman Replies and CLSA Advisory Opinions 1989*, 45-47.)

The question must be presented differently in regard to the proofs which concern the merits of the case. Before the acceptance of the *libellus*, it is not the judge's responsibility to verify whether the allegations of the petitioner are true or not. In fact, the judge may reject the *libellus* only "if from the *libellus* itself it is certainly obvious that it lacks any foundation whatsoever and [furthermore] that it is impossible that any such foundation would appear through a process" (c. 1505, §2, 4°).

Therefore, in regard to the merit, the judgment about the acceptance or rejection of the *libellus* must be made per se on the basis of the *libellus* alone and not on the basis of the eventual proofs. If from the *libellus* there emerges any possible foundation for the petition, then the judge *must* admit it, without any further examination about the merits of the case.

In this regard it is worthwhile remembering canon 1529, which clearly states, "Except for a serious cause, the judge is not to proceed to gather proofs before the joinder of issues." Such a serious cause could be the danger that later a proof could not be collected (e.g., in the case of the danger of the death of a witness) or could be collected only with great inconvenience (e.g., in the case of someone leaving on a long journey).

If from the examination of the *libellus* there does not emerge any possible foundation, then — and only then — may the judge make a very limited preliminary investigation, but only for the purpose of seeing whether there would not emerge some kind of foundation for the petition. If on the basis of such an investigation some foundation emerges, the judge then must accept the *libellus*, abstaining in this phase of the process from any further verification concerning the merits of the case.

Zenon Grocholewski [1992, revised 1993]

Canons 1528; 1530-1534; 1556-1570; and 1678

Interrogation by Letter or Telephone

May the parties and/or the witnesses be questioned by letter or by telephone?

Opinion

1. Interrogation by letter or by telephone may not be accepted as an ordinary means of questioning the parties and/or the witnesses.

a. This point is clear in the current legislation, for such interrogations do not satisfy the requirements given by canons 1530-1534; 1556-1570; and 1678 of the Code of Canon Law. This can be verified simply by looking at the canons which expressly concern the ways in which the examination of the parties and the witnesses is to be carried out (cc. 1558ff, together with c. 1534).

— The very first of these canons (c. 1558, together with c. 1534), which concerns the place in which the parties and the witnesses are to be examined, shows the intention of the legislator that the interrogation be carried out in the presence of the person doing the questioning.

The same is found in canon 1559 (together with c. 1534), inasmuch as it deals with the question of who can be present for the interrogation.

— In interrogation by letter one cannot be sure about the observance of canon 1560, §1, according to which the "individual (*singuli*) witnesses are to be questioned separately (*seorsim*)." In fact it can happen that the parties or the witnesses, in writing their depositions or testimonies, consult one another. In the same way, one cannot be sure about the fulfillment of this requirement in an interrogation by telephone, insofar as one witness might have already heard the testimony given by another witness present in the same room or speaking on another telephone extension.

— Canon 1561 (together with c. 1534) prescribes:

1) that the examination of the parties and the witnesses be done by the *judge*, or by the judge's *delegate* (cf., c. 135, §3), or by the auditor described in canon 1428;

2) that in each of these cases a notary be present, carrying out the notary's function according to the norms of canons 1567-1569;

3) that the parties, the promoter of justice, the defender of the bond, whenever they are present during the interrogation, may propose further questions (in matrimonial nullity cases, the parties may not be present, but the defender of the bond, the procurators/advocates of the parties, as well as the promoter of justice, in participating in the process, have the *right* to be present during the examination of the parties and the witnesses, "unless the judge believes that the process must be carried on in secret because of the circumstances of things and persons" [cf., c. 1678; in reference to other cases, cf., c. 1559]).

What is required by this canon — considering points 2 and 3 — cannot be fulfilled through an interrogation by letter or telephone.

— In such an interrogation there is also less certainty about the oath prescribed by canon 1562, §2 (together with c. 1534),

— and it is less possible to verify the identity of the party or the witness in keeping with canon 1563 (together with c. 1534).

— In interrogation by letter it is impossible to observe the prescription of canon 1565, §1 (together with c. 1534), that prohibits the communication of the questions to the parties or to the witnesses ahead of time.

— Canon 1566 is not observed in interrogation by letter, and its observance can be doubtful in interrogation by telephone. It requires that the witnesses "are to give testimony orally; they are not to read from written memoranda, unless there is a question of calculation and accounts."

— Canons 1567-1569, which determined the duties of the notary, also presuppose a direct interrogation.

Therefore, there can be no doubt that the interrogation of the parties and witnesses by letter or telephone does not correspond to the kind of interrogation prescribed by canons 1530-1534; 1556-1570; and 1678.

b. Such a conclusion is confirmed by the intention of the Pontifical Commission for the Revision of the Code of Canon Law. In the session of November 22, 1978, during the discussion of what is now canon 1558 — which in §3 concerns witnesses "for whom it is impossible or difficult to come to the tribunal because of distance, illness or other impediment" — one consultor proposed "that a norm be added whereby it is decreed that a judicial deposition, for a serious reason, can be taken by telephone, as long as the judge or notary certifies the authenticity of the deposition," but the proposal was not acceptable to the other consultors, "because such a norm could give rise to abuses and there could be doubts about the identity or freedom of the witness, etc." (*Communicationes* 11 [1979] 114).

Furthermore, it must be observed that the Commission justified the retention of what is now canon 1566 (cited above) in the new code for the following reason: "The canon must be retained in order to avoid those abuses which have already been detected and deplored, according to which the witnesses are not interrogated by the judge, but rather send the judge written depositions, drawn up by the advocate" (*Communicationes* 16 [1984] 66).

c. The Apostolic See more than once has pointed out the irregularity of interrogation by letter or telephone.

In this regard some decrees of the Apostolic Signatura can be cited, e.g., the case of November 25, 1988 (protocol number 20045/88 VT); the cases of March 14, 1989 (protocol numbers 19737/87 VT, 20188/88 VT, 20227/88 VT); the case of November 28, 1989 (protocol number 21183/89 VT); and the case of March 10, 1990 (protocol number 21359/89 CP), in which it is stated, "The request for a written response to the tribunal's questionnaire cannot be accepted as the ordinary way of questioning the parties and witnesses" (cf., cc.

1528-1534 and 1558-1569).

One can also find observations in this regard in rotal jurisprudence. A recent sentence *coram* Doran of March 27, 1991, in reference to an interrogation by questionnaire, speaks of "depositions and declarations made in an erroneous manner." The same sentence notes that this type of interrogation "amounts to . . . a complete surrender of the right [one should even say 'the duty'] of the judge . . . or auditor . . . to carry out, direct, and control the examination of the party or witness according to the norm of law." The sentence then indicates two consequences of such a lack of direction on the part of the judge:

1) "it often happens . . . that the depositions and declarations turn out to be diffuse, vague, indeterminate, often too wordy, and sometimes too terse (as, for example, when the response to a serious and complex question is a single word)";

2) "after an apparently useful response, there is no opportunity to ask immediately, 'who said this, when, how, in what precise words, in what circumstances, where, why,' and other similar questions, in order to provide some support for the answer given."

As a result, the sentence finds little usefulness in such questionnaires, concluding, "all these problems can be avoided and truly convincing proofs can be had by the proper use and the careful application of the method prescribed in the code for hearing the declarations of the parties and the depositions of the witnesses" (*Monitor Ecclesiasticus* 116 [1991] 552, n. 13).

In regard to the use of the telephone, a sentence *coram* Pompedda of February 27, 1984, laments: "Once the notary and twice the officialis-instructor heard the physicians by telephone, as if it were a private matter or one of no importance," observing that "it hardly befits the seriousness of the canonical process and the sacredness of marriage which is its object" (*Rotae Romanae Decisiones* LXXVI [1984] 123, n. 5).

2. Canonical legislation does not provide for interrogation by letter or by telephone even in the case of a party or a witness who is far away or for another reason cannot come to the tribunal in which the case is being heard.

a. In this regard canon 1558, §3 provides: "The judge is to decide where those are to be heard for whom it is impossible or difficult to come to the tribunal because of distance, illness or other impediment." Thus, even in reference to these circumstances, the code still speaks of an interrogation in a concrete place to be determined by the judge, that is, it still speaks of a direct interrogation according to the norm of the canons cited above.

b. Moreover, in reference to parties or witnesses who are located far from the tribunal, the code expressly provides these two possibilities:

—that the interrogation be carried out through another tribunal nearer to the party or the witness (c. 1418);

—that judges, having heard the parties in the matter, travel outside their own territory to carry out the interrogation, "with the permission of the diocesan bishop of the place they enter and at a site designated by the bishop" (c. 1469, §2).

3. Interrogation by letter or telephone is not provided for by the legislator even when a party or a witness refuses to appear before the judge to testify.

Even when considering this kind of case, the code does not mention interrogation by letter or telephone but provides that it is permitted:

—"to hear the person through a lay person assigned by the judge";

—"or to seek the person's declaration before a notary public";

—"or in any other legitimate manner" (c. 1528).

Nor should one say that this third means includes (implicitly) interrogation by letter or telephone, for:

—the expression "or in any other legitimate manner" must be interpreted in light of the two means clearly determined in canon 1528 ("through a lay person assigned by the judge" or "before a notary public") that demonstrate the concern of the legislator to proceed, as much as possible, according to the norms of canons 1530-1534; 1556-1570; and 1678.

Furthermore, one can hardly consider an interrogation in which the prescriptions of these same canons are not observed as much as possible to be another "legitimate" mode of interrogating a party or a witness who refuses to appear before the judge to testify.

It is not hard to perceive the root problem, that is, the reason for which the code does not provide for (or even mention) interrogation by letter or telephone.

4. In truth, depositions and testimonies made in this fashion have a very uncertain probative force, both for the reasons mentioned in the sentence *coram* Doran, and for the fact that they easily lend themselves to fraud, to falsification, to corruption, or just to undue interference of the advocates in the depositions of the parties as well as the interference of the parties and their advocates in the examination of the witnesses. There is no guarantee of the identity of the person who answers the telephone or of the person who really composed the written responses. One cannot exclude a fraudulent substitution of persons or the possibility that the written responses were dictated by another person. Yet the judge, in order to pronounce a sentence in favor of the petitioner, must have moral certainty (cf., c. 1608), namely that which "is characterized . . . by the exclusion of every well-founded or reasonable doubt" (Pius XII, "Allocution to the Roman Rota," October 1, 1942, *AAS* 34 [1942] 339; *CLD* 3: 607).

As a result, an interrogation by letter or by telephone could be justified only by the most exceptional circumstances.

Furthermore, depositions and testimonies made — by exception — in such circumstances must be evaluated with a great deal of prudence. The judge may not uncritically give them the same value as depositions and testimonies given according to the law, but in each individual case must accurately evaluate all the circumstances in order to determine what value to give them.

Zenon Grocholewski [1992, revivsed 1993]

CANON 1593

THE RIGHT OF A RESPONDENT TO BE CITED IF POTENTIALLY VIOLENT

In a given marriage case for nullity there exists real danger of physical harm to the petitioner and the children from the respondent in the event that the respondent knows the whereabouts of the petitioner. How can the rights of the respondent to be cited in a trial for nullity be protected when the petitioner and the advocate request that the respondent not be informed? How can the judicial vicar of the tribunal where the respondent has domicile grant consent according to canon 1673, 3° unless he has first contacted the respondent whether or not he/she has any objections?

OPINION

There are, I suppose, two basic situations envisioned in your question, one where the petitioner requests the tribunal not to give the petitioner's address to the respondent; the second where the petitioner has reason to believe that, if the respondent knows of the proceedings, the respondent will likely inflict some serious harm on the petitioner and/or the children.

In the first case, the tribunal, if asked, simply advises the respondent that the petitioner has specifically requested that the address be kept confidential. It might even help if the tribunal of marriage (c. 1673, 1°) hear the case and that the source of jurisdiction be made known to the respondent so that the respondent has no reason to believe that the petitioner lives within a particular diocese.

In the second case, I personally feel that the solution *might* be to appoint a guardian. Canon 1478 seems to suggest that a guardian may be appointed only for minors and those who either lack the use of reason altogether or at least are of diminished mental capacity. I suspect, however, that if we had a law that was written specifically for marriage cases, it would include two other

465

possibilities as well: the unlocatable respondent and the dangerous respondent. I have a new little book called *Procedures* (a kind of companion volume to *Annulments* and *Decisions*) in which I take this position: that there are *four* occasions when a guardian may be appointed: for minors, the mentally disturbed, the unlocatable, and the dangerous.

This is warranted, it seems to me, partly by the general principles of justice and equity (merely petitioning should not expose the petitioner to almost certain serious harm) and partly by the fact that the commentators on the 1917 code listed chronic alcoholism and even simple drunkenness as equivalent to mental disturbance and, therefore, as conditions that might warrant appointing a guardian (see, for example, Gennaro Sesto's Catholic University of America thesis, no. 358, 42). Being dangerous, in other words, might similarly be regarded as akin to being mentally disturbed.

However, a respondent, generally speaking, has a precious and almost sacred right to know when a tribunal is investigating his or her marriage, and that right should be curtailed only for the gravest and most exceptional reasons. I would see such a procedure, i.e., the appointment of a guardian because the respondent has been shown to be dangerous, as extremely rare.

Also, both the petitioner and the court must consider that, if the marriage is declared null, sooner or later, the respondent may well find out about it, and then what? Does the appointment, in other words, just postpone and maybe even exacerbate the problem? Sometimes yes, sometimes no; it depends on the circumstances.

If a guardian *is* appointed then, of course, the third question posed in your letter is not a real problem since the respondent is considered, in accord with canon 105, §2, to be domiciled in the diocese of the judge hearing the case (or at least of the guardian, which is presumably the same).

Lawrence G. Wrenn [1987]

CANONS 1598 AND 1626

RIGHT OF DEFENSE FOR RESPONDENT

The following scenario and series of questions were posed by a member of a European tribunal:

*The competent tribunal (*forum contractus*) accepts a case and requests the assistance of the tribunal of the diocese where the respondent lives to interrogate the respondent. The latter tribunal cites the respondent twice for an oral* *hearing, but the respondent indicates both times he is only willing to reply in writing. Then, the latter tribunal sends the respondent a questionnaire and he replies in writing in a very cooperative manner (with useful information). The tribunal then sends the questions and the answers of the respondent back to the competent tribunal. Upon the reception of this package this tribunal declares the respondent* contumax. *Hence, he loses the right to be further informed and to canon 1598. The respondent is informed of this but does not react. After all other formalities are correctly observed the case is closed. The defender of the bond hands in his remarks and says that the respondent was* contumax, *but then uses the respondent's written testimony for his argument. In the sentence the same happens: it mentions the* contumax *declarations of the respondent and then it bases its arguments also on his testimony. An affirmative decision is given.*

The case was "ex officio*" sent to second instance where the defender of the bond remarked: Since the respondent was unjustly declared* contumax *and thus did not have access to the acts (c. 1598), the right of defense was violated. Thus, the sentence of first instance was irremediably null (c. 1620, 7°). Hence, there is no need to present any remarks on the content of the case.*

Then the problems started. Why? The Code of Canon Law provides for a complaint against the nullity of a sentence, but who can complain? The parties, the promoter of justice, and the defender of the bond (c. 1626, §1) can complain to the judge who pronounced the sentence (c. 1621).

Among several canonists we discussed this question.

1. Can a tribunal insist on an oral hearing? If the respondent is only willing to answer in writing, is the judge compelled to then submit questions in writing, in order not to violate the right of defense? (The custom is an oral hearing, if necessary through another tribunal). In other words, was the contumax *declaration valid? Personally I do not think so, but how far do we have to go in accommodating people?*

2. Who is the defender of the bond mentioned in canon 1626? I think this can only be the one who was competent in the case, i.e., the defender of the bond of first instance. The defender of the bond of second instance has no right to intervene in the case in first instance. I think the defender can appeal the second instance decision on nullity of affirmative decree if the judges would give that.

3. The defender of the bond of second instance has only to look to the content of the case, not to the procedures, to see if the law was correctly applied (correct interpretation and application of, e.g., c. 1101, but not to the procedures as such). I myself do not agree with that opinion. I think the task of the defender of the bond is both to look to the procedures as well as to the content.

4. Some said canon 1620, 7° did not apply, since the respondent had participated in the case, had been given a chance to bring forward arguments, and did not protest against the contumax *declaration. So the right of defense was not violated in such a way that it constituted a denial of right of defense as mentioned in canon 1620, 7°. (See* Studia Canonica *25 [1991] with the decisions of complaint of nullity of sentence* coram Burke. *I think he would agree with me that the right of defense was violated. The case mentioned there was different, in that one of the parties presented a complaint of nullity.)*

5. How should the tribunal of second instance proceed? Should they declare by decree that the first instance sentence was irremediably null and send the case back? First instance then should publish the acts and continue from there on. What about the following argument: by law one should presume the validity of a sentence. If no party complains about a nullity of sentence, second instance can proceed and decide the case, e.g., by confirming the first instance sentence by decree. (By the way, this case from the perspective of the content is very clear: c. 1101, §2 on the side of the petitioner and that makes it all very sad; it is delaying something which was not necessary). I do not agree with that opinion, and think that if that is done the defender of the bond of second instance can present a complaint of nullity of the affirmative decree of second instance. Suppose the second instance would give an affirmative decision on the latter complaint, what should happen then? (By the way, would the parties in the meantime have a right to remarry since they can presume the validity of the sentence [c. 1684, §1]?)

OPINION

Perhaps it would be best if I began with a series of propositions or opinions.

1. We no longer speak of uncooperative respondents as contumacious but simply as absent. This is because the chapter entitled in the 1917 code as *De Contumacia* (beginning with c. 1842) is now called in the 1983 code *De Partibus Non Comparentibus* (beginning with c. 1592). In the 1983 code the word contumacy is used only in sanctionary law.

2. Lack of full access to the acts at the time of publication does not necessarily involve a denial of the right of defense, as is clear from canon 1598 itself when it says that a judge can withhold an act *cauto tamen ut ius defensionis semper integrum maneat.*

3. Nevertheless, canon 1598 binds *sub poena nullitatis.* It would seem,

however, that when the acts are not published, the sentence can be either irremediably null (when non-publication effectively deprives the respondent of the right of defense) or remediably null (when it does not have that effect). This perhaps explains why canon 1598 is not listed either under canon 1620 or canon 1622 — because it can be either.

4. It is possible for a respondent to be unjustly declared absent and still not be deprived of the *ius defensionis*. This presumably is why the code includes both canons 1620, 7° and 1622, 6°. The code envisions, in other words, that a respondent who was declared absent but should not have been has the right to claim the remediable nullity of canon 1622, 6° but not necessarily the irremediable nullity of canon 1620, 7°. Or, to put it another way, if every such respondent had an automatic right to claim that the *ius defensionis* had been denied, then there would have been no point in including canon 1622, 6° in the code.

5. Every denial of *a* right to defense does not necessarily mean the denial of *the* right to defense. Or, as Erlebach points out (*Monitor Ecclesiasticus* [1989] 508ff.) there is a difference between total and partial denial.

6. When a respondent is declared absent, the declaration according to canon 1592, §1 must be done in accord with canon 1507, §1. Canon 1507, however, expressly allows for the response to be in writing, though it also says that the judge has the right to require a personal appearance. The sense of the canon, however, is that the judge make that determination before contacting the respondent and not afterwards. In the United States, as you probably know, a respondent is regularly offered the option not only of replying in writing to the citation but also of offering written testimony as well.

7. Ordinarily the judge who pronounced the sentence is the one who examines a complaint of nullity (c. 1624).

So, having said all that, let me try to answer your questions.

1. The judge can insist on an oral hearing (assuming it does not work a basic injustice against the respondent), but it must be done before contacting the respondent and not afterwards. I gather from the case history, however, that, in the case at bar, it was done only *post factum*, i.e., after the judge's rogatory commission conveyed to the respondent, at least by implication, that written testimony (an affidavit?) was acceptable, and after the judge received the "package." This, in my judgment, exceeded the judge's competence.

2. It seems to me that it is unclear whether the defender of the bond mentioned in canon 1626 includes the defender of the bond in second instance. Since, however, the Church is loath to allow a truly invalid sentence (*a res odiosa*) to stand, I would think that those permitted to propose a complaint would be interpreted broadly in order to insure that the fewest possible invalid sentences will go unchallenged. Furthermore, even though the case is not

officially opened in second instance until that court cites the respondent, still, even before the second instance court does so it enjoys some jurisdiction over the case. So I would favor allowing the defender of the bond in second instance to propose a complaint.

The complaint should, however, be proposed not to the defender's own court, but to the first instance court to whom the case should be remanded. This is particularly true in the case at bar where the complaint was not proposed along with the appeal (c. 1625). Incidentally, I see a certain analogy here with the hearing in second instance of a *libellus* rejected in first instance. In those cases article 66, §1 of *Provida* recognized the right of the second instance defender to intervene.

3. In general, the defender of the bond in second instance has the same competence as the defender of the bond in first instance. Among those rights of the defender is the right to inspect all the judicial acts, even if unpublished (c. 1678, §1, 1°); so I would say that, in general, a defender has a right to look not just at the content of a case but at procedures as well. More to the point, however, at least the defender in first instance, and in my opinion, the defender in second instance as well, as noted above, can propose a complaint of nullity (c. 1626, §1).

4. I would want to know more facts before making a decision on this, but if the respondent offered clear and thorough information in his written response, if he made it clear that he was satisfied with that and did not wish to participate further, that he did not wish to exercise his right to rebut the position of the petitioner, and if the defender of the bond in first instance argued *pro vinculo* with reasonable diligence, then I would say that the respondent's *ius defensionis* was not substantially violated.

This is not to say, however, that the sentence was, therefore, valid, because even though it might not be invalid on *this* ground, perhaps it is, and I think probably is, on *another* ground, namely, because canon 1598 was not observed. The judge felt justified in not observing it because he had declared the respondent absent, but if, in fact, his declaration of absence was invalid, as the case history seems to indicate, then, in fact, a publication was required.

5. How should the tribunal of second instance proceed? This is complicated, but I would answer as follows. First, the defender of the bond in second instance should determine whether the failure to publish resulted in remediable or irremediable nullity. If the defender decides that the nullity is irremediable (because it deprived the respondent of the right of defense — as noted in answer to question #4, it seems to me that it does not), then he should lodge a *querela nullitatis* with the first instance court which, if it found the complaint justified, would be obliged to rehear the case in its entirety (cf., Goyeneche II: 189, and Doheny I: 520). If, however, the defender of the bond decides that the nullity

470

is remediable, he can either let the three months elapse (c. 1623), which heals the nullity, or can propose a complaint, whereupon the first instance court would again make a judgment on the complaint (according to the oral contentious process prescribed in c. 1627). Then, if it is judged in favor of the complaint, it would publish the acts and proceed to sentence. There are other possibilities, of course, but it would probably get too complicated to try to get into them at this point.

Let me just close by answering the parenthetical question at the end: can the parties remarry while the complaint is pending? The answer, I think, is no, since a complaint is, by its nature, suspensive, even though the code is silent on the matter (*CLSA Commentary*, 998 under par. 161).

Lawrence G. Wrenn [1992]

CANON 1671

CIVIL ANNULMENTS

In an article entitled "Remarks Concerning Proofs and Presumptions" in The Jurist *39 (1979), the opinion is expressed that a civil annulment decree can be confirmed for ecclesiastical effects, by a decree of the diocesan tribunal, for cases involving two non-baptized persons. Our tribunal has received the complete acts of a civil annulment which fits this description, but we have some questions relative to the opinion published in 1979.*

OPINION

1. Why does the opinion limit itself to cases where both parties are non-baptized?

The opinion was written before the new code came into effect. Under the old code the Church laid claim to judge the marriage cases of the baptized; this was an *exclusive* right to judge the marriage cases of *all* the baptized, non-Catholic as well as Catholic (cf., 1917 code, cc. 12 and 1960). So a decision by a civil court was considered to have no effect. For the non-baptized, however, the Church did not make such a claim. Therefore, it seemed that their cases were subject to civil jurisdiction.

The Church does not recognize divorce, but it does recognize nullity. In the case of the non-baptized, the Church seemed to recognize the jurisdiction of civil authorities to determine nullity. Properly understood, a civil annulment may be such a declaration of nullity. So, if a non-baptized person were previously married to another non-baptized person, but the marriage broke up and the civil courts issued a true declaration of nullity, the non-baptized person would be free to marry. No intervention of the Church was required for the Church to recognize the validity of this second marriage, since it was within the competence of the civil authorities.

Under the new code non-baptized persons seem to be subject to the same provisions as before (cf., cc. 11 and 1671).

What would be needed for a non-baptized person who has obtained such a civil annulment to be able to marry a Catholic? If the non-baptized person did not seek to use the privilege of the faith, did the Church have to repeat the work of the civil tribunal or could it recognize the effects within the Church of the annulment granted by the competent civil tribunal?

My 1979 opinion was expressed in the context of a study of proofs and presumptions. I argued that in this type of situation, the ecclesial effects of a civil annulment could be recognized by a church court. A church official had to intervene, however, to determine if the annulment were truly a declaration of nullity and not a nullifying of the marriage. If the civil "annulment" were merely a nullifying of the marriage, declaring the nullity from the moment of the decision as in a divorce, this could not be accepted by the Church as a declaration of nullity. If the civil "annulment" were indeed a declaration of nullity, it would be what the Church means by a declaration that the marriage was null *ab initio*.

A church court could make this determination in the course of a regular marriage case, using the document from the civil courts as documentary proof along with other evidence, and coming to its own declaration of nullity.

The opinion expressed in the article was that it might also be possible for the Church to declare the ecclesial effects of the civil annulment, without rehearing the entire case, given the jurisdiction of the civil courts over the non-baptized. This would be an administrative decree, much as the decree declaring the freedom to marry of Catholics who have not observed the canonical form required of them.

2. What would such a decree contain? Would the tribunal simply use the usual decree and put the civil decree in the file as it is, or would it essentially use the civil decree to create its own arguments?

As indicated above, the civil annulment could be used as the basis for arguments of the church tribunal in coming to its own decision in the case. For example, if the civil annulment were based on an impediment which the Church recognizes as binding non-baptized persons, the procedure of canons 1686-1688 could be followed, using the civil document as documentary proof. If the civil annulment were based on a defect of consent, the civil decree could be used as a public civil document and is to be trusted concerning everything directly and principally affirmed in it (cf., cc. 1540, §2; 1541). It could eliminate the need to obtain additional testimony, thus simplifying the process of instructing the case. But the decision would essentially be that of the church court.

If the second approach mentioned above were adopted, it would mean issuing a decree recognizing the validity of the civil annulment, after examining it to make certain it is based on grounds acceptable to the Church, and that these were adequately proven in the course of the civil case. The decision would essentially be that of the civil court, which the Church recognized as being within the jurisdiction of the civil court to issue and as acceptable within the Church.

As mentioned above, this second approach is an administrative action, a determination of facts to assist the diocesan bishop in making a declaration of the non-baptized person's freedom to marry a Catholic. There does not appear to be a provision in the code for this type of action by a tribunal, but it could be delegated by the bishop to make such a determination on his behalf. Diocesan tribunals are often similarly delegated by the bishop to prepare privilege of the faith cases (an administrative, not a judicial process), and in some dioceses are delegated to determine lack of form cases (again, administrative rather than judicial determinations of freedom to marry).

There are more fundamental issues raised by this question, which cannot be dealt with here. For example, to what extent is this issue affected by the Church's claim to exclusive jurisdiction over cases concerning spiritual matters or matters connected with the spiritual (c. 1401, 1°; see 1917 code, c. 1553, §1, 1°)? To what extent, under the new code, are baptized non-Catholics subject to church courts in marriage cases (cf., cc. 11; 1671), and to what extent could a civil annulment of their marriages be recognized by the Church?

Even more difficult are such questions as whether baptized non-Catholics are exempted from merely ecclesiastical law impediments (e.g., age, certain degrees of consanguinity, etc.). To what extent does the Church recognize the jurisdiction of other courts (e.g., Orthodox Church tribunals), and how is this recognition to be put into practice for individual cases?

Without going into all these issues, it would appear that at least as a source of proof in a standard marriage case, civil annulments which are truly declarations of nullity for marriages involving the non-baptized can simplify the instructional phase of the case. It may also be possible for a bishop to make use of them administratively in coming to a determination of the non-baptized's freedom to marry.

James H. Provost [1988, revised 1993]

473

COMPETENT TRIBUNAL WHEN RESPONDENT'S
WHEREABOUTS UNKNOWN

In a marriage case in which the whereabouts of the respondent are unknown, is it possible to hear the case on the basis of the domicile of the petitioner even though it is not possible to obtain the permission of the respondent's judicial vicar (it being impossible to determine who that might be — see c. 1673, 3°), or is it necessary to refer the case to the tribunal of the place of contract (in virtue of c. 1409, §2, which says that the forum of the petitioner can be used "provided no other legitimate forum is available")?

OPINION

The norms for competence in marriage tribunals are given as a separate set of norms on competence in the 1983 code (cc. 1671-1673). The law itself does not specify that these are an exception to the general norms on competence in processes (cc. 1408-1414), and canon 1407, §1 declares a judge incompetent if one of the titles in canons 1408-1414 is not present. However, such an incompetence is relative (c. 1407, §2), and the provisions of canon 1673, §§3 and 4 are clearly exceptions to the provision of canon 1407, §3 (that the petitioner follows the forum of the respondent). It appears reasonable to conclude that the provisions on competence contained in canons 1671-1673 are applications and explicit exceptions to the general norms on competence, and therefore, are to be followed in themselves when determining competence in marriage cases.

The norms for competence in marriage cases are drawn on the norms contained in Paul VI motu proprio *Causas matrimoniales*, March 28, 1971 (*AAS* 63 [1971] 441-446; *CLD* 7: 969-974). While there are some changes in the provisions of the motu proprio, it has been proposed unofficially by an officer of the Apostolic Signatura that the interpretation applied to the motu proprio may be applied to interpreting canon 1673, §§3 and 4.

In 1973 the Signatura was asked to give a pontifical indult for a tribunal to accept a case they could have accepted under *Causas* if they had been able to locate the respondent and obtain the consent of the authorities in the respondent's diocese. However, unable to locate the respondent, they could not get the necessary permission, so were seeking it from the Signatura as an exception to the general law set down in the motu proprio. The Signatura looked at the purposes for the law and determined the diocese did not need papal permission, but was already empowered to accept the case under these circumstances. (Unofficial translation of the Signatura's decree is attached.)

The same reasoning applied by the Signatura to the request in 1973 applies to the case where the respondent's whereabouts are unknown, and a tribunal seeks to employ the provisions of canon 1673, §3 (on the competence of the tribunal of the petitioner's domicile) or §4 (on the competence of the tribunal where de facto most of the proofs are to be collected, a section based on the provision of the motu proprio addressed by the Signatura's decision).

In effect, therefore, if the whereabouts of the respondent remain truly unknown after serious efforts to locate the person, the tribunal of the petitioner's domicile or the tribunal of the place where de facto most of the proofs are to be collected may accept the case and are competent even though no agreement or consent has been obtained from the judicial vicar of the respondent, it being impossible to determine what judicial vicar that might be since the location of the respondent is unknown. This is an exception to the general norm on competence, but is in keeping with the fact that the norms on competence for marriage cases are distinct and themselves represent an exception to the general norms on competence in tribunal cases.

James H. Provost [1984]

APPENDIX: TRANSLATION OF SIGNATURA'S DECREE

The following is an unofficial translation of the Signatura's decree on competence, based on the Latin text as reported in "SigAp, Decretum de foro competenti in causa nullitatis matrimonii, 6-4-1973" Periodica *62 (1973) 590-591, and in* Documenta recentiora circa rem matrimonialem et processualem, *ed. I. Gordon, S.J. and Z. Grocholewski (Rome: Gregorian University, 1977) 217-218.*

The officialis of a regional tribunal requested on March 15, 1973 a pontifical commission in order that D. Paulus might introduce his cause before that tribunal. The reason given is that all the witnesses which the petitioner can introduce live within the territory of the Archdiocese of M; however, it is not possible to apply art. IV, §1, c., of the motu proprio *Causas matrimoniales*, since the whereabouts of the respondent were not known and so it was impossible to seek the consent of the respondent's local ordinary.

The Supreme Tribunal of the Apostolic Signatura,

having maturely considered the request;

taking into consideration the investigation which has been carried out to discover the location of the respondent;

taking into consideration that the difficulties arising out of the ignorance of the location of the respondent and the consequent impossibility of contacting the respondent's ordinary would also exist more or less in granting competence by a pontifical commission, since generally it is not expedient to grant this kind of grace without hearing the respondent and the respondent's ordinary;

considering moreover that the fundamental reason for the aforesaid art. IV, §1, c, is to render the instruction of the case easier and more rapid; and the consent of the ordinary in these cases is seen more for the safeguarding of the public interest than for safeguarding the rights of the respondent; the public interest, however, can scarcely be harmed in these circumstances but rather would be promoted by the introduction of the case in a place which is suited for carrying out the instruction of the case expeditiously;

having heard the promoter of justice and defender of the bond,

decrees that the regional tribunal of M can treat the aforesaid case without needing a Pontifical Commission.

Given at Rome, from the Hall of the Supreme Tribunal of the Apostolic Signatura, April 6, 1973.

Dino Cardinal Staffa, Prefect
Aurelius Sabbatani, Secretary

CANON 1682

NECESSITY OF RITUAL BEFORE APPEAL COURT OVERTURNED AFFIRMATIVE DECISION OF THE FIRST INSTANCE

Once an affirmative decision in a marriage case has been issued in first instance, it is automatically sent to the appellate tribunal. That tribunal may issue a decision confirming the decision in first instance, or can "admit the case to an ordinary examination of a new grade or trial" (c. 1682, §2).

The problem raised in this query is that a particular appellate tribunal does not cite the parties when it admits a case to an ordinary examination, but proceeds to a decision without notifying the parties in advance. In such a circumstance, the parties have heard from the first instance tribunal that the decision was affirmative, but learn only after some time that their case has been retried in

476

second instance, and that the decision is negative. This poses serious pastoral problems in ministering to the parties.

OPINION

In order to understand an appellate tribunal's responsibilities when it admits a case "to an ordinary examination of a new grade of trial," it is helpful to review the responsibilities of a tribunal of second instance when it has accepted a case that has been appealed to it.

Canon 1628 provides the basis by which an appeal can be lodged:

> The party who feels aggrieved by a given sentence and likewise the promoter of justice and the defender of the bond in cases in which their presence is required, have the right to appeal from a sentence to a higher judge, with due regard for the prescription of canon 1629.

The wording of this canon implies that it is not proper for a tribunal of second instance simply to adjudicate a case on appeal on the same grounds as in first instance and, in effect, ignore the deliberations, determinations and pronouncements of the tribunal of first instance. Rather, the meaning of "appealing from a sentence" ("*a sententia appellandi*") should be taken as a party's being aggrieved not only of the final decision but also the procedures and determinations which have been made by the tribunal of first instance. Presumably it is these same concerns which would motivate a defender of the bond or promoter of justice to appeal from a sentence.

From this understanding of canon 1628, it would not be proper for an appellate tribunal to take as its own the issue as it was formulated by the tribunal of first instance ("whether the marriage of 'Titius' and 'Titia' is null on the grounds of grave lack of discretion of judgement") and then arrive at its own affirmative or negative decision regarding the nullity of the marriage. A more proper question for an appellate tribunal to formulate might be stated in the following manner: "whether the affirmative decision rendered in first instance by the tribunal of 'Antioch' in the case of the nullity of the marriage of 'Titius' and 'Titia' on the grounds of grave lack of discretion of judgement has been determined in accord with the norms of law and properly demonstrated."

Canon 1640 states that "at the appellate level the procedure is the same as in first instance insofar as it is applicable." Thus, those elements necessary for validity, such as the citation of all parties (see cc. 1507 §1, and 1511) and publication (c. 1598, §1), must take place.

In the instruction of an appeal, the tribunal should seek out the reasons for appeal presented by the aggrieved party, and the observations of the defender of the bond; in addition, it should study the deliberations of the judge. But an appellate tribunal also has a responsibility to examine whether or not the procedures followed by the tribunal of first instance were proper. It is altogether possible for an appellate tribunal to find itself in complete agreement with a decision that was rendered by the tribunal of first instance in favor of nullity but at the same time determine that the proposed doubt has to be answered in the negative due to a procedural error at first instance which impacts on the validity of the process.

If the issues have been joined as suggested above, a finding in the affirmative to the doubt confirms the sentence (whether for or against nullity) rendered in first instance. Should the appellate tribunal's decision not find in favor of the nullity of the marriage, the decision must be made whether or not it is proper to exercise the option available in canon 1683:

> If at the appellate level a new ground of nullity of the marriage
> is offered, the tribunal can admit it and judge it as if in first
> instance.

If a decision against nullity is based upon the discovery of a procedural flaw at first instance that can be remedied by that tribunal, it would obviously be preferable to return the case to the tribunal of first instance so that the error can be dealt with. However, if the appellate tribunal finds against nullity but at the same time detects a new or more convincing grounds which would favor nullity, it can determine either to hear the case "as if in first instance" or return the case to the tribunal of first instance giving that tribunal the opportunity of adjudicating the case on these new grounds once it has received a proper *libellus*.

If the appellate tribunal does determine to adjudicate the case on new grounds and does find for the nullity of the marriage, then the case must go to the Roman Rota (which is a tribunal of second instance's usual tribunal of appeal) for its examination and confirmation of the sentence.

This examination of procedures followed in processing an appeal provides a basis for now considering an appellate tribunal's responsibility when it admits a case to "an ordinary examination" as provided for in canon 1682, §2.

If an appellate tribunal has determined that it cannot confirm by decree a sentence rendered by a tribunal of first instance and if no appeal has been placed by either party, the defender of the bond, or the promoter of justice, the only alternative available to the tribunal is, in effect, to "appeal" the case to itself, that is, to "admit the case to an ordinary examination of a new grade of trial."

An appellate tribunal can make this determination after having considered the observations of the defender of the bond and of the parties, if there are any. The same procedures and canonical requirements which regulate the processing of an appeal must then be followed: all parties must be cited, and a joinder of issues must be formulated.

The failure to observe any formalities of law required for validity, such as the citation of the parties, would certainly render null any decision arrived at by the appellate tribunal in instances where it has admitted a case to an ordinary examination and proceeded to a decision without having contacted the parties and allowed them to participate in the process. A complaint of nullity certainly could be sought on the basis of either the failure to cite (c. 1511) or the denial of the right of defense (c. 1620, 7°).

Gregory Ingels [1989]

ANOTHER OPINION

1. The first set of canonical issues the query raises are these: is the second instance tribunal exempted from the usual requirement that the parties be cited (cc. 1640 and 1513, §1); if not, is the second instance's decision null due to denial of the right of defense (cc. 1511 and 1620, 7°)?

In order for the appellate court to admit the case to an ordinary examination of a new trial, it needs to follow all the procedures for an appeal. These include the citation of the parties and the joinder of issue. Not only the provisions of the code (c. 1640), but also the practice of other appellate tribunals — and in particular, of the Sacred Roman Rota — make this quite clear.

Carlo Tricerri, an advocate at the Rota, makes it clear in his commentary on canon 1682 that the provisions of canon 1640 are to be followed in this new examination (cf., *Commento al Codice di Diritto Canonico*, ed. Pio Pinto [Rome: Urbaniana University, 1985] 960-961).

My understanding of the situation is that even for the review of an affirmative decision (c. 1682, §2, first part) the parties are to have been notified that the sentence was issued and that they have a right to appeal, indicating that the sentence will be sent within the required twenty days to the appellate court. This notification could be taken by the appellate court as a citation, but properly speaking it is not - it is only the publication of the sentence (c. 1614: "The sentence is to be published as soon as possible with an indication of the ways in which it can be challenged . . .").

In admitting a case to a new examination, the appellate court must cite the parties and give them a chance to respond to the joinder of issue; otherwise it would seem their right to defense has been denied, and you would have the problem of irremediable nullity arising from denial of the right of defense (c. 1620, 7o).

2. The query raises another question concerning canon 1682; namely, do the provisions of this canon apply only to affirmative decisions in first instance, or

to any decision in first instance (affirmative or negative) in a marriage case.

The answer is quite clearly that canon 1682 applies only to *affirmative* decisions, and only to these when they are given in *first instance*. This is clear from the wording of the canon. Moreover, Lawrence Wrenn in his commentary on canon 1682, §2 states: "This canon, in accord with the general tenor of *Causas matrimoniales* (VIII) and the 1976 draft (c. 347), permits the ratification only of an affirmative sentence." (*The Code of Canon Law: A Text and Commentary*, ed. James A. Coriden et. al. [New York/Mahwah: Paulist Press, 1985] 1014).

His opinion is shared by Tricerri (960-961) and Juan Luis Acebal (*Código de Derecho Canónico: Edición bilingue comentada*, ed. Lamberto de Echeverria et al. [Madrid: BAC, 5th ed., 1985] 814-815), although these place their major emphasis on the fact that only first instance affirmative decisions can benefit from the possibility of ratification by decree, not the first affirmative decision (if given in a higher grade of tribunal).

Thus a negative decision in a marriage case, if it is appealed, must always be heard by the ordinary appellate process (c. 1640). An affirmative decision in a marriage case, if issued by a first instance court, can be ratified by the appellate tribunal, or can be heard by the ordinary appellate process (c. 1640). But for either negative or affirmative first instance decision, if they are to be heard by the ordinary appellate process it is necessary to cite the parties in order for the acts of the process to be valid (c. 1511), and for the right of defense to be accorded to all parties, which is necessary for the validity of the sentence (c. 1620, 7°).

James H. Provost [1989]

ANOTHER OPINION

The question is: what is the meaning of the phrase "admit the case to an ordinary examination of a new grade of trial" in canon 1682, §2? As you suggest, canon 1640, without being very specific, nevertheless provides the answer. It says that "at the appellate level the procedure is the same as in first instance insofar as it is applicable."

Canon 1640, as you probably know, is based on canon 1595 of the old code and on article 213 of *Provida*. As regards canon 1595, Coronata (III, 52, n. 1131) says that those things required for validity in first instance are also required for validity in second instance. Article 213 reads: "In the grade of appeal the Tribunal should be constituted and the court should proceed in the same method and manner as in first instance, not omitting the citation and concordance of the doubt.'' Doheny's commentary on this article (523-528) includes a list of 30 particulars required in a second instance process, including, of course, the citation.

In light of this it seems entirely appropriate to conclude that, apart from the case of a simple ratification, a citation is always required for validity in second instance just as it is in first instance (c. 1511).

If the citation has *not* been legitimately communicated then the sentence is null by reason of canon 1622, 5° and perhaps even by reason of canon 1620, 7° (if, in fact, it can be shown that a right of defense was actually denied).

For an interesting rotal decision on this first question, see the Staffa sentence of October 30, 1953 (45, 634-636).

Your second question was whether it is only an *affirmative* first instance decision that can be ratified and the answer to that is in the affirmative. That is clear from the wording of canon 1682, §2 itself, as well as from the general tenor of *Causas matrimoniales* VIII.

Lawrence G. Wrenn [1989]

CANONS 1682, §2 AND 1684, §1

PLACEMENT OF PROHIBITIONS BY SECOND INSTANCE TRIBUNAL

The second instance court of appeals has developed the practice of adding monita *or* vetita *during the course of their sessions. Is it not unusual for them to insist upon this almost as a condition for the ratification of the sentence of nullity?*

Is such a practice licit? Does it make any difference whether the second instance ordinary process is being used or the ratification procedures described in canon 1682, §2?

OPINION

While the canon cited in this question is canon 1682, §2, the more relevant reference for comment would appear to be canon 1684, §1. In this latter canon, the issue of attaching a prohibition, and by reference a warning, is specifically mentioned. Canon 1684, §1 deals with the effects of the second instance court action and states that when a first instance affirmative decision is confirmed at the appellate level, either by decree or by another sentence, the parties to the case are free to contract a new marriage as soon as the second instance decision

481

is made known to them. However, there is a famous *nisi* clause in this canon! The freedom to marry may be restricted by means of a prohibition. The origin of this prohibition is stated as either the second instance court or the local ordinary. Since the canon specifically states that the prohibition may be in the sentence or the decree of confirmation, it seems clear that the second instance court may attach such a prohibition regardless of whether the second instance ordinary process or the ratification procedure was used. In the former process, the prohibition would be attached to the sentence, in the latter, it would be to the decree.

There is no specific mention in the code about the sentence of the first instance court including such a prohibition. Therefore, it could be argued that only the second instance court is empowered to do so. Thus, it is not a question of whether or not the second instance court acts licitly in the placing of prohibitions but rather whether the first instance court does so licitly.

The first instance court is frequently closer to the case and more involved in the details of the acts of the case and the parties involved. Therefore, it may not be inappropriate for the first instance court to attach a recommendation to the sentence at the time the case is forwarded for appeal. This recommendation, addressed to the second instance court, could state the advisability, or even inadvisability, of the attachment of a prohibition or warning to the sentence or decree of the appellate court. Thus, it would not be a matter of the appellate court's adding or deleting a prohibition or warning, but rather of their considering the recommendation. Information from the court that had the most contact with the party or parties in question could include not only the reasons a prohibition is suggested (or ill-advised despite evidence to the contrary), but also the type of action that would need to be taken by the individual(s) for the prohibition to be lifted. Such information could be invaluable at a later date when a diocesan bishop or local ordinary is faced with the issue of allowing the marriage of a person who has such a prohibition. The decision about lifting the prohibition can be made more easily if the reasons that gave rise to the prohibition as well as suggested remedies were more readily available.

In every case it would seem that the placing of a prohibition should not be done lightly or "as a matter of course." The second instance court would have to balance carefully the individual's natural right to marry against a goal of protecting the institution of marriage and/or a prospective spouse.

Of course, none of what has been said deals with the even more intriguing question of the effectiveness of prohibitions, whether or not the prohibition results in the intended effect of more careful preparation and premarital counseling. (For more on these latter issues, cf., John Lucas, "The Prohibition Imposed by a Tribunal: Law, Practice, Future Development," *The Jurist* 45 [1985] 588-617) There is also the interesting interplay that occurs when the prohibition is placed by the tribunal in one diocese but the prohibited party lives in or seeks marriage in another diocese. Practical and jurisdictional questions arise in such a case but reflections on them are beyond the scope of the present question.

Barbara Anne Cusack [1991]

ANOTHER OPINION

Canon 1684, §1 affirms the right of immediate remarriage following notification of a confirming second instance affirmative decision, whether by decree or sentence, "unless a prohibition is attached to this sentence or decree, or it is prohibited by a determination of the local ordinary." Apart from this canon and canon 1685, the 1983 code offers no further reference to prohibitions. Nonetheless, in practice three authorities by office exercise competence to issue prohibitions: sole judges, collegiate panels of judges, and local ordinaries. Therefore, second instance collegiate panels could issue a prohibition during the course of their sessions. The wording of canon 1684, §1, "sentence or decree," makes it clear that the issuance of a prohibition is not restricted to the ordinary second instance procedure. However, a second instance court's deletion or revocation of a prohibition issued by a first instance court is a questionable administrative act.

As a canonical institute, the prohibition (*vetitum*) has been identified repeatedly and specifically as a personal precept (cf., John Lucas, "The Prohibition Imposed by a Tribunal: Law, Practice, Future Development," *The Jurist* 45 [1985] 596; Peter Lauzon, *The Tribunal Prohibition: Law and Practice in the Ecclesiastical Province of Louisville*, Canon Law Studies [Washington: The Catholic University of America, 1987] 49). Canon 49 identifies an individual precept as a decree. Decrees are regulated by the general norms for administrative acts (cc. 35-47). James Risk, commenting on the provision for the revocation of administrative acts (c. 47), states: "The authority competent to revoke an administrative act may be the person granting the executive power or that person's successor or superior" (Title IV: Individual Administrative Acts [cc. 35-93], in *The Code of Canon Law: A Text and Commentary*, ed. James Coriden et al. [New York/Mahwah: Paulist Press, 1985] 52).

Therefore, the authority competent to revoke a prohibition issued by a first instance judge is that judge or his successor or superior. First instance judges have only one superior: the bishop who appointed them (c. 1421). Second instance collegiate panel judges are neither successors nor superiors of first instance judges. As such, a second instance court's deletion or revocation of a *vetitum* issued by a first instance judge is a questionable if not an invalid

483

administrative act.

David R. Perkin [1991]

Canon 1686

Necessary Competence in order to
Use the Documentary Process

A Columbian couple (the man is in the USA but the woman is still in Columbia) approached their parish priest in Columbia, gave him the equivalent of one hundred dollars for him to prepare them for marriage, and eventually to witness their marriage. However, the priest repeatedly delayed the marriage. When pressured by the couple to prepare them for marriage, or to give the money back, the priest decided to witness the marriage at that moment in the sacristy with no witnesses, except perhaps an altar server. There was no record made of the marriage either in the parish or the civil register.

Clearly, this is a defect of form case and comes under the canon allowing for the use of the documentary process. The question is: Is the USA tribunal competent to use this procedure since the respondent (the woman) is outside the territory of the conference of bishops?

Opinion

In my opinion the answer has to be "no." Traditionally, a "neglect of form" case was considered to be a part of the preliminary investigation prior to marriage which established the parties' freedom to marry (cf., W. Doheny, *Canonical Procedure in Matrimonial Cases*, Vol. I, *Formal Judicial Procedure*, second edition [Milwaukee: Bruce Publishing Co., 1948] 1062-1064). "Lack of form" cases, then, would need no semblance of judicial procedure and could be processed by a pastor or someone else preparing the couple for marriage (cf., W. Doheny, *Canonical Procedure in Matrimonial Cases*, Vol. II, *Informal Procedure* [Milwaukee: Bruce Publishing Co., 1944] 582-584). Doheny is quite clear in stating that if there is any doubt about the neglect of form, the case is to be handled by way of a judicial process.

In the past we have been tempted to view any case in which a duly delegated priest (minister) and two witnesses was lacking as a "defect of form" or "lack of form" case and thus part of the marital preparation (cf., cc. 1066-1067). However, we need to be more nuanced in our phrasing. Indeed, a "lack of

484

form'' case continues to be handled as part of the process of establishing freedom to marry. But a ''defect of form'' case, as canon 1686 notes, requires the citation of the defender of the bond and in my opinion falls under the jurisdiction of canon 1673 (cf., Lawrence G. Wrenn, ''Book VII: Processes [cc. 1400-1752],'' in *The Code of Canon Law: A Text and Commentary*, ed. James A. Coriden et al. [New York/Mahwah: Paulist Press, 1985] 764).

Royce R. Thomas [1992]

Canon 1722

Imposition of Administrative Leave Against an Accused

Canon 1722 permits an ordinary to impose ''administrative leave'' on someone accused of a canonical transgression: ''To preclude scandals, to protect the freedom of witnesses and to safeguard the course of justice, having heard the promoter of justice and having cited the accused, the ordinary at any stage of the process can remove the accused from sacred ministry or from any ecclesiastical office or function, can impose or prohibit residence in a given place or territory, or even prohibit public participation in the Most Holy Eucharist; all these measures must be revoked once the reason for them ceases.'' The question is: May the ordinary impose such administrative leave during the investigative phase of the process (cc. 1717-1719) or during an administrative penal process (cc. 1720; 1342-1350), or is the imposition of such ''leave'' only permissible during the judicial penal process (c. 1721)?

Opinion

Canon 17 gives the hermeneutical rules for interpreting canon law:
The primary hermeneutical rule attends to *text* and *context*.
> ''Ecclesiastical laws are to be understood in accord with the proper meaning of the words considered in their text and context'' (c. 17a).

The secondary hermeneutical rule attends to *parallel* passages, *purpose* and *circumstances* of the law and the *mind of the legislator*:
> ''If the meaning remains doubtful and obscure, recourse is to be taken to parallel passages if such exist to the purpose and circumstances of the law, and to the mind of the legislator'' (c. 17b).

There are two schools of thought among canonists on the application of these rules to canon 1722.

485

I. The Argument from Immediate Causes

Canon 1722 is contained in Chapter II "The development of the process" and immediately follows canon 1721 on the beginning of the judicial process. The words in canon 1722 must, therefore, be understood in accord with the proper meaning considered in the light of the entire canon and its immediate context.

Therefore:

1. The ordinary referred to in canon 1722 who may impose administrative leave is the ordinary in canon 1721 who decrees that a judicial penal process is to be begun.
2. The promoter of justice in canon 1722 who must be consulted is the promoter of justice in canon 1721 who submits a bill of complaint to the judge.
3. The "stage of the process" referred to in canon 1722 is the judicial penal process of canon 1721 and not the administrative process of canon 1720 or the investigative process of canons 1717-1719.
4. The citation of the accused referred to in canon 1722 must either accompany the citation to respond to the accusatory *libellus* or may follow it but not precede it.

Canon 1728, §1 states that the canons on trials in general and an ordinary contentious trial must be applied to the penal trial:

1. with due regard for the special norms of the "title" on penal procedure;
2. unless the nature of the matter is opposed;
3. observing the special norms for cases that refer to the public good.

Hence, canons 1507-1512 on citations are generally applicable. If the petition is accepted the judge must cite the respondent to join issue within twenty days (c. 1507, §2). The accusatory *libellus* or charge is ordinarily attached to the summons, although this is at the discretion of the judge (c. 1508, §2).

The summons mentioned in canon 1722 is a summons by the ordinary to hear the reasons for administrative leave and to show cause why such leave should not be imposed and is to be distinguished from the summons to respond to the bill of complaint.

Nevertheless, it may not be issued until the judicial penal process has begun, certainly after the presentation of the bill of complaint to the judge, and probably not before the citation to join issue, at which time prescription is interrupted and litigation begins to be pending (c. 1512).

The context, therefore, demands the following interpretation.

1. Administrative leave may not be imposed during the investigative phase of the penal process.
2. Nor may administrative leave be imposed during an administrative penal

process.

3. Such leave may only be imposed by the ordinary after presentation of the bill of complaint by the promoter of justice to the trial judge.

4. The administrative leave must be revoked when the reasons cease and is automatically revoked by the judicial sentence which decides the case and which has become a *res judicata* in accordance with canon 1642, or after two concordant sentences in cases of the status of persons (e.g., dismissal from the clerical state) if appeal to a higher tribunal is not made or the appeal is rejected in accord with canon 1644.

II. An Alternative Interpretation Based on a Wider Context and the Secondary Hermeneutical Rule of the Purpose of the Law

Most civil institutions, police departments, schools, charitable organizations, place employees on administrative leave as soon as a sensitive accusation is made and during the investigation. Civil lawyers are urging the church to follow the same procedure when a cleric is accused of a transgression which could involve vicarious liability for the Church. Is this canonically possible?

A. Argument for the purpose of the canon;

Canon 1722 states that the purpose of the institute of temporary "administrative leave" is threefold:

1. To preclude scandals;
2. To protect the freedom of witnesses;
3. To safeguard the cause of justice.

But it is precisely during the investigative phase when such purposes can be met by administrative leave. Witnesses are heard during the investigative phase and their evidence presented to the accused after citation to join issue and respond to the bill of complaint of the promoter of justice. It is precisely during this investigative phase when their freedom must be protected. Once the fact of transgression has been proved, the witnesses do not appear in court personally except at the discretion of the judge. Nor are they cross-examined by the defense attorney or the accused, but only by the judge on the basis of questions presented by the accused. Hence, this purpose of the law cannot be accomplished if imposition of administrative leave is only permitted after the witnesses have been examined.

Although the investigative phase should be conducted in confidentiality with care not to endanger anyone's good name (c. 1717, §2), there are situations where the accusation is already public, or there is danger that it will become public. Scandal can only be *avoided* by placing the accused on administrative leave during the investigation. Once the investigation is complete and the bill of complaint presented to the court, the possibility of "precluding scandal" has

487

long passed. In such cases, the purpose of canon 1722 would be frustrated by preventing the ordinary from imposing administrative leave until after the presentation of the bill of complaint and citation of the accused.

The course of justice includes not only the judicial process itself, but the entire concern of the Church for justice toward the accused, the possible victim and the church community. In some cases, the Church has an obligation in justice to protect a victim from the accused. Certainly after the ordinary receives information that seems to be true of an offense which involves danger to a third party, the course of justice can only be served by isolating the accused from further contact with the possible victim until the case is resolved. Civil law could hold the Church liable for failure to protect the alleged victim or potential victims. A strict interpretation of canon 1722 prevents the Church from adequately protecting the course of justice.

B. What about the context?

The context of canon 1722 should not be so rigidly interpreted as to prevent the purpose of the law from being accomplished. The context of canon 1722 is not limited to canon 1721, but includes the entire *Part IV* on Penal Procedure (cc. 1717-1731). Hence:

1. The ordinary referred to in canon 1722 who may impose administrative leave is the ordinary of canon 1717, §1 who receives information which at least seems to be true of an offense.

2. The promoter of justice in canon 1722 who must be consulted is the promoter of justice appointed in accordance with canon 1430; "a promoter of justice is to be appointed in a diocese . . . for penal cases." In the 1917 code the promoter of justice received accusations and denunciations prior to the investigative phase of the penal process. The 1983 code omits reference to this function. Nevertheless, the 1983 promoter is responsible for providing for the public good and is available for consultation prior to completion of the investigative process.

3. The "stage in the process" referred to in canon 1722 is the entire process mentioned in the title to *Part IV, "*Penal Procedure," and includes Chapter I, the prior investigation; Chapter II, the development of the process; and even Chapter III, action for reparation of damages.

4. The summons of the accused mentioned in canon 1722 has no relationship to the summons of the judge to join issue implied in canon 1721 (in light of the canon that penal trials generally include the norms for contentious trials if applicable). The ordinary may at any time of this entire process, from the receipt of an accusation and his decree to open an investigation, to the completion of the process by decree or sentence legitimately communicated and executed, impose administrative leave.

Hence, the ordinary may impose administrative leave as soon as he has reason to believe, on the basis of information he has received, that scandal is possible and must be avoided, that the freedom of witnesses is in jeopardy and must be protected and/or that the justice concerns of the Church must be safeguarded, including not only the process itself, but possible victims, the community and for that matter the accused.

As soon as these reasons cease, the measures *must* be revoked. They automatically end by the law itself when the penal process ceases and becomes a *res judicata* or at least in the case of dismissal from the clerical state and dismissal from a religious institute (situations concerning the status of persons) the sentence may be executed.

III. Conclusion

In any event, the *dubium juris* raised by canonists on this issue leaves the ordinary free to impose administrative leave whenever necessary during *any* stage of the penal process, until such time as the legislator grants an authentic interpretation to the contrary, or until recourse in a particular case decides that such administrative leave was illegitimate. Accused clerics, other ministers or religious may always petition revision of such a decision and may demand hierarchic recourse. (Administrative leave is not a penalty; hence, recourse against such a decree does not suspend execution.) Hence, administrative leave remains in force unless the immediate superior to whom hierarchic recourse is made grants a suspension.

Finally, a compromise position distinguishes two administrative leaves:

1. As soon as a reasonable accusation is made, the ordinary may place the cleric on administrative leave until the investigation is complete, in virtue of the diocesan bishop's general vigilance over clerical continence in canon 277. He may place the cleric under precept to avoid persons who could endanger continence or to avoid places where there would be scandal. He can also require evaluation, and if recommended, treatment. During the extent of such precepts and treatment, the priest is on temporary leave from his assignment (for pastoral reasons). Such leave should not be protracted longer than necessary. A decision needs to be made by the bishop whether to initiate penal procedures, to extend sick leave for additional treatment if professionals recommend it, to declare the cleric impeded from ministry for psychological reasons or to return the cleric to full or part-time ministry as recommended by professional therapists.

2. If the decision is made to set a penal procedure in motion, canon 1722 can then be invoked during the penal trial and until its conclusion.

Bertram F. Griffin [1988, revised 1993]

489

Canon 1733

Due Process

In developing a revised set of "Due Process" norms for the diocese, the bishop proposes to declare that all who exercise administrative authority by his appointment must submit to arbitration if conciliation fails. Does the bishop have such authority? Can he mandate binding arbitrations?

Opinion

The understanding of arbitration in the Church is really a form of mediation, in which both parties agree in advance that whatever is decided by the mediator is what they will abide by. In other words, church usage of "arbitration" carries with it in this country the notion of free prior commitment by both parties. If the bishop were to mandate such arbitration, it could be questioned whether the prior commitment to arbitration of those who exercise administrative authority by his appointment is really free.

The concern of those reviewing your policy is a real one, however, and here is at least one way I have experienced it being resolved. The bishop could declare as part of diocesan policy that he encourages parties to engage in binding arbitration freely. However, if someone who exercises administrative authority by the bishop's appointment declines to engage in binding arbitration, the policy could also provide that the matter will automatically be submitted to a review panel made up precisely the same as the panel of arbitrators, and that the bishop will enforce the review panel's decision.

This alternative would mean the same procedure would be followed whether binding arbitration were agreed upon (and would therefore be enforced by the prior free commitment of both parties) or whether fact-finding and award were made by a panel acting as delegates of the bishop for resolving administrative disputes.

I hope this is not too confusing. I suggest you review the CLSA's 1991 revised report on due process, *Protection of Rights of Persons in the Church*.

James H. Provost [1986, revised 1993]

Canon 1747

Appointment of Administrator While
Pastor Has Recourse to Removal

Canon 1747, §3 directs the bishop to appoint an administrator for the parish while the pastor's recourse against a decree of removal is pending. No reference is made in the canons on the procedure for removal of a pastor (cc. 1740-1747) to the possibility of appointing an administrator during the process but prior to the issuance of the decree of removal.

In the procedure for removal of a pastor, under what circumstances would the appointment of an administrator prior to the issuance of the decree removing the pastor be canonically proper? Would such an appointment be overly prejudicial to the rights of the pastor in the process? If an administrator may be and is appointed prior to the decree of removal, to what extent may the pastor continue to exercise the office of pastor prior to the issuance of a decree of removal?

Opinion

It is unfortunate that the procedure for removal of pastors is considered by some to be a penal action and is at times actually used as a form of "penal remedy" in dealing with pastors who have abused their office or who are guilty of misconduct. In fact, the procedure exists to deal with circumstances in which the ministry of a pastor has become "detrimental or at least ineffective for any reason, even through no grave fault of his own" (c. 1740).

It is precisely because the removal of pastors is not a penal process that there is no provision such as that in canon 1722 allowing the ordinary to "remove [perhaps not the best translation of *arcere*] the accused from the sacred ministry or from any ecclesiastical office or function" during the course of a judicial penal trial.

In the present case, it is not clear what specific circumstances necessitate the appointment of an administrator prior to the issuance of a decree of removal; it would seem, however, that the questioner is envisioning a situation in which the pastor is guilty of misconduct or has acted in an abusive manner towards the faithful entrusted to his care.

While it certainly would be necessary ultimately to seek the resignation or removal of a pastor who is guilty of misconduct or abuse, the process of removal may not be the most expedient way to proceed at the outset. There are a number of options that can be considered prior to the implementation of the process of removal.

If it is certain that a pastor has committed a crime, an appropriate penalty could be imposed prohibiting the priest from exercising the office of pastor. Thus, if a pastor were embezzling parish funds, this would certainly be an abuse of ecclesiastical office under canon 1389 and could result in the application of an expiatory penalty prohibiting the priest from exercising the office of pastor (c. 1336, §1, 3°), or even depriving him of the office (c. 1336, §1, 2°) if the situation were serious enough or a source of scandal. Likewise, if a priest were guilty of the specific sexual misconduct listed in canon 1395, §1 or §2, the same expiatory penalty could be imposed or the suspension provided in canon 1395, §1, declared effectively prohibiting his exercise of the office of pastor. The decree imposing or declaring the penalty could specify the extent to which the priest in question might continue to exercise the office of pastor.

Of course, any administrative imposition or declaration of a penalty must carefully follow the applicable canons in the penal process (cc. 1717-1720); and it must be remembered that the administrative application of a penalty cannot be perpetual (c. 1342, §2). The principal purpose being served in the application of a penalty in this manner addresses the questioner's concern of removing a priest who is a clear threat or danger to his people from exercising the office of pastor prior to a consideration of his removal from the office. Once a priest is prohibited from exercising the office of pastor, the bishop can name an administrator in virtue of canon 539 to serve until the time limit of the penalty lapses or the priest is removed from the office of pastor.

Not all misconduct that would render the ministry of a pastor detrimental or ineffective is necessarily a crime in the context of canon law. For example, the sexual harassment of a church or school employee or inappropriate contact with a minor, which might have clear sexual overtones, does not necessarily fall directly under those actions to which a canonical penalty might be attached.

If the concern of the questioner falls into these grey areas of sexual misconduct, a careful consideration and application of canon 277, §3, might provide the diocesan bishop with a means of dealing with a potentially critical situation.

For example, if a number of verified reports indicate that a pastor is relating to persons in ways that are inappropriate and clearly sexual, the diocesan bishop might well judge that for his own spiritual good the pastor must be removed from a situation which gives every indication of his possibly being unfaithful to his obligation of perfect and perpetual continence. If later it is determined that the pastor is laboring under problems that cannot be remedied, the effects of this determination by the bishop would remain in place during the process of removal. Again, the decree by which this judgment is made could indicate to what extent, if any, the pastor might continue to exercise his office prior to his removal.

Every administrative act at the diocesan level admits of recourse; and in the application of penalties, recourse is suspensive, meaning that the effect of the penalty is suspended until the recourse is resolved. There does not appear to be a suspensive effect, however, in the case of an administrative judgment rendered in virtue of canon 277, §3. Nevertheless, even if the pastor in question were not to initiate recourse against these types of administrative decisions, great care must be exercised to assure that his rights are protected and that such actions are being undertaken not simply to rid ourselves "of this meddlesome priest" but to exercise the best possible care for the pastor and the flock which was entrusted to his pastoral ministry.

The questioner asks whether such actions would be overly prejudicial to the rights of the pastor during the process of removal. Certainly such actions will influence the considerations that must be made in association with a final decision to remove the pastor. It must be assumed, however, that the facts and circumstances which resulted in a determination to apply or declare a penalty or to make an administrative judgment of canon 277, §3 are clear and beyond dispute. If this is the case, it can only be hoped that the diocesan bishop and the pastors from the *coetus* of canon 1742, §1 will consider this matter in a careful, pastoral and objective fashion.

Gregory Ingels [1993]

INDEX

members of racist associations, 424-426

Schismatic church, confirmation in, 147-150

Seminary and HIV/AIDS Testing, 44-52

Sex Education, rights of parents, 32-37, 274-275

Society of St. Pius X, 147-150

Sunday obligation
anticipated Masses, 399-400
double precept fulfilled at one Mass, 397-399
fulfilling obligation in Traditionalist church, 400-407
Mass obligation, 394-395
substitution of priestless services, 395-397

Taxation
diocesan bishop and public juridic person, 408-410
parish funds, 410-416

Term of office
college of consultors, 106-109
councilors, 171
pastor, limited tenure, 19-22, 129-137
presbyteral council, 103-106

Traditional Mass Society, 23-26

Treasurer (*see* Consecrated Life)

Tribunal (*also see* Annulment, Marriage)
appeal court overturns affirmative decision, 476-481
citation of parties in second instance, 476-481
competence and documentary process, 484-485
competent tribunal when respondent's whereabouts unknown, 474-476
defect of form, 336-338
defender of the bond, 452-455
documentary process, 336-338
gathering of proofs, 459-460
interdiocesan appeal court judges, 455-457
interrogation by letter or telephone, 460-465
judges and defenders of the bond from outside diocese, 448-452
lack of form, 336-338
lay judge, 442-448
missing respondent, right of defense, 457-459
proof of freedom, 336-338
potentially violent respondent, right to be cited, 465-466
prohibitions by second instance tribunal, 481-484
right of defense for respondent, 466-471

University authorities, relationship to bishop, 225-229

Virgins, Order of
admission, 163-164
previously married persons, 165-166

Voting by telephone, 18-19

CONTRIBUTORS

John A. Alesandro, J.C.D., J.D., is chancellor of the Diocese of Rockville Centre.

John R. Amos, J.C.D., is adjutant judicial vicar of the Archdiocese of Mobile.

Jack D. Anderson, J.C.D., is a judge of the Diocese of Scranton.

Nicholas P. Cafardi, J.C.L., J.D., is dean of the school of law at Duquesne University, Pittsburgh.

Randolph R. Calvo, J.C.D., is judicial vicar of the Archdiocese of San Francisco and lecturer in canon law at St. Patrick's Seminary, Menlo Park.

Robert F. Coleman, J.C.L., is instructor of canon law at Immaculate Conception Seminary School of Theology, Seton Hall University.

Patrick J. Cogan, S.A., J.C.D., is executive coordinator of the Canon Law Society of America.

Mary Conroy, O.S.U., J.C.L., serves on the tribunal of the Diocese of Youngstown.

James A. Coriden, J.C.D., J.D., is academic dean and professor of canon law at the Washington Theological Union.

Craig A. Cox, D.Min., J.C.D., is judicial vicar of the Archdiocese of Los Angeles.

J. James Cuneo, J.C.D., is a judge in the Diocese of Bridgeport.

Barbara Anne Cusack, J.C.D., is chancellor of the Archdiocese of Milwaukee, and judge on the Metropolitan Court of Appeals.

Catherine C. Darcy, R.S.M., J.C.D., is associate judge and defender of the bond in the Diocese of Trenton.

James I. Donlon, J.C.D., is judicial vicar of the Diocese of Albany and editor of *CLSA Advisory Opinions*.

Jerald Doyle, J.C.D., is judicial vicar of the Diocese of Bridgeport.

John D. Faris, J.C.O.D., is chancellor of the Diocese of Saint Maron-U.S.A.

Donald J. Frugé, J.C.D., is finance officer for the Diocese of Austin.

George D. Gallaro, J.C.O.D., is chancellor and judicial vicar of the Eparchy of Newton.

Robert C. Gibbons, J.C.L., J.D., is chancellor of the Diocese of St. Petersburg.

Paul L. Golden, C.M., J.C.D., is associate vice president for academic affairs at DePaul University, Chicago.

502

Bertram F. Griffin, J.C.D., is adjutant judicial vicar of the Archdiocese of Portland and judicial vicar of the Interdiocesan Tribunal of Region XII.

Thomas J. Green, J.C.D., is professor of canon law at The Catholic University of America.

Zenon Grocholewski, D.D., J.C.D., is Secretary of the Apostolic Signatura.

James C. Gurzynski, J.C.L., is judicial vicar of the Diocese of Amarillo and judge of the Appellate Court for the Diocese of Texas.

Richard A. Hill, S.J., J.C.D., is professor of canon law at the Jesuit School of Theology, Berkeley.

Jordan F. Hite, T.O.R., J.C.L., J.D., is minister provincial of the Province of the Most Sacred Heart of Jesus, Third Order Regular.

Sharon L. Holland, I.H.M., J.C.D., is a staff official of the Congregation for Institutes of Consecrated Life and Societies of Apostolic Life.

John M. Huels, O.S.M., J.C.D., is associate professor of canon law at the Catholic Theological Union of Chicago.

David H. Hynous, O.P., J.C.D., is a judge of the Metropolitan Tribunal of Chicago and associate chancellor of the Archdiocese of Chicago.

Gregory Ingels, J.C.D., is judicial vicar of the Interdiocesan Appellate Tribunal, San Francisco, and instructor in canon law at St. Patrick's Seminary, Menlo Park.

Lynn Jarrell, O.S.U., J.C.D., is vice-president of the Ursulines of Louisville.

Michael P. Joyce, C.M., J.C.D., is adjutant judicial vicar of the Metropolitan Tribunal of the Archdiocese of St. Louis.

Ellsworth Kneal, J.C.D., is judicial vicar emeritus of the Archdiocese of Saint Paul-Minneapolis.

Joseph J. Koury, J.C.D., is a judge for the tribunals of the Diocese of Portland, Maine and the Melkite Diocese of Newton.

Herbert J. May, J.C.L., is judicial vicar of the Diocese of Lake Charles.

Rose McDermott, S.S.J., J.C.D., is assistant professor of canon law at The Catholic University of America and assistant editor of *Roman Replies*.

Francis G. Morrisey, O.M.I., J.C.D., is professor of canon law at Saint Paul University, Ottawa and editor of *Studia Canonica*.

John J. Myers, D.D., J.C.D., is bishop of the Diocese of Peoria.

Louis Naughton, J.C.L., is judicial vicar of the Archdiocese of Atlanta.

David F. O'Connor, S.T., J.C.D., is chairperson of the department of church law at the Washington Theological Union.

Ladislas M. Örsy, S.J., J.C.D., is professor emeritus of canon law at The Catholic University of America.

Joseph Parampath, J.C.D., is a judge in the Diocese of Bridgeport.

David R. Perkin, J.C.L., is judicial vicar of the Diocese of Nashville and adjutant judicial vicar of the Metropolitan Tribunal of the Province of Louisville.

Joseph N. Perry, J.C.L., is judicial vicar of the Archdiocese of Milwaukee and instructor of canon law studies at Sacred Heart Seminary School of Theology.

James H. Provost, J.C.D., is professor of canon law at The Catholic University of America and managing editor of *The Jurist*.

Joseph R. Punderson, J.C.D., is an official of the Apostolic Signatura.

Esther A. Redmann, O.S.U., J.C.L., is judge and defender of the bond in the Diocese of Springfield in Illinois and for the Interdiocesan Tribunal of Second Instance, Chicago.

Elissa A. Rinere, C.P., J.C.D., serves on the tribunal of the Archdiocese of Los Angeles.

Pius Smart, O.F.M., Cap., (deceased).

Rosemary Smith, S.C., J.C.D., is assistant general superior of the Sisters of Charity of Convent Station.

Royce R. Thomas, J.C.L., is a judge for the Diocese of Little Rock.

D. Timothy Thompson, J.C.L., is judicial vicar of the Diocese of Fort Worth.

Kevin W. Vann, J.C.D., is a judge for the Diocese of Springfield in Illinois and editor of *Roman Replies*.

William A. Varvaro, J.C.D., is pastor of St. Margaret's R.C. Church, Middle Village, New York and a canonical consultant.

Francis C. Wallace, J.C.L., is a judge in the Archdiocese of Los Angeles.

Ralph E. Wiatrowski, J.C.D., is chancellor of the Diocese of Cleveland.

Lawrence G. Wrenn, J.C.D., is judicial vicar of the Court of Appeals, Province of Hartford.

Gary D. Yanus, J.C.D., is adjutant judicial vicar for the Diocese of Cleveland.